New Daughters of Africa

New Daughters of Africa

Edited by
Margaret
Busby

First published in 2019 by
Myriad Editions
www.myriadeditions.com

Myriad Editions
An imprint of New Internationalist Publications
The Old Music Hall, 106–108 Cowley Rd,
Oxford OX4 1JE

First printing
1 3 5 7 9 10 8 6 4 2

A CIP catalogue record for this book
is available from the British Library

ISBN (hardback): 978-1-912408-00-9
ISBN (trade paperback): 978-1-912408-01-6
ISBN (ebook): 978-1-912408-02-3

To sisterhood,
love,
and friendship

Contents

1940s

1950s

1960s

1970s

1980s

1990s

Introduction

What a joy to be introducing *New Daughters of Africa*—a truly collaborative venture that will have an inspiring legacy for years to come! Enabling it to be assembled in record time, writers not only came on board with enthusiasm and alacrity but often steered me in the direction of others whose work they admire, lest these were not already on my radar. Altogether, more than 200 living writers have contributed work to these pages—an amazing party guest list!

A template of sorts was provided by the anthology I compiled more than twenty-five years ago, *Daughters of Africa*; yet this present volume represents something of a fresh start, since it duplicates none of the writers who appeared in the 1992 collection.[1]

New Daughters of Africa begins with some important entries from the eighteenth and nineteenth centuries—and that a limited number of names represent these periods is not to say that there are not many others whose words could have expanded the early sections; however, these few names serve as a reminder of the indisputable fact that later generations stand tall because of those who have gone before. The chronology continues in the ordering of the twentieth- and twenty-first-century writers who follow by decade of birth, primarily to give context to the generational links.

Beginning this anthology with Nana Asma'u[2] (1793–1863) signals that there are foremothers who could have occupied a leading place in any era. A revered figure in northern Nigeria, she spoke four languages and was an educated and independent Islamic woman who can be considered a precursor to modern feminism in Africa. In her "Lamentation for 'Aysha", epitomising the depth of connection that at best can be found between sister-friends, she mourns the loss of her lifelong confidante with the words:

> Know you not that love, when firmly established, is priceless?
> There is no child who could make me forget that love
> and no brother, nothing that could soothe me, not even all sorts of riches.
> ...

---

1 See a full listing of those who appeared in *Daughters of Africa* (1992) on pp. 796–7.

2 Nana Asma'u was brought to my attention, after the publication of *Daughters of Africa*, by Jean Boyd, who kindly sent me her 1989 book, *The Caliph's Sister: Nana Asma'u 1793–1865: Teacher, Poet and Islamic Leader*, and who translated much of this extraordinary woman's work, published in *The Collected Works of Nana Asma'u, Daughter of Usman dan Fodiyo 1793–1864* (edited by Jean Boyd and Beverly B. Mack).

I cry for her with tears of compassion
and of longing and sympathy for her, and loving friendship...

Sarah Parker Remond (1815–1894), abolitionist, lecturer, suffragist and much else, who leads the nineteenth-century grouping, demonstrates many of the themes and serendipitous connections that characterise this collection. A prime example of internationalism, she was born in Salem, Massachusetts (where her father had been brought as a child from the Dutch island of Curaçao), and lectured and studied in England before relocating to Italy, where she became a doctor and married. Her letter of September 1866 to the London *Daily News*, in which she waxes eloquent on "the reactionary movement against the coloured race in the United States", and castigates the social commentator Thomas Carlyle for having "claims to the gratitude of all negro haters on both sides of the Atlantic", makes one wonder how she might have reacted to a tweet by Donald Trump. Delia Jarrett-Macauley's essay "The Bedford Women" delves further into her remarkable story, along the way revealing personal links much closer to home.

It gives pause for thought that Elizabeth Keckley (1818–1907), her life bridging the nineteenth and the twentieth centuries, was describing first-hand the trauma of enslavement in her autobiography *Behind the Scenes: Or, Thirty Years a Slave and Four Years in the White House*, published in 1868—exactly one hundred years before the "mould-breaking year" that Jarrett-Macauley refers to, when "on university campuses from Paris to New York, students were protesting against the old order, against bureaucratic elites, against capitalism, sexism and racism and all forms of authoritarianism", one direct result being the birth of black studies programmes in such places of learning as Cornell, Howard and Harvard. And 1968 would be blighted by the assassination of Dr Martin Luther King in April (later that month MP Enoch Powell gave his notorious "Rivers of Blood" speech, scaremongering about mass immigration to the UK), and made notable too for the moment when at the Mexico City Olympic Games, African-American athletes Tommie Smith and John Carlos raised their fists in an iconic Black Power salute on the podium after winning medals, watched by, among others, the only black girl in Angela Cobbinah's Cornish village, who recalls: "I felt an unfamiliar emotion. Call it connection or kinship, or the bubbling of a youthful rebelliousness..."

Such connections, and bonds of kinship, actual as well as intuited, strengthen the links between contributors to this volume, and those in my earlier anthology, and those who hopefully will discover themselves in these pages or draw inspiration to continue the legacy in their own ways. There are the literal mother-daughter relationships, beginning here with Josephine St. Pierre Ruffin (1842–1924) and Florida Ruffin Ridley (1861–1943). It is especially pleasing to note the emergence as a writer of Yvonne Bailey-Smith, having raised and empowered three children (Zadie Smith and her brothers) to successful careers, and to see Attillah Springer follow the pathway of her mother Eintou Pearl Springer, a contributor to *Daughters of Africa*, and to see

Rebecca Walker, daughter of Alice Walker, achieve prominence in her own right. Exciting, too, to see work from Juliane Okot Bitek and Wanjiku wa Ngũgĩ, whose fathers' writings I have enjoyed, and illuminating to read the experience of Arthenia Bates Millican (1920–2012), mentored by a father who was mired in "stuckness" but taught by Langston Hughes about "the value of humor in literature as a means to obliterate the soreness from difficult bruises to the soul".

We each have our individual experiences of the mother-daughter relationship, some of which are shared in these pages, such as Marina Salandy-Brown's "Lost Daughter of Africa". Recognition of connection to the crucial and indelible maternal spirit is given by H. Cordelia Ray (1852–1916) in her 1991 poem "To My Mother" and in Akosua Busia's elegiac "Mama":

> She is the centre of my earth
> The fire from which I warm my soul
> The spark that kindles my heart.
> The sustenance I feed my daughter
> Is the nourishment I sucked from her once-succulent flesh
> Turned brittle-boned, held together by willpower
> Mama feeds me still—

Permeating the very personal stories in these pages is always an awareness of the wider world, and of the impact of national and international politics. As well as honouring her mother, Cordelia Ray celebrates the heroic Toussaint Louverture, leader of the Haitian Revolution expelling the French, British and Spanish armies that enforced slavery in Haiti and Santo Domingo. Effie Waller Smith (1879–1960), meanwhile, both addresses world issues in her poem "The Cuban Cause" and finds time from the perspective of the first decade of the twentieth century to praise "The 'Bachelor Girl'":

> She's no "old maid," she's not afraid
> To let you know she's her own "boss"…
>
> Of politics and all the tricks
> And schemes that politicians use,
> She knows full well and she can tell
> With eloquence of them her views…
>
> She does not shirk, but does her work,
> Amid the world's fast hustling whirl,
> And come what may, she's here to stay,
> The self-supporting "bachelor girl."

(Definitely one of the "Independent Women" sung about by Destiny's Child.)

In many ways 1992 seems longer ago than a quarter-century; yet, while much has changed, many challenges remain to impact on the publication of work by women of African descent. Who imagined in 1992 that we would celebrate the first African-American US president in 2008, and who could have predicted what would follow Barack Obama's achievement, a decade later, on the watch of his successor in the White House? Much more empowering to think of 2018 as the year former first lady Michelle Obama broke records on the publication of her autobiographical memoir *Becoming*, which sold 1.4 million copies in its first week.

In 1992, Toni Morrison had not yet been awarded the Nobel Prize. Only the following year did she become the first black woman to win that laureate, and to my mind her international celebrity had been slower to come than it should have been, given that *The Bluest Eye* was published in 1970. Since then, I had looked up to her, and was privileged to spend time with her when she was in London for the British publication of *Beloved*—I interviewed her in 1988 (recorded by then fledgling filmmaker Sindamani Bridglal, and subsequently shown on Channel 4), not long before she won the Pulitzer Prize. Toni Morrison was my beacon. In the 1960s, when I started out as a publisher, she was the only other black woman editor I knew of, the first black woman senior editor at Random House, championing books by Toni Cade Bambara, Angela Davis, Gayl Jones, Henri Dumas, as well as compiling *The Black Book* (1974), an anthology of photographs, illustrations, essays and other documents of black American life. She continued as an editor while producing extraordinary novels of her own, before leaving publishing in the 1980s to devote more time to her writing, including her play *Dreaming Emmett*, about the 1955 murder of the black teenager Emmett Till—also the subject of Bonnie Greer's contribution to this present anthology. *Beloved*, too, was inspired by a true story, that of enslaved African-American Margaret Garner, whose story Morrison discovered while compiling *The Black Book*. History "rememoried" unfailingly drives many of the stories that keep these pages turning.

In 1992 came Morrison's novel *Jazz*, the second in a trilogy that ended with *Paradise* (following publication of which I would again have the honour of being in conversation with her, at the Queen Elizabeth Hall in 1998), as well as her succinctly powerful volume of essays, *Playing in the Dark: Whiteness and the Literary Imagination*, containing the stand-out quote: "As a writer reading, I came to realise the obvious: the subject of the dream is the dreamer."

That special year 1992 also saw the publication of Terry McMillan's *Waiting to Exhale*, which remained on the *New York Times* bestseller list for months, and with the election of Bill Clinton as US President, Maya Angelou would in 1993 read her poem "On the Pulse of Morning" at his inauguration, the second poet (after Robert Frost at Kennedy's inauguration in 1961) in history to read a poem at a presidential inauguration, and the first African-American and woman.

Many accomplishments were years away, and names now very familiar and deservedly lauded were still at the starting line. Jackie Kay, current poet laureate (or makar) of Scotland, had only just begun to receive recognition and the accolades that would start piling up after the 1991 publication of her first collection of poems, *The Adoption Papers*; her additional talents as novelist and memoirist were yet to be shown to the world. Ama Ata Aidoo was on her ever-upward journey, and was two decades away from becoming the subject of a film by Yaba Badoe.

Custom, tradition, friendships, mentor/mentee relationships, romance, sister-hood, inspiration, encouragement, sexuality, intersectional feminism, the politics of gender, race and identity—within these pages is explored an extensive spectrum of possibilities, in ways that are touching, surprising, angry, considered, joyful, heartrending. Supposedly taboo subjects are addressed head-on and with subtlety, familiar dilemmas elicit new takes.

How candid and engaging is Jay Bernard's "I resist the urge to destroy my own records by reflecting on archives, how I use them, and what they have meant to me":

> I used to be a bit of a psychogeographer. All criticisms considered, I used to like the term, the ideas, and made a zine for a short time called *Psycho-geography for the Modern Black Woman*. I equated my gender with the city around me. I was not simply a woman, but a specific knot of places, perceptions, possibilities. It detailed my walks around London and men-tioned the bookshops, squats and other spaces I used to go to—Silver Moon, Index, Kennington Books, New Beacon—locations that made me make sense. Only one of those, New Beacon, still exists.
>
> Isn't that just what happens? Things disappear.

How fearlessly revelatory is Nawal El Saadawi in "About Me in Africa—Politics and Religion in My Childhood", in which she writes:

> I was brainwashed by my official education as a Muslim, Egyptian girl from the working class. In primary school the British and Egyptian teachers praised the upper-class girls, with fair white skin. My maternal Turkish grandmother despised my dark skin, which I inherited from the poor peasant family of my father.
>
> My maternal aunt used to hide my dark skin with white powder, and would straighten my hair with a hot iron. I liberated my mind from this slavery by educating myself. Also, my enlightened mother and father helped me to undo what teachers did to me.

How disarming and informational is Zuleica Romay Guerra in "Something About Me", which concludes by saying:

> I am the Cuban Revolution, I am an outcome of the process started in the sixteenth century when, weighed down with chains in the lower decks of the slave ships, brutally dropped into their own excrement, and thrown

overboard as garbage when they were on the point of death, more than a million African men and women arrived upon this island in order to keep on writing a history in which their offspring—all Cubans today, without any qualifying prefixes whatsoever—keep on with our struggles to win the fullest justice ever.

How courageous and touching is Andaiye's recollection of her amity with Audre Lorde:

> I do not remember when I wrote Audre but I did, and I remember that she answered immediately and sent me a copy of *A Burst of Light* with the inscription, "Sister Survivor—May these words be a bridge over that place where there are no words—or where they are so difficult as to sound like a scream!"
>
> And so began my friendship with Audre Lorde, around the sharing of the fear of living with, perhaps dying from, cancer. She wrote often, mostly on cards. She'd say, "I need your words too." I couldn't write too many. So I called, often. And she called too.

Lorde's is a name that recurs in other contributors' work, including that of Edwidge Danticat, Sisonke Msimang and Panashe Chigumadzi, who writes:

> It wasn't until I met the force of the unflinching stories of our mothers and grandmothers and aunts and sisters written by black women—Yvonne Vera, Tsitsi Dangarembga, Bessie Head, Ama Ata Aidoo, Alice Walker, Toni Morrison, Audre Lorde, Jamaica Kincaid, Edwidge Danticat, Maryse Condé—that I was compelled to ask more of my view of their worlds, to find an answer to the question: what did it mean to be a black woman in my grandmother's time?

Echoes and cross-references abound; the history we all are part of creating can be reimagined in many ways. Makhosazana Xaba and Diana Ferrus both pay poetic tribute to Sarah Baartman. Dorothea Smartt contributes "Poem Beginning With A Line From Claudia Rankine", and Rankine herself contributes "Making Room" from her innovative *Citizen: An American Lyric*.

In my introduction to the 1992 anthology, I concluded that "Throughout these women's words runs the awareness of connectedness to a wider flow of history, to the precursors, our foremothers. Our collective strength, like that of a chain, derives from maintaining the links."

The different ways of connecting to an African heritage is an ever-present theme, as are stories of migration, and specifically "Windrush stories", typified by the writing of Andrea Levy, whose father was among those immigrants who sailed to Britain from the Caribbean on the *Empire Windrush* in 1948, to be joined soon afterwards by her mother. To quote from Levy's acclaimed novel *Small Island*: "It was inconceivable that we Jamaicans, we West Indians, we members of the British Empire would not fly to the Mother Country's defence when there was threat."

Windrush is an inescapable reference point in the British-Caribbean nexus, whether mentioned specifically (as in Beverley Bryan's "A Windrush Story" or Selina Nwulu's poetry) or informing and permeating the creative consciousness. Stories of mothers separated from offspring, and the resultant psychological effects, inform many of the contributions.

Ifeona Fulani's essay "Three Islands, Two Cities: The Making of a Black/Caribbean/Woman Writer/Scholar" talks of how her parents' migration, "a few steps ahead of the great wave of Caribbean migrants to England in the late 1960s", led her to becoming accustomed to being "the single grain of allspice floating in the milk jug" in the course of her very British education, and of her own transatlantic criss-crossings with which so many others would find common cause.

Jamaican-born Yvonne Bailey-Smith draws on her own memories of rejoining a mother who had gone ahead to the promised land that forever beckons immigrants, laying the ground for her daughter Zadie later to muse—as she is accepting the Langston Hughes medal in New York—about the significance of "all those years I'd spent as a child in England trying to prove that I was both Black and British; that I knew their plays and poems and history, that I could get into the finest institutions of education they had to offer, that I could perhaps even add a few words to the history of their literature—that I, too, was England."

Yvvette Edwards in her short story "Security" brilliantly captures the emotions of a septuagenarian woman regarded as a foreigner worthy of deportation after half a century of sacrifice and thwarted hope in Britain. Carmen Harris, in her "Hello... Goodbye", pins her hopes on being able to recreate an identity through her father's migration story.

Sue Woodford-Hollick's "Who I Was Then, and Who I Am Now" gives another aspect of finding identity in the course of growing up in Britain, as does Simi Bedford's excerpt from her novel *Yoruba Girl Dancing*, showing the particular experience of being an African at boarding-school in England shared by many (myself included). Others who speak to the British experience include Kadija Sesay, whose formative years included being fostered (an experience in common with Patience Agbabi). Time and again, a topic that arises is the need to be uplifted by finding oneself mirrored in early reading.

Whether the journey is from a childhood in West Africa—as happened to Nah Dove—or from rural Cornwall in England's southwest—Angela Cobbinah's early life—it is London that encapsulates the Black British experience, with all its possibilities for racism, and much else besides. For Donu Kogbara, whose harrowing tale is of being kidnapped in her Nigerian homeland ("Losing My Fragile Roots"), London has become a sanctuary.

Women reveal themselves in these pages as survivors of violence and trauma. Verene Shepherd gives some valuable context in "Historicizing Gender-Based Violence in the Caribbean". A variety of partnerships and marital relationships elicit poignant writing, including Barbara Jenkins' "A Perfect Stranger", Reneilwe Malatji's "My Perfect Husband", and Catherine Johnson's "The Year I Lost".

Andrea Rosario-Gborie, whose personal commentary from the perspective of her last days of working in Hollywood has resonances for today, identifies 1992 as a landmark in other ways: the year of major rioting in Los Angeles in April, following the acquittal of four police officers in the Rodney King beating criminal trial, while in the same month in Sierra Leone, West Africa, a group of young soldiers launched a military coup that brought to power a new twenty-five-year-old head of state.

Minna Salami, introduced to feminism by her mother, acknowledges that "we are feminists because there were women before us who were feminists. What causes the sense of loss, then, is that due to the invasion of Africa, the majority of historical records of these women are missing. So when someone says that feminism isn't African, we are reminded that we do not have the historical proof to show how continuous our presence is in the continent." She quotes from my introduction to *Daughters of Africa*—"Tradition and history are nurturing spirits for women of African descent. For without an understanding of where we have come from, we are less likely to be able to make sense of where we are going." She goes on to assert: "Without doubt, it was this sense of loss that led me to Oya, who unlike any other figure in precolonial African history has expanded my purview of where I come from and of where I am going."

That restorative African feminist lineage is something Chimamanda Ngozi Adichie finds in the conclusion to her iconic essay "We Should All Be Feminists":

> My great-grandmother, from stories I've heard, was a feminist. She ran away from the house of the man she did not want to marry and married the man of her choice. She refused, she protested, spoke up whenever she felt she was being deprived of land and access because she was female. She did not know that word *feminist*. But it doesn't mean she wasn't one. More of us should reclaim that word. The best feminist I know is my brother Kene, who is also a kind, good-looking and very masculine young man. My own definition of a feminist is a man or a woman who says, "Yes, there's a problem with gender as it is today and we must fix it, we must do better."
>
> *All* of us, women and men, must do better.

Self-image is examined in numerous ways. "You will get your hair done" is the refrain in Bridget Minamore's piece, "New Daughters of Africa". Zadie Smith, accepting her Langston Hughes medal, concludes her acceptance speech, poignantly and humbly, by saying:

…I am so thankful that tonight it has stretched far enough to include a Black-British woman like me, a freckle-faced woman like me, a mixed-marriage woman like me, a green-card holder like me, an immigrant like me, a second-generation Jamaican like me, a distant but not forgotten daughter of Africa, like me. Thank you.

The importance of nomenclature is a recurrent theme. Ellah Wakatama Allfrey in "Longchase", linking her Zimbabwean heritage—specifically the saga of her great-uncle, a veteran of colonial warfare—to her own engagement with the world and the perennial traversing of borders, reflects that it is "an imprecise thing, this English naming of Africans". For the main protagonist of Chibundu Onuzo's story ("Sunita"), Toni Morrison's epiphany "that the subject of the dream is the dreamer" could not be more apt, while Nana-Ama Danquah in "Saying Goodbye to Mary Danquah" points out:

> The practice of conferring Christian, or English, names on African children was introduced by missionaries from the Western world who came to what they considered the Dark Continent for the purpose of religious indoctrination. In many cases, children were required to have Christian names in order to register and attend classes in the missionary-run schools. Usually that meant balancing an existence of duality—using one name when operating within the colonial system and using another when operating within one's native culture.

The process of translation from one culture to another is amplified when it comes to language itself. This anthology, though, of course, limited by resources, gives a rich glimpse of the dynamic range of original sources out there to be discovered. Trifonia Melibea Obono's *La Bastarda* was the first book by a woman writer from Equatorial Guinea to be published in English and I am delighted to be able to include a passage of her work, "Let the Nkúkúmá Speak", translated by Lawrence Schimel, who also provided translations of the poems by multilingual Benin writer Agnès Agboton, whose mother tongue is Gun.

The genres represented here are widely varied—fiction of different types, including short stories and extracts from longer works; essays; journalism; columns; blogs; poetry; speeches; extracts from plays and film scripts; poetry; other experimental forms… An unexpected pleasure is to read writers expressing themselves in a genre with which they are not normally associated. Who knew that Nadifa Mohamed, one of *Granta*'s "Best of Young British Novelists" in 2013, was also a fine poet? Adrienne Kennedy, best known as a playwright, contributes the memorable poem "Forget" about her white grandfather. Zoe Adjonyoh, from whom cookery writing might have been expected, delivers a memoir of her father that is indeed "A Beautiful Story".

As much as the contributors are all grouped together as writers, they are each made up of many parts, that if labelled according to the work they do would run almost the gamut of the alphabet: academics, activists, bloggers, campaigners, children's writers, critics, curators, diarists, directors, dramatists, editors, essayists, fiction writers, filmmakers, historians, journalists, lecturers, lyricists, memoirists, novelists, painters, performance artists, playwrights, poets, politicians, producers, publishers, science fiction writers, screenwriters, short-story writers, speculative fiction writers, travel writers, young adult writers…and more.

Now, as in past decades, the nature of the publishing industry has a bearing on what reaches the marketplace. In *Daughters of Africa* I touched on the importance of pioneering black publishers—including New Beacon Books (founded in 1966) and Bogle-L'Ouverture, begun half a century ago by Jessica Huntley, who responded to the 1968 "Rodney riots" that followed the banning from teaching in Jamaica of Guyanese scholar Walter Rodney by producing his book *The Groundings with my Brothers* in 1969. (Earlier in that same year Allison & Busby—the publishing company I co-founded—defied all odds by turning Sam Greenlee's subversive first novel *The Spook Who Sat By the Door* into a publishing success.) Other imprints to be remembered include the Black Ink Collective, and Buzz Johnson's Karia Press, credited with having "rediscovered" Claudia Jones by reprinting her writing. Both Jessica Huntley and I were founding members of an initiative called Greater Access to Publishing (GAP), campaigning to bring about a more multiracial publishing industry, and a 1988 article that I authored (together with Lennie Goodings of Virago) in trade magazine *The Bookseller* began with a statement by Toni Morrison that chimed with our reasoning thirty years ago, and remains relevant: "It's not patronage, not affirmative action we're talking about here, we're talking about the life of a country's literature."

Lasting change in the publishing workforce as a whole has yet to be achieved, although the aspirational mantra of inclusivity and diversity has become increasingly routine in today's mainstream and corporate industry. The category of African literature, let alone literature by women of African descent, is debatable, depending on who is doing the categorisation. Lesley Lokko in her essay "'No more than three, please!'" says:

> The tensions over classification are exacerbated by the fact that much African literature is published outside Africa, for audiences that may *include* Africans, but not exclusively, with everyone having a view on what it should be, what it should say, who can write it and who may read it. Yet the confusion and contestation are liberating. The "real" question is whether current and aspiring African writers will invent forms of their own.

Verna Wilkins, founder in 1987 of the children's imprint Tamarind Books, in "A Memory Evoked" explains what frustrates and motivates her:

Having witnessed, year after year, over more than a quarter of a century, the exclusion of Black and ethnic minority children from books aimed exclusively at children, something had to be done…

I…began working in diverse classrooms in the UK. The existing barriers that exclude children of colour from books aimed at children could start with the children. They should see themselves as the authors, editors, designers, illustrators and publishers of the future.

It was in 2000 at a publishing party that I first met Ellah Wakatama Allfrey—we could hardly have missed each other, being the only two black women present. She was at the time working at Penguin Books, and the connection we made then has been sustained through many a project. (For example, at her request I wrote an introduction to the Penguin Modern Classics edition of Bessie Head's *A Question of Power*.) Beyond that, the role she has played in mentoring others is exemplary, culminating in her taking on the laudable adventure of becoming Publishing Director of new publishing house the Indigo Press. Likewise, the indefatigable Bibi Bakare-Yusuf of Cassava Republic Press is a role model for how to grow a respected independent list.

Individual editors have an opportunity to make change happen, particularly where they lead imprints, as in the UK with Sharmaine Lovegrove heading Dialogue Books at LittleBrown, or Valerie Brandes at Jacaranda. Other ventures to applaud include gal-dem, Digitalback Books, and Knights Of, as well as such online resources as Mostly Lit, Brittle Paper, Kinna Reads, Africa in Dialogue, and James Murua's blog. Among those to whom kudos is due in the US are Amistad, founded by Charles Harris, a ground-breaking publisher in an era that also saw flourish the likes of Paul Coates of Black Classic Press, and the late Glenn Thompson of Writers and Readers.

Festivals and literary celebrations—Aké Arts and Book Festival in Nigeria, Abantu in South Africa, Mboka in The Gambia, Bare Lit and Africa Writes in London, the Bocas Lit Fest in Trinidad, Calabash in Jamaica, the Yari Yari conferences put on by the Organization of Women Writers of Africa, and the African Writers Trust in Uganda, the Harlem Book Fair in New York—have played their part in nurturing literary careers, as have initiatives such as Africa39 (represented in these pages by Chimamanda Ngozi Adichie, Monica Arac de Nyeko, Jackee Budesta Batanda, Nana Brew-Hammond, Edwige Renée Dro, Hawa Jande Golakai, Nadifa Mohamed, Glaydah Namukasa, Chibundu Onuzo, Taiye Selasi, Namwali Serpell, Lola Shoneyin, Novuyo Rosa Tshuma, Chika Unigwe and Zukiswa Wanner), *Granta*'s "Best of" lists of novelists (the British choices including in 2013 Nadifa Mohamed, Taiye Selasi and Zadie Smith, who also featured in 2003; the American choices listing Edwidge Danticat and Chinelo Okparanta), and prizes and competitions such as the Caine Prize for African Writing, winners over the years including Leila Aboulela, Monica Arac de Nyeko, Makena Onjerika, Yvonne Adhiambo Owuor and Namwali Serpell (intimations of Chimamanda's increasingly stellar talent came when she was a runner-up, in 2002 when I was a judge, pipped to the post by the visionary Binyavanga Wainaina, who used his prize money to found the influential Kenyan journal *Kwani?*), the Brunel African Poetry Prize (winners including Warsan Shire and Safia Elhillo), the SI Leeds Literary Prize, the Etisalat Prize, the Golden Baobab, and the Bocas Prize, which has showcased the gifts of Tiphanie Yanique, Edwidge Danticat, Jacqueline Bishop, as well as *Daughters of Africa* alumnae Lorna Goodison and Olive Senior.

From the Myriad First Drafts Competition, which in 2018 focused on women of African descent, came two excellent winners whom we gladly welcomed on board, Anni Domingo, with an excerpt from her debut novel *Breaking the Maafa Chain*, about Sarah Forbes Bonetta, and Rutendo Chabikwa with "Mweya's Embrace" from her work-in-progress *Todzungaira*. Mention must in addition be made of the shortlisted candidates—Christine Amede, Gila K. Berryman, Emmanuella Dekonor, Malika K. McCoy, Ethel Maqeda, Morenike May, Melita Vurden and Roxanne Young—who all, it is to be hoped, will be emboldened to keep creating.

Many glorious firsts are represented among contributors, whether Diane Abbott becoming in 1987 the first black woman elected to the British parliament, or Warsan Shire, who won the inaugural African Poetry Prize in 2013, in 2014 being appointed the first Young Poet Laureate for London, or Safia Elhillo becoming the first Sudanese American to win the George Ellenbogen Poetry Award in 2018. We must aim high and strive to break through glass ceilings and barriers; but let us be wary of the trap of remaining "the only". Ponder the words of Karen Lord: "If we want people to walk this path again, we have to tell more than facts. We must tell truths, root-deep, tree-tall testaments to understanding…"

Countries represented include Antigua, Australia, Bahamas, Barbados, Benin, Bermuda, Botswana, Brazil, Burundi, Cameroon, Canada, Cuba, Dominica, Egypt, England, Equatorial Guinea, Eritrea, Ethiopia, Finland, France, Germany, Ghana, Grenada, Guyana, Haiti, Ivory Coast, Jamaica, Kenya, Liberia, Nigeria, Norway, Portugal, Puerto Rico, St Thomas, US Virgin Islands, St Vincent and the Grenadines, Scotland, Sierra Leone, Somalia, South Africa, Sudan, Trinidad and Tobago, Uganda, USA, Wales, Zambia, Zimbabwe…

Yet the history of these regions is driven by constant social and political change—the Bahamas of Patricia Glinton-Meicholas probably connects with that of Meta Davis Cumberbatch more in terms of memory than actuality, yet she says defiantly: "I ain't goin' nowhere / this land and me is one." Nevertheless, few of us remain static forever. Deise Faria Nunes, born and raised in Brazil, and living in Norway for the past two decades, as she embarks on an exploration of Candomblé, with its West African roots, writes in "The person in the boat":

> Some fellowships we do not choose: we are born into them. Others we walk voluntarily into, with our eyes wide open, even though we do not know what will meet us on the other side.

There is legitimacy in the joy and burden of one's place of origin, the joy and burden of one's place of settlement, the joy and burden of one's adopted homeland, the affiliations rejected or chosen. I feel some native pride that Ghana is a chosen subject or destination for many who originally hail from elsewhere—Candace Allen, Attillah Springer, Sandra Jackson-Opoku and others—knowing also that I have familial ties in Dominica, Trinidad, Barbados, Bermuda, the Bahamas, Europe, America... We are universal, and it is the right of any artist to resist categorisation or the sort of pigeonholing that sets out to be restrictive and stifling. But just as naming oneself can be liberating, so we need never feel limited by labels. Explaining why she does not mind being called a black writer or a black woman writer, Toni Morrison has said: "I really think the range of emotions and perceptions I have had access to as a black person and as a female person are greater than those of people who are neither... So it seems to me that my world did not shrink because I was a black female writer. It just got bigger."

Wasafiri magazine, the literary journal that since 1984 has been a champion of black and diasporic writers worldwide (its name deriving from a KiSwahili word meaning "travellers"), marked the twenty-fifth anniversary of *Daughters of Africa* with a special issue in December 2017, a feature of which was brief testimony from a handful of writers about what their first encounters with the anthology meant to them. Hailing the milestone, Bermudian Angela Barry spoke of her thrill at coming across a contributor whose father was from her island, allowing her to feel "that I also was a daughter of Africa and that I too had something to say."

Goretti Kyomuhendo revealed: "I first encountered *Daughters of Africa* nearly ten years after it was first published—and my first reaction was that of total excitement. I carried a few copies back with me to Uganda, which I shared with nearly forty members of FEMRITE—The Uganda Women Writers Association, which I was directing at the time. *Daughters of Africa* was to become the gift that never stopped giving..." Somali novelist Nadifa Mohamed testified that her writer's block was cured as the result of a copy of the anthology being passed on to her, enabling her to follow the thread of writers "who left their stamp on the world only through the written word."

Phillippa Yaa de Villiers, who as Commonwealth Poet in 2014 performed her poem "Courage—it takes more" at Westminster Abbey, wrote: "We were behind the bars of apartheid—we South Africans had been cut off from the beauty and majesty of African thought traditions, and *Daughters of Africa* was among those works that replenished our starved minds, connecting us to the Black planet of memory and imagination, correcting the imbalance of information and awakening our own potential in ourselves... *Daughters of Africa* brings our separate spaces on the planet into each other's purview, our experiences accented by our geographical and historical conditions, a text that creates solidarity, appreciation and reminds us that we are never alone… Putting African experience at the centre of our understanding, at the centre of ourselves, we learn more about how to be together, to heal ourselves and to plan for the most fabulous future."

Edwige Renée Dro from Côte d'Ivoire talked about the fact that, as she was starting out on her literary journey, "literary columnists were talking about the rise of African writing, a wonderful fact for me even if the majority of the writing they were praising seemed to come from Nigeria. Or from anglophone Africa…" She continued:

> So here I was, heralding from a country that needed its name translated for people to have any idea, living in England and writing in English. Here I was also immersed in a literary milieu that defined Nigerian writing as African writing. What was a lacking-in-confidence aspiring francophone writer living in England to do but set her novel in Nigeria? It is during that time that I stumbled upon a copy of *Daughters of Africa* at my local library… I let out a Yes! as I recognised names like that of my compatriot Véronique Tadjo, but also other francophone writers including Aminata Sow Fall or Mariama Bâ or Marie Vieux-Chauvet with their works set in Côte d'Ivoire, Senegal, and Haiti. From that moment, I stopped the transportation of my story to a country I hadn't even been to. The writer's block lifted and my confidence returned. It was as if the daughters of Africa featured in that anthology were telling me, their daughter and grand-daughter, to bravely go forth and bridge the literary gap between francophone and anglophone Africa.

That these intrepid writers have found their rightful place in *New Daughters of Africa* is a source of immense satisfaction to me, and I trust to them as well.

The passing years since this book's ancestor, *Daughters of Africa*, appeared have meant saying goodbye to irreplaceable friends and family. My own mother, my dedicatee in 1992, had died the previous year (my father in 1981), so could not share the pleasure of seeing the project come to fruition. Many whose words graced those pages we will not see again:

> Maya Angelou (1928–2014), Toni Cade Bambara (1939–1995), Valerie Belgrave (1946–2016), Louise Bennett (1919–2006), Gwendolyn Brooks (1917–2000), Barbara Burford (1944–2010), Octavia Butler (1947–2006), Aída Cartagena Portalatín (1918–1994), Alice Childress (1916–1994), Michelle Cliff (1946–2016), Lucille Clifton (1936–2010), J. California Cooper (1931–2014), Jayne Cortez (1934–2012), Noemia de Sousa (1926–2002), Alda do Espirito Santo (1926–2010), Buchi Emecheta (1944–2017), Mari Evans (1919–2017), Beryl Gilroy (1924–2001), Rosa Guy (1922–2012), Kristin Hunter (1931–2008), Noni Jabavu (1919–2008), Alice Perry Johnson (1932–2011), Amryl Johnson (1944–2001), Marion

Patrick Jones (1931–2016), **June Jordan** (1936–2002), **Caroline Khaketla** (1918–2012), **Ellen Kuwayo** (1914–2006), **Audre Lorde** (1934–1992), **Lina Magaia** (1940–2011), **Anne Moody** (1940–2015), **Gloria Naylor** (1950–2016), **Lauretta Ngcobo** (1931–2015), **Flora Nwapa** (1931–1994), **Grace Ogot** (1930–2015), **May Opitz** (1960–1996), **Anne Petry** (1908–1997), **Carolyn Rodgers** (1940–2010), **Sandi Russell** (1946–2017), **Ntozake Shange** (1948–2018), **Zulu Sofola** (1935–1995), **Maud Sulter** (1960–2008), **Efua Sutherland** (1924–96), **Elean Thomas** (1947–2004), **Miriam Tlali** (1933–2017), **Adaora Lily Ulasi** (1932–2016?), **Margaret Walker** (1915–1998), **Myriam Warner-Vieyra** (1939–2017), **Dorothy West** (1907–1998), **Sherley Anne Williams** (1944–1999).

We mourn them, but are thankful that their words still inspire and urge us on.

Countless other writers, past and present, deserve to be celebrated alongside those in these pages, and indeed in any company, and we stand on the shoulders of many. Restrictions of space, time and resources are the blight of every fantasist anthologist.

There are those on whom the spotlight will always shine, those whom the cameras seek out, yet who sometimes yearn for anonymity. For others, to bask in reflected glory is enough, to see our sisters triumph and take curtain calls, to stand tall while giving others a well-deserved standing ovation. Yet the imagination respects no hierarchy. There will be names within these pages that are, as yet, unfamiliar to many readers but deserving of as much attention as the household names.

My ambition was and is to shine a light on as many as possible of the deserving, whether or not they are acknowledged or lauded by the gatekeepers, who traditionally single out a privileged few, seemingly never too many to rock the boat. But the boat is going nowhere if it is content to drift in stagnating water.

In November 2018, Canadian contributor Esi Edugyan added another award, a second Giller Prize, to her enviable collection. Her thoughtful and perceptive essay, "The Wrong Door: Some Meditations on Solitude and Writing", provides a caveat to the celebrity that many an aspirant craves:

> I think it would come as a surprise to most readers to learn that most writers in their middle to late careers regard with nostalgia their days of obscurity. I remember being puzzled when a writing professor sat us down and told us to savour our collegiate days, because our motives for writing would never again be this pure. We dismissed her as jaded, and longed for the days when we would see our words bound and prominently displayed in the local bookstore.
>
> … But I understand now too that what she was speaking of was a certain lack of privacy, a certain public spotlight that can begin to erode not only our artistic confidence but even motive, the very impetus for writing in the first place. I have spoken to a German writer who after publishing an

international bestseller thirteen years ago struggles to write, paralyzed by the idea of tarnishing his own reputation with an unlikeable follow-up. I have spoken to an American writer who was so badly shamed for an extra-literary occurrence that she cannot bring herself to enter again the public sphere. All of these tragedies are tragedies of exposure, and they speak to the very fundamental need for an area of silence, a room of, yes, one's own.

I feel undeterred in my proselytising for greater visibility for women writers of African descent, which until relatively recently I had thought that I began doing towards the end of the 1980s, when I began to work on compiling *Daughters of Africa*. However, while searching through the archive of papers surrounding me at home, I happened on a letter from Wole Soyinka (who in 1986 made us all proud by becoming the first African to be awarded the Nobel Prize for literature). In 1975, while he was editor of *Transition* magazine, he wrote me a letter responding to something I had said when our paths had crossed in London and I had seemingly berated him for not including enough women in an anthology he had recently curated. His warm response read, in part: "It goes to show—the proportion of women poets never did occur to me—a greater testimony to my non-sexist outlook I cannot imagine! But seriously though, it's quite true, and I am sure you wouldn't have wanted double standards applied in selection. But you are right to point it out. I know that in the next edition I will especially search for poetry by women." Thank you, Prof, for speaking out boldly against male monopoly as recently as December 2018 at the award ceremony for the prize that bears your name, which I was honoured to judge—and which was won jointly by a man and a woman—take a bow, Harriet Anena from Uganda.

Long may those handsome garlands keep coming. For my part, I award every woman—more than 200 of you—who did me the honour of accepting my invitation to feature in this anthology the Venerable Order of True African Sisterhood. May you wear it proudly! A legacy of *New Daughters of Africa* that has been facilitated by your generously waiving your usual fees is a major new scholarship at London University's School of Oriental Studies (SOAS). This will directly benefit African women, making possible a course of study free of the worry of fees and accommodation costs.

And may all who find their way to this anthology, regardless of gender, class or race, feast well on its banquet of words.

Margaret Busby

Acknowledgements

Back in 1989, I met a young editor called Candida Lacey, from feminist publishers Pandora Press, who had just brought out *An Anthology of British Women Writers* (edited by Dale Spender and Janet Todd). We talked of the need to rectify the absence of black women from the literary canon, and I agreed to take on the world single-handedly with her commissioning me to compile *Daughters of Africa: An International Anthology of Words and Writings by Women of African Descent from the Ancient Egyptian to the Present*. Then I became a sort of literary stalker. Pandora transitioned to HarperCollins, and I followed; I was right behind Candida when she moved on to Jonathan Cape, where *Daughters of Africa* was eventually published in 1992. Twenty-five years later, with the original long out of print, and Candida now publisher of Myriad Editions, along came the notion of a completely new edition.

Thank you, Elise Dillsworth, for kickstarting the idea, and thank you again, Candida, for running with it with so enthusiastically. Your hands-on commitment to *New Daughters of Africa* demonstrates everything one could wish for in a publisher. And gratitude aplenty for the dedication of the Myriad-New Internationalist team — seen and unseen — including Corinne Pearlman, Kelsi Farrington, Dawn Sackett, Emma Dowson, Anna Burtt, Charley Chapman, Linda McQueen...

Brilliant backup from the US came in the person of Stephanie Steiker, whose efforts resulted in the welcome partnership with Amistad.

I owe more than I can ever express to my siblings — George and Eileen — who have been by my side from day one, ready to help whenever and however necessary, including with translations. Other family members around the world continue to be loyal cheerleaders and keep me going in various ways—Allyson, Phyllis, Moira, Natalie, Ibrahim, Jamil, Kathryn...

Innumerable friends (which category embraces contributors too — you know who you are) and colleagues gave time, encouragement, practical help, and occasionally much-needed chocolate. To mention just a few: Pauline Melville; Burt Caesar; Joan Harris; Christopher MacLehose; Irene Staunton; Sylvester Onwordi, son of the late Buchi Emecheta; Eve Lacey; Miranda Pyne; Ike Anya; Nicola Cross; Nuruddin Farah; Lorna Goodison; Mandla Langa; the late Ernest Hecht...

How fortunate I am to have Luke Daniels in my life, providing sustenance, sharing the good times and keeping me on my toes. There is no one I'd rather go dancing with!

Which brings me to music, without which I can't function, so the soundtrack of NDOA features Aaron, Abbey, Abdullah, Ahmad, Al, Albert, Alberta, Alexander,

Ali, Alice, Alicia, Alick, Althea, Amadou, Amakye, Andra, Andy, Angela, Angelique, Anita, Ann, Anne-Marie, Antonio, Archie, Aretha, Art, Arthur, Asa, Aston, Astor, Ayanna, Baaba, Baba, Babs, Barbara, Barry, Bébé, Bebo, Ben, Benny, Beres, Bessie, Betty, Bettye, Beverley, Beyoncé, Bheki, Bi, Bill, Billie, Billy, Bob, Bobby, Bonga, Booker, Brandi, Brenda, Brian, Brook, Bruno, Bud, Buddy, Burt, Byron, Caetano, Cal, Cannonball, Carl, Carla, Carlos, Carmen, Carole, Cassandra, Cece, Cecil, CeeLo, Celia, Celina, Cesaria, Chaka, Chano, Charles, Charlie, Cheikh, Chet, Chick, Chucho, Chuck, Cissy, Clarence, Cleo, Cleveland, Cliff, Clifford, Coleman, Corinne, Count, Cuba, Curtis, Daddy, Dakota, Damian, Dave, David, Dawn, Dee Dee, Della, Denise, Denyse, Derrick, Desmond, Des'ree, Dexter, Diana, Diane, Dianne, Dick, Dinah, Dionne, Dizzy, Dobet, Dolly, Don, Donna, Donnie, Donny, Dorothy, Duke, Eartha, Ed, Eddie, Eddy, Edwin, Elizabeth, Ella, Ennio, Eric, Erma, Ernestine, Ernie, Erroll, Erykah, Esperanza, Esther, E.T., Etta, Fats, Fela, Femi, Filomena, Fontella, Francis, Frank, Freda, Freddie, Freddy, Fundi, Gary, Gato, Gene, Geoffrey, George, Gil, Gladys, Gloria, Grace, Gregory, Guy, Gwen, Habib, Hank, Harold, Harry, Hazel, Heather, Helen, Herbie, Hope, Horace, Hugh, Inez, Irene, Irma, Isaac, Ivie, Jackie, Jamelia, James, Janet, Jean, Jeff, Jeffrey, Jennifer, Jevetta, Jill, Jim, Jimi, Jimmy, JJ, Joan, Joe, John, Johnnie, Johnny, Jon, Joni, Joseph, Josephine, Joyce, Kadija, Kai, Kaissa, Keith, Ken, Kenny, Ketty, Khadja, Kirk, Kitch, Lauryn, Lee, Lena, Lenny, Leona, Les, Lester, Letta, Linda, Lionel, Lisa, Lizz, Lonnie, Lorez, Lorraine, Lou, Louis, Lucky, Lukie, Luther, Lynn, Ma, Machel, McCoy, Macy, Mahalia, Manu, Marcel, Marcia, Marcus, Maria, Mariah, Mariam, Mariza, Mark, Marlena, Martha, Martinho, Marvin, Mary, Mary Lou, Mavis, Max, Maxine, Maya, Melba, Melissa, Mercedes, Me'shell, Miatta, Michael, Michel, Mildred, Miles, Millie, Milt, Milton, Minnie, Miriam, Mitty, Monica, Monty, Moses, Mwenda, Nana, Nancy, Nat, Natalie, Nawal, Nene, Neneh, Nico, Nikki, Nina, Nneka, Noel, Nona, Norah, Norma, Oleta, Oliver, Omar, Omara, Ornette, Oscar, Otis, Oumou, Owen, Paco, Papa, Pat, Patrice, Patsy, Patti, Paul, Paulinho, Peabo, Peaches, Pearl, Peggy, Percy, Pharoah, Pharrell, Phineas, Phoebe, Phyllis, PP, Prince, Queen, Quincy, Rachelle, Randy, Ray, Rebecca, Red, Regina, Richie, Rita, Roberta, Rokia, Roland, Ronald, Rose, Roy, Ruben, Ruby, Ruth, Ry, Sade, Salena, Salif, Sam, Samantha, Sambou, Sammy, Sarah, Sathima, Sergio, Seydu, Shadow, Sheila, Shirley, Shontelle, Sibongile, Sipho, Slim, Smokey, Solomon, Sona, Sonny, Souad, Sparrow, Stanley, Stephanie, Stevie, Susana, Susheela, Syreeta, Tadd, Taj, Tammi, Tania, Teddy, Thad, Thelma, Thelonious, Thomas, Tina, TK, Tommy, Toni, Tony, Toots, Toumani, Touré, Tracy, Tunde, Tyrone, Virginia, Vusi, Walter, Wasis, Wayne, Wes, Whitney, Wilson, Winston, Wyclef, Wynton, Yemi, Yolanda, Youssou, Yvonne, Yusuf, Zoe, ZZ… (stop me when I run out of space, because I won't run out of names), ABBA…

Pre-1900

Nana Asma'u

(1793–1863)

An inspirational West African poet, social activist and scholar, who remains a revered figure in northern Nigeria, she was the daughter of the founder of the 19th-century Sokoto Caliphate. She is variously held up as an example of education and independence of women possible under Islam, and as a precursor to modern feminism in Africa. Historical narratives, laments and admonitions are among her more than 60 surviving works, written over 40 years, including a large body of poetry in Arabic, Fulani and Hausa. She wrote two elegies to her lifelong friend 'Aysha, moving expressions of personal grief ("I am desolate over losing her... my confidante from our earliest days") and revealing of the mutually supportive relationship the women shared. The Collected Works of Nana Asma'u, daughter of Usman dan Fodiyo 1793–1864, *edited by Jean Boyd and Beverly B. Mack, was published in 1997.*

From "Lamentation for 'Aysha II"

This is the poem of Asma'u, daughter of our Shaykh Uthman d'an Fodiyo, in lamentation of her friend and dear one, 'Aysha, the daughter of Umaru Alkammu.

Oh, my eyes weep liberally for my loved one
as a consolation for my grief and a companion for my gloom.
Shed copious tears for the loss of 'Aysha
the noblest of my dear ones of my age group, my friend...
This poem was written because there is no one else like her
from among the Brethren. How long my nights dwell on her.
How often she helped me to forget my own grief
and how often she helped me most kindly.
The depth of my sadness and loneliness after her death has grown
The depth of my sadness and loneliness after her death has grown
O the multitude of sorrows, the deepening of my gloom!
Know you not that love, when firmly established, is priceless?
There is no child who could make me forget that love
and no brother, nothing that could soothe me, not even all sorts of riches.
Therefore my heart withers from worrying:
sigh after sigh rises up from my grief;

Tears have continued to flow constantly
as if they would never dwindle or cease...
I cry for her with tears of compassion
and of longing and sympathy for her, and loving friendship...

Sarah Parker Remond
(1815–1894)

*Born in Salem, Massachusetts, she grew up in an educated and abolitionist household.
She became, along with her brother Charles Lenox Remond, a respected speaker
for the American anti-slavery movement, and gained wide acclaim as one of the
few Black women anti-slavery orators during lecture tours of Ireland and England
between 1859 and 1861. While in Britain, she studied the classics at Bedford College
for Women (later part of the University of London and now merged with Royal
Holloway College). She stayed at the home of the honorary secretary of the Ladies'
London Emancipation Society and was among the 1,500 signatories to a petition
requesting the right of women to vote, prepared in 1866. In her forties, she moved
to Florence, retrained as a doctor, and in 1877, married Sardinian painter Lazzaro
Pintor Cabras. She never returned to the United States and remained in Italy until
her death.*

Why Slavery is Still Rampant

Although the anti-slavery enterprise was begun some thirty years ago, the evil is still
rampant in the land. As there are some young people present—and I am glad to see
them here, for it is important that they should understand this subject—I shall briefly
explain that there are thirty-two states, sixteen of which are free and sixteen slave
states. The free states are in the north. The political feelings in the north and south
are essentially different, so is the social life. In the north, democracy, not what the
Americans call democracy, but the true principle of equal rights, prevails—I speak
of the white population, mind—wealth is abundant; the country, in every material
sense, flourishes. In the south, aristocratic feelings prevail, labor is dishonorable, and
five millions of poor whites live in the most degrading ignorance and destitution. I
might dwell long on the miserable condition of these poor whites, the indirect victims

of slavery; but I must go on to speak of the four millions of slaves. The slaves are essentially things, with no rights, political, social, domestic, or religious; the absolute victims of all but irresponsible power. For the slave there is no home, no love, no hope, no help; and what is life without hope? No writer can describe the slave's life; it cannot be told; the fullest description ever given to the world does not skim over the surface of this subject. You may infer something of the state of society in the southern states when I tell you there are eight hundred thousand mulattoes, nine-tenths of whom are the children of white fathers, and these are constantly sold by their parents, for the slave follows the condition of the mother. Hence we see every shade of complexion amongst the slaves, from the blackest African hue to that of women and men in whose cheeks the lily and the rose vie for pre-dominance. To describe to you the miserable poor whites of the south, I need only quote the words of Mr. Helper, a Southerner, in his important work on slavery and the testimony also of a Virginian gentleman of my acquaintance. The five millions poor whites are most of them in as gross a state of ignorance as Mrs. Stowe's "Topsey" in *Uncle Tom's Cabin*.

The free colored people of the northern states are, for no crime but merely the fact of complexion, deprived of all political and social rights. Whatever wealth or eminence in intellect and refinement they may attain to, they are treated as outcasts; and white men and women who identify themselves with them are sure to be insulted in the grossest manner.

I do not ask your political interference in any way. This is a moral question. Even in America the Abolitionists generally disclaim every other ground but the moral and religious one on which this matter is based. You send missionaries to the heathen; I tell you of professing Christians practicing what is worse than any heathenism on record. How is it that we have come to this state of things, you ask. I reply, the whole power of the country is in the hands of the slaveholders. For more than thirty years we have had a slaveholding President, and the Slave Power has been dominant. The consequence has been a series of encroachments, until now at last the slave trade is re-opened and all but legitimized in America. It was a sad backward step when England last year fell into the trap laid by America and surrendered the right of search. Now slavers ply on the seas which were previously guarded by your ships. We have, besides, an internal slave trade. We have states where, I am ashamed to say, men and women are reared, like cattle, for the market. When I walk through the streets of Manchester and meet load after load of cotton, I think of those eighty thousand cotton plantations on which was grown the one hundred and twenty-five millions of dollars' worth of cotton which supply your market, and I remember that not one cent of that money ever reached the hands of the laborers. Here is an incident of slave life for you—an incident of common occurrence in the south. In March, 1859, a slave auction took place in the city of Savannah. Three hundred and forty-three slaves, the property of Pierce Butler—the husband of your own Fanny Kemble—were sold, regardless of every tie of flesh and blood; old men and maidens, young men, and babes of fifteen months—there was but one question about them, and that was decided at the auction-block. Pierce Butler, the owner, resides in Philadelphia, and is a highly-respected citizen and a member of a Church. He was reputed a kind master, who rarely separated the families of his slaves. The financial crisis took place, and I have given you the result to his human property. But Mr. Butler has in no wise lost caste amongst his friends; he still moves in the most respectable society, and his influence in his Church is so great that, with other members, he has procured the removal from the pulpit of Rev. Dudley Tyng, who had uttered a testimony against slavery; and in that pulpit, the man who now preaches, Mr. Prentice by name, is the owner of a hundred slaves. Such is the state of public opinion in America, and you find the poison running through everything. With the exception of the Abolitionists, you will find people of all classes thus contaminated. The whole army and navy of the United States are pledged to pursue and shoot down the poor fugitives, who panting for liberty, fly to Canada, to seek the security of the British flag. All denominations of professing Christians are guilty of sustaining or defending slavery. Even the Quakers must be included in this rule.

Now I ask for your sympathy and your influence, and whoever asked English men and women in vain? Give us the power of your public opinion, it has great weight in America. Words spoken here are read there as no words written in America are read. Lord Brougham's testimony on the first of August resounded through America [On August 1, 1859, Lord Brougham addressed a London gathering, including Sarah Parker Remond, in observance of the anniversary of West Indian emancipation]; your Clarkson and your Wilberforce are names of strength to us. I ask you, raise the moral public opinion until its voice reaches the American shores. Aid us thus until the shackles of the American slave melt like dew before the morning sun. I ask for especial help from the women of England. Women are the worst victims of the Slave Power. I am met on every hand by the cry "Cotton!" "Cotton!" I cannot stop to speak of cotton while men and women are being brutalized. But there is an answer for the cotton cry too, and the argument is an unanswerable one.

Before concluding I shall give you a few passages from the laws of the slave states. By some of these laws, free colored people may be arrested in the discharge of their lawful business; and, if no papers attesting their freedom can be found on them, they are committed to jail; and, if not claimed within a limited time, they may be sold to pay the jail fees. By another law, any person who speaks at the bar, bench, on the stage, or in private, to the slaves, so as to excite insurrection, or brings any paper or pamphlet of such nature into the state, shall be imprisoned for not less than three nor more than twenty-one years; or shall suffer death as the judge decides. I could read such laws for hours, but I shall only add that in Maryland there is at present a gentleman in prison, condemned for ten years, because a copy of *Uncle Tom's Cabin* was found in his possession. The laws are equally severe against teaching a slave to read—against teaching even the name of the good God.

The Negro Race in America

To the Editor of *The Daily News* (London), 1866

Sir,—Will you allow me to say a word in reference to the reactionary movement against the coloured race in the United States? It seems almost like trifling to write a short letter upon a subject so important, and teeming with so many facts, to prove that a new leaf is now being turned over in the history of the negro, and that there is a reaction; a most intense reaction, against that race in the United States. What is the principal cause of the political conflict now going on? Never has there been more at stake than the present position of affairs involves. Why does the conflict assume such gigantic proportions? Why is it that reconstruction has become so exceedingly difficult? Why is it that party spirit is now reaching a height almost, if not quite beyond, any political struggle known even in that country so accustomed to political conflicts. Why is it that in so many of the States neither the freedmen nor their friends find any longer suitable protection? Why is it that the only really liberal newspaper that was published at New Orleans is now discontinued? What was the cause of the riot at New Orleans? Why were the men who served the country in her hour of need shot like dogs? There is but one answer, and one source from which all these difficulties emanate—slavery in the past and its hateful remnants in the present. The Southerners and their Northern allies are determined that the black race shall not be recognised, shall not receive justice. They are determined to prevent the consummation of emancipation, to make freedom almost nominal. Reconstruction cannot be permanently settled until hatred of the coloured race is kept in check or exterminated. No one who has kept pace with the history of the coloured race can hope to re-educate a nation at once: therefore the only remedy is to check this hatred, made up of fashion, prejudice, and intense ignorance. This is the prolific source of the struggle between the contending political parties. The combatants may or may not recognise this fact. It assumes many many shapes, puts on and off at pleasure such a variety of costumes, adapts itself to almost all circumstance with so much skill, that at first only its victim can defeat it. Fresh hatred seems to have been added to the old stock, and then taken complete possession of the Southerners and their Northern allies. The same elements animated by the same spirit which produced the civil war, starved Northern prisoners, and then assassinated the President when he became the firm friend of the slave population, now desire to gain new political strength. The Southern chivalry now demand that all their former slave population shall be represented in Congress, instead of the three-fifths representation which they formerly possessed. What bold injustice! Deny a race their civil and political rights and then endeavour to use them as an element of political strength to degrade them. Should they obtain this, perhaps another generation would pass before the consummation of emancipation. Many republicans are deserting their principles, and joining the ranks of the enemy. Who can foresee the result of the coming contest? It may be that another fiery trial awaits the tried but faithful friends of the republic. A share of the same feeling of hatred towards the coloured race can now be most clearly seen in the minds of many Englishmen, of whom Mr. Thomas Carlyle is the best representative. He has special claims to the gratitude of all negro haters on both sides of the Atlantic. I know of no man who could so consistently be the defender of Mr. Eyre and the Jamaica massacre as Mr. Carlyle. It seems to be a most congenial occupation. He does his work con amore. The name of Mr. Thomas Carlyle, the literary leader of public opinion, has been for many years synonymous with all that is ungenerous and wantonly insulting to the negro race. His position as a literary man has given him the power of influencing the minds of the young. The same influence has been for many years a weapon in the hands of our enemies for adding deeper and more scornful insults. Negro haters on both sides of the Atlantic have again and again repeated his offensive insults, and his outspoken hatred in his recent letter against a race because they chance to be of a darker hue than himself is a fit offering to the spirit which seeks to defend might against right. Why Mr. Carlyle considers it his duty to attack a defenceless race with such hatred and passionate fury is a problem which I leave his many admirers on both sides of the Atlantic to solve.—I am, &c.,

Sarah Parker Remond
Florence, Sept. 19

Elizabeth Keckley
(1818–1907)

Born into slavery, she eventually bought freedom for herself and her son in St Louis, moving in 1860 to Washington DC. There she became a successful seamstress, creating an independent business based on clients who were the wives of the government elite. In 1861 she met Mary Todd Lincoln, wife of newly elected president Abraham Lincoln, and was appointed her personal dressmaker and dresser, becoming an intimate witness to the life of the First Family. In 1864 she founded the Contraband Relief Association, an organisation providing support for recently freed slaves and sick and wounded soldiers. After the American Civil War (1861–65), she wrote an autobiography, Behind the Scenes: Or, Thirty Years a Slave and Four Years in the White House *(1868), described by its publisher as a "literary thunderbolt", from which the following extract is taken.*

Where I Was Born

My life has been an eventful one. I was born a slave—was the child of slave parents—therefore I came upon the earth free in God-like thought, but fettered in action. My birthplace was Dinwiddie Court-House, in Virginia. My recollections of childhood are distinct, perhaps for the reason that many stirring incidents are associated with that period. I am now on the shady side of forty, and as I sit alone in my room the brain is busy, and a rapidly moving panorama brings scene after scene before me, some pleasant and others sad; and when I thus greet old familiar faces, I often find myself wondering if I am not living the past over again. The visions are so terribly distinct that I almost imagine them to be real. Hour after hour I sit while the scenes are being shifted; and as I gaze upon the panorama of the past, I realize how crowded with incidents my life has been. Every day seems like a romance within itself, and the years grow into ponderous volumes. As I cannot condense, I must omit many strange passages in my history. From such a wilderness of events it is difficult to make a selection, but as I am not writing altogether the history of myself, I will confine my story to the most important incidents which I believe influenced the moulding of my character. As I glance over the crowded sea of the past, these incidents stand forth prominently, the guide-posts of memory. I presume that I must have been four years old when I first began to remember; at least, I cannot now recall anything occurring previous to this period. My master, Col. A. Burwell, was somewhat unsettled in his business affairs, and while I was yet an infant he made several removals. While living at Hampton Sidney College, Prince Edward County, Va., Mrs. Burwell gave birth to a daughter, a sweet, black-eyed baby, my earliest and fondest pet. To take care of this baby was my first duty. True, I was but a child myself—only four years old—but then I had been raised in a hardy school—had been taught to rely upon myself, and to prepare myself to render assistance to others. The lesson was not a bitter one, for I was too young to indulge in philosophy, and the precepts that I then treasured and practised I believe developed those principles of character which have enabled me to triumph over so many difficulties. Notwithstanding all the wrongs that slavery heaped upon me, I can bless it for one thing—youth's important lesson of self-reliance. The baby was named Elizabeth, and it was pleasant to me to be assigned a duty in connection with it, for the discharge of that duty transferred me from the rude cabin to the household of my master. My simple attire was a short dress and a little white apron. My old mistress encouraged me in rocking the cradle, by telling me that if I would watch over the baby well, keep the flies out of its face, and not let it cry, I should be its little maid. This was a golden promise, and I required no better inducement for the faithful performance of my task. I began to rock the cradle most industriously, when lo! out pitched little pet on the floor. I instantly cried out, "Oh! the baby is on the floor;" and, not knowing what to do, I seized the fire-shovel in my perplexity, and was trying to shovel up my tender charge, when my mistress called to me to let the child alone, and then ordered that I be taken out and lashed for my carelessness.

The blows were not administered with a light hand, I assure you, and doubtless the severity of the lashing has made me remember the incident so well. This was the first time I was punished in this cruel way, but not the last. The black-eyed baby that I called my pet grew into a self-willed girl, and in after years was the cause of much trouble to me. I grew strong and healthy, and, notwithstanding I knit socks and attended to various kinds of work, I was repeatedly told, when even fourteen years old, that I would never be worth my salt. When I was eight, Mr. Burwell's family consisted of six sons and four daughters, with a large family of servants. My mother was kind and forbearing; Mrs. Burwell a hard task-master; and as mother had so much work to do in making clothes, etc., for the family, besides the slaves, I determined to render her all the assistance in my power, and in rendering her such assistance my young energies were taxed to the utmost.

I was my mother's only child, which made her love for me all the stronger. I did not know much of my father, for he was the slave of another man, and when Mr. Burwell moved from Dinwiddie he was separated from us, and only allowed to visit my mother twice a year—during the Easter holidays and Christmas. At last Mr. Burwell determined to reward my mother, by making an arrangement with the owner of my father, by which the separation of my parents could be brought to an end. It was a bright day, indeed, for my mother when it was announced that my father was coming to live with us. The old weary look faded from her face, and she worked as if her heart was in every task. But the golden days did not last long. The radiant dream faded all too soon.

In the morning my father called me to him and kissed me, then held me out at arms' length as if he were regarding his child with pride. "She is growing into a large fine girl," he remarked to my mother. "I dun no which I like best, you or Lizzie, as both are so dear to me." My mother's name was Agnes, and my father delighted to call me his "Little Lizzie". While yet my father and mother were speaking hopefully, joyfully of the future, Mr. Burwell came to the cabin, with a letter in his hand. He was a kind master in some things, and as gently as possible informed my parents that they must part; for in two hours my father must join his master at Dinwiddie, and go with him to the West, where he had determined to make his future home. The announcement fell upon the little circle in that rude-log cabin like a thunderbolt. I can remember the scene as if it were but yesterday;—how my father cried out against the cruel separation; his last kiss; his wild straining of my mother to his bosom; the solemn prayer to Heaven; the tears and sobs—the fearful anguish of broken hearts. The last kiss, the last good-by; and he, my father, was gone, gone forever.

The shadow eclipsed the sunshine, and love brought despair. The parting was eternal. The cloud had no silver lining, but I trust that it will be all silver in heaven. We who are crushed to earth with heavy chains, who travel a weary, rugged, thorny road, groping through midnight darkness on earth, earn our right to enjoy the sunshine in the great hereafter. At the grave, at least, we should be permitted to lay our burdens down, that a new world, a world of brightness, may open to us. The light that is denied us here should grow into a flood of effulgence beyond the dark, mysterious shadows of death. Deep as was the distress of my mother in parting with my father, her sorrow did not screen her from insult. My old mistress said to her: "Stop your nonsense; there is no necessity for you putting on airs. Your husband is not the only slave that has been sold from his family, and you are not the only one that has had to part. There are plenty more men about here, and if you want a husband so badly, stop your crying and go and find another." To these unfeeling words my mother made no reply. She turned away in stoical silence, with a curl of that loathing scorn upon her lips which swelled in her heart.

My father and mother never met again in this world. They kept up a regular correspondence for years, and the most precious mementoes of my existence are the faded old letters that he wrote, full of love, and always hoping that the future would bring brighter days. In nearly every letter is a message for me. "Tell my darling little Lizzie," he writes, "to be a good girl, and to learn her book. Kiss her for me, and tell her that I will come to see her some day." Thus he wrote time and again, but he never came. He lived in hope, but died without ever seeing his wife and child.

I note a few extracts from one of my father's letters to my mother, following copy literally:

SHELBYVILE, *Sept. 6, 1833.*
MRS. AGNES HOBBS.

Dear Wife: My dear biloved wife I am more than glad to meet with opportunty writee thes few lines to you by my Mistress who ar now about starterng to virginia, and sevl others of my old friends are with her; in compeney Mrs. Ann Rus the wife of master Thos Rus and Dan Woodiard and his family and I am very sorry that I havn the chance to go with them as I feele Determid. to see you If life last again. I am now here and out at this pleace so I am not abble to get of at this time. I am write well and hearty and all the rest of masters family. I heard this eveng by Mistress that ar just from theree all sends love to you and all my old frends. I am a living in a town called Shelbyville and I have wrote a greate many letters since Ive beene here and almost been reeady to my selfe that its out of the question to write any more at tall: my dear wife I dont feeld no whys like giving out writing to you as yet and I hope when you get this letter that you be Inncougege to write me a letter. I am well satisfied at my living at this place I am a making money for my own benifit and I hope that its to yours also If I live to see Nexct year I shall heve my own time from master by giving him 100 and twenty Dollars a year and I thinke I shall be doing good bisness at that and heve something more thean all that. I hope with gods helpe that I may be abble to rejoys with you on the earth and In heaven lets meet when will I am detemnid to nuver stope praying, not in this earth and I hope to praise god In glory there weel meet to part no more forever. So my dear wife I *hope to meet you In paradase to prase god forever * * * * * I want Elizabeth to be a good girl and not to thinke that becasue I am bound so fare that gods not abble to open the way * * * ***

GEORGE PLEASANT,
Hobbs a servant of Grum

The last letter that my mother received from my father was dated Shelbyville, Tennessee, March 20, 1839. He writes in a cheerful strain, and hopes to see her soon. Alas! he looked forward to a meeting in vain. Year after year the one great hope swelled in his heart, but the hope was only realized beyond the dark portals of the grave.

Josephine St. Pierre Ruffin
(1842–1924)

Born in Boston, Massachusetts—to a father of French and African descent from Martinique, and a mother from Cornwall, England—she was a publisher, journalist, civil rights leader, suffragist and editor. She helped form the American Woman Suffrage Association in 1869, wrote for the black weekly paper The Courant, *and was a member of the New England Woman's Press Association. In 1894 she founded the Women's New Era Club, an advocacy group for black women, and also started and edited* The Woman's Era—*the first national newspaper published for African-American women—which called on black women to demand increased rights for their race, at the same time as promoting interracial activities. In 1895, she organised the National Federation of Afro-American Women, and on 29 July that year convened the first National Conference of Colored Women in Boston, an unprecedented gathering attended by representatives of 42 nation-wide black women's clubs.*

Address to the First National Conference
of Colored Women, 1895

It is with especial joy and pride that I welcome you all to this, our first conference. It is only recently that women have waked up to the importance of meeting in council, and great as has been the advantage to women generally, and important as it is and has been that they should confer, the necessity has not been nearly so great, matters at stake not nearly so vital, as that we, bearing peculiar blunders, suffering under especial hardships, enduring peculiar privations, should meet for a "good talk" among ourselves. Although rather hastily called, you as well as I can testify how long and how earnestly a conference has been thought of and hoped for and even prepared for.

These women's clubs, which have sprung up all over the country, built and run upon broad and strong lines, have all been a preparation, small conferences in themselves, and their spontaneous birth and enthusiastic support have been little less than inspiration on the part of our women and a general preparation for a large union such as it is hoped this conference will lead to. Five years ago we had no colored women's club outside of those formed for the special work; to-day, with little over a month's notice, we are able to call representatives from more than twenty clubs. It is a good showing, it stands for much, it shows that we are truly American women, with all the adaptability, readiness to seize and possess our opportunities, willingness to do our part for good as other American women.

The reasons why we should confer are so apparent that it would seem hardly necessary to enumerate them, and yet there is none of them but demand our serious consideration. In the first place we need to feel the cheer and inspiration of meeting each other; we need to gain the courage and fresh life that comes from the mingling of congenial souls, of those working for the same ends. Next we need to talk over not only those things which are of vital importance to us as women, but also the things that are of special interest to us as colored women, the training of our children, openings for boys and girls, how they can be prepared for occupations and occupations may be found or opened for them, what we especially can do in the moral education of the race with which we are identified, our mental elevation and physical development, the home training it is necessary to give our children in order to prepare them to meet the peculiar conditions in which they shall find themselves, how to make the most of our own, to some extent, limited opportunities, these are some of our own peculiar questions to be discussed. Besides these are the general questions of the day, which we cannot afford to be indifferent to: temperance, morality, the higher education, hygiene and domestic questions. If these things need the serious consideration of women more advantageously placed by reason of all the aid to right thinking and living with which they are surrounded, surely we, with everything to pull us back, to hinder us in developing, need to take every opportunity and means for the thoughtful consideration which shall lead to wise action.

I have left the strongest reason for our conferring together until the last. All over America there is to be found a large and growing class of earnest, intelligent, progressive colored women, women who, if not leading full useful lives, are only waiting for the opportunity to do so, many of them warped and cramped for lack of opportunity, not only to do more but to be more; and yet, if an estimate of the colored women of America is called for, the inevitable reply, glibly given is: "For the most part ignorant and immoral, some exceptions, of course, but these don't count." Now for the sake of the thousands of self-sacrificing young women teaching and preaching in lonely southern backwoods for the noble army of mothers who has given birth to these girls, mothers whose intelligence is only limited by their opportunity to get at books, for the sake of the fine cultured women who have carried off the honors in school here and often abroad, for the sake of our own dignity, the dignity of our race and the future good name of our children, it is "mete, right and our bounded duty" to stand forth and declare ourselves and principles, to teach an ignorant and suspicious world that our aims and interests are identical with those of all good aspiring women.

Too long have we been silent under unjust and unholy charges; we cannot expect to have them removed until we disprove them through ourselves. It is not enough to try and disprove unjust charges through individual effort that never goes any further. Year after year southern women have protested against the admission of colored women into any national organization on the ground of the immorality of these women, and because all refutation has only been tried by individual work the charge has never been crushed, as it could and should have been at the first.

Now with an army of organized women standing for purity and mental worth, we in ourselves deny the charge and open the eyes of the world to a state of affairs to which they have been blind, often willfully so, and the very fact that the charges, audaciously and flippantly made, as they often are, are of so humiliating and delicate a nature, serves to protect the accuser by driving the helpless accused into mortified silence. It is to break this silence, not by noisy protestations of what we are not, but by a dignified showing of what we are and hope to become that we are impelled to take this step, to make of this gathering an object lesson to the world.

For many and apparent reasons it is especially fitting that the women of the race take the lead in this movement, but for all this we recognize the necessity of the sympathy of our husbands, brothers and fathers. Our women's movement is woman's movement in that it is led and directed by women for the good of women and men, for the benefit of all humanity, which is more than any one branch or section of it. We want, we ask the active interest of our men, and, too, we are not drawing the color line; we are women, American women, as intensely interested in all that pertains to us as such as all other American women: we are not alienating or withdrawing, we are only coming to the front, willing to join any others in the same work and cordially inviting and welcoming any others to join us.

If there is any one thing I would especially enjoin upon this conference it is union and earnestness. The questions that are to come before us are of too much import to be weakened by any trivialities or personalities. If any differences arise, let them be quickly settled, with the feeling that we are all workers to the same end, to elevate and dignify colored American womanhood.

This conference will not be what I expect if it does not show the wisdom, indeed the absolute necessity of a national organization of our women. Every year new questions coming up will prove it to us. This hurried, almost informal convention does not begin to meet our needs, it is only a beginning, made here in dear old Boston, where the scales of justice and generosity hang evenly balanced, and where the people "dare be true" to their best instincts and stand ready to lend aid and sympathy to worthy strugglers. It is hoped and believed that from this will spring an organization that will in truth bring in a new era to the colored women of America.

H. Cordelia Ray
(1852–1916)

Born in New York City to Charlotte Augusta Burrough and abolitionist and newspaper publisher Charles B. Ray, she had six siblings (one of her two sisters, Charlotte E. Ray, was the first Black American female lawyer). She graduated from the University of the City of New York with a master's degree in pedagogy, but gave up working as a teacher in order to write. After an 1876 memoir of her father, she published her first poetry collection, Sonnets *(1893), which opened with a poem celebrating her mother. Demonstrating an engagement with Black politics, Ray dedicated the sonnet below to Haitian revolutionary leader Toussaint L'Ouverture (1743–1803). Her subsequent book,* Poems, *was published in 1920.*

Toussaint L'Ouverture

To those fair isles where crimson sunsets burn,
We send a backward glance to gaze on thee,
Brave Toussaint! thou wast surely born to be
A hero; thy proud spirit could but spurn
Each outrage on thy race. Couldst thou unlearn
The lessons taught by instinct? Nay! and we
Who share the zeal that would make all men free,
Must e'en with pride unto thy life-work turn.
Soul-dignity was thine and purest aim;
And ah! how sad that thou wast left to mourn
In chains 'neath alien skies. On him, shame! shame!
That mighty conqueror who dared to claim
The right to bind thee. Him we heap with scorn,
And noble patriot! guard with love thy name.

To My Mother
January 1, 1891

Sweet Mother! rare in gifts of tenderness!
Thou who didst nurse my child-life into bloom,
And for each native grace made ample room
To blossom in love's light, —how can we bless
The Power that gave thee to us! In the stress
Of life's great conflict, what could e'er illume
Its mystic shadows and its deepest gloom,
Like smiles and loving words from thee! No less
Than widest sunshine is thy sympathy.
O precious Heart! so rich in sacrifice.
And—boon beyond compare—supremest love,
May Heaven's choicest blessings rest on thee.
Rarer than jewels of the costliest price!
And Peace brood o'er thy path like calmest dove!

Florida Ruffin Ridley
(1861–1943)

Born in Boston to pioneering parents—writer, civil rights leader, and suffragist Josephine St. Pierre and George Lewis Ruffin, the first black graduate of Harvard Law School and first black judge in the US—she too became an activist, involved with founding the Woman's Era Club and the National Association of Colored Women's Clubs, and one of the first black public schoolteachers in Boston, as well as having a literary career as journalist, essayist, writer of short stories and editor of the black woman's newspaper The Woman's Era. *In the latter capacity she was the only female contributor to a feature on manners in* The Boston Globe *on May 27, 1894. Days earlier, an open protest letter she had written to visiting English writer Laura Ormiston Chant appeared in the same pages.*

Our Manners—Are They Bad?

Without doubt the Americans have not generally the finished manner which characterizes some other nations; that they are not lacking in the foundation of good manners, the kindly heart, is also without doubt; but what the influence is that has brought about a certain poverty in the outward expression of an inward grace it is difficult to say. Even the black man with his traditional courtesy has succumbed to the hidden influence, and is now seldom seen bestowing his genial and elaborate bows upon all alike—he is even dropping his old epistolary style which was so delicious in its affluence.

Some say that in this latter day Americans are too busy after the material things of life, and that they have little faith in devoting time to anything that has not a marketable value: others believe that their naturally honest and independent spirit has revolted against the tendency to degrade manners into mannerism and to bow down to a conventional code.

Doubtless there is some justification for both these beliefs, and, as far as the latter is concerned, who of us has not been astounded at the way common sense and common kindness are sometimes prostrated before rules of etiquette? A beautiful, but, as some would say, overbred girl was the source of much amusement to me upon a rainy day. She was about to take, unknowingly, a seat in an open car, which had become very wet from the rain. I attempted to detain her, but she was so shocked at my lack of breeding in addressing a stranger that she deliberately sat down in the water and tried to administer a deserved rebuke by turning upon me a cold, but decidedly shapely, shoulder. Before this I had though Rev. E. E. Hale's story of the girl in the car who preferred to lose her bundle rather than pick it up at the suggestion of a man who had never received an introduction to her something of a joke, but now I know it is true.

Whatever the causes which prevent a more general use of the outward signs of cultivation, American women can and do congratulate themselves that in this country the relation between men and women generally is that of real dignity and true courtesy. For all this, a tendency to discredit the proper and legitimate cultivation of manners is to be regretted. True cultivation is never lost. It makes the coarse man presentable and the fine man irresistible, and lack of attention in this direction is apt to lead before long to a deterioration of standard. Witness the number of excellent people who characterize that fine, manly and altogether delightful little fellow, Lord Fauntleroy, "as a prig." There are already too many who mistake boisterousness for manliness, who call that in a girl which is "pertness," "brightness," and who forget that gentleman is a gentle man.

After all, the surest and truest way to measure people is by their children, and tried by this test can we really and truly put a great big NO after the question, "Are our manners bad?"

If we could but draw a veil over the lack of reverence and deference to elders, and over the intrusiveness of the average American child! It is hard to criticize our own, but sometimes it is best that it should be done.

Doubtless we are in a transition state. After a time, when we shall have become better acquainted with ourselves, we shall have thrown off that which is superficial and burdensome in the accepted code of manners, and shall present as an example to our children a people almost ideal in manners, a people who are free to give full expression to their kindliness of heart, who believe in the value of a current form of intercourse, but who do not mistake form for substance. I believe there is now a chance for criticism of our manners just because we are, unconsciously perhaps, struggling towards that end.

Protest Against Lynch Law

Dear Mrs. Ormiston Chant,

One year ago this month the members of the Woman's Era club of Boston were privileged to have you address them as a body. The occasion was the first public meeting of the club, and besides yourself, Mrs. Lucy Stone, Mrs. Cheney, Mrs. Diaz and Mrs. Spaulding spoke.

It is safe to say that of all these noble women and fine speakers no one did more than yourself in strengthening the impulse to good works, in giving fresh inspiration toward right living,

Your name and that speech has been to us a refreshing memory. Think, then, the shock it has occasioned us to hear that through your efforts a resolution at the national conference of the Unitarian church denouncing lynching was defeated.

We feel assured, and do truly believe, that you opposed the resolution from a high moral standpoint, but we also feel assured that your position on this subject is the result of influences entirely one-sided, and that you will at least be interested to hear "the other side."

We, members of the Woman's Era club, believe we speak for the colored women of America. We have organized, as have our women everywhere, to help in the world's work, not only by endeavoring to uplift ourselves and our race, but by giving a helping hand and an encouraging word wherever they may be called for.

As colored women, we have suffered and do suffer too much to be blind to the sufferings of others, but naturally we are more keenly alive to our own sufferings than to others, and we feel that we would be false to ourselves, to our opportunities and to our race, should we keep silence in a case like this.

In the interest of common humanity, in the interest of justice, for the good name of our country, we solemnly raise our voice against the horrible crimes of lynch law as practiced in the south, and we call upon Christians everywhere to do the same or be branded as sympathizers with the murderers.

We here solemnly deny that the black men are the foul fiends they are pictured; we demand that until at least one crime is proved upon them judgment be suspended.

We know positively of case after case where innocent men have died horrible deaths; we know positively of cases that have been "made up;" we know positively of cases where black men have been lynched for white men's crimes. We know positively of black men murdered for insignificant offense.

All that we ask for is justice, not mercy or palliation—simple justice.

Surely that is not too much for loyal citizens of a free country to demand.

We do not pretend to say there are no black villains; baseness is not confined to race. We read with horror of two different colored girls who have recently been horribly assaulted by white men in the south.

We do not expect that white women shall feel as deeply as we. We know of good and high-minded women made widows, of sweet and innocent children fatherless by a mob of unbridled men and boys "looking for fun."

In their names we utter our solemn protest. For their sakes we call upon workers of humanity everywhere, if they can do nothing for us, in mercy's name not to raise their voices against us.

Florida Ruffin Ridley,
Secretary, Woman's Era Club, Boston, May 19, 1894

Effie Waller Smith
(1879–1960)

Born in the rural mountain community of Chloe Creek in Pike County, Kentucky, she was the child of former slaves Sibbie Ratliff and Frank Waller, who ensured that their children were well educated. She attended Kentucky Normal School for Colored Persons, and from 1900 to 1902 she trained as a teacher, then taught for some years. Her verse appeared in local papers, and she published her first collection, Songs of the Months, *in 1904. That same year she entered a marriage that did not last long, and she divorced her husband. In 1908 she married Deputy Sheriff Charles Smith, but this union was also short-lived. In 1909 she published two further collections,* Rhymes from the Cumberland *and* Rosemary and Pansies. *She appears to have stopped writing at the age of 38 in 1917, when her sonnet "Autumn Winds" appeared in* Harper's Magazine. *She left Kentucky for Wisconsin in 1918.*

The "Bachelor Girl"

From *Rhymes from the Cumberland*

She's no "old maid," she's not afraid
To let you know she's her own "boss,"
She's easy pleased, she's not diseased,
She is not nervous, is not cross.

She's no desire whatever for
Mrs. to precede her name,
The blessedness of singleness
She all her life will proudly claim.

She does not sit around and knit
On baby caps and mittens,
She does not play her time away
With puggy dogs and kittens.

And if a mouse about the house
She sees, she will not jump and scream;
Of handsome beaux and billet doux
The "bachelor girl" does never dream.

She does not puff and frizz and fluff
Her hair, nor squeeze and pad her form.
With painted face, affected grace,
The "bachelor girl" ne'er seeks to charm.

She reads history, biography,
Tales of adventure far and near,
On sea or land, but poetry and
Love stories rarely interest her.

She's lots of wit, and uses it,
Of "horse sense," too, she has a store;
The latest news she always knows,
She scans the daily papers o'er.

Of politics and all the tricks
And schemes that politicians use,
She knows full well and she can tell
With eloquence of them her views.

An athlete that's hard to beat
The "bachelor girl" surely is,
When playing games she makes good aims
And always strictly minds her "biz."

Amid the hurry and the flurry
Of this life she goes alone,
No matter where you may see her
She seldom has a chaperon.

But when you meet her on the street
At night she has a "32,"
And she can shoot you, bet your boots,
When necessity demands her to.

Her heart is kind and you will find
Her often scattering sunshine bright
Among the poor, and she is sure
To always advocate the right.

On her pater and her mater
For her support she does not lean,
She talks and writes of "Woman's Rights"
In language forceful and clean.

She does not shirk, but does her work,
Amid the world's fast hustling whirl,
And come what may, she's here to stay,
The self-supporting "bachelor girl."

The Cuban Cause
From *Songs of the Months*

What was it caused our nation
To take up arms 'gainst stubborn Spain?
Was it to only conquer her
That she might praise and glory gain?

Or was it territorial greed,
That she might richer be?

Or was it beneficial
To her on land or sea?

Oh, no, not these, not these at all
Did ever cause this war;
For it was something nobler
And holier by far.

It was for suffering Cuba,
'Twas for her liberty
To save her from the Spanish yoke
Of awful cruelty.

Who then would dare to say: "Don't go,"
To relatives or friends, "And fight for rights and freedom
'Till Cuba's suffering ends."

1900s

Meta Davis Cumberbatch
(1900–1978)

Although born in Trinidad, she spent most of her life in The Bahamas, where she became known as the "Mother of the Arts". Her parents sent her to England to study medicine, along with her two sisters, but she chose to follow her passion for music instead, graduating from the Royal Academy of Music in 1925. She married fellow Trinidadian Dr Roland Cumberbatch, and when he accepted a post through the Colonial Medical Service in The Bahamas they relocated there. A pioneering cultural activist, she taught piano, gave recitals and lectures, wrote poetry, plays and essays, and was a catalyst for an annual national arts festival. "A Child of Nature (Negro of the Caribbean)", one of her most celebrated poems, appears in Complete Works of Meta Davis Cumberbatch *(edited by her grandson Peter D. Maynard, who also wrote the 2010 companion volume* Great Awakening: Meta Davis Cumberbatch*).*

A Child of Nature
(Negro of the Caribbean)

Shackled? No shackles can bind me!
Enslaved? I am free!—
I roam the fields, pluck the flowers,
Spend with nature happy hours,
Bare my body to the sun,
Share its rays. Leap and run
In sheer abandon. Seeking fun,
In little things much joy I find.
Nature is to me quite kind.
The air, the sky, the land, the sea,
Fruits in season are all there for me.
The moon, it shines and lights my way
It bridges night-time into day.
With dancing feet and voice to sing,
Passing joys to me they bring.
Much within my breast I yearn,
And many are the things I learn,
I live, I love, I laugh, I sorrow.
Each day brings with it tomorrow.
I toil, I labour for my bread.

For shelter for my weary head.
Yet lazing under a shady tree
I feel the world belongs to me!
With mocking laugh and look of scorn,
You seek to crush a child free-born!
You captor vile who would enslave me; –
You are shackled. I am free!

Arthenia Bates Millican

(1920–2012)

Born in Sumter, South Carolina, she was a poet, short-story writer, essayist and educator. She was encouraged to write by her Baptist minister father, her first poem appearing in a local paper when she was 16 and still at school. She earned a BA in English from Morris College (1941) and an MA from Clark Atlanta University (1948), where she studied under Langston Hughes, becoming his protegée. She went on to earn a PhD from Louisiana State University (1972), with a thesis on James Weldon Johnson. Her teaching career spanned four decades, culminating in her holding the position of Professor of English at Southern University, Baton Rouge, until she retired in 1980. Her writing appeared in many journals and she published two collections of stories, the acclaimed Seeds Beneath the Snow *(1969) and* Such Things from the Valley *(1977), as well as a novel,* The Deity Nodded *(1973).*

The Autobiography of an Idea

The purpose of this essay is to support the premise that an idea is born, nurtured, and raised to maturity just as an individual is. That idea is death, the cessation of life—or death-in-life—as the sole source stream in a writer's world. That idea was/is a gift. For me, it is a second-hand gift, because I was influenced by a certain group of writers via the influence that this group exerted on my first mentor in creative writing.

I received the ideas pandered by my mentor from many writers, even Paul Laurence Dunbar, the first professional African-American poet, and the American poet Edgar Allan Poe, but more readily from the pre-romantic writers of English literature. Some of the pre-romantics belonged to the eighteenth-century Graveyard School of writing. Back-story reveals that my mentor occupied his mind with the thoughts of others to buttress the "brutal dilemmas" of his own existence, dilemmas that had in part faced the writers of his favorite literary works, especially Robert Burns and Edgar Allan Poe. Catherine Haich, after experiments and experiences with spiritualism, expresses the view in her book *Initiation* that "…it is possible to receive the thoughts of another human being" (90). After years with Sweet Mary by "Sweet Afton," the tragic child bride Annabel Lee, the "Raven" quoting "Nevermore," and the man without a country (but with a "dead soul") sauntering the deck of ship after ship, mumbling, "I can never say again, |This is my own native land,"[1] I became an initiate of "tragedy" as my mentor envisioned it, and was eventually baptized as a true believer.

---

1 Edward Everett Hale (1822–1909), a clergyman and author, wrote the realistic story "The Man Without a Country".

My mentor was my father, Calvin Shepherd Jackson (1880?–1947) of Winsborn, South Carolina. He became my mother country as a writer. His spirit, his consciousness, his thoughts permeated my being so completely that it is fair to say that he was my god from 1923 to 1930. This man, who became a Christian minister, believed in the efficacy of fate. His classical studies at Benedict College in Columbia, South Carolina, in the field of Greek literature introduced him to the Greek mind/ spirit that held fate as the grand arbiter in human affairs. He never came to terms with the idea that Jehovah God could man the affairs of the being created in his own image with justice and mercy. He, somehow, did not ingest the ideas that, though the tragic hero moved to catastrophe because of his flaw in character, he maintained his moral courage and spiritual prowess. A line from Calvin's poem "The Apple Man" reads: "All my themes become discord." Since Calvin was my god, I worshipped at his shrine of "tragedy," unconsciously bringing a predilection for doom and gloom into my stories and verse.

When Lance Jeffers, the revered African-American poet, read my short stories in the mid-1980s, he said in a letter, "Several of your stories are realistic tragedies. There is often in 'Rena' in *Such Things from the Valley*, 'Silas,' 'Little Jake,' and 'Runetta' in *Seeds Beneath the Snow*, that element that sobers and brings tears to the eyes."[1] My few faithful critics have never become tear-struck on reading my fiction,[2] although they do note some characters who are struggling to alleviate inordinate justice. Lance, however, set me thinking.

I knew Aristotle's "imitation of an action" definition of tragedy. I knew about Shakespeare's tragedies. But Lance's words came across to me as "What have I to do with Hecuba?" in terms of my having an affinity with tragedy as a writer. Me? Tragedy? Then, I remembered Linda's conversation with her sons in Arthur Miller's *Death of a Salesman*. Her inference that a small boat has as much need for a harbor as a large one shows us the "brutal dilemmas" in the life of the humble man, whose life counts as well as the life of a mighty ruler. The death of Linda's husband Willie Loman is a metaphor of fallen humanity. For the first time I was moved to examine my own stories to see why my people were always falling. I was surprised to learn that my characters of note were set to fall.

In 1990, I found "My Last Affair," a short story that I wrote in the spring of 1947 in Langston Hughes's class when he was guest professor of creative writing at Atlanta University. My father had died a few weeks before that spring semester started, so I was full of grief because I had wanted my father to visit the Oxford University of the South, the Atlanta University system.

Hughes tried to market "My Last Affair" with no success. He said that people coming from work were reading the magazines he approached. He said a tired

---

1 My Jeffers file was misplaced during one of the hurricanes in Baton Rouge, Louisiana.

2 Several reviewers have made pertinent remarks about my works, but the "faithful critics" are Charles Rowell, Jerry W. Ward, and Rita B. Dandridge.

person would not want to deal with a forlorn character who could find no way out of depression. Hughes could see that he had provoked me. He asked, "Arthenia, aren't you happy about anything?" I failed to understand his ignorance in regard to my need to suffer. Had not the people who influenced my father been "blessed to suffer"?

Celeste, the protagonist in "My Last Affair," apes my sorrowful experiences as a dethroned "debutante" of sixteen. She is determined to (and with the help of a sister, an aunt, and an uncle does) attend her Senior Class Day Reception even though her mother had commanded her to stay at home. But her mother arrives on the scene and demands that she leave the reception while teachers and students look on with surprise.

The popular song of that season, "My Last Affair," is her favorite, and it becomes more precious to Celeste as she dances to the time (her first dance) with the Romeo that she sights with one eye (a tall, skinny, half-fed-looking youth). She is the "old apple man" whose theme has become discord once her mother crashes the scene. Her heart sings as she trails her mother back to the house before sundown:

"Tragedy just seems to be the end of me, my happiness is misery, this is my last affair." Actually, it was a first glimpse for the girl into a world where young people wore pretty dresses, new hairstyles, whole suits—dark suits, white shirts and ties— just to sit down to eat good food, cake, ice cream, drink punch, and dance.

As I read over and over again in 1990 the sentence "This is my last affair," I began hearing my father's voice speaking of the 1927 flood: "We will drown; we will starve, there is no way out. God has broken His promise by destroying us again with water instead of fire." Tragedy? The father who was god appeared to me now as an "inevitable pessimist." Hopefulness is essential to tragedy, but fate had deleted that element from his book of life.

Then Langston's voice became clear. I could at last buy Lance's idea of the "realistic" in my stories. Hughes told me to examine my own life as a black person, and to deal with African Americans in my milieu and with the tenor of their lives. He stressed the value of humor in literature as a means to obliterate the soreness from difficult bruises to the soul. My father now became a man in my view, not my god of seven years in our West Street home in Sumter, South Carolina.

"Striking incongruities" claimed Calvin's consciousness when he was a Benedict College student in the 1890s. And he had, in a way, found his Langston Hughes. His English teacher, an Anglo-American lady from New England, asked Calvin to stay after class one day. She asked: "Calvin, did you write this?"

"Yes, Miss Livingston," he replied.

She did not allow them to say "Yes, mam."

"My boy," she continued, "God has given you a gift. Always write."

He did, though most of his writings are lost, and he never published a word. Like Hughes, this woman became a friend to her students. When she learned that he was an orphan working to secure an education, she asked all of her friends to use his hack services.

Calvin would have a different experience with his mathematics teacher. This prominent African-American minister became his role model, the kind of man that he would be as an educator. He gave his students assignments that required hard, laborious preparation. The assignment that determined whether or not a senior would finish his term was the main conversation at the preparatory school. This was Calvin's challenge for excellence. He fought sleep until late in the night to work the algebra problems. He passed his work in certain that he had won his professor's respect. He would graduate.

Calvin waited with "bated breath" to hear the words of praise. The professor had asked him to remain after class.

"Calvin, I kept you after class to reprimand you for stealing the problems from your roommate. He solved the problems and you became the copycat. You will not graduate."

"No, sir," Calvin replied, "my roommate was out on the town; I did the problems."

The Reverend Professor smiled down on the so-called offender and said, "Do you think I would take your word against that of your roommate? He is somebody's son."

Calvin knew that he was a child of fate—a cursed being. Legend has it that his father Primus, who was named for a saint, became a living devil in life. Through some deed, it is believed that he brought down a curse on his progeny.

In 1981, the Calvin Jackson heirs joined the Jackson clan with roots in Winsboro and Fairfield County, South Carolina, in a sizeable gymnasium in Philadelphia. It was full of people. I met ministers, educators, artists, land barons, entrepreneurs—you name it. But no one would call the name of Primus Jackson. I faced this impenetrable barrier to self, the backstory of my existence that Calvin had known, no doubt, most of his life.

Robert Bly explains "stuckness" as a paternal phenomenon: "The wound a man receives from his father, or from life, [hurts]. Through that hurt, his way of dealing with the world was damaged. He is enveloped in a mood of "stuckness'" (71–72). Bly's *Iron John: A Book about Men* was/is a gift. It is a second-hander. The father, Bly continues, "does not exist, as the hero through his heroism nor through his invincibility, as the warrior does, but he exists through his wound" (73).

I realize that this "stuckness" my father experienced is, through him, a part of my experience. Finding the evidence of the experience is another task to assume as I examine my canon rife with the old influence—especially in *Seeds* (1969, 1973, 1975) and *Valley* (1977).

"Striking incongruities" exist in my life. Conflict is an eternal verity.

I understand why my father wrote, "And all my themes become discord." But I have kissed the darkness hello. And as I move, I search through that darkness for the most brilliant fight.

Works cited

Bly, Robert. *Iron John: A book about Men*. New York: Addison-Wesley, 1991.
Haich, Elizabeth. *Initiation*. London: Allen and Unwin, 1965.

Barbara Chase-Riboud

A US-born visual artist, sculptor, novelist and poet, she attained international recognition with her first novel, Sally Hemings *(1979), which imagines Hemings' life as a slave, including her now historically proven relationship with President Thomas Jefferson. The book won the Janet Heidinger Kafka Prize and sold more than one million copies. She is also the author of the novels* Valide: A Novel of the Harem *(1986),* Echo of Lions *(1989),* The President's Daughter *(1994), and more recently* Hottentot Venus *(2003), which humanises Sarah Baartman, a Khoikhoi woman who was exhibited in 19th-century freak shows in Europe. Chase-Riboud's poetry collections include* Memphis & Peking *(1989) and* Everytime a Knot is Undone, a God is Released *(2014). Her numerous honours include the Carl Sandburg Prize for poetry and the Women's Caucus for Art's Lifetime achievement award. In 1996, she received the French Ordre des Arts et des Lettres.*

Ode to My Grandfather at the Somme 1918
For James Edward Saunders (1898–1966)

He stands a solitary figure in
Dark brown and khaki along the Somme trenches,

Wearing the uniform of the Union dead
On the foreign soil of the Western Front,

Himself a foreigner in his own homeland
A ferocious volunteer in the 366 Infantry Regiment

Of the segregated all-Negro volunteer division raised
From the depths of the Black Philadelphia ghetto,

A lonely steel-helmeted figure, erect in a field of blood
Having traversed the Atlantic in an American vessel

Just like his great grandfather
170 years before except this time not

In the ship's hole in iron chains but chained nonetheless
To America's destiny and the idea of patriotism

In a useless war that freed no one,
Changed nothing nor set any human goal

Nor any value on human life which will result
Only in engendering World War II

Separating this war from the next war
As *The Great War*, killer of an entire generation

The boy stands wondering what is great
About a war in which both sides are

Cannon fodder for the guns of the other
And white men fight for a hollowed-out hill

As a respectable excuse for one million dead,
In awe the French called the Black soldiers *Men of Bronze*,

While generals tried out their new maiming machines
And mustard gas made its entry into war's Hell.

The boy carries a just issued machine gun
And a vacant-eyed black-goggled canvas gas mask,

No protection from the searing pain of
Poison gas outlawed by the Geneva Convention.

Mercenary bombs burst in countless numbers
Blowing off arms and legs around his muteness

Like scarlet oak leaves fluttering, splattering
On the rich, brown French soil

In a senseless, useless White Man's War
That has claimed 4 million dead on both sides

The boy stands in never-dry leggings,
Binding 26 days of mud and mold,

Dead skin that must be scraped off
With the bayonet of his gun in order to stand

At attention resisting the fog of deadly gas,
Believing that the duty to die for one's country

Was his duty as a Negro and his right as a citizen
Even as he was despised as being unfit to wear

The uniform he wore or shed the blood he shed
For years afterwards coughing blood from burned lungs

I remember the brown syrup on a lump of white sugar
That kept his breathlessness at bay, his only medication,

That and his veteran's pension and the right to a
Military burial but not the right to march with

American troops down the Champs Elysées in triumph
Among the flags and the confetti, a Yank like all the rest,

Revered by the French as the victors of the Armistice
And the savior of European peace and civilization,

Safe for those same Europeans who had enslaved his
Great-grandfather but never safe for him neither along the

Somme, nor in Paris, nor in Philadelphia, nor for that matter
Safe for democracy, the vote, the labor union, the working man.

Returning home to my grandmother Lizzi, struck dumb with joy
That it was over, over there but just beginning over here.

And our surprise in 1966 to learn that
Our silent patriarch was a hero.

Who had the right to a military funeral with honors
And the cannon salute he never received from the French.

Who had never revealed what had happened to him over there for
How can 1,000,000 cadavers be conceived within one square kilometer?

The folded flag rests in my arms, his faithful granddaughter's
The last tribute to the last *Bronze Man of the Somme*.

Nawal El Saadawi

Born in Egypt, she is a medical doctor, a leading feminist activist and an internationally renowned writer of non-fiction and fiction. Once banned from public speaking and imprisoned under President Sadat, she is founder and president of the Arab Women's Solidarity Association, co-founder of the Arab Association for Human Rights, and is an outspoken campaigner against Female Genital Mutilation. Her extensive body of writing— including plays, memoirs, novels and short stories—is studied in universities across the world. She has received three honorary degrees, the North-South Prize from the Council of Europe, the Inana International Prize in Belgium, and the Seán MacBride Peace Prize. She lives in Cairo and continues to write in Arabic. Her numerous works in translation include Woman at Point Zero *(1982),* God Dies by the Nile *(1984),* Memoirs of a Woman Doctor *(1994) and* Love in the Kingdom of Oil *(2001).*

About Me in Africa—Politics and Religion in my Childhood

In my childhood I did not know that Egypt is in Africa. The Egyptian government under King Farouk did not consider Egypt as part of Africa. They followed the British colonizers, who divided Africa into Black and White. Divide and Rule has been the main plan of any colonizers throughout history.

To exploit people, you must veil their minds, and create conflicts and wars between them. This is happening today in our life as happened in earlier societies.

Religion is the best tool to veil the minds of people and divide them. The Egyptian educational system followed that of the British colonizers and contained many racist, patriarchal, religious, and capitalist ideas.

I was brainwashed by my official education as a Muslim, Egyptian girl from the working class. In primary school the British and Egyptian teachers praised the upper-class girls, with fair white skin. My maternal Turkish grandmother despised my dark skin, which I inherited from the poor peasant family of my father.

My maternal aunt used to hide my dark skin with white powder, and would straighten my hair with a hot iron. I liberated my mind from this slavery by educating myself. Also, my enlightened mother and father helped me to undo what teachers did to me.

To weaken the human mind you need an absolute power in Heaven and on Earth. Obedience must be the rule, to God, the King or the President. In Ancient Egypt, God *was* the King. In fact, "God's power" was created by the statesmen or the politicians to conceal the King's domination and exploitation. Throughout human history, political economic power was the origin of all religions. Obedience to God is inseparable from obedience to the ruler. The idea of secularism, or of separating religion from state, is misleading. No state can control its peoples without their submission to God's Will, which hides their submission to the government or ruler.

Democracy and secularism are deceptive words, among others, masking the politics behind religion. The post-modern, so-called, Daesh, El Quaida, Taliban, Boko Haram, Muslim, Christian, Jewish state, and all other religious fundamentalist states or groups, are political imperialist capitalist powers, created by global-local colonizers under the name of God.

When I was a primary school student during the 1940s, I noticed that King Farouk, who was head of the state and the army in Egypt, had more power over the Egyptian people than God and his Prophet Mohamed. However, the British general of the invading army in Egypt had more power over King Farouk and the Egyptian army and government. My father told me one day that the British army had surrounded the palace of King Farouk and threatened to kick him off the throne if he did not obey the British order to appoint El Nahhas Pasha as prime minister of the Egyptian government.

Al Azhar, the highest Islamic power in Egypt, could not defend the King, though its top Islamic sheikhs declared every Friday, in all the country's mosques, that His Majesty the King was protected by His Majesty God and His Prophet from all evils, and that he, the King, would rule Egypt for ever, never to be de-throned unless by God's Will.

I asked my father this question: "How can the British Will be above God's Will?" My father replied that no human will can be above the Will of God, but God can use the British colonizer or any human being as a tool to punish our king Farouk, who was corrupt and unjust.

In July 1952, while I was a student in the medical faculty, King Farouk was overthrown by the Free Officers Movement led by Nasser. My father said that God used Nasser and his group as a tool to realize God's Will. It became clear to my mind that, in reality, the only Will working is that of the state and the army.

In fact, religion is needed today, as in all times and places, to transform the human being into a tool in the hands of the dominating global-local powers. Today we use the new word "glocal" to show that the global and local are inseparable.

My father died in February 1959; he did not live to witness the big defeat of Nasser in June 1967, but the top Islamic sheikh declared that the defeat was God's Will, not the Will of the British-French-Israeli-American powers. He considered Nasser a communist atheist secular dictator and that God had punished him.

Nasser died in September 1970 and the new ruler, Sadat, opened the doors of Egypt to American-Israeli goods, he signed a peace treaty with Israel, changed the constitution to declare Egypt an Islamic state, and named himself The Believer, The Father. Sadat would start his speeches with God's name—Allah—and end with the Prophet Mohamed's name.

The leaders of the Muslim Brotherhood were released from Nasser's prison and were encouraged to hold political and religious posts. Women and even female children started to wear the veil. In September 1981 Sadat imprisoned all opposition leaders, men and women, who criticized his policies, including myself. I was accused of being against Sadat and God.

I used to see God in my dreams when I was a child. He was inseparable from Satan the Devil. When I started my childhood diary, both of them, God and Satan, were always together. I could not separate them in my imagination or in reality. Imagination was inseparable from reality. When God resigned in any of my novels, Satan had to resign. And when Satan resigned, God had to resign.

It was not my fault. Since I started reading the three monotheistic holy books — The Qur'an, the New and Old Testaments—I have found God and Satan together all the time. I was severely punished by political-religious powers because I did not separate between God and the local-global President.

Anyway, I stopped hiding my dark skin very early in my life, since I discovered that Egypt is in Africa, not in the so-called Middle East. In fact, I never use the term Middle East.

December 2017
Cairo, Egypt

Adrienne Kennedy

Influential as a playwright and memoirist, she was born in Pittsburgh, Pennsylvania, and raised in Cleveland, Ohio. She draws on myth, autobiography and history to explore issues of race, kinship, and violence in her work, which has been produced, read and taught internationally for more than six decades. She is best known for her one-act play Funnyhouse of a Negro, *which was written in 1960, the year she visited Ghana, and won an Obie Award in 1964. Other notable works followed, including* The Owl Answers *(1965),* A Rat's Mass *(1967),* A Beast Story *(1969), and* June and Jean in Concert *(1996), earning her many prestigious honours, among them a Guggenheim fellowship (1967), an American Academy of Arts and Letters award in Literature (1994), the 2003 Anisfield-Wolf Lifetime Achievement Award, the PEN/Laura Pels International Foundation for Theatre award (2006), and an Obie Lifetime Achievement Award in 2008. Her most recent play,* He Brought Her Heart Back in a Box, *premiered in 2018. In November 2018, she was inducted into the US Theater Hall of Fame.*

Forget

I met my white grandfather a few times.
of course he lived on the white side of town.
he sent his chauffeur who was black and his name was Austin
in a black car to

my grandmother's house to get us.
my mother wanted my brother, herself, and me to walk
but he insisted.

we went to his house.
his white wife wanted us to go in the back
door,
but he insisted we come into the front.

full of contradictions,
he sent my mother and her half-sister to college,
bought them beautiful things

but still maintained the distance. they called him
by his surname and he never shared a meal with them.

we sat in his parlor twice.
he was slightly fascinated by my brother and me.
he said something like you all have northern accents.
he was interested in our schooling in Cleveland.
he was interested in the fact that people
said I was smart.

at that time the thirties and before the WAR
he owned a lot of the town

and had three children by black women.
my mother's mother was fifteen, worked in the peach orchards.
like the South itself, he was an unfathomable
mixture of complexities,
these are two generations of white men
removed

who went all the way to Africa to get SLAVES,
quite mad.

I was lucky enough to spend a day and evening in his
and his family's house. built about 1860
where he was born…his father was the town's first bank owner.
the house, white, wooden in weeping willow trees
down a long archway.

by 1940, when I visited, the house had one usable
room, the rest all boarded up
and was lived in by black COUSINS
of his Negro family.

despite her Atlanta Univ education and marrying a Morehouse man
and making a nice life in Cleveland,
my mother found it impossible to say her mother's name.
and impossible to call her father by anything but his
surname.
she used to say to me when I was a child,
Adrienne, when I went to town to get the
mail, they would always say
here comes that little yellow bastard.

Andaiye

Guyanese-born, she has been described as a transformative figure in the region's political struggle, particularly in the late 1970s, '80s and '90s. She has devoted most of her adult life to left and women's politics in the Caribbean and internationally. She was an early member of the Executive of Guyana's Working People's Alliance with (among others) Walter Rodney and worked alongside him as he wrote A History of the Guyanese Working People: 1881–1905. *She was a founder of Red Thread women's collective, and served on the Regional Executive of the Caribbean Association for Feminist Research and Action (CAFRA). Later, she was associated internationally with Women of Colour in the Global Women's Strike. A cancer survivor twice, she was a founder of the Guyana Cancer Society and Cancer Survivors Action Group. She has published articles and chapters, mainly on women in Guyana and the Caribbean, and continues to support organising for radical change.*

Audre, There's Rosemary, That's For Remembrance

For Audre Lorde (1992)

I met Audre Lorde toward the end of 1988 at the Caribbean Association for Feminist Research and Action (CAFRA) meeting. I was chairing (they call it facilitating) a session. CAFRA members were being—as usual—disorderly, and why not? I was in my best head-teacher mode. Audre came in late. I recognized her face from the back cover of books, but I had to make a point; she was late. I asked her to identify herself. She said, looking a little surprised (she was not humble): "Audre Lorde." I led the acknowledgement by thumping the table. She acknowledged the recognition with a slight raising of the eyebrow, a ducking of the head.

A short time after, I was asked if I could be interviewed with Audre. I agreed. It took some time to get the interview together. When I was free, I heard she was tired. When she wasn't, I was busy. I wasn't trying to be difficult. I hadn't read the cancer books; I didn't know about her struggle with cancer. Eventually we did the interview at a table (I think; my memory is bad) in a room full of people and smoke. I think, too, I was smoking myself. As I said, I didn't know she had cancer. And I didn't know I had cancer.

Somewhere in the next six months I learned she had cancer. Somewhere in the next six months—on International Women's Day, 1989—I learned that I, too, had cancer.

I remember only fragments of what happened over the next few days. I remember being at my father's house and people coming in, the women breaking the silence of awkwardness by asking me what I needed washed or ironed or bought for the hospital; the men, not socialized into housework, having nothing to break the silence. I remember my friend, Jocelyn Dow, taking me to see a play that was on in celebration of IWD: *For Colored Girls Who Have Considered Suicide/ When the Rainbow Is Enuf*. I remember going to the home of another friend, Alice Thomas, where I cried and Alice said, "Done, done, never mind, the diagnosis probably wrong." Mother words. I remember yet another friend, Nesha Haniff, saying angrily that we all know Guyana's medical services had fallen apart so why were we so stupid as to believe they could read any slides? I remember my father sitting with Jocelyn making arrangements for me to go to Canada for the diagnosis to be checked, even as he denied the possibility it might be right. I remember him calling my mother, who was in England, and who did what she did best—pretended she was coping well; how was her daughter? I remember my brother, Abyssinian, calling to say that he would leave his job in New York (as he did) and come wherever I would be, to be my nurse (as he was). I know I spoke during those few days, too, to other women who became major supports; the thing I call not yet a women's movement called in.

I do not remember when I wrote Audre but I did, and I remember that she answered immediately and sent me a copy of *A Burst of Light* with the inscription, "Sister Survivor—May these words be a bridge over that place where there are no words—or where they are so difficult as to sound like a scream!"

And so began my friendship with Audre Lorde, around the sharing of the fear of living with, perhaps dying from, cancer. She wrote often, mostly on cards. She'd say, "I need your words too." I couldn't write too many. So I called, often. And she called too.

West Indians are a people who, for good or evil, express the serious as joke, so across all my weekly and monthly phone calls with Audre in four years, here's what I remember most sharply.

I was well into my treatment and had developed a reputation as a person who was dealing well with cancer and chemotherapy. And I *was* brave. I knew from reading that the drugs I was using would cause me to lose my hair. I arranged to shave it all off when it began to fall. I was determined that I would be in control. Every time I went for chemo I vomited my guts out, then, vomiting over, called for soup with pigtail, which my Aunt Elsene or mother made. I watched people watching me with pity—hair gone, cheeks deformed by steroids—and managed to laugh. My friend Karen de Souza, a photographer, would come from Guyana to visit me and climb up high to take pictures of the sun shining on my head and my cheeks, so that (she said) I could see later where I had been and acknowledge the journey. I genuinely found that funny. At least she assumed there would be a later.

I was brave until the day I was told I had to lose several teeth, which, given the teeth I had been losing since childhood, meant that I had to get a plate.

A plate, teeth in a cup, at night; worse than cancer, a metaphor for old age. I went back to the home where I was staying with my friend Elsie Yong, entered my bedroom, closed the door, climbed into my bed, went into the foetal position and lay.

Somewhere within this—the same day, next day?—Audre called.

"Hi, girlfriend," she said.

"Hi," I muttered, the first time I had ever felt or sounded not glad to hear her voice. She chatted and then eventually asked what was wrong.

I said, "I have to take out teeth and get a plate and soak it in the night like old people." One breath, whining.

I heard a noise like a person who hadn't managed to get her hand over the phone before she giggled. Then Audre said, "I lost my two front teeth. Which teeth are you losing?"

"The remaining ones on the right side," I answered.

"Oh, that's bad," she said. "But not as bad as front teeth."

I sucked the teeth I had left.

"Listen," she said. "You know I'm supposed to be so brave? Well, when I lost my two front teeth I felt worse than when I lost my breast. I mean, you don't have to show your breast or use it every minute, but your teeth!"

I giggled, then said, "But this is it. This is the end. This is teeth in a cup, in the night. The end of..."

"No," she interrupted. "Here's what I do. In the night, I go into the bathroom and close the door, firmly. I take out my two front teeth. I brush the teeth in my mouth, then the teeth in my hand. Then I put the teeth in my hand in my mouth. I go to bed. Now, if you have expectations (and, girlfriend, you and I might seem to have different expectations but they're really the same expectations), you wait till the expectations are met or if none are forthcoming you raise some..."

I giggled.

"Stop interrupting," she went on. "After your expectations are met (she/he approaching, you approaching), you wait for the right moment (she/he asleep) and you take out your teeth (if you think you must) and place them strategically under your pillow."

I giggled.

"Girlfriend, you put them there so you can get at them quickly if any further expectations come up. And if they don't, in the morning you get up, take them quickly from under the pillow, go to the bathroom, close the door firmly, brush the teeth in your mouth then the teeth in your hand, put the teeth in your hand in your mouth and you're ready to meet any further expectations..."

"OK, OK, OK," I giggled. "OK."

It occurred to me then, it occurs to me now, that the story had been made up out of whole cloth. But what does that matter?

A few times Audre called me because she needed to find company in the place she was in. When the alternative therapy that had helped her stay alive for so long wasn't shrinking her liver tumor anymore or even keeping it the same size, the question was whether finally to take chemotherapy even though she was tired of carrying her life every day in her hands.

"Girlfriend," she inquired, "tell me about methotrexate."

I answered; she hummed.

She asked, "You think I should take that, you who've felt it?"

I tried a balancing act: I wanted her to take anything that might keep her alive; I wanted to support her in her determination not to switch gears from a form of therapy that was about strengthening the immune system to one that could destroy it; I wanted her to take poison if poison would keep her alive.

We spoke when after she had taken the chemo her locks had fallen out and she asked, "Do you understand thin with bloat?"—because she had lost weight while parts of her body had grown fat.

She called when, for love of those for whose love of her, she was considering more chemo, although her heart and her body and her mind said no. And all she asked of me, at those moments, was that, as a person in a place similar to hers (although never the same), I would listen to her weigh options I had weighed and tell her the truth of what I had discovered, so she could use that in her weighing of the options.

A person in a similar place. For we were never, Audre and I, "sister survivors", surviving in the same place. No one else I came to know who had cancer had travelled such a road, from breast cancer to liver cancer to ovarian cancer. From mastectomy to hysterectomy. From a person who started like the rest of us with little knowledge of cancer and its treatment to a person fully informed about the disease and the options for treatment; from a person just living to a person having to make decisions every day about what to do or not to do just to live, who found the courage to choose a road with no one ahead to guide her—no person who had chosen that road and walked it for so long through such pitfalls and reached the places she wanted to be.

Audre told me, as she told countless others, that I should write—a diary entry each day, poems. I didn't.

When Gloria said Audre had died, I thought (I didn't know what else to think) I would write her a poem. I couldn't. I wrote, "I want you in this world." Nothing else. What I meant was that although I believe she will always be in this world in her children, her partner, her blood and non-blood sisters, all her life's work, I wanted her in this world—at the other end of a phone or postcard, talking about the loss of teeth and hair, about bloating bellies and cheeks and Bush and the Gulf War, about where she was going/had been to see an eclipse of the sun, about why something I had written was OK but not good enough because I had chickened out on homophobia, about why she would forgive me that (for a while) in the face of CNN images of Rodney King, Ethiopia, Brazilian street children, the thing they call "black-on-black violence" with its origins in white-on-black violence, in New York, DC, the townships of South Africa. About living with and dying from cancer. About her loving me and I, her.

For I loved her, this woman who came so late to my life but whose death leaves a void in the centre of my life.

Audre, there's rosemary. That's for remembrance.

Joan Anim-Addo

From Grenada, she has long championed Caribbean writers, particularly black women to a wide public and academic audience. She is the Director of the Centre for Caribbean and Diaspora Studies, Goldsmiths, University of London, where she continues to teach and inspire students. Her publications include a libretto, Imoinda *(2008), which re-imagines the life of a woman sold into the Atlantic slave trade, the poetry collections* Haunted by History *(2004) and* Janie Cricketing Lady *(2006), and a literary history,* Touching the Body: History, Language and African-Caribbean Women's Writing *(2007). Her co-edited books include* Caribbean-Scottish Relations *(2007), and* I am Black, White, Yellow: An Introduction to the Black Body in Europe *(2007) and* Interculturality and Gender *(2009). She started Mango Publishing in 1995, and is the founder-editor of* New Mango Season, *a journal of Caribbean women's writing.*

Ashes, She Says

We do not—and I mean not—touch the computers today. We listen. I use "we" to include those of us whose lives these days are being recorded so much of the time. Still, we mindlessly provide data by one means or another. Right? Think social media, for example. Aha! That means you, I believe. And you. You, too. Yes, she smiles. And me? I'm as guilty as the rest. But what I'm inviting you to do is to put your finger on the link to today's question: where do we find significant data from earlier times? She taps at the lobe of her right ear, holds up a handful of printed sheets and, her shoulder against a pillar crammed with cable, reads to her class:

It all happened before this place, before this time, long before you were born. And I forget so much. You see, memory has been tortured out of me. They tell me that I've never lived such a life, that I'm deluded to talk of Princes and Kings, palace and courtiers. They might just be right. I myself can't trust a memory that produces lives so different from those we know so well here. Besides, my head's too full. Too much has happened. Take what you want of this sorry tale and throw away the rest, mash it underfoot, like sand. Perhaps like ashes. Yes, ashes. Minutes, hours, days, a whole life time burnt to ashes.

At first he touched me with words. Words alone, mark you. Words, light and airy, words like bubbles dancing in morning sunlight. In that place before here, the surprise of his words made me look at him again, search his face, simply because I had never heard words behave like that before. Not that I could remember, anyway. Words that gurgled. Words that tickled. Words that sounded like I'd always known I'd hear them, at once familiar, at home, and magic. And all was just a matter of wonder to me. I looked and as I looked, I found that I'd caught his eye. I suppose we had, by some magic, ensnared each other.

Sister Historian, her head full of locks and thoughts of times gone by, pauses. She surveys the class seated behind computers, like robots trained only to input. Why do they always allocate her a computer room? She momentarily considers surveillance and control.

And why do you insist on hearing this tale? True, it might have a prince and even a sleeping beauty of sorts. But there the similarity ends. The cast of characters is too large. The setting is too diverse. And as for time, forget it. There is no unity. Quite the contrary. Besides, it'll never do you any good, believe me. Look what good it did me.

You think I'm deliberately avoiding telling you. No. Then again, perhaps yes. More than that, I don't understand why you want this stuff torn from my head where I've finally, and at bitter cost, laid it to rest. But maybe this day had to come, despite time, cavernous and mournful, time like tangled ancient undergrowth. Well, so be it.

Our eyes met. I suppose it was a matter of fate. Fatal. Our eyes met. Finally, in my father's remembrance, since I was obliged to greet him, I did. Then he said something stupid, I recall. In truth, I was ready for something stupid from him. So there you are, he straight away gave me the gift I expected. He said something like, "You've changed." Now, if there's anything worse than being told by every other person in the world that you've changed—when you are simply unaware of having changed—it's being told those words by a toad of a male, when you're convinced that you're looking at one you despise and loathe, utterly.

"Since we last met you are so changed," I think he said. Puke! Vomit! Puke! Whether or not those were his exact words, the end result was fury on my part. So, I let him have it, as we say. That was that and that is that because my mind's gone blank now. Go and trouble someone else with your insatiable demand for stories, Missy His-story—anna. Vexation beats in my heart now, because what you need to know is that we have no past. This is all we have: hell here on earth, without name, without past, with an impossible future. What more is there to tell, dammit?

The young teacher, dressed in recycled African Dutch wax prints, watches Jayden plunging his Afrocomb into bleached hair. He buries it deep so that the metal teeth are barely visible. She ponders his future, waggles a finger at him and reads on.

His words were the tinkle of bells, the ripple of gentle waves homing towards the shore, a drizzle at dawn, the shiver of sunset touching the sea. We talked and talked. He was happy; I was happy. We promised to go to the palace, where we would live happily to the end of time. Wooduf, doof! Story done.

So why are you waiting and looking at me like that? Oh, and I forget! The curse of the children of Ham. A solid explanation almost forgotten. That's why you see me here in rags, a fallen princess, fallen woman, husbandless, impossible mother. And still you want me to speak of love. Was there any such thing back then? Is there such a thing now? Ai! There is no end to this world's madness.

Then again, his words, as I said, held me. Out of words we built a craft that held us both tight. Safe. Or so we thought. Poor me. How mean and foolish I was, then. Utterly. If I'd known what lay ahead, I'd have rushed to meet him, not hidden myself away when I knew he would call. I should have snatched every second. It might have added one more day of happiness to a life that has been not much more than drought, really. Go, take your chance. You're young only once. Choose to be happy for however long it lasts. I didn't. It's enough to make me trace that trail to Carib's Leap. There, to feast eyes on rocks like the teeth of giant reptiles, shudder at the frothing waves. And jump. Why don't we? Why don't we in this hell take the leaper's solution? Story done.

Each boy, outdoor jacket zipped up despite the regulated room temperature, has stopped fidgeting. Out of habit, Chantelle is desperately trying to catch an eye. Anyone's. She tugs at Jayden's sleeve, then slowly leans on him, all the while glancing up at their teacher. Jayden's resistance strains to breaking point until the teacher locks eyes with him. She beckons to him, points him to her chair and speaks directly to him. There is much for us to consider, Sister Historian says, as we embrace the topic of enslaved women and strategies of survival. She reads on.

You see me turning this way and that. It's because sometimes I'm convinced others stole our happiness. Sometimes, though, conviction deserts me. I mean, we were two desperate people who should've nodded recognition and gone our separate ways, run hard in opposite directions. Maybe then none of this would've happened. Evidence: we didn't like one another from the beginning. He didn't care for me. I didn't care for him. There was a moment of madness. We were both bereaved. We let stuff go to our heads. True, passion walked with madness for a few sweet moments. Sweet. Truly. But the rest has been sorrow, straight and simple. That's the crux of it. I don't know how to speak of happiness here. I know nothing whatsoever of happiness.

Ah! But I could tell you about tears. Ever wondered where the water comes from to fill the ocean washing the other side of this island? Watch these eyes. They've watered every space they've lit upon since before time, when we left those shores. And I wept before that with joy. I should've fallen on a borrowed spear. You see, words are no friends of mine. It's why I prefer silence. In that respect, this place suits me. Lesson number one: silence. Everybody chewing on silence. You don't speak, nobody worries there might be a problem. They studying you and your silence. In silence. Always. As if they have time for your worries on top of their own! Still, they read your face, your eyes, the droop of your shoulder, the heaviness of your body as you move through space from here to there. They read the quality of drag on your feet. They studying you. From the tones and textures of your moving there's nothing they cannot tell. Man sleep in your bed? They can tell. Master at he nastiness again? Your child join the disappeared in dead of night? They can tell.

But as soon as you open your mouth, people start to worry. O Lawd, she goin' bring trouble on we head. Now, what to say if anybody ask? I tell you, taking on the habit of silence was a helluvva difficult thing when I first came to this place. Okay, the whole world was upside down. When people should be speaking up, they clamp down. When for them to shout, they eyes rolling. Little strangled sounds escaping into kiss teeth. I couldn't understand at all when I first came. As soon as speech fell from me, "Gal, shut you mouth!"

Was a hard lesson, especially as it was pure grieving had kept me silent. And there's the rub. I suppose I would have opened my mouth long before. Grieving shut me up; grieving saved me blows. Hadn't seen it like that before.

But he loved words. Words he rolled on the tongue, shaped them, honed their edges and sent them coursing through the air. His words filled my ears, my waking moments, my dreams. I heard his voice as I fell asleep. I heard his words in my dreams. I heard him as I woke. Ah! Wonderful for a while. I would laugh out loud so many times and there wouldn't be a single soul present.

He was funny, you see. Without effort; without setting out to make a single joke. How I loved that! Thought myself in paradise on earth. Now, words? I curse them. I'll tell you: words are loud farts in the wind. They assault a passing nostril, if luck would have it. They blow this way and that but mostly they go unnoticed. If we sniff them, we turn our noses up for a few seconds and that is that. Yes, I was once soundly hexed by words. Those days when his voice would not go away. The same with his touch. That too; I curse the memory of his touch. Of course it was a different story then.

Did I tell you that my father was a warrior? Now, this I can truly say, hand on heart: those two cared for each other. When Papa was at home, he would visit. I guess he was the son Papa never had, that everyone wished for. I've had time enough to think of this. He loved Papa. Papa died. I was all that was left. No, that's not the truth. It's despair in masquerade. True, they were like father and son. Closer than most fathers and sons. True, we were both lost souls after Papa died. True, we saw each other with new eyes. Maybe we should've run in our different directions. Maybe we were too headstrong. Maybe we should've listened to the advice of others.

Soon time passed too quickly with each other. We had an understanding. If what we felt for each other was magic, we didn't care. We were prepared to live and die with it. We laughed. We laughed a lot.

So tell me about my eyes, Missy. Do they sparkle? No? Ha! Suppose I said he spoke always of my eyes, of my spirited ways, what would that tell you? Suppose I said we knew then, back in that place, that what we felt was an enchantment alert to the sap of trees, the trembling of leaves, the tender rays of moonlight, what would you say? Madness, right? Who knew that fire would follow? Fire, and now just ashes. It's all that's left. Go. Take any happiness you can. There is a time to come when you'll find only ashes left. Ashes, settled and cold.

Sister Historian clears her throat and addresses her class: I did not promise that our data will offer any easy answers. Think, though. Is this "testimony" about one individual slave woman? The overall question we are addressing is this: were these victims or strategists? She drops her voice. Do not reach for the keyboards. Today's input is of a different kind. It used to be called a conversation.

Simi Bedford

Born in Lagos, Nigeria, to parents who had come there from Sierra Leone, she was schooled in England and went on to read Law at Durham University. She worked in London as a model, in publishing, as a broadcaster, TV researcher/producer, and as a movie locations manager. She has three adult children and lives with her ex-husband in Southern France. She is the author of two novels, the autobiographical Yoruba Girl Dancing *(1991), from which the following extract is taken, and* Not with Silver *(2007), a historical novel focusing on mid-18th-century West Africa, and on her own ancestral history. She is the proud grandmother of five.*

From *Yoruba Girl Dancing*

A party of English explorers was trekking along a narrow jungle path in single file, sandwiched between their African bearers. The African bearers were clearly nervous, the ones in front rolling their eyes fearfully and the ones bringing up the rear jumping out of their skins at every turn. The explorers, with not a hair out of place, were on their way to find Tarzan. He was the only one who knew the jungle well enough to lead them to the treasure, which, according to the map left by a previous explorer, was buried in a virtually inaccessible part of the jungle. It could only be reached by crossing impossible terrain inhabited by hostile natives and dangerous animals.

Suddenly, up ahead, from the thick and impenetrable undergrowth, a terrifying thrashing and bellowing could be heard. The native bearers promptly downed their loads and disappeared to safety. I used to think that this was prudent behaviour on their part as they obviously knew the place and were familiar with the dangers and knew the best thing to do to avoid them. Now I bitterly resented their behaviour, because this kind of sensible precaution was considered cowardly in Croydon and, more to the point, the disapprobation rubbed off by association on me, the only representative of the black races in the whole of Thornton Heath.

The noise in the undergrowth reached a crescendo and one of the fleeing natives (you could depend on it every time) caught his foot in a tree root and fell heavily to the ground, rolling his eyes frantically and gibbering in fear. Whereupon the heroine, the only woman in the group, and who had previously shown no interest whatsoever in the bearers, unaccountably rushed to the native's assistance just as a huge, rampaging, mad bull elephant thundered through the dense vegetation into the clearing. The fallen native, galvanised into action by this terrifying sight, freed his foot and slunk off into the greenery with a hideous expression on his face, leaving the heroine to her fate. She, instead of running away, stood still, screaming, while the infuriated animal, ears flapping and trumpeting with all its might, lunged at her, determined to run her down. Certain death only seconds away, the hero came leaping to the heroine's defence and, with unerring aim, shot the elephant cleanly between the eyes, then dropped the gun in time to receive her fainting in his arms.

At that very moment, Tarzan burst onto the scene, calmed down the troupe of elephants, who were following behind the mad bull, and led the whole party off to the safety of his place for rest and recuperation before the next week.

Only one thing was certain and that was that the natives would not come out of it well. If there was danger, they could be relied upon to disgrace themselves and run away, leaving the hero and heroine and anyone else from England in the lurch, or else perish horribly. Considering that the jungle was their home, the natives were exasperatingly accident-prone. Hosts of them disappeared down the gullets of countless crocodiles, were crushed by rhinos, mauled by lions and strangled by snakes with no one to mourn their passing. My fate mirrored theirs in the games we played, I was thoroughly fed up with these celluloid Africans, ditto the Red Indians. They could carry on rolling their eyes and coming to grief week after week, but this African in Thornton Heath was going to do something about her situation.

"Gerald," I said, as he was tying me up prior to lowering me into the snake pit at the side of the compost heap in Wilf's garden, "why do you think it's always the natives who get eaten by the animals? After all, they've lived all their lives in the jungle, you'd think they'd have learnt a few tricks by now."

"You would think so," said Gerald. "Maybe it's because they haven't got any guns."

"I don't think that's the reason," said Roger.

"Why do you think it is then?" Gerald asked him.

"I think it's because white people have got more brains," said Roger.

"That's right," agreed Doreen.

"Not all Africans are stupid," I said indignantly, "I've got just as much brains as you have."

"It's only in the films," Wilf said.

"Yeah, they're only stories," said Paula. "Are we going to get on with this game or what? If you don't hurry up and finish tying her up, Gerald, I'll get cramp in my leg waiting to be rescued here forever." Paula tossed her long blonde hair.

I could see that reasoning wasn't going to change things. I would have to try something else.

"Wilf," I said, "I think it's very unfair that you always get the smallest parts to play."

"Elephants and rhinos aren't small."

"You know what I mean."

"Yeah, I suppose so."

"Just because you're the smallest and I'm the youngest we get the worst."

"I don't see how we can go against Gerald."

"We could play other games."

"What other games?"

"King Arthur and his Knights of the Round Table, for instance."

"Uh-huh."

"It'd be more fun to play a knight than an animal or a native."

"Might be."

I left him to think about it. He wasn't persuaded in a day but eventually he agreed. We laid our plans in secret and when the occasion arrived we were ready.

"Remi," Gerald shouted, "off we go, put the baggage on your head and lead on."

"I'm not carrying it on my head," I said.

"Oh, all right, carry it anywhere you like, but lead on."

As I led on down the narrow alleyway and pushed open the gate into Roger's garden, in the dense undergrowth beyond the hedge the pawing and thumping of some mighty animal could be heard. The noise reverberated like thunder through the jungle, and sure enough Wilf came charging around the hedge bellowing and raging, straight towards the native bearer, who, with what I hoped was unimpeachable dignity, laid down the luggage, and with unerring aim struck the rhino just above the horn. With equal dignity the rhino buckled to the ground beneath the astonished gaze of the explorers.

"What do you think you're doing?" yelled Gerald.

"I have killed him with my spear," I said.

"What spear? You haven't got a spear," Doreen said.

"Natives usually carry spears," said the rhino from the ground.

"As for you, what did you fall down for?" Gerald said furiously. "Get up and shut up."

Wilf arose and came to stand beside me. "We have decided," he said, "that we're not going to play these silly games any more. She," he said, nodding his head at me as I stepped closer to him, "is fed up with being a native all the time and as for me I only ever get to play animals or Red Indians. I'm fed up too. You can play by yourselves."

Our knees quaking, we passed through the gate and out of Roger's garden.

Gerald was unforgiving. I took to following Uncle Theo around instead, working beside him on the allotment, carefully weeding the little section he set aside especially for me. I strongly suspected that Uncle Theo carried out secret work on my bit, because it always looked healthy and flourishing when I arrived for the holiday, and kind of wilted and dead by the time I returned to school, having forbidden Uncle Theo to lay a finger on it during the time I was at home.

"Uncle Theo, do you think of me as a darkie?" I asked him.

"No, of course not, I think of you like any other child, like my granddaughter."

"You really don't think of me as a darkie?"

"No, I do not," he said, carefully raking the soil around his leeks.

"Doreen says I'm a darkie and that English people don't like darkies."

"She's just talking daft. Sensible people don't think that way; as far as they're concerned people are people, they like them for what they are."

"What am I then?"

"Like I said, you're a child, quite a nice child for most of the time."

"What will I be when I grow up?"

"You'll be an African, a coloured person."

"Why a coloured person?"

"Because, I suppose, you're not white," Uncle Theo said.

I studied him carefully as he turned back to his raking. His skin was scarlet from the sun, his eyes were emerald green and his little pointed teeth were green too.

I thought, Grandma would have said this man is talking nonsense. Mind you, it was becoming increasingly difficult to imagine what Grandma would have said. I was beginning to think that she and Aunt Rose and Patience and Alaba were all figments of my imagination.

Wilf and I met by the lamppost outside his gate. He said he thought that if Gerald and the gang continued to ignore us we might have to revise our position, which was that they needed us more than we needed them. I reassured him that though Gerald was a great man of action—he could jump on and off trams when they were moving, wangle us into the cinema or the swimming-pool without paying and melt the ice at Streatham Ice Rink with the power of his blades—he was very short on imagination; he depended on Wilf and me—they all did, I pointed out—for the refinements we supplied in our games. We'd all be back together soon, I predicted. I was confident because Gerald depended on me for something else that Wilf knew nothing about. I read to Gerald every night before I went to bed. He loved stories but, as Aunty Betty said, though he could manage the *Dandy* and the *Beano*, he was no reader. We had stopped at a particularly exciting point in *Treasure Island* and I knew he was longing to get back to it.

"So you reckon we should hang on a bit longer?" Wilf said.

"Yes, I think so," I replied and hurried in…

At breakfast the next morning Gerald told me ever so casually to be sure to be ready to accompany him as usual to Saturday morning pictures. He said it between shovelling in mouthfuls of porridge; winter or summer, it made no difference, Gerald began the day with a saucepan of porridge. I took my time walking out of the room but once outside the door I raced up the stairs to prepare.

We called in on Wilf on the way to the cinema. He was so happy, he didn't look where he was going and was nearly run over when we were crossing the road all strung out in a long line. Roger only just managed to haul him back in time.

Walking back home, Gerald, again ever so casually, said that maybe we should think of some new games to play. I put forward King Arthur and his Knights of the Round Table, which I was reading at school and Wilf suggested Martians from Outer Space. He and I both knew that he would never be King Arthur but he could be a knight, which all the books said was a noble thing to be, and, as for Martians, well, there was no reason for Doreen to look in my direction. Martians, as everybody knew, were green.

Nah Dove

A transatlantic womanist and Afrocentric theorist of Ghanaian and English heritage, she has lived in Ghana, Nigeria, Canada, the UK and the US, where she was awarded her PhD, which focused on African culture, women and education. She has written articles, book chapters, encyclopaedia entries, and is the author of the 1998 book Afrikan Mothers: Bearers of Culture, Makers of Social Change. *Her other accomplishments include involvement in developing African-centred and Afrocentric schools. She is a proud mother and grandmother and, although retired, continues to volunteer and consult as well as learn and grow.*

Race and Sex: Growing up in the UK

Africa

Once a young girl danced beneath the African sky
and the sun kissed her bones.
She saw her reflection in the lake
and understood her spiritual connection.
She never betrayed her mother Africa.

It might be confusing to the reader that I consider myself to be a person of African descent although my father was African and my mother European of Jewish lineage. I remove myself from the label of mixed "race" that is grounded in the patriarchal belief that there are several "races" of humanity, largely identifiable through colour. The whitest women and men are superior to the yellow, red, brown and Black-skinned women and men. Although women are considered inferior in each category, they exist in the same hierarchy with each other.

There is one race. The Mitochondrial DNA proves that we are all related to one African woman. It is wretched that in more recent human history the less melanin-ated have designed and invested in the falsehood of white superiority, whether through advantage or ignorance, disrespecting, debasing, demonising and betraying the light of their dark ancestry.

The label of "mixed race" privileges people like me in that whiteness separates us from Blackness or ethnicity because we "appear" closer to the "white" and are therefore perceived to be superior to darker-skinned people. This historical, religious, social and materialist belief is globalised and normalised through cultural conquest. The origins of racism and other heinous inequalities lie firmly in the subjugation of woman by man, the societal basis of existence. If this relationship is unjust, nothing can be right.

Now, at the age of seventy-two, I see that culture has taken a critical role in formulating reasons for the constructions of human inequalities throughout the world. My formative years were spent in Africa and I was schooled in the UK.

After arriving in London, although a child, I was both fascinated and horrified at the English ignorance and the perpetuation of lies and myths about Africa, its people and its culture. This terrifying experience gave me an insight into the minds and culture of European people. Conceptualising diversity in European and African cultures is problematic; after all, Africa was conquered using the same patriarchal methods by Europeans and Arabs; Africa's resources lie in their coffers.

My father first worked as a sweeper for the London Underground until he joined a dental practice. We lived in a small run-down infested flat in East London. We were all poor, but I soon discovered that the hostility shown to me as a "darkie", "blackie" and "nig- nog" was neither confined to me nor East London.

The fight to survive was both physical and mental. Name calling and fighting in the streets was a regular threat to my life and the lives of my brothers. I fought mostly with white boys, although was often intimidated by the girls. The boys were quick to get into physical attacks. My aggressors feared me as though I were an animal—unpredictable. The white boys fought me to show off their bravery. Whether these fights were in school or on the street, no one defended me. My brothers and I were alone. The agony that I felt was not from the pain of being kicked in the stomach, or punched in the face or head, or even wiping the blood and spit from my face or hair, it was at having no defence against the belief that I was less than human, posed a threat, and was certainly not a girl. I understand the internal damage to a young psyche forming in this cultural milieu of rampant racist hostility without the protection of the foundation that I had acquired through my prior knowledge and experience of Africa.

Similarly, racist encounters happened to my father. I had seen him come home bloodied on more than one occasion. One day when I was about seven years old, whilst walking with my father in a park, seven (possibly more) white teenagers of around sixteen or seventeen years old called my father obscene names and threatened him. My father picked me up and placed me on the side of the path on the grass verge under a tree and turned to defend himself. The youths surrounded him. He was able to cause some considerable damage before they ran away in fear. My father took my hand and we proceeded to walk on, amidst stares. This event had a tremendous effect on me because it gave me the confidence to fight to survive. I was in awe of my father because he was brave, humble, dignified, handsome and intelligent. To my mind, he was so much better a human being than those who believed that he was less human than they. I witnessed my gentle mother, a white woman who in the 1950s married an African man—betrayer of her culture—humiliated, called foul names and spat upon.

Quite soon, I understood that in order to be treated with any kind of respect and sensitivity one had to have blond hair and blue eyes. I went through what so many of us struggle with even today, some de-melanin-ising their skins. My existence was always under some kind of threat and I remember how I sobbed to my mother of my dilemma. My mother assured me, "You are beautiful just the way you are." It was small comfort at the time but in fact, those words sustained me all of my young life. It helped when my mother informed me that "those who smiled at you as little ones are the ones who will later hate you."

I learned that racism was not limited to London. Once, while my mother was washing me in the tin bath in the living room just before bed-time, I was watching television (our family had television early, we mostly watched the news); a discussion on apartheid was taking place. An Afrikaner expert on African intelligence claimed that head-size indicates the size of intellect. He was justifying the idea that African people could not rule themselves when so-called independence movements were rising. I remember getting upset. My father helped put these ideas in the context that it was the general belief of white people everywhere. It seemed so ludicrous, I could not understand how such ideas could be believed when they were so blatantly untrue. It made me angry and hurt and I felt the sadness of my father and African people everywhere. One day on the radio news a "Negro" in the US South who had been accused of raping a white woman, was being dragged out of a prison cell with the help of officers. We could hear the man's head hit every stone step on the way to being lynched by the mob. I cried but understood so clearly that the injustices happening to me were so minor compared to what was happening to my people. In some strange way, it served to strengthen rather than weaken me.

After wanting to be white, it became important to be recognised as a girl. Even when I wore a dress I was referred to as "sonny boy". It is true to say that my abuse at the hands of white boys led me to believe that I was not considered a female because white girls did not get threatened or bullied openly the way I was. The fact that I had to fight seemed to further relegate me to being less than feminine. Although there were girls who fought, they usually fought each other until I was older. For me being of African descent outweighed my sexuality amongst my peer group.

Ironically, older men did not feel the same way. By the time I was thirteen, at least thirty white men had exposed themselves to me while I was going to and from school, the library or the shops in the many places that I lived. Mostly they wore big coats. Even though I wanted to be viewed as a girl, this type of act was puzzling. It happened even while walking with my brothers whom I protected always. There was certainly an awareness of my biological makeup. These men never attempted to touch me, some smiled, grinned, or nodded a polite hello and some proceeded to ejaculate. If invited into cars, I would carry on walking or if on a bus or train would move to another seat. I was frightened and afforded no respect outside that of being an object of lust.

I was too ashamed to speak of this to my parents or my white girl friends. It was years later when I found that it happened to other Black women. Rape was also a clear and present danger. One might imagine that I wore very short skirts and was well developed physically. In reality, my clothing was very conservative, I wore dresses or uniforms below my knees and heavy brown or black lace-up shoes, which I hated, and white ankle- or knee-length socks. By the time I was thirteen, I was into ya-ya skirts like my peer group. The question of my femininity in European society was part of the abusive and racist environment that I had to survive in and I saw it as that at the time.

This same hostility existed inside the classroom. When bullied the perpetrator would often escape punishment while I would receive an admonishing about my attitude. In truth I developed an attitude about the unfair treatment that I received. In one secondary girls' school that I attended, a white South African geography teacher continually gave me lower grades than I deserved. In frustration I drew and coloured a beautiful map for a friend who received an A. Although I never received a good grade I had the satisfaction of knowing why. Whenever I was asked to read derogatory statements about Africa and African people I refused and was made to stand in the hallway. I spent considerable time there during her classes and earned a reputation as a trouble-maker. The stories are too numerous, suffice it to say that my experience was mild compared to that of many others even to this day.

When my children attended school, the psychological services had gained a massive foothold in the school system. The focus had moved from the white poor to the Black. Any perceived challenge to the psycho-social racism of teachers became a child's behavioural problem. It was said that I had a chip on my shoulder. In reality, I did not acquiesce to unfairness easily which posed a threat to the "order". This spoke more to their mind-set than mine. Later, these experiences enabled me to have insights into the realities of children of African descent often thought to have innate behavioural problems. Generally, my parents had little to do with my school life and were unaware of some of the problems that I faced. I studied hard at home and was expected to gain As and was punished if I did not.

My father always kept me informed about the politics of white supremacy. When I was sixteen he returned to Ghana and we corresponded regularly. He sent me a newspaper photograph of white mercenary soldiers in Angola with African heads impaled on their bayonets. His influence had a profound effect on me as it enabled me to take away the focus on my individualistic concerns and place my problems in a wider global context which helped me survive school; life even. On my last day of school, I spat on the building and walked away.

My children led me back to the school environment and to my own studies. I had very light-skinned children. People often believed that I was a child carer or nanny to my own children. A concern was the false portrayal of Africa and the invisibility of African world achievements in the school syllabus. Little had changed since my childhood except that there were more of us. Our melanin cannot protect us from the imposed debased, demeaned and demonised ideas about Africa and her people. The dehumanisation of my image and identity naturally affected the development of my children's perceptions. It was critical to counteract the attempt to alienate my children from me. Thus, I became involved with the Supplementary School movement. "Education" would thus become a battleground for truth against lie in the international African-centred and Afrocentric school movement that I would be a part of. Personally, I wanted my daughters and son and other girls and boys to grow up to respect and recognise their relationship to their African ancestors and fight against racism, sexism and all injustices.

Bonnie Greer

Born in Chicago, the eldest of seven children, she has lived since 1986 in the UK, where she is best known for her significant role as a cultural critic. She is a playwright (winner of the Verity Bargate Award), author, critic, broadcaster and Chancellor of Kingston University, London. She was formerly Deputy Chair of the British Museum, and has served on the boards of RADA, the London Film School, and Theatre Royal, Stratford East. Her plays include Munda Negra *(1993), about black women's mental health problems,* Dancing on Blackwater *(1994),* Jitterbug *(2001) and the 2008 musical* Marilyn and Ella, *and have been produced on BBC Radio and in the West End theatre. Her first novel,* Hanging By her Teeth, *was published in 1994, and her other books include the memoirs* Obama Music *(2009) and* A Parallel Life *(2014). She was awarded an OBE in 2010 for services to the Arts.*

Till

I am looking at the papers my late Auntie Ree left me. They have been meticulously bound and sealed.

She left the following instructions:

"Read my notes and then write something in response to these notes. While you read, play Chaka Khan and Miles Davis duetting on 'Human Nature' at Montreux, 1989. Then that 1969 video of Miriam Makeba asking people 'how can your enemy write your history?' Read first. Then write your thing."

And so I will.

Notes on a Work About Vengeance

Short sharp.

The description of Emmett Till and his death and the coffin and how Auntie Ree's mother (Grandmamma) came home determined to kill a white man and how she (Auntie Ree) took up that call herself and hooked up with Jackson Pollock in New York and learned about his work and worked him to the point where he was in that car looking for her but he had two other girls (white girls) in there and then hit the tree.

But he was on his way to her: my Auntie Ree.

Auntie Ree's Notes and Thoughts

"I knew one thing about Jackson Pollock and it is this: I understood what he was doing. And I knew that he wanted to be the receptacle of my vengeance. So I worked in a dime store, even though I could have been a teacher. Even a painter like him because that was in me. But I decided to go to New York City, find him, and use my beauty.

What else do you do when you discover that you are the Angel of Death?

Let me begin with the facts, the roots of my journey of acceptance: Emmett Till, a teenage "Negro" as they called us, was murdered in Mississippi at the age of fourteen, after doing what they called flirting with a white woman. That summer of 1955.

Till—from where I'm from: Chicago—was visiting his relatives when he spoke to twenty-one-year-old Carolyn Bryant, the married proprietor of a small grocery store.

A white woman.

Several nights later, her husband Roy and his half-brother J.W. Milam went to Emmett's great-uncle's house. They took Emmett away to a barn. They beat him up badly, pulled out one of his eyes, then shot him through the head. Then they took his body to the Tallahatchie River, tied a seventy-pound cotton-gin fan around his neck with some barbed wire and threw him in the river.

They found him three days later. They returned his body to Chicago.

His mother, Mamie, wanted a public funeral with an open coffin. So that the world could see his water-bloated and mutilated body.

That picture you'll find wrapped up in black cloth next to my writing is the picture I took of his body.

Child, you could smell that boy's corpse two streets away.

Younger than me, and you know, at that age you don't expect people to die.

Death and that smell. Like somewhere inside you knows what it is even if you've never smelled Death before.

It took me burning down the playground of my old grade-school to get that smell out of my nose.

I didn't mean to kill the junkyard dog who slept in it. I didn't know. I didn't know.

I left my First Holy Communion rosary for him.

In the cinders.

I stared at it there.

The cinders looked like splashes, drips-errors on the floor.

Like Christ all twisted up.

Chaos.

Maybe that was my first connection to Mr Jackson Pollock and his art and way of life.

And the things Jackson told me about that painting called "The Scream".

My dear niece, did you know that the sky in it is red because a volcano erupted: Krakatoa, in Java, thousands of miles away from the painter of that painting? And that volcano was the loudest noise ever heard on earth at the time.

And, too, I've come to see that we coloured, we Negroes, become alive because of what's happened to us. What we have witnessed. And what we will do with the happenings and the witnessing. Especially us women.

Before that, we're just invisible.

After Till, I decided to become visible.

As simple as that.

Simple.

My attempt at Auntie Ree's notes. CHAPTER ONE

1955. Late summer. South Side of Chicago. The Black community—the Ghetto.

The body of murdered African American teen Emmett Till lies at the biggest funeral home in the community. Murdered in Mississippi while visiting relatives because he had spoken to a young white woman. The Klan came for him.

The uproar over his murder is massive and kick-starts the next phase of the Civil Rights Movement.

Musicians sing his praises; preachers preach; etc.

And the queue to see his body stretches for almost a mile in the hot late summer sun and heat.

Sheltered, eighteen-year-old convent school girl, Dido Pygmalion Brown joins the queue, defying her parents who want to keep her sheltered. She can smell the body two streets away. Till's mother had refused to have him embalmed. She wants everyone to see the real thing.

People start dropping out of line because of the stench.

Dido feels strangely empowered.

She moves past an old bluesman serenading the crowd. Later on, he comes to where she works and tells her that she inspired him to make a new composition; he made it the very night of the Till funeral. He called it "The Angel of Death".

"I'm keepin' it till I see you again," he sang to her.

Dido sees the body. It is horrible, and people are fainting and getting sick all around her.

She overhears the story of what happened to Till—how he went to the local penny-store to get some candy; how he made a cheeky remark to the cute white girl who sold liquorice sticks to him; how there was a knock on the door of his grandmother's house at midnight; how masked white men came for him; dragged him to a barn; put his eye out (for not looking down when talking to a white person); beat him to death, and threw his body into the Tallahatchie River. After his grandma found him, Till's single-parent mom insisted that his mutilated and rotting corpse come back to Chicago—and that the whole world sees.

Two days later, the Blues Man comes back to the store Dido works in and serenades her with his "Angel of Death" blues. Suddenly he asks her to come to his apartment. Dido has never done anything like this before, but she accompanies him. It is pristine and also like a voyage behind the Looking Glass: baroque furniture; ancient books and scrolls; a figure of Nefertiti.

She looks out of the window and in the back is what looks like a cemetery. He tells her that all of the women in his family are buried there. He asks her to take off her clothes and stand before him. She does it, even though she has never been naked before anyone, except her mother.

The Blues Man gives her a New York City address. He tells her that she has to go there. She has work to do for Till.

Dido returns to her nice, orderly middle-class home. Her father is a doctor, her mother a society queen.

A few days later, Dido goes to the cotillion for black society girls. It is stifling; unreal; phony. She tries to talk about Till to her stuck-up fellow debutantes, but they'd rather talk about boys, dresses, cars, money, etc. When her name is called to "courtesy to the cake"—a ritual adopted from English Society (the cake represents the Queen)—Dido stands up and tips over the table, knocking the cake, the champagne, all of it over. She walks out into the night.

Dido makes her way to the Blues Man's apartment to tell him that she's leaving, but she sees him carried out on a stretcher. He's dead. The neighbours begin pilfering his apartment.

An Old Woman comes in and fires a pistol in the air. She announces that she used to be in a Wild West show, and before that she had lived in Paris, France. She'd met some women there who had taught her how to shoot. She turns to Dido and tells her to get going. Then the Old Woman turns and shoots as many as she can. In the pandemonium, the police arrive and shoot her dead. Her last words are: "Harriet Tubman said: 'I freed as many slaves as I could. I could have freed more, if they'd known they were slaves.'"

Dido sleeps surprisingly soundly that night, waking occasionally to hear bits of the panic-conference her parents are having about her.

She leaves without them knowing it, taking a small bag. She sweet-talks a white man into letting her get on a train bound for New York City. He talks about his life—its futility, his fears. She listens. He buys her food and drink. The black porter looks at her disapprovingly. Dido tells him in a loud voice that she is not a prostitute. The porter asks her if she knows that Mr Barker, the white man, is a regular and that he has five children and a wife on Long Island. Dido tells him that a white man named Pygmalion freed her mother's ancestors, and that he had come from Long Island.

Dido eats well and drinks well and listens well on that train.

As the train pulls into NYC, the man asks if he can kiss her. She allows him.

Walking through Grand Central, trying to find her way, she notices a small crowd. She goes over and it's the man from the train. He looks at her, smiles and dies. He's had a heart attack. The porter glances at her with a look of wariness and respect.

Dido makes her way to an address in Greenwich Village. It's above a soul food restaurant. She is greeted by the waitresses dressed in frilly pink dresses, serving plates of soul food. There's a juke box blasting away and what looks like a stage behind a huge curtain. She is given a uniform and told to start serving. Dido has never served food in her life, and she messes up, but soon gets the hang of it. All of the customers are Greenwich Village types.

She is introduced to Gency, the Boss.

Gency is in her middle thirties; very beautiful. She has a withered arm that she hides in her sleeve and black eyes like night diamonds. Dido asks Gency what happened to the Blues Man who had directed her to New York.

Gency replies simply that his time was up.

After her shift, Dido is taken to Gency's apartment, where she will be temporarily housed. If she does well, she'll move to the main restaurant located on 125th Street, Harlem.

Gency's apartment is even more elaborate than the blues singer's back in Chicago. When Dido asks where all the furniture, the books came from, Gency replies: "Paris. About 1871."

Dido tells Gency that her name is unusual.

Gency repiles: "It's short: for 'Vengeance'."

Dido is the fried-chicken maker. Her chicken is exquisite, and this surprises her because she is an indifferent cook. She calls her parents who are frantic with worry. They beg her to come home. She listens. She hesitates.

She walks through Central Park against all warnings. It is dangerous; dark; primeval, but she loves it. She returns and rings her parents. She tells them that she has to stay. She has work to do.

One day Gency tells her that she is promoting her to the main restaurant. Dido tells Gency that she did not come to New York City to cook.

Gency tells her that this is exactly why she came, and that she cannot turn back. She has walked through the Park and must now go over to the River.

Dido does as she's told and takes a walk to the East River. For a moment, she thinks that she might throw herself in. But she sees the body of Emmett Till.

Floating along.

Till.

Jane Ulysses Grell

A teacher, poet and storyteller in the African-Caribbean oral tradition, she was born and grew up on the Eastern Caribbean island of Dominica. She has worked extensively with audiences of all ages and cultures, and was teacher-secondee to BBC School Radio, advising on its multicultural content, as well as writing and presenting. She is a regular contributor as writer and reviewer to scholastic publications, and has had work included in several poetry and prose anthologies. Her books include, for children: A New Life in Britain *(Macdonald Educational),* Dr Knickerbocker and other Poems *(Hawthorn Press),* Mosquito Bounce *(Papillote Press); and for adults,* Praise Songs *and* White River Blues *(both published by Papillote Press).*

Whatever Happened to Michael?

From his balcony on the seventeenth floor of a London tower block
an old black man sits flying paper planes.
He launches them with great dexterity
then through thick binoculars he follows their descent
and smiles with satisfaction as they zigzag crazily to the ground.

From the top of his mountain on Montserrat
Lord Vulcan too amuses himself
sitting on his haunches in a state of undress
leaning forward to perform such an unmannerly display
of belching, throat clearing and spitting
that the devil himself would cringe.

I knew a man named Michael once, who had but one ambition
to build a "back home" island dream house of his own
high up on a hill, with the sea as his front lawn
wild woods as his back yard and mountain ranges for a fence
and he did.

With his lifetime's savings and his own two hands
he built this house
now nothing but a faint memory, blurred by billowing black smoke
the sulphuric smell of red hot ash and the acrid taste of volcanic soot.

Now as I watch this frail Elder while away his days
from the confines of this concrete height, I remember Michael
and cannot help but wonder…whatever's become of him?

Queen of the Ocean Rose

Her retirement home is the Ocean Rose, perched on the crest of a smug plateau;
a pink and white pearl, gleaming in the white-hot sun.
It's early morning as she steps out unto her verandah, warm tiles under bare feet
waves of well-being tingling up her spine.
Two slender palms guarding the front lawn swish their heads in greeting
while gaudy crotons dance their splendour.
From the mango tree within her reach, a gentle rustling of leaves,
exuberant bird song and…a seductive scent.
With tentative fingers she lifts and parts the dark green leaves
to discover…oh joy!—a blushing, fully ripened fruit.
And right there in her night dress, in full view of a winking sea and approving
     mountains
she sits on the stone steps; sits her down to breakfast
not on bacon and eggs nor milk and cornflakes
but on her first mango of the season.
She savours the pulpy treat, as sticky yellow juice runs down her chin
she sucks slowly, a carefree, country girl again
and unbelievably,
—Queen of the Ocean Rose.

Rashidah Ismaili

Born in Cotonou, Benin, she married at 16 and moved to the US with her husband. She studied music, then went on to obtain an MA in social psychology. After separating from her husband she worked to support herself and her son while doing graduate studies, earning a PhD in psychology. A poet, fiction writer and playwright, she participated in the Black Arts Movement in New York in the 1960s and was a member of the Umbra collective of young black writers. Her poetry collections include Cantata for Jimmy *(2004) and* Missing in Action and Presumed Dead *(1992). Her* Autobiography of the Lower East Side: A novel in stories *was published in 2014. She has taught at Wilkes University and Rutgers University and has served as the associate director of the Pratt Institute Higher Education Opportunity Program and as vice president of Pen & Brush, an arts organisation for women. She lives in New York City.*

Dancing at Midnight

She waited in the hushed night silence of her house. An obstacle at her door lest someone sneak in while she dozed. Satou was sleepy and there were long periods of time when she lost consciousness. But, when she remembered the tears and cries of her friend, shivers went up and down her spine. This should not have been, because all the students at her new school envied her. She had travelled to Paris and New York with her family. She had actually lived in America and seen Him—M.J.—Michael Jackson, on stage!

She had posters of Him and His Sister. Janet was all over her room. She'd seen lots of great stars in New York. But her little circle of friends here only cared about Michael, Janet and maybe Latoya. In fact, last week, at her friend's coming out party, she was so moved by her tears and the pathetic way she walked and sat stiff in her seat of honour, that Satou threw her favourite (well almost) poster of Him in the heap of gifts.

The eyes of her friend were filled with incredible pain. A deep sadness seemed to haunt her and an aura of dejection hung about her. Later, Satou was allowed to see her in the company of her friend's aunt. They had developed a secret language so they were able to set up a secret meeting. After much cunning and with great courage, Satou crept up to the window of Oumou's room. Her head slowly rose to get a better view. Safe, no one inside with her.

Satou rapped on the window three times and then slowly lifted it. She raised it enough to slide over the ledge and into the small bedroom. Oumou lay listless and sad on the bed. All around her were cards and other gifts celebrating her fourteenth birthday. She took no interest in them. There was a huge basket of bon-bons from a very prestigious store in France. Satou knew it well because she used to take the metro there from her father's flat for special treats. At the moment they offered little comfort to Oumou. In fact, all these displays of congratulations and so on only made the moment more tragic.

Satou sat quietly on the bed. She took Oumou's hand in hers and watched the huge tears fall down her lovely dark cheeks. Satou had always envied her dark copper skin and "Fulani" braids. Now her hair was done up in a ceremonial way, showing she'd "had her bath". They spoke slowly, quietly. Satou knew she could only stay a short while because someone might come in and there would be a tremendous price to pay for breaking the taboo. She, an unclean girl visiting a newly bathed girl.

Back in her own room, Satou was racked with uncontrollable shivers because she was actually a year and a half older than Oumou. Like her friend, she too had lived almost all her life outside of Home. Coming back when her father had his annual leaves, returning had always been something she looked forward to. She and her mother shopped for months in preparation for the gift giving that was ritualistic, mandatory. All her relatives would come to see them. Children in the yard, grown-ups in the parlour. The veranda would be overflowing with shoes. But now, a hard rock of dread sat in the bottom of her stomach, immobilizing her.

Oumou had tried to describe her ordeal. The shock of a knife and then the space between it and pain. But each time she got the words to unroll themselves, the spool around which they were threaded fell off. Got lost and rolled around, caught up in small bits and pieces of details that seemed at the moment, irrelevant.

Oumou's parents had agreed not to have her bathed. For almost four years they'd not been back. Oumou's aunt and sister to her mother's mother, had argued that it was required. There had been a great fight. Her parents, she thought, had won. Then on a day when her parents went to Ouagadougou for a conference, her cousin came to take her to spend the three days with her. At first Oumou was happy to get away from her aunt because she was afraid of her.

They travelled by car to the house. It had been a long time since she'd been up-country. The air was moist and signalled the rainy season. When they arrived, her cousin's mother came out to greet her. There were several other girls around her age there as well. Shortly after she'd fallen asleep that night, someone came into the room where she and her cousin slept. It was dark so she couldn't see the face clearly. The face said simply, "It is time."

That was it. All that was said. Oumou's cousin got up quietly but she cried out. Fought the hands pulling her. She was held tightly and marched out back to the yard. There the other girls were huddled together. Cloths wrapped around them. Teeth chattering in the night-chilled air. Then slowly as she heard the singing, she understood. They were all going to the river to be bathed.

Oumou really couldn't say more because she was still in shock. But when she was returned to her aunt's house the night before her parents got back, her elder aunt came to sit with her. She sat reciting the Holy Words. She told her she, Oumou was a good clean woman. Most of all she, her aunt had done her duty to their clan and her God. That the house of S— would not be disgraced by having an unclean girl entering womanhood. Then she recited the names of all the women of her line. Oumou said her aunt took off her amber and silver necklace and put it around her neck. Kissed her on both cheeks and called her sister. Her aunt promised she, herself would keep her clean and all would be well. When she was married into a fine family, her parents would thank her.

Well, that is not what happened. Her father called the police and they went to her cousin's house to arrest her, his wife's aunt, and the driver of the car. After much negotiating, the charges were dropped. Oumou's parents booked a flight on the next plane back to Paris. Oumou said she would never come back to Africa again. Never! She tried to cry but for now her body was heaving without tears. Her water had dried.

Satou had promised to try to sneak back if she could to see her. Leaving, as she came, by the window, she had raced back to her house. It was the fear of a similar thing happening that made her say she'd never go up-country with anyone other than her parents. But then she had no cousins up-country. However, she did have an elderly aunt who wanted her cleansed. Satou's parents were friends with Oumou's and knew they were afraid as well. Satou's mother stayed very close to her.

Satou could only sit and feel the anger rise up in her. Anger and fear had come to spoil her vacation. That her friend Oumou was hurting and she could not help her made her sadder. Lost in her thoughts of Oumou's red-raw stitches and the oozing mess that was once her vagina etched indelibly in her mind she suddenly felt the presence of someone standing in the doorway. "Come, Missy, it's time." Oh, God! Satou panicked, jumped to her feet. "No!" Her scream pierced the house. Her mother came running. Soon she was wrapped in her mother's arms, safe.

Satou's mother continued to rock her. The bewildered servant stood by quietly. She asked them again to the table. "Madame, Missy, it is time. Supper is on the table." She turned and left the room. Silence followed her.

At dinner the conversation was light. Then just as she began to relax, there was a knock on the door. Satou froze. Her father went to answer. She held her mother's eyes. Her mother smiled but her back was straight and eyes alert. Then her mother's shoulders softened. Her father's laughter eased the tension that gripped them. When he came back his belly laugh entered the room first. He and his cousin, who was his best friend, came back in holding hands. Oh, she had forgotten this. In Europe and New York, one never saw men holding hands. Only if they were lovers, and then the men were timid.

"Good evening, my little wife." He always called her that. Satou loved it. His wife was her favourite aunt. Although he is her father's cousin, in the African tradition they are brothers. That is how it is here. Her father calls him cousin/brother. So he is her uncle and his wife is her aunt.

"Good evening, Uncle," Satou answered and held her cheek for his kiss. He smelled nice and his shirt made crick-crick sounds as he bent over her. Uncle sat and joined them for coffee and a dish of fruit. It was nice to listen to her parents and uncle as they talked and ate. Satou watched their faces and thought of funny words to add to the end of each sentence. She made one so funny she almost laughed out loud.

"So, Satou." Uncle turned to her. "How does that sound to you?"

She was so involved in her game she hadn't heard him speak. "What, Uncle?"

He smiled. "A party. We're going to have a party at our house." Her first thought was to say "great". But then, when she thought about Oumou in bed, she felt sad and guilty. Somehow the prospect of fun seemed out of place.

Uncle must have read her thoughts. He took her hands. "I know how you feel but it is for her, Oumou. We are going to dance her all night. Dance all her pain and sadness away." That sounded great. "I would like that very much. But, will Oumou be able to move?" "Well that does not matter so much. We will dance all around her. We shall dance her."

Later that night she lay awake remembering Oumou's face. Satou thought of the aunt and how and she cried when Oumou's mother abused her. The aunt said it was her duty to their tradition. She said she'd carried out the law their customs demanded. She said she had fulfilled her obligation to her God and her people. The aunt had no idea of the laws other than clan. She never realized how close she came to being imprisoned for what she'd done. Ahh Africa, as Mama says, Satou sighed.

In spite of the party and all the attempts to make them happy, she knew that she'd never forget the look on Oumou's face. When she said she'd never come back to Africa, Satou heard the pain and sadness. She prayed that at the party, when they danced her, Oumou would smile again. That she, Satou, would help her smile again. *Oh*, she thought lying back, hearing the night noises and breathing the scented cool air, *I love dancing.*

Margo Jefferson

Born and raised in Chicago, Illinois, she is a Pulitzer Prize-winning cultural critic, journalist and essayist. Her essays have appeared in many journals and anthologies, including the New York Times Book Review, New York Magazine, *the* Washington Post, O, Oprah Magazine, Vogue, The Believer, Guernica, The Best American Essays of 2015, The Inevitable: Contemporary Writers Confront Death, Best African-American Essays 2010, The Mrs. Dalloway Reader, *and* The Jazz Cadence of American Culture. *Her first book was* On Michael Jackson *(2006) and she is also the author of the memoir* Negroland *(2015), which won the National Book Critics Circle Award for Nonfiction, The Bridge Prize, The Heartland Prize, and was shortlisted for the Baillie Gifford Prize. She lives in New York and teaches in the Writing Program at Columbia University.*

My Monster

Supple, wily monster of mine.

You wait for one of those mornings when I wake up thinking ill of myself in a fretful, petty way. I've been in too many discussions about the pros and cons of Botox and facelifts. A young woman at the gym told me how terrific I looked, then added *I wouldn't think you were more than—* and threw out a number higher than I would have wished.

I go to the kitchen. I can't find the mug I want. I go to the bathroom. The container that holds my sterilized cotton balls is stuck. I'm furious: what did Carmen do, when she came to clean yesterday—did she break the mug and not tell me? How did she close the container so tightly I may have to take a screwdriver to it? And I'm seized by a thought:

If I were a white slave mistress this is the moment I'd call her into my presence, rail, slap her, throw an object—maybe the container—at her and warn her she'd be whipped if it happened again.

Maybe if I were a high-handed white woman in New York City, I'd chastise her sharply the next time she came here. If I were angry enough, maybe I'd fire her.

Maybe if I were a high-handed woman of color—black, brown or beige—I would do the same thing. And decide to hire a white cleaning woman so I could feel less guilty about my tone.

I get the container open with no screwdriver and no damage to my nails. It had probably tightened when Carmen polished it. I find the mug, which I'd left in the dishwasher, on the shelf where it belongs, with the other mugs.

If I'd called Carmen and spoken sharply to her, would I apologize now? On the phone or in person? If I apologized, would she stay on? I know she needs the work. So how would we proceed? Would we perform our old cordialities or adapt slightly—she more distant or more anxiously obliging, I more distant or more strenuously *gracious*.

Monster says, we're done with that. Let's move on. Today you're going to feel blocked and impeded, a coward in work and love; resenting duty; suspecting pleasure. It's time to blame your parents, and to do so properly you must be artful and nuanced. You must be literary.

You send me to a quote from the wise and balanced Willa Cather.

"Always in every family there is this double life…secret and passionate and intense… Always in her mind, each member is escaping, running away, trying to break the net which circumstance and her own affections have woven around her…"

I try my own more lethal variations.

"Daddy dearest I hate you, I'm through." Allusions to Sylvia Plath are overused, says Monster.

"My dead mother gets between me and life." Romaine Brooks, says Monster. Not bad, but too general.

My parents enthralled me. My mother's ubiquitous charm, my father's artful dignity —they enthralled me.

Monster says: Your mother didn't love you enough to want you less than perfect.

Monster says: You father didn't love you enough to prefer your company to his depression.

Monster says: You've worked hard, you've left your mark. Maybe it's time to die. You're past the prime you wasted so much of. Why don't you join your parents? Imagine their faces as you walk towards them. They'll cry out oh Margo, we're so happy to see you.

Then I realize that if any of this were possible—this Sunday School fantasy of an afterlife— they would be furious. My mother would cry: How dare you waste your talents and achievements like this? All our work. My father would look at me in silence, unutterably disappointed by this failure of honor and character. And they would join arms, turn their backs and walk slowly away. Holding their heads high.

Barbara Jenkins

Born in Trinidad, where she still lives, she began writing in 2008 and her debut publication, Sic Transit Wagon and Other Stories *(2013), was awarded the Guyana Prize for Literature. Her stories have won the Commonwealth Short Story Prize Caribbean Region in 2010 and 2011; the* Wasafiri *New Writing Prize; the Canute Brodhurst Prize for short fiction, the Caribbean Writer; the Small Axe short story competition, 2011; and the Romance Category, My African Diaspora Short Story Contest. In 2013 she was named winner of the inaugural Hollick Arvon Caribbean Writers Prize. Her first novel,* De Rightest Place, *was published in 2018.*

A Perfect Stranger

We were not always like this. I mean us, we two. Like this—this one, past the best-before age of three-score and ten; and the other, crystallised dust in a jar, lying in a teak box on the dressing table.

Close your eyes to the sagging skin, the drooping frame, the sparse, man-cut, greying hair and see beneath the girl of twenty-one that you first laid eyes on one Easter weekend, half a century ago, in a granite building atop the hill of a mid-Wales seaside town. And I will see you too, risen from under your blanket of crisp rose petals, faded photographs, curling, grief-filled cards, the yellowing, passionate, desperate notes, written too late.

The first time I saw your face, the world I knew before fell away. I closed my eyes to capture your image, to hold it behind my eyelids, to gaze at it inside my head. I never wanted to lose sight of you ever again.

You remember where we were that day? It was at the men's hall of residence, where, over the four-week Easter break, third-year students, like you, putting in the extra slog before finals, stayed locked into their little cliques of focused swots, away from the aimless overseas students, like me, with nowhere to go in their vacation time, with little to do but drift around the only welcoming space, an open hall of residence, to carry on moaning in an unending circuit of longing about back home in Uganda, back home in Nepal, back home in Trinidad.

Back home in Trinidad was the conversation between the two men and me as we limed in the room of the one who was in his final year—he was later to marry a Welsh girl and stay on; the other was a second-year student, bound for a life of success as a diplomat. When the good-natured teasing about how awkwardly I was coping with the strangeness around me took on what I felt was a somewhat more judgemental tone, I flung a pillow at one; he retaliated, I flung it back, harder this time, and it quickly became a pillow fight which I was losing. I left the room with a hurt head and even more hurt feelings.

You know something? Many years later, when you were long gone, I was with our son at a post office in Port of Spain and who should come in but the by then retired diplomat who, when introductions were made, said to my son, "If it wasn't for me, you wouldn't be here." At which our son gave me a surprised "what have you been keeping from me" look and the diplomat, seeing his expression, laughed and said, "Don't worry, you're the image of your father. What I meant was, your mother, a friend and I had a fight when we were students and, after she ran away from us, your mother met your father."

I stumbled to the bathroom—communal baths and showers—closed the door to a bath cubicle, sat on the edge of a bathtub and cried. At first the tears were about the fight, about the unfairness—two ganged up against one—then about being away from anyone who belonged to me—no letter from home for a few weeks, then about the disappointment of no daffodils fluttering and dancing beside Windermere where I had just been on a fortnight's geology field trip, and about not being able to go up Scafell with the climbers, and that disappointment merged into feeling wretched about my lack of foresight in failing to book a room for when I returned—it was the Easter weekend and the office of the only hall available was closed for business, so there I was, the unofficial and clandestine guest of those two fellow-Trinidadians with whom I had been stupid enough to pick a fight. Not genteel tears rolling silently along damp cheeks, I was sobbing uninhibitedly—loud and hard, full of rage and self-pity.

"Are you all right?" A man's voice came over the partition wall from the adjoining cubicle.

I hadn't stopped to think about whether I was alone. I caught my breath and strangled a sob before it could come out of my throat. I didn't dare say a thing. There was a silence, too, from the neighbouring cubicle, but I could feel a listening presence. I feared even to breathe, lest my breath made a snuffle that could be heard.

"Are you all right?" Softer now, some uncertainty had edged into it.

I was still silent. I wished the owner of the voice would think he had been mistaken. That he had imagined hearing someone crying. I couldn't leave, I had nowhere to go. I couldn't go back to my friends. I had no room of my own. In the two cubicles, there was a listening silence that lasted many minutes. Then I heard a swishing and splashing noise, bathwater sloshing against the sides of the bath, followed by a loud whoosh and the noise of water falling from a height. I could work out that the person had stood up in the bath and the noise was the water falling off him. The plug was pulled, water gurgled away. Listening hard I picked up noises like a body being rubbed dry and the slap of slippers on the tiled floor. I heard the click of a bolt being pulled and felt relief; I was certain that my neighbour would just mind his own business and go away. The rap at my cubicle door was soft, but I was startled and didn't answer.

"You're not going to do anything you will regret, are you?"

Such worry was in the voice that I had to say something.

"No. I'm not."

"Would you like to talk?"

When I opened the door, did I stare at you? You didn't stare at me even though my face was red, eyes red, nose runny, cheeks wet. But could you sense what I was thinking? I think now that you sensed even then that I could love you, a perfect stranger for ever, for you came into the cubicle, closed the door and sat next to me on the edge of the bath. You leaned back, turned on the tap and wet a corner of the towel that you slipped from over your shoulder. You wiped my face with the damp corner and dried it. You sat next to me and asked me nothing. We sat in a long silence. I breathed in a new fragrance from your skin—sandalwood soap, I learned later. I looked down at my hands folded in my lap, at your hands also folded in your lap—long slim fingers, dark hair springing from the backs of your wrists. I looked at your feet, slim and pale in soft, beige felt-looking slippers and at mine, bare and brown, stirrup straps of the chocolate-coloured stretch pants hooked under the insteps. The way you were gave off a sense of security, of completeness, of knowing how to do things the right way, of understanding your world, the one into which I had stumbled, blindfold, picking my way around in error and confusion. I was embarrassed that I had made a fool of myself and had to be rescued. I didn't dare look at you for shame. After a while, you took my hand and said, "Whatever it is, it's not that bad." You were wearing your fawn dressing gown—it served you well for at least a decade more—and from a pocket you took out a black and gold tin of cigarettes. You shook out two. You lit both and passed me one. We sat and smoked. The sweet molasses-flavoured Balkan Sobranie calmed and relaxed me. You crushed the glowing gold tips in the lid of the tin, put the blackened stubs in your pocket and closed the tin. You looked into my eyes. I looked into yours for the first time. Green, flecked with gold.

"Are you going to be all right now?"

"Yes."

NomaVenda Mathiane

A South African writer, she has had a long career as a journalist. She covered the June 1976 Soweto student uprising for The World *newspaper, a white-owned but black-run publication dealing in township events and some national politics. When, in 1977, 19 black organisations including* The World *were banned, she briefly worked for the* Rand Daily Mail *as a freelancer and later joined* The Star. *In 1984 she joined* Frontline *magazine, part of the alternative press, and brought to the publication a Black perspective, writing a column called "Asiwona amaphixiphixi" that dealt mainly with day-to-day township activities at a time when the political situation was volatile. Some of her work was published in the US as* South Africa: Diary of Troubled Times *(1989), and a similar collection,* Beyond the Headlines: Truths of Soweto Life *(1990) was published in South Africa. Her book* Eyes in the Night: An Untold Zulu Story *was published in 2016. She is now retired and writing fiction.*

Passing on the Baton

In January 1879, the British army attacked the AmaZulu people on the slopes of the Isandlwana mountains in Natal, north of Zululand. A young mother accompanied by her two daughters aged ten and three fled their home and hid in the mountains for the duration of the war, which lasted about eight months. When they came out of hiding at the end of the war, their home and land had been usurped by the invaders and her husband had died. For months, the woman and her children wandered aimlessly in the valleys and gorges of Zululand, searching for kith and kin, eking a living from roots and rats, braving the harsh environment, the scorching Natal sun and the torrential Benguela rainstorms. They slept in treetops during the day, hiding from wild animals, and journeying at night time.

A miraculous encounter with another clan led to their ultimate reunion with members of their family. However, the coming-together would be short-lived, as culture and tradition stepped in to alienate the young woman and her daughters from the family and render them unwelcome in the fold. Once more, mother and daughters would be homeless, up until she relented and agreed to a marriage of convenience with a farm labourer who worked and lived on a farm owned by a cruel Hollander.

At this point, the ten-year-old was now a well-developed girl; the farmer, who was master of all that inhabited his grounds, thought he had the right to the ripe young woman. But she would have none of it, and literally fought off the advances of the farmer, physically hurting him. She was forced to abscond from the farm, leaving her mother and sister behind, never to see them again.

However, in her quest for freedom and belonging, somehow, the universe and her ancestors led her to a wonderful woman living in a village in Dundee, in Zululand. The woman took my grandmother in, loved her and treated her like her daughter.

Later, Grandma was betrothed to a Christian gentleman and sired nine healthy children—five boys and four girls—one of whom was my mother.

Like my grandmother, Mother also married a Christian gentleman and they too were blessed with nine children. Our mother, who was deeply rooted in African values of respect for human beings and anything that walks on the earth, sang us songs that told the stories of the brave AmaZulu kings and warriors. She taught us the importance of love for family, close and distant. She believed that the most important words in life were "Hello" and "Thank you", and that holding grudges against those who had wronged you was a useless emotion. She taught us to appreciate the beauty of languages, particularly IsiZulu, through which she was able to communicate our culture and traditions, while telling us about the power of prayer. She prayed every night and mentioned each and every one of us. Later when we had children of our own, their names were added to her list of people to pray for.

When Mother died, the first thing that came to my mind was the realisation that her passing on meant that the glue that had held the family together was gone. I also realised that there would be nobody to pray for me and my children. But more than that, I was made aware of the fact that the hour had come when my generation had to take on the mantle of being the shepherd of the fold.

The reality of what lay ahead brought about an inexplicable panic to me. Where would I begin? So much had happened in my country. Our lives had changed in ways that even we could not understand.

While all sorts of questions went through my mind, I was suddenly transported to the year 1990, a time in my life when as a journalist I had been part of a group of writers who had travelled to El Salvador in South America at the height of the war, to witness the elections in that country.

One morning, as we drove to a polling-station, we were ambushed by the rebels and taken to their headquarters in the bush. As we sat, black and white journalists, veterans and young writers, waiting to be interrogated by the rebel leader, I thought I would not come out of that place alive. At that significant moment when my mind was in torment about the situation I was in, my gaze fell on the ground. I scooped a handful of sand and toyed with it. The soil looked and felt different from what I was used to. Even though we were kept in the most verdant part of the country, surrounded by trees, big and small, that soil looked different. It appeared to be grey and dry. It was not dark and damp like the soil back home. Maybe, that was only in my head. I let the sand run through my fingers and thought: "So this is the soil that will cover my remains!" I could feel my heart beating loud and fast, yet my fear was not of death. As a journalist practising in South Africa, death was part of the package. My fear was of the aftermath of death—how would my soul travel back to Africa? What kind of ancestor would I be, interred in a grave so far away from home?

Coming out of my reverie of El Salvador to the realisation that I was now responsible for imparting values to my offspring and the many youngsters I would meet in the course of my journey through life was daunting. South Africa today was different from yesterday when we knew what we were striving for. The bond that held us together as Africans seemed to have snapped as we grappled with the here-and-now and tried to make sense of the new world.

Yet I had to steer the ship of the family in murky waters. The sea was rough and I was without a compass. How was I to navigate the waters when the language we had used for generations was becoming obsolete? Overnight, young people had become strangers whose values we could not fathom; we simply could not get through to them. They were in another world—the world of technology. And in between, they were chasing after their Eldorado and plastic dreams.

It took me some time to realise that I was not alone in this dilemma, that many of my peers, who like me, are proud of their children and their grandchildren, were also concerned about their offspring, who seem not to care to bask in the sunshine of our love. Our grandchildren are up and about, texting on their mobiles even at the dinner table. As for the girls, they have denied us the pleasure of passing over to them our skill of knitting cornrows in their hair. We have to contend with the long artificial hair they wear. When travelling in their cars, one must persevere, and risk a heart attack, as one listens to the incomprehensible recitals of weird so-called poetry that they regard as music coming out of the stereo. I am not expecting them to play Handel's *Messiah* or the Mormon Tabernacle Choir, Barry White, Miles Davis, Miriam Makeba or Hugh Masekela; I know that is yesterday's music to them. But, for crying out loud! Is there no artist in this world who can save our grandchildren from the death of the art of good music?

As if that is not enough, what happened to a good family get-together, where a tasty and sumptuous home-cooked meal would be served and we would reminisce about the good old days? Restaurants don't quite cut it. The worst moments are when there is to be a family wedding. Gone is the fanfare of aunts and uncles getting together to prepare for the great day of the uniting of two families. Old ladies are no longer given the opportunity to impart advice to the bride-to-be on how to be a good wife. Old people have to take a back seat and listen to the wedding planners' directives. Oh, cry the beloved country!

However, in spite of everything, I am determined not to give up. I will continue to try to impart the values that my grandmother, mother and the many others before them instilled in us. We must teach the young to know that one has to make time for old people, to be gentle with children, to love animals, and above all, to respect the ground they walk on.

Somehow, I have to find a way of getting through to them, to tell them of the trials and triumphs of my grandmother. I have to tell them of the great African kings who fought hard to save their kingdoms. I will tell them of how the British abducted Cetshwayo, the Zulu king and took him to England to parade him before their Queen Victoria, because Cetshwayo's spear-wielding regiments had lynched the gun-toting British army at Isandlwana. I have to tell them about Robben Island, about Nelson Mandela, Robert Sobukwe and the many men who languished on that island

and suffered because of their quest for freedom. I have to tell them about the great African women who kept the homefires burning while their men were jailed and killed. Women such as Albertina Sisulu, whose husband Walter was with Mandela on the island and whose son Max and daughter Lindiwe were somewhere in exile. Two sons remained behind with her: Lungi, and Zwelakhe who was banned along with their mother. I will tell them of a woman in Mzimhlophe township who lost three sons on the one night when hostel inmates clashed with township residents.

And, more than that, I have to devise a means to make them realise that soon they will have to take on the baton and lead the family and the country forward. I owe it to them.

Broadacres, Johannesburg.

Elizabeth Nunez

Originally from Trinidad, she migrated to the US after high school. Her memoir Not for Everyday Use *won the 2015 Hurston-Wright Legacy Award and her 2016 novel* Even in Paradise, *a contemporary take on Shakespeare's* King Lear *set in the Caribbean, was called "A dazzling epic triumph" in* Kirkus. *Her other novels are* Boundaries *(NAACP Image Award nominee);* Anna In-Between *(PEN Oakland Award and longlisted for IMPAC International Dublin Literary Award);* Prospero's Daughter *(2010 Trinidad & Tobago One Book selection);* Bruised Hibiscus *(American Book Award);* Beyond the Limbo Silence *(Independent Publishers Book Award);* Grace; Discretion *(shortlisted for Hurston/Wright Legacy Award); and* When Rocks Dance. *She co-edited* Blue Latitudes: Caribbean Women Writers at Home and Abroad, *co-founded the National Black Writers Conference, and was executive producer of the Emmy-nominated CUNY-TV series* Black Writers in America. *She is a Distinguished Professor at Hunter College, CUNY, teaching Caribbean Women Writers and Creative Writing.*

Discovering My Mother
From *Not for Everyday Use*

Quite accidentally I discovered that my mother read books. I didn't think she did. I thought her only interests were domestic, all related to her children, her home, and her social circles. It turned out, however, that she had read my first novel, *When Rocks Dance*. I hadn't expected her to. Years ago, I had left the novel for my father. He never read it. As far as I know, he never read a single one of my eight books. When I found out my mother had read *When Rocks Dance*, I gave her my next two novels,

Beyond the Limbo Silence and *Bruised Hibiscus*. She read them too and was full of praise for me. I was her favorite author, she said.

As the past and the present became more and more indistinguishable to my father, my mother continued to blossom. Soon I was sending her the manuscripts of novels I was working on. She became my most enthusiastic fan, offering me observations that ultimately found their way into my final drafts.

My older sister Yolande was not surprised when I told her that our mother read my novels. "Mummy used to be a voracious reader," she said. She told me that Mummy would have her running back and forth to the library to get books for her. Within days after she borrowed one book for her, my mother would want another. "Eventually, I'd bring her stacks of books," Yolande told me.

How had I missed this? How had I never seen my mother reading a book? What had happened? Had I simply taken for granted that men were intellectually superior to women and so it would not be surprising that my mother's interests did not extend beyond the domestic affairs of her home and the activities of her circle of friends? And yet I had ambitions for myself. I wanted to be more than a mother and a wife; I wanted to be a writer. I had read Virginia Woolf. I wanted a room of my own and the means to be independent.

The women's movement had not yet reached our shores when I was young, before I left for college in America, but I had a grandmother who entertained artists and intellectuals in her home. She was good friends with Beryl McBurnie, who would later be awarded the Order of the British Empire (the OBE) for the playhouse she founded, the Little Carib Theatre, which survives today as a showcase for local playwrights, actors, visual artists, dancers, and musicians.

I must have been ten years old when I first met Ms McBurnie. She strode into my grandmother's drawing room wearing a shockingly bright multicolored cotton dress, shocking because I was accustomed to seeing women of Ms McBurnie's social class in the more muted colors of the English dresses we imitated. But splashed across Ms McBurnie's dress were the vivid colors of our tropical flora and fauna: reds, oranges, yellows, greens, purples, blues. Soon Ms McBurnie began expostulating on the bold plans she had to form her own dance group and theater company. She was tired of all those English jigs and Scottish reels she had been taught at school, she declared. She wanted us to sing and play our own music and perform our own dances; she wanted to validate what she heard in the country from the people who were largely untouched by the British influence: the Africans, Caribs, French, Spaniards, Portuguese, many of them speaking a sort of patois, African words and rhythms laced with English. She talked about one of her concerts where her dancers performed a market scene shouting out the names of our local fruit: sapodilla, mango, pommerac, pomme cythère, chenet.

At nine years old my reading had been largely confined to the books of the English writer Enid Blyton. I was consumed with the adventures of English boys and girls my age who picnicked on beaches without coconut trees, eating cucumber sandwiches and all sorts of exotic fruit—apples, peaches, pears, grapes—as they solved mysteries that eluded adult detectives. I used to do my best to emulate them, but try as I might, I never seemed able to develop a taste for cucumber sandwiches and always found the beaches where I had my picnics too hot to wear a cardigan. After I heard Ms McBurnie, my imagination expanded. Cucumber sandwiches, apples, peaches, pears, and grapes didn't seem so special anymore, and I found myself being given permission to dream up picnics at the beach with pelau, coconut water, tamarind balls, pomme cythère, and mangoes.

I knew about other women, my aunts' contemporaries, who were challenging the roles traditionally assigned to females. Audrey Layne Jeffers, another of my grandmother's friends, founded the Coterie of Social Workers, and together with other women, established homes for the elderly, for the blind, for "women in distress", and nurseries for babies. Leonora Pujadas McShine—Leo, as she was familiarly known—organized the first League of Women Voters in Trinidad. My aunt Pearl, while still in her thirties, founded the Negro Theatre Workshop in London and was an agent there for artists of color.

So my ignorance of my mother's interest in books cannot be blamed on prejudices I inherited about the inferiority of women. Perhaps I was so brainwashed by the myth of Nunez intellectual superiority that I chose to be blind to much of what my mother did and said.

My mother told me the story about the first time she felt belittled by my father. I was in my fifties when she told me this, old enough to know better, and yet I was alarmed that my father would have dared to give voice to suspicions I had harbored, when I was a child, about her limited intellectual capacities.

It was true, my mother said: she had not been a reader. In fact, before she was married, she had never read a book from cover to cover. Then, one day, as she was talking idly about some social event that had taken place, my father snapped at her: "For God's sake, Una, is that all you can talk about? Educate yourself! Broaden your interests. At least read the newspaper!"

The irony, though, was that the newspaper was the most my father ever read, with one exception. He got a kick out of the novels of P.G. Wodehouse. After a day at work having to endure the arrogance of his British colonial bosses, little gave him as much pleasure as laughing at the buffoonish Bertie Wooster. But he never progressed beyond Wodehouse, or the newspapers (the cartoons were his favorite). My mother, on the other hand, took his admonishment to heart. When I discovered she had read my first novel, I gave her not only my other novels, but also novels by my favorite authors, novels that before my father began to withdraw from the world I could not imagine she was capable of appreciating or understanding. Within weeks she devoured Jane Austen's *Pride and Prejudice*, Gabriel García Márquez's *Love in the Time of Cholera*, V.S. Naipaul's *A House for Mr. Biswas*. (I would not count Naipaul among my favorite authors, but *A House for Mr. Biswas* is as close to a masterpiece as a novel can get.) She read Naipaul's *A Way in the World* too, a novel I found difficult to digest, but she was intrigued by it and had lots of questions for me.

I dared to introduce her to my love of opera. I took her to see *Master Class* on Broadway, that backhanded homage to Maria Callas. Callas is at the end of her operatic career. She has lost her voice, her lover has abandoned her, and now she teaches opera hopefuls at Juilliard. She is angry, her voice shrill and strident, her young students cowering under her criticism of their slightest mistakes, and yet in the background we hear that miraculous voice that awed the world and made millions worship her.

My mother sat forward in her seat, her eyes glued to the stage. Was it the savagery of time marching indiscriminately onward, reducing us to shadows of our former selves, that had moved her, or regret for the person she could have been had her life not been circumscribed by eleven needy children and fourteen pregnancies? She wanted me to play arias by Callas when we got home, and as Callas's voice swelled throughout my house—"Casta Diva," "La Mamma Morta," my favorites—my mother and I bonded in a way we never had when I was young and living in her home. She returned to New York for the Christmas holidays, and I had no trouble persuading her to come along with me to Carnegie Hall to hear Handel's *Messiah*, though I warned her it was hours long. She sat transfixed through the entire program while my father, who comes from a musical family and played the violin as a boy, paced the corridors long after the first intermission had ended.

I want to think my father recognized this change in his wife and that their conversations had deepened beyond the mundane as they grew older together. If this was true, my mother, too, must have missed our father's searing intelligence that had made our world less chaotic, more ordered, safe. How frightened she must have been when he swirled butter in his tea, or when he insisted on going alone for the long walks he loved to take through the maze of streets in their neighborhood, wielding a stick to keep the stray dogs at bay. He always returned, but it must have been harrowing for my mother, waiting, as the minutes ticked away. She reacted in the only way she could. She buried her fear so deep that she was able pretend it did not exist. She chastised my father when he returned; she blamed him for making her miserable; she called him a selfish old man who cared only for himself.

If only she could see him now when I tell him that the funeral director has agreed to allow us to come to the funeral parlor later in the morning. He is sitting up on the bed, eyes alert, the old intelligence shining out of them. In a voice crisp, clear, strong, he thanks me. "I can't wait to see her," he says.

If my mother were here now she would know that she was right: she had not lost him. Behind that jumble of memories in his brain, he has kept a clear space for her. He has never forgotten that he loves her.

Verna Allette Wilkins

Born in Grenada, she was the founder in 1987 of Tamarind Books, and is the author of 40 picture books and eight biographies for young people. Her books have featured on BBC Children's TV programmes and have been included on the English national curriculum. The many awards she has received include the British Book Industry Decibel Award for Multicultural Publishing and an honorary doctorate from Newman University, Birmingham in 2014 for her work as a champion of children's literature. With a mission to redress the balance in publishing output, she writes books that give children of colour a high and positive profile. A moment that will remain forever in her mind is when, during a school visit in the UK, a young black girl said to her, "I always wanted to be an author, but I didn't think I could be one until I met you today!"

A Memory Evoked

Calypso! The subject of the email message from my sister in Baltimore led me to a video link. To click or not to click! I had loads of work to do. It was the middle of a very busy day preparing for a school workshop—"Writing Books For Children, With Children" —the very next day, but the sweet smell of the ruby-red mango ripening in my fruit bowl had already put me in the mood to indulge warm memories of home, memories of the Caribbean that conflicted with a cold, grey, London winter seeping into my room. A little light music would surely do me good. I clicked.

The calypso's title was "Fork Up the Beaches" by the calypsonian Scorcher. The title evoked the island in the sun I missed so much. My room, overlooking a bleak, suburban North London road, was filled with an infectious melody and the tintinnabulation of steel-band rhythms.

Calypso is multidimensional. Calypso can be unpredictable. It is the politics of the working people of the Caribbean islands, put to a catchy tune. The double-entendre that is calypso's stock in trade means that for all its easy danceability, its flip side may well be serious naughtiness. Or, naughtily serious business. Calypsonians give themselves fabulous names. Roaring Lion, Lord Melody, The Mighty Spoiler, Lord Executor, just to name a few. So when I heard Scorcher cheerfully begin, I knew there was more to this title than met the ear. It was a protest song despite the rollicking tune. The jaunty lyrics, combined with the scent of mango in the room, pulled me back more than half a century.

Back to a tropical sea sparkling in the bright sun, resplendent with small boats bearing big names. *In God We Trust, Crewed Structure,* and *No Fear*—bobbing about near the shore. Further out to sea, larger vessels and visiting yachts have dropped anchor. Their owners sit in beach bars, swim or snorkel in the gentle morning sun. The miles of white recumbent beaches receive the waves, lapping, foaming and receding. Inland, there are hundreds of trees of various shapes and sizes. Stretching higher than all others are the stately palms which wave their skeletal branches in the soft breeze.

I drift back into the cold and listen to Scorcher's powerful lyrics stating strongly that the beaches belong to everyone. He sings that if the rich incomers cut off access, the local people should destroy the beaches.

The Caribbean is the fantasy of would-be lottery winners. Here is the place where rich foreigners buy land near the beaches and build elaborate homes. They build high fences to cut off large areas around their elegant residences to keep the local people as far away as possible. This allows for private beach parties, and as some local folk have argued, skinny-dipping in the daytime and unmentionable carryings-on when the sun dips into the far horizon. This urge for privacy means that locals on and around the beach areas are not welcome. Neither are the fisherwomen who come to the beach from the hinterland. These women walk for miles, carrying large woven baskets. They sit on the beach, in the shade of the wide-leafed manchineel trees and wait for the fishermen to bring in the morning catch. As the fishermen arrive bare-chested and weary from hours at sea, the women rush forward to buy enough fish to fill their baskets. They make a small profit selling the fish as they walk back home, their heavy baskets balanced securely on their heads with pads of twisted cloth. In their brightly coloured dresses, vivid in the morning sun, they walk slowly all along the beach and all along the road, calling out the list of the catch they carry. The barriers that the rich beach dwellers built prevented the fisherwomen from doing their trade. They were forced to make hazardous detours, bypass potential customers and worse yet, the fish would begin to rot in the harsh midday tropical sun. Livelihoods lost.

These desperate fish-sellers turned to my father for support. My father was a political animal. He was head of a large school. A number of his pupils were poor. He created a breakfast club so that the children could have a bowl of porridge made from locally ground cornmeal. This was accompanied by plates of warm buttered "bakes" which set the children up for the day at school. Downstairs in our family home, which was the converted old school house, my father ran evening classes in literacy for adults. He was active in the Union of Teachers and fought for the rights of the young men and women he helped train to become teachers. Parents of children at his school and many in the community came regularly for his advice and support. Faced with the barricades on the beach, the fisherwomen too, beat a path to his door. They needed his help. My father rose to the occasion. He donned his pith helmet. He saddled his horse, and off down to the beach he went. He waited for the women to load their baskets. "Just follow me," he said quietly.

I carry a vivid memory of him on his horse, followed by a line of women balancing laden baskets on their heads. He charged forward, waving at the fence builders. "These barricades are illegal. This is common land. It belongs to all of us."

He summoned a group of young men looking for some action. "Come on, lads! Go on! Take these barriers down!"

They set to, ripping poles out of the ground and smashing fences, shouting as the barriers fell. The fisherwomen walked through, triumphant while the incomers barricaded themselves inside their lavish dwellings.

Three and a half thousand miles away, and more than half a century later, the jaunty steelband music reminded me of my island in the sun but the lyrics of Scorcher's calypso told a painful story. He sang of the same atrocities that my father fought against, more than fifty years earlier. Then, the incomers were building holiday homes near the beaches, but now the international hoteliers had arrived as well, with the encouragement of the government trying to boost the tourist trade. The situation seemed worse than ever. Scorcher's absolute frustration and anger at the continuing injustices and abuse of power rang out in his calypso— "Fork Up the Beaches"—dig them up with forks.

As the steelband rhythms died away, I was aware, more than ever, of the influence of my father on my own life. Scorcher's words brought clarity. I realized why, after twenty-five years as a publisher of children's books, I have abandoned the role. Having witnessed, year after year, over more than a quarter of a century, the exclusion of Black and ethnic minority children from books aimed exclusively at children, something had to be done. Ongoing countless proclamations from publishing houses which set up apprenticeships, and mentoring schemes to address the problem of "the lack of diversity in publishing" made no noticeable difference. So many conferences, charters for equality and training. So many initiatives. So little discernible improvement. Barriers to including children of colour in publishing remained. I had to take a different path.

I walked away from being a publisher and began working in diverse classrooms in the UK. The existing barriers that exclude children of colour from books aimed at children could start with the children. They should see themselves as the authors, editors, designers, illustrators and publishers of the future. An illustrator, editor and I work together to demystify the entire process of how books are made. So far, working in suburban and inner-city schools we have produced two beautiful picture books that have children of colour as the main protagonists. The children contributed and were involved in the entire process from the idea to the finished product. On both occasions, they chose to write with me about their school trips. They had all the knowledge they needed about these. My Caribbean childhood experiences of a trip to the seaside was so very different. I learn so much from these workshops.

Abdi's Day is a story about a young Somali boy on his first seaside trip, travelling from his diverse inner-city school, across the English countryside to the seaside. *A Visit to City Farm* tells of a school trip to a farm in the middle of the city, with llamas and many exotic creatures, surrounded by city skyscrapers. An enjoyable experience for all of us. The children were involved in the entire writing, editing and publishing process, *"hands-on"* from the first rough notes to the final edit. They contributed and were involved in the writing, they witnessed and worked with the illustrator on her roughs all the way to her finished artwork. They were fascinated by the design process and checked the final proof sheets from the printers in China. To hear even reluctant readers shout, at the launch, "This our book! We did it!" was heart-warming.

I thank my father for opening my eyes to change and empowerment. He was a brilliant storyteller and the best and most hilarious raconteur I have ever known. I thank Scorcher for bringing memories and music to warm my spirits on a cold North London day, and I thank the children who, with support, will change publishing forever. The programme grows.

Another chilly day in London and I gasp at the list of emails to be tackled. A quick scan picks up one from the Caribbean. I click. This time it is not a Calypsonian calling for desperate methods to ruin the beaches because of exploitation and greed. This time it is:

> **Hotel Developer Forced to Demolish Walls on Grand Anse Beach**
>
> After weeks of outcry on local radio and social media platforms, with petitions signed by hundreds of locals, the developers of Silver Sands Resort have finally bowed to public pressure and were forced to demolish the wall that was built on the beach to cut off access to local people.

That beach is where my father protested physically so many decades ago. That beach where Scorcher sang out loud in desperation was at last rightfully claimed. The local people could finally walk freely and enjoy their own island in the sun.

Sue Woodford-Hollick

A former investigative journalist and current affairs producer for Granada Television and founding Commissioning Editor of Multicultural Programmes for Channel 4, she is now a businesswoman (the founder and co-owner of Little Garden Day Nurseries, a London-based childcare company) and consultant with wide-ranging experience in broadcasting and the arts. She spent nine years as Chair of Arts Council England, London, has chaired and been a trustee of numerous other arts organisations, including Tate Members, Index on Censorship, Talawa Theatre Company, the Theatre Museum and Free Word, and recently retired from the international board of AMREF, Africa's largest health NGO, based in Nairobi. Currently a trustee of Complicité Theatre Company, Reprieve, Music for my Mind, and Chair of the Stuart Hall Foundation, she is also a passionate supporter of Chineke!, Britain's only majority black and brown classical orchestra. She was appointed an OBE in 2011 for services to the arts.

Who I Was Then, and Who I Am Now

This is a story about secrets and lies. I kept it under lock and key for most of my life, allowing only a few carefully curated strands to be unravelled by my closest family and friends.

Until several years ago…

My youngest daughter Abigail, then a new mother, is a radio producer specialising in programmes for women. One day she put my new grandson down for a rest, gave me a cup of tea and placed her tape recorder assertively before me: "Mum, tell me everything…what was your childhood really like?"

No one had cornered me in this way before and Abby, an ace interviewer, is very direct. As a mother of three daughters, and as a grandmother, I finally realised that it was time to speak openly about *my* mother and *my* grandmother. Of who I was then, and who I am now.

★ ★ ★

I was on my own, always on my own, in a small, mock-Tudor terraced house in Streatham, South London, with Auntie May and Uncle Dick. They seemed *very* old. Uncle Dick was a kind, patient man who loved cricket. He had real charm, a lady's man way back when. Auntie May, a small nervous woman, was Irish-Catholic, very strict. She was always complaining and seemed desperate for middle-class respectability. I remember her compulsively washing and re-washing the net curtains at the front of the house. She didn't seem to like me. I don't know why. They had a daughter, my "Auntie Joan", who was twenty-six years older than me and lived on the other side of town with her husband Rob and three children. I saw them from time to time. When we did meet, Joan was friendly and seemed to like me. I quite liked her.

In those years, the 1950s, I felt different and I *was* different: never allowed to do any of the things other children did. If I looked out of the window May would be furious: "Come away from there at once!" A knock on the front door and I was rushed to the back of the house, as if I was a fugitive. A number of times I was hidden in a cupboard under the stairs and forced to stay there until the coast was clear. It was dark inside and I'd panic, even though I was given an ice cream once when I came out.

I had one friend, Heather, the girl next door. She was five years older than me. Sometimes Auntie May and Uncle Dick would drive us to the sea, near Brighton, for an outing. On the way home, as we approached the house, May would burst out, "Get down, Susan. Get down now!"

You'd think it was an air-raid! I would immediately duck down on the floor in the back of the car so none of the neighbours would see me. Heather told me recently that she thought this was very odd.

It was a hidden childhood for a long time. Did I ever ask why? Not really. "Good little girls" didn't speak up in those days. They barely even spoke. In post-war Britain, people felt lucky just to have survived. Adults didn't ask deep questions; children certainly didn't. I did finally find the courage to ask Uncle Dick, about my "mummy" and "daddy".

After a long pause he answered: "We adopted you because your real parents couldn't look after you."

End of conversation. I assumed my birth parents couldn't look after me because they were dead and I grew up firmly believing I was an orphan.

May said to me once: "If we hadn't taken you in, who knows where you would have been? You should be grateful." They had saved me from the orphanage.

From then on, I started to call Auntie May and Uncle Dick "Mummy" and "Daddy".

But there were gigantic elephants in the room…the colour of my skin!…the kinks in my hair! I wasn't conscious of being black and no one ever said I was, but people must have speculated that I was probably the illegitimate child of a black man (possibly an American GI) and a white woman. Oh, the shame of being a "half-caste bastard" in white, genteel South London. No wonder I was hidden. No one in my world looked remotely like me.

But in truth, even I had no idea what I looked like. Never allowed out without a "bonnet" covering most of my face, secured with a bow tied under my chin. Whatever I wore had to have long sleeves—my skin must never get any darker from the sun. My frizzy hair was straightened—and fell out a couple of times because of the chemicals.

To cope with my isolation, I escaped to the library and the tennis court at the end of the road as often as I could. Girls at my convent school called me "Sooty" and I kidded myself that it was affectionate. After all, everyone was watching a popular, long-running children's television series *The Sooty Show*, featuring a small, mute, cute yellow bear.

Boys were less subtle when it came to racist taunts and called me "baked potato" to my face and "a touch of the tar brush" behind my back.

But I was tough—cocooned by Catholicism and protected at school by Jesuit nuns who believed that women were every bit as good as men. If the abuse became too much, I fantasised an exotic back-story for myself: I was the daughter of an African prince or a powerful Arab sheikh. I would be fine until I could escape.

Which I did—a gap year in Cameroon, West Africa, teaching at another convent school. It was there that I finally realised that I was a "daughter of Africa". I loved everything about Africa and I still do—the heat, sounds, smells and most of all, the people. I feel completely at home wherever I am in Africa. Then I went to the University of Sussex to read English. Dick died while I was at university and after that I rarely went back to South London.

I was working in Manchester as a television journalist, presenting and reporting on a nightly news programme. One evening, after the show, Joan rang to tell me that my adopted mother May had died.

Her funeral was a miserable affair—blinding wind and rain on top of the South Downs. Just the three of us: Joan, her husband Rob and me. Mummy / Auntie May had no friends. Later, Joan and I sat in her cramped apartment above her failing sweet shop. Her husband Rob had gone to bed. A bottle of whiskey sat on the table between us.

I sat silently as Joan spoke in a tone I hardly recognised.

"I'm your real mother. May was your grandmother. You're not adopted. You were never adopted!"

I was shocked.

"I've wanted to tell you for a long time. May wouldn't let me. I had to go along with her. She sent me away in secret to have you and she made me give you to them. Told me to marry the person I was engaged to…I had no options. Your father was from Trinidad … in the RAF. He is Black."

Black? Why did I never suspect this? Suddenly the identity I had forged over more than twenty-five years was shattered. I wasn't who I thought I was. But, incredibly, I did have a living mother and father!

I learned my father's name: Squadron Leader Philip Louis Ulric Cross, DSO, DFC, nickname "Black Hornet". An RAF navigator who commanded No 139 (Jamaica) Squadron. Charismatic, gorgeous, exceptionally brave and very black. She had been in love with him. He was a war hero, recognised as probably the most decorated West Indian of World War II. He became an eminent jurist and diplomat. Not quite the prince or sheikh I had dreamt of as a child, but not far off!

He had tried to visit me once when I was very little. Uncle Dick opened the door, took one look at him and told him never to come near his daughter, or me again. Illegitimacy was scandalous in respectable households; prejudice against black people was extreme. The combination of the two was unthinkable.

I was also shocked when she told me I had met my father when I was teaching in Cameroon during my gap year. I remember at the time being told someone "very important" from the government wanted to meet me. I was taken to a house and introduced to the most extraordinary man I had ever met. I wrote to Joan to tell her. I named him and explained how handsome and captivating he was—sadly he was married. Airmail letters took a long time to fly between Africa and the UK especially back in 1963. I received an almost instant reply: "Whatever you do, keep away from this man. I was engaged to him once. Don't have anything to do with him!" There had been a strong connection between the then Attorney General of Cameroon and the teenage gap-year student. I had never understood why he insisted on meeting me. And now I was being told that he was my father.

I was stunned and the whiskey bottle was almost empty.

I told my mother that the lies had to stop, and if she didn't tell her family the truth, then I would. To her credit, she did so. Her husband, Rob, didn't take it well, but her children were unsurprised.

★ ★ ★

Suddenly the baby alarm went off with a jolt. My grandson had woken up and needed feeding. Abby turned off the tape recorder. I'd only told her half the story. I hugged her and the baby and drove home, emotionally exhausted.

That conversation with Joan happened almost fifty years ago but it had a profound effect on my life. I had grown up feeling "out of place". I had no sense of identity, race or culture. I knew I wasn't white, it didn't occur to me that I was black, and the word 'bi-racial' was unknown. I never understood why I felt so at home in Africa or when I was surrounded by people of colour. It was a huge relief to know the truth.

Thankfully, the shame and guilt of illegitimacy that existed more than sixty years ago when I was a child has virtually disappeared from Britain. Racism has not, but to be bi-racial in London today is not unusual and it's not a scandal. The town I grew up in is now brimming with people of colour, many of whom look like me.

I try to forgive my mother and grandparents for hiding me away, but it's difficult. I understand they were a product of their time, but I'm not sure I can entirely forgive. Our past is our future, and part of me will always be the black child called Sooty at school, whose identity was erased because of white people's shame. I shall always carry some of that toxic guilt. And I know I've also handed some of it down to my three daughters, however hard I tried not to. A painful, heavy burden I carry. Mothering is hard when you haven't had much yourself. I am proud that they are strong, confident, feminists and I hope they will be able to forgive me. We don't communicate enough because I still find it so hard talk about my past. They have a right to know my story.

Postscript

In time, I traced my father, Mr Justice Cross, and met his extended family. We became close, and he was an adoring and much loved "Grandpa Ulric" to Abby and her sisters. We all love his daughter, my sister Nicola— "Auntie Nicky". I also found a son Ulric didn't know he had: my half-brother Richard, who is just three weeks older than me!

It was a long, sometimes painful journey. And there are many more rich stories left to tell…for another time and place.

Diane Abbott

Born in London to parents who were Jamaican migrants to Britain in the 1950s, she has built a distinguished career as a parliamentarian, broadcaster and commentator. After attending Harrow County Grammar School, she went to Cambridge University where she obtained an MA in history in 1973, and subsequently worked as a journalist. She was a Home Office trainee, Race Relations Officer for the National Council for Civil Liberties, a reporter with TV AM and Thames Television, Public Relations Officer with the GLC and head of Lambeth Council's Press Office. Active in community politics, including OWAAD (Organisation of Women of African and Asian Descent) and the Black Media Workers' Organisation, in 1987 she became the first black woman ever elected to the British Parliament, as Labour Party MP for Hackney North and Stoke Newington. Her 2008 speech on civil liberties won The Spectator *magazine's "Parliamentary Speech of the Year" award and further recognition at the 2008 Human Rights awards. She has served on a number of parliamentary committees and held shadow ministerial positions. She is founder of the London Schools and the Black Child initiative.*

The Caribbean

2 December 2004

Diane Abbott (Hackney, North and Stoke Newington) (Lab): I am grateful to have an opportunity to speak in this important debate…

As someone who has been a Member of the House since 1987, I want to begin by saying that there is no doubt that since the mid-'80s the Caribbean region has slipped down the Government's agenda. That is to take nothing away from the indefatigable efforts of former Ministers in previous Governments and this Government or the indefatigable efforts of Baronesses Amos and Scotland, friends of mine who have worked very hard in the other place [the House of Lords] to represent the interests of the region. Whatever Heads of Government tell Ministers over cocktails, they tell everyone else that over the past two decades the region has slipped down the agenda.

I do not blame any particular Government for that. There are historic trends; the end of the Iron Curtain and of the Cold War meant that regions that were once cockpits of the Cold War fell from the attention of the United States, and to a lesser extent that of the UK. With the rise of the Asian tigers and the emergence of the massive economies of Taiwan, China and Korea, our economic focus has moved. The importance of Eastern Europe and Russia has led attention, capital flows and economic interest away from the region to other parts of the world.

Undoubtedly, the Department for International Development's otherwise laudable emphasis on helping the very poorest countries has been at the expense of allegedly middle-income countries such as Caribbean countries. It is regrettable that the region has dropped down the Government's agenda. It is regrettable philosophically because of the historic links between the region and Britain and because of the existence of large and passionately engaged Caribbean communities in all our great cities. It is also regrettable practically.

I come to this debate having spent the morning at a conference on gun crime organised by the Metropolitan police. I am sure that Ministers appreciate that in a globalised world we face globalised crime and globalised social disorder. Ministers cannot pursue policies in relation to trade liberalisation, and the so-called modernisation of the public sector, which will inevitably lead to job losses in the region, without that having an impact on security and crime issues right here in Britain.

If people sneeze in west Kingston, we catch a cold in Hackney. The criminals are as globalised as any multinational company. I regret that for all the energy that Ministers put into security, crime and drug issues, they do not link it to their trade liberalisation policies and modify them accordingly. Of course change has to come—to bananas, to sugar and to the whole region—but the pace of change and the ability of the countries to draw down funds to manage that change is crucial if this is not to result in social disorder and dislocation in that region, which directly impacts on us here in London.

I am sure that Hon. Members will forgive me if I return to sugar, because it is a major issue. People are very unhappy with how things have developed... These new proposals on sugar—whether they are in technical breach of the Cotonou agreement or not, they certainly breach its spirit—specifically reconfirm the importance of preserving the benefits of the sugar protocol.

Although I may not say this over cocktails with Ministers, as far as the region is concerned, the new proposals on sugar and the precipitate slashing of the sugar price are a breach of faith...

People were promised money and aid in relation to bananas, but until now they have not been able to draw down even a fraction of that money, nor do they want to repeat that experience with sugar.

For Ministers, trade issues are in some sense abstract, as they have to fit in with a wider Government agenda. Perhaps Ministers think it is enough to say that change must come, but I remind Hon. Members of the economic, social and psychological importance of sugar to the region. We are, after all, talking about sugar islands that were the jewels of the British Empire precisely because of sugar production. The structures of the societies on those islands—their economies and internal social relations—are still based on the world that sugar made. Those economies are still major employers of unskilled and semi-skilled labour.

The Minister will probably tell me about diversification, but I want to know how an unskilled sugar cane worker in Portland, Jamaica, is going to diversify and become a computer programmer. That is the reality that people across the region face, not just in Jamaica, but in St Kitts and Nevis and elsewhere. Ministers talk too glibly about diversification without considering the reality of the work force that they are trying to diversify and the work available.

Ministers must also remember, when they glibly talk about diversification, that there is no major political party in the sugar-producing islands of the region that does not have its political base in the sugar unions. What politicians are being asked to do is turn to their bases and say that an economic structure and source of work and prosperity that has been relied on since the beginning of those island societies is going to go, and go much more rapidly than anyone anticipated at the time of Cotonou.

Let me remind Ministers that those sugar industries were originally constructed as suppliers to the metropolitan market. Unlike British beef producers, they do not enjoy sizeable domestic purchasing bases, which is one of the things that makes the current price proposal so untenable. Let me also repeat that most countries want to diversify. They do not want to rely on the same economic and social relationships that existed in the eighteenth century.

There is sufficient surplus land and labour to diversify, albeit not at the expense of the industry. Having been a Member of the House since 1987, I have seen Ministers with responsibility for the Caribbean come and go, but there is a list of large-scale experiments that the Caribbean islands have entered into in an attempt to diversify their agricultural production for the large and lucrative US market. Many of those experiments have failed, owing to all sorts of structural difficulties.

When Ministers talk about diversification, they also ignore the fact that in most islands the structure of the economy, small populations and underdeveloped internal and international transport militate against the establishment of new businesses. Where there are communications structures, people have realised that they could, for instance, move out of bananas and into other crops. But guess what—up to now, how would they have transported those new crops to Europe and America? The answer is on a banana boat. If we smash up the banana industry, we also smash up the transport infrastructure with which the agricultural produce of those islands could be moved about as a whole.

There is a lack of joined-up thinking among International Development Ministers about diversification. Ministers also need to remember that the economic pressures affecting sugar are also hammering other industries, such as bananas and citrus.

...When pressed on the sugar question, Ministers will tell us that it is all about British consumers and that they want them to have cheaper sugar. Consumers in Hackney call me for lots of reasons, but they do not call for cheaper sugar. Let us be clear: consumers in Britain or Europe will not benefit from lower sugar prices. The main beneficiaries will be an oligarchy of sugar producers in Brazil and the large sugar-using industrial manufacturers.

What will be the social consequences of a precipitate collapse of the sugar industry?

The people in the precise categories of the labour market that the sugar industry employs are not those who will find it easy to diversify into new industries. They will not just grow ganja—if they were growing ganja alone, that would be one thing—but we will see an accelerated drift of young men from the rural areas of St Kitts, Jamaica and elsewhere to the big cities, where they will find themselves involved in criminality and then fan out into international crime between New York, London and the region. That is the consequence of trade liberalisation if sufficient thought is not given to the transition.

Ministers must start to link their concern about security with trade policies and aid and development issues.

As I said at the beginning of my remarks—I speak as one who has been a Member of the House since the mid-1980s—there is no question but that the region has, although not through the fault of any particular Administration, gradually slid down the agenda of Her Majesty's Government. We can see that. People protest and talk about the UK-Caribbean Forum. That is very nice. They talk about visits by junior Ministers—it is always a treat to have such a visit—but we can see that the region has slid down the Government agenda when we look at the institutional arrangements in DFID [the Department for International Development] and the Foreign Office for dealing with the Caribbean.

…Let me say this on the dangers of fragmentation: most people in the Chamber may not remember or have learned about the history of the West Indies Federation, but when Britain sought to oversee the move to independence of different Caribbean islands, the original idea was that they should form part of that federation, because it was clear all those years ago that individual islands and dependencies would find it difficult to impact on international institutions, let alone the British Government.

Those countries, led by Jamaica under Alexander Bustamante, resoundingly rejected the idea of the federation, but as we move into the twenty-first century the islands of the region need to act more collectively and to have a common view on issues…

The region is building and reinforcing its common institutions and is trying to take more of a common view on issues. Here in Parliament, it is wonderful to have a multiplicity of groups, but in the context of making an impact on Ministers, the more that we can move together in a common organisation the better.

It is regrettable that the region has moved down the Government's agenda, but it will never move down the agenda in the hearts and minds of those of us whose parents and grandparents came from the region immediately after the Second World War. I constantly urge diplomatic representatives here to do more to harness the passion and concern of the Caribbean diaspora because, as well as building up the parliamentary work, that would be an important weapon to help the region.

On the weekend of Hurricane Ivan, I remember sitting with friends watching the news bulletins hour by hour. We all had friends, family and villages of which we were thinking. I would like to see a time when the institutional arrangements in DFID and the Foreign and Commonwealth Office, the funding, the concern, and the approach to trade matters reflect in their understanding of Caribbean issues the genuine love and concern that so many of us have for the region.

Candace Allen

Born and raised in the northeast US, she has lived in London since the 1990s. She is the author of the novel Valaida *(2004) and of* Soul Music: The Pulse of Race and Music *(2012) and a freelance contributor to* The Guardian *and the BBC World Service. She came to writing after 20 years working as an assistant director on feature and television films, and later as a screenwriter. She was a founder of Reel Black Women, a professional organisation for African-American women in film and was the first African-American woman to be a member of the Directors Guild of America. "That First Night in Accra" is from a novel-in-progress.*

That First Night in Accra (1974)
(Part of a work-in-progress novel)

A Friday night, some three weeks after she'd arrived. Hot. Hot that screamed for hammocks and frosty lemonade, which weren't to be had, or regular water pressure for showers or regular electricity for fans, so what she'd done was adjust: discarded the New York shoes that were constantly filling with sweat, cut back her billowing 'fro. Since her arrival Ghana had been about adjustments, some of it annoying, most of it exciting, but all of it simply prelude.

For Alex Walker, Ghana wasn't the Motherland of myth and recent discovery, nor the inspiration of prideful identity that had been spine to her college years. So single-minded was her attention to her goal that mere surrounding white noise *black noise*? had been this country, this continent, this city, until, after almost two years of nothing more tangible than constant, obsessive, heart-rending and confusing thought, the reason for her entire being stood right across the room.

The tiny club full to bursting. Spirits high to the Afrobeat, psychedelic funk that had been the unexpected soundtrack of her last three weeks. Everyone wanted to be James Brown, it seemed, stomping and grinding down the house rather than elegantly swaying to the Highlife sometimes played at civil rights-oriented parties in the early '60s to raise funds in Westchester County for all those valiant freedom-fighters way down South. *Even her Daddy pulling himself upward, swaying his hips slowly to those pride-filled beats, but all eyes on her Mama, undulating with the grace of a* gazelle and Alex wanting so much to move with such grace, to receive such admiring regard if only just once. Pretty please, God, just the once? Alex could see that David knew people in the club as he greeted brothers and bartenders with handshakes and nods, ignored the courtship displays of several sisters, to stand alone, Coca-Cola in hand.

His hair was neat, clipped far shorter than it had been at school, no beard, an irregularity in his right cheek she hadn't seen before. More beautiful even than her memory of him. The club's small yellow bulbs reflecting round his brow like a halo. Dressed in form-fitting grey slacks and an open-necked cotton shirt not bought at a market stall, the cut too perfect, the fabric too fine.

She inhaled somehow, exhaled as well, without drama, steadying her nerves. She'd travelled more than five thousand miles for this moment, but she hadn't made a beeline. Starting with her roommates, Emma and Akuwe, she'd danced. And he'd watched. *Like folk had always watched her Mama.* She felt rather than saw him watching, all the hairs on her body antennae processing his every move. He'd danced once with a persistent admirer then stopped and watched some more. They'd let the room's ebbs and flows move them together. It took less than one hour but more than a half. Long sessions with Akuwe and Emma had prepared her for this night.

"*Think Pam Grier, Alexandra! 'They call her Coffy, and she will cream you!' Yes? You are a warrior. Do not waver! In your veins runs the blood of market mamas, the true queens of Africa, my sister, who can conquer all manhood with the quiver of one buttock!*"

Four years Alex's senior, Akuwe was unconvinced that any man was worth all this trouble, but she and Alex had bonded during their bibliographical hours. Akuwe was very pleased that Alex hadn't come to Ghana trying to be African. It was all Akuwe could do not to spit on the sandals of Negro Americans on their pilgrimages to the Motherland, thinking and playing they were "African".

"*It might as well be Halloween! Mixing Yoruba and Fante into fairy tale characters; and the drama at the slave castles! Yes, it's difficult this history. I don't deny it's difficult, but please, a friend of mine, a tour guide, told me that just last week some man tore off his shirt, tried to bar all white people from entering then bring the building down like some deranged Superfly Samson. If the Good Lord was watching He was having quite a laugh.*"

Alex wasn't like this. Alex had a purpose to her journey, as Akuwe had had her purpose in braving the snows of Indiana for higher education. "*Among ignorant peasant farmers who thought me some form of lower ape. You block their foolishness out. You get what you came for.*" Alex had come a very long way to get this man, a display of stamina that Akuwe admired, and she wanted Alex to win. Pink-petal-cheeked, Emma was more the romantic, but a practical one who'd learned, the hard way, that doormats invite foot traffic.

"*Akuwe is right, Alex. You've been here three weeks and not hunted him down. He works for Slocumbe so he knows that you're here. Your not pounding on his door and flinging yourself at his feet will have confused him. And remember, you are beautiful! What I wouldn't give for those legs of yours and that neck! He will see you and he will surrender!" followed by an embarrassed giggle with which Alex had empathized far more than had been useful.*

She'd managed her heartbeat with the dance. Much of her adrenalin had been pumped out with perspiration, not all but enough that her hands were reasonably still, her eyelids not twitching. When she and David were finally face-to-face she'd maintained a steady gaze. Emma and Akuwe had melted away.

They'd done without the superfluous intros. There'd been none of that "You? Here?" nonsense. They both knew why she was there.

"Hello," he'd said. Without a smirk, without the sense that he was doing her a favour just by speaking to her, with pleasure, understated but undeniable. He'd been happy to see her, and surprised at his happiness. It was not her imagination. It was real. She could see this.

"Hello," she'd replied. Thirsty after all the dancing her eyes had fastened onto his bottle of Coca-Cola, a distraction in aid of her poise.

"Take it," he said. "I'll get a couple more. Should they add rum?"

"Yes, please." She could feel her new friends' barely suppressed cheers and guttural admonishments somewhere beyond her to the right, but she'd ignored them, turning instead to look at the open door, even her breath, keep her heart from smashing through its cage. She'd felt at once that her senses were on high alert yet much around her was behind a veil. When he'd returned with their drinks he'd nodded towards the door.

"Shall we?" he'd asked.

"Good idea," she'd replied.

Outside, Accra. Bodies milling in limited light, music, not just from the club, from tinny transistor radios of various sizes, a live band across the street, another but one street away, all the beats complementary somehow. Voices keying upwards in celebration of a night's promises good and bad, the smell of kabobs and wood smoke, diesel fuel and human funk. Clean for the most part, for a night on the town, but sweating bodies without deodorant, in loose cotton garments, minimal body hair, slightly acrid; with an overlay of overripe everything including bodily wastes. The drink generous and the rum ramming into her stomach like panic.

"You know the bartender?" she'd asked.

"I've been here a time or two," he'd replied. "You need a cushion?"

"I better," she'd replied. With a smile that did not quiver.

The kabob seller's broad grin was missing three front teeth, with the rest more yellow than white. "You not from 'round here," he'd said, looking her way after David made the order.

"Is it so obvious?" she'd asked.

The seller's nod and all his movements were at one with surrounding beats. "Yes, but you are very welcome, my sister! Where you from? New York?"

"Yes, New York. How'd you guess?" she'd said laughing. How wonderful to laugh with David at her side.

"Because you got the flare, my sister! You got the style! 'New York, New York. The Big Apple!' The Last Poets, we know them here, very wise, very wise, and you one lucky man, my brother, to have a New York sister like this!" and as he handed over the kabobs, "Very welcome home!" Moving off to allow the seller to serve the clean-cut white man waiting behind them, for the first time, Alex felt maybe that might be true.

The eating of kabobs delayed in-depth conversation, that and the enormity of being in his presence at last. Alex had felt calm when there was no precedent for calm. A snippet of T.S. Eliot flit in and out of lamp-light, the sense of being in and out of time. Because in all the world Alex was where she wanted to be. That moment, standing in the street across from the Club Ambassador, that first moment of feeling with him, of having achieved more than at any previous second in her entire life by getting here to his side; far more than the academic fluency that took her to the College, far more than the painting with which she had won a state-wide competition her high-school junior year, far more than the diploma that to some was a prize to frame and display but for her was lying unperused on a dusty shelf in Harrison, New York; and the wall about him almost permeable.

She'd smiled into that space, not at him, and felt only barely a dollop of kabob juice rolling down her chin. David had produced a handkerchief. Her hands had been full with kabob and drink; but he'd managed to clean her chin. Softly. The magic in the touch rather than the prestidigitation. Her heart now tugging wildly and never-before-seen questions in his eyes. *"So, it's really you here?" "Did I ever really see you before?"* Her lungs on fire, expanded to explosion, she wanted to throw her arms around his neck, wanted to scream; but sense told her that any acknowledgment of this change in his eyes would cause it to flee forever. She'd cooled the fire with rum and Coke. "Are you 'very welcome home' here?" she'd asked.

"It's where I am," he'd replied, "where I could go and where I am." He'd nodded towards the club. "You want to go back in?"

"I've danced enough," she'd said.

"Your friends?" he'd asked. She'd shaken her head and he'd summoned a taxi. They didn't touch or speak in the ride to his small bungalow, allowed the sounds and smells of Accra to burnish the fullness between them.

His bungalow was set back from the street. Banana trees muffled the night sounds of modern Accra but the switches and coos of its nature remained. Where his off-campus apartment had been a chaos of books, posters, record albums and scattered clothing, he now lived in another style entirely: immaculately clean, spare of objects. A table with a lamp, a well-made bed. Nothing on the walls. A few books, *The Invisible Man*, Chinua Achebe's *Things Fall Apart*, some detective novels in French, Fanon in both

English and French, an English-French dictionary, what looked to be scientific tracts on mining; a small cassette player, a few tapes: some Miles, Cecil Taylor, his Ornette Coleman, of course.

Ornette Coleman had seemed more noise than anything else at school. She'd never been able to distinguish Ornette's ups from his downs, but in this sparse bungalow Ornette was making far more sense and, standing in that small space out of known time and place, the music's questing and weaving projectiles were sounding absolutely right.

He'd opened the few windows to release some of the day's stifling heat, taken a beer and a Coke out of a cooler. She'd pointed at the Coke but rolled its bottle across her forehead before taking a drink. He'd approached her from behind and done the same with his beer along the nape of her neck, causing her to gasp. He'd turned her around and kissed her gently. They'd swayed a bit to the rhythms beneath and between Coleman's notes. He was wearing a ring that she hadn't seen before, heavy, African. She could feel the pressure of its form on her back beneath his hand, the ripple of his muscles beneath her hand; then he'd taken away her Coke, placed it carefully on a counter.

A different man.

The David Prescott she had followed to Accra had never cared about her pleasure before, nor had she considered her satisfaction a priority. If truth be told, she had been unsure what pleasure meant, the vague stuff of love songs, lascivious comments, embarrassed giggles, nothing concrete, let alone liberating, nothing that she'd known she needed, nothing she knew enough about to want. Who was this man who had trembled as he'd plied and explored her, who'd rested his cheek against hers with care that she didn't smother? A different man, this David. Perhaps a man who needed her? As he never ever had in school…

Yaba Badoe

A graduate of King's College Cambridge, she worked as a civil servant in Ghana before becoming a general trainee with the BBC. Her debut novel, True Murder, *was published in 2009. Her short stories have been published in* Critical Quarterly, African Love Stories: An Anthology *(2007) and* Short Stories: Southern African and Beyond *(2009). She is an award-winning documentary filmmaker whose credits include* The Witches of Gambaga *(2010) and* The Art of Ama Ata Aidoo *(2014). She was nominated for a Distinguished Woman of African Cinema Award in 2014.*

Aunt Ruby and the Witch

I'm listening to the radio. An old woman on my favourite FM station is swearing that she had just embarked on her night travels—a round trip from Accra to Kumasi—when her magic failed and she plummeted to the ground. "That's why I am standing here naked, young man. I was caught out."

"How long does the journey usually take you, Nana?"

"In the spiritual realm, Accra to Kumasi is no time at all. Not like in the old days, when the train took three hours at least. In the spirit, I'm there just like…" The old woman snaps her fingers.

I turn the volume of the transistor radio up and imagine the eyes of the cub reporter widening at his scoop: a woman, a self-confessed witch, marooned on a roundabout in Osu. And he, the first reporter on the scene, is interviewing her.

"Ask her which asylum she's escaped from," I prompt him. "Offer to escort her home."

He doesn't.

"Now, if the train were still running," says the old woman, "I'd take it to Kumasi to visit my sister. But with things as they are, what am I to do? No money for tro-tro or state transport. I have no choice, young man, but to go from place to place the only way I can."

"But, Nana, witchcraft is evil."

"Then, for my sake, petition the President. Tell him to mend the railways so I can use them again. Have you ever been on a train, young man?"

"No, Nana."

"Not even the link from Accra to Tema?"

The young man sighs. He's too young to have felt the surge of an engine as it hauls carriages over tracks; too young to have seen the foliage of rain forest as it clambers overhead. The first time I saw it—a forest thick with trees I could not name—unable to see the sky, I marvelled as the train snaked through shadows. Bark slithered past my eyes: leaves, creepers and never-ending trees.

The forest is gone now, cut for timber. Fragments of track are still in place; fragments of a journey to Kumasi to visit an aunt, who insisted on living in the "Garden City", while her husband, my uncle, pined for her in Accra.

Aunt Ruby met me at Kumasi Station, and swept me along, her arm in mine, to show me her city. First stop, her seamstress.

"Take a good look at her," Ruby said. "I want you to choose a style that flatters her. And you shall make the garment out of this." She picked out a bail of cotton cloth and flung it across a work table: a profusion of pink hibiscus against a turquoise sky.

Ruby spun me around and looked me over. I was shy, angular, unwilling to straighten my back to display my budding breasts. "My dear niece," she said, "after a week with me, you will feel the magic in your blood."

That evening, Ruby put on a record in the sitting-room of her bungalow, a home she'd built for herself after her first marriage failed. The gramophone needle squeaked, then a burst of highlife music shook the room. Ruby danced, rolling her hips at a song dedicated to her.

Ruby—priceless gem among women!
Whenever I see your face,
My heart leaps and I can't help but laugh.

She jiggled her body, dragged me to my feet, and we danced to her song a second time. Her buttocks and hips rippled, as if she held the secret of joy between her thighs. And the secret was hers; hers alone.

My uncle was Ruby's third husband.

I remember Ruby dancing, and that gift she gave me. The turquoise and pink cloth, sewn into bou-bou, whirling about me as I turned, admiring myself in a mirror.

"You see," Ruby smiled. "You have it too. We all do. Magic."

Seven years later, Ruby left my uncle.

I can't help wondering, as I listen to the old woman on the radio, if Ruby would have stayed married to him if she'd been able to travel by night between Kumasi and Accra. My uncle and aunt are dead now, but I still have the bou-bou and the memory of trees that towered over railway tracks.

"Do you mean to tell me, young man," says the old woman, "that you've never travelled by train? Hmm! You young people of today know nothing about magic.

Yvonne Bailey-Smith

Born in Jamaica, she came to the UK at the age of 15. A qualified social worker and family and systemic psychotherapist, she has worked with children and families for more than 40 years in various statutory and voluntary sector settings. She has been writing poetry and short stories for as long as she can remember. Her first short story was published in the late Dorothy Kuya's magazine New Impact *as were some of her poems. She contributed a chapter to the publication:* Helping Families in Family Centres: Working at Therapeutic Practice *and is the co-author of the publication and accompanying video* Baby & Me, *aimed at supporting and helping women who suffer from postnatal depression to develop a good bonding experience with their infants. Now retired from full-time employment, she works part-time as a psychotherapist and also undertakes freelance parental consultancy for the Young Minds charity. The following piece is an extract from her novel-in-progress,* The Day I Fell Off My Island. *It tells the story of a young girl who becomes a reluctant immigrant following the death of her grandmother.*

Meeting Mother

The next time I saw my mother I was fourteen years old.

The giant aircraft had landed with a jolt at London's Heathrow Airport and raced down the tarmac as though it had no intention of stopping. I had taken the deepest of breaths and offered up a silent prayer, overwhelmed with relief that, for the second time on the long journey, I and my fellow travellers had made it back to earth alive in a machine that was seemingly only held up in the sky by great puffs of white cloud. I had barely stirred on the entire journey. We had made our first stop somewhere in America for refuelling. Only then had I stood up, rather shakily, to make a trip to the bathroom; while the aircraft was in the sky, I had feared that any extra movement would be enough to bring it tumbling to the ground. I couldn't relax while so many people were moving aimlessly up and down the aisle like yoyos, possibly risking the safety of us all. The hostesses had fussed and constantly asked passengers if they were OK. Of course no one was OK! We were all trapped! I had refused all offers of food and took only tiny sips of water to avoid any further toilet visits. When we finally landed in London, my hamstrings were so tight I was unable to stand up straight for some hours.

The pretty yellow-haired hostess had been patient and kind, trying in vain to reassure me. "Think how lovely it will be to see your mum and dad again," she offered.

To which I responded crossly: "I don't want to see her and my father don't live in England." Each time she gently mopped the tears that came like rainfall, another torrent would cascade down my anguished face.

The room where I waited for the immigration lady to complete the pages of different-coloured forms for my entry into the UK was dank and cold. My blue and white cotton dress offered little protection against the bitter winter chill. My knees shook and my teeth chattered as my skinny body struggled to cope with the cold that invaded every inch of it. I tilted my head as far back as I could in a determined effort to stem further tears but came they did, accompanied by loud uncontrollable sobbing. I felt as though I had fallen off my island with no way of ever getting back. When she eventually returned my British Overseas Airway Corporation ticket I focused on the word "minor", wondering over and over again what I had done to find myself in such a terribly bleak and daunting place.

"Ready to go, Erna? Your father is waiting for you."

Oh, dear God, I thought, *please don't let it be the ugly Satan Devil man.*

"Where is my mother?" I demanded.

"It's your father who has come to collect you, dear. Maybe your mother stayed behind to prepare a nice welcome for you."

I screamed soundlessly. I was thousands of miles from everything I knew. I was now in this cold foreboding place full of strange people who all looked and talked funny. I didn't want to be here in this England place. Something in the faces of the strangers told me that they didn't want me here either. I felt like the girl in the middle of the "ring of roses", only the circle was made of thorns. To complete my misery, my mother had sent the person I disliked most in the entire world to collect me.

Unhappiness took hold of my body, coming in rapid waves of feverish heat. I didn't look at him as I climbed into the back seat of the clapped-out Ford Cortina, ignoring his suggestion that I sit in the front. As the car trundled noisily along, I peered into the darkness where I made out row upon row of grey houses squashed together, all with little front yards. Dense black smoke billowed from the chimneys. We travelled in silence along roads made of asphalt just like the ones on my island. Not a hint of gold anywhere!

The jalopy came to a halt outside a house that looked exactly like all the others we had passed. The front yard sloped down to what I first thought was some kind of gully but turned out to lead to rooms in a lower area that I later learnt was called a "basement". Why would anyone want to live underground? Surely that was a place for the dead! Above the enormous black front door stood another three storeys of heartless red bricks. The ugly Satan Devil man turned a key. The door swung open into a hallway that felt even colder than outside. My nostrils were suddenly filled with all kinds of unfamiliar smells, not all of which were pleasant.

He ushered me into the large living-room, every square inch of which was taken up with ornaments and plants. An aviary of plastic birds had prime position on a low glass table, while a huge rubber plant, a money plant and an oversized Busy Lizzie in full bloom took pride of place in a corner. Small china animals were spread across every surface that could accommodate them. Every creature on the planet seemed to be represented in this one room. The wallpaper, carpet, curtains, rugs and sofas all boasted different clashing patterns in shades of orange, red and brown. Finally, I sat down and stared at the flickering little black-and-white screen of the television set.

"Your mother gone to Brixton to get food shopping," the ugly Satan Devil man volunteered. "She should be back in the next half or so. I suppose you can't wait to see her," he muttered.

I didn't respond. I sat and waited.

Suddenly the front door slammed shut. I had not heard it being opened. I immediately sprang to my feet. My mother walked past the open living-room door, pushing a huge Silver Cross pram. Inside, seated facing each other, were two very fat baby girls, dressed identically and obviously twins. Walking sluggishly behind her were three more children, a girl and two boys. They were all slimmer than I remembered. Patsy still had very short hair but apart from that she looked different, her face no longer like a child's, but resembling that of a much older person to whom life had already been unkind. The boys no longer had their sticking-out bellies; now some of their bones stuck out in places that should have been covered by more flesh. My mother parked the pram at the far end of the corridor, leaving the twins strapped in. I could hear them babbling away to each other.

"Hello, my dear, I am glad you arrived safely."

My mother looked much as I remembered from her visit to our village. Her head was covered in a flowery scarf, secured under her chin. I could see that the wisps of hair that escaped from underneath were not her own, but a wig. She was wearing a thick brown coat and big black wellington boots.

I didn't respond to her greeting, afraid of giving the impression that I was actually happy to be there.

"Cat got your tongue, child? You know it's rude not to answer when an adult is talking to you!"

I smiled weakly in her direction, but no words would come out.

"You must be tired," she said. "The plane journey is a long something." She smiled broadly, appearing genuinely happy to see me. She patted me on the head and disappeared into a room further along the corridor.

I had imagined that when my siblings and I saw each other again we would all be overjoyed. The scene that had played out in my head was of the four of us rushing into each other's arms, laughing loudly, with lots of rapid-fire talk as we tried to catch up on all our lives. Instead we just stood in the corridor and stared at one another.

My mother soon reappeared and, without warning, she offered a prayer.

"I thank you, my God Jehovah, for delivering this child safe into our hands. Amen."

Her prayer did nothing to help create conversation. Instead I found myself thinking of my island...waking up to the crowing of cockerels, the many bird songs, the orange glow of the sun as it lifted gently above the horizon, the morning dew, the lushness, the vibrancy of the colours, the early morning banter of the adults and children in my village.

In the living-room I sat near the glowing gas fire, which turned out to be the main source of heating in the entire house. The children plonked themselves on the other side of the room, from where they continued to stare at me out of three pairs of sad-looking eyes. From time to time I would look away and concentrate instead on studying one of the half-dozen framed pictures of Jesus that represented the only art in the house. I wondered how it was that Jesus was always white, even on my island where the population was mainly black. Surely he should at least be a "Mulatto"...

"Your food is ready." My mother's voice broke into my reverie.

My siblings were out of their seats at lightning speed. I followed them into the bathroom. The pitted walls were painted a glossy pink with a hint of purple. A thin layer of multi-coloured lino covered the floor. Frozen icicle stalagmites hung from the top of the window frame. We took turns washing our hands, the ice-cold water causing me to wince and jump back from the cracked sink

In the dining-room I tried hard to ignore the cat-litter tray that sat in a corner with its display of recently excreted faeces. I gingerly sipped some sweet tea. The food on the table looked familiar but tasted unfamiliar. When I realised that I was screwing up my face with every mouthful, I said in my most convincing voice:

"De people dem give mi plenty food on de plane." It was the first time I had spoken since leaving Heathrow.

Suddenly there was hysterical laughter around the table.

"She sounds really funny. They must speak really funny in your country," Patsy said. The boys giggled their agreement.

They must speak really funny in your country. I repeated the comment in my head. They had apparently already forgotten that it was their country too. How could they not know that it was they who sounded funny with their new way of speaking?

It was the middle of November and the cold was piercing. On my first morning in England I woke at 7 a.m. to a grey day, which remained resolutely cold and grey until I curled up in the ice-cold bed in the freezing room at 8 p.m. that evening. Day and night morphed into one.

The pattern remained the same for many months, and I still had not figured out how to address the two adult strangers I was being forced to live with. I noticed that even the children who had lived with our mother and their father for the past four years did not appear to have a name for either of them. To attract our mother's attention they would touch her somewhere on her body. None of them spoke spontaneously to their father.

I decided to adopt the same tactics. I would simply ignore my mother's husband. I was on my own now and was going to have to sort things out for myself. Grandma Melba was no longer around to protect me.

Angela Barry

Bermudian by birth, she lived abroad for more than 20 years—in England, France, The Gambia, Senegal and the Seychelles—before returning to Bermuda, where she has primarily worked as a lecturer since the 1990s. She holds a PhD in Creative Writing from Lancaster University, for which she worked on cross-cultural projects, reflecting her connections with the African diaspora, and her work has been published in journals including The Massachusetts Review, The Bermudian *magazine,* The Caribbean Writer *and* BIM: Arts for the 21st Century. *She is the author of* Endangered Species and Other Stories *(2002) and* Gorée: Point of Departure *(2010), which was nominated for the 2012 International IMPAC Dublin Literary Award and in 2013 won the Brian Burland Prize for Fiction. In 2017 she received a Lifetime Achievement Award from the Bermuda Arts Council.*

Without Prejudice

Susan had a clear view of Claridge's foyer. Its sweeping staircase, crystal chandelier, and ornate tubs of billowing white roses. Beneath the great doorway she saw a young black girl. She seemed angry. Bristling. She was looking straight at Susan, who touched her pearls and blinked her eyes. The roses faded. The livid face of the stranger was still staring at her. The girl strode towards her, high heels clicking on tile then muted by plush carpet as she wove between the buzzing tables.

"Hello. I'm Esi." The voice carried the South London vowels Susan hated. "And presumably you are…"

By then, Susan had made her assessment. The distasteful accent was coupled with precise syntax. This girl was not quite what she'd expected. No ripped jeans. No visible tattoos or piercings. But…despite Susan's discreet email warning her about appropriate attire, here she was, loud and conspicuous. At Claridge's! Nothing refined about those primary colours, nothing subtle about that look on her face. But Susan was ready. With a studied smile, she got up and extended her hand to the first blood relative she'd ever met.

"Susan." Her hand was left floating untouched in the space between them.

"And you are…" the girl repeated, eyes flashing, "my Aunt Abena. My mother's sister. You know. The sister you treated like shit."

Susan sat down, stunned by the immediate attack. She'd hoped that the first half-hour would be spent talking about university entrance and such. But no. She tried to focus. On what? The skinny body, the blazing African scarf or the tight coils of hair standing about the face… She settled on the girl's skin—black, gleaming and pulled tight across sharp cheekbones—the way hers had been thirty-odd years ago. She'd hated it then, and that thought steadied her.

"Sit down, Esi. Please don't make a scene."

For the first time, Esi's armour seemed to slip. Her face was stamped with "Bugger off!" but her hands nervously pulled a large manila envelope from her bag. She continued to stand, immovable, while deft servers manoeuvred around her. Finally, she ripped open the envelope, causing a few tea drinkers to glance at them.

"My mother wanted you to have these. That's why I'm here." Still standing, Esi took out the first document and in a quiet hiss said: "Her last will and testament."

She slammed it on the table. "Your birth certificate. Your real one. See? Republic of Ghana!" It too landed with a thump.

Susan was certain she heard a disapproving murmur from the other patrons, and prayed that they didn't include anyone from the College.

"This is my personal favourite." Esi waved the paper about. "Your letter. The one that made your sister give up. It was this, not the cancer that killed her!"

"I…killed…" Susan's mouth hung open.

"There!" Esi said, satisfied. "I've kept the promise I made to…my…mum." Esi dropped into the chair, breathing heavily, her face crumpled.

"May I take your order, ladies?" The server smiled at them, oblivious.

Susan pulled herself together. "We'll have the traditional tea. With Assam and Darjeeling." She looked at Esi, who seemed to be weeping. How to survive this impossible encounter? Susan decided to think about her twenty-first birthday, in this same room. She'd been wearing her new pearls, just like Emily's. A mother-and-daughter occasion. The memory soothed her like a sweet balm.

When the server returned, Esi sat, revived and fascinated, as he brought the sumptuous "traditional tea" of finger sandwiches, scones and cakes. Such artistry! Relieved, Susan gestured towards the table but Esi shook her head. "No cow's milk. No processed flour. No white sugar."

A choking fury flared in Susan's chest.

"But I will have tea," the girl added. "I like loose-leaf tea."

Susan mustered a smile. "Try the Darjeeling." Picking up the jade and white teapot, she said, "Shall I be Mother?"

Esi's face hardened, her mouth twisting into an ugly line. "Are you trying to impress me with all this?" Her out-flung arm encompassed the universe of Britannia. "You are nobody's mother!" Esi spoke in an intense whisper. "Too late! Too late to know your own mother. Long dead! And, worst of all…" She retrieved the documents. "Too late to know the sister who was at your side every minute of your life until you were taken. Who searched for you for years. Years! Who never stopped loving you! And when she found you, what did you do?" Esi snapped open the paper with the words *Without Prejudice* boldly printed at the top. "I know it by heart." She cleared her throat and put on a poncy accent:

> Miss Akua Acqueh, while I acknowledge the possible biological connec-
> tion between us, there can be no relationship. Enclosed is a cheque
> for £500 to cover the cost of five years' worth of stamps, courier fees,
> surveillance and any other means that you have used to stalk me. Your
> letters to me must now cease or I will place this matter in the hands of
> my solicitor. Yours faithfully, Susan Matthews.

Something in Susan cracked. It wasn't the words themselves but the hideous caricature of herself being played out before her.

"I am… You may not…" She started again. "I am Susan Matthews. The only child of Emily and Roland Matthews of 14 Vicarage Lane, Kendal. Both of my parents are deceased."

"I guess you think you look like them," Esi sneered.

Susan's heart contracted and all she could say was, "I have no memory of anything or anybody before Mother and Father."

"You were four years old. I remember when I was four!"

"I have no memory." The teapot was heavy in Susan's hand. Heavier still was the weight of the life she remembered. The Sunday roast. Walking holidays in the Lake District. The Christmas pantomime in Manchester. The shadow memories came too.

Cruel jibes in the playground. Emily struggling with her hair. The times she caught Father looking at her, as though bewildered by her presence at his table. Father…and his vicious dogs…

"No memory," Susan murmured, fighting for control. She filled two cups and passed one to Esi, saying in a low voice: "My mother…Emily…always told me that my life began when I came to them. Your mother's letters told another story. But it was just that. A story." She raised her eyes. "Nothing to do with me."

Something in Susan's voice made Esi look at her.

"I'd never wanted to know about…before." Susan's face twitched. Then the words burst from her. "I wanted to know even less when your mother started to write." She stopped. "How the person who gave birth to me…abandoned me in some African village with…"

Esi grasped Susan's hand and squeezed hard. "Wrong! That 'person' left her children—you and my mother!—with her family. She came to England…for everybody. For a better life." Esi's grip was crushing. Its aggression pushed Susan away from afternoon tea into a waking dream, the girl's words washing over her, dimly heard.

"…became a hospital cleaner…shared a cold-water flat…the walls of her room black with damp…three years before she could send for you and Mum…"

Susan felt she was drowning but, despite her terror, didn't want Esi to stop. For the first time ever, she wanted to break down the wall that separated her from her early life. She closed her eyes. Maybe something from the past, some message, some buried ancient thing would come to her. Perhaps she would remember her childhood and the feel of a burning sun.

"…when you and Mum came, things got worse. Two more mouths to feed. No-one to look after you…"

Susan felt only the cold English air. Perhaps she would see again that African sunlight. But her sealed lids kept all light out.

Esi's tale continued. "The perfect solution…foster care, for a few months…until she found a decent place. She handed you over because my mum was fourteen and could work."

Or perhaps she would hear the ocean's thunder. But all she heard was:

"So you disappeared, Abena…and were rescued, by a couple with money…took you up North and decided to keep you."

Perhaps she would hear rain drumming on those zinc roofs she'd read about. She waited. This time her own voice was saying, "I don't remember."

At the same moment, Esi said, "Gran signed the adoption papers."

Silence.

The server came, topped up the teapots and went away again.

Esi released her grip and Susan noticed Esi's thin fingers, prominent knuckles and flat nails. So much like her own. The girl gathered her things and put a photo next to Susan's teacup.

"You and Mum."

Susan picked it up, trembling a little. A grainy black-and-white picture of two girls—one tall and thin with Esi's face, the other, small, sitting on the bigger girl's narrow hip, their heads turned to each other. Both were smiling.

She shook her head and gave it back with a quick "Sorry."

"Thank you for tea, Aunt Abena." They both looked around. The famous hotel was still there.

"Surreal," muttered Esi, putting the photo in her bag. She leaned in to Susan. "You don't even remember when your mum and mine came to get you? How could you forget that?"

"I told you!" Susan's blood boiled. "I have no memory of that time!"

Esi wound the brilliant scarf around her neck. *"Akwadaa yerafo."*

"What?"

"That's what Mum called you. 'Akwadaa yerafo'." She slung her bag over her shoulder. "The lost child."

With that, Esi was gone.

Susan felt unable to move yet unable to stay. She managed to pay the bill and headed to the ladies' room. In the foyer, an expensively dressed guest was in heated confrontation with a uniformed employee, demanding full rights of entry for her large, restless Alsatian. "Tell me why he can't! Tell me!"

Upset and disoriented, Susan climbed the staircase and wandered around the first floor. She finally found a ladies' room. Who was that woman in the mirror? And those eyes so full of rage and fear…whose were they?

She straightened her back and walked towards the stairs. Suddenly, a loud barking! Her heart began to race. Over the landing, she saw the dog, straining, tugging at the leash. She heard his angry barking at someone she couldn't see.

Susan began to sweat. Beads of perspiration gathered at her temples. She was shaking. Suddenly she realised that Esi was in the foyer, caught up in the fracas between the dog's owner and the hotel staff. And the dog kept on barking.

Esi looked up and saw Susan.

It was then that the buried ancient thing came back to her. She is a child again, playing in the upstairs bedroom. Father's in the garden. Both Alsatians start to bark. She pulls back the window curtain. The dogs are straining on their leads. On the other side of the high chain-link fence, two black strangers, women, one wearing a head-tie, are standing. Calling out. Father shouts back at them in the hard voice she knows. The big woman with the head-tie starts shouting and gripping the fence. Father unleashes the dogs. They attack the fence, lunge at the intruders. The head-tie woman jumps back, knocking down the tall young one. Father turns away; the dogs quieten. But the head-tie woman is back. She is wailing, shaking the fence, getting a foothold, trying to climb over it. The dogs rush forward, barking, snarling, throwing themselves against the fence, their bared teeth threatening the woman's fingers, tearing her coat. Crying out, the young one points up. To her window. Suddenly, the window curtain is closed and her mother carries her away. On her cheek, tears mingle with the smoothness of her mother's pearls.

The child screams.

"AKUA! ONUA! AKUA! AKUA!"

Before Susan collapsed on the hotel floor, her screams could be heard throughout the building. When she finally opened her eyes, Esi was there with several members of the hotel management, anxious to bring this disruption to an end. Susan watched as Esi took charge.

"Thank you so much. If you could please get us a taxi, I'll take my aunt home."

Tears were still rolling down Susan's cheeks as the taxi wove through the early evening traffic. Despite an immense weariness, she forced herself to speak. "Why did you come back?"

"I forgot to give you the picture." Esi took it out of her bag. "It's the only thing Mum really wanted you to have."

But Susan wasn't looking at the photograph. She was looking at the hand that was so much like her own.

Linda Bellos

Born in London, England, to a Jewish mother and Nigerian Catholic father, she has been engaged in politics since her early teens, becoming involved with Black liberation and lesbian/feminism when attending Sussex University as a mature student. She accomplished many firsts in the 10 years after graduating, including being the first Black woman to join the Spare Rib Collective, be leader of Lambeth Council, and treasurer of the Africa Reparations Movement, UK. She is currently re-engaging in community politics following the death of her partner of 15 years, and is working on the first volume of her memoirs. She remains proud of her heritage and considers oppression not a competition but a spur to making the world a better place for all humans, if we can hear each other. She is the proud mother of two children.

Age

Late in 1987, I stood before a gathering of people who had invited me to address them. It was not the first time that I had been invited to speak to a community group, and I have in years since spoken to many more. But what was memorable about this meeting was that I was faced with a group of elderly African and

Caribbean people, and it was the first time I had noticed what had previously been missing from my life.

I was born in London in 1950; at that time, though I was not to realise it for some years, I was one of a small number of Black people to have been born in Britain. The significance of being in such a small minority does not, of course occur to a small child. It was only later, with the perspective of distance, that I have been able to look at the true significance of events in my own life. With a shock I realised that my own parents, plus those of my friends and peers, were by necessity young(ish). At the time they seemed old, but most of them would have been in their twenties or thirties when we were born.

When my dad came to England from Nigeria in 1942, his own parents were dead; even had they been alive, it is doubtful they would have been allowed to follow him to Liverpool at the height of the war, or afterwards. When he moved to London in the late 1940s and married my mother, he socialised with other Nigerian men. Many, like him, had married European women and, naturally, they were of a similar age. As a consequence, I did not come across Black people with grey hair, neither did I have the opportunity to learn from the experience and maturity of African elders.

When I finally became aware of what I had missed, it occurred to me how much this absence symbolised the problematics of racism. In the mid-1980s, when the campaign for racial equality was most prominent and (in my view most successful) there were many in both the Conservative and Labour parties who argued that racism would disappear if we (Black activists) would stop drawing attention to it; indeed, they positively urged us to adopt a colour-blind approach. But my revelation had demonstrated to me the weakness of colour-blindness. White people had and needed older people. It would be impossible to imagine the British without any grandparents, picture the House of Commons or House of Lords without those over sixty. It is, of course, not merely a matter of how old people look, it is the continuity and experience that they represent which is significant. And yet, for the communities from the Caribbean and Africa we had to establish homes and families and, ultimately, communities without elders. The immigration rules meant that only the economically active were accepted, our older "dependants" were often not. This was the period when we came here in significant numbers, in the 1950s and 1960s. We did so, or at least our parents did, without many of the social support systems which we now rightly consider essential to survival.

And yet, survive they did. In the face of subtle and unsubtle racial discrimination, in a country in which it was near impossible to find decent accommodation, or fair wages; our parents, my father included, set up shops, churches, and sometimes schools, which began to address our cultural needs. In other words, in addition to moving to a new, cold and sometimes hostile environment, our parents met their own cultural needs and those of their children (to some extent) without the support or help of their parents. Indeed, it did not occur to me until recently that they were of course sending money "back home" because the legacy of British rule did not run to pensions.

I am myself now in middle age, so I am naturally sensitive to issues of old age in a way I was not when younger. Maybe it is that I have recently attended several funerals or memorials of elderly Black African people. Lord Pitt's memorial service in Westminster Cathedral saw us celebrating the long life of a man who achieved respect and admiration in his lifetime. This contrasted with the funerals of young people who had died at the hands of the police or street racists, or more recently at the hands of their brothers. There is, to my mind, something rather good about attending the funerals of old people who lived long, fruitful and varied lives. It offers an opportunity not only to celebrate that life but also gain a tangible sense of our having a history. Grey hair in some ways represents the notion of history as well age and experience.

One of the things which for me has underpinned racism, and which was most evident during the Windrush Celebration in 1998, is that we are a people without a history, just as Africa was a Continent without a history. Windrush was presented as the point at which we arrived in Britain, having apparently had no history prior to 1948. Grey hair speaks to me of generations, and generations speak to me of ancestors or wisdom—in other words, of history.

My own father, like others of his generation, did not expect to die here. He came to better himself, and he came to serve the motherland at a time of war. Things did not turn out as he would have hoped and expected. He did not, for example end up a rich man able to support his family and friends back home. So, in disappointment and shame, he stayed in England. He died in the UK, on the 17 January 2000.

While I celebrate those of our elders who are returning, buying or building that long-dreamed of home, there is also the recognition that most of our elders are staying here. This means that there will be Grey Heads for our young people to see and learn from, a real sense of continuity and history. The other important side of this reality for me is that the services that our parents paid for and worked in now need to be changed to incorporate their needs. What I mean here is that our elderly may need "multicultural" social services provision, which is sensitive to their needs. In the mid-1980s, when Councils such as Lambeth began to provide multicultural meals on wheels, they were attacked as "Loony Left". These days not even the *Daily Mail* would think that it is acceptable for social services departments to leave elderly Caribbean, African and Asian people hungry, offering only traditional British food. (I have no idea whether, since privatisation, culturally sensitive food is provided by the private sector who now provide the services which councils used to provide.)

My own father was the only African man in the nursing home that was his last home. The reason I chose that home for him when I could no longer care for him was that others had a few Black residents but not as many African staff. As his Alzheimer's had progressed, he had lost control over whether he spoke English or Yoruba, so there being staff who could talk to him in his own tongue was important. The same was true for many other Black people. We hear a lot about new research and campaigning which is being carried out in response to changing demographic patterns, with older people representing a larger percentage of the population; some of these people are Black and from other ethnic minorities; they may have needs which are specific to their cultural background, whether it be food, religion or bathing. In looking at our elders' needs, an awareness of cultures and ethnicity is essential. It is not merely political correctness that makes me insist that care or nursing homes take on board that not all their residents want meat and two veg, with suet pudding and custard to follow.

I never thought I would allow my parents to be put in a home, and no doubt they would have had some of the same concerns. For both my parents, the idea of a home that was not one's own was too close to the idea of a workhouse. Even though my father had spent the first twenty-five years of his life in Africa, he knew and feared the poor provision for older people in Britain. It was not just the legacy of Poor Laws which made me reticent about old people's homes, it was more that I had grown up with stories from Africa, where older people were venerated, where the idea of putting them out of their homes was utterly alien. My mother too, had similar views about the responsibilities of children towards their aged parents. Nursing homes were no more a part of my view of family relationships than sending my small children away to boarding school would have been. And yet when my father's Alzheimer's had developed to the extent that he had become a danger to himself, I had no hesitation in finding a nursing home for him. In other words, the reality of the situation made me jettison the rhetoric and deal with the needs of my own father, which I could not, despite my best endeavours, satisfy on my own. I do not feel guilty about my father, and I have long since come to the realisation that to try to care for him myself would have been more about me than about him. None the less, there were real difficulties with him being in a nursing home that I had not anticipated.

It should have come as no surprise that most of the other residents were white, but I failed to consider their racism. These were people who, now in their old age, were plagued by the fears and anxieties of Alzheimer's, and some of these fears were triggered by me, my father and the Black staff. Violet, who seemed sweet and charming, could, in a moment, become vile and venomous. It was strange, almost surreal for my father to have to tolerate even such low-level verbal racism.

The nursing home was my father's home, it was a safe place in a world that was otherwise hostile or, at best, confusing to him, and at one level he coped with the offensive comments made from time to time by the other residents. There was no doubt in my mind that he both heard and understood what was being said. He gave each speaker a careful and thoughtful look and said nothing. It struck me that his dignity was as intact as it had been during those early years in England of overt and rampant racism. He may have had Alzheimer's but that did not mean he was stupid. What bemused me about his situation, and no doubt that of other isolated Black people, is that when they are old, at their most vulnerable they may be exposed to more overt racism than when they were younger. I do not wish to exaggerate the extent of racism in old people's care provision, and from what I have seen first-hand, it varies from home to home. In London, where many of the staff are themselves African or Afro-Caribbean, perhaps that sense of isolation is not so real as in locations where there are a few Black residents but no Black staff. Given the nature of Alzheimer's in particular, and old age in general, older Black people need to feel safe and protected, yet these are often tough people, who have survived separation from home—building new lives amidst blatant racism and discrimination. By retirement age, a bit of offensive language is not a big deal.

It is I who felt most offended on my father's behalf but, like him, I said nothing. Partly this was because I knew my father could cope, partly because the old white people who made racist comments couldn't be persuaded to change the habits of a lifetime. Ironically, it is the African notion of respect for one's elders that enabled me to cope with the everyday racism in my father's home. I saw those old people, white and wrinkled as my father was black and wrinkled, as people who had histories, as people who had learned either to hate and fear or to feel superior to people of African origin. In their older years, they too were vulnerable and neither I nor my father felt threatened by their words. I know that many Black staff feel the same. They can return to their own homes and families after each shift; they have a strong sense of both their own identity and that the old must be respected because of their age.

I have often found a deep irony in the ways in which we Black people are asked to assimilate into British society and culture. This seems to include the way that British people treat their old folk. Even as a child born in England, I know enough from my father to know that shutting older people away and treating them with disrespect is not a universal practice, and that maybe African and Asian people can teach Britain something. Now I have even more reason to believe this to be true. My father's generation may be the first older African, Caribbean and Asian people to die here in numbers, leaving their children and grandchildren to remain in Britain. Consequently, we may make a cultural contribution which adds something positive to British life. As we grow older and ourselves reproduce, we may be seen less as immigrants and more as settlers. We will make an impact on pensioners' groups and in nursing home management. It is not just about Black faces being seen to be present in more areas of British society than hitherto; more significant may be how African, Caribbean and Asian attitudes to ageing are incorporated or, should I say, assimilated.

I wonder what this society will look like when a generation of Black people born here have parents and grandparents from whom to learn and from whom advice and guidance can be gained. I know that such a sense of continuity did not exist for my father or for many others from Africa and the Caribbean. They made do without Grey Heads, but they retained the memory of them back home. It is we, who grew up here in the 1950s, 1960s and 1970s who did not have that benefit and may not have even noticed it was missing. Now, I know what I have missed and am pleased and nourished by the sight of old Black people. Ageing for me is like completing a circle.

Marion Bethel

From Nassau in The Bahamas, she is an attorney, poet, essayist, filmmaker, and human and gender rights activist. She has published two poetry books, Guanahani, My Love, *which won the Casa de Las Americas Prize in 1994, and* Bougainvillea Ringplay *(2009). In 2012 she produced the documentary film* Womanish Ways: Freedom, Human Rights and Democracy, The Women's Suffrage Movement in The Bahamas 1948–1962, *which chronicles the journey of the enfranchisement of women and the significant contribution of this suffrage movement to the larger civil rights, majority rule and independence movements in The Bahamas. She serves on the United Nations Committee on the Elimination of Discrimination Against Women (CEDAW).*

We Were Terrestrial Once, Maybe

the sand feels sandy   & loose
until my bone & muscle   grow heavy
my sight short   my breath
shorter

small waves now lap   at my mouth   & against my slit
I am   out of my head   with the smell   like fresh seaweed
of our glide   deep & slow   our belly-to-belly glide
south to the Tongue of the Ocean   off the Andros shore
where I lost you   dizzy   with sonic ringing
bang & buzz   now deep in my ear
calling me to shore

if in this merciful light-headedness
my heart is a cork   playful   light with laughter
afloat   out there   with you   leading you   oceanward
understand my love   there is nothing here   but beach & shore
(maybe a once-upon-a-time home)   & the crushing weight
of flesh   without water

the too-blue sky   a mirage of ocean   just above
teases me   I no longer   feel the sun   burn my skin

we flukeflapped   for love   & flipperflopped
in the deep deep   where we breached   for each other
& dipped & dragged our flukes   like drunken oars
off the Nantucket shore   while the tourists gasped

the deep deep is so so far away   muscular tail flaps away
& an oh so slow deep swim   in easy drag & glide   with you
In pitch col.   & utter blackness   your whale breath
in my lungs

thankyou for the guard of honour   our humpback podmates
you bring   to steer me back   to you   outlandish my love!
I would if I could   just roll over   roll to you   roll all over you
& suck   another barnacle   & another from your throat
eat squid   from your tongue   I hear you   your whalesong
a dirge above the rest

& you my love   you still point your nose   to the shore
you would   I know this   if you could   drag
drag & drag some more   the last bits   of my imploded flesh
back back   back to the deep.

Of Cowrie Shells & Revolution

I
In the marketplace of once upon-a-time
cowrie shells tell and trade their own story
the flooding of stalls with kola nuts
the ascent of salt & copper
the currency of silver & bronze
and an uprising of gold.

II
I never wore the cowrie belt
you gave me
a gift from Kenya.
Three rows of thirty shells
a broadhipped sling of ninety lips and fine teeth
threaded together
in serrated chorus
of daily Yes-es.

I packed and unpacked it
at every port of call
after long periods of rest
in apartment drawers,
a sullen stowaway
in trunks and boxes.

Oh, yes! I was very African then
headwraps afro and daishikis
full of black powder & marxist too!
Cornforth's Theory of Materialism in hand.

But the sea-green leather strip
of cowrie shells was too too wide & long
for my rational hips—
a black-is-beautiful clash
with my dialectic pose—
a primary contradiction!

III
This gift to me
more worthy of the waist
of a daughter of Yemaya
possessed by the bass drum.
It was not fit for a socialist and lover
of Al Green's "Let's Stay Together" in falsetto.

Draped over outstretched arms
you brought it—a deaconess's stole
a sling of Mau Mau grenades
or a snake in concertina.

You wrapped the belt around me
your fingers in touch
with each and every lip.

IV
I come to the belt now
some thirty years later.
I rip out one row
of dryrot thread
& the cowries explode
in relief.

I know now some
of what you divined
through these shells
that gift day.
A straitjacket of snakeskin

translucent & cool
yet not sloughed enough
on time.

I was unwilling
in the late '70s
to stop and listen
to the sacred story
from the whorled lips
of a fine-toothed shell
that housed once
upon-a-time
a sea snail.

Nina 1984
(Ronnie Scott's Jazz Club)

You have no mercy reliving
"Mississippi Goddam"
before our eyes.

I cannot imagine the '70s
without your drumroll voice
singing of a new world
coming ushering the good
news out of the church into
the jazz & blues clubs.

You say: "I would rather have been
a classical pianist."
I do not question
your loose vibrato longing.

I want to rock you
hush that sultry prophecy
to rest.

You hold down those jazz & blues keys
until the dogs stop snapping & snarling
and until the water hoses run dry.

Nina, your voice is still now
still the balm in Gilead.

Tanella Boni

Translated by Eileen Busby

Born in Abidjan, Côte d'Ivoire, she pursued university studies in Toulouse, France, and at the University of Paris (Sorbonne), where she obtained a PhD. Returning to Côte d'Ivoire, she became Professor of Philosophy at the University of Cocody-Abidjan, served as President of the Writers' Association of Côte d'Ivoire from 1991 to 1997 and organised Abidjan's International Poetry Festival from 1998 to 2002. During the political strife in Côte d'Ivoire, from 2002 onwards, she lived in self-exile in France. She writes poetry, novels, short stories and children's literature. In 2005, she received the Ahmadou Kourouma Prize for her novel Matins de couvre-feu. *Her first full collection of poems to be translated into English (by Todd Fredson) is* The Future Has an Appointment with the Dawn *(2018).*

One Day Like No Other
(Excerpt from an unpublished manuscript)

My story begins one March 8. It is said that March 8 is the day of women whose presence is forgotten for 364 days. March 8 is the only day of the year when women are visible in the public square. Issa, my baby, accompanies me to the scene of a march. I usually take don't take part in any demos. I flee crowds full of sound and fury, where words flow freely, words signifying nothing. My job as a school teacher gives me the right to speak in public, but I express myself so rarely. I don't usually say what I believe and what I think.

There's no such thing as a silent teacher, but silence heats my blood because I am an angry woman. More than once a day, I have a rage in my gut. I wonder how I hold up in front of my students. I probably forget I'm in a class, in a public place. Then I build sentences that make sense, my words come freely; of course, I don't talk about myself, I talk about others. I want to tell stories. Everything seems to run like clockwork. Now, by necessity, the school is closed. I have no idea when classes will reopen. I don't have time to be bored, even if the war does not end and chaos persists around me. To deceive the anxiety lurking in the shadows, I walk with a notebook. And I note down a few sentences. This time, I want to tell what happens to me, what I see, what I hear.

About nine o'clock, in a common courtyard where there are only women, I go to the meeting place. At the entrance, two young girls, sentinels in sportswear, are keeping watch. These are the bodyguards trained at the police academy or in a private club. And I imagine they are there for a good cause. They search all those who arrive. There is no time for *Hello*, or the endless *salaams*. As soon as I see the girls, I hear:

—You seem to be a pregnant woman—come let me check you!

—Do you have anything to declare? adds the other.

They come near me. One lifts the cloth that covers the baby's head. She smiles.

—What's his name?

—Issa!

—A beautiful baby boy. He's asleep. My name is Estelle—

—And I'm Nani. We provide security.

I am far from being a round woman and I'm not expecting a child. Not anymore. My baby is nine months old. I'm strong, certainly, but mostly armoured. I wear on my body what matters in my opinion. What cushions blows from batons and would undoubtedly deflect the trajectory of an untimely bullet. These objects piled on my belly and my chest will serve as a bulletproof vest if needed. But this is all so ridiculous…

—You know why we look under the cloths? adds Nani.

—I have no idea. Probably to make sure we haven't come here with a gun or something else, to stir things up…

—You got it, said Estelle. You see, belts are the new fashionable games, apart from the usual much talked about objects.

—Belts? What for? I asked, surprised.

They saw my banana belt, which is my handbag.

—Don't worry, said Estelle, feeling the bumbag. I know you have nothing in your belt except a penknife, a stinging object or nail clippers, those little things that are so effective for scaring off a troublemaker…

—We are talking about homemade bombs exploding in the markets and on the streets. These devilish things can kill hundreds of people in a second as you know, said Nani.

—Women carry bombs on their bodies, adds Estelle, when they obey the orders of those who have lost their heads and who drug them. Well, you know what I mean. Even very young children don't escape their grip…

—Yes. I see…

—Good. Let's get on with business. We have placards over there, on the table. You choose what you want. There are also squares of white sheeting and pieces of cardboard. You have what is necessary to write and express your anger.

Nani comes to see what I'm doing.

—Is that all you're writing? asks Nani.

—I have a hard time expressing myself…

—It will come on the spur of the moment! she says.

I move away from them. While women of all ages flock to the scene of the demonstration, I head towards those who are speaking loud and clear, gathered under a big mango tree planted at the other end of the yard from Estelle and Nani.

They look at me suspiciously.

—You, you're not a spy, by any chance?

And, stung to the quick, I react without thinking.

—Why?

—We've never seen you at any of our meetings!

—Leave it. She's already been searched at the entrance…

—Welcome!

The one who interrupts the words of her colleague doesn't want to know who I am or where I come from. It was one of the committee members. Among the crowd, no one knows me. I'm not wearing a women's activist cap. In fact, I'm not one of them. Here, among the crowd, I'm in another territory that is not mine. There is no shortage of sidelong glances and whispers. I'm the stranger who intrigues everyone, with my baby that I should have asked someone to look after before coming to this unsavoury place. Yet I see so many mothers with babies in their arms or on their backs, some of them younger than my Issa.

Around me float boubous and white scarves. Incense and other scents pleasantly perfume the crowded street. In the distance, I see women in black and red. Then the procession visibly grows, joined by very young girls and girls in short dresses. Very coquettish grandmothers, wearing boubous or multicoloured cloths, come out of their homes and join the march. In the middle of the procession, naked women, with kaolin-tattooed bodies and faces, form a group that does not go unnoticed. These clay-marked bodies speak a clear language that I cannot translate into words. I am not in front of a blackboard on which all the letters are legible. I realise that I am uneducated as soon as I leave my classroom and I mingle with a crowd that has a different alphabet to offer passers-by.

In our world, sign interpreters are numerous. Because they understand the language of the traditions, they predict that the appearance of naked women in the street is a prelude to great misfortune, and they hasten to say so. Thus, onlookers observing the procession metamorphose into sign readers. Planted on the sidewalks, on both sides of the street, they move at times, while chatting cheerfully.

In the procession, no one takes note of the presence of the foreigner that I am. We march together. Each of us is convinced that it is for the common cause, the only good cause. This cause, we don't know what it is, even if one has the impression of touching it, of living daily in its grip. I look at the signs parading before my eyes. There are so many associations, NGOs, various groups that are concerned about the lives of women, their problems in relationships, their professional integration, all the violence they suffer, the exclusions of which they are victims. I imagine that violence among so much violence is nothing but harassment on a daily basis. Where a grain of sand seeps into an ordinary relationship. The little word assassin spoken on the street or in the workplace. This little word that shouldn't be said, slowly descends in your memory of a woman, bothers you all day and, when evening comes, gives you insomnia. And worse, the damage to the dignity of your body pressed against a wall, wedged between two doors. How to explain this rage that lives in your body and your memory of a woman while weapons crackle, and your city sinks under piles of filth?

Things feel even more confused when those closest to you—husband, friend, son, brother, father—do not make the task easy.

That's why I'm here. Why all these young girls, mothers and grandmothers are here, I'm sure.

"Find your own place, find it clearly before a war, like a child's game, don't let it disturb your sleep." Mother's words.

It's my common cause, because life is like a beautiful net in the middle of which we swirl around. To find one's place. That's why we sing in unison, whatever our differences.

I sing. It is balm to my heart. I don't remember the last time I sang. I forget, indeed, that I can sing loudly, provided I have the strength to not see the chaos that surrounds me. This chaos that constantly brings me back to the harsh realities of the moment.

Pots, calabashes, wooden spatulas and other improvised instruments enter the dance to accompany the songs and slogans disseminated by loudspeakers. Then the music becomes thunderous. And the first shots, crossing the hubbub at its peak, break the joyful atmosphere. No one knows where this deafening noise comes from, accompanied by an infernal stench.

The head of the procession was sprayed with tear gas. It reminds me of the years when all schools, in full uproar, went down the streets. This time, it is women, out of nowhere, who move the streets. But the method of punishment for the unruly does not change, from one year to the other. In this world, no peaceful march is acceptable. The tear-gas bomb is the first response, heralding the imminent arrival of lethal weapons.

Some wounded fall. There's a stampede on the road where the speakers take time to shut up. To hold on, my heart must cling firmly to life. No one is immune from a heart attack. A few of the zealous continue chanting slogans to the rhythm of gun-fire and bursts from sub-machine-guns. The group eventually breaks up. This is the unplanned end of the rally that has not reached the party stage. It's a missed celebration that ends in a fishtail, in total confusion.

Journalists arrive and film some scenes of violence. Women have the courage to speak between shots, cries and tears. A trellised shadow passes before my eyes. I'm already on the pavement on the other side. I run as fast as I can. I wander for a good part of the morning. Issa, who has felt nothing of the unfolding drama because he was sleeping peacefully, wakes up. He brings me back to reality. He wants to know where he is, if he can play on the floor, if he can crawl on all-fours and stretch his legs as he has learned to do in recent weeks. But it's too late. I keep him on the bed of my back while he gesticulates. The area is cordoned off and I don't know where to go.

Beverley Bryan

Jamaica-born, she migrated to England as a child to join her parents—a part of the "Windrush generation". She was a member of the British Black Panthers in the early 1970s, and later helped found the Black Women's Group and Organisation of African and Asian Descent (OWAAD), which shared similar radical views. With Stella Dadzie and Suzanne Scafe she co-authored The Heart of the Race: Black Women's Lives in Britain *(1985), which won the Martin Luther King Prize. In 1992, she returned to Jamaica to join the University of the West Indies (UWI) as a lecturer in educational studies, eventually becoming Professor of Language Education. She has been a consultant on language and literacy policies to the Jamaican Ministry of Education and other Caribbean governments, as well as serving as a member of the United Nations Literacy Decade Experts' Group. She was also the Caribbean Coordinator of the Caribbean Poetry Project, a collaboration between UWI and the University of Cambridge that worked to increase the visibility of Caribbean writers in the UK.*

A Windrush Story

The night before Marva left for England she had a strange dream. In the night's eye she dreamt of birds flying, and from her own bed, she saw herself dip and flow over a crystal quivering blue-green sea. As she moved high and soared against the sharpening air, all fears and doubts about the path ahead sloughed from her. Here and now, she was supreme, no longer an anxious and confused twelve-year-old. Suddenly a cloud, imagined, flitted… The hawk hovered, and the slowly flapping wings cast a long shadow that seemed to blot out the sun. The knowledge that she was only dreaming stilled her fears so that she could calmly assess this new danger. Such tranquillity filled her sleeping self with wonder. Even as the hawk stiffened, and its body swerved ready to swoop, another distant voice emerged:

"Kwik! Kwik! Chickin 'awk wi get yu!"

She jumped and fell to the floor. Her little cousins, Delcy and Loris, continued to sleep peacefully on the bed above; no one else in the house had been disturbed. The only sounds that she heard were the competing choirs of crickets and tree frogs. Wanting nothing to disturb her further, to remind her of the journey tomorrow, she concentrated on the night-time chorus and slipped into a, now, dreamless sleep.

That morning, she overslept but was shaken out of her slumbers by Delcy and Loris playing noisily over her grandmother's insistent voice:

"Marva, is how yu stay so late? No mek mi haffi trow some liks pan yu tail."

With Mammie's presence, the fears and shadow of the night returned, and yet Mammie was sounding as though this was just an ordinary departure. Not that after losing her husband, she was also about to lose her eldest grandchild and be left with five younger ones to manage until it was their turn to be "sent for". But Marva, who knew the whole truth, simply said:

"Yes, Mammie, a hear yu."

She took in the straight back, with one hip hunched high under the folds of the long, faded dress. Again, the tightness in Marva's chest and an urge to confirm the knowledge that burdened her, that made the prospect of leaving so overwhelming.

It went back to the conversation she overheard as she rested by the concrete stilts that raised the front of the house, quietly mourning the death of her grandfather. Reverend Matthews' voice had come drifting down:

"It's a great shame she has to leave, Madda Cole…so soon after… Tings moving faas in England, but couldn't the bigger one stay back? You don't know when…"

Mammie's voice came back sharp but heavy: "No, Reverend! Is di laas chance Lucille have. Marva have to go. Jackson know how tings stay…keep Lucille mind fram it. The Lord will provide."

And so shadows came and lengthened like the hawk. Part of her wanted to go—not to carry water from the stand pipe again; to use toothpaste and soap all the time and not just when parcels came. But most of all to see her parents after nine years: to have those hazy faces become solid and real.

And now Marva turned and faced her grandmother. The eyes grown grey and glazed with age gave nothing away except the bustling activity that drove her.

"Chile, don't dawgle. Ready yuself."

The morning Marva left, all the leading figures of Priestman's River came with their last-minute messages for family in England, as was the custom. Among them, Teacher Parker came with a letter for his brother, who had hardly been heard of since he gave up his farming lands at Pampey Gate. Reverend Matthews came and gave his customary Bible. Then came Gaddy Beck inspecting the going-away outfit, the puff-sleeved, two-streamer dress she made for every child in the district who left for foreign lands. Mammie received them, dressed in her best dark-rose pink crepe, conversing with Gaddy Beck, who would watch the children until she came back from the airport.

Then in the distance the horns of the bus, Carlton Express, growing louder as it shuddered to a halt on the grass verge. All was pandemonium. But Mammie mounted the bus slowly and the other passengers made way for her progress.

Marva looked out of the window to her young cousins, who were now beginning to understand the finality of the occasion. As the bus geared up they began to sniffle—Loris, Nordal, Hugh, and Delcy lifting baby Errol. And when it swerved off, belching smoke, Nordal and Hugh ran behind, waving desolately.

Marva stored that memory and added the passing scenes of grey stone walls, topped by the golden love bush and the pastures that reached out to the variegated blue horizon of sea. On and on, through districts she hardly knew—past Fair Prospect, to Manchioneal, and then to sleep.

It was not until they reached Town that she woke with a start to the frenzied orchestra of horns tooting as voices swirled around. Mammie moved slowly down the steps of the bus, ignoring the vendors, but making sure a side-boy was there to help with the case across the busy road to the next bus. This much grander vehicle moved smoothly and swiftly out of the flat peninsular landscape to PALISADOES AIRPORT, signalled on the bare, square building ahead. Once inside the airport reception area, Mammie left her, while she went to process the travel papers. Marva felt a kind of anticipation over-riding fear and dread. This was heightened when Mammie came back with a lady exquisitely dressed in a lemon two-piece suit, white gloves and cloche hat with a small veil.

"Marva, Miss Clover here will go wid yu—tek yu to Lucille. She will be at airport." Miss Clover was a church sister from Hope Bay leaving domestic servitude to join her children's father before she too could send for them. Like her fashion, she was bright, airy and talkative:

"Hello, Miss Marva. We'll soon leave. Ai, ai, no cardigan?! Inglan soo soo cold." She stopped when she found her answer: "Yu madda will bring sumting to airport."

Mammie hovered, because now this was it.

Trepidation, longing, dread: everything came to Marva, feeling her grandmother's softness for the last time: "A wi….wi come back soon. Soon, soon, Mammie."

"Yes, mi chile." Mammie looked at her sadly, steadfastly: "A so it mus go, Marva. Mi wi manage… Gawd bless…." Her voice began to falter. "Jus don't figet yu Mammie."

Her voice told Marva she was ready to accept her future, as she wanted her grandchild to accept hers.

There Marva stood, the young girl starting her life, facing the old woman maybe ending hers. They didn't need to say anything because both had silently acknowledged what they knew. The tears simply slipped silently down and on to her arm.

All Marva could manage was: "A wi come back soon…"

The night before Marva came to England, Lucille could not sleep. The anticipation and dread for her daughter were too much. She left her husband to sleep off the tiredness of a ten-hour shift cleaning railway tracks. Her six months of pregnancy made it hard to rest, especially with the continuing nausea and the news of her mother's illness. Jackson had not managed to keep it from her. Long after the passage was booked, she had accidentally found Mammie's letter to him, carelessly tucked behind the family portrait photo. So now Marva was on her way. Lucille pulled herself heavily out of bed and to the kitchen, trying not to wake the tenants in the house. She took the packet of tea from the blue locker and measured out the spoonful needed for her brew. As she stirred, she went back over all the plans for the future that had led them to this moment.

When news had spread that England was a place you could go to get more than farm work, it was just a matter of saving the money bit by bit, with help from Brother Freddie, who went first, and Jackson with his post-office job and a little farming. And they came and worked on the railway, the buses, the hospitals and in factories—glad of the opportunity to work and send for the next one. Now the British Government seemed determined to keep out Jamaica people. All the talk of "vouchers" and fresh papers had made them realise they had to do something to get their child to them.

Sending for Marva was not a hard decision. Even now with news of her mother, it seemed clear that maybe this was the last chance. The alternative made Lucille shudder. After all the insults, the rudeness and the one-roomed living—now mercifully over, with the house in Clapham—to swallow all that battering in the cold, and then return with nothing but more children? People would just look and laugh, wondering what happen to the big house England people say they were coming back to build.

No, things would get better. Once she had the baby, she would be back in the factory. Marva would be able to help a little. Lucille smiled, thinking of the daughter she had left nine years ago. How would she know her? She had no photograph. How big was she? Would the cardigan she was taking to the airport fit?

Then she heard Edith, her friend and best tenant, coming in from her night shift on the railway. Edith would look after the boys while she and Jackson went to the airport. Edith's brother had sent the money for her and then her gentleman Joe had sold his land, borrowed his mother's savings and taken the boat with Lucille. Edith and Joe still had no children, but she heard them every night busy trying. With Jackson awake now, she bathed in the cold bathroom with the sluggish geezer—happy still that it was theirs and that there was no one to rap impatiently and hurry her along in her heavy pregnant state.

A sharp knock on the front door told her that her brother Freddie was here ready for the airport. He was the first in the family to reach England, the one who sent for her and allowed her to send for Jackson. Now she hurried, not wanting him to find something to complain about, but also eager for what was to come. As she reached the front-room door, she heard Jackson's final words: "…not when she pregnant." Then she knew that Freddie and Jackson shared the truth but decided today would not be the day for the reckoning of her anger: it was her daughter's day and she needed her strength to meet her. Instead, Lucille turned back to Edith and the instructions for her still sleeping sons.

By the time they reached the airport in Freddie's new saloon, Lucille's spirits were lifted. They joined the other Jamaicans waiting for passengers. Freddie hailed a few who were past tenants of his. The minutes stretched on, until a burst of activity told them the arrivals were coming through. The colour and the warmth of those clothes further lifted Lucille. She scanned the crowd expectantly. Then she saw the woman in the two-piece lemon suit holding the hand of a serious-looking young girl who wore a familiar dark pink dress. Miss Clover brought her to Lucille, who rested her hands on each shoulder:

"Marva, let me look at you good."

The girl was thin and straight but not too unhealthy. *Thank you, Mammie.* Aloud: "You looking well. The cardigan jus about fit. By the way, how she stay?"

Lucille saw her daughter's face in tortuous movement and pulled her close:

"Is alright, Marva. A know. A know… Me an yu father will mek it up to yu."

Marva hugged that promise for the future: "Yes, Mamma."

It was enough for the time being—to feel the shadows lifting and fading:

"Yes, mi chile, mek wi go."

And then out together, towards the chill air. And home to the newly arrived telegram from Gaddy Beck, lying patiently on the table, waiting their return.

Angela Cobbinah

A UK journalist of many years' experience, she started her career with the North London Press and went on to become a founder member of the independently owned Camden New Journal. Her interest in Africa led her to work for Concord magazine in Nigeria as a features writer during the days of military rule and, on her return to England, for a wide range of African publications. She then joined the BBC World Service, before becoming a production editor and reporter-at-large of News Africa magazine, which saw her re-visit West Africa. In 2007 she became co-editor of Black History 365, an award-winning magazine that was both a response and a challenge to Black History Month. She now works as a freelance writer and editor and is features contributor to the Camden New Journal, Islington Tribune and West End Extra stable of newspapers, with an interest in local history, the arts, health and housing. She is also production editor of Africa Briefing magazine. She lives in London and has two children and three grandchildren.

Black Tracking

I was sixteen when I first spoke to a black person. By this I do not mean the two other black kids who attended my school, as we spent all of our time avoiding each other, and I don't mean the Pakistani boy, who was fostered by a local family one summer and kept on being referred to as my "long-lost brother".

When I tell you that I grew up in Cornwall, you'll understand. Even now it seems one of the whitest places on earth. As the only black girl in the village, my isolation was made worse by the fact that my mother was Hungarian, so obviously different that she might as well have come from another planet, too. Sure, I had friends but while they were preoccupied with boys and clothes and reading the latest *Jackie*, I was trying to work out my place in a world that had just been rocked by the black power salute at the 1968 Olympic Games. I watched that, and I watched the funeral of Martin Luther King, and I felt an unfamiliar emotion. Call it connection or kinship, or the bubbling of a youthful rebelliousness, it was something I knew I could not talk about with anyone else.

My father, Jimmy, was from Ghana and had been sent to England to study public administration in the 1950s, one of a select group of people being prepared to take over the reins of government come Independence. Once he completed his course, he had to return home to take up a job. I was three months old. My mother, a midwife who had settled in Britain after the war, declined to go back with him as there was the not inconsiderable problem that he already had a wife and four kids. Their parting broke my mother's heart, but she never had a bad word to say about him and always called me Korkoh, my Ghanaian grandmother's name.

He kept in touch until I was eight. I still have that last telegram he sent me from Tarkwa, the mining town in which he lived: "Many Happy Returns, Korkoh, love Daddy". One day my mother saw a picture of a pathetic group of political prisoners in the *Sunday Express*, victims, it claimed, of "African dictator" Kwame Nkrumah. My mother swore that Dad was one of the prisoners and that was why we no longer heard from him. She placed the cutting in a drawer and occasionally would take it out and gaze at it sadly. I would not find out whether she was correct until many years later but for now all I had for a father was his smiling photograph on the front-room wall and my mother's fond memories of him.

We lived in Torpoint, a nondescript town on the other side of the river from Devonport Dockyard in Plymouth. Plymouth was in Devon, which might as well have been a foreign land. Torpoint was solidly Cornish, with only me and a few other kids betraying roots of far-away places—Mercedez from Cyprus, Ted and Mary from Ireland and Mark and Sofia, whose dad came from Malta. Mark had black hair and olive skin and like me was described as a "darkie". As a small kid, I was aware of being different but this did not unduly preoccupy me. My mother was able to provide all the security and love I needed and I thrived in the fresh sea air and rolling green countryside.

When I was around twelve, though, it seemed as though a cloud suddenly descended on my world. I had a feeling that adults were looking at me strangely out of the corner of their eye, or giving each other knowing looks about me. I felt uncomfortable and afraid, but when I told my mother she told me not to be silly. I knew she didn't understand. A spate of Keep Britain White slogans around the town filled me with more dread.

There were two other black kids in the school in higher years who came from surrounding villages. But I can't remember saying a single word to either of them or vice versa. It's as if we instinctively knew that any coming together would have been viewed negatively.

I was clever and good at sport, so people looked up to me. But I was always on my guard, ready to deflect remarks about coons and the like—"Oh, we don't mean you, Angy." If teachers were aware of the difficulties I was experiencing they didn't show it. Once, during a dance and movement class when I kept being out of step with the rest, the PE mistress bellowed: "What's the matter with you, Angela? You people are meant to have such rhythm!"

So I muddled through, taking pleasure in being near the top of the class and breaking athletics records. But I was on the outside looking in, tiptoeing around in the shadows, trying not to draw attention to myself since my very presence got everyone's heads turning. My friends fulfilled my need for companionship but the people I felt most comfortable around were those who also saw themselves as outsiders, like Hazel who was still hurting from having to give up her first child for adoption.

When I was sixteen my periods suddenly stopped, as if the constant assaults on my psyche had disrupted my physical balance. I didn't tell my mother, who now felt like a stranger to me. It was the local library that proved to be my lifeline. Here I sought out books that could offer an explanation for my predicament. I read George Orwell's *Coming Up for Air* several times, finding common ground with its middle-aged protagonist's disillusionment and loss of innocence. I avidly read anything about human psychology. Eric Berne's *Games People Play* was another favourite. Over time, I came to the conclusion that there was nothing wrong with me, but a lot wrong with "them". They were not only mean-minded and emotionally dishonest but also plain stupid. Armed with this knowledge, I became rude and difficult in sixth form, making no effort to fit in except with a little band of rebels who played truant and listened to Leonard Cohen. That year my form teacher wrote in my report that I needed psychiatric help. What a fool, I thought as I tossed the report in the bin to save upsetting my mum.

The library was running out of books for me, so I began visiting the big one in Plymouth. Not being a member, I couldn't borrow books so would spend hours reading them there and then. One day, I spied a black man at one of the study tables, writing in a very concentrated fashion. I cast aside my usual shyness and approached him. He seemed pleased to see me too, set aside his fountain pen and shook my hand, introducing himself as Prince. As it seemed obvious we had a lot to talk about and people had begun to frown in our direction, he suggested we go to a nearby café. His suit looked a bit threadbare but he walked with a dignified air, briefcase in hand. He was about thirty yet described himself as a student, saying he was writing a book. "It's all in here," he said, taking several exercise books of neatly written script from his case to show me. As to the book's subject, I was unclear, but it contained his views on philosophy and life in general. "I believe I am ahead of time," he declared.

Prince certainly sounded erudite, enunciating his words carefully as they tumbled forth. He talked as if addressing a large crowd. But he was genuinely interested to hear all about me too, his ears pricking up when I told him my father was from Ghana.

"The first African country to shake off the colonial yoke," he exclaimed. "We prefer self-government in danger, to servitude in tranquillity—thus spoke the late great Kwame Nkrumah," he added with a flourish. "You have great antecedents."

And he proceeded to give me a history lesson: "The white man came to Africa with a Bible in one hand and a gun in the other. They made us pray, and by the time we opened our eyes they'd taken our land. We should have known better, my child, because long before that they had used the gun to enslave us."

What part of Africa did he come from? I asked.

"I come from St Lucia, indisputably the most beautiful island in the Caribbean; my forefathers came from the Motherland before being taken away in captivity." In an attempt to erase their guilt, white people spread the lie that black people were inferior, he stated. "But they are always looking over their shoulder, afraid that we will rise up and punish them. So they always want to put us in our place. My book touches on all these things, which is why it probably won't ever be published," he added darkly.

The last bit of the puzzle was falling into place, I thought excitedly. Of course, I knew the colour of my skin was central to my predicament but now I realised it was part of a much bigger picture. I was eager to find out more.

We met up at the library the following week, once again falling into a deep conversation until Prince suddenly got up saying, "Now, Angela, you must come home and meet my wife."

He lived on one of Plymouth's most notorious estates and his flat was pokey and cluttered. His wife was sitting at the table beneath the dim light of a forty-watt bulb, the two forlorn-looking toddlers beside her completing a miserable tableau.

Melsa came to life when she saw me, giving me a broad smile, saying Prince had told her all about me. "Now we mus' feed you up with some good soul food," she said, going into the kitchen.

Later, during a meal of chicken and rice, she advised me to move to London when I finished my A-levels. "You need to be among you own people. There's nothing for you here. Look at we," she gestured at the flat.

I couldn't help feeling that Prince himself may have contributed to his family's plight since he seemed to spend most of his time in the library.

The next time I was with Prince we were making our way to Torpoint. At our last goodbye he had announced he wanted to meet my mother, who was now waiting for us with a meal of Hungarian-style fried chicken and home-made noodles. I've no idea what she thought as she welcomed my much older friend into her home and, looking back, I am amazed at her open-mindedness. But the evening proved a great success. Prince was particularly charming, congratulating her on doing such a fine job of bringing me up and listening sympathetically to the story of my father's disappearance.

"Your mother's a fine woman," he said, as I took him back to the ferry. "The Magyars have always been real fighters. Make sure you look after her when you grow up; don't do like these English kids."

A couple of weeks later I received a letter from him in his neat, even handwriting saying that he and the family had had to suddenly move back to London, though he didn't explain why. Melsa and the boys sent their love. I never heard from Prince again but did not feel sad. I regarded him as a good fairy who vanished once he'd accomplished his mission. My periods had resumed and I felt a lot happier.

Then came a school trip to London to see *Carmen* at the Coliseum. As soon as I got off the train at Paddington, black people seemed to be everywhere, smiling at me, winking at me; one even tried to chat me up, much to the amusement of my mates. I was in heaven.

Within a year I was boarding the train to London again and soon it would be a hop, skip and jump to Ghana, where I would go in search of Jimmy. It was to be quite an adventure.

Carolyn Cooper

Born in Kingston, Jamaica, she is a literary scholar and author who studied in Jamaica and Canada. A Professor of Literary and Cultural Studies, she was instrumental in establishing the Reggae Studies Unit at the University of the West Indies and founded the annual Bob Marley Lecture. She is the author of books including Noises in the Blood: Orality, Gender and the "Vulgar" Body of Jamaican Popular Culture (1993) *and* Sound Clash: Jamaican Dancehall Culture at Large (2004). *She writes a weekly column for the* Sunday Gleaner *and is a consultant on culture and development, as well as having been a broadcaster and host of television programmes. In 2013 she was awarded the Jamaican national honour of the Order of Distinction in the rank of Commander "for outstanding contribution to Education".*

Finding Romance Online in 2018

On the very first day of the new year, I signed up for membership on the Singles Club 876 website. I'd read about Everton Tate's clever idea in last Sunday's *Gleaner*. Mr Tate's smiling baby-face promised honesty, if not expertise. Looks can be very deceiving on the world-wide Anansi web.

I've taken a very old-fashioned approach to this business of romance: waiting for Mr Right Now to just show up. But I have concerned friends who've decided that I must help him to find me.

A year ago, one of them gave me a crisp US$20 bill to register on Match.com. I know you usually get what you pay for. And I really didn't think I needed a man I could get at that cut-rate price. An executive search was more my style. I thanked my friend for her gift but told her I wasn't going to use it as intended.

Managing Powerful Women

Another friend decided to take matters into her own hands. She got in touch with a man she thought would be ideal for me and asked if he would consider inviting me on a date. She was so distressed when he told her he couldn't "manage dem powerful woman". And he's a magistrate!

To be fair to him, I don't think he meant "manage" in the literal sense of the word, as in this dictionary definition: "be in charge of, run, be head of, head, direct, control, preside over, lead, govern, rule, command, superintend, supervise, oversee, administer, organise, conduct, handle, take forward, guide, be at the helm of."

I suspect that the magistrate meant something more complex. It wasn't so much that he felt inadequate at management. It was more a self-protective suspicion that he, himself, might be subjected to management. Forced to negotiate the terms of the relationship! So-called powerful women have a mind of our own. And we expect to be able to use it even in romance.

What I think the magistrate meant by "manage" is "cope with". Having to take into account the needs and desires of a powerful woman! This is, in fact, the very opposite of being in charge of. Of course, "managing" a certain kind of woman can be both quite challenging and rewarding. But some men will never find out.

Seemingly Self-Confident Man

Without the help of my concerned friends, I began "talking" to a seemingly self-confident Jamaican man who is a professor at a brand-name US university. The conversation didn't last very long. He soon told me, in all seriousness, that he was shocked to discover that a relative of his, who lives in rural Jamaica, knew about me. And he didn't want to be with a woman in the public eye.

The professor could have come up with a better excuse. In the age of the Internet and cell phone, connectivity across all media is the norm. And there are no communication barriers between town and country. In 1993, Desmond Allen, founding editor of *The Observer*, asked me to write a weekly column. He promised to make me a household name. It was actually a threat. Look how him mash up mi love life!

Seriously though, far less accomplished men than the magistrate and the professor have no reservations at all about managing powerful women. What I admire about the typical Jamaican man is his absolute confidence in his masculinity. From yu name man, yu can get any woman! They really believe it.

There's a nice young man at Hellshire Beach who always greets me affectionately. I make a point of calling him "Son". You think that would deter him? Not at all! He recently told me, "Miss Cooper, no bodder wid di 'Son' business. We a go get married next year." Another young man told me with great self-assurance that I wouldn't have to worry about going out with him to social events. As he put it, "Me know when fi keep my mouth shut."

Staying Focused

According to the *Gleaner* report, the registration fee for Singles Club 876 is US$25–35. That's not much more than for Match.com. But I've now conceded that cost and value are not always identical. When I went to register, I was a little concerned about a couple of punctuation errors:

> The Singles Club 876's sophisticated, we pride ourselves in providing the most exclusive singles-orientated Dating services for establishing long-term, committed relationships.

I reminded myself to stay focused and not get distracted by minor details of style: a bright apostrophe mark pretending to be half of a verb and an out-of-order comma taking the place of a full stop. In matters of the heart, it's character that counts; not punctuation skills.

I signed up and immediately got an email with this subject heading: "We have received your response for Club Membership Registration Form." I considered offering to help Mr Tate with copyediting. But mi catch up miself. No corrections; just romance! I'm waiting for the vetting process to be completed. I hope to be matched with a sensible man. No fool-fool magistrates or professors!

Patricia Cumper

Born in Jamaica, she studied Archaeology and Anthropology at Cambridge University. Returning home after graduation, she became an award-winning playwright with work produced throughout the Caribbean, in the US and Canada. Back in England in the 1990s, she worked for the UK's largest Black-led theatre company, Talawa, as writer, script reader, tutor, director and dramaturge, and artistic director from 2006 to 2012. She has won awards for her work in radio drama with the BBC, for both original series and adaptations of the work of others (including Andrea Levy, Alice Walker, Zora Neale Hurston and Toni Morrison). She is the author of a novel, One Bright Child *(1998). Her recent play* Chigger Foot Boys, *about black soldiers in the First World War, was performed in London in 2017. She is a Fellow of the Royal Society of the Arts, a trustee of the British Museum, and in 2013 was awarded an MBE for services to Black British Theatre.*

Just So Much a Body Can Take
A short film

INTERIOR. EVENING. THE HALLWAY OF ETHEL'S HOUSE

Ethel Gordon stands in the hallway of her small house, the phone cradled between her shoulder and her ear, as she carefully dries her hands on a dish towel. The living room, which we can see over her shoulder is a little untidy, but not remarkably so. It is too early to turn on the lights, just about that time when shadows are beginning to fall.

ETHEL: ...so how long you think you going to be? Das right. You remember di address? You write it down?... Good, good, I waiting on you.

She hangs up the phone, then looks at a small cut on her hand. She presses the dish towel over the cut and when she looks at it again, it has stopped bleeding. She begins to walk determinedly up the stairs, dishcloth over her shoulder, her age showing in her steps.

ETHEL: Wonder what dis ole house going to do withouten me fi haunt it? So much years a life live in dis one said place, so much years a drawing breath: never t'ought I would leave it dis way, but what to do, eeh? What to do.

She passes a sepia-coloured picture of herself and her husband on her wedding day at the top of the stairs and touches it gently as she stops to look at it and catch her breath a little.

ETHEL: Twenty-four-inch waist. You used to be so proud a mi twenty-four-inch waist, eeh, Donville? Used to take you hand and span it mek all you friends see how mi shape nice. Say dat mi pretty like money, pretty like money.

She goes into her bedroom. The bedspread is chenille, the dresser generously spread with hand-crocheted and starched doilies. She takes a brown, hard-shelled suitcase down from the top of the wardrobe and lays it on the bed, opening it. In it she finds a yellowed page of a newspaper at least twenty years old. It is folded to reveal an ad for cheap flights back to Jamaica. She crumples it up and throws it on the floor.

ETHEL: 'Bout we going to go back home. Always talking 'bout how we going to go back home. Build a likkle house fi wiself pon di half acre you inherit from you uncle. Build wah, eeh Donville? (*kisses her teeth*) Build wah?

(*sings a revival hymn as she packs*)
Mother, the great stone got to move,
Mother, the great stone got to move.

Mother, the great stone, the stone of Babylon,
Mother, the great stone got to move.

As she sings, she begins to pack the suitcase. Her hands work with the expertise of years, folding precisely, piling neatly. She is not taking a great deal with her and she soon finishes packing. She looks around the room.

ETHEL: And I don't even know if I am sad to be going. England is mi home still, but mi navel string never bury in dis country. Sometimes mi skin so hungry fi di sunlight even after forty, fifty years, it feel like it a go mad me... The great stone got to move...

She takes off her housedress and selects a church dress from her closet and puts it on. We glimpse a bruise on her shoulder. She changes her shoes then selects a hat and puts it on top of the suitcase which she closes. She smooths the bedcover and tweaks a doily into place.

ETHEL: Must call Ruby and ask her to come sort out all dis after mi gone. See who want what and give di rest to one a dem charity shop. (*laughs*) All dese years mi putting so many tings away for safe-keeping... (*shakes her head*) Still, s'm'ody will find use fi dem...

She picks up the suitcase and hat and carries them out of the room and down the stairs. She stops at the bottom of the stairs, takes a deep breath to make herself stronger, then enters the living room, lifting the suitcase over an obstacle as she does. There is a large old couch with antimacassars, an armchair by the window; photos line the mantelpiece. There is a painting of a tropical scene on the wall, faded silk poinsettias in a vase.

   Ethel straightens the cushions on the sofa, then puts the suitcase on it and opens it. She crosses to the fireplace and takes up several of the photos as if to pack them, then sees the one that is on top and stops to look at it. It is Ethel as a young woman in Jamaica, shading her eyes from the sun. She stops to touch the face in the picture: smiles.

ETHEL: So hungry for the sunlight, is like it a go mad mi... Who is dat girl? When was I dis young girl?

She lays that photo in the suitcase and looks at another. Her wedding day. Outside an English town hall. She young, pretty, happy; Donville standing straight, allowing himself a small smile, pride radiating from him. She puts it into the suitcase too then notices that her hands are shaking. She looks at them, almost puzzled, observing herself.

ETHEL: Donville shake like a leaf dat night, our wedding night. Him never know dat I know and I would never tell him. Shaking like him heart going jump outa him chest every time him ease himself over to my side a dat old bed...

She clasps her hands together to stop them shaking. Her face is closed, almost blank. She throws a quick glance, immediately regretted, towards the door of the room. Squares her shoulders and crosses back to the fireplace to pick up another couple of photographs. She finds one that she has stuck behind another in the frame and pulls it out. She crosses to the old armchair and sits in it, staring at the picture, then out through the net curtain to the street. The photo falls from her fingers and we see it is a picture of a young man, big afro and bell bottoms, giving a black power salute. He is angry, defiant.

ETHEL: Yu have pickney and you love dem cyan done. Yu watch dem grow and you try guide dem…maybe what was di right ting for me, living with mi granny in Portland, was not di right ting fi a black boy growing up hard… Do what is right and keep you counsel, dat is what my granny always used to say, but what relevance dat have to my son? How dat help him when dem chase him to beat him, how dat can cool di anger when him see injustice round him every living day? Di anger used to talk in him, dem days. And dat everlasting rasta music every day…all day… Wonder if mi did have a daughter, tings woulda turn out different? Some say dat a girl child woulda do better… A dis said same chair Donville was sitting in when him see Ronald coming to di door. Trouble, Ethel, him say to me, Trouble in wi son face.

She gets up slowly and goes to put the photos in the suitcase.

ETHEL: Trouble, yes. Every last penny weh wi save to go back to Jamaica it take to fight dat charge in court. GBH and the old wretch weh accuse him sure dat dem going to convict a black man? Not my son, not Ronald. Mi and Donville mek up wi mind dat dat was one black man not going to die in no prison under no mysterious circumstances. The lawyer smile and lick di plate clean. Donville have to take on guard work a di building site when dem was building dat new supermarket to finish pay him. But Ronald never go to jail. Him walk free from dat court and das when my boy turn the corner and start make life for himself. Never look back from dat. Donville tell him, you see: living well is di best revenge. Nutting hurt a racist more dan to see a black man prosper…

She takes up photos of her son, now a middle-aged man, with his wife and children. Individual photos of her grandchildren, a drawing one of them has done with the words "For my gran, from Janet" written across the bottom. She puts them in the suitcase too.

ETHEL: No point worrying dem just yet. Better to call Ronald when mi reach there… when mi reach there.

She goes back to sit in the armchair, closing her eyes and breathing in deeply.

ETHEL: Bay rum. Donville always used to use it when him come in out a di rain. Just to smell it remind mi a when mi used to reach home after my shift a night time and see di two a dem—Ronald sitting pon di chair arm—di two a dem concentrating pon di boy's homework like nutting could be more important... Bay rum. Even after yu dead and buried, mi still smell yu, see yu, feel di breeze at mi side every day dat you gone... Ruby tell mi dat she spread yu ashes in a yam field in Christiana, just like you ask, so you suppose to be at rest now...

Tears begin to roll down from under her closed eyelids and she sits quiet, bowed, for a minute. Then she digs a handkerchief out from under her bra strap and wipes her eyes. There is a dried bloodstain on the handkerchief. She goes back to the mantelpiece and takes from pride of place a large, silver double frame in which there are two photos of Donville: as a police constable in Jamaica, chest forward and smiling, and in his British Rail cleaner's uniform, looking dour.

ETHEL: Poor mi husband. Just come off di boat and step up big and bright to di police station, tell dem dat him want work as a policeman. Jesus had more hope of saving Satan's soul dan Donville have to get dat job... Di way dem look at you, di way dem talk to you...is like when you step on glass: cut you so deep, so quick... Sometimes it never heal. Sometimes it just never heal...

She takes up a flat case from behind where the photos were. She opens it. Finds it is empty. Closes it, opens it again and sees it is empty. Her face changes completely and is contorted in blind anger. The case falls from her hands because they are shaking, claw like, so violently. She turns and looks directly at the corner to which she has only glanced before. She strides across and below eye level, rummages about, muttering darkly to herself as she does so. We realize that the room is not untidy so much as damaged.

ETHEL: Di one ting I have to 'memba him by...di one nice ting dat him get for all the years and yu fink yu have di right to it... You know how long mi watch mi husband suffer, you know how long him no laugh, him no talk, him just work, and work, and work... Not a blast, yu hear mi...you no have no right to dis!

She hauls a gold watch into frame, wiping it clean with her handkerchief before restoring it to its case. The act of doing so calms her. She closes the suitcase with the photos, puts on her hat and goes to sit by the window in Donville's armchair. She is holding the watch in its case to her breast as she sits, very upright, her suitcase at her heels. As the camera pulls away from the fragile, old lady sitting at the window, the room is revealed as torn up, as if in a terrible struggle. The blue lights of an approaching police car begin to show through the window as we finally pull far enough out to reveal the body of a young thief, lying across the entrance to the living room.

Stella Dadzie

Born in London to an English mother and Ghanaian father, she is an educationalist, activist, writer and historian. She is best known for her involvement in the UK's Black Women's Movement, being a founding member of the Organisation of Women of African and Asian Descent (OWAAD) and co-authoring The Heart of the Race: Black Women's Lives in Britain *with Suzanne Scafe and Beverley Bryan, which won the 1985 Martin Luther King Award for Literature. The book was reissued (with a new foreword by Lola Okolosie) in 2018. She has written widely on curriculum development and good practice with black adult learners, and the development of anti-racist strategies with schools, colleges and youth services.*

Do You Remember?

Do you remember
my sister
those dark November nights
when we listened to the world
and sought to right its sorrows
with our clenched fists?

Do you remember
those languid summer days
when we raised our placards high
and sang sweet songs of freedom
so sure that history
was on our side?

The world's cruel burdens
weigh heavy still
and time may have tempered
our youthful dreams
yet we have come at last to know
a deeper truth

For it is people
not ideals
that are transient
and freedom's spirit lives
imprisoned in the shy smile
of a hungry child

and in a fierce, enduring love
that conquers fear

December 1992

Roots

I am an ancient oak
Twisted, gnarled, permanent
indifferent to the passage
of time

I am amber and gold
russet and sage
bone-white
blood-red
moss-green

I am rain-blanched and sun-bleached
and where once I was scorched
by lightning
I am an angry charcoal black
with keloid scars

Solid and thick-girthed
my thighs resist
the fury of the elements
yet remain vulnerable
to the footfalls
of passing strangers
they twist and turn
charting new paths
into the rich, dark earth that nurtures me
they burrow deep
seeking life's sustenance
and other treasures

My skin is rough and weather-beaten
rain-lashed
wind-smoothed
with many unexplored places
secret nooks

colonised by teeming armies
whole cities that strive
beneath a protective bark
hidden crannies
where shy, itinerant seeds
once took root
and burst forth in a celebration
of reckless beauty
dark, barren places
where I was once torn
limb from limb
and nothing more can grow

When I was a sapling
exploding with energy
and purpose
I chose to make my home
by the river
where her calm, impassive face
could mirror my growth
her music a soft, sighing lullaby
soothing me
as I sleep

When the sun parches the earth
sapping my strength
she revives me with cool water
from her own abundant store
her gentle waves
caressing
my aching feet

Her gift is an orchestra
with many players
drums and violins
a choir of joyful singers
rousing me from my slumber
as they herald the dawn
of each new day

Time is my armoury now
scudding clouds keep their watch

as the changing seasons
present new horizons
healing wounds
renewing old paths

Tomorrow I shall be here still,
wiser and sturdier than before
I have withstood the fury of thunder
the rage of forest fires
I know
my life-force
will prevail

And if by chance
an ax should fell me
should I succumb
to the vengeance of the hurricane
or the slow, creeping stealth
of nature's wrath
I shall sink gratefully into the earth
that has sustained me
returning my gifts
so that others
may grow to touch
the sky

Anni Domingo

Growing up in Sierra Leone, she attended school in Freetown, and went on to further education in the UK, where she first trained as an actor and a teacher of speech and drama, obtaining a BA in Drama and English. Later she obtained First-Class BA degrees in Literature and Humanities and an MA in Creative Writing, and was awarded an honorary doctorate in 2018. She has worked extensively in theatre, radio, TV and film, both acting and directing, as well as teaching English, Drama and Creative Writing. Her company, Shakespeare Link, takes workshops to schools and colleges and she has written workbooks on Shakespeare. She has also written poetry and short stories. Her poem "The Cutting" is published in the text of Bullet Hole, *a recent play about female genital mutilation in which she played the lead role. She was joint winner of the 2018 First Drafts competition with an extract from* Breaking the Maafa Chain, *her debut novel.*

From *Breaking the Maafa Chain*

Fatmata
Prologue
December 1846

Stripped of everything but our black skins, our ritual scars, our beings, we were tied together in rows and jammed into another *djudju* pit, packed in so close no one could move. We lay on our sides, rough wooden boards hard against our bare skins, rubbing our shoulders raw, chained to the living and to the dead.

I knew then what fear smelt like. It was the smell of grown men, groaning, sweating, and stinking. Fear was women crying, wailing, and calling on the ancestors to save them and their children before they were lost to *mamiwata*.

The noise in the cramped space swirled around, hitting the wooden sides of the swaying ship, drumming thoughts and fears into my mind. I heard chains rattle and whips crack as the sails flapped, boards creaked, and ropes stretched. I heard the howls of those beside me, those above me and those below me. I heard the call of the *Ochoema*, the bird of parting. It held me tight before fading into the darkness.

Through tears, I saw everything that had been. There in the back of my eyes, way back, were the spiritless bodies of my mother Isatu, my father Dauda, Maluuma, mother of my mother, Lansana, my father's first son, all gone to the land of our ancestors, without due honour. My heart ached for Salimatu, my sister, my mother's child, captured too and sold, to Arabs? to the white devils?

Deep inside of me I heard drums beating, talking, calling, and shouting out my name, Fatmata. I listened as my words, my thoughts, my life, were beaten into my bones, into my smell, into my flesh, for all times and tried to push away the pain, from the raw mark of slavery burned into my left shoulder.

Oduadua, god of all women, help me. I must remember, I will remember, I do remember. Hear me, Fatmata, for this is my story.

Salimatu
Chapter I
July 1850

At the water's edge, Salimatu could not move. The wet sand held her tight, refusing to let her go. The white devil picked her up and she stiffened in his arms. His smell was strong. It filled her nose robbing her of the sweet smell of the pawpaw and palm trees that lined the edge of the land. Salimatu shut her eyes, not wanting to see the mark she had left in the sand, not wanting to see it washed away as if she had never been there. She made no sound as the white devil, Captain Forbes, walked her into the ocean. She neither squealed with delight nor cried out, as fear, like a huge bird, swooped down and clutched at her inside. She had learnt to be silent.

They had been together now for a full moon cycle and she was no longer frightened of him. But the ocean terrified her. Fatmata had told her, a long time ago, that *mamiwater*, the goddess of water, lived in the big river and was ready to swallow those who disturbed her sleep. And here was the river in front of her, waiting for her.

"Do not be scared," the Captain said, sitting her down on the plank seat, in the middle of the canoe. It rocked and the rowers, big and strong, their bodies shining with sweat, steadied it with their oars, before pulling away.

"You're safe," said Captain Forbes. "These Kroomen know how to get their canoes over huge waves even better than my sailors."

He had said it, safe, the first time she had met him. She had not understood his words then. She had not wanted to go with the white devil, afraid that she was going to be his sacrifice instead of King Gezo's. Fatmata had warned her that people like him, people who looked skinless were *djuju*, so she shrank from his touch, from his smell. He had smiled, picked her up and carried her away from the "watering of the ancestors" ceremony. She had trembled and pissed all over him. Her white garment steamed and dried and smelt in the sun but he did not put her down. He took her to the missionaries, Reverend and Mrs Vidal.

"But what are you going to do with her?" asked Reverend Vidal.

"Take her to England with me."

"Is that wise, old man?" Reverend Vidal asked.

"I'm sure we can find a place for her in the Mission school," said Mrs Vidal. "If she is bright she could help teach others in time."

"King Gezo has given her as a gift to Queen Victoria. 'From the King of the blacks to the Queen of the whites,' that's what he said. It is not for me therefore to decide her future. I will take her with me and hand her over to the Admiralty. May I leave her with you until *The Bonetta* sails in a few weeks?"

"Those markings on her face are tribal, you know," said Rev. Vidal. "It means she is the daughter of a chief. There could be trouble."

"I'll come for her as soon as we are ready to sail."

"What's her name?" asked Mrs Vidal.

"I don't know," said Captain Forbes. "But if I'm taking her to London she had better have an English one. What about Sarah? That was my mother's name."

"Sarah. In Hebrew it means Princess." said the Reverend, nodding.

"Sarah, it is then," said the Captain. "Sarah Forbes and Bonetta, after the ship."

That was a moon cycle ago. Now, sitting in the canoe, Salimatu stared hard at the shore fading into the distance. The sun on the white sand hurt her eyes, filling them with tears she refused to shed. Once on the big ship that would take her to England, the tears would flow, for how could she then find her way back to Talaremba? She reached for the side of the canoe and tried to stand.

The Captain grabbed her. "Sarah, hold on or you'll fall in."

Maybe Fatmata had been taken across the big ocean too. Was not that what Ma Ayinde had told her the first time the Minos, the King's women warriors, had come for Seyi and Memuna.

"Where are they taking them?" she had asked as the two women, dressed in white, were dragged away, screaming, from the compound.

"They have been chosen as sacrifice for the 'watering of the grave' ceremony today," said Ma Ayinde, her voice low.

"Why don't they use goats and chickens?"

"To honour the King's ancestors? No. When they put white on you, it means your time has come. All of us in this compound," she said, waving her hand around, "will wear white one day and be sacrificed as part of the ceremony."

"When King Gezo bought me from the Arabs, he said I was safe here."

"Child, you have a lot to learn."

"My sister will come find me."

"You have been here three rainy seasons, has she come? When they take us as slaves, we are either killed, sold again and again to the Arabs or to the white devils. They take us across the big water, never to return," said Ma Ayinde, with a bitter laugh. "Your sister is gone. If she is not dead or sold to the Arabs, she will be far away across the big, big waters. Don't know which is worse."

Salimatu had never seen the "big water", the ocean, before and here was water as far as her eyes could see. As they sat in the canoe, the water raced towards them, attacking, roaring, hungry. Just as she thought it would swallow them alive, it backed away slithering and sliding, hissing, only to come rushing back with greater power. It was like an animal with two heads that went both ways. Water splashed her face, she licked her lips and her eyes widened with surprise. It tasted of salt. On the long journey to Abomey she had learnt that salt was important, not just for cooking but for buying and selling. Did the white man have so much salt they could put it in all this water? Another wave hit the canoe and she let go of the side. Her gloved hand plunged into the furious ocean.

Salimatu pressed her wet hand to her chest. Her inside beat fast and underneath all her English clothes she could feel her *gri-gri* pouch tied with a string, around her neck. Inside it was her blue glass and a piece of her "white cloth", her *ala*. They will protect her. That's what Fatmata had said. She wished she could remember more of the things her sister had told her as they walked through the forest after they had been captured. She had eight harvest seasons now but she had seen only four harvest seasons then. Everything was fading away.

Before she could think about it any longer there was a shout. She looked over her shoulder and the ship, a huge thing, was there rocking and swaying, as if trying to shake everything off, like a big dog trying to get a monkey off its back. Memories came then of Madu and Jaja, her mother and father, as the ship rose high above her head, its poles and ropes cutting the sky up into small sections. Did they reach right into the sky? Could she climb up, squeeze through a hole in the sky and reach Madu and Jaja? To ask them . . . what? Was Fatmata up there too? Before she could catch the memories and hold them, they drifted off like smoke. She bit her lips to keep the words in.

A rope-ladder was thrown down from the ship. The canoe danced as the Captain began to climb the ladder with her in his arms. Shutting her eyes and trying not to breathe in the Captain's smell, she clung on, till rough, hard hands, reached down, grabbed hold and took her from him. She still was not used to wearing so many clothes or shoes that hurt her feet. The sailor put her down, her feet slid on the wet deck and she reached for a rope to steady herself.

Captain Forbes rushed away, waving his arms about, shouting, telling the sailors what to do. The men called and whistled, pushed and pulled, their bodies, shiny with sweat, hauling up boxes and barrels. There were many men, running all over the ship, fast and busy, like ants, pink ants, building a nest. She had to keep away from them. Ants can sting.

One man rolled a barrel close by and she jumped out of the way, falling into the side of the ship. It was wet and she wriggled as she felt the water soak through her clothes. The movement of the ship made her stomach toss and turn. Above all the noise of the ship the call of the *Ochoema*, could be heard.

The wind blew her hat back and stroked her face. She smiled for it felt like it used to when Fatmata blew on her face and said, "Salimatu, I'm part of you and you are part of me because we have swallowed each other's air. We will never be lost to each other." She knew then that Fatmata had travelled on these waters. Why else had she come to her like this? She put her hand to her face and through the thin, now wet gloves they had made her put on, she felt the markings that had saved her.

She felt a hand on her shoulder and she turned around.

"Come, Sarah. You cannot stay here."

She shook her head. "Not Sarah," she said, tapping her chest, "Salimatu. Me Salimatu."

"No. I've told you. Sarah." He pointed at her. "You are now Sarah Forbes Bonetta," and tapping his chest he said, "Captain Forbes, I'm Captain Forbes. You understand?"

She tightened her lips but did not reply.

Bernardine Evaristo

A British-Nigerian writer, she has published eight books of fiction and verse fiction exploring the African diaspora and numerous other performed and produced works. She is also a literary critic, editor and writer for BBC radio. Her many awards and honours include an Arts Council Writers Award and a NESTA Fellowship Award for her 2001 verse novel The Emperor's Babe, *which was also a* Times *"100 Best Books of the Decade", and was adapted into a BBC Radio 4 play. Her 2013 novel,* Mr Loverman, *won the Jerwood Fiction Uncovered Prize and the Ferro-Grumley Award for LGBT Fiction in the USA. In the 1980s she founded Britain's first black women's theatre company, Theatre of Black Women, and has since founded many other important diversity arts initiatives. She is Vice Chair of the Royal Society of Literature, Professor of Creative Writing at Brunel University London and she was made MBE in 2009.*

On Top of the World

I flew in across a sea packed with ice floes, the sky overcast but the sun shooting rays through the clouds like the dawn of creation, and arrived at surely the smallest airport in the world—an outsized shed stuck in a clearing of slush and gravel. There was seating for five inside and a middle-aged Inuit woman with a smile that responded rather than offered. She didn't ask for my passport. She knew for sure I'd be returning home. Everyone did. England was equatorial compared to this most northerly part of the world where summer stabilized at just below freezing and winters plummeted to minus twenty.

Soon enough the helicopter was ready to take me on the last leg of my journey to a village for which it was the only access to the outside world, storms permitting—it and a ship that arrived yearly to off-load essentials like pre-fab houses, satellite dishes, vitamins and dried fruit. Nothing grew there except summer berries. The diet was, by necessity, carnivorous: seal, hare, polar bear, narwhal, muskox.

We took off across the mountains, the propeller whirring noisily as its blades chopped up the sky. The other passengers' chatter annoyed me. I scowled. They politely turned away. I looked down at the earth beneath my feet where snowy mountains dipped and peaked and I fought the urge to activate the emergency lock and make the most dramatic exit—to free-fall with an exhilarated, fading-away scream.

An hour later we landed on the top of a hill side. The small village of Ittoqqor-toormiit swooped up from a frozen fjord, its wooden bungalows all bright reds and yellows, prettily offset by a whole winter's-worth of snow.

I trudged to the waiting taxi—a skidoo, best suited to a village with no roads, just icy, undulating pathways. The young driver wore a padded orange jumpsuit and beckoned me to climb aboard. I sat behind as he hurled the beast bumpily along with no regard for his novice passenger. I tried to complain but he feigned deafness, which was the story of my life. It was mid-morning, the village was deserted. Packs of sledge-dogs chained up outside houses started howling like wolves as we zoomed past. There was no market here, only one store, no bars, no cinema, no Internet café or bingo hall. Just a school, a hospital, a police station.

We quickly arrived at my guide's house, Isa, he who would lead me out into the wilderness. A stout man, in his mid-fifties, he had deep-set eyes which required probing to see behind, something I wasn't prepared to do. He spoke in broken English and I was soon attired in bulky Arctic fashion: size nine boots to accommodate four pairs of woollen socks, thermal leggings, two pairs of fleece trousers underneath sealskin ones, a fleece jacket, a sealskin parka with fur hood, earmuffs, hat, scarves, goose-down mittens, and goggles. I felt as clumsy and heavy as a yeti, yet never more ready for my journey into the greatest unknown.

Isa led me out to his sledge and thirteen dogs who were straining at the leash. I kept my distance, as instructed, as he began to untie them from a long chain and hook each one up with bright green rope so that they spread out before the sledge in a wide fan. They went wild then, barking, jostling for space, desperate to set off, the strongest dogs were tugging at the helm. The sledge had a low sloping backrest against which I sat on bearskin which covered luggage, tents and sleeping bags. Hooked over the back were grubby plastic buckets containing the kitchen which was, basically, a kerosene fire and a single saucepan. Isa sat up front, between me and a tiny white boat where our provisions were stored. I was exposed to the elements and the seating was uncomfortable, but I didn't mind.

Very quickly Isa was issuing orders to the dogs who began charging off across a fjord that was as interminable as an ocean. I couldn't believe I was there, finally, that for thousands of kilometres northwards, there were no other humans, only an ice cap three thousand metres deep which was pushing the land back into the sea with its weight. And beyond that lay the Arctic Ocean and the North Pole.

We travelled across the frozen desert and out onto the sea ice which resembled frosted glass. It was scary at first. Far below I could hear the hollow rumble of water. When the ice was flat, the dogs raced ahead, tongues panting, releasing themselves on the job. It was a vision of flying, smelly excrement and jets of urine which formed beautiful, fluorescent-yellow flowers in the luminous snow. Sometimes the snow was so deep the dogs almost slowed to a full stop, or we came upon frozen waves which rose up in large, jagged lumps where the tide had pushed up against snow and solidified. The sledge ran over them and landed with a spine-shattering bump.

Sculpted icebergs a hundred feet high were always somewhere to be seen on the horizon. Calved from glaciers years ago, they sailed slowly downstream in summer, getting trapped in ice in winter before the melting water released them again. I never got used to the crystal-clear visibility which made everything appear nearer than it actually was. Icebergs half a day away looked like I could sprint there in a mere twenty minutes. On sunny days the ice was so bright it was blue.

I drowned in the cold voluptuousness of it all, feeling the space in my head open up. I didn't wash for five days but to my surprise I barely noticed. We boiled snow for drinking water. It was delicious. I didn't miss anyone or anything. How could I? This was the world as it should be—without mankind. This was the trip of my life and I would never feel such harmony again. This was my new beginning. I would not crave an afterwards.

Back home I called my local high road "The River of Phlegm". I needed a wet suit just to wade to the post office. I'd begun to wear surgical gloves to avoid contact with the sticky residue of soiled fingers on shopping baskets, toilet handles or café tables. Then I stopped using public transport altogether. I had a little run-around, for sitting in traffic jams, mostly, to and from work. For two hours every working day I'd be trapped behind smoking exhaust pipes, assaulted by a cacophony of impatient horns in the kind of free-for-all jazz improvisation designed to give you a major headache. I'd be hypnotised by the rain dance of my leggy, knobbly-kneed window wipers. My "not waving but drowning" window wipers. Left, right, *squeak*. Left, right, *squeak*.

That was life before the letter plopped harmlessly through my letter box one Saturday morning a month ago:

Elizabeth Ekundayo/ As you are aware/ complaints/ due process/ and so we have no option/ terminate your contract…

After fifteen years of seeing the same faces every morning. The same friendly faces, I later realised. The people who heard my words, if not my thoughts.

Liking the cold is not in my DNA, but I'd been drawn to Greenland for years, to its emptiness. It was so different to the England I knew, where nobody really knew me, and the Nigeria I didn't know, where my father had returned before I was born, two years before my mother died. I was not protected from the people I was told to call my parents. A plaything. I escaped at sixteen. I made my way.

On the sixth day, Isa hunted seal at the tide-crack, where the frozen sea met the flowing sea. He waited patiently, lying prostrate with his rifle for the head of a seal to bob up. When it did, he shot it. A soft plop making it flip onto its side. Blood gushed into the water, staining it red. The Inuit believe that an animal agrees to be killed. They enter into a contract with the hunter.

He got into the boat, rowed out and brought the seal back. He gutted and skinned it, throwing chunks to the slathering dogs, who devoured it in seconds. He cooked seal-ribs for dinner, accompanied by powdered mashed potato, our staple vegetable. It was a fine meal.

There's an extended twilight here. It won't get dark now until winter, when it stays dark for months. In summer the sun doesn't set for months. This is the in-between time. This is spring. I shiver in my silver bubble tent. It must be minus twenty degrees. Isa sleeps in his tent on the other side of the dogs who are chained in a long line which is staked at both ends to prevent their night-time inter-canine battles. They're used to me now, so they don't create havoc when I appear outside my tent. We're camped in front of a glacier. Spread out before me is an Arctic beach, stretching out to infinity.

The snow is so dry and flat it's like sand. An iceberg shaped like a ship rears against the sky. This is how I imagine the moon to be—so isolated, so strange, so utterly devastating.

I have removed my sealskin outerwear and put on my trainers. I won't get very far in them, but I want to walk awhile, towards the iceberg, which is miles away. My footprints will be a record of where I have gone. If the ice doesn't melt they might still be here next winter, and the next one, and the one afterwards. There's a thought. Still here, somewhere.

The cold will numb my feet first, then creep up through my limbs and freeze me in the act of walking. I will become the most extraordinary ice sculpture. I will become one with the planet I came from. This is how I've long imagined it.

Diana Ferrus

Her poetry collection, I've come to take you home, *was published in 2010. She is currently working on three collections of poetry, two in Afrikaans and one in English. She has attended numerous festivals locally and overseas. She is well known for her poem, "I've come to take you home" which was instrumental in the repatriation to South Africa of the remains of Sarah Baartman, an indigenous South African woman who was taken to Europe under false pretences.*

I've come to take you home

A tribute to Sarah Baartman (written in Utrecht, Holland, June 1998)

I have come to take you home—
home! Remember the veld,
the lush green grass beneath the big oak tree?
The air is cool there and the sun does not burn.
I have made your bed at the foot of the hill,
your blankets are covered in buchu and mint,
the proteas stand in yellow and white
and the water in the stream chuckles sing-songs
as it hobbles along over little stones.

I have come to wrench you away—
away from the poking eyes of the man-made monster

who lives in the dark with his clutches of imperialism,
who dissects your body bit by bit,
who likens your soul to that of satan
and declares himself the ultimate God!

I have come to soothe your heavy heart,
I offer my bosom to your weary soul.
I will cover your face with the palms of my hands,
run my lips over the lines in your neck,
feast my eyes on the beauty of you
and I will sing for you
for I have come to bring you peace.

I have come to take you home
where the ancient mountains shout your name.
I have made your bed at the foot of the hill.
Your blankets are covered in buchu and mint,
the proteas stand in yellow and white.
I have come to take you home
where I will sing for you,
for you have brought me peace,
for you have brought us peace

Glossary:
Buchu — a herb used by Khoi-khoi people for medicinal purposes
Mint — a herb also used for medicinal and cooking purposes
Proteas — the national flower of South Africa
Veld — wide open space

A woman's journey to sanity

Past Wellington, past Worcester and Wolseley —
the monstrous peaks loom openmouthed.
The faces in windows whisper and mock —
"I have his report", she wants to scream,
but the wind in the fields
through the Soutpansnek
denounces the verdict again and again —
"It's not what she says, but what she does."

Bosluiskloof and Brandrivier,
Porterville and Pietersburg,
the rivulets chuckle in secret song—
"The woman in slippers seems quite insane",
"Look not at my feet but in my eyes",
but her diary lines are splashed against
the overgrown hills of Wiegenaarspoort—
"It's not what she says, but what she does."

In Swanepoelspoort where the sun means hurt,
the heavy oak trees have stories to tell.
They beg her onwards to Steytlerville,
but her voice sounds hollow in defeated response—
"Please guide my feet to Sewe Weekspoort,
for my heart feels dead and my eyes are cold"
and her traces shout in the Rosebergpass—
"It's not what she says but what she does."

Through Dysselsdorp, De Rust and De Aar,
the lush green fields of the Sederberg,
water from the heavens sucks in the earth
and a woman without slippers and hospital gown
dances victorious to the dying sun—
"What matters the content of a doctor's report",
the echoes of her voice reaching the stars—
"For it is what I say and what I do!"

At the feet of the mountains in the Hex Vallei
and in the unspoilt walks of the Houwhoekpass,
(so goes the story of the indigenous ones),
roams the spirit of a woman brave in her heart
and when the earth goes dark with thunder and fear,
her voice lights up in the heavens,
"Hear not the call of the treacherous ones,
who sneak around and swindle your soul.
Listen to the beat of your heart,
hear the music, follow the sound—
know, where your journey's bound."

Saartjie's cry

Oh mother, I am not me,
my soul has been lost in this journey.
Here where the clouds hardly leave the sky
the sun never appears to kill the lie.
Oh mother, it is not just my soul they've torn apart—
It is oh mother my very heart!
They call me savage, they call me whore,
they call me names I have not heard before!
It's only in the dark of the night
that the drink in the bottle makes my body all right.
In my dreams I see our mountain with its foot in the bay,
I see our springbok, our eland, our wildebeest at play,
how we run up the hills so steep,
go dive for fish in the ocean so deep—
and I cringe oh mother, I die
to think we are all caught up in this lie.

When next you do the dance to our sun,
please remember your forgotten one.
Hold your hands up high to the sky,
send me the wings so that I may fly.

Nikky Finney

*Born in South Carolina, within listening distance of the sea, she is a child of activists,
and came of age during the turmoil of the civil rights and the creative renaissance
of the Black Arts movements. At Talladega College, nurtured by Hale Woodruff's
Amistad murals, she began to understand the powerful synergy between art and
history. She is the author of five poetry collections—*Head Off & Split, *which was
awarded the 2011 National Book Award for poetry;* On Wings Made of Gauze
(1985); *Rice (1995);* Heartwood (1997); *The World Is Round (2003)—and also
edited* The Ringing Ear: Black Poets Lean South *in 2007. She co-founded the
Affrilachian Poets, a group of black Appalachian poets. The many awards she has
received for her work include a PEN America Open Book Award and the Benjamin
Franklin Award for Poetry. She holds the John H. Bennett, Jr, Chair in Creative
Writing and Southern Letters at the University of South Carolina.*

Auction Block of Negro Weather

The eye wall was human. Black skin could not take off running from this surge & convergence. Legal tender built & brewed this storm into a quick moving cell of half-goodbyes and twisting outstretched arms. A father's wailing mouth turned up to the night sky was forever. A mother's eyes sunk below the county's water line world without end. One three x three vortex of epic ongoing drowning. Forests of human oak razed by the zephyr-force winds of banknotes. Family trees broken leaf by leaf then scattered by the winds of profit. Ten million fingers and toes divided up for chicken change. No hats or scarves or wings issued for the highly skilled wearing black skin. Beloveds, the elements, out in the elements. Low tide. Lightning strikes touching the ground where they stood waiting to be sold. Screams pushing the air unmeasured. Six million eyes and arms in whirling disbelief unravelling from each other. High tide. *Goodbye Lovey*. A deluge of wind is made by the mouths of children being sucked away. Women are opened like bank vaults, their gold coins snatched. Jerome is made to bare his teeth. Boy & girl twins are pulled north and south like sweet fruit on a stem. Hope is ground into a powder that will later be worn around the neck for good luck. Fathers sew their own eyes shut for what comes next. Salt streams each face under the fat and cumulous Negro clouds gathered. Holding her tiny wet hand his long-drawn monsoon begins. Her feet are caught running off the wooden stump straight into the air. *Don't forget me, Benna*. His voice, her barometer, drops in the dew as he disappears in the back of a wagon. Told not to turn & wave. He waves & turns until she is only a black dot in a torn white dress. Amina grows wings that stretch and bear up against the sight of daughters chained around the same feet she rubbed with rabbit oil the night before. *You will never be out of my sight*, Rose promises the dust in the shape of a son trailing the back of a horse. Jocko and Juju go colorblind when they finally arrive in South Carolina, the rows of cotton there are long squalls of blue and green. A handsome woman stands in the middle of hurricane force winds, her ten-year-old daughter is being led away by a man with a whip whose zipper keeps flying open. The weather vanes of their sweet tobacco breath still hover in every public square of every city of the Republic. *I was here* they remind us if we dare lift our eyes to dare look their way. The promise of their stolen lives crumbled in between the joists and the starlight of the jet stream. A handsome people who arrived with broken hearts, punctured lungs, liver spots. A lovesome people, who arrived with belly buttons and blackberry moles, who came slew footed, left-handed, cried easily, or not at all. A red-blooded tribe who tried to run away, endured, and molded a nation out of infested swamps, impassable timberland, and eye wall after eye wall of hate. It was cataclysmic. There was water everywhere. Their easy-on-the-eyes hearts pushed back against the sheets of water that kept coming.

Ifeona Fulani

Caribbean-born, she holds an MFA in Creative Writing and a PhD in Comparative Literature, both from New York University. Her published work includes an edited volume of essays titled Archipelagos of Sound: Transnational Caribbeanities, Women and Music, *a collection of short stories titled* Ten Days in Jamaica *(2012), a novel,* Seasons of Dust *(1997), and scholarly articles and reviews, most recently in* Atlantic Studies, Caribbean Quarterly, Frontiers: A Journal of Women's Studies, Small Axe *and* The Caribbean Review of Books. *She is currently working on a novel provisionally titled* Verna's Dream. *Her research interests are Caribbean literary and cultural studies, literatures of Africa and its diasporas, transnational feminisms, urban cultures and writing. She is a Clinical Professor in the Global Liberal Studies Program at New York University.*

Three Islands, Two Cities:
The Making of a Black / Caribbean / Woman Writer / Scholar

I am one of those Caribbean people whose journeys have criss-crossed the ocean, my travels on two continents shaped by the dynamic flows of the black Atlantic—that triangular zone theorized by Paul Gilroy, constituted by cultural currents as well as literal movements by black people. I migrated to London, UK, from Jamaica when I was three. My parents went ahead, leaving behind me, aged eighteen months, and my six-month-old sister, intending to send for us both once they were settled. They left us with my Aunt Cindy, Mother's older sister, who had no children of her own. I had a serious accident when I was three and my aunt no longer wanted to keep me. My parents sent money for my fare and I flew to London on a BOAC plane in the care of Miss Ida, a cousin of my father.

Because my parents were a few steps ahead of the great wave of Caribbean migrants to England in the late 1960s, in primary school I was the only black pupil. In grammar school I was one of three. At Nottingham University I was the only black undergraduate in the Faculty of Arts. I was accustomed to being the single grain of allspice floating in the milk jug, so that didn't phase me. What was difficult was having to read English literature from Beowulf to Eliot and no further. I was alienated from the texts I studied and from my instructors, who were mainly white, upper-class and very self-regarding. In my undergraduate courses and seminars I read nothing that related to my personal experience.

At that point in my life my black identity was defined in relation—and sometimes opposition—to the white/English people and culture around me. My home environment—people, décor, food, values—was unadulterated in its Jamaicanness. But Jamaica itself was an abstraction; my parents had nothing good to say about the place, though, paradoxically, they clung fiercely to Jamaican ways.

An avid reader, I joined the public library on my own initiative when I was seven, by faking my mother's signature on the membership application. I spent hours immersed in books thereafter. As a teenager I liked to write and won a prize at grammar school for a short story, but I did not think of becoming a writer. I studied English at university, but did not dream of teaching at university level. The marginality of black cultures in Britain, the absence of black writers, histories and subjects from British curricula, left black Britons of my generation without literary reference points or models. When I was growing up there were a few well known black writers, such as Chinua Achebe, but they were men. I did not read a novel by a black woman till I was in my twenties—*Brown Girl, Brownstones* by Paule Marshall. As for black academics, decades later there are still only seventeen women professors in the UK. I left university, took a job at the British Council, married and moved to India, where I lived for two years—but that's another story.

Coming to Writing

By the 1980s the wave of writing by African-American women that gathered momentum in the 1970s began to have an impact in the UK. The books, their stories and their authors were a source of inspiration for young black women like myself. *Sula*, *The Salt Eaters*, *The Women of Brewster Place*, I devoured those novels. They were about people to whom I could relate, their authors role models for young black British women who dreamed of becoming writers: Alice Walker, Toni Morrison, Gloria Naylor, Toni Cade Bambara and, of course, Paule Marshall. But they were in America; in the UK we did not have access to any space that encouraged or nurtured black writing and literary talent.

That changed somewhat in the 1980s, following uprisings by black youth in Brixton, Tottenham and Birmingham. The 1981 Scarman Report on those uprisings recommended (among other things) that provision be made for the cultural development of black youth, as well as for more leisure and recreation facilities, and skills training. Progressive metropolitan councils such as the Greater London Council invested in the development of arts centres for ethnic minority communities. Literary presses, such as Virago and the Feminist Press, that published women writers now included a handful of Afro-Caribbean and Black British writers on their list—Joan Riley and Andrea Levy, for example.

In my thirties I had a novel "cooking" in my brain but no idea how to go about writing it and, if I'm honest, deep doubt that anyone would be interested in reading anything I wrote. The novel in my head was about two generations of a Jamaican family settled in London. My family, my relatives and our experiences as black people in London were the original inspiration, but I observed that other people I knew and their families experienced similar challenges and pressures, had similar stories to tell. The desire to write combined with a sense of being marginal, even invisible in London and in England, influenced my decision to take leave from my job in London and return to Jamaica. I wanted to live on the island where I was born, even if only for a while, and I wanted to write that novel, which meant I also needed to know the place my characters came from.

Moving to Kingston, Jamaica

I had been back to Jamaica only once since I was three and that was the year before I made the move. My parents never went back and never encouraged me to do so; they had nothing good to say about Jamaica, or their parish, St Elizabeth. To them, Jamaica meant hard life, hard work and poverty. My mother's sister, and my favourite aunt, Veena, who had arrived in London shortly after me—returned to Jamaica and had settled in St Catherine, in a housing development near Spanish Town. My plan was to stay with her until I found a place of my own—I wasn't sure where or how. I was travelling on a current of faith. A Jamaican friend from London had also returned and was living in Kingston and my first weekend on the island I took the bus to visit her. She had been invited to a party on the Saturday night at the house of a lecturer at the University of the West Indies, in College Common, Mona, and she was eager to attend, to meet new people and to network. The party was at the home of Carolyn Cooper, who, it turned out, had a room to rent, the former helper's room at the side of the house that was quite private and had its own shower. A few days later I moved to College Common, where I stayed until I found a studio apartment in Kingston.

In Carolyn's house I was in my ackee; I was surrounded by an expert selection of books by and about Caribbean, African-American and African people, books from the postcolonial canon, books in the black intellectual tradition: the Black Atlantic in book form. I was drawn into a vibrant literary culture centred on UWI; I made new friends who were lecturers, writer, poets, artists. I was lucky; at the time I thought I could feel ancestral hands on my shoulder guiding me towards the people who soon became my friends. Many of them are still my friends.

After one year in Jamaica I returned to London, resigned from my job and sold my house. My father thought I'd spent the year smoking marijuana and had lost my mind. (I had done neither.) I returned to Jamaica and I wrote the novel that had been cooking in my head, titled *Seasons of Dust*, over a period of two years. That novel draft helped me secure a place in the 1995 Summer Workshop for Caribbean Writers at Miami University. Many of the people in my Caribbean creative community I met at that workshop; I was there with Kezia Page, Donna Aza Weir Soley, Danielle Legros Georges, Dahlma Llanos Figueroa. On the faculty were Olive Senior, Lorna Goodison, Eddie Baugh, Gordon Rohlehr, Antonio Benitez-Rojo—a stellar faculty. I still tell people that Olive Senior was my first Creative Writing Teacher. A fellow participant who was a student in the Creative Writing Program at NYU encouraged me to apply to join the MFA program, which I did and I was successful. I went to NYU with a *New York Times* Creative Writing Fellowship. Even now it seemed miraculous that my first writing workshop at NYU was taught by Paule Marshall.

Coming to New York

Looking back, that entire period seems golden, magical. In Jamaica—in Carolyn's house—I had met a writer from New York who was doing research at UWI, and who had worked in an agent's office in NY. That was how I found an agent and, shortly after, a publisher for *Seasons of Dust*, before arriving at NYU for the creative writing program. I was grateful for the funding and for the time and space to write, as well as for the feedback on my work that the workshop structure promoted. Also positive—exceptional, actually—was the experience of working with stellar instructors: Paule Marshall, Edwidge Danticat, Chuck Wachtel. But my experience could illustrate Junot Diaz's critique of creative writing programs quite well—#SoWhite—except for two other students from the Caribbean—Angie Cruz from DR and Ana Menéndez from Cuba. But, to be fair, white students did not overtly "other" my work; that was left for the world-famous Irish author, who commented on the dialogue of characters in one of my stories saying: "People don't talk like that!"

Resistance or a negative reaction to my writing soon became the response I anticipated from white folks in the US literary world who had difficulty seeing beyond stereotypes of Caribbean people. I did not fit an obvious niche. When my agent shopped my novel around editors and publishers, the responses she received ran the spectrum from: "These characters aren't believable" to: "What would the audience be for this book?" "Is she Caribbean? Her characters don't seem Caribbean."

Eventually, *Seasons of Dust* was picked up by an independent black publisher, Glenn Thompson. His press, Harlem River Press, no longer exists; it folded in the early 2000s, along with many other small presses, leaving black writers and others who are perceived as marginal by the publishing mainstream facing decreasing possibilities of seeing our work in print. And in the US, Caribbean writers are even more marginal; we are exotica, even to many African-American readers.

I had planned to return to Jamaica after completing the MFA, to build a house on a piece of land I'd bought in Highgate, St Mary, just before leaving for New York. However, one of my literature professors persuaded me to apply to NYU's PhD program in Comparative Literature; Kamau Brathwaite was teaching there, Ngũgĩ wa Thiong'o and Sylvie Kandé were there also, but I was hesitant. But it was lucky for me that I did submit an application, because the financial crisis in Jamaica in 1997 and the ensuing devaluation of the Jamaican dollar drove the cost of building a house way up and out of my reach. News of the crisis and the offer of a fully funded place in NYU's Comparative Literature Department arrived at around the same time, making the decision easy. I was advised against the PhD and warned that doctoral studies would encroach on my writing. I published two short stories while a graduate student, and a volume of short stories, *Ten Days in Jamaica*, twelve years after completing my MFA. Teaching full time left very little time for creative writing.

But I have no regrets. My studies have enabled me to do work that I love: teaching, researching and writing about Caribbean and African literature. And in the breaks between semesters, I write fiction.

Patricia Glinton-Meicholas

A Bahamian poet, cultural critic and author, she was the first winner of the Bahamas Cacique Award for Writing (1995) and recipient of a Silver Jubilee of Independence Medal for Literature (1998). Her many books include short story collections such as An Evening in Guanima *(2013) and* Lusca and Other Fantastic Tales *(2017), the novel* A Shift in the Light *(2001), three volumes of poetry and several works of satire. Her poetry appears in* Across Borders, Poui, Womanspeak *and* Yinna. *Her monograph on Bahamian folktales appears in the Encuentros series of the IDB Cultural Centre, Washington, DC. Her extensive writing on art includes* Bahamian Art 1492–1992, *the first comprehensive work on the subject (with Smith and Huggins). She is Vice President of Creative Nassau, and co-host of the Creative Nassau weekly radio show on Island 102.9 FM.*

Remembering, Re-membering

My name was scraped from the register
of the griot's tongue
and fed to sharks, whose memory is short
except for blood
and long ago, my captive member
was wrenched from the sweetness of yours.

Remember me
I'm the pricking of memory in your loins.
Press your ear against my breast
hear your drums pulsing still in my blood
let their throbbing send your heart racing
past coffle and castle
beyond forced couplings in foreign lands.
Strip away the long cloak of separation
rend my bodice of bondage
shred the rough girdle of shame.

Grip me once again
in your baobab arms
bind me with the lianas of your heart
bathe me in your potent Congo
cradle my head again
in the thick savannas
of your seething breast…

Call me yours again
re-member me
grow me a griot's tongue to tell ancestral tales
give me warrior's legs to leap the rough Atlantic chasm
and arms to embrace the freedom that is mine by right.
Let me, with heart and hands wide open
grasp your immensity
let my roots plunge into your soul's soil
knitting an indissoluble re-union.

Slavery Redux

We who cut teeth on promises of paradise
frolic to the flute of a star-striped piper
gyrating on the sword's edge
of geopolitics.

We eat, drink, sing and dance
lulled by the illusion
of benevolence on call
to drive us home from heedless revels
drunk on the over-proof rum
of self-delusion.

Revels grow cold
and soporific melodies
pledging endless summer, sky juice
and year-round junkanoo
will forge us new chains and manacles
with small hope of emancipation.

Woman Unconquerable

I am woman
reputed rib from Adam's side
assigned voiceless subordination
relegated to the role of sidekick
servant to penile supremacy
daily peeling the mazorca
jaw frozen in rictus

knees locked in genuflection
of unnegotiated servitude.

Yet, here I am
refusing reduction
head unbowed, tongue unchained
resisting devaluation
of self-forged new coinage.

I'm "Third World" woman
mistress of the alchemy of hunger
daily spinning life from straw of scarcity.
Is ancient Japanese kaprang[1] I ride
we two daily mounting insurrection
braving pothole, detour and downpour
fighting fickleness of two-faced economy
all on shame-brand, threadbare tires
her joints creaking a duet with mine
in ready-to-retire sisterhood.

I am a witch of Gambaga
by the twin spells
of custom and spite
transmuted
from wife, wise woman, mother
into poisoner of mates, minds and wombs
Satan's doxy, covert holder
of his proxy for evil
my fate steered by the compass
of a dying fowl's wings.

Yet, scrawny yard bird that I've become
I scratch up sustenance from the dust
conjure up purpose and cling
rotten tooth and bony claw
to life.

I am every woman
I pay passage but never reach

---

1 Bahamian Creole word meaning "broken down vehicle", e.g. bicycle or motorized vehicle. Used among British airmen during World War II as a verb signifying "crash".

the market called "freedom"
my fruit spoiling in fetid cage
and claustrophobic crate
shut in and shut out
by tariff, quota
disease and domination
ignorance and interdiction
my flight to higher heights
often hijacked, shot down.

But still, I am, I live
a woman, mistress
of unconquerable convictions.

Now, meet this sister
steel forged in magma-spilling mountains
tempered in chill Tongue of Ocean depth
bold Atlantic/Caribbean woman
hands akimbo
liberal and bent on liberation
broad of beam, deep of voice
brave and feisty for days
raucously refusing
to travel bound again
below deck again.

Go ahead, Lords of Fraud
and tainted tenure
repossess the kaprang
foreclose the shack
cancel my right to community
refuse note and certification
cancel permit and visa
invoke self-interested sanction
trample on my aspirations
slam your door in my face.
Like loa-duppy-jumbie-sperrit
I'll haunt your dreams.

Dis me nah! Caribbean Buttercup
colonizer of roadside ditch
conqueror of desolate ground

queen gilding a glorious kingdom
from a stinking, ancient rubbish heap.

I ain't goin' nowhere
this land and me is one.
Deny me rain and I run wild
prune me and I'll coppice
rip off my blooms and I'll reseed
root me up and I'll spring back
to flourish in your face.

Carmen Harris

Born in Kingston, Jamaica, she migrated to the UK at the age of five. After graduating from London University (BA Hons, Sociology), she worked variously as a writer in fringe theatre, as a sub-editor for Chic Magazine, *as a corporate scribe, and a children's author before becoming a professional TV scriptwriter. She used the pen-name Lisselle Kayla, during which time she wrote two series of her own original primetime BBC1 sitcom,* Us Girls *(the first such in the UK for a black female writer). She went on to work in many professional writing genres including radio, children's and drama, with 10 years as a core writer for the popular BBC1 soap* EastEnders. *She is the author of several books, among them the 2015 self-help/autobiography* Sh*t Happens, Magic Follows (Allow It!).

Hello… Goodbye

It was the year 1962. I was a skinny, dreamy, thumb-sucking five-year-old, about to leave my homeland with my mother, two brothers and sister. Unusually, we were to travel by plane, the height of privilege in those days. At least, compared to the thousands of other Jamaicans making the same journey by sea, taking up to twenty-two days to reach the shores of the Mother Country. Six months previous, in preparation for our migration, we had moved from our home in Kingston to live with my Aunty Hilda and her family in Annotto Bay. Now, the long-awaited day had finally arrived. Amid the tears, the farewell hugs and kisses, as we embarked on our sleepy night-time journey back towards Kingston, the capital, a whole banana was tucked into each child's hand. I immediately decided that I would not eat mine. I would save it as a gift for my father, that mysterious figure who had gone ahead of us to that mythical land called England to materialise his dream of social and economic self-improvement for the family. His absence had amounted to a lifetime in my young universe. Being just three years old when he'd left our tropical island, I'd virtually forgotten who my father was. I announced my noble intentions to my brothers and sister and to my annoyance they decided that they, too, would save their banana. Possessing the instincts of an only child, I was always caught short by the careless intrusions of my siblings into my inner life. My grumpiness didn't last long, for I needn't have worried. One by one, both brothers and my sister eventually succumbed to hunger and temptation and, by the time we reached Palisades Airport, all they had to show were three empty skins. I, however, clutched my yellow fruit to my chest with an intense loyalty. During my sleep on the plane, several times I felt my mother gently prising open my grasp and, each time, I awoke with a start to tighten my hold.

After an eternity of sleepless and sleep-filled hours, our BOAC flight finally landed at Gatwick Airport. As my siblings and I, dressed optimistically in flimsy sunny frocks and khaki shorts, stepped onto the tarmac and shivered in the chilly May winds, I was still clutching my banana. Inside the terminal building, a tall, caramel-skinned man wearing a brown suit and a felt hat, broke through the crowds and strode confidently towards us. I'd spent many hours dreaming of the exact moment, and now that it had arrived, I froze, unsure of my next move. But as soon as I felt myself swooped into the air, nestling in my father's embrace, I remembered to wave the triumph of my gift. My father chuckled. A mixture of pride and joy, it seemed. It didn't for one moment occur to me that it would be at the blackened, oozing mess, sticking to my palm…

I was often frustrated, felt somewhat cheated, by my father's existence in the UK. This was the man who decided from early on that I was bright enough to become a lawyer. Yet, when single-parenthood forced me to take a dreary clerical officer post in the GPO's *Yellow Pages*, he was appalled two years later by my proud announcement. My daughter was now five and I had been accepted by London University to study Sociology. I'll always remember that look, not of admiration, but of terror that I might have taken leave of my senses. *"What? You going to leave you good-good job in de Post Office?"* he gasped. Where the father of my dreams was bold and gregarious, mine was not only socially coy, but cautious, meticulous, suspicious. Perhaps he had always been like this, for I have heard stories of my mother being the real force behind my father's earlier entrepreneurial endeavours in Jamaica as a tailor, radio technician, Panamanian labourer and freight distributer at the Kingston wharf. Or, perhaps, due to frustrating early migrant experiences in the UK, he felt compelled to adapt to a new reality, one that required dampening passions and abandoning dreams of the future. Watching him consume a meal probably summed up everything there was to know about my father's approach to living. No matter how welcome the offering, each meal was a ritual that began with a sigh, as though the arrangement of food before him was yet another one of life's testing trials. Next, he would give a little sniff, as if strengthening his resolve, before proceeding to dissect the portions on his plate into neat surgical morsels. Once these were in the mouth, he would close his eyes to the sound of his masticating dentures, most probably counting each mouthful to a precise number of chews. Sometimes, like a cow ruminating on grassland, he would literally fall asleep over the task, till a clean plate was eventually accomplished. That's not to say he didn't enjoy food, he was an interested grocery shopper and, for a man of his generation, a surprisingly competent cook; but an ingrained apparent joylessness forbade him from fully indulging in life's pleasures.

I hear my assessment of him and a part of me cannot help but wince, for when we find fault with a parent, our irritation may have more to do with seeing a reflection of our own selves in their image. It was much later in life when I learned that I could expand the boundaries of my "personal space" without feeling exposed or threatened; when I decided it might be more affirming to roll with others' "playful" punches than coil inside and take umbrage; when I discovered that my authentic self could be found in laughing long and hard. This is in direct contrast to my younger years when I was accustomed to being hailed as the "serious" one, the humourless one, the one who lived more naturally in the head than in the world. Not a bad description of my father, as it happens.

Though it was difficult to admit, my father and I had our similarities. When he died, some twenty years ago, one of the more useful traits I inherited from him came to the fore. Faced with the double wardrobe and chest of drawers full of dead-man's clothes and the stack of old documents and paperwork that my father had left behind, my siblings blanched. I, however, immediately rolled up both sleeves, relishing the opportunity to process my grief through the fastidiousness of creating order. My father would have been proud.

But I was being driven by a second, more urgent motive. Here was my chance to examine forensically the man behind the buttoned-up colonial mask; retrospectively to meet my father on equal terms. Halfway through the clear-out, I came across a battered old suitcase that I remembered from my childhood as first belonging to my mother. It was covered with a thin film of dust, suggesting it had lain unopened for quite some time. With excitement, I raised the lid, inhaling the decades-old nostalgia of the island years. Putting aside a few musty items of clothing, my eyes fell upon a rubber-banded collection of miniature diaries that had been stowed in the bottom, dating back to the late '50s. My heart beat in anticipation. If I had failed to understand my father in life, I reasoned, surely now in death, his inner being would be revealed to me.

I sat down and didn't draw breath till I had examined every single page of all twenty diaries. Disappointment was like a heavy door casting its dark shadow, before slowly closing on me forever. Each one of the diaries, written in my father's deliberate cursive style, was an unreflective account of the minutiae of his everyday life: work rotas for the night shift, various doctor's appointments, dates the insurance man called, when the gas meter was due to be emptied, etc. Whatever heartfelt longings and unrequited desires my father had nursed during his lifetime, he had carried them to the grave as efficiently as he had once cleared a plateful of food.

Sandra Jackson-Opoku

Born and raised in Chicago, she is the author of the American Library Association Black Caucus award-winning novel The River Where Blood is Born *(1997), and* Hot Johnny (and the Women Who Loved Him) *(2001), which was an* Essence *magazine Hardcover Fiction Bestseller. Her fiction, poetry, essays, reviews and travel articles appear in the* Los Angeles Times, Ms. Magazine, *the* Literary Traveller, Transitions Abroad, Rolling Out, Soul of America, *and many other outlets. With poet Quraysh Ali Lansana she coedited the anthology,* Revise the Psalm: Work Celebrating the Writing of Gwendolyn Brooks *(2017), a* Chicago Review of Books *Nonfiction Finalist. Her work has earned such honours as the National Endowment for the Arts Fiction Fellowship, the Coordinating Council of Literary Magazines/General Electric Fiction Award for Younger Writers, a Ragdale Foundation US/Africa Fellowship, a William Randolph Hearst Research Visiting Fellowship at the American Antiquarian Society, a Roots Fellowship at the University of Virginia at Charlottesville, and several awards from the Illinois Arts Council and Chicago Department of Cultural Affairs.*

Boahema Laughed
From *Gods Gift to the Natives*

Bags were packed, belongings sold, tickets bought and planes boarded before it occurred to me that it might be a mistake. That in leaving Africa we were repeating the ancient rite of dispossession our ancestors had made. A modern Middle Passage, Diaspora's children having returned to the Motherland, only to forsake her once again—this time voluntarily.

The aircraft taxied leisurely, as if to taunt us with reminders.

Kwesi, foolish man. See what you go leave behind-o?

Palm trees waved and whitecaps boiled off the Atlantic as drops of rain began to pelt the window. The plane seemed to rear on its hind wheels and sniff out the sudden storm before heaving itself into take-off. The airport, the city of Accra, the long beige ribbon of Labadi Beach, all retreated into the distance as we moved across the blue-gray Atlantic. I thought of all that would be lost at the end of this journey. Our spacious, mud-splattered bungalow. Our web of friends and adopted family. Our daughter's African accent.

I found myself absentmindedly fondling the worn, pitted surfaces of my father's old pocket watch. I clicked the lid open and shut in a familiar rhythm until I glanced guiltily in Alma's direction. She called it my obsessive-compulsion. Whenever she caught me at it, she'd say: "Your OCD is showing." I couldn't imagine how she kept up with the latest American psycho-babble. It must be her subscriptions to all those women's magazines.

I was relieved to find her snoring lightly, and feasted on the sight of her. Though my wife hated me to watch her sleeping, I always found her enticing in repose—full lips slightly parted, bosom rising and falling, her features relaxed and languid.

My gaze strayed to a woman moving gracefully down the aisle, a smile on her face and a basket of hard candy in her outstretched hands. An Alma wide awake might read lewd ogling into my glances, rather than fleeting admiration of a lovely young creature with cornrowed hair and gold earrings. The kind of woman Boahema might grow into, were not this journey interrupting her African childhood.

The flight attendant caught me watching and stopped at our row. "A sweet for the little one, sir?"

A "been-to", no doubt. She looked African but spoke with a decided British accent. Her pear-shaped breasts lifted as she leaned across Alma's sleeping form to offer a handful of wrapped mints.

"No, thank you," I declined, hand raised. "Our daughter doesn't eat candy."

"Just something to suck," she whispered conspiratorially, pressing unwanted sweets against my upraised palm. I found myself thinking of other things one might want to suck, then chided myself for being a filthy old lecher, my child sitting beside me no less.

The flight attendant turned back and winked, as though she could read my dirty mind. "The cabin pressure can be hard on children's ears."

While my wife slept, my daughter wept. Alma snored against my right shoulder on the aisle seat, Boahema sniffled against my left shoulder at the window. I didn't realize she'd been crying until I felt a warm, damp spot seeping down my sleeve.

"What is it, baby?" I hugged her to me, accidentally dislodging Alma's head from the other side. "Tell Papa all about it."

My daughter seemed ashamed to be caught crying. She batted her eyes furiously, clutching to her chest the bedraggled rag doll that had become her security blanket.

"Nothing, Papa." Boahema burrowed her face into my arm. "Something is irritating my eye."

I took her gently by the chin and tilted up her heart-shaped face. Blew softly into one eye then the other. I kissed my fingertip and smoothed it against each eyelid, dabbing the tears away.

"No more irritation," I whispered. "Everything's going to be alright."

Though really, there was no guarantee. I unwrapped a mint and popped it into her mouth.

Boahema had been happy about our move to New York, more excited than either Alma or myself. She'd been three years old on our last trip to the States, too young to remember much of the visit. Now her six-year-old imagination conjured up an endless revelry of ice cream and television, video games and the expensive designer sneakers the been-to's sent back home to their African relatives. The very things we'd been trying to escape in the first place.

I didn't know if it was the unsteady rocking of the plane or the onset of homesickness that made Boahema bite her lip and breathe a ragged sigh.

"Papa, I'm sleepy."

"Rest yourself, child." I offered her my shoulder. "Warmest pillow on the plane."

"But it's wet," she protested, as if she hadn't caused the damage. I took a folded handkerchief from my pocket and spread it on the damp spot.

Boahema snuggled against me once more, eyes blinking with sleepiness. I could feel her jaw working as she sucked hard on her bit of candy.

"A bedtime story," she murmured.

Alma the poet should have been a more likely bedtime griot. I was the journalist, the practical one. Yet somehow, I fell into the habit of reading Boahema to sleep at night. She soon began requesting *anansesem*, folktales about the trickster spider, Ananse. I exhausted my store of tales and would have to go scrambling for more, collecting them from friends and colleagues. It had become a bedtime ritual.

"*Mmofra, mmofra*," I chanted. "Attention, attention. What is your pleasure, Miss Omobowale?"

She tilted her head, considering. "I want to know about a family that takes a long, long trip."

"I don't know any Ananse stories like that."

"You make it up," Boahema demanded.

I don't know what brought slavery to mind. Certainly not the most appropriate subject to entertain a homesick six-year-old, yet I found it prickling the tip of my tongue and tumbling from between my lips.

Boahema never knew any difference between herself and the African children she had grown up with. Words like *slavery*, *racism* and *minority* had not been in her vocabulary. It seemed as good a time as any to broach the subject.

"Not everyone who left Africa flew on planes. Some people left through the Door of No Return."

"A magic door? Like when Kwaku Ananse went to visit the Sky God?"

"No, baby. Ananse tales are fables. This story is real."

"The No Return Door is real? Where?"

"All up and down the West Africa coast. Elmina, Cape Coast Castle, a little island called Gorée."

"What is the meaning of this word, Gorée?"

"I really don't know, baby."

"You do," Boahema insisted. "It means you must 'go away.' Go 'way you, bloody fools!*" She was mimicking one of our elderly neighbors. The little English Mrs Acheampong knew were insults hurled at her boisterous grandchildren.

"Now, Boahema," I scolded. "Is that a nice thing to say?"

"Go 'way you," she repeated, giggling. When Boahema was tired she became giddy. "Papa, have you been to Go'way Island?"

I glanced guiltily at Alma's sleeping form. "Only once, long before I met your mother. An old friend once had a gig there, a singing engagement. Not many people lived on Gorée before the Europeans came. Africans found it rather inhospitable."

"In a hospital bowl?" came a sleepy grunt. Boahema was fighting to stay awake.

"In*hospitable*. It means it wasn't a good place to live. No fresh water. Not much in the way of creature comforts."

"It doesn't sound anything like New York."

New York had become Boahema's paradigm of paradise.

"It was like New York in one way. They're both places where people are good at selling things."

"Like Central Market in Kumasi?"

"Except on Gorée Island and other places like it—and this will be hard for you to understand—what they sold were people."

I waited, expecting innocence to evaporate before my eyes.

"People? Sold in a market?"

Then Boahema laughed, bless her heart. A laughter so shrill and sudden the people in the row ahead turned back, startled. Her mouth was wide open, the disintegrating mint still on her tongue. She soon began to cough and I made her spit the mint into my hand.

"Papa," she chortled. "You said this was a *real* story."

"Lord, do remember me," I murmured, relief like cool air on my face.

"What happened to the people then?"

"The ones who passed through The Door of No Return? Well, they weren't happy to leave, but something was taking them away from their home."

"*Go 'way you*. Were they chasing a story too?"

"Say what?"

Her response was a gaping yawn, a baby bird begging for food. Boahema's eyelids fluttered like butterfly wings as she drifted off to dreamland. I wouldn't get to chant the ritual closing lines:

This is my story I have told
If it be sweet, or if it not be sweet
Take some for yourself
And let some come back to me.

Boahema would not be awake to hear it, even if I knew how the story ended.

Donu Kogbara

Born in Nigeria, she is a print/broadcast journalist and communications consultant. She has worked for the BBC, Sky TV, the Sunday Times, The Guardian, Economist Intelligence Unit, *Shell and various Nigerian government organisations, including the Ministry of Transport and the Presidential Oil/Gas Sector Reform Implementation Committee. She writes a weekly column in* Vanguard, *a leading Nigerian newspaper, and is currently working on an environmental remediation project via the British Department for International Development. She has one child. Her hobbies are reading, eating good food, watching quality TV, talking, listening to 1970s music and travelling.*

Losing My Fragile Roots

Kidnapping is the most intelligent and justifiable crime…if you come from the wrong side of the tracks in a developing country that has a predatory ruling class and extremely weak policing system.

Domestic-level armed robbery—once the main occupation of the most forceful hoodlums in Nigeria—makes much less sense. You break into someone's home, waving lethal weapons. You tell everyone to lie on the floor face-down while you ransack the joint; and you leave with a bit of cash and sundry used goods—cars, TVs, jewellery, phones and so on—that you can usually only sell for a pittance.

It is much more lucrative to steal a person "of substance" as well as—or instead of—the above items of limited value, knowing that, nine times out of ten, his/her family will gladly pay you a sizeable ransom and that there is a very good chance that you will never be caught.

At the crack of dawn on 30 August 2015, I was shaken awake in my bedroom in Port Harcourt—a city in the troubled oil-producing Niger Delta region on Nigeria's southern coast—by gun-toting youths. I was then frogmarched to a waiting jeep and driven to a quiet cove, from which I was transported in a speedboat to a fisherman's hut that was precariously balanced on stilts in a swampy mangrove islet.

The hut was in a totally deserted section of the Atlantic creeks. I was held prisoner for thirteen days. There were nine of them, the kidnappers, and one of me.

Three years have elapsed since my sister paid a ransom to get me out of that dangerous mess. And I have so much to say about the actual (terrifying yet fascinating) experience of being incarcerated…in the middle of nowhere with a bunch of loquacious kidnappers—some sane and essentially decent, some drug-addled and psychopathic—who were happy to share their personal histories, their political views, their anger, their sadness, their anxieties, their dreams, their failures and their rationales for turning to crime.

It was all so weird, contradictory, complex and ambiguous. There were interesting and amusing conversations. There was warm emotional bonding. There were numerous rape and murder threats.

There were times when I was respectfully addressed as "Madame", affectionately addressed as "Maleh" ("Mum" in their native Ijaw lingo) or "Auntie" (they were indeed all young enough to be my sons or nephews).

There were times when I was treated like the hated representative of a grasping, ridiculously pampered and heartless elite that has abused the powers it inherited from British colonialists in 1960 and has ignored, oppressed, cheated, impoverished and killed the masses for decades.

There was a day when some of them competed, in a sweetly childlike manner, to impress me with their culinary efforts and asked me to give the surprisingly tasty dishes they had cooked marks out of ten.

There was a day when the worst of them—two alcohol and narcotics addicts who sometimes descended into sadism and lewdness when they were high or inebriated—sniggeringly brushed aside objections from their colleagues, hogtied me like a slaughtered animal being ferried to market in a traditional African rural setting, hung me from the hut ceiling by my wrists and ankles and beat me so savagely that my eardrum was ruptured and I was sure that I would die.

The actual experience of being an abductee was a very, very big deal. I was damned lucky to emerge alive and un-raped; and no day passes when I don't clearly recall certain details. It's like having the same movie constantly replaying itself in your head. And, to me at least, it isn't at all strange that it is not a horror movie throughout.

Alongside painful flashbacks, there are memories of camaraderie, great jokes and uproarious laughter…memories of touching acts of kindness…memories of feeling sorry for brutalized boys who said they became outlaws because they were sick of being powerless victims…and memories of enthralling discussions that taught me a lot about alien existences scarred by injustice, neglect and hunger.

They called themselves "soldiers" who were waging a war on the upper echelons of society; and I admired them for fighting back.

My friends have concluded that I am completely screwed up because, as one of them exasperatedly puts it, "you sound as if you miss those evil gangsters and as if you were often happy in their bloody hut". And it is possible that I am indeed mad as a hatter and warped and suffering from Stockholm Syndrome, a psychological phenomenon that makes captives illogically identify with their tormentors, sometimes to the point of vigorously defending them.

I cried when I was told that my kidnappers had been caught and summarily executed at the end of 2015. I suppose that tears were an inappropriate response, given that they had hurt me and confessed to murdering, sexually assaulting and torturing several abductees and law-enforcement officials.

"You should be furious with those thugs and *very* relieved that they have been eliminated," said the pal who told me they were dead.

Nevertheless, the anguish they inflicted on me was only part of an immensely complicated story; and I prefer to think I am not deluded but simply capable of being forgiving and objective under pressure. I also reckon that the whole thing about illogically identifying was a two-way street, in the sense that my jailors succumbed to whatever the hitherto un-named flipside of Stockholm Syndrome is. They gradually and grudgingly concluded that I was, despite my privileged background and irritating inability to speak proper pidgin English, an OK Person and Good Sport who didn't deserve misery.

So instead of cynically saying something like "Well, you would say that, wouldn't you, you posh fake bitch?" when I told them I was ashamed of my class and understood why the likes of them kidnapped the likes of me, they gave me the benefit of the doubt.

And they wound up feeling guilty. Even the sadistic psycho addicts got to a point where they could no longer look me in the eye, and left me alone and even gruffly paid me a couple of compliments.

Meanwhile, most of them apologised to me and said they wished they could continue to hang out with me when I was released.

One offered to work as my driver and bodyguard, if I was willing to forgive and promise to not report him to the authorities. Another planted a shy kiss on my cheek when he said goodbye on the dark Friday night when I was finally returned to the real world.

But you know what, Dear Reader? What happened inside that hut was far less devastating than what has happened subsequently.

For a start, my ear never fully recovered from the bashing it received; and I don't hear as clearly as I used to.

Furthermore, my once vibrant, sharp-witted and indomitable mother literally lost her mind shortly after I regained my freedom and now sits listlessly slumped on sofas, silently enduring an ailment that a psychiatrist has described as "trauma-induced pseudo-dementia". That said, many octagenarians have dementia and my poor old mother is not the only member of my extended family who has it and might have got it anyway, even had I not been kidnapped. So I don't, to be honest and selfish, count her mental deterioration as the most devastating thing that has happened in recent years.

What has upset and destabilised me most is the fact that I felt compelled, after the kidnap drama, to exile myself from my roots and family home in Port Harcourt, a marvellous structure built by my stylish late father and lovingly renovated by me.

My parents bitterly regretted sending me and my three siblings to English schools because we became unrepentantly Westernised Londoners, acquired very foreign partners and flatly refused to move to Nigeria. Then, aged thirty-nine and inspired by various factors, including a desire to please my parents—who were feeling very sorry for themselves and whining interminably about being abandoned in their dotages—I suddenly decided to give the whole Land-Of-My-Ancestors thing a go, which was how I wound up living in the parental residence in Port Harcourt.

I am a member of the Ogoni tribe. Ogonis are domiciled in Rivers State. Port Harcourt is the capital of Rivers State, which is multi-ethnic, populated by minorities and part of the Niger Delta. Rivers State is one of thirty-six states and produces a lot of the petroleum that has made the Federal Republic of Nigeria wealthier than most African countries. Nigeria prides itself on being the "Giant of Africa."

I did my best to juggle and embrace the often conflicting narrow ethnic, wider state and even wider regional, national and continental loyalties that all Nigerians are expected to juggle and embrace. And, despite being profoundly and unashamedly Eurocentric by nature, I was making serious progress and had mastered the challenge of figuring out why ethnic/tribal loyalty tends to be prioritised over wider loyalties, even by sophisticates who have genuine chums everywhere and were educated abroad and are citizens of the world and rarely or never visit their ancestral villages.

When I was dragged out of my bedroom in the late summer of 2015, aged fifty-five, I had already done a decade and a half of struggling to meaningfully (and simultaneously) connect to my Ogoni, Port Harcourt, Rivers, Niger Delta, Nigerian and African identities.

The kidnapping abruptly truncated this process of me trying my darndest to find my feet in a tough and tricky terrain that has battled with serious security problems and toxic gang activity for years.

Now, I am too spooked to spend significant amounts of time in Ogoniland, Port Harcourt, Rivers State or any Niger Deltan location. Which is a tragedy, from my point of view…partly because I have been a Niger Deltan activist and advocate for nearly two decades. I have robustly complained about the fact that the Niger Delta produces most of Nigeria's wealth but gains almost nothing in return. Unemployment is rife because jobs and business opportunities go to grasping bigwigs from elsewhere. Youngsters like my captors can't earn a living via legal activities. Pollution generated by oil exploration and production has destroyed our farms and fishing fields.

I have lost my self-confidence and no longer feel able to stick around to vocifer-ously join those who make a habit of protesting on behalf of the dispossessed—and the protestors really need help because there are not many Nigerians who can be bothered to push for reforms.

Also, before Port Harcourt became a place that scares the hell out of me, I had created a wonderful support system comprising talented health professionals, beauty therapists, seamstresses, food suppliers, and so on. Now I don't get to see these angels who put smiles on my face, made me great outfits, straightened me out when I had backache...

I no longer get to keep my poor widowed mum company. I can only nervously visit her for an hour or two at a time.

The bottom line is that I am just so sad and so tired of life and missing the cosy existence I carved out for myself in Port Harcourt...and the house I beautified in my own image and regarded as a sanctuary.

I guess the worst thing the kidnappers did to me was make me lose the ability to feel comfortable around my fragile roots, and cast me back into the realm of people who don't fully belong anywhere.

Ah, well. Never mind. Loss is part of human existence and Africa was never my main gig, to be truthful. I do, at least, still have good ole London...which represents about seventy per cent of who I really am; and makes me feel safe.

1 October 2018

Andrea Levy

Born in London to a father who sailed from Jamaica to England on the Empire Windrush *and a mother who followed him soon after, she grew up Black in what was still a very white England. This experience gave her a complex perspective on the country of her birth. In her mid-thirties she began writing the novels she had always wanted to read, that reflected the experiences of Black Britons. She has been a recipient of an Arts Council Award and her second novel,* Never Far from Nowhere *(1996), was longlisted for the Orange Prize.* Small Island *(2004) was the winner of the Orange Prize for Fiction, and of the Whitbread Novel Award, the Whitbread Book of the Year award, the Orange Best of the Best, and the Commonwealth Writer's Prize.* The Long Song *(2010) was shortlisted for the Man Booker prize and was awarded the Walter Scott Prize for Historical Fiction. She has written short stories that have been read on radio, published in newspapers, and anthologised. She has been a judge for the Orange Prize for Fiction, Orange Futures and the Saga Prize. She still lives and works in London.*

From *Small Island*

Let me ask you to imagine this. Living far from you is a beloved relation whom you have never met. Yet this relation is so dear a kin she is known as Mother. Your own mummy talks of Mother all the time. "Oh, Mother is a beautiful woman, refined, mannerly and cultured." Your daddy tells you, "Mother thinks of you as her children; like the Lord above she takes care of you from afar." There are many valorous stories told of her, which enthral grown men as well as children. Her photographs are cherished, pinned in your own family album to be admired over and over. Your finest, your best, everything you have that is worthy is sent to Mother as gifts. And on her birthday you sing-song and party.

Then one day you hear Mother calling—she is troubled, she needs your help. Your mummy, your daddy say go. Leave home, leave familiar, leave love. Travel seas with waves that swell about you as substantial as concrete buildings. Shiver, tire, hunger—for no sacrifice is too much to see you at Mother's needy side. This surely is adventure. After all you have heard, can you imagine, can you believe, soon, soon you will meet Mother?

The filthy tramp that eventually greets you is she. Ragged, old and dusty as the long dead. Mother has blackened eye, bad breath and one lone tooth that waves in her head when she speaks. Can this be that fabled relation you heard so much of? This twisted-crooked weary woman. This stinging cantankerous hag. She offers you no comfort after your journey. No smile. No welcome. Yet she looks down at you through lordly eyes and says, "Who the bloody hell are you?"

"Okay, Gilbert, you have gone too far," I can hear you say. You know I am talking of England—you know I am speaking of the Mother Country. But Britain was at war, you might want to tell me, of course she would not be at her best.

Some of the boys shook their heads, sucking their teeth with their first long look at England. Not disappointment—it was the squalid shambles that made them frown so. There was a pained gasp at every broken-down scene they encountered. The wreckage of this bombed and ruined place stumbled along streets like a devil's windfall. Other boys looking to the gloomy, sunless sky, their teeth chattering uncontrolled, gooseflesh rising on their naked arms, questioned if this was the only warmth to be felt from an English summer. Small islanders gaped like simpletons at white women who worked hard on the railway swinging their hammers and picks like the strongest man. Women who sent as much cheek back to those whistling boys as they received themselves. While even smaller islanders—boys unused to polite association with white people—lowered their eyes, bit their lips and looked round them for confirmation when first confronted with a white woman serving them. "What can I get you, young man?" Yes, serving them with a cup of tea and bun. A college-educated Lenval wanted to know how so many white people come to speak so bad—low class and coarse as cane cutters. While Hubert perusing the countryside with a gentle smile said, "but look, man, it just like home," to boys who yearned to see the comparison—green hills that might resemble the verdant Cockpit country, flowers that might delight as much as a dainty crowd of pink hibiscus, rivers that could fall with the same astounding spectacle of Dunn's river. And let me not forget James, perplexed as a new born, standing with military bearing surrounded by English children—white urchin faces blackened with dried snot flaking on their mouths—who yelled up at him, "Oi, darkie, show us yer tail."

But for me I had just one question—let me ask the Mother Country just this one simple question: how come England did not know me?

On our first day in England, as our train puffed and grunted us through countryside and city, we played a game, us colony troops. Look to a hoarding and be the first to tell everyone where in England the product is made. Apart from a little argument over whether Ford made their cars at Oxford or Dagenham, we knew.

See me now—a small boy, dressed in a uniform of navy blue, a white shirt, a tie, short trousers and long white socks. I am standing up in my classroom; the bright sunlight through the shutters draws lines across the room. My classmates, my teacher all look to me, waiting. My chest is puffed like a major on parade, chin high, arms low. Hear me now—a loud clear voice that pronounces every p and q and all the letters in between. I begin to recite the canals of England: the Bridgewater canal, the Manchaster-to-Liverpool canal, the Grand Trunk canal used by the china firms of Stoke-on-Trent. I could have been telling you of the railways, the roadways, the ports or the docks. I might have been exclaiming on the Mother of Parliaments at Westminster—her two Chambers, the Commons and the Lords. If I was given a date I could stand even taller to tell you some of the greatest laws that were debated and passed there. And not just me. Ask any of us West Indian RAF volunteers—ask any of us colony troops where in Britain are ships built, where is cotton woven, steel forged, cars made, jam boiled, cups shaped, lace knotted, glass blown, tin mined, whisky distilled? Ask. Then sit back and learn your lesson.

Now see this. An English soldier, a Tommy called Tommy Atkins. Skin as pale as soap, hair slicked with oil and shinier than his boots. See him sitting in a pub sipping a glass of warming rum and rolling a cigarette from a tin. Ask him, "Tommy, tell me nah, where is Jamaica?"

And hear him reply, "Well, dunno. Africa, ain't it?"

See that woman in a green cotton frock standing by her kitchen table with two children looking up at her with lip-licking anticipation. Look how carefully she spoons the rationed sugar into the cups of chocolate drink. Ask her what she knows of Jamaica. "Jam- where? What did you say it was called again. Jam- what?"

And here is Lady Havealot, living in her big house with her ancestors' pictures crowding the walls. See her having a coffee morning with her friends. Ask her to tell you about the people of Jamaica. Does she see that small boy standing tall in a classroom where sunlight draws lines across the room, speaking of England—of canals, of Parliament and the greatest laws ever passed? Or might she, with some authority, from a friend she knew or a book she'd read, tell you of savages, jungles and swinging through trees?

It was inconceivable that we Jamaicans, we West Indians, we members of the British Empire would not fly to the Mother Country's defence when there was threat. But, tell me, if Jamaica was in trouble, is there any major, any general, any sergeant who would have been able to find that dear island? Give me a map, let me see if Tommy Atkins or Lady Havealot can point to Jamaica. Let us watch them turning the page round, screwing up their eyes to look, turning it over to see if perhaps the region was lost on the back, before shrugging defeat. But give me that map, blindfold me, spin me round three times and I, dizzy and dazed, would still place my finger squarely on the Mother Country.

Juliana Makuchi Nfah-Abbenyi

A Cameroonian-American who was born and raised in Cameroon, she earned doctorates from the University of Yaoundé, Cameroon, and McGill University, Canada. She is Distinguished Professor of English and Comparative Literature and Assistant Dean for Diversity in the College of Humanities and Social Sciences at North Carolina State University. She is the author of four books and many other publications, writing fiction under the pen name Makuchi. "Woman of the Lake", her short story about the 1986 Lake Nyos disaster that wiped out entire communities in Cameroon, was nominated for the Pushcart Prize. In 2016, she became president of the African Literature Association.

Home is where you mend the roof

SUNDAY, 2 A.M.
I'm jolted out of sleep. I do not recognize the number. "Hello." Silence. I hang up.

My home phone rings again. I say, "Hello." Twice. I hang up again. Who's calling me from Africa? I know it's not a Cameroon number. The 242 country code looks familiar but the number my caller ID displays isn't my brother's. My iPhone interrupts my thoughts. "Hello." The connection holds. Still no answer on the other end. I hang up. My son opens my bedroom door. Who is it? he asks, standing in the doorway. He has that look on his face. Many an African immigrant to the United States would recognize that look. That dreaded 2 a.m.-phone-call-look; the albatross around our necks. I don't know. I don't recognize the number, I say. Why don't you call them back? he says. I shrug, slowly pulling the sheets up to my shoulders. Whoever it is will call back, I say. Are you sure? Maybe you should call them, Maku. He gives me one last glance and gently shuts the door. Someone's about to ruin my spring break, I mumble, pulling the sheets over my head.

I want to go back to sleep. Five minutes later I grab the home phone and hit redial. "We're sorry your call cannot be completed as dialed." I slam the phone down on the nightstand; grab my cell phone and hit redial. "Hello." My brother's voice; crystal clear. Relief.

"My brother! How are you?"

"I'm fine."

"Are you back from South Africa?"

"Yes."

"How was the trip? How was Cape Town?"

"Everything went well…but I'm calling because I have bad news…"

"Someone's dead."

"Yes."

"Who?"

"Fr. Sylvester."

"When?"

"This morning. I just got off the phone with Timothy. Timothy called me yesterday. Not long after I got back. He told me Fr. Sylvester was sick. I called and talked to Fr. Sylvester for twenty minutes…"

My forty-one-year-old brother, Rev. Sylvester Nsemelah Nfah, died in his bed, sometime before dawn on Sunday March 3, 2013, in Bamenda, in the North-West Region of Cameroon.

That 2 a.m. call brought anguish to my bed in Raleigh, NC, as people in Bamenda were rising to a new dawn and getting ready for mass.

News of the death of a loved one unsettles even the most laid-back immigrant once it reaches its destination somewhere in America. It is the one thing that has the power to disrupt the structured sense of place that African immigrants cultivate, whether as permanent resident aliens or as naturalized citizens. When one is thousands of miles away from what used to be home, one expects, one day or another, to hear about a sudden death, for it is said that no one in Africa dies of natural causes.

This is of course the psychological mask one dons in the pretence that a loss in the family is one more occasion for celebrating life, no matter. I wear this shield in the hope it would protect me from the heartache; from that invisible accusing finger that blames faraway calamities at home on my abandonment; to my quest for personal fulfillment.

One brother dies, then a second, then a third, and now a fourth brother joins the group of siblings departed. And my shield endures yet another crack. It is as if I have to begin all over again.

I moved to Raleigh, NC in June 2006. I have slowly, in the last seven years, been making Raleigh home. I was even becoming blasé about the success of this project.

And all it takes is a phone call, this one in the dead of night while I am ensconced in the warmth of my comfortable bed, to shatter any illusion of that neat separation between home there and home here.

Feelings not of loss but of helplessness abound. You wish you were a character on *Star Trek*. You yearn to say "Beam me up, Scotty!" In the blink of an eye, I'd be right there in Bamenda, standing side by side with my dad and siblings, crying in each other's arms, dashing from neighborhood to neighborhood making preparations, having heated arguments—sometimes calmly, sometimes screaming, sometimes laughing—over who has done what, and who was supposed to do what and who hasn't done what and who needs to do what.

Twenty-first-century globalization lulls us into believing one can simply reach out and touch someone else; someone in America can reach out and touch someone in Bangladesh; someone in China can reach out and touch someone in Cape Verde, so the experts quip. News of Sylvester's death tells me otherwise. Scotty's *Enterprise* cannot come to my rescue; I can't reach out and touch my brother. The global village is only a theory; at this moment it is exposed as a lie.

And I find myself forgetting, even resenting, all the good things I like about Raleigh; those things that have made Raleigh home. The State Farmers Market, for one. A place that gives me intense joy; that stirs warm feelings in me akin to the kiss one hurriedly steals from a new lover before rushing off. Seven years on, and I still can't believe this market is open every day of the year! Driving to the State Farmers Market on Saturdays always fills me with anticipation of what I might find, besides fresh fruits and vegetables, once I get there.

I have no illusions I'd find ethnic African foods. For such items, I go to specialty grocery stores or visit the summer produce stands at the flea market on Capital Boulevard. These alternative food outlets are far from my mind as anticipation grows once I turn left from Nazareth onto Centennial Parkway. As I drive closer to the market, I imagine throngs of people already busy shopping; people from all walks of life strolling from one stall to the next, some in pointless banter, some lingering to chat with the farmers about their produce even as other buyers wait patiently for their turn.

I always smile when I turn left onto Centennial for the simple fact that were I in Cameroon, once I made that turn, I would have heard the market come alive, if not before. West African markets are boisterous venues where people interact with such emotional abandon you can hear the market from miles away. One hears African markets before seeing and experiencing their pulsating intoxication. You can hear it beckoning, calling out to you, calling your name, inviting you to partake, even for a brief moment, in the joy of living on this planet. A cacophony of voices ignites a rush and propels one's steps to this theater of human drama.

That is why I am always drawn to Building 4, the Truckers Building, tucked away at the far end of the Farmers Market, where produce is sold in bulk; where one can split a box of tomatoes with a total stranger. "Want to split?" "Sure." Nothing's more fun.

Building 4 is also the go-to place for brown skins and immigrant faces. These faces lure me even when I don't need to buy in bulk. On Saturdays, as I make my way through a crowd of brown people from many walks of life, I secretly fixate on those faces from home. It is a common practice among immigrants to play this silent game. The blank stare that says you can pretend to be American all you want but I can tell you are an African: your clothes, your hair, your walk, your bearing, that bone structure, those facial marks, the way you rotate that mango on the tips of your fingers, the way you squeeze that pineapple with your thumb, index and middle fingers…they all betray you.

My ears reach for their voices; for the tone and the pitch. Voice. Language. Two things that give it away, arousing competing thoughts in my head. That Pidgin English is definitely West African, probably Liberian. That one is obviously Nigerian. Those francophones over there are definitely sub-Saharan Africa; they're probably Congolese. Those two are without a doubt Senegalese. I walk closer. Sometimes, I say, Hi. Sometimes I get a cheerful response; sometimes not. Sometimes I am engaged in a spirited conversation in which we compare notes about what country we are *originally* from and what the political climate is like *back there*. We chat about how long we've been here; we skillfully avoid the taboo question, *What do you do here?*

But when one person volunteers they're here just biding their time, planning for when they'll return home, For Good, we burst into hysterical laughter, recognizing we've heard the same bullshit many many times before. You know that ten, twenty, thirty years later, you will bump into this going-home-for-good talker and you'll likely hear them say it all over again. We recognize this as our acknowledgment that despite the envy of all those we left back home; despite it all, immigration is experienced as a form of impoverishment. It is a state of mind that frames and defines an immigrant's relationship with their sense of place, their sense of belonging in America…

I realized while writing this piece that I cannot write about Raleigh, North Carolina, without recalling Hattiesburg, Mississippi. My first semester in a full-time tenure-track position at the University of Southern Mississippi ended with the news of the death of my sibling, the fifth of ten children, in Yaoundé, Cameroon. A first. Unfamiliar territory. I was so traumatized by the death of my brother, Ezekiel Takumberh Nfah, that I locked myself in my apartment for an entire week, never stepping foot outside. I wrote "Mourning…in distant lands", a poem, that captured my raw emotions; that poked holes in my belief that I had made the right decision to come to America. I later used the poem to dedicate my book of short fiction, *Your Madness, Not Mine: Stories of Cameroon*, to my younger brother, Ezekiel…

I had never in my life felt so alone until I answered that 3 a.m. call in my Hattiesburg apartment on December 26, 1995. I have experienced a familiar helplessness with Fr. Sylvester's death; that is one ingredient a distant death never changes for an immigrant, but this time, I have not felt alone. I have not been alone. Flowers, calls, emails from friends and colleagues remind me of that fact; abundant gestures of concern and love from my children and family remind me I am not alone; members of the Triangle Cameroon Association holding a wake in my house to coincide with the wake in Cameroon remind me I am not alone.

Two years ago, the UN Conference for Women came to NC State. I was on "The New South" panel with women who shared insights on immigration and the changing face of the South. When Regina Wang of the *News & Observer* interviewed me at the conclusion of the panel, I told her that "I hope it's a place where I can live and thrive, where I can bring something positive and receive something positive back." I used to obsess over what home is, what home means, where home is, but when I read Isidore Okpewho's foreword to my book, *The Sacred Door and Other Stories: Cameroon Folktales of the Beba*, I relented and learned to take comfort in his words: "Makuchi may lament…that leaving her native Beba home in Cameroon has removed her from the warm, familial environment in which the tales in her collection were originally told, or that she has not succeeded in recreating with her children the traditional context of cultural education in which she was raised. But she is bringing that education to a larger, universal audience that includes her own children here in North America who, in time, will come to recognize that—to paraphrase an old Igbo (Nigerian) proverb—'Where you mend the roof, there is your home.'"

Tess Onwueme

A Nigerian-born playwright, scholar and poet, she rose to prominence writing plays with themes of social justice, culture and the environment. She uses the theatre as a medium to showcase historically silenced views and shed more light on African life. In 2010, she became the Professor of Global Letters at University of Wisconsin-Eau Claire. A Nobel Prize in Literature nominee for 2016, she has won several international awards, including the Fonlon-Nichols award, the Phyllis Wheatley/Nwapa award for outstanding black writers, the Martin Luther King, Jr./Caeser Chavez Distinguished Writers Award, the Distinguished Authors Award, and the Association of Nigerian Authors Drama Prize which she won for her plays The Desert Encroaches *(1985),* Tell It To Women *(1995),* Then She Said It *(2003) and* Shakara: Dance-Hall Queen *(2006).*

The Runaway's Daughter: A Diary

I sat there. Limp. Gazing into night's misty face. The sky had a black eye and couldn't stand it. She vanished. The stars, too. Washed their gleaming celestial hands off the sky that stooped sour and spewed his dirt into the gaping hole in my eyes. What remained was a dark hole poked in the eyes of day, filled with silence. I must find my way in it. My mother too—trying to ignite her way with a patch of light, forged from the flickering yellow oil lantern in her hand. My snoring brother Nosike was secured with the "*Oja*" woven sash and wrapper around what used to be her robust ebony frame. Her handful of wrappers were sopping bread loaf in water, furtively laid now in a ratty wicker basket. Waiting…waiting by that rickety door.

That treacherous door! Wish you had the nerve to swing up close and hold her back! But you've always been a coward. You can't even boast of a key. Any key. To lock her out of that world that she's headed into now. Door, just find an excuse…any excuse to lock her in. But the traitor-door has conspired with all to rob me of her, my mother!

The loaded basket will take center-stage on her bare head. I envy the scruffy cargo, now her chosen companion, and not me. I look out. See the moon. Like a shy new bride, trying so hard to shine through the dark deluge of our world. The stars surrounding her look dull.

"Baby, it's time." She breathed hard as she tucked me gently into her bosom with the thickset arms that I wished I could remain glued to for life. Just to be a tag in my mother's arms was all I needed in my world now to survive. A tag to somebody I know, my mother.

"Baby, it's time… I'm ready. Come see me off," her hushed voice pleaded. At the mere mention of time, my bladder burst open, yielding its loaded contents, held tight since the evening cockcrow when Mama whispered to me that night was coming. That she'd have to hurry to cook okro soup for me, before her journey. Because it was time…Why does time have such a stranglehold on my mother? Who can arrest it? Papa? But where is he? Who is he? I don't even remember his face. Never saw him since my toddler years when they say the pretty man sailed to England to drink tea with Her Majesty the Queen. I need him. Now! Somebody tell Papa to come kill this thing they call Time that is about to take my Mama!

For many market-weeks, since Mama started stuffing my calabash with her clothes that she stole away from the scorching eyes of in-laws in our endless trudge to Iyi-Ada stream, she's been loading me with secrets; whispering in my six-year-old ears that she was preparing to run away. She said I must never tell anyone.

My body turned jelly in Mama's trembling hands as she folded me into her bosom, humming magic lullabies to steady me, before prising open the wounded door of our hut. With the load rooted firmly on her head, my baby brother lodged on her broad back, and me dripping wet in her arms, she lingered in that spot, humming those enchanting tunes. Outside, the night habitués were at play: crickets, owls, frogs and rodents with other nocturnal associates busy calling their lovers for the mating season and clan supper. Night's zillion sounds.

But suddenly Mama stopped humming. She set my reluctant feet down. Turned her back against the door. Took her first step. Marching away and never looking back, as her kind eyes, like wet tar glinting in the dark, prodded me. Silence stood between us. And would soon be my sole companion. For so long, I'd held on to silence: my prop…my anchor—with no Mama, no Papa, no Bro… Aaaah! Silence had claimed me young and wedded me. I had no voice: I had no choice. My fumbling feet followed with my heart racing. Into the night. With darkness blooming, yawning in our faces. But she was resolute. Each step provoked a million icy fingers clawing me with chills, seizing my spine.

"I'm cold. Scared, Mama. Please, don't go. Stay!"

Her portly legs sag but will not abort her mission. They press on. Still holding on to her load with one hand, the other stretched to pull me along as I stood shuddering beside her cooking hearth with much smoke and no fire. Her hand enveloped me. Tight. Tighter in that arm as she breathed hard into me, anointing me with her scent. Her fresh coconut breath stuck in my face. Soothing. Warm. I'd carry that with me far—especially when I was afraid. Years later, when I'd trip and fall—as I did so many times—and whenever I was losing myself, her soothing breath would guide me back in the way. We had reached the front gate of my primary school. Here, Mama broke into my thoughts.

"Malio, I know you like school."

"Very much. That's where I get to really play with my friends…"

Mama stopped, turned me to face the school. "Child, listen: That school is your father. Your mother. Your life!" She nailed each word. "I pray they let you continue…" she sighed.

"Who, Mama?"

"Your father's people." Silence seized my tongue. "And, Baby, you know Mrs Onoh?"

"Yes, Mama. Isn't she the trader who sold you the cloth for my school uniform?"

"Yes. I haven't paid her…"

"So, should I return the uniform to her?"

"Oh, no! She wouldn't even take it. Just tell Mrs Onoh that… Tell her that I'll pay her some…day."

As she spoke, I fingered the thick khaki uniform that was already smiling at the seams around my waist. It was the only dress I had—apart from the one I regularly wore to school. Mama had made both uniforms from Mrs Onoh's fabric. She'd spread the long piece of cloth on the floor and asked me to hold one end while she cut it into pattern pieces with her cooking knife, sharpened on the whetstone. Grandfather Nnady also used that knife for shaving our hair, Nosike, me, with all the other children of the kindred. Mama stitched the pieces together with the black thread that women normally used in plaiting their hair. The khaki dress matched my small body. I was in love with it. I didn't have to be flogged anymore by the headmaster who forbade colored dresses in his school. It made me feel so proud that after weeks of being sent home from school, I had not one but two dresses. I walked tall!

"Yes, Mama. I'll tell her."

"Great girl!" she cooed and pumped my hand as she pulled me closer to her. Years later, I'd look in the mirror and see her sleek blue-black body standing firm, like a soldier on guard. This guard of honour in my heart, my mother! Talking.

"Baby, it's okay to be afraid sometimes. But don't you ever let fear conquer...control you. I've learned that along the way. And I'm still on my journey. Life! Ah!" she chuckled.

"Mama, what is...this journey? When it will end?"

"Ma-liii-jeeem." She stretched each syllable, planting every strand of it in my head and heart. "Ma-li, *who knows my journey? Nobody can tell...*"

"But...Mama...it's...not my fault, is it?

"What, Baby?"

"That you're leaving... Is it?"

"Child, how can you say that?"

"Mama, because sometimes when you were angry with me—like that day I cooked the only okra you had for soup with my playmates—you dragged me to the farm and beat me. Very hard. Yelling that it was because of me you were suffering. If it wasn't for us your children, you said, you'd have left this bloody place long ago. That is what you said, Mama..."

"Stop!" her throat bubbled with tears. "I'm sorry. Forgive me," she sobbed. "Child, I was lost. Confused. Frustrated. Didn't know what to do..."

"But you want to run away and leave me. Why?"

"I have...adult...matters...I com...committed... Marriage? Aaaah!" she took a deep sigh.

"Adult matters? What are they, Mama? Tell me. You're keeping secrets from me now, when you've always called me your handbag."

"Handbag?" She chuckled. "Child, you're much too young to know. Someday, you will understand. Just wait till you grow up. But one truth I know: I will not lie to you."

"But you're leaving me and won't tell me where you're going?"

"Leave you? Never!"

"And you'll come back to me?"

"To you, yes! Always. Carry you with me...in me...yes!"

"And you will come back for me?"

"Hmn...Some...day."

"When?"

"Soon. All I can tell you now is that I will try. I'm just going where life takes me. But I will come back. Always. To find my bearings. *You*, my children are...my bearings. So help me. I need you." She slumped under a tree. "And even now as I go away," she continued, "remember this. You are not alone. Remain strong. Whatever they ask you to do, *work hard*," she drilled into me. "Your dinner is in the forest. It never comes to you. You must go fetch it. Above all, stay humble. For obedience and humility go far. But don't give up your dignity. Hold on to it! You hear me?"

"Yes, Mama." I was still soaking in her words, when she suddenly exclaimed: "Oh, dear! You've come too far already. I must take you back…to the village. Come! Let's go." She pulled me along as she made a roundabout turn. I could see we had left the village far behind. The only other wayfarers on the dusty track were the sheep in their nightly chewing and stargazing. We passed by them in silence, continuing our aimless march until Mama realized that she had gone too far. Then she'd sound her alarm note. Again!

"Mali, we've gone too far now." Back to where we began.

"Don't leave me, Mama!" I shrieked.

"No, child. I must go…" She began to pull away, but I stuck to her like lint.

"Baby, it's too late. For you…for me… Night is here. You'll walk me only a few steps back?"

"Yes, Mama. I promise." I rushed into her arms. Tears had taken possession of us. Fears too. We couldn't see. Salty canals ran down our faces. We staggered back and forth. My mother would see me off, then she'd take me back to the village. And again, I'd see her off. Back on that dusty pathway. To that *Nowhere* and *No Place* that she called *Her Journey*. We went far on this back-and-forth circle of the interminable journey on the road I had no name for. Then the cycle was finally broken.

A howl unleashed into Night's monopoly tore up the silence, injecting new chills into me. And Mama too. She froze. For a moment. Only a moment. For nothing could deter her now. Nobody. Nothing. Not even the night.

"We need to part now, Baby. Go back!" Then Mama turned around swiftly. Her feet pointed back in the direction of the village she was fleeing—as if that was where she was heading. With measured steps, backwards, Mama started walking away. Finally. One. Two. Three. Four. Five. Six. Seven steps. I stood there, counting her steps. Searching, tracing her footprints, now shadows in the dark. Till I lost count. And she kept moving. Moving. But I wouldn't stop counting. Couldn't. Shoeless, she walked backwards. Yes, backwards! So her footprints wouldn't register the direction of her escape; as she said her mother taught her.

My mother is…going. Going. I can't hold her any longer. I can't hear her any more. I just stand there. Gaping. Her shadow stretches, longer, and longer. Fading into the night that stretched into eternity. I shut my eyes. Tight.

When they tore open, an eclipse ruled. The Moon. Red. Bloody Moon. Sucking and licking night's ravenous tentacles. In my head, I saw Mama's shadow, vanishing. Her feet pounding my heart. Still. Until night swallowed them. I could see her no more. My mother's gone! Gone! I know it: *Loss is what you have but can only keep and feel in your mind's eye!*

Zuleica Romay Guerra

From Havana, Cuba, she is a social investigator, writer and professor. Author of the titles: Studies of the Public Opinion in the Downfall of the Cuban Neo-colony *(2012);* Eulogy of the Althaea or the Paradoxes of Raciality, *which was winner of a Casa of the Americas Award (2012); and* The Pillories of Memories: Impression of Slavery in the Cuban Social Imaginary *(2015) which won the Cuban Language Academy Award. She is co-author of articles and essays published in domestic and foreign publications and a lecturer in universities in several countries. She is a member of the Latino American Studies Association, LASA; of the Latin American Board of Social Sciences, CLACSO; and of the Cuban Committee of the Route of the Slave.*

Something About Me

Some time ago, at an international event on cultural tourism in London, one of a trio of British businessmen commented on my black and almost symbolic presence among the Cuban leaders negotiating future tourist relations with the island. Wasn't the presence of just *one* black person within such a representative group of people evidence that the Cuban Revolution had not succeeded in eradicating racial discrimination?

"Forty-six years of revolution cannot erase 400 years of slavery," I replied.

And I began a detailed exposition of my life story, in which my earliest memory is of the figure of Crecencia Santa Cruz, the only one of my great-grandparents whom I met, when she was more than eighty years old and a victim of Alzheimer's. In our apartment, during many hot nights, Crecencia would deprive us of sleep with her hair-raising cries of horror, loudly begging not to be beaten. Her inner return to childhood, the paradoxical privilege of senior citizens, had taken her back to the slave barracks where she was born, and to who knows to how many episodes of ill treatment, either as victim or as powerless onlooker, which even in the latter days of her life her mind could not forget

I spoke to those Englishmen about my grandmother Elena, a militant fighter for the People's Party in Cuba, about which she took unconditional pride. She was the very first person to explain to me that just through personal endeavour and total adherence to the Revolution she could reverse the historic disadvantage that four consecutive centuries of exclusion left as a legacy for the disempowered and excluded in this country. "Your aunt," she insisted, "who believes she is always right because she happens to be a school teacher, claims that slavery was abolished in 1886; but, my daughter, the truth is that it was indeed Fidel who removed our chains."

I referred to my father who, when he was only eleven years old, began to work washing cars in order to contribute to the family's meagre income, until his natural intelligence enabled him to rise within the working hierarchy to become first of all a blacksmith, and later on a car mechanic. My father—who took part in the July 1953 attack on the Moncada Barracks as a paramilitary adventure, and was able to understand his own role by reading Castro's "History Will Absolve Me", on his own and secretly—was the first in the family to be honored for academic results, and during a very cheery Sunday lunch we celebrated his graduation from elementary school (sixth-grade).

I told them how books initially came into my household as bait to keep us children in our beds when we refused to take a mandatory nap at noon And how books became our main spiritual nourishment, within a family that almost instinctively managed to tell the difference between chance and opportunity. My father encouraged in us the need to read, and he led us, compelled by the fraternal competition that gradually became staunch commitment, to graduate one at a time from university classrooms. Today, my father, whose calloused hands can still handle a drill skillfully, as well as a metal polisher, shows off our higher education diplomas with great pride, and he deliberates on political and ideological battles as might a teacher, a journalist or any other like-minded intellectual, concurring with our own existence as a sovereign country that has provided him with knowledge, and the capacity for analysis and argument.

I explained that this process had not taken place in the same way in every single Cuban family. The January 1959 victory of the revolutionary movement made the dream of equal opportunities in all spheres of social life come true, but the possibility of identifying opportunities and taking advantage of them was directly connected to individual accumulation of experience. At the family level, lifestyles and ways of being are simply absorbed and reproduced, and it is not at all easy to alter them, or escape from the intertwined network of habits in a close social environment. That is why, since the very first day and the very first actions, the emancipating endeavour of the Revolution was aimed at the social setting, so as to transform people's living conditions, both materially and spiritually.

The Revolution, in a matter of barely two years, demolished the economic, judicial and political foundations upon which 400 years of slavery were so staunchly built, after which those original symbols, the shackle and the clamp, had been replaced by marginalization and exclusion from the social fabric for a majority made up of all ethnic groups and all skin colors. After the collapse of Batista's tyranny, that marginalization and the instruments of discrimination were suppressed; but stereotypes and biases are way too old and deep, and they continued by being trans-ferred through the phenomena of social osmosis inherent to all human society, and settled into general consciousness because of the persistent inertia at the bottom of the pool, where things were less susceptible to the changes brought about by the swift currents on the surface.

These stereotypes and biases—finding different expression in both those discriminated against and those doing the discriminating—link action and reaction in a way that can only be uprooted by making a revolution *within* the revolution itself in a permanent and conscious way, so that ever more increasingly ethical values, supported by solid education, wide culture, and a steady spirit of justice, may be the compass guiding the behavior of the people.

Since the very beginning of the forging of Cuban nationality, suicides, revolts, runaways, and rebel hideouts in the woods bear witness to our resistance against all manner of enslavement. However, we need to understand that ever since the basic freedoms were gained five decades ago, the overcoming of racial discrimination has been a lengthy process—with predictable periods where there were setbacks, sustained in the midst of radical social transformation and consolidated over time.

So I wrapped up that political-entrepreneurial conversation in London with an immodest but very truthful assertion: I am the Cuban Revolution, I am an outcome of the process started in the sixteenth century when, weighed down with chains in the lower decks of the slave ships, brutally dropped into their own excrement, and thrown overboard as garbage when they were on the point of death, more than a million African men and women arrived upon this island in order to keep on writing a history in which their offspring—all Cubans today, without any qualifying prefixes whatsoever—keep on with our struggles to win the fullest justice ever.

Andrea Rosario-Gborie

An African-American television and film producer and reporter in both the US and Africa, she was born in France, and has travelled extensively throughout the US, Europe and Africa. She studied Sociology at Boston University and received a BSc. Throughout her career she has worked for organisations including Reuters News Service, Voice of America, 20th Century Fox and Disney. Among other achievements, she acted as talent coordinator for the cultural festival PANAFEST '94 in Ghana, which brought together musicians, performing artists, writers and intellectuals from the African continent and the diaspora. During the 1990s she worked as a television producer/reporter covering the war in Sierra Leone continuously from 1995 to 1998, and the issues and events associated with that conflict. She currently resides in Washington, DC, where she works as a software engineer.

1992

As has so often happened, the police have assaulted and beaten yet another Black man to within an inch of his life and gotten away with it. In this case, the police officers who beat Rodney King were acquitted on 29 April 1992 by an all-White jury in nearly all-White Simi Valley, California. They were cleared of committing any crime at all, although the incident had been filmed by a civilian and sent to a local television station, the footage clearly showing King being beaten repeatedly during his arrest for speeding. The news of the jury's decision caused an immediate response in the predominately Black community of Watts that quickly spread into the Black and Latino communities in and around the Los Angeles metropolitan area.

Coincidentally, eight thousand miles away in the tiny country of Sierra Leone, another uprising had taken shape, although I didn't know it at time. I lived in another universe that day, so far away from what happened in West Africa and yet so close to the seeming endless suffering for people of African descent. I didn't yet know that for me the Los Angeles riots marked the start of what would be the most important part of my life journey.

For the first time in American history, rioting was not confined to an area of the city that could be contained. The mobile telephone revolution and the twenty-four-hour news cycle of cable television news had changed the way people communicated, no longer relying on the media of the past—the television news hour, newspapers, landline telephones—to keep informed about what was happening. The cell-phone generation made it possible to communicate instantly with anyone, no matter their location. With access to round-the-clock news people could watch and communicate in real time as the riot grew and spread throughout the county of Los Angeles. From the Wilshire District to the San Fernando Valley, the general population didn't have to be at home to get a phone call. The cellular revolution had begun and this was one of its first major unintended consequences.

As people in Los Angeles began calling friends and family, telling them to come to X location to get a new refrigerator, television, and so on, news helicopters hovered overhead and broadcast the looting and mayhem. Law enforcement had no idea how to respond. The previously established policing policies of surrounding and controlling rioters in their immediate location, which had been very successful in the past, were powerless against this new threat. Riots broke out in pockets all over the city of Los Angeles, even moving into Beverly Hills.

It was on that day that I realized I was never going to be successful in Hollywood. Looking back, I see that I was lacking so many things, in addition to facing the institutionalized racism that was still so prevalent in the Hollywood system.

My final job in the Hollywood system was working at 20th Century Fox in the music department as the music licensing coordinator. There is one event that sticks out in my mind that happened while the studio was producing *The Five Heartbeats*, a film by African-American director Robert Townsend. The vice president of the department, Elliot Lurie, had to fire the composer on the film and to replace him they chose Stanley Clarke, a great bassist, composer and innovator who, with classically-trained jazz pianist Chick Corea, had formed one of the greatest jazz-fusion groups of all time, Return to Forever. I absolutely adored Clarke's music and respected his talent. He was entirely capable of composing musical scores for the movies, but it was, and still is, an uphill battle for Black composers to get work in Hollywood. A chosen few, and none of them people of color, got most of the composing work in the Hollywood system—no matter which studio produced the film or television series. A meeting had been organized outside my office one day where several executives spent much of the time trading innuendos and jokes about Black people—including the director Townsend and the film's producer, Loretha C. Jones—"not having what it takes" to make a successful Hollywood film, with no regard for the fact that I was sitting close by and could hear every word. I was invisible to them, like *The Spook Who Sat by the Door*. Anyway, Jones and Townsend's *The Five Heartbeats* was a big success and the soundtrack and musical score by Clarke was even more successful. I wonder who is laughing now?

The 2015 hack attack of Sony Pictures and the racist emails that were revealed from two of its top executives shows that little had changed in Hollywood since 1992.

There were many hit television shows and films being produced on the 20th Century Fox lot at that time. *LA Law*, *Doogie Howser MD*, *The Tracy Ullman Show* and *The Simpsons* were just getting started, along with the show that I worked on most, *In Living Color*. My job was to clear music that was used on these shows, and *In Living Color* used more music from African-American recording artists than any show, with the exception of *Soul Train*, and made so many people famous. The Wayans Brothers and sisters, Jennifer Lopez, Rosie Perez, and Jim Carrey all became superstars because of this show and I am proud to have been a small part of making that happen.

Still, Hollywood had a long way to go when it came to diversity behind the scenes for film and television making. I was moving up in the Music Department. I had my own office, which had actually been Marilyn Monroe's dressing-room back in the 1960s. Had I stayed the course, I probably would have continued to grow there, but somehow I knew that my destiny lay elsewhere. I was one of maybe six African Americans working on the lot at 20th Century Fox in some area of television or film production. There were three of us in the music department; the others were working in human resources or as executive assistants. There were no producers, directors, script supervisors, development executives that were Black people. No Black people in the Film Workers Unions were the grips and gaffers or light and sound professionals either. The lot was a union house and one had to be sponsored to get into the union. I didn't see that changing at all in the future.

So let's just admit that I had a chip on my shoulder when the Rodney King incident happened and during the trial of the police officers. But one thing is for sure, it is the advent of the digital age that changed everything. Now that people had their own affordable video equipment for the first time the world could see what we knew was happening to Black and Latino people at the hands of the police on national television.

When the riots started after the trial acquitted the police officers who were charged with Rodney King's assault, I was at work. The television was on in the conference room and there was a news helicopter circling the intersection where poor Reginald Denny, a white construction truck driver, was pulled from the cab of his vehicle during the riots and was being beaten in the street. Luckily for him, some compassionate Black folk in the neighborhood protected him from the mob. The last thing I wanted was for any innocent person to be hurt as a result of the verdict in the case, but that is indeed what happens when a system of justice breaks down. People lose faith in it and bad things happen.

That was the day I quit my job at 20th Century Fox. I just quit.

I remember watching the mayhem on the television in the conference room, and my crazy boss—who was known for periodically losing his temper and tearing up his office when something pissed him off—saying to me that I was not like those people on the screen, I was different. The whole weight of institutionalized racism suddenly just bore down on me. I had had enough. I could not understand how this man who behaved so inappropriately could manage to keep his job when no Black person could ever have got away with the things he did at work. After two years I had had more than enough.

The studios all closed early that day, as reports of rioters moving up Wilshire Boulevard toward Beverly Hills persisted. As I left the lot and turned onto Century Park West, I saw young Black people in cars with signs that read "No Justice, No Peace!" Other Black people in their cars were thrusting up fists in the Black Power sign as a show of solidarity, while White people started putting up the tops on their convertibles and rolling up their windows. I drove home through the canyon roads to avoid the traffic. When I reached Benedict Canyon I was struck by the fact that the very wealthy people who lived at the top of the passes were all out in their gardens and streets, casually watching the city burn, so totally unafraid from that vantage point.

I made it home to Sherman Oaks in the San Fernando Valley, and that area seemed to be without incident until later that evening, when we began to hear reports on the news that rioting was breaking out in the San Fernando Valley as well.

I didn't then know of the extraordinary coincidence of events unfolding that very day at the same time: that some eight thousand miles away the tiny country of Sierra Leone in West Africa, also founded in slavery, was being violently transformed, just like Los Angeles. A group of young army officers, most of them in their twenties, had overthrown the deeply corrupt and indifferent government that offered them very little in the way of economic opportunity or justice. These young men—like the young men rioting in Los Angeles—had lost faith in a system founded in slavery and colonialism. Many of the African Americans in Los Angeles had arrived after the 1861–65 American Civil War and during the Jim Crow era, when racial segregation was enshrined in law in the Southern US, and saw California as a land of possible opportunity, just as many repatriated enslaved Africans saw Freetown, Sierra Leone, as a land of opportunity in a world that loathed people of African descent.

When I arrived in Sierra Leone two years later I would find a country that had been transformed by rebellious young Black men. It was certainly not perfect, but they had managed to create something never seen before on the African continent: the possibility of change.

1992 would pave the way for so many of my future experiences. I felt deeply that there was so much more that could add meaning in my life. And, indeed, so many things were to happen in 1992 that I could never have imagined, from a friendship with Stevie Wonder to the most important and meaningful relationships in my life. Just from that friendship with Stevie Wonder I would come to travel throughout Africa, to Cameroon, Ivory Coast, Ghana, and eventually to Sierra Leone.

But it was 1992 that pointed me towards all my future milestones. It was also the year that *Daughters of Africa* was first published—a year that transformed my life to one filled with adventure, romance, trauma, and countless other happenings, experiences and emotions that I have yet to write about. A year that was to lead to stories still untold, and as Maya Angelou said in *I Know Why the Caged Bird Sings*, "There is no greater agony than bearing an untold story inside you."

Marina Salandy-Brown

Now living in Trinidad, where she was born, she drew on her background in publishing in the UK, as well as 20 years as an editor and senior manager in BBC Radio, to found in 2011 the NGC Bocas Lit Fest, the annual literary festival that has revitalised the world of Caribbean literature. Since 2005 she has also contributed a weekly commentary column to the Trinidad and Tobago Newsday. *She has been awarded honorary doctorates by the University of Westminster and the University of the West Indies in recognition of her work over the years as a prize-winning journalist, programme editor and senior manager dedicated to the development of culture and the arts. She is a member of the British Council Arts Advisory Committee and is a Fellow of the Royal Society of Arts.*

Lost Daughter of Africa

Massa! Massa! Rua ina zua.

The strange words, fragments of a forgotten language, fall off the tongue of my ninety-seven-year-old mother. We are sitting at the breakfast table on the patio of our home in Cascade on the southern Caribbean island of Trinidad, reminiscing.

Massa! Massa! The rain's coming.

It is all that my mother remembers of the Hausa she heard spoken during the first seven years of her life while growing up in northern Nigeria. But the memories of her birthplace are vivid, unlike the events of yesterday or maybe even five minutes ago. The few faded, now sepia-coloured photographs that have endured from the early 1920s help me visualise her in that environment, but they do not contain the menacing hyenas, the curious giraffes or other frightening wild animals that are most etched in that memory of early childhood.

In the 1980s while back in Trinidad and visiting my nonagenarian grandmother, for the last time before she died, as it turned out, the old, pale-skinned lady, whose paper-thin, brown-spotted face, arms and hands bore the proof of a lifetime of damage from sun-exposure, broke out in a peel of laughter. I had boasted to her about my sojourn in Ghana. I too had been to Africa.

As we say here, mouth open, story jump out. My grandmother regaled us in fluent Hausa with tales of her time on that forbidden continent. My uncle and his family, with whom she lived, were as amazed as I was by this new bit of history, by the acknowledgement, finally, that my grandmother had an African past.

She had been a constant in my life until the age of seventeen when I left Trinidad for life in London. She had never revealed that she spoke any language other than English, French [patois] and Spanish. She taught me to count in those three European tongues before I went to school at the age of four; the rest was her closely guarded secret.

All questions about the finely worked, brightly coloured leather artefacts that hung in the privacy of her and Grandpa's bedroom, away from prying eyes, were ignored. The intriguing, large, ivory-coloured ostrich eggs that sat in simple mountings on her tallboy, next to her glass bottles of scent; the two, no-longer-labelled rum bottles, full to the neck with gold dust, that stood mysteriously on the wooden ledge; the fly chasers with tails of silky, shiny feathers that my child's eyes had never seen elsewhere on my island were too much of a draw for me, even though they were out of bounds. I would sneak in whenever I could to feast my eyes. From the time I became aware of them until I was aged seven when my grandfather died and mysteriously they all disappeared, I tried in my childish way to know more about these extraordinary objects. I was always diverted, my questions left unanswered by my grandfather. My grandmother berated me for being too curious and warned of the dangers of asking too many questions. Children should be seen and not heard. That thick leather strap named Toby that my grandfather kept within easy reach to right any childhood wrong kept my tongue in check, but not my fascination with the provenance of those objects.

For my mother, Africa was an open secret. The word Nigeria would pop up occasionally. She told me when I commented how much I loved the large, cushioned, wicker chairs that furnished the Victorian-style gallery of my great aunt's Port of

Spain house that they had come with my grandparents from Nigeria. I remember looking at them differently, as if they had landed from the moon. I remember, too, the surprise I felt to learn that my mother was an African by birth. It was hard to understand why she was not very much darker, but even more incredible to me was that her two younger sisters were also African by birth when their skins were the colour of porcelain and their hair hung loose like any white or Indian person's.

They never had much to say about their Nigerian childhood. For the youngest daughter of this Edwardian Caribbean family the memory lay too deep in her infant subconscious. Her older sister preferred not to remember because the threat of having her tongue cut out for uttering a single word of her childhood language stayed with her. But my mother, a reluctant rebel because of her brown skin and dry, unruly hair, was the one who clung to that sense of coming from somewhere else. She never concealed that she came out of Africa, but somehow I knew it was not something I should broadcast widely, if at all.

In 1921 when my mother was born, Nigeria and Trinidad and Tobago were part of an Empire in which free movement of people was a reality. My grandfather, who worked in the highly prestigious railways, was recruited by the British to go to Nigeria around the start of World War I to be involved in the management of the expansion of the railways there. In 1920 he returned to Trinidad, married my grandmother and set sail to Liverpool, where they changed ships for Nigeria. He was posted to northern Nigeria, first in Zaria, where the two older girls were born, then to Ilorin, where the youngest was born in 1925. West Indian godfathers were chosen for all three daughters as new friendships formed, although upon returning to the Caribbean easy and fast travel between islands was impossible and friendships faded.

In 1927, my mother's grandfather, born of privileged English-French parentage dating back to 1645 but whose first marriage to her mixed-race grandmother got him disinherited and not allowed re-entry, despite a second more acceptable marriage, was on his deathbed and my grandparents returned home with their elegantly clothed little princesses from whose mouths a now inadmissible language would occasionally emerge. They were considered beauties, but the language they sometimes spoke was not. All foreign languages were unwelcome among the multi-ethnic arrivals in this British colony where the King's English had to be the standard, and an African language was especially unacceptable. Any admission of a link to Africa by a person of colour was to open oneself to disadvantage.

In the 1920s, slavery had been abolished fewer than a hundred years earlier in the English-speaking Caribbean and was only about sixty years in the past in Cuba. Ideas of racial inferiority and superiority were the norm. Each shade of skin colour indicated a natural place in the hierarchy for jobs, schooling and personal advancement. The closer to Africa, the further away from God, one might say, in a society where whiteness was taught as being "next to Godliness", where kinky hair and every darker hue of skin stigmatised one as being less far from barbarity. My mother's natural advantage of a fierce intelligence and a world-class operatic soprano voice was neutralised by her physical features that clearly revealed her mixed ancestry.

As the effect of the economic crash of the 1930s made itself felt all over the Americas, including Trinidad and Tobago, my grandparents travelled to Venezuela to work in the administration of the oil industry, leaving behind their three daughters in the care of their mother's extended family. It was then that my mother and her siblings learned about race and opportunity. Her younger, very pale-skinned sisters soon recognised that they were more valued, and my mother learned of cruelty, becoming their Cinderella. She was often made late for school by being sent to run errands, only to be physically punished by her teachers for tardiness. Her unruly hair lacked the careful handling that it needed and led to her being unfairly chastised by teachers and to play truant as a result.

She was the sister called upon for household duties and deprived of playtime. Her wellbeing went unnoticed so that she had no help in dealing with the sores from mosquito bites on her calves that stuck to her woollen socks. One morning she was pulled from her bed before dawn and marched into a cold, outdoor shower that caused pneumonia and a near-death experience. Deeply stressed by the physical and emotional violence, she took to biting her nails down to the cuticles, for which she was made to eat chicken droppings, to kneel on a grater and to suck bitter aloes. Memories of happy days in Africa soon faded. She hardly remembered what pure, innocent joy might be.

This beloved but lost daughter learned that she needed guile to divert the worst of her suffering: she resorted to telling untruths when necessary and hiding her real thoughts and feelings, she set traps to hurt those who made her life a misery, but she endured and focused on her escape: she shone at her convent school and once her miraculous talent for singing was discovered she became the musical showgirl of the Catholic nuns.

Her adult life followed a similar pattern. The success of her professional life contrasted with the difficulties of a personal life that was full of injustice and disappointment, but she remained defiant, resolute. I sometimes call her an African warrior. The toughness and the lightly veiled anger frightened me when I was a child. Today, that indomitable core is undiminished, and I must find ways not to let it dwarf me.

None of this is visible to the outside world, for my mother is the sweetest, most poised and elegant little lady this side of the Atlantic.

When television news reports from Nigeria appear I say, "There, Mum, your countrymen."

To which my mother often replies, "I'd love to see Africa again."

I tell her that she would not recognise it nearly a hundred years later and that she should be content knowing she is the oldest Nigerian in Trinidad and Tobago, possibly the Caribbean.

In "Baa Baa, Black Sheep", Rudyard Kipling's autobiographical short story for children published in 1888, the author describes how as young children he and his sister were sent to England from India to live for five years with a retired ship's captain, his wife Auntie Rosa and their bully of a son, Harry. Auntie despises the boy and calls him Punch; she dubs his sister Judy, but treats her warmly. Soon Punch becomes known as Black Sheep and can do nothing right. He is beaten constantly and tries to avoid the violence by telling lies and committing small acts of vengeance. In his tale Kipling constantly referred to his new abode as the House of Desolation.

Kipling's story of an unforgivable episode in a child's life always seemed to echo my mother's. The ordeal marked him and her forever. "Baa Baa, Black Sheep" ends with Punch setting a test that happily proves the love of his mother, who returns and saves him, and he asserts that from now all will be different. But Kipling is not sure:

> Not altogether, O Punch, for when young lips have drunk deep of the bitter waters of Hate, Suspicion, and Despair, all the Love in the world will not wholly take away that knowledge; though it may turn darkened eyes for a while to the light, and teach Faith where no Faith was.

My mother's eyes have always tried to focus on the light, and as she approaches a century of life and experience, Faith has slowly dimmed the sharp memory of loss.

Sapphire

Moving to New York in the 1970s from California, where she was born, she became involved in the Slam Poetry movement, writing, performing and eventually publishing her work. She is the author of two collections of poetry, Black Wings & Blind Angels *(1999) and* American Dreams *(1994), and of the* New York Times *bestselling novels* The Kid *(2011) and* Push *(1996), which was the inspiration for the Academy Award-winning movie* Precious. *She has performed her work in venues in North America, Europe, Africa and South America. She has said of her work: "A major focus of my art has been my determination to reconnect to the mainstream of human life a segment of humanity that has been cast off and made invisible. I have brought into the public gaze women who have been marginalised by sexual abuse, poverty, and their blackness. Through art I have sought to center them in the world."*

From *Push*

I was left back when I was twelve because I had a baby for my fahver. That was in 1983. I was out of school for a year. This gonna be my second baby. My daughter got Down Sinder. She's retarded. I had got left back in the second grade too, when I was seven, 'cause I couldn't read (and I still peed on myself). I should be in the eleventh grade, getting ready to go into the twelf' grade so I can gone 'n graduate. But I'm not. I'm in the ninfe grade.

I got suspended from school 'cause I'm pregnant which I don't think is fair. I ain' did nothin'!

My name is Claireece Precious Jones. I don't know why I'm telling you that. Guess 'cause I don't know how far I'm gonna go with this story, or whether it's even a story or why I'm talkin'; whether I'm gonna start from the beginning or right from here or two weeks from now. Two weeks from now? Sure you can do anything when you talking or writing, it's not like living when you can only do what you doing. Some people tell a story 'n it don't make no sense or be true. But I'm gonna try to make sense and tell the truth, else what's the fucking use? Ain' enough lies and shit out there already?

So, OK, it's Thursday, September twenty-four 1987 and I'm walking down the hall. I look good, smell good—fresh, clean. It's hot but I do not take off my leather jacket even though it's hot, it might get stolen or lost. Indian summer, Mr Wicher say. I don't know why he call it that. What he mean is, it's *hot*, 90 degrees, like summer days. And there is no, none, I mean *none*, air conditioning in this motherfucking building. The building I'm talking about is, of course, I.S. 146 on 134th Street between Lenox Avenue and Adam Clayton Powell Jr Blvd. I am walking down the hall from homeroom to first period maff. Why they put some shit like maff first period I do not know. Maybe to gone 'n git it over with. I actually don't mind maff as much as I had thought I would. I jus' fall in Mr Wicher's class sit down. We don't have assigned seats in Mr Wicher's class, we can sit anywhere we want. I sit in the same seat everyday, in the back, last row, next to the door. Even though I know that back door be locked. I don't say nuffin' to him. He don't say nuffin' to me, *now*. First day he say, "Class turn the book pages to page 122 please." I don't move. He say, "Miss Jones, I *said* turn the book pages to page 122." I say, "Motherfucker I ain't deaf!" The whole class laugh. He turn red. He slam his han' down on the book and say, "Try to have some discipline." He a skinny little white man about five feets four inches. A peckerwood as my mother would say. I look at him 'n say, "I can slam too. You wanna slam?" 'N I pick up my book 'n slam it down on the desk hard. The class laugh some more. He say, "Miss Jones I would appreciate it if you would leave the room right NOW." I say, "I ain' going nowhere motherfucker till the bell ring. I came here to learn maff and you gon' teach me." He look like a bitch just got a train pult on her. He don't know what to do. He try to recoup, be cool, say, "Well, if you want to learn, calm down—" "I'm calm," I tell him. He say, "If you want to learn, shut up and open your book." His face is red, he is shaking. I back off. I have won, I guess.

I didn't want to hurt him or embarrass him like that you know. But I couldn't let him, anybody, know page 122 look like page 152, 22, 3, 6, 5—all the pages look alike to me. 'N I really do want to learn. Everyday I tell myself something gonna happen, some shit like on TV. I'm gonna break through or somebody gonna break through to me—I'm gonna learn, catch up, be normal, change my seat to the front of the class. But again, it has not been that day.

But thas the first day I'm telling you about. Today is not the first day and like I said I was on my way to maff class when Mrs Lichenstein, the principal, snatch me out the hall to her office. I'm really mad 'cause actually I like maff even though I don't do nuffin', don't open my book even. I jus' sit there for fifty minutes. I don't cause trouble. In fac' some of the other natives get restless I break on 'em. I say, "Shut up mutherfuckers I'm tryin' to learn something." First they laugh like trying to pull me into fuckin' with Mr Wicher and disrupting the class. Then I get up 'n say, "Shut up mutherfuckers I'm tryin' to learn something." The coons clowning look confuse, Mr Wicher look confuse. But I'm big, five feet nine-ten, I weigh over two hundred pounds. Kids is scared of me. "Coon fool," I tell one kid done jumped up. "Sit down, stop ackin' silly." Mr Wicher look me confuse but grateful. I'm like the polices for Mr Wicher. I keep law and order. I like him, I pretend he is my husband and we live together in Weschesser, wherever that is.

I can see by his eyes Mr Wicher like me too. I wish I could tell him about all the pages being the same but I can't. I'm getting pretty good grades. I usually do. I just wanna gone get the fuck out of I.S. 146 and go to high school and get my diploma.

Anyway I'm in Mrs Lichenstein's office. She's looking at me, I'm looking at her. I don't say nuffin'. Finally she say, "So Claireece, I see we're expecting a little visitor." But it's not like a question, she's telling me. I still don't say nuffin'. She staring at me, from behind her big wooden desk, she got her white bitch hands folded together on top her desk.

"Claireece."

Everybody call me Precious. I got three names—Claireece Precious Jones. Only mutherfuckers I hate call me Claireece.

"How old are you Claireece?"

White cunt box got my file on her desk. I see it. I ain't that late to lunch. Bitch know how old I am.

"Sixteen is ahh rather ahh,"—she clear her throat—"*old* to still be in junior high school."

I still don't say nuffin' she know so much let her ass do the talking.

"Come now, you are pregnant, aren't you Claireece?"

She asking now, a few seconds ago the hoe just *knew* what I was.

"Claireece?"

She tryin' to talk all gentle now and shit.

"Claireece, I'm talking to you."

I still don't say nuffin'. This hoe is keeping me from maff class. I like maff class.

Mr Wicher like me in there, need me to keep those rowdy niggers in line. He nice, wear a dope suit *every* day. He do not come to school looking like some of these other nasty ass teachers.

"I don't want to miss no more of maff class," I tell stupid ass Mrs Lichenstein.

She look at me like I got three heads. What's with this cunt bucket? (That's what my muver call women she don't like, cunt buckets. I kinda get it and I kinda don't get it, but I like the way it sounds so I say it too.)

I get up to go, Mrs Lichenstein ax me to please sit down, she not through with me yet. But I'm through with her, thas what she don't get.

"This is your *second* baby?" she says. I wonder what else it say in that file with my name on it. I hate her.

"I think we should have a parent-teacher conference Claireece—me, you, and your mom."

"For what?" I say. "I ain' done nuffin' I doose my work. I ain' in no trouble. My grades is good."

Mrs Lichenstein look at me again like I got three heads or a bad odor coming out my pussy or something.

What my muver gon' do I want to say. What is she gonna do? But I don't say that. I jus' say, "My muver is busy."

"Well, maybe I could arrange to come to your house—" The look on my face musta hit her, which is what I was gonna do if she said one more word. Come to my house! Nosy ass white bitch! I don't think so! We don't be coming to your house in Wesschesser or wherever the fuck you freaks live. Well I be damned, I done heard everything, white bitch wanna visit.

"Well then Claireece, I'm afraid I'm going to have to suspend you—"

"For what!"

"You're pregnant and—"

"You can't suspend me for being pregnant, I got rights!"

"Your attitude Claireece is one of total uncooperation—"

I reached over the desk. I was gonna yank her fat ass out that chair. She fell backwards trying to get away from me 'n started screaming, "SECURITY SECURITY!"

I was out the door and on the street and I could still hear her stupid ass screaming, "SECURITY SECURITY!"

"Precious!" That's my mother calling me.

I don't say nothin'. Mrs Lichenstein ain' the only one noticin'. My mother been staring at my stomach. I know what's coming. I keep washing dishes. We had fried chicken, mashed potatoes, gravy, green beans, and Wonder bread for dinner. I don't know how many months pregnant I am. I don't wanna stand here 'n hear Mama call me slut. Holler 'n shout on me all day like she did the last time I was pregnant. Slut! Nasty ass tramp! What you been doin'! Who! Who! WHOoooo like owl in Walt Disney movie I seen one time. Whooo? Ya wanna know who—

"Claireece Precious Jones I'm talkin' to you!"

I still don't answer her. I was standing at this sink the last time I was pregnant when them pains hit, *wump*! Ahh wump! I never felt no shit like that before. Sweat was breaking out on my forehead, pain like fire was eating me up. I jus' standing there 'n pain hit me, then pain go sit down, then pain get up 'n hit me harder! 'N she standing there *screaming* at me, "Slut! Goddam slut! You fuckin' cow! I don't believe this, right under my nose. You been high tailing it round here." Pain hit me again, then *she* hit me. I'm on the floor groaning, "Mommy please, Mommy please, please Mommy! Mommy! Mommy! MOMMY!" Then she KICK me side of my face! "Whore! Whore!" she screamin'. Then Miz West live down the hall pounding on the door, hollering "Mary! Mary! What you doin'! You gonna kill that chile! She need help not no beating, is you crazy!"

Mama say, "She shoulda tole me she was pregnant!"

"Jezus, Mary, you didn't know, *I* knew, the whole building knew. Are you crazy—"

"Don't tell me nothin' about my own chile—"

"Nine-one-one! Nine-one-one! Nine-one-one!" Miz West screamin' now. She call Mama a fool.

Pain walking on me now. Jus' stompin' on me. I can't see hear, I jus' screamin', Mommy! Mommy!"

Some mens, these ambulance mens, I don't see 'em or hear 'em come in. But I look up from the pain and he there. This Spanish guy in EMS uniform. He push me back on a cushion. I'm like in a ball from the pain. He say, "RELAX!" The pain stabbing me wif a knife and this spic talkin' 'bout relax.

He touch my forehead put his other hand on the side of my belly. "What's your name?" he say. "Huh?" I say. "Your name?" "Precious," I say. He say, "Precious, it's almost here. I want you to push, you hear me momi, when that shit hit you again, go with it and push, Preshecita. *Push*."

And I did.

Claire Shepherd

Born in Bequia, St Vincent and the Grenadines, she came to England as a child with her parents in 1960. She later became involved with the Keskidee Centre in Islington, the first Black Arts Centre in London, doing theatre arts. She studied at Goldsmiths College, University of London, obtaining a BA in Anthropology/ Sociology and an MA in Communications, Culture and Society. She worked as a journalist on several of the first Black British newspapers, including the West Indian

World, Caribbean Post, Voice *and* Caribbean Times, *and has written for a number of other publications, among them* African Woman, Happy Home *and* London Arts. *She was also a researcher on a number of documentaries, including* The People's Account, *a film commissioned by Channel 4 from Ceddo Film and Video Workshop on the 1985 uprisings in Birmingham, Brixton and Tottenham. She currently spends time between London and St Vincent.*

Unforgotten

As I write this in St Vincent and the Grenadines, where I was born during the colonial era, it is "Black History Month" in the UK, where I spent much of the past few decades. It is also one hundred years since the end of the First World War, and it is hard not to revisit the contributions made by African and Caribbean people to the British war effort.

An estimated one million people died in East Africa alone during the First World War when thousands of African and Caribbean people went to war to defend the interests of their colonial masters in the trenches of Europe and even more gave support from their homelands.

More Africans were economically worse off by the end of the war in 1918 than in 1914 at its outset, and to date there is still no comprehensive record of the names or ranks, and of the thousands of African and Caribbean men who gave their lives no names appear on memorials. Their sacrifice has been largely forgotten.

The role of Africa and the Caribbean in the First World War has generally been overlooked and untold for decades by western colonial historians. Was this "turning a blind eye" by accident or amnesia or by carefully crafted intentional design?

In recent years, through the diligent efforts of African and Caribbean historians and researchers, together with the observance of Black History Month—October in the UK—there is an increasing interest in excavating African and Black British History, accompanied by social movements calling for reparations for slavery and colonialism.

There is a growing awareness of some of the true horrors and brutality of colonial rule and of the immense contribution made by people of African heritage to Europe, notwithstanding the often violent European aggression in Africa during the nineteenth century conducted against African societies to enslave people and later to conquer territory—resulting in the "Caribbean" people.

A couple of years ago I was part of a group visiting the Imperial War Museum in London for a session on the involvement of Africa and the Caribbean in World War I, a session that was illuminating on a number of levels. My initial thoughts and reaction on entering the building were that this institution was created as a monument to war, and the Imperial War Museum through its war memorabilia largely tells the stories of white people's experiences of modern war from WWI to conflicts today. But in the interpretation of texts, whether through words or the artefacts collected and displayed at the museum, what truths are really told about the now independent ex-colonies and their contributions?

The group who visited the museum on the day in question had an opportunity to discover for themselves the story of the war through the eyes of people in Britain and its acquired Empire, both on the home front and the fighting fronts, and through this gain a better understanding and personal insight into how the war started, why it continued, how the Allies "won", and the war's global impact that still reverberates today.

The Great War was a drain on many African countries, which never fully recovered from the horrendous effects. Removing young men in their prime from their role in agricultural production to serve as soldiers and carriers created many local problems, increasing the need for women to take over in many cases. These countries remain "under-developed" today.

My visit was eye-opening for several reasons. First, it was a unique opportunity to see film clips and to touch some of the 1,300 objects drawn from the Imperial War Museum's First World War collections—the richest and most comprehensive in the world. These included weapons, uniforms and equipment, diaries and letters, keepsakes and trinkets, photographs, and art. Each object displayed gave a voice to the person who created them, used them or cared for them, revealing stories not only of destruction, suffering and loss, but also of endurance and innovation, duty and devotion, as well as comradeship and love.

However, to be candid, the "comradeship and love" so glowingly described in parts of the literature of the Imperial War Museum appear not to have touched the many Africans who were still subject to the social psychology of colonialism yet sacrificed their lives for white Europeans.

As we thumbed through the memorabilia, including dozens of written cards and photographs with descriptions of the people and their situations in Africa—what we saw and felt repeatedly was a nascent racism and the lack of any deep knowledge or understanding of what Africa's role in this largely European escapade truly was.

It is argued that not since the American War of Independence had such a huge number of people of African descent been involved in fighting for Europeans. But what is not commonly known is that most of these "volunteers" were used as "beasts of burden"—forced recruits used to carry the heavy weapons and supplies needed by the Europeans, and to do other menial work—although by necessity some were at the heart of battle. The majority of these men were poorly fed, given substandard food with which they were not familiar and for which they had no stomach.

As World War I progressed, more than a hundred nations worldwide joined the conflict, with seven African territories directly involved in the fighting, including: (Belgium) Congo, (British East Africa) Kenya, (German East Africa) Tanzania, (Northern Rhodesia) Zambia, (Nyasaland) Malawi, (Portuguese East Africa) Mozambique, and Uganda. Millions of people on the African continent made the ultimate sacrifice for the Europeans by losing their lives. The precise number who lost their lives for the British Empire, and were among the estimated overall total of 40 million who died, is still undocumented.

With hindsight, we can say that the fighting started in Africa, with, and because of, the Berlin Conference of 1884, when representatives of some thirteen European countries, and America, began the carving up of the African continent—without any African being present: no political leader, no delegate, nor ambassador from Africa was at the Berlin Conference. The Berlin Conference regulated European colonization and trade in Africa, and is usually referred to as the starting point of the "scramble for Africa"—the occupation, division, and colonization of African territory by European countries that led to the partitioning of Africa and in effect began the competition among Europeans countries, who avoided warring with each other over Africa.

This European imperialist push was motivated by three main factors: economic, political, and social. The goal was to dominate the African peoples completely, with each of the countries who sat at the Berlin Conference taking a slice of the continent and its incredible resources.

By the outset of World War I most of Africa was under the control of various colonial powers, for trade and profit and also because of prestige. The spoken and tacit understanding was that the duty of the Europeans in Africa was not to fight each other, but to keep control of the Africans.

War, as most of us now recognize, is a multi-national industry where huge profits are made and lives are lost in the thousands. Yet many of us are still rather naive about the huge financial profits and other material motivation involved.

Glenford D. Howe, author of *Race War and Nationalism: A Social History of West Indians in the First World War*, in his PhD thesis "West Indians and World War One: A social history of the British West Indies Regiment" (University of London, 1994) documents the involvement of the colonies.

He states that "15,600 men of the British West Indies Regiment served with the Allied forces. Jamaica contributed two-thirds of these volunteers, while others came from British Honduras, British Guiana (now Guyana), the Leeward and Windward islnds of Trinidad and Tobago, Barbados, Grenada, St Lucia and St Vincent. Nearly 5,000 more men subsequently volunteered to join up, and so by the outbreak of war in 1914, centuries of alienation and the suppression of the remnants of African cultural practices, and the proliferation of British institutions, culture and language, had created staunchly loyal Black Britishers in Barbados and other colonies."

The expression of support for Britain from the West Indian population was therefore, "not surprisingly, quite overwhelming", according to Howe: "Donations were often made in spite of severe hardships. Gifts to the value of several thousand pounds were contributed by the colonies to the war effort; these included sugar, rum, oil, lime, cotton, rice, clothing, log wood, and aeroplanes. A total of eleven ambulances and adequate funds for their maintenance were donated, and approximately two million pounds sterling was given to the British government and charities. These donations were made in spite of severe hardships caused by major increases in the cost of living throughout the region which occurred with the proclamation of war." A 2008 report in *The Guardian* by Simon Rogers noted: "The islands donated some £60m in today's money to the war effort—cash they could ill afford."

Howe points out that this generosity was sometimes contested locally, as when the Grenada liberal newspaper *The Federalist* described it as "extravagance" on the part of the local legislatures. And while "it is claimed that even Marcus Garvey encouraged young Jamaican men to join the war effort…in several colonies including Trinidad, Grenada, Jamaica and British Honduras, a number of people of African descent later adopted the position that it was 'a white man's war' and therefore black people should not get involved."

There were also ambiguous feelings among some white people about the involvement of Africans. According to one source some whites thought "it would be dangerous to train African men…to fight, in case they might rise up and use it against the colonial powers".

After the war, African delegates were not welcomed to take part in the 1919 Versailles Peace Conference, so "Africa's demands were not represented and the continent received no rewards for its contribution and neither were the efforts of the men and women who served mentioned".

There was, in the UK, no memorial dedicated to commemorating the contributions to victory made by more than two million servicemen and women from the Caribbean and Africa in both world wars, until the initiation of a project by the Nubian Jak Community Trust, which set out to remedy the neglect and oversight. In 2017, in Windrush Square in Brixton, London, an African and Caribbean War Memorial was finally erected to honour the brave men and women who fought for Britain in the wars, and a growing movement continues today, to have "colonial history" taught in schools in Britain and elsewhere.

By contrast, and sad to say, in St Vincent and the Grenadines, we still have a statue of what is clearly a white man standing erect on a plinth near the Central Market in Kingstown that was unveiled on 11 November 1925, and was erected in honour and in memory of those who fell in the First World War, stating: "To the glory of God and in memory of the sons of Saint Vincent who gave their lives for King and Country in the Great War, 1914–1918". Yet, controversially and ironically, an obelisk stands at Dorsetshire Hill outside of the city in memory of Joseph Chatoyer, Carib chief, and first National Hero of St Vincent and the Grenadines, who died in 1795 in the course of leading the indigenous resistance against early European colonists. That is a history deserving of being claimed from the margins.

Verene A. Shepherd

A social historian, and the current Director of the Centre for Reparation Research at the University of the West Indies, she is author, co-author, editor, co-editor and compiler of a number of books, including: Women in Caribbean History *(1999);* Engendering Caribbean History: Cross-Cultural Perspectives *(1995);* Livestock, Sugar & Slavery: Contested Terrain in Colonial Jamaica *(2009);* Maharani's Misery: Narratives of a Passage from India to the Caribbean *(2002) and* I Want to Disturb My Neighbour: Lectures on Slavery, Emancipation and Post-Colonial Jamaica *(2000). Her most recent book is* The Gibson Relays: History and Impact on Jamaica's Sports Culture and Social Development *(2017). She is host of* Talking History *on Nationwide 90 FM in Jamaica, and a member of the UN Committee for the Elimination of Racial Discrimination (CERD).*

Historicizing Gender-Based Violence in the Caribbean

My father's house was full of female slaves, all objects of his lust; amongst whom he Strutted like Solomon in his grand seraglio, or like a bantam cock upon his own dunghill... By him my mother [Rosanna] was made the object of his brutal lust...

—Robert Wedderburn, *The Horrors of Slavery* (1824)

After abusing me with every ill name he could think of, and giving me several hard blows with his hand, he said 'I shall come around tomorrow morning at twelve on purpose and give you a round hundred.' He kept his word... He tied me up upon a ladder; Benjy stood by to count them for him. When he got weary he rested, then beat me again. An earthquake interrupted, and in the confusion, I crawled away, my body all blood and bruises.

—*The History of Mary Prince* (1831; 847)

These two startling quotations—one from 1824 by Robert Wedderburn whose father owned plantations in Jamaica; and the other from 1831 outlined by Mary Prince, enslaved in Bermuda and Antigua before being taken to England, where her experience of enslavement was used to fuel the anti-slavery cause—are apt because a long historical view of the contemporary scourge of domestic and gender-based violence is necessary to link the past and present.

These flashbacks from the nineteenth century, these references to the totality of the exercise of male power over women in the form of rape, sexual exploitation, verbal abuse, physical violence, threats, cruel and inhumane treatment and general female unfreedom—all illustrate the Caribbean region's long genealogy of gender-based violence, which has been defined in the 1993 UN Declaration on the Elimination of Violence against Women as any act that results in, or is likely to result in, physical, sexual or psychological harm or suffering to women, including threats of such acts, coercion or arbitrary deprivations of liberty, whether occurring in public or in private life. In 1995, at the Fourth World Conference on Women in Beijing, the UN expanded the definition to include: violations of the rights of women in situations of armed conflict, including systematic rape, sexual slavery and forced pregnancy; forced sterilization, forced abortion, coerced or forced use of contraceptives; prenatal sex selection and female infanticide. It further recognised the particular vulnerabilities of women who belong to minorities: the elderly and the displaced; indigenous, refugee and migrant communities; women living in impoverished rural or remote areas, or in detention.

What circumstances in history brought us here? The answer is embedded in our past. During the period of slavery, gender-based violence normally encompassed three sets of acts:

a) Physical, sexual and psychological violence occurring as part of human trafficking and perpetrated by crew against women and girls on the Middle Passage, when captive Africans were shipped to the New World as part of the Atlantic slave trade.

b) Physical, sexual and psychological violence, including battering, sexual exploitation, sexual abuse of females in the household, and violence related to exploitation on the plantation and other spaces during the slavery period.

c) Physical, sexual and psychological violence perpetrated in the home against men and women and children in the post-colonial period and at times condoned by law enforcement officials.

Gender-based violence also has roots firmly embedded in patriarchal ideologies that continue to have contemporary manifestations. Historically, as now, sexism, power and hegemonic masculinity were features of patriarchal societies, combined with notions of a gender hierarchy, race/ethnicity and class. In addition, religious orthodoxy, gender inequity, the lack of education around gender relations and the economic situation in which many men find themselves today feed the problem, as they empower men and keep women subordinate.

Research has shown that violence is instrumental in maintaining those power relations, and that men are responsible for most of the systematic, persistent, and injurious violence against women and under-report their own experience as victims.

From the fifteenth to the nineteenth century, such power was manifested in various forms of violence over indigenous, enslaved and later indentured labourers. From the late nineteenth through to the twentieth century, the Victorian gender order, along with the male-as-breadwinner ideology, clashed with women's claims to socio-economic and political power to act as justification for violence. This link between violence and power has been highlighted by the UN Declaration on the Elimination of Violence against Women (1993), which states:

> ...violence against women is a manifestation of historically unequal power relations between men and women, which has led to domination over and discrimination against women by men and to the prevention of the full advancement of women, and that violence against women is one of the crucial social mechanisms by which women are forced into a subordinate position compared with men.

Feminist theory holds that it is impossible to sever gender from power and hegemonic masculinity; that gender is implicated in the conception and construction of power. In most places, men possess more economic, political, domestic, and overall decision-making power than women. Understanding, on a basic level, the fact that violence follows power in a social context is a building block to being able to adequately address it. Women have not traditionally had the same access to the resources associated with power. For example, inheritance law used to favour male heirs, thus denying women economic resources of power.

Within this discourse, masculinity is a social construct based on male/female power relations, also operating in the private sphere in the division of labour. But when economic and social factors are not aligned with these embraced roles, the result is conflict, at times leading to gender-based violence.

What fed this violence in the past and propelled it into our present? In general, gender-based violence has its roots firmly embedded in the history of colonialism, and more specifically the conquest of the indigenous peoples who inhabited some Caribbean countries; in the trans-Atlantic slave trade and African enslavement; in a slave society that was characterised by racism, ethnocentrism, classism and discrimination against women in both field and house; in Asian indentureship; in a post-slavery Victorian gender order played out in the exercise of male power and in patriarchal ideologies that continue to have contemporary meanings and manifestations.

Violence linked to power relations was gendered from as far back as the development of civilizations. Colonialism in the region did not begin the global practice, though it provides a useful starting point for its introduction in the Caribbean. Gender discrimination operated in indigenous societies. In the islands called the Greater Antilles, the Taino people believed that men should be the rulers; the power holders and the warriors. Europeans perfected this system, but added racism and ethnocentrism to it, exploiting indigenous women in gender-specific ways, including trafficking, and rape.

Under African enslavement, women's bodies became the site of power contestation. Any esteem attached to being an enslaver derived from the power that he or she could exercise over the bodies of his/her enslaved chattel; and this was sanctioned by laws that allowed white men and women to exercise intimate power through punishment, torture and control. In drawing up and enforcing such laws the enslavers in the Caribbean, like those in the rest of the Americas, created their own version of slavery. They invented from scratch all the ideological and legal underpinnings of a totally new slave system.

This violence was manifested in the invasion and capture (of lands and peoples) in the Caribbean, the forced kidnapping and trafficking of Native Caribbean peoples and Africans, the chaining and shipment of Africans in inhumane conditions, the throwing of live African male and female captives overboard (as happened in the case of the 132 jettisoned from the British ship *Zong* during its voyage to Jamaica in 1781), the sale and branding of Africans on the plantations, the sexual harassment of women, rape and other forms of violence on the Middle Passage and later on the ships with indentured Indians, flogging and degrading punishment of field slaves and enslaved domestics and murder (including during and after armed conflicts).

Once in the Americas, women were enslaved in large numbers and subjected to various forms of exploitation and control, being categorised as property and forced to work without wages. Indeed, women served an essential ideological function: enslavers appropriated their reproductive lives by claiming their children as property to eventually perform unwaged labour; and used their blackness as justification for making them reproduce the status of enslavement, unlike white women who could only reproduce free status, even if black men fathered their children. On sugar plantations, women weeded, planted, harvested, worked in the factories (where many lost fingers while feeding cane into the mill), and generally contributed to the productive processes. They laboured in enslavers' residences as domestics and nursed the sick in the hot houses. They worked in coffee, cotton and sugar industries and supplied food, especially to the urban areas. Men had a wider range of tasks and were dominant in the supervisory and plantation management fields. So in a sense they were co-opted into the patriarchy.

As field labourers (and as domestics and concubines) women's bodies became the site of power contestation. Plantation labour placed great physical strain on them; and any infraction of the slave codes or the law of the black slave-driver was followed by severe beating and other forms of physical abuse of the enslaved female's body. In fact, the history of slavery demonstrates that many confrontations between female slaves and managers arose from contradictions between "women's roles as mothers and as workers—which were intensified by growing labour exploitation after the abolition of the slave trade." (Lucille Mathurin Mair, *A Historical Study of Women in Jamaica 1655–1844*, 2006, p. 59)

In addition to the arduous physical field régime and severe whipping, enslaved women were open to sexploitation. Neither colonial statutes nor slave codes invested enslaved women with any rights over their own bodies, but rather, transferred and consolidated such rights within the legal person of the enslavers, who thus claimed violent access to enslaved women's bodies, and to the sale of enslaved women's bodies on the sex market.

Much of the evidence of violence against women resides in the documents generated by men; but a few narratives generated by women, such as the enslaved woman Mary Prince, survive. Prince recounted the violent punishment inflicted on her fellow enslaved Hetty, who while pregnant, was tied to a tree and flogged till she was streaming with blood, with the consequence that "poor Hetty was brought to bed before her time, and was delivered after severe labour of a dead child".

Acts of violence against the black woman were facilitated by the fact that the law until 1826 gave the enslaved female no protection from sexual attack. When women resisted, they suffered severe punishment. Violence against women continued in the post-slavery period, with the ruling classes' attempts to recreate the actions and mentalities of slavery. Colonisation cemented British and African gender systems, which became even worse after emancipation, when jobs became gendered, along with wages, rewards and positions in the workplace. The male-as-breadwinner ideology was promoted by the elite and the church, accompanied by ideas about women's place being in the house. Women have struggled against this domestication ideology for a long time and the struggle for gender equality in all spheres of life continues.

There are no sides to this debate, only the move to halt the protracted violence that sears the souls of all those involved. This, then, is our history. It is time to leave this violence in the past, learning from it, so that we do not repeat it.

To the women who batter men and boys, I say, their bodies do not belong to you. You do not have the right! To the men who batter women and girls I say, their bodies do not belong to you. You do not have the right!

It took an earthquake and migration to end it for Mary Prince: what will it take for you?

SuAndi

Originally a performance poet, her field of work has expanded into live art, writing narratives for exhibitions, one-act plays, and keynote speaking. Her writing is embedded in her cultural heritage—she was born in Manchester, her mother from Liverpool and her father from Nigeria. She has published collections of poetry including Style *(1990),* Nearly Forty *(1994),* There Will Be No Tears *(1996), and* I Love the Blackness of my People *(2003), and her work has appeared in various magazines and anthologies. She has written two librettos,* The Calling, *and* Mary Seacole, *which toured Britain in 2000. Her acclaimed production* The Story of "M" *is offered in the A-level English Literature syllabus. She says, "I am constantly pushing against the barrier of racism in my writing, but it is cloaked in humour and*

the celebration of humanity in all its shapes, colour and laughter." She received an
OBE for her contributions to the Black Arts Sector and an honorary doctorate from
Lancaster University. She is a Creative Writing Fellow at Leicester University and the
freelance Cultural Director of the National Black Arts Alliance.

Intergenerational Trauma

My father first walked the earth in Warri
his feet sinking into the hot mud of Nigeria's Delta State
then one day, as other men launched fishing boats
he sailed far away.

Why, I don't know
he never told me
I never asked
Africa and Manchester offered no parallels
so, we never had that conversation.

My father never talked of the past
I never asked
What did you do in the war, dad?
What was your home like?
Do I look like your people?
Can you see your mother in my eyes?
The way I walk, argue, am
I a female version of you?
The same height as your father?

Words never spoken
only silent responses.

My father never said when
the white man came:
but I know he knew.

Summers, we would visit his old master
exchanging our terrace house
for a large white detached in Surrey
where my father cleaned—
a servitude repayment for our visit—
while I was forbidden to
touch, speak, play, do anything
without first asking permission.

Strange white people, I thought.
"Snobby bastards," said my mother
when I returned home
"Where do they think this is?
It's not bloody Africa."
Her temper flaming her cheeks
to match the copper of her hair
"Andi," she'd say
"Slavery is over;
Get over it."
What did she mean?

I never asked, she
never explained.

Schools for my father were
glorious European opportunities.
He spared nothing to buy
my uniform, my shoes
a too large briefcase
copies of the same books that teachers
gave out daily in class.

Strange, that I had to leave the classroom
to begin my education, tutored
via overheard conversations
documentaries, radical articles
orators from Marcus Garvey to Malcolm X
even though neither had a penchant for white people.
But no matter how I broadened my knowledge
I still loved my mother
nothing was going to change that.

Now my mouth was full
of words my brain had memorised:
colonialism, lynchings, detention
apartheid, segregation
civil rights, Black Power
and always
slavery.

What did my father know?
That the Yoruba were favoured for their strength

but whipped long to curb their independence
that Ibos stolen in their thousands
found an inner power to walk on water.
And the Ijaw from Warri
who speaks of them?

Not, certainly my father.
except sometimes
when the silence was so loud
my ears would ache
I would turn to him
and he, looking far into the distance
seemed oblivious to the tears
washing his cheeks
flowing under his chin
flooding his heart.

In that moment, my father
was no longer the man I knew
he was in that moment,
the man I didn't know
filled with ancestral spirit.

My family came down from my grandfathers'
grandfathers, generations who never imagined
life beyond the Forçados River:
conquered, shackled, bartered
sold, imprisoned, abused
demonised, throttled, burnt,
flogged, criminalised, castrated
executed under the law.

The trauma of the new
the wicked, the evil
filled my father
so that he could not speak
and I never asked why
why
before he died
was he called Thomas?

Under my right eye
I have an indentation

in the exact same place
as my father's peoples' ritual scarring.
Some days when I look at it
it seems more prominent
like it really is a scar
but I can barely make it out
through my tears.

Aroma of Memory

There are ladies
of a certain age
hair coiffured silver-grey to wig-black
or the corn-rows of back-home childhood
that I hug.
I smile, lean in
wrapping my arms across shoulders
once held straight
letting my hands travel
the spine of years.
I breathe the heavy perfume
of clean living
and a scent unnamed
that lingers in the smartness
of their clothes.
In this moment
I am like a young buck
tempting this loveliness with
guile and flirtation
words that in their speaking
wash away the years
rekindling her bloom of youth.
They giggle at my innuendo
a little naughty, never rude
for I am not church
no Miss-name falls from my lips.
To me they are sweetness
"Sisters of Joy" to my vision.
On a dull English morning
they are "Praise to heaven"
for crossing my path
and the wickedness of accusation

that I have caught them slyly
heading to a discreet liaison.
I tut-tut-tut my way through
this tête-a-tête.
I have to avoid tasting them
my lips heavy with face powder
coconut lotion.
I leave
waving away the greyness
of the day.

Charlotte Williams

From Wales, she is currently Professor of Social Work and Associate Dean of the School of Global, Urban and Social Studies at the Royal Melbourne Institute of Technology in Australia. Her extensive writings on issues of migration, race and ethnicity in social welfare practice include the recent books Critical Multicultural Social Work: New Perspectives and Practices *(2019),* Social Work and the City: Urban Themes in 21st Century Social Work *(2016),* Social Work in a Diverse Society *(2016), and* A Tolerant Nation? Revisiting Ethnic Diversity in a Devolved Wales *(2015). Her contributions to post-colonial studies include her 2002 memoir,* Sugar and Slate, *exploring her Welsh-Guyanese heritage and diasporic identity, which was named* Welsh Book of the Year *in 2003, the co-editing of* Denis Williams: A Life in Works, New and Collected Essays *(2010), regular contributions to* Planet *and* Wasafiri, *and publication in* Tangled Roots: Stories of Mixed Race Britain *(edited by Katie Massey). She received an OBE in the Queen's 2007 New Year's Honours for services to ethnic minorities and equal opportunities in Wales.*

Small Cargo, from *Sugar and Slate*

I am six years old. "We're going on a boat to Africa," Ma has announced. I tell Ann Morgans and Diane and Mrs Jones fach[1] who lives on the corner and they nod like when I said, "I'm going to Auntie Maggie's on Saturday." That's the way it was. Nobody we knew from within our small community had travelled.

We sailed there by cargo ship the first time. A paint-peeled ocean-goer called the *Prome*; soft white letters printed on a charcoal background. It must have been to-ing

---

1 Welsh: literally "Little Mrs Jones", but used as a term of endearment.

and fro-ing this ancient marine route for years by the time it carried us outwards from Liverpool dock. Ma glanced over her shoulder but kept going. Wales was behind her now and she could only move forward as she had done many times before. In the sweep of her skirts we were voyaging to a different world. Dad had already been in Africa for one lonely year when he sent for us. Just Ma and four small girls made our family then; *teulu bach*.[1] Just a small cargo on a big ship.

There is a curious intimacy about these cargo passages that one doesn't experience on passenger liners. A few cabins on loan to a handful of purposeful passengers for three weeks or so. Over hundreds of years small cabin-loads of explorers, missionaries, those in the service of the Colonial Office and their families have been transported in this way, their stories and their histories becoming intertwined by these sea crossings. They are the people who opened up the connecting routes; the ones who crossed the maps drawn out by Church and Empire. From 1868 Elder Dempster had a fleet of steamers following the infamous route to and from the Dark Continent. In later years we would travel to and from the coast of West Africa aboard luxurious dazzling white passenger liners; the *Apapa*, the *Accra*, the *Aureoll*. But at first we went cargo to the Sudan. It is surprising how you first notice difference as a child. A missionary family travelled with us on the passage I am remembering now. They were heading out to work in old Omdurman. They were noisy, and unlike us they spoke proper English. The mother had a loud challenging voice like a teacher, her mouth opening long and wide with every word. The father wore long socks with sandals, the type worn by older men today. He had too many words in his mouth as I remember and overly explained everything to their three children who all looked and dressed exactly the same, in the way English children did. Then there were some very pale nuns, white as their starched collars and some stiff foreign office people with world-service accents going to Aden. One of their group was a younger man, a fresher on his first tour to what must by then have been the vestiges of the colonial administration; part of the mopping-up job I suspect as Nkrumah brushed out the pink paint on the map of Africa. "Creative abdication" the British called it. Only pieces of these memories come to me now, pieces that shaped me. The memories don't fall out in nice neat lines as they seemed to do when there weren't so many of them.

We move out across the Bay of Biscay where the storms lash the sides of the ship and pitch and turn us till we all lie down seasick for three days. Then into warmer waters and warmer days when schools of dolphins appear and swim alongside the ship, a happy squeaking escort that brings our entire passenger group out onto the deck. The crew put up a makeshift canvas swimming pool on the rear deck. I can smell the wet tarpaulin now, filled daily with salty sea water which moves in rhythm with the waves in the huge wide sea, so that we are tossed and showered and bobbed and ducked until we will never again misjudge the power and the perils of the ocean. The missionary children are not allowed to participate in the fun but content

---

1 Welsh: "small family".

themselves instead with standing nearby and staring. I can smell the ship's ropes and the bleached wooden decks. We find some hessian quoits that we wear as heavy armlets or anklets in our small-girl play, and we sing a Welsh song about a saucepan and a cat that scratches *Johnny bach*.[1] The wooden rails of the ship's sides taste of the sea. Everything tastes of the sea. "Why do you have to put everything to your mouth, Cha?" Ma is saying. "*Ych a fi*".[2] I'm not listening, only tasting and feeling.

There are areas of the boat barred to us. Over the rope boundary we can see oily black pulleys, coils of rope, rusting pieces of machinery and the sailors—rough sailors, the engine wallahs, the deck hands and the cooks and cleaners taking a cigarette or just emerging from the underworld to squint a few minutes daylight. They are on the other side of things from us. They are very different from the smartly dressed officers who change from their blues to tropical whites and from whites-long to whites-short as the voyage takes us towards the Mediterranean. We spend whole days out on the decks, hair fuzzy and free, skin colour changing from pale to mellow browns. And by night we sleep in the belly of the ship lulled to sleep by the hum of the engines and the creaking of the old boat's aching structure as she rolls with the waves. We are suspended, with the echoes of our forefathers rumbling below.

Ma is happy on the sea. She prefers to travel this way. She likes these voyages; both the drift and the drive of them are part of her make up, carried along with a helplessness she courted. "Why did you bring me here?" she would demand of Dad in the months to come. Yet this passage was part of her own inner drive to move out from under the claustrophobic pile of slate that was her birthplace. I would come to know her as sacrificer, sufferer, survivor. She had a steel will that had pushed her away from all the chapel goodness, the village small talk, from the purples and the slate greys that invaded her inner landscape. In its wake came a fatalism that she could not shake off. It haunted her. But she was suited to the slow acclimatisation in the space of the voyage. The place between somewhere and elsewhere was so right for her.

Ma was never good in small spaces. I imagine myself small again, flung back into those snatches of memory that make up my Africa. Just once we fly to Africa and there are goody bags with BOAC written on them for all of us. The insides of Ma's hands are red and there are beads of sweat sitting quietly on her nose. We are boarding the plane which has a cold grey outside that looks like it will taste of pencil lead. There are lots of waiting people and bags ahead of us and it seems as if there may not be room for us. A woman with a loud English voice says "Excuse me," and pushes past Ma to the front of the boarding queue. Ma just ups and grabs her by the neck of her blouse and starts to shake her like a piece of washing. "Bloody *Sais*,"[3] Ma says. "Just who do you think you are, Queen of the Cannibals? How dare you.

---

1 Welsh: "Little Johnny".
2 Welsh: "Ugh!"
3 Welsh: "Bloody English!"

How bloody dare you." Thumb in mouth, I try to shrink myself into the folds of her skirts. Ma is in a complete rage, shouting and flapping her arms. Beads of sweat have broken out on her top lip too by now. Eventually the captain comes to see what the problem is. "See that one," she says to him, "She thinks she can treat me like a dog, putting on airs like she's somebody." Lots more "How bloody dare you's" and "Who do you think you are's" follow before she can be pacified. The captain calls Ma "Ma'am" very slowly. He tells her that they are first timers to the colonies and they don't know anything about Africa or about coloured people and so she lets it go, for now at least.

This battle would be part of what we were and what we would be, although I can't say I knew at that stage of my life what the battle was about. I guessed, like Dad said, it was because Ma was Welsh and she wasn't taking orders from anybody. But she was beautiful at sea. The cool openness on the decks, her wild beauty matching the elements; the blue of the waves and the blue of her eyes. Africa had called for Dad and now he was calling for her; Kate sweetheart, his love and his mentor. He loved the rhythms and poetry of her thoughts. Her ideas fell together like jazz, the blue notes resonating across the staves with their own logic, defying the predictable sequences and the rudimentary facts. He would not be without the magic that was her. She was shaping him; her mind was his umbrella and beyond this umbrella he dared not step. *"Paid poeni Denis bach*[1]… Everything will be fine," she would say. She provided such spiritual security for him. She was our backbone.

Behind them they left London. The London of John Nash, Wyndham Lewis and Elgar that very gently nudged them away with all its imperialist assumptions and its contradictions. That London would never be the same after the Picasso exhibition in the V&A took the country by storm, the influences of Africa cutting through the canvases like a knife. A London of immigrants. Sam Selvon's London; a cold, grey and miserable motherland.

There had been much pillow talk about the move out to Africa. They had discussed it over and over again, trying to anticipate the future. It could have been different. They could have stayed on in London; things were going well. Dad had a teaching job at the Central School of Art and several major exhibitions behind him with excellent reviews. I have a scrapbook from this time that Ma must have put together. Wyndham Lewis wrote in *The Listener* about a "brilliant newcomer"—his huge canvases hanging on the walls of the Gimpel Fils gallery bursting with colour and symbolism. Dad had painted *Human World*. It was magnificent, painted in equatorial reds, yellows, ochres and greens with tree-like people standing and glaring with large threatening eyes as if the Empire might stand up and strike back. It was pure savagery confronting civilisation. When I read the old fragment of *The Listener*, I saw all those assumptions that pushed them away; all those assumptions that lay deep in the lines.

---

1 Welsh: "Don't worry, Denis dear."

In spite of the fact that Denis Williams speaks with an unmistakable Welsh accent, he is a Negro. But because of the Empire-building propensities of the Briton of yesterday he is British for he comes from British Guiana. Georgetown, the capital city, is where he lives. It is anything but the jungle: there are splendid boulevards lined with blood-red trees, a fine hotel (for Sahibs only), a busy port. The Negroes are tennis and cricket playing Negroes; Milton and the other national poet Shakespeare, is what they are brought up on, but especially Milton.

How could this country have held him with all its double speak? Wyndham Lewis was a Welshman, Ma told us later. "He was the one who said that the coloured men of London were all boxers and sailors and that we should move on," she said.

But Ma and Dad rubbed along the edges of a very glamorous London, moving in circles that included Francis Bacon, Lucien Freud and other equally well-known artists. Dad was artist-in-residence at the Slade for a while. He became the interesting chap to have at parties; a curiosity, a poodle, the comfortable stranger. Ma was not so easy. She was Welsh and uncomfortably different. "You're the English one," she used to say to Dad, knowing in her heart that she was the real dark stranger.

Their real life was a small cramped flat in Oxford Road, where Dad hung up his smarty-boy suit on the back of the door at night and set to work painting whilst Ma's wages from a job in a book warehouse kept them going. At night the West Indian chaps dropped by; Michael Manley, Jan Carew, Wilson Harris, Forbes Burnham were all regular visitors. Gathered in that small space they talked about imperialism, about colonialism and independence. They were the Caribbean writers and artists and future leaders with visions and big thoughts, not boxers and sailors. They were planning a different world. And the stuff of their talk was the destiny of their own countries and news of Africa and Nkrumah in his fight for independence. That was their struggle; they were not concerned with their position in the motherland. For them the motherland was only ever to be a temporary host, so although they knew the colour bar, they didn't need to take it on. They knew it was difficult to get lodgings and in many a bar they would be told, "Sorry but we don't serve you chaps in here." But it was all very polite; so very polite and so accepted.

When Welsh and Irish girls came to London looking for work they found the same lodging houses willing to let them in as the coloured chaps. It was Mrs Dovaston who took in Katie Alice and found Denis on Kilburn High Street and invited him back for tea. Ma said Mrs Dovaston's own granddaughter Josephine was a black girl and that her father had played the piano for Paul Robeson in America. I suppose she liked having coloured people round the house for Josephine's sake.

So Ma and Dad became lovers, eventually married and moved on. That's how we began to learn about movement. It was movement that was home. Home was not a particular place for us in the very early years. Home was Ma. We arrived into an exile; into a state of relocation that was both hers and his. And the journeys were more than physical journeys. They were travels across worlds of thinking, across generations of movements. These boat stories and seascapes, I now know, are part of a collective memory lying buried below the immediate moment...

Makhosazana Xaba

A South African anthologist, essayist, poet and short story writer who has published two collections of poetry, these hands *(2005) and* Tongues of their Mothers *(2008), and has featured in numerous anthologies. She won the 2014 Nadine Gordimer SALA Short Story Award for her book of short stories,* Running and Other Stories *(2013). She holds an MA in Creative Writing and is currently a Research Associate at the Wits Institute for Social and Economic Research writing a biography of Helen Nontando Jabavu. She worked as a women's health specialist with national and international NGOs in the areas of women's rights, gender and anti-bias training and violence against LGBT communities. In 1986, she went into exile where she trained as an MK cadre and a journalist, worked as a broadcaster on Radio Freedom in Lusaka and returned in 1990 with the African National Congress Women's League. Initially she trained as a general nurse, midwife and psychiatric nurse.*

#TheTotalShutdown: Disturbing Observations

"Wear black with a touch of red and comfortable shoes." This was the suggestion placed on the right bottom side of the poster advertising the intersectional women against gender-based violence march planned for 1 August 2018. Black is the colour of mourning for many South Africans, I know; I understood wearing mourning. I was not sure about the significance of the colour red but that was not going to stop me from participating.

On that Wednesday morning I remembered the suggestion and dressed appropriately: in a flared long-sleeved, polo-necked black dress, black pantyhose, black shawl and black head wrap. My touch of red was my ankle-length fake leather, comfortable boots. I was not preparing for the high-level Pretoria March, where the marchers were planning to hand over the memorandum of demands. I have grown more claustrophobic with age and avoid crowds. I was ready for the lunch-hour gathering in Braamfontein, a few blocks from my office.

I left the office with a colleague twenty minutes before the start. We walked comfortably in the sunny but cold ever-populated streets and arrived at the rendezvous to find just under twenty people. In no time the numbers had grown, and the singing of struggle songs had begun. We spread ourselves right around the De Korte intersection of four, one-way (westward) lanes and two, two-way north–south lanes. As the cars started hooting with impatience to drive through, we stood aside to let them pass. But the more hooting and speeding we witnessed, the more sense it made to simply block the roads. And, we did.

As we stood there singing, now blocking all the cars, I was appalled as I witnessed the rampant violence of men. They hooted even louder and for longer. They threatened to drive through us—by now I had taken a position, with others, bang in the middle of the four-lane one-way, De Korte Street. Some drivers opened their windows, screamed and insulted us. The most repeated screams being "Step aside!" and "I want to drive through" and "I have a meeting to attend!" At some point I decided to give the inner circle my back and dared to face these drivers. I wished I had brought my phone so I could take pictures. I looked at them, on all four lanes while holding firmly the hands of my sisters on either side. It was not only the drivers in the front cars just behind us who were screaming, even the ones up to three rows back were doing the same. I spotted only one woman driver who just sat there, with her phone in her hands. I looked at these men in shock.

The irritation on their faces!

If irritation could kill…

The anger!

If anger could enact the disappearance, an instant erasure of an object in front of it…

The shouting!

If shouting could remove a body and place it where it desires…

The hooting never stopped. Neither did our singing. The grasp on my hands on either side felt stronger. I found that comforting because looking at these drivers, these men, had disturbed me so much I was relieved in the knowledge I was held, firmly, on both sides.

As I turned around to face the inside of the circle, one young man on rollerblades managed to find his way between two women and, in a macho-look-at-me-style, rollerbladed his way through the circle in a southerly direction. The speed with which he moved made the women just give way for him. They freed their hands, stepped aside and watched him whizz through and down the road. They rejoined hands afterwards.

I had expected the drivers to respect our protesting presence on the road. I expected them to—if they had not heard of it—turn on their radios and find out why women were on the streets, singing struggle songs, midweek. I expected them then, if indeed they were in a hurry, to call the people they were to meet and let them know they were running late. Listening to the news would have assured them that the demonstration was scheduled to last for an hour. I expected the drivers, these men, to sit in their cars and wait, until the demonstration was over. Instead, we forced them to wait. And *they* protested as they waited.

As soon as we cleared the road they put their cars in speeding gears and drove away. Some continued to scream insults at us through the windows. And yes, some were in business suits and ties.

Such is the violence of men in South Africa.

In a country some have labelled "the rape capital of the world", where all forms of gender-based violence—violence against women and girls; sexual violence (including gang rape and rape of elderly women); sexual harassment; intimate partner violence; violence against LGBTIQ+ persons (including "corrective rape" of lesbians); domestic violence; and structural violence—are rife, it seems trite that I should be writing about this observation. The murder rate of women shot up by an alarming 117 per cent between 2015 and 2016/2017 as recorded by Statistics South Africa in its report, *Crime against Women in South Africa*. This is but one of the numerous shocking statistics about gender-based violence in South Africa.

But, I continue to expect men in the streets of Braamfontein, Johannesburg, to be civil and behave like decent human beings! Surely there is something wrong with this picture. My denial is no longer justifiable. Why do I expect men who are guilty of the range of violations I list above to behave differently—respectfully—during a lunch hour of an ordinary working day, a Wednesday? What does my hope to humanize them mean? I have lived and experienced violence from men all my life. I was a fool to think that the older I got (read "physically less attractive to men") the less of a "target" for violence in public spaces I would become. Nothing has changed. It would appear that the default presentation of men in South Africa is violence. I continue to walk the streets and pavements in fear for my life because now I am a target of a special kind: *because* I look older.

The #TheTotalShutdown March by intersectional women against gender-based violence, on 1 August 2018, has been written about; detailed information is easily accessible. Similarly, the demands women made to President Cyril Ramaphosa are firmly on the table. He has been quoted repeatedly as he assured women that the summit (one of the demands) on Gender-Based Violence will be held soon.

In all my years of feminist activism I avoided working directly on violence against women. The closest I got to it was via two avenues. First, the work we did on women's health. Second, the poetry I have written. Thankfully, it is now being used at universities in South Africa and I continue to get feedback on how it allows students to speak up. In my firm belief that I do not have the personality to work in the "VAW sector"—as we called in in the 1990s—I have admired and respected women who did, including, more recently, the young women who are standing up, unafraid and ready to face the enemies: our sons, brothers, fathers, uncles, grandfathers and boyfriends.

Our enemies, our people!

My colleague Pretica Singh and I talked about this unrecorded violence from men as we walked back to the office an hour and a half later. This is the violence that the South African Police (SAP) and Statistics South Africa neither record nor report on. It does not show up as a category in their statistics. This violence that my body has failed to forget! This is the violence that clearly springs from intense hatred and disregard of women as human beings, deserving of respect. This ubiquitous violence we are forced to breathe in and out each time we navigate our way through public spaces.

I have begun to wonder whether my expectation of men can, in fact, be viewed as complicity. I am reminded of how I have never had the courage to ask my two brothers if they have ever raped a woman. I am not ready for their answers. Does this too make me complicit? Is it most disturbing to acknowledge that our violators are our people?

Tongues of their mothers

I wish to write an epic poem about Sarah Baartman,
one that will be silent on her captors, torturers and demolishers.
It will say nothing of the experiments, the laboratories and the displays
or even the diplomatic dabbles that brought her remains home, eventually.
This poem will sing of the Gamtoos Valley holding imprints of her baby steps.
It will contain rhymes about the games she played as a child,
stanzas will have names of her friends, her family, her community.
It will borrow from every poem ever written about her,
conjuring up her wholeness: her voice, dreams, emotions and thoughts.

I wish to write an epic poem about uMnkabayi kaJama Zulu,
one that will be silent on her nephew Shaka, and her brother Senzangakhona,
It will not even mention Nandi. It will focus on her relationship
with her sisters Mawa and Mmama, her choice not to marry,
her preference not to have children and her power as a ruler.
It will speak of her assortment of battle strategies and her charisma as a leader.
It will render a compilation of all the pieces of advice she gave to men
of abaQulusi who bowed to receive them, smiled to thank her,
But in her absence never acknowledged her, instead called her a mad witch.

I wish to write an epic poem about Daisy Makiwane,
one that will be silent about her father, the reverend Elijah.
It will focus on her relationship with her sister Cecilia
and the conversations they had in the privacy of the night,
how they planned to make history and defy convention.
It will speak the language of algebra, geometry and trigonometry,

Then switch to news, reports, reviews and editorials.
It will enmesh the logic of numbers with the passion that springs from words
capturing the unique brand of pioneer for whom the country was not ready.

I wish to write an epic poem about Princess Magogo Constance Zulu
one that will be silent on her son, Gatsha Mangosuthu Buthelezi.
It will focus on her music and the poetry in it,
the romance and the voice that carried it through to us.
It will describe the dexterity of her music-making fingers
And the rhythm of her body grounded on valleys
mountains and musical rivers of the land of amaZulu.
I will find words to embrace the power of her love songs
that gave women dreams and fantasies to wake up and hold on to
and a language of love in the dialect of their mothers.

I wish to write an epic poem about Victoria Mxenge,
one that will be silent of her husband Griffiths.
It will focus on her choice to flee from patients, bedpans and doctors.
This poem will flee from the pages and find a home in the sky.
It will float below the clouds, automatically changing fonts and sizes
and translating itself into languages that match each reader.
This poem will remind people of Qonce that her umbilical cord fertilized their
    soil.
It will remind people of uMlazi that her blood fertilized their soil.
It will remind her killers that *we* shall never, ever forget.

I wish to write a poem about Nomvula Glenrose Mbatha,
one that will be silent on my father, her husband, Reuben Benjamin Xaba.
It will focus on her spirit, one that refused to fall into pieces,
rekindling the fire she made from ashes no one was prepared to gather.
This poem will raise the departed of Magogo, Nquthu, Mgungundlovana,
Nanda, Healdtown, Utrecht, kwaMpande, Ndaleni and Ashdown,
so that they can sit around it as it glows and warm their hands
while they marvel at this fire she made from ashes no one was prepared to
    gather.

These are just some of the epic poems I wish to write
about women of our world, in the tongues of their mothers.
I will present the women in forms that match their foundations
using metaphors of moments that defined their beings
and similes that flow through seasons of eternity.
But, I am not yet ready to write these poems.

Pre-1900

1900s

1920s

1930s

1940s

1950s

1960s

1970s

1980s

1990s

Leila Aboulela

Born in Cairo to an Egyptian mother and a Sudanese father, she grew up in Sudan and moved to Scotland in 1990. Between 2000 and 2012, she lived in Jakarta, Dubai, Abu Dhabi and Doha, then returned to Aberdeen, where she still lives. She was awarded the first Caine Prize for African Writing in 2000 for her short story "The Museum", which was included in her collection of stories Coloured Lights. *Her other publications include* The Kindness of Enemies *(2015);* The Translator *(UK, 1999);* Minaret *(2005);* Lyrics Alley *(2011), fiction winner of the Scottish Book Award; a collection of short stories* Elsewhere, Home *(2018), which won the Saltire Fiction Book of the Year; and* Bird Summons *(2019). Her work has been translated into 15 languages.*

A Very Young Judge

My best friend, Leena, laid down the law regarding clothes: no green with blue, no checks with stripes, sandals and handbags must match. "The first thing I look at in a man," she said, "is his shoes." We were eleven at the time.

She was my companion during the long years of puberty when womanhood loomed ahead of us fractured and out of reach. I visited her almost every day. Her house was more feminine than ours, her father more indulgent. He had a sheepish smile and smelt of lemony, expensive cologne. I watched as Leena stroked his scalp. With him she became a cuddly girl again, her mother taking time from an almost continuous regime of grooming to look up and smile. It was neighbourhood gossip that Leena's mother went for regular massages. This, in my austere household was viewed as the height of decadence.

In the playground, I smoothed down my new Eid dress, loving its loose softness and flowers. Leena studied me and said, "It makes you look pregnant!" When I stuck to her advice, she sighed and complained, "You're so repetitive."

Her comments about other's scruffiness and vulgar tastes made me laugh. "He looks like he hasn't had a shower today!" she would say, or "Her ears are too big for her head." Or she would make pronouncements such as, "An ugly couple will have a beautiful baby" and rattle off the names of acquaintances to prove her point.

Once on our way home from school, stepping out from the grocer, we saw Leena's father and a woman getting into the back of a taxi. The woman was in tight trousers, a black T-shirt sliding off her shoulders; she shimmered with gold dust and crimson, her hair twisted to one side to show long jingly earrings. Leena and I stood on the pavement and stared as they drove off.

When we started walking again, Leena's voice was calm and objective, "My father is a womaniser but he has good taste." I thought Leena would make fun of the woman's greasy lip gloss or even call her a slut. Instead she turned to me and frowned, "You really must do something about your bushy hair. Are you competing with Einstein?"

She was ruthless about her own looks. Every pimple was dealt with without mercy, every excess hair removed. She wore a wide belt under her clothes in order to slim her waist. Even when she dressed casually, it was deliberate and thought-out. The right jewellery, the right shoes, her hair done in a different style, the look innovative and well-matched. Unlike me, she hated our school uniform. Nothing pleased her more than meeting girls outside school and checking out how they dressed. Or the few events when we were allowed to come to school out of uniform.

We attended a Catholic missionary school in which most of the students, like us, were Muslims. It was the best private school in Khartoum but Leena took a dislike to the nuns. Their white habits depressed her, their cultivated plainness was alien to her soul. "Worst of all," she would snap, "are the pretty nuns. What a waste!"

Once she asked me, "Who do you think is the most beautiful girl in our class?" I nominated the popular, glamorous ones, including her. But she snorted and chose instead a studious Ethiopian refugee on a scholarship. The girl was without the benefit of fancy clothes or trips to the hairdresser. I was taken aback. Leena could scramble and find a gem. She cared enough to look beyond the obvious.

So I gathered my courage and asked for her judgment. I made a mistake when I begged, "Leena tell me the truth, the real truth. Am I pretty?" She passed her sentence on me. Her ultimate assessment. That was when I first started to want to break free from her.

It was for aesthetic reasons that Leena rose against the girls who started to wear hijab. Leena was no less religious than any of us, but appearances were her territory, her unchallenged area of expertise. The first girl who came to school with her hair covered caused a stir. Unlike the rest of us, she was wearing a long-sleeved white shirt and her navy pinafore had been adjusted to reach her ankles. The nuns weren't happy. It was a violation of the dress code, they said.

In break, Leena dragged me to the hijabi girl. She tapped her on the shoulder and spoke out loud, "Tell me, when your hair is your best feature, why do you hide it and emphasize your big nose?"

The nuns moved to expel the girl but there were now new government policies, which sided with the hijab. A missionary school in a Muslim country would always be vulnerable. The teachers turned a blind eye to the new taunts of the schoolyard. And Leena made the most of this. She got bolder as the popularity of the hijab spread, sometimes drawing these girls out in heated arguments, once even tugging a veil off a junior's head. I was always with her, her best audience, her side-kick. I didn't protest when she spread a rumour that girls who wore hijab would never get married. I didn't stop her when she drove a younger one to tears.

In the school-yard, I walked next to her, conscious of her grooming, her self-conscious air, her aura of fashion. But I was already plotting to match blue with green. To wear the same thing more than once, and move away from her jurisdiction.

Sade Adeniran

Born in London to Nigerian parents, she was taken back to her father's village in Nigeria at the age of eight, and spent her formative years living with her grandmother in Idogun, Ondo State, before returning to the UK. She has written for radio, theatre and film but is best known for her debut award-winning novel Imagine This, *which won the 2008 regional Commonwealth Writer's Prize for Africa. She is also a filmmaker, and has written, produced and directed several short films that have screened at various festivals around the world.*

The Day I Died

I am guessing you don't know who I am, because I've yet to do anything remarkable with the life God gave me. But most importantly, you don't know who I am because the 14th of April 2014 was the day I died. That was the day they came for us. It was around 11:30 p.m. I was asleep at the time, but I heard the gunshots in the dream I was having. The sharp *tat-tat* had no place there, but I ignored the sound and carried on dreaming. I can no longer remember what that dream was about. All that has stayed with me from that night is the waking nightmare my life became.

The moment the rough hands of the man shook away my sleep, the sweet dream disappeared into the place of loss. The horrible smell from his unwashed body made my stomach give him the *tuwo shinkafa* I ate earlier. It went all over his holed-out muddy boots. I might have kept it in my belly if not for the gun slammed into my stomach when my legs failed me. I heard Amina lose hers too. She was my arch-enemy because of the many disagreements we'd had over things that small girls fight over. She hated me mainly because I was smarter than her; she came second to my first in all the subjects we studied.

My favourite subjects were Biology and English. However, in that moment of sharing our undigested dinner with our Boko Haram captors, neither of us was thinking of the study of living organisms or how to use a conjunction in a sentence. At that moment in time, petty grievances were set aside as we both wondered if we would ever see our families again. Others wailed and as our eyes met across the dormitory filled with frightened children, we briefly became friends, allies, the enemy of my enemy. We finally had something to unite us. We had been fighting over rubbish all school year and became staunch allies over regurgitated *tuwo shinkafa*.

I don't know if our friendship would have lasted, but for a little while we bonded over a minor victory, which was of little consequence. But it is these little things that my mind clings to, because the other things, I cannot speak of or bear to remember.

I do not know what happened to Amina, she was braver than me and the rest of the girls. She ran, I did not. Shots were fired after the few who were brave enough to run. I do not know if they survived or if they died in the bush surrounded by nothing but trees, but in my moments of hope, I liked to think they made it back home and that help would soon be on its way. I imagined my father, Bible in one hand and the holy cross in the other, coming into camp and begging for my release. We had plans; he had plans for me.

The first girl in his family who would go to university and become a real doctor. My mother did not agree, she wanted me to marry, to become someone's wife. It was not what I wanted, neither was becoming a doctor, but going away to university would allow me the chance to see more than our village.

What I wanted more was to see those places I only read about in the novels I ploughed through. To taste the food I saw them cooking on the television. The only programmes my father watched were the foreign cooking programmes, so they were the only ones me and my younger sister watched. I try not to think about her. If not for the fact that she was ill that week and had gone home to get well, she too would have been in school and my parents would have lost both their children. There is not much comfort in this for me, but at the same time it is a good thing.

I did not want to die; what I did not know was that I was already dead. I curse Boko Haram with my last breath, I pray for them to feel a tenth of the pain I have suffered, the pain I know my mother has suffered and will continue to suffer until the day she goes to her ancestors. I want to wish ill on their families and if they have daughters, I pray for what happened to us to happen to them. But as I say these words, I know that it does not make me a good Christian. I have prayed for deliverance, for rescue and for mercy, but the bitterness on my tongue is more bitter than bitter leaf. Where is God? Hours turned into days and the days into months and the months into years. And still there is no rescue, no deliverance and no mercy. My father will not be coming to collect me. When there is an absence of hope, there is an absence of life, and so my death is all but certain, this I do know and this I can finally control.

My father would tell me that it is a sin for a person to take their own life, but if that life has already been taken, then surely God will let me into heaven? I wanted to live, but two stillbirths sealed my fate. The husband I did not want has divorced me and I have become a wife to many. When I felt the new life stir within me for the third time, I did not know who it belonged to. What I did know was that I could not continue. They call me a witch because of the dead babies. It is true, I did not want any child to survive, how could I? Could I truly love a child born of rape? I felt nothing but hatred towards the man they forced me to marry. I cooked, cleaned and performed the duties of a wife; the one thing I would not do was renounce my own religion. It was the last piece of home I could cling to, they had taken everything else.

The times they took my body, I removed my mind and escaped to other places. I imagined myself arriving at university and graduating with my proud father in the audience clapping and celebrating my success. I imagined myself in a fancy restaurant in Lagos eating *suya* with a knife and fork. I imagined myself on an aeroplane, high up in the heavens and as close to God as an ordinary person can get.

These imaginings floated through, but I was never able to hold on to them for very long. They were always vague and with no definition. I'd never been beyond our village and the school gates, so the picture of my graduation contained just the family dressed in our Sunday clothes posing outside our house for photos. The restaurant where I ate *suya* with a knife and fork looked like Alhaja's house. Her husband is the richest person in our village and their house has an indoor kitchen. So the restaurant looked like the inside of their house. It made no sense, but it helped pass the time.

I could not picture the inside of an aeroplane because I've never seen the inside of one. So instead I imagined floating in the clouds in a car with wings. This car also managed to resemble Alhaji's car. The only difference: the wings; and instead of the boring black, it was a tomato red, which made it stand out against the clouds. My body was theirs but my mind was mine and it soared and explored. I stopped screaming when I realised that only made it worse. So I became silent and thought of flying cars and eating suya with a knife and fork.

I also thought of the times I fought with my younger sister. Two years my junior yet she failed to show me the proper respect due an older sister. We argued over silly things at home, like whose turn it was to sweep the room or wash the plates. As the elder, I of course delegated my share to her when I could get away with it. But when she came to school, I was her protector. I would not let the seniors treat her like their housegirl. Hafsat Umar wanted her to wash and iron her school uniform every day. That was not really an issue; the problem was that Hafsat had a habit of staining her uniform and getting palm-oil out of her clothes was a challenge my sister failed to meet. So Hafsat naturally had to punish her, but she went too far, which is why I stepped in. We have not spoken since that incident; even here in our misery she still holds a grudge. As one of the many who have converted to Islam, she is in a different group, but that has not stopped her adding more misery to my existence. It was she who started calling me a witch, all because I made her eat sand. I wished I had knocked out her teeth at the same time; that way she would not be able to smile her fake smile each time she sees me.

Next time she smiles her smile that covers the grudge she holds against me, I might tell her that the husband she is now clinging to spends time on top of me, so she has nothing to be happy about. I stopped believing in miracles a while ago and the truth is I am tired and I am beyond damaged. In a village where gossip livens the daily chores, I know I can never go back and be normal again. They still talk about Mr Mohammed who killed his first wife because she refused to accept his second wife into their home. Something that happened before I was born, and fourteen years later it is still a topic of conversation. So I can imagine the loud whispers, I can imagine the stares of family, friends and everyone else. My future is gone, stolen.

I am no longer bitter or angry, what I am is just tired. I have gone from cursing them, their children and their grandchildren, to accepting that this is my fate. The great things my father planned will only ever exist in my head. I can no longer dwell on what could have been. I wanted my life to matter, I wanted to make a mark in the world, to do good, to be great, to be somebody beyond the confines of our village. I have now made my peace and it will be all over in the morning. The sun will no longer rise on my pain.

I write this, because maybe one day this letter will be found and it can be read to my father, mother and sister. I want them to know that I fought for as long as I could, but I was not strong enough. My wish is that one day they can forgive my weakness. I really wanted to go to university and learn. There were things I wanted to do, places I wanted to see. I wanted to build a house for my parents that had an indoor kitchen, so my mother didn't have to carry firewood on her head when we ran out of kerosene for the stove. I wanted to have a job that did not include having babies, cleaning or cooking.

As I look around camp at girls like Hafsat who have accepted their fate, I question my own sanity. My life for the last two years could have been better, if only I had accepted life in the bush as my reality. But I rejected it, it was not my portion, it was not my blessing. When I was twelve my mother told me it was every woman's dream to marry, have children and look after her husband. It was not what I wanted and Father did not want that for me either. So he sent me to school because he understood that I wanted more, and he wanted more for me. My mother never finished primary school and never left the village, so she did not understand the importance of education, but she gave in and let me go. Despite what has become of me, I am grateful for the things I have learned.

Father is well travelled; he's been abroad, he's been to Lagos and Abuja and has seen many things. When we were little, he would come back from his travels with pictures of people and places. As you enter our room, there is the picture he took of the burial place of Jesus, he took it when he went to Jerusalem for a conference or something. For hours I would stare at it and imagine what it would be like to fly in an aeroplane and visit another country.

It pains me that I am giving up, that I will never again see their faces. I will never again fight with my sister, argue with my mother or disobey my father who had a thousand rules about what we could and could not do and a cane to set us on the right path when we did not listen. I will use my last prayer, hoping that this message finds them, that they know I did try to get home, but after they kept me tied up for several days, I stopped trying. Am I a coward? I do not know how to fix the emptiness, the brokenness. I do not know how to lose the pain that is wound so tightly around my body like a wrapper.

There are times I look around camp and things seem so normal. At first we were constantly on the move. They did not want to risk capture, but as the months passed we moved less and less, until we finally settled here. During the day, the men go off with their guns as if they are going to their farm to harvest corn. Sometimes they come back on the same day, sometimes days later, with provisions, but never anything that makes our lives comfortable.

I have to forgive them, because it is the only way I can be at peace. I accept what is and what has been, not because I want to, but because I have to. Please do not judge me too harshly. You do not know who I am.

Patience Agbabi

Born in London to Nigerian parents and fostered in a white English family in North Wales, she is a poet whose work links high art with popular culture. She read English at Oxford University and completed an MA in Creative Writing at Sussex University. She became prominent on the London spoken word circuit in the early 1990s. Her work has been featured on TV and radio and she has toured extensively in the UK and abroad with the British Council. Her poem "The Doll's House" was shortlisted for the Forward Prize for Best Single Poem 2014. Her fourth collection of poems, the critically acclaimed Telling Tales *(2014), is a contemporary, multicultural remix of* The Canterbury Tales.

The Doll's House

The source of the wealth that built Harewood is historical fact. There is nothing anyone can do to change the past, however appalling or regrettable that past might be. What we can do, however, what we must do, is engage with that legacy and in so doing stand a chance of having a positive effect on the future.

—David Lascelles

Art is a lie that makes us realise truth.

—Pablo Picasso

Welcome to my house, this stately home
where, below stairs, my father rules as chef:
confecting, out of sugar-flesh and -bone,
décor so fine, your tongue will treble clef
singing its name. Near-sighted and tone-deaf,
I smell-taste-touch; create each replica
in my mind's tongue. My name? Angelica.

This is my world, the world of haute cuisine:
high frosted ceilings, modelled on high art,
reflected in each carpet's rich design;
each bed, each armchair listed à la carte.
Come, fellow connoisseur of taste, let's start
below stairs, where you'll blacken your sweet tooth,
sucking a beauty whittled from harsh truth…

Mind your step! The stairway's worn and steep,
Let your sixth senses merge in the half-light…
This muted corridor leads to the deep
recesses of the house. Here, to your right,
my father's realm of uncurbed appetite—
private! The whiff of strangers breaks his spell.
Now left, to the dead end. Stop! Can you smell

cinnamon, brown heat in the afternoon
of someone else's summer? This rust key
unlocks the passage to my tiny room,
stick-cabin, sound-proofed with a symphony
of cinnamon; shrine to olfactory
where I withdraw to paint in cordon bleu,
shape, recreate this house; in miniature

All art is imitation: I'm a sculptor
of past-imperfect; hungry, I extract
molasses; de- and reconstruct high culture
from base material; blend art and fact
in every glazed and glistening artefact
housed in this doll's house. Stately home of sugar.
Of Demerara cubes secured with nougat.

Look at its hall bedecked with royal icing—
the ceiling's crossbones mirrored in the frieze,
the chimneypiece. The floor is sugar glazing
clear as a frozen lake. My centrepiece
statue of Eve, what a creative feast!
A crisp Pink Lady, sculpted with my teeth,
its toffee glaze filming the flesh beneath.

The music room's my favourite. I make music
by echoing design: the violet-rose

piped ceiling is the carpet's fine mosaic
of granulated violet and rose,
aimed to delight the eye, the tongue, the nose.
Even the tiny chairs are steeped in flavour
delicate as a demisemiquaver.

Taste, if you like, sweet as a mothertongue…
See how this bedroom echoes my refrain:
the chairs, the secretaire, commode, chaise longue,
four-poster bed, all carved from sugarcane;
even the curtains that adorn its frame,
chiselled from the bark, each lavish fold
drizzled with tiny threads of spun "white gold".

The library was hardest. How to forge
each candied volume wafer-thin, each word
burnt sugar. In the midnight hours, I'd gorge
on bubbling syrup, mouth its language; learned
the temperature at which burnt sugar burned,
turned sweet to bitter; inked a tiny passage
that overflowed into a secret passage,

the Middle Passage; made definitive
that muted walkway paved with sugar plate,
its sugar-paper walls hand-painted with
hieroglyphs invisible as sweat
but speaking volumes; leading to the sweet
peardrop of a stairwell down and down
to this same room of aromatic brown

in miniature. Here, connoisseur, I've set
the doll, rough hewn from sugarcane's sweet wood:
her choker, hardboiled sweets as black as jet;
her dress, molasses-rich; her features, hard.
This handcarved doll, with sugar in her blood—
Europe, the Caribbean, Africa;
baptised in sugar, named Angelica,

has built a tiny house in Demerara
sugar grains secured with sugarpaste,
each sculpted room a microscopic mirror
of its old self; and below stairs, she's placed

a blind doll with kaleidoscopic taste,
who boils, bakes, moulds, pipes, chisels, spins and blows
sugar, her art, the only tongue she knows.

Agnès Agboton

Translated by Lawrence Schimel

*Born in Benin, she is a multilingual author and storyteller now living in Catalonia,
Spain. She has published two bilingual books of poetry in Gun (her mother tongue)
and Spanish:* Voz de las dos orillas *("Voice of the Two Shores", 2010) and* Canciones
del poblado y del exilio *("Songs of Village and of Exile", 2009) Her other titles
include* Más allá del mar de arena *("Beyond the Sea of Sand", 2005) and* Na Miton.
La mujer en los cuentos y leyendas africanos *("Na Miton. Women in African stories
and Legends", 2004), plus books on African food and collections of African legends.
She represented Benin at the Poetry Parnassus at the London 2012 Olympics. Her
poems in English translation have appeared in* Modern Poetry in Translation *and*
Wasafiri.

1.

Here, where time
seems to have stopped.
Here, where the land
is abandoned,
sacrificed daily
to useless memories
and heroic songs.
Here, where blood
seems fruitless.
Here, in the stillness
of the cemetery,
I've still found
the steady gaze
of crushed eyes,
I've listened to the words
of a stiffened tongue.

30.

Through their veins flows
night and morning
and in all their gestures
the dance is born.

I counted, one by one, their fingers
now far away,
I approach its skin of foam
and I saw that look
ignite in their eyes.

The dance is born, yes,
the dance is born.

I then saw how, in them,
two continents sprouted.
Their steps were white,
all their complaints were black,
those words.

The dance is born, yes,
the dance is born.

I now take refuge in their arms,
the new shoots,
with the sun at one extreme
and dark scent in these leaves
I curl around.

The dance is born, yes,
the dance is born.

Who will stop those rivers?
Who will channel that wind?

It is already an enormous flow
that lifts those bodies,
through all their veins flow
the nights and the mornings.

And they are a dance, yes,
they are a dance.

Omega

I am afraid that one day we might sink
into the sadness of a rainy afternoon
and our lives, now forever damp
from defeated and daily tears,
might never find
the strength with which we lift them today,
sadly,
steadfast in the search for a new dawn,
recreated from a word,
perhaps a sparkle.

                (Always a small thing,
                  never nothing.)

The sadness of a rainy afternoon
that sometimes invades your eyes;
and sometimes spills from your mouth
and from my own.

The sadness of a rainy afternoon
that binds our hearts
with sad (lulling)
ties of hopelessness and sleepiness.

The sadness of a rainy afternoon
on which we masturbated our minds
and our hearts.
NO.

Let us rise up again…,
there are other eyes in search of the hidden sun.
Other hands try to tear away
the clouds that cover it.

In other hearts
the weariness has been defeated.
NO.
I am tired, my love…, and I am afraid.

Ellah Wakatama Allfrey

Born in Zimbabwe and raised there and in the US, she has lived in England for more than 30 years. The founding Publishing Director of The Indigo Press, London, she has judged numerous international literary prizes including the Man Booker Prize, the International Dublin Literary Award, the Caine Prize for African Writing, the Commonwealth Short Story Prize and the David Cohen Prize. In 2016 she was Visiting Professor and Global Intercultural Scholar at Goshen College, Indiana, and served as a Guest Master for the Gabriel Garcia Marquez Foundation fellowship in Colombia. She is a former Deputy Editor of Granta *(2009–13) and former Senior Editor at Jonathan Cape, Random House. She was series editor of the* Kwani? Manuscript Project *and the editor of* Africa39 *and* Safe House: Explorations in Creative Nonfiction. *She sits on the Advisory Council of Art for Amnesty, and the boards of the Caine Prize for African Writing, the Jalada Collective (Kenya) and the Royal Literary Fund and is a patron of the 9Mobile Literature Prize. In 2011 she was awarded an OBE for services to the publishing industry.*

Longchase

When I look online, I do not find my great-uncle Michael Kanerusine's name on any of the websites my research brings up—not even those that claim "ninety-seven per cent accuracy". I know he fought in the Second World War. That's one fact. It could be a matter of confusion over his surname, I tell myself. As a people, we identify primarily by clan, totem and then father's name. Perhaps the surname that has eventually become the "official" family name isn't the one he enlisted under. It's an imprecise thing, this English naming of Africans—seeking to determine equivalences in kinship patterns, to define what constitutes "family" and inheritance. It can never survive the translation from one culture to the other.

I am keen to find some verification of my great-uncle's war record because my memories of his presence remain vivid from childhood and I realise, now that I want to pin down his story, there is no one from his generation that I can ask. Lucia, my grandmother and Michael's older sister, died seven years ago and though we spent much time together during my visits to Zimbabwe, we always had so much else to talk about. So much to laugh about. And now, every time I speak with my mother about him, the story changes.

Here's what I do know. Over a million black African soldiers from the British Commonwealth served and fought in the Second World War and after. My great-uncle's regiment, the Rhodesian African Rifles (RAR), was formed in 1940 with many of its troops recruited from the rural areas—leaving their homesteads and farms for battlefields in Europe, North Africa and East Asia. Some volunteered, some were conscripted, some went at the behest of their local chiefs. I know that in 1944–45 soldiers from the RAR were in Burma. Later, after the war, in 1951, I read, they fought in Egypt during the Suez Crisis. In 1956 they were deployed to Malaya.

One final fact: in April 1981, following Zimbabwe's independence from colonial rule, the RAR was disbanded along with the other regiments of the Rhodesian armed services, replaced by the formation of the Zimbabwe Defence Forces.

I have always been fascinated by these soldiers. When I first lived in London thirty years ago, my boyfriend's grandmother gifted us her flat in Sloane Square—a temporary home for our gap year after she had moved to a nursing home and was waiting for the flat to be sold. As I wandered this incredibly posh neighbourhood I kept seeing old men dressed in smart scarlet red coats with brass buttons and black trousers with a single red stripe piped along each outside seam. I asked about them. They were Chelsea Pensioners, retired soldiers who lived at the Royal Hospital Chelsea—a Christopher Wren building commissioned by Charles II and completed in 1629. The Royal Hospital offers a home for British Army veterans who are without family in their final years. Although I never quite drummed up the courage to speak to any of these old men, I would stare and then smile my most welcoming smile if they looked up and noticed me. I know now that some pensioners are women but the ones I remember seeing were all men. And they were all white. Where, I wondered then—as I still wonder now—were the black and brown veterans? What happened to them and were they as cared for, as recognised, as honoured?

The men of my mother's maternal clan are tall, strong-boned and handsome. They are powerful and lithe with dark skin and long limbs. Well, my mother says, when I ask about her uncle's enlistment, we are vaRozvi, you know. He would have volunteered. There was a war; he wanted to go show his spear. She adds, with a sidelong glance at my father: They were the lords—the fighters, the rulers. It is a family joke that my father "married up", his own origins and ancestry not nearly as exalted as those of his wife. *Her* people once had an empire. They were a fierce, aggressive people whose rule included the south-western plateau of what is now Zimbabwe, and at its zenith extended west towards Botswana and south to north-eastern South Africa. The empire lasted from the late 1600s well into the 1790s when severe drought and stirrings of rebellion from within and without brought about its gradual decline. They are a people who still carry this history with pride. Their totem, Moyondizvo, deviates from the general ascribing of a single animal totem for a clan. I cast about for a translation that captures both the meaning and the spirit: moyo—the heart; ndizvo—that is it; that is the truth…the heart that is true. The Rozvi are "the true heart"—a totem that embraces all others. Or, as I am sure my mother would put it, subsumes all others.

These are my mother's mother's people, and although the tradition of patriarchal inheritance would frown on me claiming too much of this history for myself, I am proud of these forebears who were successful farmers, rich in cattle and famous for building cities of stone, for their pottery and, in 1693, for defeating a Portuguese militia which sought to gain control of their gold mines. They traded copper, gold and ivory with Arab merchants and—especially important to me as I try to piece together Michael's story—they were known as cunning military strategists, developing the "cow horn formation" of battle that Shaka Zulu would later employ against the British. The Moyondizvo praise song exalts Jengetanyika—the keepers of the land; Kudanga kusina chinoshayikwa—the abundant kraal in which nothing is found wanting. We are warriors, my mother says—sitting up in her chair. And although history books credit the Kingdom of Mutapa as the builders of Great Zimbabwe, the city that gives my country its name, my mother has always shrugged this off. The Mutapa and Rozvi empires ran concurrently and, she is quite clear about this, the books have it wrong. *We* built those houses of stone.

This is the lineage of Michael Bhasvi Kanerusine. Mu'soja of the Rhodesian African Rifles. Sekuru Toro, the Tall One. Great-uncle Longchase. Moyondizvo. The True Heart. I do not have his rank and, besides a general idea of what his cohort *would have* done during the war, I know nothing about his wartime experiences. I can only imagine the journey he would have taken as a nineteen-year-old from Ruzane village, Hwedza, Southern Rhodesia. But as I stole glances at the old men in their Royal Chelsea Hospital uniforms, and later as a commissioning editor searching for writers who could tell the story of the soldiers I longed to know more about, it was his memory that nudged me on.

My great-uncle would have looked stunning in that red coat.

Let me begin with what I remember. The story my late brothers, my sister and I told one another.

One day my mother's uncle arrived at our home in Tynwald, Harare. In my memory it is not long after independence, the early 1980s. We lived in a rambling single-storey house set on five acres in what had, merely years before, been a whites only neighbourhood on the southern outskirts of the city. Michael Kanerusine was my grandmother's younger brother, the fifth out of ten children. Although our home was a regular stopping point for relatives visiting from the rural areas, including those from Ruzane village, we children had not met him before.

He was an imposing presence—long and lanky with big hands and huge feet. My sister Mavhu remembers how she and our younger brother Nhamu would follow him around the garden, always making sure not to get too close or to bother him as our mother had warned that he had a temper. He gave us a hard time, my mother says when I ask her about this. She tells the story of how he got drunk one day and lay down to sleep on the railway line that ran near our house. He just slept right there on the railway tracks, she sighs. Luckily, some neighbours recognised him and brought him home.

He had gone to fight King George's war and when he finally made it home he said he had come back from Burma. But what took you so long? Ndangandiri kuhondo. Ndangandichiri kuuya. I was at war. I was still on my way. Sometimes he spoke of being in Algeria, in Angola, Uganda… He mentioned Germany and Russia. One story was that he had participated in a powerful ritual to ensure he would not be killed in battle, that he would survive the war. But the vow he had to make to the ancestors in return for their protection was that he would never again see his parents. By the time he returned, they were already dead.

In the story my siblings and I told each other over the years, Toro's sojourn with us marked this eventual return home some thirty-five years after the soldiers who fought in WWII would have been decommissioned. We imagined him journeying from the far north, across a continent, stopping along the way as history swept by with world-changing movements of independence, new governments and national identities. *I was at war. I was still on my way*. It is a story of epic adventure and daring and I have always wanted to believe that I carry his spirit in my heart, have always wanted to be as fearless in my adventures. What better ancestor to claim than one, a colonial subject, who had boldly gone into the world and chosen for himself the timing and manner of his return? I think of the ease with which I cross borders with my dark red British passport and wonder what it must have meant for a young (and then not so young) man from a Southern African village making his way, over a period of more than three decades, across our vast continent. In our minds, Toro became a giant.

Amma Asante

Born in London to Ghanaian parents, she is a BAFTA award-winning writer/director who began her career as a child actress, appearing as a regular in the popular British school drama Grange Hill. *In her late teens, she left the world of acting and eventually made the move to screenwriting with development deals from Chrysalis, Channel 4 and the BBC. Two series of the urban drama* Brothers and Sisters *followed, which she wrote and produced for BBC2. The film* A Way of Life *was her directorial debut (she also wrote the screenplay), garnering newcomer nominations from the London Film Critics' Circle and* Evening Standard Film Awards, *and winning 17 international awards for writing and directing and Newcomer Awards for writing and directing from the BFI London Film Festival and the prestigious South Bank Show Awards.* Belle, *her second feature film, received widespread acclaim and earned her nominations for various awards worldwide.*

The Power of Defining Yourself

Figures revealed by the Women's Media Center in New York showed that, across a five-year period ending in 2012, of the 500 top-grossing movies, only two had black women directors attached to them—that's 0.4 per cent. So I'm thinking, now, back to the night before I was about to set foot on the set of the first movie I directed. I was absolutely terrified, and my fear pivoted around the fact that I knew I wasn't what was expected of a director. I didn't fit the industry model, full stop. I wondered how I was going to lead my all-male crew, who were also all white, how I was going to instil confidence in them and get them to believe in me, so that I could end up with the film that I had written on screen. After all, I knew they had never worked under anyone like me before; you know, my shape, my flavour.

I realized, essentially, that society had created the very world I wanted to work in as one that, statistically, did not include me. And that society, by its own boundaries and perceptions, had created me to be somebody who didn't fit into the category of what filmmakers were generally expected to be. Yet I felt like a director, and I knew I could craft stories onscreen and connect those stories to audiences. Still, the figures don't lie. The statistics did not tally in my favour. Essentially, my definition of me didn't match the definition that society had bestowed upon me.

It begs the question: who defines you? Society, or yourself? Is society's opinion of who you are, who you can be, what value you have, what you can achieve in life—is that more powerful and important an opinion than your own? If you say you are a writer, for example, and you have something valuable to contribute to the literary world, but reviewers and critics say you're not a great writer, then whose truth wins? And whose truth is most likely to determine your future as a writer?

Well, for me, the answer is really simple. It's whichever you choose to believe. I have this idea. Since we can all dream a far bigger dream for ourselves than society ever could, what would happen if we all decided we were going to actively define ourselves and allow that definition to govern everything, over and above anything that society could define or indicate for any of us? How would that influence our lives?

The question of who defines us comes up in everybody's life at some point. It doesn't have to be about race or gender, necessarily. For me, the question embedded itself long ago. I grew up down the road from Brixton at a time when it was being so negatively defined by society, and defined in a way that it didn't authentically see itself, that it practically imploded in its struggle to be heard. And, with an older brother, who was still a teenager at the time, I experienced how it felt for some that they were living in a police state. Yet I also witnessed how Brixton refused to be marginalized and criminalized, as it rose up during the riots of the 1980s and rejected the definition of the existence it should have by society's standards.

Defining yourself outside the realms of society is not easy. It's such a fascinating subject to me as a writer and director that it has risen to the fore of every single project I have ever worked on, and probably every single project I will ever do. I think the reason is because it's so complex, and what's so hard about it is to recognize when your choices and your direction in life are being influenced by society's perhaps more restricted ideas of who you should be.

You know, when the mirror image of what society is suggesting to you doesn't reflect the person you really feel you are. Or, even worse, when the untrue image that's coming back to you does feel real, because the messages and the influence can be so subtle that it's easy to dismiss. You know, "This is just the way things are supposed to be." That's what you tell yourself.

Think about how many used that argument when it came to the trans-Atlantic slave trade, or against women who demanded the vote, or even today, when it comes to gay marriage. Think how many institutions and organizations use outdated, antiquated, biased rules to maintain the status quo, sometimes an unjust status quo: "We've been doing this for x number of years, so we can't change it now, it's tradition." That's a word they like to use, "tradition". For me that sounds *un*evolved, to not move forward because something is tradition.

Yet when society is acting to prevent you reaching your goals and your dreams, that's precisely the time you have to truly remember who you are. The reason I believe that is because today none of us emerge from just one single world. We are all a combination of many worlds put together. And sometimes, when you are at the junction of many worlds, society considers you a contradiction.

Growing up down the road from Brixton, I experienced the common story of constantly being asked: "Where are you from?" I would say: "Well, actually, I was born here in London." Then I would be harangued: "No, but where are you really from?…"

And, interestingly, I would go back to Ghana to visit both my grandmothers, with my mother during summer vacation, and I would be told: "Well, you're not really Ghanaian, because you're too English." It got to the point where at this junction I was at, I didn't know which pathway to go down. Because, if I took one pathway, it would be rejected, if I took another pathway, that would be rejected. In many ways it felt like society was defining me as an outsider.

And I say again, this doesn't have to be solely about race or gender. We're all at the junction of many worlds. It can concern race, class, sexuality, so many different things today. I wonder if there is anyone who, at some point in their life, hasn't been identified outside of the realms of where they see themselves, or at some point hasn't felt like an outsider. I don't think it should be about having to pick one pathway over another. I shouldn't have to pick being British over being Ghanaian, or being Ghanaian over being British. Because, ultimately, I am a product of both. Both those cultures reside inside me. And it shouldn't really matter if that's not normal to society.

It's not so much about a collision of worlds as it is a combining of worlds. And it really shouldn't matter whether society defines it as normal or not. As the late Dr Maya Angelou would say, if we are always trying so hard to be normal, how can we ever know how amazing we can be?

Now, bringing to bear your definition of yourself in society, I know, can be hard. There are all sorts of things: beauty ideals, gender expectations for both men and women, racial profiling, class prejudice, these are all examples of how we can be thrown off-base in terms of knowing, understanding and defining who we know we truly are. I am thinking now about the guy who wants to stand in his truth when it comes to his sexuality, even though his community or his religion might expect something different of him. Those who define themselves as beautiful but society tells them they are not, and I think to myself that at those points exactly, when society is telling you that you are not who you feel you are, that's the time that you have to understand the power of what it means to define yourself. It may be the difference between whether you may be happy or less happy in life, a failure or a success in life, but most importantly, conscious or unconscious in the story of your own life.

I think back now to finding my way originally in the business of film, and being told so often: "It's very hard to sell Black movies with a Black protagonist." Yet there are enough movies today that have defied that and shown that to be untrue. But regardless of whether that was just opinion, or whether that was perception, or whether it was truth or not, I realized that if I was going to move forward in the business, I was going to have to try to find a way of working out what the obstacles were, and find a way to negotiate those obstacles.

What I learned is that when you truly embrace who you are, and all the worlds that you come from, when you bring those sensibilities to a previously closed-off world, you move society forward. When we move into other worlds, we touch people, we impact people, and when people change, then society has to as well. For me, the value of embracing all the worlds that exist in you is that those of us who are able to do so have an insight that shows us why colliding worlds on the outside are not a bad thing. Because when worlds meet, progress can follow; the mother who may run a Fortune 500 company, the son of a cleaner who becomes a doctor, or think about the first African-American children to set foot in the all-white schools after segregation was abolished, those are all people that inspire me to do what I do.

I'm thinking now about the women who do make their way in the male-dominated world of film-making, and what we realize about those women is that when they are able to break into that world, they make an impact. The British Film Institute released figures between 2010 and 2012 that show that although women were still under-represented in terms of independent film-making, they represented a significant percentage when it came to successful films. People love their films. That's what I mean by saying that when we have the courage to move forward into other worlds, we have the impact to change them.

It takes me back to the story I started with: stepping onto the set of my first film. A few weeks before I was about to shoot that movie, a film executive came up to me and said: "Well, you're not going to step on set with your big high heels on, are you?" As if me coming on set with high heels was going to be the thing that established me as a woman in a man's world. For the record, I don't direct in high heels, and I didn't direct my first film in high heels, except for the last day; I always make that a tradition now. But I did celebrate my love for heels in one way. The logo of my company is essentially a high heel and appeared with my company name at the end of that film. You see, I believe in leaning into our identity, not leaning back. And high heels are definitely a part of my identity.

But I believe the part of me that loves high heels and loves being a woman is every bit the part of me that is able to write movies, direct movies, and deliver movies. Just as the part of me where Africa meets Europe is the very part that gives me my unique yet universal eye. You see, I believe every industry, every business, every society, requires fresh eyes to open new windows on old concepts and unseen worlds, to bring new perspectives to the universal experience.

The journey for me of defining myself is an ongoing experience. I work at it every day. But if you ask me today: "Who are you, Amma? Where are you from?" I can tell you this: I am a black British woman. I am proudly born of Ghanaian parents. And I am a screenwriter and a movie director. Now, how will you define you?

Michelle Asantewa

Born in Guyana, she migrated to the UK to reunite with her mother. Her interest in African traditional spiritual practices and cultural identity prompted her to do a PhD on the Guyanese Comfa ritual. She set up Way Wive Wordz Publishing, Editing and Tuition Services to accommodate a range of learning and creative aspirations. Her publications include the novels Elijah *(2014),* Something Buried in the Yard *(2018),* The Awakening and Other Poems *(2014), her PhD thesis* Guyanese Komfa: The Ritual Art of Trance *(2016) and* Mama Lou Tales: A Folkloric Biography of a Guyanese Elder *(2016), which are self-published through Way Wive Wordz.*

Rupununi affair

I had made up my mind to marry Catherine, a local Wapishana girl. I imagined a simple ceremony before I took her to England and arranged a more elaborate reception. My mother would naturally object, as much to her kind as her age. You see, Catherine had recently finished high school and I had long passed the season of enviable attraction for any English girl whom my mother would prefer I chose for a wife. My means were moderate despite the company, whose affairs it was my job to oversee in this godforsaken part of the world, expeditiously making good on their investment. I believed Catherine would be sensible about it, the opportunity being what it was.

The heat had become intolerable, as it always did after a few months. At such times I returned for the coolness of the English air before I could again face the ferocious sun and the locals, who were not all so repugnant. Of all the places I'd seen of this ghastly region, the Rupununi was the loveliest; I particularly loved their women. As for the Negro coquettes and wily East Indian women in the city, their hard, pleading smiles, canoodling atop foul obscenities and lewdness wore me out. They begged for everything without remorse or shame as though they were owed the entire earth.

We had arranged to meet at the usual place, a small creek a little out of view from the thatched mud houses and somewhat shaded from the wretched sun. One of the biggest houses belonged to her father, the Toshao. I found it curious that he had electricity whilst the other houses didn't. At night many relied on the stars and the moon when it was full for light outside—not everyone carried torches, I suppose by choice or lack of means. Indoors, kerosene lamps glimmered, imposing a kind of antiquated tranquility I grew to appreciate.

Catherine's skin had a golden sheen and was gloriously soft. Her face was majestically framed by thick, dark hair that flowed to her waist. Like the other Wapishana women and girls her calves were magnificently sturdy—though I confess I wished she had less than her share of muscles, perhaps with the delicateness, if not the fairness English ladies were blessed with. It's true she differed in passion and sensuality, which I found lacking in the girls back home. As for her lovemaking, this was beyond compare—I couldn't complain.

At last Catherine arrived at the creek. She wasted no time removing her clothes and slipping into the cool dark water, which was barely deep enough for her to stand fully without revealing her breasts. From our first encounter, she had given herself to me with a sort of calm grace. I sometimes took her sharply, however, my hand vigorously cupping her mouth as though I feared she might scream. She never screamed, but responded to my fierce gestures and jabs by sucking my fingers as though she was gorging on a mango. Our lovemaking lasted a few minutes but it was always remarkable.

We had spread our clothes to make blankets on the edge of the creek, our bodies being dried by the sun.

"How do you stand it?" I posed after a while, instead of asking the intended question of marriage.

"Stand what?"

"Not you, I suppose. Your father. Your people? How do *they* stand being, you know, *ruled* by the others?" My eyes were closed. She didn't say anything, so I continued.

"Those on the coast—the Negroes. The *other* Indians."

"Oh," was all she said.

"Don't you…I mean…you know, think it strange? It's your country, after all, and you don't *govern*. You don't have *power*?"

"Oh. Is been that way a long time," she said slowly, with an air of finality.

"Catherine, darling…Catherine…I…" I had worked out the proposal very well in my head but suddenly became unnerved and couldn't understand why. I firmed up my resolve somehow and went on.

"Catherine, I'd like us to be married."

I peeped at her to check her face. Her eyes were closed, her hair splayed like seaweed on the ground. I became a little impatient because she didn't immediately respond.

"Come now, darling. What do you say?" She opened one eye, which reminded me of an old horse we had when I was a boy. It had fallen brutally one day, stabbing one of its eyes against a stray piece of wire and was blinded. My parents kept a patch on the eye to stop me having nightmares.

"How long we been sexing?" she asked suddenly, a finger slowly circling her breasts. She knew I hated it when she used that word, but I had become less infuriated by it after I decided we'd be married. I felt she would outgrow those awful habits. I wondered why they bothered inventing words when there were already adequate ones in the English language they could use. I knew I was needlessly working myself up, the question was illegitimate.

"Catherine, don't you know how long we've been…how long it's been?"

"Less than a year, nuh?"

"What of it?"

"You think sexing for not even one year is love?" She was a child, I reminded myself. She was playing games, the way all natives played games to mask their deviant motives. I had believed Catherine wasn't like that, so why?

"Oh, Catherine! Don't you want to marry me?" I hated the awful pleading in my voice but couldn't help it. I hoped she wasn't wise to it. She had again closed her eyes, one hand angled across her forehead.

"I don't know, English." I had long given up expecting her to call me by my name but regretted how impersonal it was for her to call me "English" as everyone addressed me this way. I knew it was not out of fondness, but acrimony.

"Don't you love me?" I leaned up to face her fully.

"Love ain' have nothing to do with sexing, English." Her tone was nasty, some part of me wanted to strike her for being unusually presumptuous.

"Is it only sex for you then?" I asked sternly. It would soon be dark and I had little time to convince her to marry me. All those arrangements to be made, and she was playing the fool.

"I ain' know," she said, with that annoying lilt in her voice. I resigned myself to drop the proposition for another day, maybe away from her village, if we could get away without discovery.

"You are so beautiful—I suppose you have your share of suitors," I said, hoping she couldn't detect how unsettling this all was for me. She giggled and rolled towards me, her breasts cushioning against my arm. She stroked the rim round my nipples, rousing me again. I closed my eyes; my head tilted a little further back, my body arched in grand expectation. We made love again and I released after a good deal of strain compared to her rapid, excitable and frequent bursts of pleasure. I was certain I wanted her for my wife.

"Catherine, I love you very much. You do know that, don't you? I want to take you to England. I leave in a few weeks." She said nothing. "A small service—you know—formalities and all that can be arranged here. We'll do something bigger when we get home." I resolved that her silence needn't mean resistance, it might instead be fear.

"I have a small fortune to boast of. Of course, I'll square things with your father. My family are a good sort too. From Dorset. Ah, Dorset! When you see Dorset… England is so big, though, we can live wherever you like." I felt her turning away. I must have been right, she was afraid. I touched her shoulder, tugging it towards me as gently as my patience allowed.

"What's the matter, darling? There's nothing to be afraid of." She rolled towards me. She opened her eyes widely as if startled by her own exalted rumination. She shivered, too. The sun had by now started to go down, but it was still hot. She began to smile again but looked somehow far away, as though being compelled by some profound memory. Her face took on a strange look. It made me feel awkward and suddenly embarrassed by my nakedness. She stood up and prised her dress from beneath me.

"England is big?" she asked in a flat tone.

"Yes. Remarkably so!"

"And Guyana is what?"

"What about Guyana—is that what you mean?" She was standing over me, her dress now covering her naked body. She tucked her hair up tightly, clasping an elastic band over it.

"Guyana ain' big? Rupununi, Aishalton big." It struck me that she perceived Aishalton to be comparable to Dorset, perhaps England. I began to imagine her bewilderment when she saw the grand coasts and beautiful beaches in Dorset, let alone England, our rivers and lakes much less meagre than the pitiful overrated creeks she was used to. I gave a little chuckle in anticipation of that revelation.

"Why you laugh, English?" At this interjection I noticed the sun sinking more deeply and a frightful shadow appeared on her face.

"Well, Catherine, Aishalton is a lovely, quaint place, with a few juts of mountains, large trees overbearing with the sweetest fruits I've ever tasted, large open plains and so forth, but how little it compares to some of the places you'll see in England." She became silent. I became nervous, though I couldn't say why.

"Darling, what's the matter? I thought you wanted us to be married?"

"You tink cause we been sexing I love you? I know wha England is, English. It have a ugly Queen wha' rule da world but living on a small island." She stopped, but I could tell she was not through. With a long gulp of air that seemed to come from some place deep within her, she snapped—"Yoh forget to say Guyana gah plenty gold too, English."

I hopped to my feet, not before I had observed how the sun's changed position now made her face appear rough-looking and ugly.

"Catherine, I apologise if I've hurt your feelings. I didn't mean to." I didn't want to say anything else; the apology didn't seem proper but rather like the bleakest burden ever forced upon me.

"You know nutting about my feelings. I nat going wid you to Englan'. I ever tell you I wan' go Englan'? Guyana is where I baarn an' grow."

I could not think of what to say momentarily. I managed to lick my lips and wiped a trace of perspiration from my forehead.

"I'm sorry, Catherine. You're right. Guyana is all those things but it's not…well, this is about us, you and me."

"You nat going see me again, English. Don't ever come back here. Go back to Dorset an' leave me alone. A big man like you must know sexing is nah love." She released a peculiar shriek before stomping away.

I watched her as she ran towards her home, certain I heard laughter trailing behind her. The evening had closed in on me. I was still naked, flies intermittently brushed across my face. I wondered if I should chase her and slap sense into her. My legs felt subdued, however, and I stood there awhile feeling like a forlorn statue. I could remotely hear parts of a song she was singing.

"…I love the Rupununi…land of natural beauty…where the Kanaku mountains…" I turned, my heart feeling heavy and constricted. I dreaded the long, dark drive to Lethem where I had my room. I could still hear baleful echoes of her song. I vowed then that when I returned to this wretched place, as I was bitterly fated to do, it would be strictly for business. This propitiation I declared before those ominous mounds they called the Kanaku.

Sefi Atta

Born in Lagos, Nigeria, she currently divides her time between Nigeria, England and the United States. She is the author of the novels Everything Good Will Come *(2005),* Swallow *(2010),* A Bit of Difference *(2014) and* The Bead Collector *(2019); the short story collection,* News from Home *(2010); the children's book* Drama Queen *(2018); and the play collection* Sefi Atta: Selected Plays *(2019). She was a juror for the 2010 Neustadt International Prize for Literature and is a judge for the 2019 Caine Prize for African Writing. She has received several literary awards, including the 2006 Wole Soyinka Prize for Literature in Africa and the 2009 Noma Award for Publishing in Africa. In 2015, a critical study of her novels and short stories,* Writing Contemporary Nigeria: How Sefi Atta Illuminates African Culture and Tradition, *was published by Cambria Press.*

The Cocktail Party

Ashake and Debayo Dada had a cocktail party at their Ikoyi house the other night. It was supposedly to celebrate their eighteenth wedding anniversary, though I suspected their real reason was to show off their new swimming pool. Ashake had ordered her invitations from my greeting-card shop, and dictated the exact wording she wanted: "Chief and Mrs. Adebayo Dada request the pleasure of your company", and so on. She'd also added a recently invented family crest, which should have stated: "Est. 1976". My shop manager had delivered the cards to her weeks ago, and I was still waiting for her to pay me.

Ashake was my daughter's godmother and we'd known each other for years, so we weren't about to fall out over money. When we were girls, she was called Sumbo. Ashake, her praise name, meant "the pampered one". Her mother was a union leader of the women who attended my father's church and had several informal titles conferred by them. She was most popularly known as Iya, which translated to "Mother" in Yoruba. Ashake and I must have been about ten years old when she walked up to me after church, as my mother was greeting hers, and said, "You're lucky to have a mother who is as gentle as a white woman." I, being equally naïve, considered that a compliment.

I later recruited Ashake as a food thief. Yes, we were in a gang with other Saint John's girls. We would sneak into Ikoyi Cemetery to steal cashews from the trees. We would hoist Ashake up because she had long arms. Her underwear was never clean and she had an odour of stale urine about her, which we ignored for the sake of solidarity. One day, a caterpillar fell on top of her head. She screamed, we dropped her and scampered off. She limped back home, where Iya beat her for disgracing her family.

Without an education, Iya managed to see her children through secondary school and they all became successful businessmen and women. They were proud of her reputation, including Ashake, who nonetheless claimed that the Oba of Lagos had bestowed Iya's titles on her.

Ashake often lied about her background and I had some idea why. As the eldest daughter in her family, she had been sent to a boarding house in Lagos run by a woman who taught girls etiquette after they'd finished secondary school. If their parents didn't have the means to further their educations, she prepared them for work and marriage. She had no children of her own, so her students became her adopted daughters. Her mission was to turn them into refined young ladies. Ashake must have taken the experience to heart because shortly after she left the boarding house, she dropped her name Sumbo and started lying. She said her father was a pharmacist. He was a herbalist. She said she took a Pitman's course in London to train as a secretary. She never did. She said her husband, Debayo, graduated from Harvard with a degree in engineering. I'd only ever heard that he had attended a university in Ohio, and assumed it was one of those that issued honorary diplomas in return for a donation.

Debayo was a well-known businessman, who had somehow managed to wangle directorships with several foreign companies. His business adversaries accused him of buggering his way to the top. Ashake herself was said to practise juju, which wouldn't have surprised me. Iya may have been a member of Saint John's, but she was also a regular at the local *babalawo*.

I did occasionally wonder if some of the rumours about the Dadas were embellished. People either worshipped or despised them. Tunde was fascinated with them. He hailed them "the lord and lady of the manor", to their delight. Whenever they invited us to a function at their house, he would hurry me up. He couldn't be bothered with the gossip about them, but observing their excesses firsthand gave him much pleasure.

We got to their house that night, and he asked their gateman if he could park in their driveway. The gateman said guests were not allowed in.

"What about those cars?" Tunde asked, pointing at five Benzes stationed on their gravelled driveway, all black.

The gateman said they belonged to Master and Madam.

"Wonders will never cease," Tunde said, smiling.

I begged him not to embarrass me.

The Dadas' house was huge, with Greek-style columns. A steward in a white uniform showed us into their sitting room, which had a beige marble floor, beige damask curtains, gilt-edged mirrors and crystal chandeliers. The whole place was beige, sparkly and full of Nigerians in colourful traditional attire. There were a few expatriates around. Ashake had insisted her invitations state the dress code was cocktail wear. Tunde and I were in traditional attire. So was Debayo, who wore a white lace *agbada* with a red-and-gold cap. Ashake herself was in a full-length red satin gown that contradicted her own dress code. She was heavily made-up, but I could tell her face had lightened a shade. I'd heard that she got chemical baths in London to bleach her skin. She had voluntarily denied that to me, swearing her complexion was natural, though I remembered a time when she was darker than me.

"My very good friend," she said in Yoruba.

I hugged her, genuinely pleased to see her again. As Tunde went off with Debayo, she took my arm and led me around her sitting room, introducing me to people, some of whom I already knew. She flashed the ruby-and-diamond ring Debayo had bought her.

"The rubies are from India," she said.

I said they were beautiful.

She tilted her head, admiring the stones. "I'm not sure where the diamonds are from."

I said it didn't matter. She should just enjoy her ring.

She had new furniture as well, faux Louis Quinze sofa sets, also in beige. She pointed at a blown-up photo of her family in a gilt frame on the wall.

"We took that at Christmas," she said.

"Where?" I asked.

"Jackie Phillips."

Jackie Phillips was a celebrity boxer turned photographer. His studio photos were superb, but they didn't come cheap.

The Dada boys had grown into handsome young men. They looked like Debayo in the photograph, dressed in their suits and ties. They were in English boarding schools and during the holidays were either at the polo club or at their beach house on Tarkwa Bay with friends who were similarly placed. The whole lot of them were known as *omo olowo*—children of the rich. Poor things, they were so indulged by their parents that you couldn't help but sympathise when they ended up taking drugs or getting drunk and crashing cars because no one had taught them when enough was enough. I knew this only because Ashake often bemoaned her sons' hectic social life, to other mothers' annoyance. I couldn't be resentful of her, no matter what she did or said. I wasn't embarrassed for her, either; there was no point. She didn't care what other people thought.

We had a few mutual friends and as we passed through the house I found myself slipping into my usual polyglot party greetings: *"Ciao." "E wo lese?" "Comme ci comme ça."* Expatriates enjoyed a Nigerian greeting; Nigerians loved a European one. They were mostly people from the business community. Tutu, a woman who had several directorships, was there. She had qualified as a chartered accountant at a time when only Nigerian men did, and was always the lone woman in the company of men. She stood with a group of them, in a black shift dress, swirling her brandy as they smoked cigars. She was divorced from her first husband and separated from her second, who had accused her of adultery. Arin, a gold-jewellery millionaire, was there as well, resplendent in traditional regalia. So was her husband, a chief, who had fathered children by several other women he supported. He and Arin lived together, practised juju together, but kept their finances separate.

Were there any normal, happily married couples at the party? Of course there were, together for ten, fifteen, twenty years, with no major problems I'd heard about. But they were indistinguishable from the rest, who looked just as normal without captions to suggest otherwise. The husbands: drinks too much; occasionally manhandles his wife; may have impregnated his wife's younger sister. The wives: on Valium; not permitted to do a thing without her husband's consent; beaten on a regular basis.

Ashake and I parted ways and I circulated, encouraged by the James Last Orchestra's instrumental version of "Soley, Soley". Tunde was busy slapping Debayo's back and looking as if he couldn't contain himself.

It wasn't a cocktail party; it was a feast. The drinks were followed by a buffet of dressed crab, shrimp salad, avocado salad, fried rice, jollof rice, coconut rice, roast chicken, and some pasta dish I couldn't identify. That was merely part of the European continental spread. The Nigerian spread included barbecued goat, peppered snails, and *egusi* with pounded yam. I started with the dressed crab and proceeded to the shrimp salad. By the time I got to the peppered snails I was full, but the food kept coming, and so did the wines and spirits. I had some Châteauneuf-du-Pape, followed by a little Baileys Irish Cream, which I'd been meaning to try since it came out. It reminded me of Bols Advocaat: far too sweet, yet I couldn't stop drinking it.

The Nigerian guests ate and drank, unaware of the waiters. The expatriates were more polite, yet deliberately brief. We all appeared to be mixing but, on close inspection, there were Nigerians who couldn't be bothered to talk to expatriates, and expatriates who would rather stick to their own kind. The Lebanese and Indians mingled with everyone. There was a Nigerian couple who only spoke to expatriates to prove—well, I didn't know what, and an English fellow who was so pleased to be in the presence of Nigerians, he shook hands with every single one of us.

After dinner, we all gathered in the sitting room with champagne flutes to toast the Dadas. Debayo declared Ashake the love of his life and they danced to Frankie Valli's "Can't Take My Eyes Off You". I had to admire them. They were unusually affectionate for a Nigerian couple, and united. Even when they argued, they referred to each other as "honey", "sugar", and all manner of sweet food. I'd been with them on such an occasion, the details of which failed me because they were so trivial. It was hard enough trying to keep up with their terms of endearment. She, for instance, saying, "Honey, your head is not correct," and he replying, "Sugar, I'm warning you for the very last time not to insult me."

The toast over, they launched their new swimming pool to Cliff Richard's "Congratulations". Debayo made everyone stand behind Ashake and count from ten downwards, then she cut a red ribbon tied across the sliding doors, which led to the veranda.

The Dadas lived in an Ikoyi neighbourhood that wasn't designated for government housing. Consequently, it had smaller plots. But they had built such a huge house in theirs that there was hardly any room for a back garden. We walked into what used to be their sons' playground, now replaced by the swimming pool, which was so small it could pass for a paddling pool.

Tunde nudged me and whispered, "How can anyone swim laps in that?"

We stood around the edge so we could see the bottom of the pool, where the Dadas' new family crest was depicted in blue tiles. All I could think of, when I saw the crest, were the invitations that Ashake had ordered from me.

"I don't know," I muttered. "But someone had better pay me my money."

Gabeba Baderoon

A South African poet, she is the author of four poetry collections: The History of Intimacy *(2018);* A hundred silences *(2006), which was a finalist for the University of Johannesburg Prize and the Olive Schreiner Award;* The Museum of Ordinary Life *(2005); and* The Dream in the Next Body *(2005).* The Silence Before Speaking, *a volume of her poetry translated into Swedish, was published in 2008. She received the DaimlerChrysler Award for South African Poetry and has held numerous fellowships internationally. She earned a PhD in English from the University of Cape Town, and is currently an Associate Professor of Women's, Gender and Sexuality Studies and African Studies at Pennsylvania State University.*

I forget to look

The photograph of my mother at her desk in the fifties
has been in my purse for twenty years,
its paper faded, browning,
the scalloped edge bent then straightened.

The collar of her dress folds discreetly.
The angle of her neck looks as though
someone has called her from far away.

She was the first in her family to take
the bus from Claremont
up the hill to the university.

At one point during the lectures at medical school,
black students had to pack their notes, get up and walk
past the ascending rows of desks out of the theatre.

Behind the closed door, in an autopsy
black students were not meant to see.
the uncovering and cutting of white skin.

Under the knife, the skin,
the mystery of sameness.

In a world that defined how black and white
could look at each other, touch each other,
my mother looks back, her poise unmarred.

Every time I open my purse,
she is there, so familiar I forget
to look at her.

Old photographs

On my desk is a photograph of you
taken by the woman who loved you then.

In some photos her shadow falls
in the foreground. In this one,
her body is not that far from yours.

Did you hold your head that way
because she loved it?

She is not invisible, not
my enemy, nor even the past.
I think I love the things she loved.

Of all your old photographs, I wanted
this one for its becoming. I think
you were starting to turn your head a little,
your eyes looking slightly to the side.

Was this the beginning of leaving?

War Triptych: Silence, Glory, Love

I. Accounting

The mother asked to stay.
She looked at her silent child.

I was waiting for you.

The quiet of the girl's face was a different quiet.
Her hands lay untouched by death.

The washer of bodies cut
away her long black dress.

Blue prayer beads fell
to the floor in a slow accounting.

The washer of bodies began to sing
a prayer to mothers and daughters.

The mother said,
who will wait for me.

II. Father Receives News His Son Died in the Intifada

When he heard the news, Mr Karim became silent.
He did not look at the cameras,
nor at the people who brought their grief.
He felt a hand slip from his hand,
a small unclasping,
and for that he refused the solace of glory.

III. Always For The First Time

We tell our stories of war like stories
of love, innocent as eggs.

But we will meet memory again
at the wall around our city,

always for the first time.

Doreen Baingana

A Ugandan, her story collection, Tropical Fish, *won an AWP Prize (USA, 2004), and a Commonwealth Prize (2006), and she has twice been a finalist for the Caine Prize for African Writers (2004 and 2005). Her recent honours include a Rockefeller Bellagio Residency (Italy, 2017), and a Miles Morland Scholarship for African Writers (2014). She has also published two children's books, as well as fiction and essays in numerous international journals. A former Managing Editor at Storymoja Africa, and former Chairperson of FEMRITE, she co-founded and runs the Mawazo Africa Writing Institute, based in Entebbe, Uganda.*

Tuk-Tuk Trail to Suya and Stars

You venture into the dark, and it looms over and crowds your every space, thick, even pushes into your earlobes like cotton wool, this hazy yellow darkness choked with harmattan dust. You are boxed in by solid air and you must breathe it in. You enter a tuk-tuk, the most rickety vehicle ever made, as if banged together from the spare parts of small cars, circa 1960 Austins, say, and old saucepans panel-beaten into shape, all loosely held by rusted nails and chains and placed on top of what was once a three-wheeled motorbike, now an ungainly carriage with a snub metal nose. You sit on plastic, which is easy to wipe of dust, but clings like a kid to your sweaty thighs. All the tuk-tuks are painted orange to compete with the river of dirty sand called the road—haze, heat, rush, animal-like hoots and horns. Orange to shock your eyes into seeing.

Still, it provides the miracle every vehicle does: to move, all you have to do is sit, or rather grip desperately, as there are no side walls or doors. The breeze is a blessing; it strokes your cheek and whispers in your ear that you can breathe, it's okay, but not too deeply. No, your lungs cannot suck air out of dust as fish do out of water. This dust that covers everything in a fine grey layer, gauze-like, sticky.

You realize as you climb into the tuk-tuk that with cars you settle quickly, assured that the solid metal case will protect you from the rush of the busy street, the intense heat and light, the potholes underneath, the direct hit of any accident. For a while, driven from A to B, you have the pleasure of giving up responsibility and you sink gratefully into the cushioned bowl of the back seat. Not in a tuk-tuk. You sit, yes, but unsupported, holding tight to the rusty rail, sweaty fingers slipping as you are shaken from side to side like jelly, shaken inside out. You are in a blender, a coffee grinder, an angry machine that jostles and jangles you. It sets your stomach churning and everything in it is squeezed and kneaded and turns to shit, straining to escape with every hard bump, your ass clenched tight. Oops, you piss in your pants as the tuk-tuk driver swerves to avoid potholes the size and shape of dried ponds. His dark ball of a head bobs in front of you as he does the same desperate bouncing you do: the tuk-tuk dance.

It's not all dance. It's real danger, as each swerve to avoid falling into a pothole leads to a motorbike coming straight at you. It's as if the whole point of being on the road is to almost crash into the next car, okada, bicycle, just missing by a thread's breadth to show off your skill, saying, We're here, full-limbed, we ain't dead yet, okay, here we go again! Respect is only for huge lumbering lorries, ancient blind dinosaurs that will not, cannot swerve out of your way, so you slow down and slide to the side: a momentary bow of acknowledgement.

You hiccup.

Everything else rushes at you, even the dusty, smoking yellow night, a living thing, a sister to the street, which is not a straight line but a maze. Is it really lit by candle light? Yes, and lamps, lanterns; words that sound so Medieval but are very much here and now, gleaming, grinning like a mouth with missing teeth. What gapes through the yellow-black gaps? What flashes past your dust-teared eyes? Endless shacks made from wooden planks and strips of corrugated iron slapped together, as ugly as a rubbish dump, that form a long crooked line that hugs the crooked road. The kiosks are filled with the cheapest that Nigeria and China have to offer: shiny nylon shirts, brightly coloured packets of Sunlight soap, curry powder, St Louis cubed sugar (all the way from France?), brand new bicycle wheels wrapped tightly around with white, black, and blue polythene strips and hung up on a pole in a pattern of open-mouthed Os, TVs and electric fans, dirty jars of chewing-gum, and shelf upon shelf of brightly coloured packages and boxes, with sacks of grain below. To you it's all jumbled up, but obviously there's some kind of order because it is repeated at every single kiosk, each guarded in front by a fire and frying-pan where starchy snacks bubble and pop.

Your eyes rove on. Bare bulbs reveal a family of half-naked babies and toddlers crawling and playing among the wares. No sissy eight-o'clock-it's-bedtime-let's-take-you-home, no; it's finally cool enough to be outside. Parents are splayed on plastic chairs nearby, their patterned akara prints showing boldly through the dusk after winning the day's competition against the sun. Some men are manly enough to wear lace, long shirts and trousers of it, while the women boast headscarves shaped like huge birds' open wings, and they all, all have cheeks lovingly scrawled by deep tiger claws, three on each side. A grandma sits wide-legged, her long skirt pulled above the knee as she leans over a red basin, peeling or washing, you can't tell which. Skinny yellow legs, chicken-like. Your shock is as fleeting as your tuk-tuk ride, and on you go, onwards, since you can't join the family.

There is a point to your night-time tuk-tuk journey: suya.

You stop by an open street stand, called there by a bare bulb swinging and shining like goodness over a huge enamel plate, as wide as a wheel, piled high with meat, as every plate should be. A cow's healthy thigh becomes a hunk of raw flesh, cut into thin slabs that are caressed and squeezed and pampered with ginger, curry powder, salt, who knows what other spices, and chili pepper, of course—this is Nigeria after all—coated with palm oil and groundnut paste, pierced with a skewer and, crying red tears, thrown over the fire to roast. What you get is thick, meaty, fire-red butterfly wings spotted with yellow chili seeds: suya.

The cook is a tall, heavy, dark man whose sweating forehead—as if more drama were needed—is speckled pink and grey. Either hot oil splashed up and seared off his skin, or he was born that way, and this somehow makes your meat spicier. His long-fingered hands are deft from years of slicing and spicing and roasting; his fingers, faster than your eyes, perform a light dance you watch greedily, because this meat is for you, as are the added ginger powder and chopped raw tomato and onion on the side. Who cares what your mouth will smell like tonight, tomorrow? You also refuse to think of the garnish of germs that have been squirming and feasting, shitting and multiplying all over your meat just before it is once again sizzled hot over the smoking charcoal. Your share is diced up and wrapped in newspaper, and of course it doesn't matter to you which chief or senator's face or subsidy scandal will soon be soggy with grease.

Back in the tuk-tuk, your load (their word for baggage, pronounced "loot") held tight in one hand, the other grasping the tuk-tuk railing, you race, jiggle, bounce, shake, rattle your way back, now in search of beer, a Star, the coldest, crispiest, liquid opposite of suya—its perfect partner.

You go somewhere with fuji and juju music and not too much light, The Club, whose design and décor is "abandoned building", and whose toilet is the rubbish-strewn back yard. An irritated rat scurries away as your piss just misses an empty Sprite bottle, but the grey-brown sand between your feet generously accepts it.

All this is preamble. You sit, eat, and suddenly your mama's *Don't talk with food in your mouth, you!* makes sense. Chew, sip, love, and be silent. Give in, as Pépé kisses your lips and stings your tongue and bites you in the belly; makes you groan with his intensity. Sick love, the kind that's so bad for you, you can't give it up. Once you've had suya, like sex, you can't not have it again. When you become dictator, you will decree that all food must burn tongues and curdle stomachs, must shoot a hole through the head like Pépé's cool green cousin, Wasabi. Food must announce its way down your throat, through your curled tunnel of intestines, circling and gurgling, and finally, kiss again your sweet asshole. So this is what nerve endings are for.

Spicy hot is sweet: a tongue and mind twister, a dark Iseyin street.

Ellen Banda-Aaku

Born in Zambia, she is a writer, radio drama producer and documentary film-maker from Zambia, based between Zambia and the UK. She has published seven books for children and two novels and has produced a radio drama and film documentary. Her first book for children, Wandi's Little Voice, *won the 2004 Macmillan's Writers Prize for Africa. Her short story "Sozi's Box" won the 2007 Commonwealth Short Story Competition in 2007. Her work has appeared in anthologies published in Australia, South Africa, the UK and the US. Her first novel,* Patchwork, *won the Penguin Prize for African Writing and was shortlisted for the 2012 Commonwealth Book Prize. In 2012 she was awarded the Zambia Arts Council Ngoma Chairperson's Award for her achievements in the field of literature. She is patron of* The Pelican Post, *a charity dedicated to donating books to schools in Africa.*

87 Tangmere Court

My father insists on holding my hand. His grip is so strong I feel my fingers numbing in the red gloves Mama bought me from the secondhand shop on the high street. We're hurrying along the walkway that cuts across the green on the estate where

Mama lives. At the metal door Dad presses number eighty-seven and says, into the intercom, "Mum, it's me."

The door buzzes open and we walk to the lift. Dad is still holding on to my hand, half-humming, half-grunting a tune I can't make out. I think like me he feels as if there's a heavy stone in his stomach because I know this is not what he wants for Mama.

We step into the lift, I press five and the doors slide shut. Scattered on the floor are chips—the thick-cut ones sold in fish-and-chip shops. There's also a flattened Coke can and a small puddle. The lift smells of pee as it does on Monday mornings; by midday when the cleaners have been it will smell of the hospital where Papa's body was taken after he died. I shake my hand free of Dad's to pull off my glove and somehow I drop it in the puddle.

"Leave it," Dad says reaching for my hand again.

I've ridden in this lift lots of times since I was a baby. My earliest memories are of Dad lifting me to press button five. As I grew a little older, I stood on tiptoe to reach it. Now I am taller than the number pad.

Dad takes deep breaths before rapping his knuckles on Mama's front door. It flies open instantly and Mama stands before us with a wide smile.

"You're in good time!" Mama is in good spirits. Dad exhales and releases my hand.

That Mama is ready is a good sign. Her white hair is tucked away under a short black afro wig and she has on her beige coat with a chocolate fur collar buttoned up to her neck.

The inside of 87 Tangmere Court is as warm as an oven, but Mama's flat no longer smells of freshly baked bread or fried plantain. That all changed the day she put a pot of rice on the stove to boil and then went out shopping on the high street. She returned to smoke billowing from the kitchen window and blackened walls. The house smelt of burnt rice for weeks. Then Uncle Simi removed the stove to stop Mama cooking.

The landing is empty apart from two black bulging suitcases. Papa's black umbrella hangs on the rail. It's strange to see Mama's place empty. Till today, it was full of furniture and boxes of stuff to take back home.

I follow Mama into the living-room, only then noticing she has her navy shoes on the wrong feet. I turn to Dad as his eyes too fall on the shoes. Neither of us says anything.

Mama's living-room looks spacious without the thick navy curtains, the heavy bookcase stacked with big books, the sofas and side-tables, the television stand and the gold-framed portraits on the wall. Only the navy carpet with yellow diamond shapes that Uncle Simi hammered to the floor remains, and in the centre of the room a small table on which Mama's handbag is perched.

Mama is talking nonstop. She's been listening to the radio and there's a build-up of traffic so we might have to leave early for the airport. Airport? My stomach churns. I realise why she's in high spirits. Dad keeps very quiet. Mama carries on talking. She's decided to leave the wall clock and the welcome mat for the next occupants. The new tenants will probably appreciate a copper clock shaped like Africa because it's different. "I can always get another one. There are plenty back home," Mama says.

Dad grunts gently in response, not wanting to agree or disagree.

From the balcony he carries in two plastic chairs with rusty metal legs. For years they have lived stacked on the balcony, until a lightbulb needs changing or the ceiling painting, or there are more visitors than sofa space. He asks Mama to sit, and he sits heavily on the chair splattered with dried paint. He keeps checking his watch. I fear Mama will notice and be anxious.

"So should Papa and I expect you at Christmas?" Mama asks, looking at me as she used to before. Today she seems both the old and the new Mama: she remembers me but has forgotten that Papa is no longer with us. I've settled myself on the carpet with my back against the radiator.

"Yes, Mama," I say brightly, though something flutters inside my tummy.

Dad shifts uncomfortably without looking at me. His right leg is shaking, as if he's in a hurry to go somewhere.

"Great!" Mama picks up her handbag and starts rummaging through it. "Your Papa will be pleased to see you," she says, taking out a set of keys. "Here they are. I thought I'd lost them."

"Mum, you won't be needing those," Dad says.

The Africa-shaped clock chimes ten, distracting Mama. "What time will the car be here?"

"Any minute now," Dad says.

A lump forms in my throat. Soon we'll be leaving 87 Tangmere Court. I can't imagine never coming here again. It's been Mama's home for years.

She and Papa moved in twenty years ago when he was exiled from his country. And from the moment they arrived in the UK, she was planning for the day she would return home. To her house with six bedrooms and two living-rooms, one the size of the entire floor area of the flat. Her house with its five acres of land where she grew Chinese cabbage and tomatoes and spring onions and sweet potatoes and maize, depending on the time of the year. Home where she said the sun shone fiercely twelve hours a day and children younger than me weave between cars selling sachets of iced water from metal basins balanced on their heads. For twenty years Mama bought stuff to take home, "when the cruel dictator who kicked your Papa out of the country is no longer in power," she always said.

It's hard to believe I am seeing the water stain on the ceiling for the last time. It's a stain Uncle Simi has painted over, year after year, but it returns after a few months. The yellow starfish stain reappeared even after Mama took the council to the Arbitrator, who ruled that she be paid for the inconvenience of having to repaint since the council wouldn't fix the leak in the flat above. But the last time Mama didn't seem to notice. That was about the time she started to change. The change was gradual but

I noticed first because I spent a lot of time with her. Her place was near the school I went to, so I saw her every day.

"Strange how?" Dad asked when I said that Mama was behaving strangely.

I told him she kept forgetting things.

"It's called old age," Dad said, laughing. "One day we'll all get there."

Now two years later, Dad knows it's something more serious than old age.

"By the way," Mama asks again, "did you confirm my arrival time to your father?"

Dad grunts and mumbles something.

"Or will it be Mususu picking me up?"

Dad's leg shakes more at Mama's mention of Mususu, whom I know about from her stories of home. He was the loyal family driver who risked his life for his employers. Mama told of how she and Papa one night hid hunched under two big upturned drums in Mususu's small kitchen as soldiers tore through the main house looking for Papa. When they didn't find him they left and a neighbour kindly offered his car. It was Mususu who drove Papa and Mama six hours to the border so they could escape to the neighbouring country.

"I've bought Mususu a shirt and a watch," Mama says, forgetting that she lost contact with Mususu over ten years ago. "Let me open the case to show you."

"It's OK, Mum." Dad stands and glances at his watch. "There's no time."

I managed to convince Mama and Papa that at nine years old I was grown-up enough to walk to and from school by myself. I had begun to feel embarrassed at Mama turning up at the school gate in her hat and long coat, sometimes with Papa. They looked odd among the other children's parents, who wore jogging bottoms and trainers, and occasionally while waiting smoked or used the F word.

Mama said the UK was not like home, where children were safe, and polite, and respected elders. But Mum insisted I was old enough to walk on my own. "Tell your mother," she said to Dad, "that in every part of the world, there is peace and danger. Kondani is growing up. They can't go on treating her like an egg."

So on Mum's orders, Dad convinced his parents to allow me to walk home alone.

One day six months later as I let myself in after school, I heard Mama talking. She was on the balcony tending her plants. I went into the living-room and there was Papa sitting rigidly in his high-back chair. His black skin had a grey tinge. He had a dot of froth in the crack of his mouth on both sides. Other than that, he could have been sleeping.

I had never seen a dead man but one look and I knew for sure Papa was dead. And right there in the living-room, I felt warm pee trickling down my legs.

I didn't know which to do first: tell Mama that Papa was dead, call Dad, or go to the bathroom. I decided to call Dad. Still wearing my backpack, I stepped over Papa's outstretched legs, picked up the cordless phone and took it to the bathroom. As I closed the door I could hear Mama talking to herself on the balcony.

I dialled the emergency numbers in the order Mama had stored them on her phone. Dad didn't pick up. Uncle Simi did. I whispered that Papa was dead but Mama didn't know. He told me he was on his way and would call an ambulance. He asked me to go downstairs and sit with a neighbour.

After Papa died, Mama would grieve one day, act as if he were alive the next. Mum enrolled me in a school nearer to our house.

I saw Mama one Saturday a month when it was Dad's turn to deliver food from a woman hired to cook for her. We would pack the lunchboxes into Mama's freezer. She complained that the food was too oily, too salty, too dry, but her children were adamant; she was not getting her stove back.

The visits to Mama made me sad. The two things she loved most, Papa and cooking, had been taken from her and I think it made her confused. She would laugh at things that were not funny and get angry at small things. Then one Sunday Dad and I passed by to visit.

Dad was halfway through taking off his coat, when Mama asked, "Junior, who is this child?"

I will never forget the shock on Dad's face. He pulled his coat back on and, not even checking the fridge, excused himself to go to the shop to buy milk. Left me with Mama, who eyed me suspiciously. She did not ask about school. Or tell me not to hunch my back because ladies sat up straight. She didn't tell funny stories like the one about once imagining she would marry Mohammed Ali or Nelson Mandela but in Papa ended up with Ali and Mandela rolled into one, so stuff them both. That day Mama did not talk to me.

When Dad returned, his eyes were red. He put the milk in the fridge and told Mama we were leaving. As we walked to the lift, Mama called Dad back. She stood in the doorway and pointed at me:

"The girl has stolen my TV remote. It was on the table, now it's gone."

Dad looked from her to me. "Mama, this is Kondani!" Dad spoke loudly, his face creased in frustration. "You know she wouldn't take anything without permission!"

I worried that the neighbours would come out. I didn't want them to know what was happening to Mama. I pleaded with Dad that we leave.

We left her standing defiantly there, arms folded across her chest.

Dad, Aunt Malaika and Uncle Simi had conversations that ended with: *Well, let's wait and see*. Because sometimes the old Mama returned and all would be well.

They argued over what to do. Dad wanted her to stay in her flat where the familiarity would comfort her; a live-in carer could be hired. But Aunt Malaika felt Mama would be lonely and suggested Mama stay with her. The brothers disagreed; Aunt Malaika was never at home, so Mama would be alone anyway. Then Mum upset Dad by suggesting Mama was put in a care-home. Dad said homes were not African. That would be like abandoning Mama. People would say they had failed to look after their mother.

"Who minds what people think?" Mum said. "It's about her being somewhere she can be cared for."

Late one night the police knocked on our door. Mama had been found wandering in the streets. She couldn't remember her address but asked the police to call her son. Luckily she remembered Dad's name.

After that incident Mama's children were forced to come together to resolve the situation.

In the living-room Mama is rattling on about home and things she's bought for Papa when the doorbell rings. Dad springs up, grabs one of the cases and starts wheeling it out. He asks me to wait with Mama, who announces that she needs the bathroom.

As I wait, I look around one last time. I remember the flat with light-blue walls, then white, then cream. I go into the bedroom that used to be mine. A last look through the window. The view has changed; new apartment blocks and parking spaces have shrunk the green play area.

Dad returns for the second case and we exit 87 Tangmere Court for the last time. We troop along the corridor, me carrying Papa's umbrella, Dad wheeling the case and Mama now wearing a hat atop her wig, her shoes still on the wrong feet. We enter the lift, for the last time. It smells of bleach and my glove is gone. The lump in my throat grows bigger. I wonder if Dad feels the same way.

Uncle Simi gives me a bear hug when we get to where he is parked. He delves into his pockets for something to give me, a habit he has not outgrown even though I'm a big girl now. He hands me half a roll of mints. Dad embraces his brother. They are so different. Dad tall, slim, clean-shaven; Uncle Simi like a big teddy bear, with long thick dreadlocks that used to irritate the old Mama.

A white lady steps forward and introduces herself. "And you must be Mercy," she says to Mama.

Mama smiles, "Hello, are you accompanying us to the airport?"

There's a silence. Uncle Simi and Dad avoid looking at one another.

"Kondani, say goodbye to Mama," Dad urges. I'm not sure if I see tears in his eyes.

Mama looks at me the way the old Mama did. "Be a good girl, OK? I can't wait for you to come and see for yourself what I've been telling you about home." She squeezes me against her soft wool coat, then lets go and says with a smile, "Don't worry. When you come, Papa and I will meet you at the airport."

I nod. Grunt gently. Like Dad, I don't agree or disagree. Today she's more of the old Mama than the new one. It worries me because the old Mama may realise what's happening.

That she's not going home but to a place where she can be cared for.

Suddenly, after months of praying for my old Mama, I want the new one. The new Mama who doesn't know that she will never go back home. Because I think it's best for Mama not to know.

Ama Biney

A Pan-Africanist scholar-activist with more than 20 years' teaching experience in the fields of African history and politics, she has taught courses in African history, Caribbean history and African American history. She is the author of The Political and Social Thought of Kwame Nkrumah *(2011), and compiled* Speaking Truth to Power: Selected Pan-African Postcards of Tajudeen Abdul-Raheem *(2010) with fellow Pan-Africanist Prof. Adebayo Olukoshi. She was editor of the Pan-African weekly electronic newsletter,* Pambazuka News *from 2012 to 2014. Currently she is an independent scholar engaging in Steve Biko's mantra of writing what she likes.*

Creating the New Man in Africa

Imagine a poster with the words: "New men wanted in Africa!" Most people would find the statement amusing, but that is what Africa urgently needs. This specific demand has to be part of a radical transformation in attitudes and outlooks that the continent must undergo, alongside fundamental socio-economic development as the twenty-first century continues to unfold.

Thomas Sankara, the Burkinabé revolutionary who was committed to socio-economic and political change in his country, had the courage to state that the waging of revolution would also "upset the relations of authority between men and women and force each to *rethink the nature of both*" (emphasis mine). He was also correct in declaring that "… the revolution cannot triumph without the genuine emancipation of women." Equally, I would like to argue that the revolution cannot triumph without a transformation in the thinking, mentality, attitudes, or consciousness of African men/boys. And for that to happen, we need to address male domination in African societies.

Human beings are taught not to question male domination. Both boys and girls are socialised into accepting that boys are to be loud and girls are to be quiet.

Boys can be angry and aggressive and girls are allowed to cry and show a "soft" and nurturing side.

Boys can be inquisitive and ask questions, while girls are expected to be passive and submissive. Boys and men cannot cry, for that is being "emotional", which only girls and women are allowed to be. These are some of the gendered stereotypes and expectations of how boys/men and girls/women are expected to behave in Africa (and around much of the globe). In academia, the term employed to describe this phenomenon of male superiority and female inferiority is "patriarchy".

In Africa, many cultural expectations are ingrained through socialisation and unquestioned cultural customs and practices to reinforce patriarchy and gendered expectations. Patriarchy is a system of ideas that intersects with other forms of domination such as class, homophobia, sizeism and racism. Patriarchy is invisible; it is like the air we breathe in that we do not recognise or feel its presence; yet it surrounds us and is unconsciously (and consciously) ingrained in our thought patterns and actions. Patriarchy manifests itself in Africa in many ways, such as the predominance of male political leaders, despite African Union protocols and the fact that several African parliaments, including Rwanda, Mozambique, Uganda and Senegal, have a large number of female parliamentarians. Men continue to disproportionately occupy top leadership positions; the bulk of agricultural work in Africa is carried out by women in the rural areas and it is women who dominate the informal economy, while the "formal" economy is dominated by African men. Conflict in Africa, particularly war, is waged by men and when we see images of peace negotiations it is two men from opposing sides and not women that we see shaking hands. Women are absent in photo-ops in all peace negotiations (unless it is a woman who is behind the camera taking the shot? But I doubt it). Yet, who creates and fuels war?

We need, therefore, to creatively "rethink"—as Sankara urges us—the nature of what it means to be male and female. But more importantly, we must begin to bring up our children differently in a de-patriarchal manner, in which we do not, for example, scold boys for crying and girls for being "tom-boyish" or "too forward" in being outspoken in their views in school or outside of school. This will be a long-term undertaking that takes courage and commitment by parents, educators and the community.

Rethinking the nature of "male" and "female", or "depatriarchalizing society", also requires men who are genuine and serious about radical transformation to re-evaluate their own behaviour and thought patterns in respect to empathy and ethical considerations. For most African men (to generalize here) are consciously or unconsciously under societal and cultural pressures to conform to some notion of a "hegemonic masculinity"—that is, an African man is aggressive, strong, competitive, in control, dominant and active. These are cultural ideas that are variously expressed in the myriad diverse cultures that make up the African continent. Girls/women are expected to embody the socially valued behaviours of being nurturing, emotional, subordinate, passive, gentle, and receptive.

In order to create new African men, a process of consciousness-raising, or the journey of men increasing their self-awareness of patriarchy or male domination, is one that has to operate on a number of levels. It must operate on a societal level, whereby those progressive elements in the media, the church, mosque, trade unions and other institutions take up the issue not only in rhetorical policy declarations but in their actions and training within their institutions. Another level is that of the family, as the social unit in which human beings are born. The family needs to socialise boys and girls differently. This extends to the wider extended family and peer group who are also very influential in legitimating negative and positive behaviour, norms and values.

It will involve men/boys having the courage and confidence to confront the sexist/patriarchal views and attitudes of other boys and men, whether openly or on a one-to-one basis. An example of this is when men/boys hold each other accountable for their language and behaviour. Such men need to provide new models of what a "real man" looks like, i.e. not one who is "macho", "tough", "silent" and unable to express his emotions. Related to this is the fact that such men/boys should embody emotional literacy. Generally, most men lack emotional engagement, emotional caretaking and relational skills, which are too often qualities and skills relegated to the domain of women. Hence, boys/men growing up are only able to express rage and anger, which often lead to domestic abuse and violence, and in countries where there is conflict it is channelled into armed militaries and rape/sexual assault of women (as in the DRC and elsewhere).

New men are able to experience empathy, to care for others, show compassion and discuss their emotions openly. The African-American cultural critic and feminist bell hooks defines a "feminist masculinity" as comprising "integrity, self-love, emotional awareness, assertiveness" and relational skills. The adverse impact of patriarchy is that men and boys are forced to wear a mask concealing their inner selves and denying their emotions. The requirement by a patriarchal and capitalist society compartmentalizes the psyche, thoughts, and actions, thereby creating schizoid humans. In the Western world, for example in the UK, this has led to a high incidence of mental illness and suicides among males.

Since there is no blueprint for creating a new non-sexist, anti-imperialist, anti-capitalist world, our strategies will be based on an evolving basis of theory and practice. One first and crucial step must involve men remaining silent and genuinely listening to the women around them.

Malorie Blackman

She has written more than 60 books for children and young adults, including the Noughts and Crosses *series of novels (*Noughts and Crosses *won the Red House FCBG Children's Book Award as well as being included in the top 100 of the BBC Big Read),* Cloud Busting *(winner of the Smarties Silver Award, 2004),* Thief *(winner of the Young Telegraph/Fully Booked Award, 1996),* Hacker *(winner of the WH Smith's Children's Book Award, 1992, and the Young Telegraph/Gimme 5 Award for best children's book of the year, 2005).* Her latest book is Chasing the Stars, *a science-fiction thriller. She is a scriptwriting graduate of the National Film and Television School. As well as writing original and adapted drama scripts for TV, she also regularly wrote for CBBC's Byker Grove. In 2005, she was honoured with the Eleanor Farjeon Award in recognition of her distinguished contribution to the world of children's books. In 2008, she was awarded an OBE for her services to Children's Literature. She was the UK Children's Laureate for 2013–15.*

Letters

Dear Daughter,

Well, here we are again. Another letter. I've written a number of them now, all waiting for when I'm no longer here but you still are. So many times, I've wanted to sit you down and just talk to you about anything and everything. Talk until my throat is hoarse and my lungs are burning, but I'm too old for that and you're too young.

So here's the compromise. A book of letters. With my love. And in this particular letter, I want to share with you the worst day of my life which was simultaneously the best thing that ever happened to me.

It happened one evening when I was eighteen. Midway through the first term of my first year at college. I'd never been away from home that long before and I was loving it. I was already broke, about fifty pounds to my name to see me through the rest of the term but what did that matter? Course apart, I was enjoying myself and nothing but good was going to rock my world.

Until one evening in early October, when everything changed. I sat on my bed in my room as a pain like an iron band around my waist began to grip and tighten. And with each moment, the band grew tighter, slicing into me.

Agony, intense and crippling soon squeezed my insides. Relentless. Excruciating. Burning fingers of pain licked through me like nothing I'd ever felt before.

Looking back at that moment, I struggle to remember anything else about that day. What had I had for breakfast? For lunch? What had I done with my morning, my afternoon? The rest of the day isn't just a blur, it's a blank. The memory of that date doesn't start until the slow, fiery grip of the pain in my insides as the October sun began to set outside my window.

I searched through my desk drawer for some painkillers—aspirin, paracetamol, anything would do—even though I knew I didn't have any and it was futile. But maybe my guardian angel would place some in there and I could persuade myself I'd just forgotten about them. Nothing doing. Frustrated, I slammed the drawer shut. Pain dictated that every action, sound, even the light was shard sharp, hard, amplified.

Flinging open my room door, I staggered across the hallway to my friend Lorraine's room and banged on her door. We occupied the last two rooms opposite each other at the end of the corridor. The hall of residence that was now our home was basic to say the least. Tiny all-purpose bedrooms contained only a single bed and a desk and the bathroom and toilets were located at the far end of the corridor.

Lorraine's door finally opened.

"Lorraine, d'you h-have any aspirin?"

The pain that was gripping me from the lower abdomen up had reached high enough to take hold of my voice, stifling my words until they were barely a whisper.

"Lori! Are you all right? No, I'm sorry, I don't have any," Lorraine said, her eyes growing wider with concern. "Are you okay?"

I nodded my way through the obvious lie. Hands against the wall, I tried to make it back to my room. Two steps, then I turned, sliding down the wall as my body gave in and gave out and the pain took over completely.

A series of images after that. A scream. People. Paramedics. Lifted. An ambulance. Lights flashing—through the windows? Sirens? Wheeled into hospital. People standing over me.

Until I was lying on a bed, my head slightly raised and doctors and nurses bustling around me. I was in control of nothing.

Mr Sing, one of the surgeons standing over me, said to his colleague, "It's unusual to see this disease around here."

Around here? What was he talking about? *Who* was he talking about? What was going on?

I tried to speak but there was something hard in my mouth. I spat it out, glancing down at the rubber block that hit my chest then rested still.

"What disease? What disease?" I asked.

Looking back, the memory of the shocked faces, the stunned silence around me still makes me smile.

But not on that date and not for a long time afterwards.

"We weren't talking about you," said the other surgeon, Mr Crew. "We were talking about someone else. Another case."

A quick nod from Mr Swift to someone behind me. A nurse picked up the rubber bung from my chest and pushed it back into my mouth. Glances and silence between those around me.

They're lying.

Even in my spaced out state I knew that. I wanted to ask more, but the room began to fade.

Darkness.

Silence.

Nothing.

Until the following afternoon.

Lorraine came to visit me. She sat down by my bed and watched me as I tried to suppress yet another cough which felt like it would surely rip out my stitches, tearing my abdomen in two.

Lorraine took a deep breath. "Lori, they took out your appendix."

Did they? Nice of someone to tell me. A doctor had yet to sit down and speak to me about anything. I hadn't had a conversation with anyone medical since my arrival. At least that explained the pain in my abdomen and the stitches.

Lorraine took a deep breath. "Look, Lori. You do know you've got Sickle Cell, right?"

I stared at Lorraine. "I've got what?"

"Sickle Cell. The doctor told me you have Sickle Cell."

Sickle Cell... Something I'd barely even heard of. What was it? What did it mean? And how dare they tell Lorraine without telling me first? How dare they?

Eventually Lorraine left and I lay still, my eyes closed, shell-shocked.

That's how I fell asleep.

That's how I woke up.

My eyes still closed, two words laced with shards of glass and rusty nails spun round uncontrollably in my head.

Sickle Cell...

Voices—

A bed away but approaching. I briefly opened my eyes only to shut them almost immediately. A male doctor and a female nurse stood at the foot of my bed.

"Ah, yes," said the Doctor. "Interesting case."

"The Sickle Cell patient?"

"Indeed. She had her appendix removed yesterday. It's a shame about this one. With her Sickle Cell, she'll be dead by thirty."

Jesus Christ—

Dead by thirty.

I lay in the bed, and it was like having my neck in a guillotine, waiting for the blade to fall. All I could think was I'm going to die—before I'm thirty years old. And at eighteen, thirty suddenly didn't seem so far away after all.

The clock was ticking.

Maybe that's the moment I developed a real loathing for the sound of ticking clocks and watches. Listening as they count down the hours, the minutes. Count down my life.

For years after that, it became all about making money. Getting a good job. Travelling the world. It wasn't until my mid-twenties that I realised my priorities were skewed.

What good would money do me when I was dead?

And, Daughter, do you know the thought that terrified me the most?

Kicking the bucket and knowing that for all the good I'd done in the world, I might as well not have been born at all. Time for not just a career change but a life change, but what to do? Maybe I should go back to my old dream of being a teacher? But would I have the stamina? Or maybe train to be a nurse? But dealing with other people's vomit and poo? Nah! I wouldn't be good with that aspect of the job.

With the very few years I reckoned I had left, I wanted to do something meaning-ful with my life, something that would make me spring out of bed each morning and greet the day with smile. Something that wasn't just for myself but for others too. Something that would allow me to connect and communicate with others.

I knew I needed to do something more creative, more fulfilling. But what?

Writing.

Daughter, when I tell people that I wrote eight to ten books over the course of two years and received eighty-two rejection letters before a publisher finally said yes, I'm always met with gasps of amazement and I get asked, what kept you going?

Well, I had nothing to fear because I had nothing to lose. I was going to try and get published right up until the day I died. I realised in my twenties that there is something worse than failing and that's being too afraid to even try.

I'm lucky. I found the perfect career for me—challenging, creative, fulfilling. An author.

Now here's the thing: if it hadn't been for the doctor and nurse at the foot of my bed stating I would be dead by the age of thirty, I'd still be in computing. I'd've hit the glass ceiling long ago and would be biding my time until I retired. I'd be miserable with wondering if I could've done something else, something *more* with my life.

If it hadn't been for that doctor and nurse at the foot of my bed stating my life was going to end, my life wouldn't have begun. I would've been operating on auto-pilot. Life is too precious to go through it on auto-pilot.

So what I thought for too many wasted years was the very worst day of my life—overhearing that I was going to die…well, it turns out it was the very best day of my life.

It made me unafraid to take a chance, to take a risk for something better, something *more*. It made me stubborn enough to never take no for an answer. It made me fearless enough to not take on board those who would tell me no, or I couldn't, or I shouldn't, or what I wanted wasn't for me.

Now here's the thing, only two things are guaranteed in this life. Taxes—unless you're a large conglomerate with good accountants—and death.

So, Daughter, here are some of the things I have learnt over the years and some of the things I know to be true:

Never let anyone persuade you that being kind is a weakness. It is not.

Never let yourself be persuaded that money, power, possessions are more important than friends and family, love and sharing your life unselfishly. As Octavia Butler said in *Parable of the Talents*— "Kindness eases change. Love quiets fear."

Never let anyone persuade you that ignorance is the new smart—it most assuredly isn't.

Be suspicious and more of those who would treat the gaining of knowledge and learning as something only the privileged few should have or can enjoy.

If you fall down or get knocked down seven times, get up eight.

As Denzel Washington said: "Without commitment, you'll never start. But more importantly, without consistency, you'll never finish."

Never believe you're too old or know too much to learn more.

Cultivate friends who embrace the real you, not the show you.

Be wary of friends and lovers who are more interested in what you have around you, rather than who you are inside.

Don't live your life on or for social media. It will mess up your head.

Don't forget to look up at the sky once in a while and watch the clouds or wonder at the stars.

Don't forget to stop and smell the flowers.

Don't be afraid to bathe in the laughter of children, don't be too afraid to shed and share tears.

Enjoy life. It's not a dress rehearsal.

Live.

Akosua Busia

Dividing her time between Ghana, where she was born, and the US, she is well known for a range of work that includes being an actress (notable for her role as Nettie in the Stephen Spielberg film The Color Purple, *based on Alice Walker's novel), a novelist (*The Seasons of Beento Blackbird, *1997), a screenwriter (*Beloved, *the 1988 film adaptation of Toni Morrison's Pulitzer Prize-winning novel), a poet/ lyricist ("Moon Blue", recorded by Stevie Wonder) and a director (*The Prof: A Man Remembered*). She is the youngest daughter of the Right Honorable Dr. Kofi Abrefa Busia, former Prime Minister of Ghana, and former First Lady, Mrs Naa Morkor Busia, to whom the following poem is dedicated.*

Mama
April 5th, 1924–January 17th, 2010

She is the centre of my earth
The fire from which I warm my soul
The spark that kindles my heart.
The sustenance I feed my daughter
Is the nourishment I sucked from her once-succulent flesh
Turned brittle-boned, held together by willpower
Mama feeds me still—
She lives—
For us—
She lives

For we cannot bear to see her ascend
Not yet—we will not let her go
Therefore frail-bodied
She calls upon the force with which she once uprooted trees
Replanting them in richer ground to revive them strong
With holes in her bones and nails like steel, painted blood-red
She digs into tomorrow from
Scratching hot tar she carves a road for us to travel
"Walk," she tells us, knowing she has prepared the way.
Celebrating her seventieth birthday we had praised the Lord for her
youthfulness
Fearful now to lose sight of her we bid her lead
"Lord take her not," we pray.
On our behalf she forges forward—out-striding her three-score-years-and-ten
Onward she climbs—
We follow
Eighty claims its toll, she pays with her black hair
Her change is grey—I stroke it—feather-soft between my fingers
Her earth-red scalp yields tender to my touch
I scratch it to her purring
Strand by strand I will her to stay with us from grey to silver-white
Leave us not yet
For still I clutch the strings of your apron
Electric-blue—embroidered with flowers, veiled in white lace
Bought in Mexico, or was it Holland?
I hold in memory to its ribbon
Follow your ample hips swaying in the kitchen
Fleshy and alive as your scones on the rise baking in the oven
Concocted from milk gone sour
You have made something edible of me
I sing you your favourite: "Ave Maria"
"Beautiful," you coo
From the dungeons of political exile you bring forth only goodness
You are Ghana sunshine in a frigid world
The unfamiliar cold made you sniff
But that did not stop you
Frosty foreign winters freezing soil rigid did not stop you
Bunions aching in feet of ice
Did not stop you planting a garden from day to dark
Seeded in pitch-blackness in a once rubble-d yard
In a Cotswold village in Oxfordshire, England
You made vibrant flowers scream full bloom

Evergreen trees, we as children challenged with our height
Now reach tall as houses
Fruit-trees spread branches so deliciously laden
Strangers trespass your garden to witness how you sprinkled nature
And commanded it to grow
Never too exhausted to water those you love, I am cultivated by your sweat
Drop by drop you formed my core
I drank holy secrets from the umbilical cord from which you fed me.
In Heaven I will remember all mysteries and find you
You will be my first knock-knocking on a door
I will know your house by the exhilarating scent of clean washing hanging on
the line
For like fragrance of frankincense and myrrh clinging beneath your skin
Freshness has followed you from country to country, house to house
I will know you, Mama
From the sweet sound of your ever-singing praise songs
To the tufts of mud falling from your Dutch clogs in which you gardened
To the click-click of your black-lacquered walking-stick
I will know you
Your health restored—your cane no longer necessary for balance
You will use it to beat-beat rhythm on the streets "paved with gold"
When you march to witness Jesus pull me home
I will know you
Even if your two wedding rings have fallen off
The one Papa took you with
And the one you took off his dead finger to wear until death no longer parts you
Even without those worn bands of gold looping loose below your shrunken
knuckle
I will know you
For I cherish you too much not to know you
I am branded by every firm press of your iron
Your body bearing down to make straight the untidy creases of my life
Papa's clean fresh-pressed pyjamas warming nightly in the airing-cupboard
Bore testimony of your diligence
He will have waited thirty-forty years and more for your arrival
But I am persuaded that seeing the need of us his children
And your children's children
He will be glad you stayed to steady us
He always rested assured
You would look after us
With all your mind
With all your heart

With all your soul
With all your flesh
Even your bones bent on our behalf
Lips, to lips, continent to continent,
They speak of you the same
"Dignified" "Elegant" "Wise" "Gracious"
Grace be unto you, Mama
You are loved
I know you
From the beginning of time
You are love
Everlasting
I will know you
Forever...

Juanita Cox

Born in Nigeria to a Ghanaian mother and English father, she moved to the UK in 1980 and worked for many years as a personal assistant before attaining a BA in Caribbean Studies with Mass Communications from the London Metropolitan University. Her interest in the Caribbean culminated in a PhD on the novels of Guyanese author Edgar Mittelholzer. She is editor of Creole Chips *and Other* Writings *(2018) and has contributed poems to a collection on black womanhood called* Songs of Yemaya *(2015). The poems here were mostly written during 2014–15 while she was living between a coconut estate in the Pomeroon and a residency in Georgetown, Guyana. She currently lives in London and is co-founder/producer of* Guyana SPEAKS *(UK), a monthly forum that offers invited speakers to share their passion for all things Guyanese.*

Guyana Poems

Revolution Lovers

Female frigates ride rising warm currents.
Soar in an arrow of Ms against
Dour dulled-skies. Heads, beaks, bellies and
Breasts powdered white, turn eyes; give accent

To black plumed frocks, and long forked-tails that trail
Magnificent wings like kites in Guyana come
Easter-time.

And a kiskadee freshens up for her partner:
Bathing only in the best pool, she swoops low,
Quick splash-tousle of feathers, she swoops out,
Perches on the greyish-brown back of a poolside
Chair, polishes her beak against the hardened
Plastic until it gleams; sends out a high-pitched
Screech like a straight-tubed saxophone fine-
Tuning itself for practice at the Sea Wall bandstand.

Her pretty feet, hint of waffle-brown, pad along
Terracotta brick-edge. Two glasses of coconut
Water, two straws, two dainty hands and I know
She's dreaming bottles. High walls of painted glass,
Vivid red, maybe. Like her toenails.
And swirls of gold, maybe. Like her hair.
She's a beacon of life, she's his Haitian muse,
His revolution lover.

Stabroek Spring Tide

The view from the Sea Wall,
Yesterday,
Barren endless flat expanse
Of cracked mud plates, deflated
Lavender-pink sails:
Dying men-of-war, purple tentacles
Unsprung by noon.

Tonight silted brown,
The pullulating sea slashes
Against Georgetown's defences,
Lashes over. Passersby
And the days full of bravado,
Drenched.

Wombs of turbulent bracing
Air are strong with scent of salt,
Siphonophores, fish and crustacea.
Mosquitoes are held at bay.

In the blank of night, a plastic bag
Flaps in frantic frip-fret, frip-piti-he,
Frip-fret-frip-piti-he. Rapt crapaud
Sing in high-pitched chirrup
'longside the slap-slash of now
Emboldened sea

The new moon, in occult syzygy, smiles sparingly,
A fishing man ties nylon string and hook 'round chicken's head.
Milk white egrets huddle like blossom in nearby trees,
Filigree plumes blowing like delicate clouds on the move.
Hungry rice-eaters rest their back against pebble-dashed wall,
And find warmth.

All are braced in buoyant expectation.
All know what dem boys say:
"Moon ah run till daylight ketch am".

Akawini Nights

On those nights when the moon reveals
nothing but a thin crocked smile and my eyes
(open or closed) see nothing but a sea of
blackness, the cool sheets of my bed
tip me gently into the cooling black waters
of the Akawini creek and as I float downward
little friendly fish nip at my skin.

And wata getting cold like crab dog's nose.
"Wata wata, yuh guh yuh wata here."
"Berbice?" "West Coas', West Coas'!"
"Come buy yuh no scale fish, here.
One fuh hundred dolla."

The ungodly darkness delights.
Wata running over my naked skin
an' I sinkin' deeper. Legs
entangle with slippery
reeds and lotus flower.
Wata Mamma asks:
"Is wha' yuh doin'? Come
Le' me comb yuh hair."

A black beetle crashes into the side of my face.
Jolts me awake.

My body
drenched by the (s)welter of the night,
an' I itchin' bad.

Mr Loverman tightens his grasp,
his long arms protective. Nothing disturbs his sleep.
I sigh. He snores.
Gently.

Along the Sea Wall

The sun shafts the shore
Parched tongues of cracked-clay
Plead in sibilant whisper:
"Lil' moisture nah… Lil' moisture nah…"
In cruel tease the ocean tosses a wave
And a shoal of silver fish that flail in the heat of living
As the sea with sleight of magician's hand
Leaves them stranded.

While the Fire in Kitty Rages

Early morning grey
A parakeet calls its tropical song,
A London bus thunders over cracked
Asphalt and sends shivers down the spine of a house
While the fire in Kitty rages.

A tired road separates Fat Boy in boxers
From the licks of yellow that laugh at
Black night and set five wooden homes howling.
He holds his hose flaccid:
Its mouth facing hard ground,

Dribbles.

Devastated,
A young woman hugs harried
Belongings, her wet tears dry
Stains on burnt wooden bones
Collapsing. In the warm, under velvet red blanket
Sipping hot coffee from a mug
Tight curls twist into helpless plaits,
Nausea seeps through my body.
How to comprehend the incongruent
Comfort of a cat curled by waking feet,
The folded lip of a long list of shopping
When a parakeet calls its tropical song

While the fire in Kitty rages.

Nana-Ama Danquah

A native of Ghana, she is the author of the acclaimed 1998 memoir Willow Weep for Me: A Black Woman's Journey Through Depression, *and the editor of the anthologies* Becoming American *(2000)*, Shaking the Tree: A Collection of New Fiction and Memoir by Black Women *(2003), and* The Black Body *(2009). She has taught and lectured at many notable institutions, among them the University of Ghana and Antioch College, and has written for publications including the* Washington Post, *the* Village Voice, *the* Los Angeles Times, Allure, Essence, *the* Africa Report, *the* Daily Graphic *and the* Los Angeles Review of Books. *She divides her time between Accra, Ghana and the Coachella Valley in Southern California.*

Saying Goodbye to Mary Danquah

> *It is not a balanced equation if all languages must come to English to mean something.*
> — Ngũgĩ wa Thiong'o

"Nana-Ama!" my mother called out. "Come meet one of your cousins."

We were in Accra, at a family gathering—a wedding or funeral or naming ceremony, I can't say which; they all blur into what, essentially, seems like the same memory of delicious platters of food and an endless array of new kinfolk whose names and exact relationship to me I no longer even try to keep track of. Except this time. This time would be different. This introduction would leave me speechless.

I went and stood beside my mother. She placed a hand on my back, just below my right shoulder. "Nana-Ama," she said, almost giddily, "this is Mary Danquah. And Mary, this is Nana-Ama."

I was instantly confused, thrust into what felt like an alternate reality. I blinked slowly, allowing my lids to stay down for a moment or two longer than usual, then I looked at my "new" cousin. For a moment, I half-expected to see my own face staring back.

"I'm sorry...um...did you...what...um...Mary Danquah?" I mumbled, unable to decide which of my many questions to ask first.

She nodded, said hello.

"That's my name, too," I blurted, drowning in the awkwardness of the moment. Not once in my forty-something years had I ever met another Mary Danquah.

★ ★ ★

In 1973, at the age of six, I emigrated to the United States of America to be with my mother, who had been living there for three years, and my father, who had only recently arrived. One of the many changes that came with living in a new country was the acquisition of a new name. Even though in private, and in the company of other Africans, my parents continued to call me Nana-Ama—my traditional, cultural name—when introducing me to anyone else, they used my Christian name, Mildred. I was not used to being called Mildred.

The practice of conferring Christian, or English, names on African children was introduced by missionaries from the Western world who came to what they considered the Dark Continent for the purpose of religious indoctrination. In many cases, children were required to have Christian names in order to register and attend classes in the missionary-run schools. Usually that meant balancing an existence of duality—using one name when operating within the colonial system and using another when operating within one's native culture.

Mildred was as far removed from my reality as anything could be. I was being called a foreign name in a foreign country by foreign people. It was ill-fitting, and I wore it uncomfortably, resentfully, woefully. It was like sharing a body with a complete stranger. Mildred was an old white woman in Hampstead who enjoyed a proper fry-up—baked beans, tomatoes, blood pudding, triangles of heavily buttered toast—not a Ghanaian girl transplanted to Takoma Park, Maryland, who craved aponkyenkrakra with fufu.

Americans tend to be lazy-tongued, preferring brevity over all else, including beauty. They tend toward names that are familiar and monosyllabic: Sam instead of Samantha, Beth not Elizabeth, Hank for Henry, and Tim not Timothy. Many immigrants to America adopt English names or Anglicize their own. Itzak is transformed to Isaac, Ekaterina to Kate. Chang Kong-Sang becomes Jackie Chan. I didn't want Nana-Ama to become anything else. I wanted to remain who I was, who I'd always been. That, unfortunately, wasn't a viable option.

The children I went to school with weren't just mean, they were hateful. They felt as certain of their superiority as Americans as they did of my supposed inferiority as an African. And they never let me forget it. I was teased mercilessly, called a monkey, an "African booty-scratcher," asked if I had slept in trees back home, and told on a regular basis to "go back to Africa." Imagine if in the midst of all that, I'd asked my terrorizers to call me Nana-Ama!

* * *

It never occurred to me that I could change my name until one of my classmates mentioned something about looking forward to marriage in adulthood in order to drop a surname she disliked. That's when the idea of finding a name to replace Mildred took hold and I began exploring possibilities for reinvention.

The lists I made were ordered alphabetically. Beginning with "A", I jotted down names I thought acceptable, thought I could tolerate, perhaps even learn to like. I listened to their rhythms, the particular cadence people used when saying them. I turned each letter over and around in my mouth, letting my tongue glide over the smooth edges of its vowels. I tried to avoid names with sharp, hard consonants, and names that were an obvious magnet for bullies.

The first name I fell in love with was Amanda. I heard it one day while watching television. A father, square-jawed and towering, had been teased by his daughter, a raven-haired girl with Shirley Temple-style curls. Afterwards, he said, "Oh, Amanda," through an exaggerated smile, then used his fingers to softly brush the girl's bangs from her forehead. There was such tenderness in that scene. We had an Amanda in our school whom everyone liked. She wasn't in my class, but during recess, when we were all outside, I watched the other kids speak to her, their voices carrying the sound of each syllable until it started turning into song.

I'd often pretend that those were scenes from *my* life, that the father in the program was talking to *me*, gently patting *my* afro-puffs; that *my* imaginary circle of friends was singing *my* name in perfect harmony, as though we were in a musical. There were so many things about that name, Amanda, that reminded me of my own name, the one I'd quite unceremoniously been stripped of. Rhythmically, they are the same: *ah-MAN-dah* and *nah-NAH-mah*. They have the same three-syllable beat and, with the exception of "d", all of the letters in Amanda are also in Nana-Ama. I think that's why I didn't, in the end, choose Amanda. I didn't want to be called a name that would forever remind of me of my original name.

Next were the names that began with "z" which, perhaps because it's the last letter in the alphabet, seems to throw a shade of mystery onto everything in which it appears. It wasn't hard to envision myself as a Zelda, Zoe, Zora or even Zeva. Ah, but those names commanded attention; they were bold, the exact opposite of what I was convinced I needed: an ordinary name that would blend in, bring an end to the teasing and make the pain of being me—heavily accented me, dark-skinned black girl me, African me—miraculously disappear.

Eventually, I just returned to my own given names. You see, I had not just one but two Christian names. In addition to Mildred, there was also an English middle name: Mary.

The name felt too deeply rooted in religion for someone such as I, who has always entertained doubt. Nevertheless, I changed the spelling to Meri to make it uniquely my own. For years, that name served me well; it enabled me to move through American society without the additional scrutiny and xenophobia that comes with having a name that's "different", "funny", "difficult to pronounce", a name that announces one's origins.

Meri is a well-constructed persona, a person my circumstances forced me to become. Whereas I despised Mildred, I am rather fond of Meri, but she doesn't reflect the whole truth of who I am, the image I see in the mirror, or the internal voice I hear when I put pen to paper. Because of that, when I began my literary career I published as Meri Nana-Ama Danquah. A few times in my young adulthood, I had tried to do away with Meri altogether but was advised against it by editors, colleagues, and friends. "Nana-Ama is just too…" each one said, citing one or more of the reasons that had previously sent me running in the direction of Meri.

* * *

I don't know the meaning of Mary. It occurred to me while writing this essay to look it up, but I didn't because, frankly, I don't have a burning desire to know. I imagine there is a beautiful story to its origin, one that probably predates the Biblical anecdotes we know of the Madonna and of Magdalene. There's a story behind every name, a narrative much longer than the simple adjectives often given by way of translation, in which so much is often lost.

Tennessee Williams wrote that "the name of a person you love is more than language." As I grew older and less compromising in my love of self, I began to see each reason I had been given for needing an English name for the lie it was. How can Schwarzenegger be easier to pronounce than Nana-Ama? If Americans can learn the proper pronunciation of Liev, Bogosian, Sinead—then why not Nana-Ama? My name also has a significance that surpasses language. It holds its own power and makes its own magic. It ties me to a land, a history, a lineage.

Sometimes we look back on our lives and despite the difficulties of our journey, despite the many times we faltered, it seems as though we were destined to be exactly where we have arrived. As an African writer, it feels strangely like a rite of passage, this decision to dispense with the use of an English name. Chinua Achebe was once Albert. Kofi Awoonor was once George. Ama Ata Aidoo was once Christina. Buchi Emecheta was once Florence. Now I, too, am my authentic self again.

Who best to define the parameters of your authenticity than you?

After I decided to drop Meri and use only Nana-Ama, the first person I told was my friend and mentor, Ngũgĩ wa Thiong'o. We were at lunch, speaking of Africa, specifically of dictatorships and the need for philosopher-kings.

"I don't think Meri is such a bad name," he said with a shrug.

"I hear what you're saying, James," I responded, not missing a beat. I had deliberately called him by the colonial name he was given at his baptism but had very publicly and emphatically rejected as a young writer. We both laughed, and when our eyes met I knew he understood.

★ ★ ★

Mary Danquah is round-faced and soft-spoken, with a presence that stands firmly in its space. We laughed, exchanged pleasantries, expressed shock about sharing the same name.

"I only borrowed it for a bit," I teased.

Just before we said our farewell, I could feel the part of me that had, for so long, been Meri Danquah preparing to leave with her. My cousin and I embraced like two women who knew their meeting was kismet.

"Bye, Mary," I said as she was walking away, her stride purposeful. She turned, waved.

"Bye, Nana-Ama."

There was something about the way she said my name, with pride, with certainty, that made me suddenly feel weightless and free.

Edwidge Danticat

Born in Haiti, she moved to the US when she was 12. She is the author of several books, including Breath, Eyes, Memory *(1994, an Oprah Book Club selection),* Krik? Krak! *(1996, a National Book Award finalist),* The Farming of Bones *(1998),* The Dew Breaker *(2004),* Create Dangerously *(2010), and* Claire of the Sea Light *(2013). She is also the editor of* The Butterfly's Way: Voices from the Haitian Dyaspora in the United States, Best American Essays 2011, Haiti Noir *and* Haiti Noir 2. *She has written six books for children and young adults,* Anacaona *(2005),* Behind the Mountains *(2002),* Eight Days *(2010),* The Last Mapou *(2013),* Mama's Nightingale *(2015), and* Untwine *(2017), as well as a travel narrative,* After the Dance *(2002). Her memoir,* Brother, I'm Dying, *was a 2007 finalist for the National Book Award and a 2008 winner of the National Book Critics Circle Award for autobiography. She was a 2009 MacArthur fellow.*

Dawn After the Tempests

I was heading to Grenada at the same time that the island was hosting the State of the Tourism Industry Conference, one of the region's largest gatherings on the subject. Though the conference was planned before Hurricanes Irma and Maria devastated many Caribbean islands whose economies rely heavily on tourism, the timing seemed prescient. Indeed, on the conference program I scrolled through on the plane were discussions focused on disaster preparedness as well as recovery and rebuilding. I was not going to the conference though, because I am not a tourism expert.

The people sitting on either side of me on the plane were not tourism experts either. They were tourists, two young American couples on their honeymoons. After listening to them exchange wedding stories, I turned to the poet and essayist Audre Lorde's "Grenada Revisited: An Interim Report", an essay she wrote a few weeks after the 1983 United States' invasion of her parents' homeland.

I had read Lorde's essay many times before—it's the last chapter of her seminal 1984 collection *Sister Outsider*—but I wanted to read it again before seeing Grenada for the first time.

That we landed at Maurice Bishop International Airport, which is named after the former Prime Minister of Grenada who was assassinated six days before the start of the US invasion, might have intrigued Lorde. I felt her begin this journey with me as I walked down the airplane steps, the sun that is only this sparkling bright in the Caribbean beaming down on my face.

"The first time I came to Grenada I came seeking 'home,'" began Lorde's essay of her 1978 visit. She had flown into the now closed Pearl's Airport in Grenville on the northeastern coast of the island. Back then, there was one paved road, she reported. Now, there are many smooth and winding ones through lively neighborhoods as well as tree-covered hills.

Among Lorde's most striking recollections was seeing Grand Anse Beach, not the hotel-lined miles of white sand that attract both locals and tourists, but the busy thoroughfare that runs alongside it.

She saw: "Children in proper school uniforms carrying shoes, trying to decide between the lure of a coco palm adventure to one side and the delicious morning sea on the other."

I, too, saw children, dozens of them on either side of the street one morning. Most of the children wore traditional uniforms, white shirts and blouses and plaid skirts or dark or khaki shorts or pants. They huddled together chatting and giggling, not paying attention to the dark blue sea on one side or the colorfully painted houses and buildings in the hills on the other. These children reminded me of children you would see heading to school in my native Haiti, or most other Caribbean islands, their range of black and brown skin glistening in the sun. The older ones kept their younger siblings at their side, even as they climbed into public transportation minivans and buses.

I went in search of more of those "vivid images" in Lorde's essay and, besides the school children at Grand Anse Beach, there was Fat Woman-Who-Fries-Fish-In-The-Market. I did not see her inside the turquoise-and-white square building downtown. She was not standing near the massive fish laid out on slabs waiting to be gutted. Nor was she by the smaller ones piled into buckets out front.

The fish market smelled predictably like the sea. The buzz of the customer and buyer exchanges was a lot more subdued than I expected. Not all the vendors had customers. The market's relative calm on a Friday afternoon reminded me how small Grenada is. The island is 120 square miles and has about 100,000 residents.

That night while pondering all this in my hotel room at the Coyaba Beach Resort, I parted the curtains and looked for a full moon to turn the beach outside "flash green". October is perhaps the wrong time of year for this. Lorde had seen the sand turn green in April. There was no full moon, but I slept with the sliding door to the terrace open so I could hear the waves gently grazing the shore.

I am not a good tourist. I can easily evoke for myself the worst-case scenario in any type of travel situation. I have immigrant guilt about taking time off. I am a bad swimmer. I am self-conscious in bathing suits, so most of my tourism is done through books. But because of my writing, I am invited to quite a few places and whenever I can I go.

I was in Grenada, which was largely unaffected by the hurricanes, to receive an honorary degree from the University of the West Indies Open Campus. Unlike UWI's brick and mortar campuses, the Open Campus is a virtual one. The 657 students in my graduating class hailed from all over the English-speaking Caribbean. They earned their degrees online. Only 139 graduates would cross the stage though.

Not all the graduates always travel to the Open Campus ceremonies, my hosts from the University of the West Indies told me. However, this year there were students who wanted to come to their graduation in Grenada but could not. Most of the graduates travel from other countries for the Open Campus ceremony, which takes place in a different location each year. Many had homes that were damaged or destroyed. Some lost loved ones along with everything they owned.

I was told the story of one graduate from Trinidad who stayed home because she had donated her plane ticket money to relief efforts in Dominica, which has UWI's most devastated campus. Some of the students from that campus are still unaccounted for.

Hurricane Maria struck Dominica, the southernmost of the Leeward Islands as a Category 5 storm on September 18. Dominica's Prime Minister, Roosevelt Skerrit, whose own roof collapsed during the storm, later told CNN: "Our agriculture sector is 100 percent destroyed. Our tourism is, I would say, about 95 percent destroyed."

In front of the supermarket across from the Coyaba Beach Resort were blue barrels lined up to collect food and other urgently needed supplies for Dominica. At The Beach House Restaurant, just north of the airport, where I attended a pre-graduation cocktail party the night before the ceremony, the young female singer entertaining us with classic soul, as well as Caribbean covers, reminded everyone to drop something in the basket that would usually hold her tips. This time the funds would go to Dominica.

I have never been to Dominica but now I wish I had. This is not just born out of a desire to see a place "before." Before the devastation, before the storm. I am from a place, Haiti, that constantly evokes nostalgia in the people who have seen it, lived in it, and loved it "before."

This longing for before always saddens me because it makes the present seem even worse. But I still wish I had seen Dominica before, in part because it is the birthplace of one of my favorite novelists, Jean Rhys. The places that Antoinette, Rhys' doomed narrator in *Wide Sargasso Sea*, longs for have flaming sunsets and rivers so clear that you can see the pebbles at the bottom. They have moss-covered gardens filled with orchids, hibiscus and flamboyants, which are illuminated at night by fireflies.

This is one of the ways I have imagined Dominica, along with what I have seen in travel guides: its high mountain peaks, forts, lush rain forests, reefs, gorges, lakes and water falls.

Dominica is also home to Xuela Claudette Richardson, the narrator of Jamaica Kincaid's novel *The Autobiography of My Mother*. At fifteen, Xuela was taken by her father to Roseau, the capital of Dominica. Roseau, Xuela finds—like a lot of places in the Caribbean—"had a fragile foundation, and from time to time was destroyed by forces of nature, a hurricane or water coming from the sky as if suddenly the sea were above and the heavens below."

"The second time I came to Grenada," Audre Lorde wrote in "Grenada Revisited", "I came in mourning and fear that this land which I was learning had been savaged, invaded, its people maneuvered into saying thank you to their invaders."

Lorde's second visit was in late 1983, after then US president Ronald Reagan had deployed Marines to the island. Reagan declared that he wanted to prevent a "Soviet-Cuban" colony from taking root in Grenada and protect American citizens on the island, many of whom were students at St George's University School of Medicine.

I visited St George's University, whose students and officials, Lorde pointed out, later denied that they were ever in danger. The school, which is no longer just a medical school, but also covers other disciplines, is an island unto itself, with its many salmon-colored buildings, massive water tanks, security personnel and buses. All over the campus are breathtaking views of True Blue Bay, the point where the Caribbean Sea and the Atlantic Ocean meet.

If Reagan was so interested in seeing democracy flourish in the Caribbean, Lorde wondered, why did the US government support Haiti's Jean-Claude Duvalier and his repressive regime? She also mentioned Puerto Rico.

In 1897, she wrote, "US Marines landed in Puerto Rico to fight the Spanish-American War. They never left."

Puerto Rico was as devastated by Hurricanes Irma and Maria as Dominica, Barbuda and the US Virgin Islands. I have not been to Puerto Rico either. I have only visited it in books, particularly through the eyes of young Esmeralda Santiago in her memoir, *When I Was Puerto Rican*.

I imagined the guavas that she taught me and other readers to eat at the beginning of her book being no longer able to grow, the fields they came from deep in the countryside flattened, and the families that farmed them struggling to stay alive without food or clean water.

I watched an interview with the tireless mayor of San Juan, Carmen Yulín Cruz Soto, and heard echoes of Audre Lorde in her voice.

"There is nothing that unites people more anywhere in the world than injustice," the mayor said. "We have to get food, we have to get water or else we are being condemned to a slow death. It may be easy to try to disregard us. It may be easy because we are a US territory and a colony of the United States. But we're a people, damn it."

The blessings of our islands are also our curse. Our geography gives us year-round sun and beautiful beaches, but more and more in the age of climate change, we are on the front line of destruction.

"We are a people" seems to be what we have been saying for generations to all our colonizers and invaders who seemed intent on destroying us. And now more than ever, Mother Nature, too.

We are a people, the Arawaks and Taínos might have said, even as they died trying to prove it. We have even inherited the word for hurricane, huracán, from them.

"Much has been terribly lost in Grenada," Lorde wrote at the end of her 1983 visit, "but not all—not the spirit of the people."

The spirit of the people is also captured in this poem I have been carrying with me for years before coming to Grenada. It was written by the Grenadian poet and short story writer Merle Collins.

"We speak," she wrote in "Because the Dawn Breaks", "for the same reason that the thunder frightens the child

that the lightning startles the tree …"

The people of the Caribbean speak, the poet wrote, because we "were not born to be your vassals."

Yvonne Denis Rosario

A storyteller, poet, librettist, columnist and researcher, born in San Juan, Puerto Rico, who holds a PhD in Puerto Rican and Caribbean Literature and a Professorship at the University of Puerto Rico, Río Piedras campus. She presided over the PEN Club of Puerto Rico International, Inc. 2012–13, and sits on the Board of the Institute of Puerto Rican Literature. The author of Capá prieto *(2010),* Bufé *(2012),* Delirio enlazado *(2015) and* Sepultados *(2018), she is finishing her studies in Archaeology with a thesis about the search and footprint of the Maroons.*

the roach and the rat at the library

1930:

—It is a cockroach and a mouse!

—They are harmless animals. The children will like them said Pura Belpré to Barbara, her fellow librarian.

—I think you are wasting your time.

—You will see, time will tell

—Good afternoon. The fumigators are here!

—Good, go right ahead said the receptionist. I would like you to thoroughly inspect the children's room. I think I saw some insects there. Many people come here daily and we want to be sure that there are no undesired visitors, it would not be proper, she said smiling.

—Some must be immune to the poison. I am not surprised, there are more mice than people, even though I come every month, he said jokingly.

—Please go right ahead then.

—Mrs Belpré, the exterminator has just finished. He inspected the area, fumigated and did not see anything at all, said the receptionist.

—Obviously, they did not come out to be seen just because he arrived, he smells like insecticide. It is only when I am here that they come out.

—I believe you, although in truth I have not seen anything.

—Look, look, there they go, shouted Pura.

—Where? Barbara also shouted as she arrived at that very moment and looking at the same place Pura was pointing to.—The only one who sees them is you!

—Yes, that is true. She left with a smile on her face.

1921:

Pura Belpré had arrived early. She was there because she had read in the newspaper that they were looking for a person who spoke both English and Spanish to work at a branch of the New York Public Library on 135th Street in Harlem. The Hispanic community was growing and they needed personnel who understood both languages.

When she discussed the details of the job description with Professor Mary Gould Davis, she told her to apply, even though she had not finished her studies as a librarian. After sending her paperwork, she received a telephone call for an interview. Although doubtful, she was here.

Upon arriving at the old building, there was nobody at the reception desk. She waited for a few minutes. She rose and knocked on the door with a sign that said: Director. She heard a voice that said: "Come in."—And you are…—the conversation in English that began would prove just how well she managed.

—Pura Belpré, the visitor responded, and at the Director's gesture accepted an invitation to take a seat.

—Mrs Belpré, I am the director of this Public Library, Lindsay Adams. I was waiting for another person, perhaps my secretary was confused. What can I help you with?

—I came to—

—The places for maintenance employees have been filled, the director interrupted. If you leave your paperwork, I will gladly refer it to the person in charge.

—Mrs Adams, I came to interview for the position of foreign assistant in the library's children's room.

—I understand. What we are really looking for is a person who speaks Spanish. Are you qualified?

—Of course, she said very confidently.

—I believe your resume and recommendations are right here—after searching her desk and finding them, she examined them at great length.—Apparently there was a mistake, excuse me. Are you from Cidra, Puerto Rico?

—That is correct, and I know how to speak Spanish perfectly—she stopped speaking in English and continued the conversation in Spanish.

"Vine los Estados Unidos cuando era adolescente…"

—I am sorry, I do not know how to speak Spanish—she stopped her immediately.

—I was saying that I came when I was a teenager—she said, returning to English quite naturally—By then, I had studied at the Central Superior School in Santurce, Puerto Rico, and I started my university studies on the island. I came to the United States for my older sister's wedding, and I have not yet returned. I am interested in working at this library.

—Your academic record and credentials are favorable. I must consult with the Board of Directors and the Office of Personnel before giving you an answer. I must also interview other people.

—When can I find out if I have been chosen?

—We will call you; we have your information and we will let you know as soon as a decision has been made. Thank you very much and good afternoon.

—Good afternoon.

After waiting around a month, Pura Belpré was chosen to occupy the position at the New York Public Library. She was the first Puerto Rican to obtain this position. Eventually, she became director and was in charge of the Children's Room.

January 6th, 1935:

—I think you are wasting your time. So many years studying to become a librarian and you dedicate yourself to reading children's stories. If Mrs Gould Davis, who insisted so much on your learning, knew what you were doing she would be so disappointed!

—I like narration and children's stories. In Puerto Rico, there is a great storytelling oral tradition.

—Children need to read, that is why they come to the library, which is why the books are stored in the room right next to them. You manage the library, take advantage of that and teach them to appreciate books.

—I will do it. Do you know what? I just finished writing a story based on the folk tales of "Martina, the little roach" and "Perez, the mouse". My story is called "Perez and Martina".

—Your thoughts always surprise me. Perhaps that is why they confused you with a maintenance employee, Barbara reminded her.

—They will like it, you will see.

—Excuse me, Director Belpré—interrupted her foreign assistant.

—Tell me, she said, turning towards the door.

—The children do not fit in the hall.

—Well then, remove the chairs and fit them in on the floor. Thus, we will have more space. Today is the celebration of the Day of Epiphany, and that is why there is so much commotion.

—Every time more and more children come.

—I know, I know, but it is the only way to read them the stories and tales of Puerto Rico. Their parents are Puerto Rican, do not forget it, and their first language is Spanish—

—Respectfully, Madam, are you going to continue using that cockroach and that mouse to entertain the children? Don't you think that they are somewhat disagreeable animals, unhygienic and rather battered?

—Mildred, I have used them as a narrating source for many years. Do not forget, the cockroach is "Martina" and that the mouse is "Perez". It works. You yourself affirm that more and more kids come each time. Are you forgetting how beloved is Mickey Mouse from Disney, even by adults?

—But this is a public library and not an amusement park.

—The mice are very agile and the cockroaches survive. The symbolism is important for those developing minds.

—Their countenances are so ugly. How can you hold them without feeling disgust? They are quite deteriorated.

—The children like them. They stay focused, entertained, and that is the important thing.

—I do not understand your education method.

—Come, let's go, I hear the voices of the little ones. Are there enough candies? We must be ready. Can you bring me Martina and Perez?

—I do not want to touch them, you will pardon me, but I cannot. They disgust me. Mrs Belpré, you always request the same thing and my answer continues to be the same: NO.

—It is ok. I cannot believe how scared you are of a couple of puppets.

Yvvette Edwards

A British East Londoner of Montserratian origin, she is the author of two novels—A Cupboard Full of Coats (2011) and The Mother (2016)—as well as having written a number of short stories published in anthologies and dramatised on radio. Her work has been nominated for many literary awards in the UK and USA, including NAACP Image Awards, the Commonwealth Writers' Prize, the Man Booker Prize, the International IMPAC Dublin Literary Award and the Hurston-Wright Legacy Award. She was a judge for the inaugural Jhalak Prize for Writers of Colour and mentors emerging writers for the National Centre for Writing. She has described her hobbies as including "reading, writing and pursuit of the perfect carrot cake".

Security

Merle noticed the security guard the moment she stepped through the entrance of Penny World: a tall, heavy-set white man, mid-forties, who had positioned himself on top of a barstool at the front of the store to have an unobstructed view of customers entering; and she knew he'd clocked her, because he stood up straightaway, trying to make the action seem natural by generally surveying the store, as if that had been his intention all along, and it surprised her, the anger she felt—hot and rapid, erupting inside her chest like a volcano come to life—surprised her at a time when she was upset with so many other things, proper problems with longevity attached, that this incident, when she'd just popped out to pick up some Sure deodorant and a roll of clingfilm, was the blow that finally swept her over the edge.

Her flight was tomorrow morning at 11 and arrangements had been made to pick her up at 5 a.m. so she didn't miss it. She'd bought the suitcase last week, had to, because the only one she'd ever owned was the one she'd brought with her when she made the six-week boat journey from Jamaica to England in June 1964, which had for years been reclining on top of her wardrobe, the metal handle broken, clasps defunct, reduced in status to a storage container, nothing more. She'd not been back to Jamaica since arriving here, had never gone on holiday abroad, never had need of a passport, and here she was, at the age of seventy-eight, making the journey back with a suitcase from Cheap Cheaper Cheapest that had a zip that kept catching when she tried to close it, and brittle wheels that clattered noisily behind her, after she'd paid for it and hauled the brand-new empty thing home.

She'd packed—probably overpacked—it, and it sat open on her bed, just waiting for the Sure deodorant to be put inside. Once she'd done that and wrestled again with the dodgy zip, the clingfilm would be wrapped around the suitcase to give her the greatest chance of making it to Kingston, on this, her first journey back, with her dignity and its contents intact.

The security guard wore a dark clean-pressed uniform and a flat black army cap pulled so low on his head, it almost touched the thin-rimmed frame of his large mirrored glasses, and he had the restless air of the American coppers Merle had seen in Hollywood action movies, lounging on the bonnet of a police car, impatient to use their gun. Ordinarily, she would've picked up a basket to put her goods in as she walked around, held the basket high and visible, would've kept it on the opposite side of her body to her handbag, in the hope of conveying the fact that she was an honest person who'd never shoplifted a thing in her life; but today her anger prevented her doing that. A voice in her head whispered a sentence she was too polite to dream of saying aloud, but it so perfectly synchronised with her mood, she nearly smiled: *Let him kiss out me backside.*

She knew the deodorants were shelved on Aisle 4, and the clingfilm on Aisle 5. The most direct route was to cut across the front corridor between the tills and the aisles, but she decided against that. Instead, she began walking the length of Aisle 1, stopping in front of shelves filled with nuts and dried fruit, stealing furtive glances upwards in the direction of the store camera fixed to the ceiling, in a manner she hoped looked very suspicious. She picked up some pistachios, examined the package, turning it over as though reading the information on the back, even though what was written there was in another language. She didn't check in the direction she had just come, didn't need to, because she knew the security guard had followed her. She felt him the same way she had felt him watching and following her around on previous visits. She peered up again at the camera, then away, put the packet back on the shelf, and carried on walking.

Seventy-eight years of age, and with the neat and tidy way she always dressed and carried herself, were she a stranger trying to work out what kind of person she might be, the word that would have come to mind is *church*. Despite this, in the fifty-four years she'd been living in England and spending her money in shops with security guards, she'd regularly been followed around like a thief.

Forty-one of those fifty-four years she'd worked as a care assistant in homes for the elderly, spoon-feeding geriatrics, dressing and undressing them, giving herself back problems that plagued her to this day, from lifting them in and out of bed and bath, on and off seats, toilets, floors; cleaning their dirty behinds and infronts, their soiled bedding, while acting like it was just sticks and stones to have them tell her they didn't want her black hands touching them, their food, their cutlery and medicine cups. She'd been watched with suspicion by those same people she'd looked after, watched as she mopped up all manner of nastiness, as if the only reason she dressed in the uniform her employers issued, wearing gloves and carrying a mop and bucket, was to rob them of the little shekels in purses and wallets they hid under mattresses and at the back of their drawers. And had she harboured any grudges against them? Nope. She had not. After all that, she'd still given them kind words on Mother's Day and birthdays and Christmas, when no family or children or friends from old times arrived to share their special day; doled out comfort in their isolation, smiles to stony faces, and fellowship in their final hours when they would otherwise have been alone.

Merle dawdled as she approached the end of the aisle, handling products she had no intention of buying, touching everything she felt like, without a backward glance. Then, as she rounded the corner, out of the security guard's sight, she began marching briskly, nearly but not quite running, careful not to slip or trip and mash up her seventy-eight-year-old body, hurrying only as fast as she could manage safely, because if she injured herself, they'd probably say she'd done it on purpose to avoid the flight, and God alone knew whether after all the years of paying National Insurance contributions from her wages, she'd be entitled to treatment from the National Health Service. She scurried determinedly down Aisle 2 and around the corner so she was back in Aisle 1, continued swiftly along it, then for the second time rounded the top, slowing only when she spotted the security guard a few feet ahead, facing away from her, body alert, his head pinging back and forth like a meerkat, no doubt wondering where the old lady had vanished. She stopped immediately behind him, and as he turned around in confusion, Merle picked up a column of fifty disposable cups and stared at it, trying to calm her breathing, while joyfully basking in the vibe of his astonishment at discovering the woman he'd been following was now behind him.

Coming to England had cost Merle her son. She hadn't realised she was trading motherhood for the Motherland. George was only eight when she'd left him in the care of Uncle Backfoot, travelled on a ticket she'd begged and borrowed to pay for—then had to pay back—with no job or place to live, just the knowledge she was welcome and would have opportunities, the chance to make something of herself, earn a decent living, provide a future for George; security, hope. It was supposed to be for a couple of years, just long enough to save up, return home, and build a little house for them both, with a small store or rum shop or cooked food served out front. But she'd underestimated how hard it would be, how long it would take just to get her oneself on her feet, never realised till she arrived here, in her scanty island dress and thin jacket, that no provision had been made for them, that she'd be subjected to so much resentment, at job interviews, in council offices, on the doorsteps of houses with rooms to rent. She had moved home so frequently, it took nine years to fulfil the five-year residency requirement to apply for local council help with housing; and by then George had grown up without her, and full of resentment. They hadn't spoken in years. He lived in the States with grandkids she'd never seen.

As the security guard began walking away, Merle put the disposable cups back on the shelf and followed. She knew he knew he was being followed; she could see the strip of neckback between his hat and his jacket collar getting redder with every step. When he paused for a moment, probably hoping she'd continue past him, she stopped too, picking up a tea towel that unfurled as she held it to reveal an image of the Houses of Parliament printed on cheap cloth. At the periphery of her field of vision, she saw the security guard turn towards her as if about to speak, but he said nothing, just spun on his heels and started walking again, and she did too. He went right at the bottom, towards Aisle 3, and she tailed him, coming to an abrupt halt as she almost collided with his stationary body waiting around the corner. He was almost two feet taller than she was. Merle glared up at him and saw herself reflected in his mirrored glasses as he stared back.

She said, "It doesn't feel very nice, does it?"

The security guard's voice was deep, bassy, tinged with a strong accent that Merle couldn't narrow down further than Eastern European. He said, "My job, stop steal."

The fact of his accent broke her; she didn't know why. It made no difference to what had happened, to this latest affront. Was it because despite being new to the country, he'd been endowed with the authority to treat her like a criminal? Did she feel because he wasn't British, he didn't have the right? Or because until he opened his mouth he'd been able to pass, to silently position himself within the system like a native, whereas fifty-four years on, she was still being made to feel like a foreigner? Now a foreigner officially.

She said, "Well you won't have to worry about this woman stealing ever again. You'll be happy to know, I'm being deported." She thrust the tea towel she was still holding into his hand. She stepped around him and walked directly to Aisle 4, fiercely concentrating as she willed herself not to fall apart. She was confident there'd be plenty of deodorant in Jamaica, just not that they'd have Sure, her brand of choice. She picked up four of the roll-ons, remembered how hot Jamaica was, then took two more. The eruption in her chest was relocating to her head, which throbbed now, but she knew would soon begin to pound. She made her way to Aisle 5 to find the clingfilm.

At the till, after she had paid for her items and packed them in the carrier bag she'd brought along, she noticed the security guard was sitting on his barstool again, and realised she'd have to pass him on her way to the exit. She'd decided to just ignore him, but as she approached his perch, he gave her a smile and she was unable to interpret what it was meant to convey. Solidarity? Pity? Glee?

Her pace slowed, but she did not stop. Reflected in his glasses she saw a proud old lady, head held high. Her voice was steady as she spoke: "It's me today, but tomorrow, they'll be back for you."

Zena Edwards

Born in London, she has been a multidisciplinary collaborative poet for more than 20 years as a writer/poet, performer, educator and creative project developer since graduating in Drama, Media and Communications Studies from Middlesex University and studying at the London School of International Performance Art. Her practice and passion is writing poems, articles and blogs for social and environmental issues, race and power, and also mentoring young and emerging artists. She is the Creative and Education Director for Verse in Dialogue (©ViD), an umbrella social enterprise that produces projects focused on live literature, creative inter-generational community engagement and wellbeing, transformational learning and liberatory practice.

In A Walthamstow Old People's Home

They keep showing up out of the blue
Fuzzy edged figures shaped like ghosts of memories

your eyes are still 20/20, even at 96, sharp, bright brown,
Now rimmed with pale blue yesteryears
your curdled dreams, clouded in 1950s sepia dementia, so
you have to keep asking the same question, "What' your name again?"

In amongst the others you sit
a young old man, native Nevis citizen, England bound
a tailor's profession proudly tucked under your arm
like a broadsheet—perfect and important like folded wings—
Hawk hunting a new life under the protection of a Motherland beckoning
you fledgling, sure of the uncertainty
of migrating, certain of your manhood

Took some time settling in
Enough time to sever ties
enough to know when you've been lied to
at least on the sunny turtle back island
you could walk slow
Too much sun to rush,

The nurse whispers, "He hasn't eaten much,"
Here the mortal hush
something rustling.
a reminder, a soft alarm
like the syrupy resonance of a familiar calling,
a hunger, a wondering— "Back 'Ome".

Back then
never knew
how you were gonna get back home
just held a spirit
that wanted forward
Knew there were doors to treasures that swung open inward
And your ambition is mighty currency and curiosity knocks loudly
And England knew, you opened up, let it in
Gave it home, it the migrant
You welcoming…

Now, amongst the others
the other fragile catacombs
whose chairs are positioned to face a TV

who sit so still so still, so as not to disturb the dust
you see them, familiar strangers who smile as they approach you
—your daughter and her child, they say.

You talk and they listen
and you know you forget things but they don't seem to mind
besides they feel warm and want to know you
they feel like home

and every time they make their farewells, you tell the girl child,
"Look after your muddah" and that you thank them for coming
cos you're not long for this world, you're just waiting,

"Waitin' on di Lawd.
Waitin' on di Lawd to call me.
To call me to come Back 'Ome"

Four (and then some) Women

In tribute to Nina Simone. For Sara Reed
  Both mothers, both women with mental unwellness

Writing art in a pleasant land
about how an Archipelago's children
would bleed back into the pipelines
stories that pummel our identities
like we are punch bags of pigment

our skin, an invitation
to be interacted with violently,
an unbroken contractual continuum
we hand no hand writing in

What sounds did your body make?
Did it call to an ache of the centuries,
of chains clinking on the auction block
Now clanking keys in prison cell locks
An ugly chime of time.
          How to make it stop?

What melodic possibilities
Did your skin make to him?
The ones that Nina sings?

>   (Kiddies practised the strum of his prejudice
>   upon a black woman's body
>   England's uniformed Brave
>   told us what we always knew.)

And I wonder did Officer Kiddie take a bow
when the curtains of inevitability
were drawn aside
only to trail another veil
stitched to its wake

Sarah's long sleep
is crimson secrecy after seconds
till we only see her silhouette on pages for a day
denial falls like a dusk of muffled thuds under scuffling feet

Listening to Nina Simone sing Four women this morning
Peaches appeared beside me at my kitchen sink
Had to grab the edge to steady myself
Clasped my throat to find the breath snatched from it

Peaches said her name over and over—Sarah Reed. Sarah Reed. Sarah Reed…
She said "My name was never meant to be swallowed sweet,
And neither is this Sister's."

There are no words with sugar on top to talk about
the beating of flesh
the sinking of blood in ocean depths
the splatter on urban streets
like signatures that spell delete

I have no candy coated metaphors
for the mental gore and shock
of the body rent from its psyche
to be smashed open and left raw.

11th January cold in a cold prison cell
2nd February—#sayhername through the twittersphere
8th February—the first vigil

I had not yet shed a tear for the deaths
my social media timeline had fed me
I was angry, technically.

So many had marched for "black lives in the US matter"
So few, why so few knew that it was time to march for Sarah?

Humanity stretched thin between the pauses
as the black women and girls went up to the coughing loud hailer
one after another and another and another and another
on this cold cold night
Gave account of the uncounted Sarah Reeds

My body wanted to walk away
hands and feet frozen, but above that biting sting
was the frightening bruising
that rose to the surface of my skin
As their words sank in
          "I am a black working class woman
                    who has suffered from mental health"

Lost my way to Holloway
walking down dead ends, roads of empty warehouses
a North London girl, who knows these streets
like she knows the meaning of mallet pulses her temple
who wanted to deny the needle on the record
that would scratch out that sample

          i am a black working class woman who has suffered from mental health
          i am a black working class woman who has suffered from mental health

As these women spoke
My feet forced me to stay, hands snap the thread
for the key around my bent neck,
opened the doors and go inside her cell

and just for a moment
see all of her
sit beside her
our breaths made misty tears of frost
for a lost child and Nina's guttural squall—"Peaches!"
could be heard along the steely cold walls

#SayHerName   Sarah Reed
#SayHerName   Sarah Reed
#SayHerName   Sarah Reed

And deep, deep down in me
I feel
she would have thought
in there,
she would have thought
she might see
her last days.

What does it mean
            to hold that question inside you?

Aminatta Forna

Born in Scotland, she was raised in Sierra Leone and the UK, also spending periods of her childhood in Iran, Thailand and Zambia. Her novels are Ancestor Stones *(2006, Hurston-Wright Legacy Award),* The Memory of Love *(2010, winner of the Commonwealth Writer's Prize),* The Hired Man *(2013) and* Happiness *(2018). In 2002 she published a memoir of her dissident father and Sierra Leone,* The Devil that Danced on the Water. *She is the winner of a Windham Campbell Award and has been a finalist for the Neustadt Prize, the Orange Prize, the Samuel Johnson Prize and the IMPAC Award. Academic positions she has held include Professor of Creative Writing at Bath Spa University, Sterling Brown Distinguished Visiting Professor at Williams College in Massachusetts, and currently Lannan Visiting Chair of Poetics at Georgetown University. She was appointed an OBE in 2017 for services to Literature.*

Santigi

Santigi was a foundling. Or at least Santigi was as close to being a foundling as you can imagine. None of us, not even Santigi, knew his origins. He knew the name of the village where he was born but had never been back there. He did not know the names of his mother or his father. He called himself a Loko, for the reason that he understood the language, which was his only tie to his beginnings. "Santigi, the Loko," we'd call him and he would bang himself on the chest and say "Loko!"

My step-mother Yabome's first memory of Santigi was when he met her off the train from school. At that time Santigi had come to live in the house with Yabome and the grandmother who raised her. At that age Yabome never thought to ask where Santigi had come from, and when her grandmother died the old lady took whatever knowledge she possessed with her. It was rumoured that Santigi's mother had borne him alone, had left him with neighbours while she went to find work scratching for diamonds in the eastern mines, that she had died there. When she failed to return the neighbours had given her young son to the old lady to raise. The story makes some kind of sense, but still it is hard to imagine, in a country where kinship is everything, where ties of allegiance are what binds, in a small country where everybody knows everyone else and their business, that a woman could be so alone. As for Santigi, if you asked him, all he ever told you was that he was a Loko. He made my step-mother Yabome his family. When she went away to Scotland to college on scholarship and came back, Santigi was waiting for her. And when she married my father, Santigi came along too.

Nobody knew how old Santigi was. In her first memory of him, of being met by him off the train from her boarding-school, my step-mother would have been twelve and guessed him to be a few years older, perhaps sixteen. In those days we had cousins living with us whose school fees my father paid. My father was a medical doctor, a politician and activist, with a high regard for learning, he had ambitions to raise the academic standards of his family, having been the only one of his generation to go to school. His father, a Regent Chief, a wealthy farmer and landholder, was a man who believed in the old ways and held modernity in contempt, thus he had sent none of his children to the new mission and government schools, with the exception of my father for the reason that his mother (my grandfather's sixth wife) was dead. Even then, he did so under duress and in answer to a mandate from the Paramount Chief that each family submit one child to the new mission school in the next village. Yabome's father, on the other hand, who had been a merchant who traded in gold, was possessed of unusual foresight for the time, and had made sure every one of his children went to school and to university. It was a story repeated all over the old world, the aristocracy, holding on to outdated modes of thinking and tied to the values of the land, only to be overtaken by the rising middle class. Santigi wanted to go to school but my father said he was already too old. Instead he sent Santigi to adult education classes at night. Often when I came back from school in the afternoon

Santigi would sit next to me at the dining-room table while I did my homework and copy out the questions and answers into his own exercise book.

If life had gone on in that way, maybe Santigi would somehow have realised his dream to go to college, though I don't remember his ambitions being taken particularly seriously. His enthusiasm for learning was not, it seems, matched by aptitude. And even if it were, it would not have helped, for all our lives were about to change. By 1970 Sierra Leone was a nascent dictatorship, a one-party state was on the rise. My father was arrested and jailed for his opposition to the prime minister. Our household was scattered. The cooks and stewards, the driver—all departed. My cousins went back to live with their families. Mum, my sister and brother and I went into hiding and then into exile in London, where we would stay for three years.

Only Santigi stayed on. Living in the empty rooms of our house, he guarded our possessions against thieves and every week he went to the Pademba Road Prison where my father was being held. Santigi brought my father food and clean clothes and took away his washing, returning it ironed and folded the following week. In times like those, loyalty is hard to find, and Santigi earned our family's loyalty in return for his. But to me, looking back, what he did was more powerful than mere loyalty. Violence was on the rise, our home had been stoned by political thugs; those same thugs raided newspaper offices, threatened journalists, university professors and lawyers, beat up anyone who dared to oppose the prime minister in his determination to become president-for-life. All our household staff had been held and detained at CID headquarters, my step-mother too, and Santigi. Santigi had been badly beaten.

As he waited at the prison gates Santigi would have been taunted by the guards, I am sure, as were the prisoners themselves. His visits to my father were an act of loyalty and of courage; they were also an act of resistance. Like the Mothers, now the Grandmothers of the Plaza de Mayo, who come out every day in Buenos Aires to march in memory of their disappeared sons and daughters, so Santigi came every week to the prison gates to remind the authorities that my father was not forgotten.

When my father was released—taken to the prison gates and let out without warning—he had no money for a taxi, but a passing driver recognised him and gave him a lift. When he arrived home, there was Santigi. It was Santigi who cooked my father's first meal as a free man.

In the year that followed, the pleasure of being reunited, of my father's freedom made us giddy. We danced to that year's hit, "Kung Fu Fighting", we sang and we punched and kicked the air. We, the three children and our older cousins: Morlai, Esther, Agnes and of course, Santigi.

Santigi got religion around that time and changed his name to Simon Peter and then to Santos. He carried a Bible around, and he also talked about his dream of becoming a photographer, even though he had never owned a camera. I would, in my university years, buy him a camera and for a while, he would have a small booth where he took portraits. But all that was some years off.

A year after being freed, my father was arrested again, this time on charges of treason. A year after that he was executed.

Our landlords gave us notice, Mum had trouble finding anyone who would rent her an apartment or give her a job. When she eventually succeeded in both, she didn't earn enough money to look after all of us and Santigi, too. Santigi found work elsewhere, and came every Sunday to wash our clothes, even though Mum couldn't pay him. He told me often that he would keep coming until the day I graduated from university. And he did.

In time Mum remarried and Santigi was given a job as head steward in the new household. But by then he had begun to drink. He had one failed marriage and then another; each produced a daughter. He named the first Yabome and the second Memuna Aminatta after my sister and me. He showed little interest in either girl. Eventually Memuna Aminatta's mother met a man who made her happy and she disappeared from our lives. Santigi's first wife Marion married again too, but remained a friend to Santigi, although it's hard to say whether he deserved her loyalty. What it was he was searching for at that time, I don't know. He dyed his hair with boot polish and when he sweated in the heat, the polish ran down his face. He insisted he was younger than he was, until he knocked so many years off his age that, if he were to be believed, he would be younger than my step-mother and soon almost as young as my elder brother, on whom he certainly had twenty years.

Santigi became a figure of fun among the children in the neighbourhood. And he kept on drinking. He remained trustworthy in every way, except one. When my parents were out, he helped himself to the contents of the liquor cabinet. He frequently turned up to work intoxicated and, after several warnings, my step-father lost patience and Santigi was suspended.

He did everything to win his job back. In Sierra Leone there exists a custom whereby a person of lower status who has offended a person of higher status will appeal to someone of equivalent or, better still, even greater status than the offended party, pleading for that person to intercede on their behalf. To "beg" for them, is what we say in Creole. In the decades he had lived and worked with my family Santigi had met dozens of people of influence and remembered them all. Now he visited their homes, waiting patiently for an audience. He explained the circumstances of his suspension, persuaded each of his contrition and asked them to "beg" my step-father on his behalf to lift the suspension.

My step-father would tell the story amidst much laughter, how for weeks to come at every cocktail party, lunch or dinner he attended, every restaurant he entered, it seemed, somebody came up to him to discuss Santigi's case. My step-father remained adamant, however, until one day he attended an international banking conference. As the delegates gathered, the governor of the state bank approached him and asked to have a word. My step-father thought the governor must have something confidential to discuss. They stepped aside. In a low voice the Governor said: "It's about your steward, Santigi…"

Santigi was found a job as a messenger in the offices where my step-father worked. The job gave him a decent income and a pension, and removed him from the dangers of the liquor cabinet. He still dyed his hair and now wore dentures too; he also lied on his application form about his age, partly perhaps out of vanity, but no doubt believing this might give him an advantage. What it meant was that he was obliged to continue working well after his retirement age.

Santigi would live to see the country all but destroyed by war, and survive the invasion of Freetown by rebel forces in 1999. When I returned home in 2000, he was there to greet me. I kissed him and he seemed overcome with shyness. I wrote of him and my cousin Morlai, who was there that day to greet me too, in the memoir of my family that I published two years later: "I remember them both as confident lads: the flares, the sunglasses, the illicit cigarettes, the slang." Santigi didn't say much during our reunion. He watched and listened awhile as Morlai and I laughed and chatted; then, picking up the pair of chickens Morlai had brought me as a gift, he slipped away to the back of the house. When I published the book a launch was held in Freetown, at the British Council. It was a formal occasion, as book launches in Sierra Leone generally are. Santigi turned up drunk. I gave him his own signed copy. He kissed it and he slapped me on the back and he kept on slapping me on the back, hearty blows, even when I was trying to sign books.

I saw Santigi a good few times over the years to come, he would visit when I was home, not once was he sober. Mum didn't want me to give him money, she said he spent it on moonshine, so I gave the money to Marion for his daughter Yabome instead.

Santigi gave up his little house in Wilberforce and started moving from one rented room to another. He had retired by then and Mum could no longer contact him at the bank. She lost track of where he lived, but not entirely; if too many months went by she always sent for news, and somebody somewhere could always tell her Santigi's whereabouts. He came to visit less often.

It's strange how some people's stories always end the same way. A possible clue comes from my cousin Morlai, who began to drink at the same time as Santigi: after my father's execution. "It felt like we were going back into the darkness," he told me. My brother told me that years ago he helped Santigi clear out his little house in Wilberforce, and among his possessions were dozens of pictures of my father, from snapshots to photos torn from newspapers.

A near-death experience while drunk shocked Morlai into sobriety. He married and had children. He grew back into himself, stronger this time. Today he's a successful businessman and although those things that happened to our family meant Morlai was never able to finish college, all his own children have done so.

For whatever reason, even though we loved him, for Santigi redemption never came.

On my last visit home to Freetown I arrived to discover Santigi had had a stroke two weeks earlier. In the weeks that followed, Mum and I tried to get him moved to a care home, but he died before that could happen. So we bought him a coffin and all his neighbours chipped in to buy him a suit from the secondhand-clothes stalls at Government Wharf. I had never seen Santigi in a suit. I asked Mum what he looked like. She laughed softly, and told me he looked good. I was back in England on the day of his funeral. I couldn't go so I sat at my desk and I did what writers do. I wrote this instead.

Danielle Legros Georges

Born in Haiti, she is a writer and translator, the author of two books of poetry, Maroon *(2001) and* The Dear Remote Nearness of You *(2016), which won the New England Poetry Club's Sheila Margaret Motton Book Prize, and the chapbook* Letters from Congo *(2017). She is also the editor of* City of Notions: An Anthology of Contemporary Boston Poems *(2017). She is a Professor at Lesley University and is Boston's second Poet Laureate.*

Poem for the Poorest Country in the Western Hemisphere

O poorest country, this is not your name.
You should be called beacon. You should

be called flame. Almond and bougainvillea,
garden and green mountain, villa and hut,

girl with red ribbons in her hair,
books under arm, charmed by the light

of morning, charcoal seller in black skirt,
encircled by dead trees. You, country,

are merchant woman and eager clerk,
grandfather at the gate, at the crossroads

with the flashlight, with all in sight.

Lingua Franca with Flora

In spite of all who would renounce petals
the petals come: *chèlbè*[1] some, shy some,
no dirt will hold them back. Planted
in dirt, and drawing from dirt, they explode
hot-pink, burst red, blown clean in the trade
winds that sweep down like a Moorish lover;
washed clean, darkened by Caribbean Sea rain:
these creeping bougainvillea.

And hibiscus flower, still delicate, still fleshy,
returning constantly to the Haitian day
he was stripped like a god of his name:
Rose de Chine. To the day he was brought low
to blacken shoes, made show his black blood
in the shine on the boots of American Marines,
1915.[2] He, now named *choublak*, spilling
dark tears for tea.

But who can deny the sly *chevalier de nuit*?
Night's knight, who blooms only at night,
unbolting his tiny white flower, perfumed,
redolant. Intoxicant known to those
who travel the night, and the night into day
down the worn trails to town, down the hills
for something, for life; known to those who
cut deals with ominous lords, with the devil
himself. All pinned by his lance.

It is he this girl picks to sweeten her dress
as she *will* emerge a goddess; in a rinsed
azure shift, after birdbath in alley
with enamel tin cup and tan bucket.
She will go boldly to her love who will
whisper to her in a schoolboy French
learned before he quit school; before life
swallowed him—and to seal their accord
(for there *is* a deal being made), in the gravity
of Creole, *wi cheri, wi—tout sa'm genyen se pou ou*,
yes darling, yes—all I have is yours.

---

1 *Chèlbè*, Haitian Creole for showy.
2 "of American Marines, 1915", a reference to 1915–34 US military occupation of Haiti.

A Stateless Poem[1]

If you are born, and you are stateless,
if you are born, and you are homeless,

if your state and home are not
yours—and yet everything you know—

what are you? Who are you? And who
am I without the dark fields I walk upon,

the streets I know, the blue corners
I call mine, the ones you call yours...

Who am I to call myself citizen, and
human and free? And who are you

to call yourself landed and grounded,
and free. And who is judge enough?

Who native? Who other?

And who are we who move so freely
without accents of identification,

without skin of identification, with
all manner of identification. With

gold seals of approval. With stamps
of good fortune. With the accident

of blameless birth. Who are we to be
so lucky?

---

1 "A Stateless Poem" addresses a September 2013 ruling by the Dominican Republic Constitutional
   Court that stripped citizenship of Dominican-born persons without a Dominican parent, going
   back to 1929. The majority of persons affected are Dominicans of Haitian descent.

palimpsest dress

rests on
a hanger—silver
shape
meaning
to be
shoulders—
whose neck
stems, bends
about a bar
that hold the armoire up

palimpsest dress
bias-cut
diasporic
(travels well)
hand-sewn,
hems, darts
(suitably)
to the stole's
left, the bustier's
right

palimpsest dress
which type of woman
slips you on
ink-spot
and all?

Songs for Women

I will there be no women here
who would circle red-
dressed, ruby-hearted,

glass-cut. If there be flowers,
then the bloom of cyclamen
awned in green's glowing
night-vase, night-shade,

wild in wind. Sin be the will
to descend, humming-bird still,
steal the fire's sound, take note

and return it. Let song be
the skin of a glimmering,
unsettled, razing, belly-deep
in the strike of match and band.

Be the belly, the pepper-pot.
Come close just to drop it.
Slide 'til the notes are a scaffold,
ash-flicked, unphoenixed.

musing

the muse licks her own tongue
pens rhymes for her own pleasure
dips her quill
mind stick
in dark ink
of her skin

and sits at a large bureau
thinking

Wangui wa Goro

She is a translator, writer, poet, academic, cultural curator and editor, best known for her scholarship as a theorist, critic, practitioner and promoter of translation, including its practical applications. She considers herself a cultural ambassador and advocate. She has spent over 40 years promoting and nurturing literature as an academic, through translation, criticism and curation in different parts of the world. Her friends consider her to be the quintessential transnational global Pan-African, feminist Afropolitan, which, though she finds hilarious, she relishes.

Looking down from Mount Kenya

Where do you hope to join my life
Flowing
Not like a river
But as torrents and currents of the tide

Buffeted by multitudinous waters of change
Going back and forth?
Lapping up the high and low banks
Dazzling the plains with luminous floodings
Awash against the orange-red sky of our history?
Where?
Do you and I
Merge as minor or major (con)tributaries
To the great sea—
Vast ocean of change?
Or where do we become engulfed by other tides of the past
Of victory and of shame.
And what futures unforetold, then and now?
What do we become?
Droplets of vapour
Carried under the translucent sky
To descend on unsuspecting blossom of spring-tide freedom
As a dewdrop—inseparably defiant;
Or swallowed by the parched earth of our desert(er)s
Or a hailstone in the tropical storm?
Here we stand poised to (e)merge
Like Gikuyu and Mumbi
In a world of numerous possibilities
Drawing from history
And awed by the great expanses of the earth, the sea and the sky
That are our future
And which hold promises of infinite, infinite
Possibilities…

London, 1997

Kitamu
(A sweet thing, in Kiswahili)

Sweetness here
Is untranslatable.
Delicious?
Sugary?
Saccharine?
Bitter even?
Where it is never clear

Whether it is black, strong
Decaf or white

The heart melts
The mind moulds
The coffee burns
The tongue lies
The missed hiss
In the complicated kiss
As cup meets lip
And it is neither hot nor cold
And the blend does not tell
From where it comes
Along the fissures
Of the region
Valleys
Mountains
And crevasses
In Kilimanjaro
Kenya
or along the Niles
Blue or White
Is always
A question
Of the gaze
And the mind
And the heart
And the winds
Which buffet souls
To cross those troubled waters
Home
The smell of home
Brewed
In a hotel
sweet pot

Kitamu, 2013

Nouvelle Danse on a Rainbow's Edge

The party is over, I know you naked now unmasked
The glitter and swagger in blood-lusted drunkardness
Falls with each step.

Sometimes you twirl and whirl
your powered lies around my innocence,
Making me believe that you love me,
That what you do is for my good

Yet, from time to time, your mask slips
And I catch sight of the gnarled glimpse directed at me
As you plunge and plunder
Plunder and plunge

So we dance,
Hips gyrating, heat sweltering
Round and round and round
Young and old together
Until the crack begins to show
In the falter of your step
Staccato, two three
I twirl
You stop
And I dance, dance, dance a new dance
Round and round and round and away from you
As the glitter beneath my feet flies, in Kenya:
57, 63, 68, 86, 2007..., one to one
I could hold you and guide you
In a modern dance
But why should I?
Or find you a new partner
Who will stretch your step, I
But why should I?

For now
Just for now
This has to be my dance
Alone
Refining each new-found step
Rediscovering the mystery of my own beat
Of wonder-dance

Of women-together dance
That lifts us to higher ground
I dance, dance, dance
On
And on
And on

Dance on you may
Or watch me
In this moment
Of my dance
Alone

1989

Zita Holbourne

*A British trade union, community and human rights campaigner and award-winning
activist, she is also an author, visual artist, curator, poet, vocalist and writer. She has
performed on television and radio and at a wide range of events including the National
Diversity Awards, Glastonbury Festival, the Houses of Parliament and the TUC, and
had the honour of writing and performing a tribute poem for the official UK Memorial
Service for Nelson Mandela. She has been published in a range of anthologies, is the
author of* Striving for Equality, Freedom and Justice, *and regularly writes for a range
of national and specialist journals on social justice, human rights and equality issues.
She won the Positive Role Model for Race Award at the National Diversity Awards in
2012, was listed as one of the top ten African and Caribbean Women of the Year in
2013 and was a finalist and one of five people's choice poets in the Manorlogz Xtreme
Spoken Word Contest in 2013. Her work has been recognised by the United Nations
and she is part of the UNESCO coalition of Artists for the General History of Africa.*

I Died a Million Times for my Freedom

My Freedom was not gained in a day, a month or a year
To achieve it I had to overcome both sorrow and fear
I walked across continents and centuries
Many times stumbling, falling down on my knees

I died a million times for my Freedom

Not a day passed when I wasn't grieving
But I never gave up, never stopped believing
That I would reach the destination called Freedom
Sometimes I cried for my Freedom

Other times I died for my Freedom
My body and soul became my own Queendom
The ground beneath my feet never there long enough to call home
Constantly I ventured to uninviting pastures unknown

I died a million times for my Freedom

Be it one century or one year
I could sense Freedom always near
The scent of sweet liberty permeated my nostrils
I etched songs of Freedom in my mind that became my gospels
Strong and defiant, never forgetting proud roots
Passed through DNA to my womb's precious fruits

I died a million times for my Freedom

Sometimes I was taken, sometimes I was used
Other times I was tortured and abused
My tears of sorrow deepened the sea
Broadening the divide between Freedom and me

Rebellion gave me hope and determination
My resistance knew no boundary or limitation
I bore the scars of my captivity
Like tribal marks of identity

I died a million times for my Freedom

When I was held back physically
I charted the route to Freedom mentally
In order to keep journeying towards my goal
The map of Freedom was imprinted on my soul

Between the stench of bodies decayed
And so many promised loyalties betrayed
I caught fast breaths of sweet fresh air
I could taste Freedom drawing near

I died a million times for my Freedom

When I couldn't run I walked
When I couldn't walk I talked

Promoting the very concept of Freedom to all who would hear
Convinced that Freedom could be reality if only they would dare

To claim it as their right
They could bring it into sight
When I could no longer walk, I rested
Learning that if I invested

In my own physical and mental well being
I would never stop believing
That Freedom could be mine
And when I finally arrived the sensation was divine

I died a million times for my Freedom

Even though I was wearied by centuries of oppression
Aged beyond my years by sadness and depression
Weathered from exposure to extreme elements
Frail from multiple abuses and resentments

I embraced my Freedom like an old lost friend
And refused to release my grasp for fear it would end
I died a million times for my Freedom
I died a million times for my Freedom
I died a million times for my Freedom

The Injustice of Justice; Extradition

She was born in the land of the ancestors, raised in the city of Angels, lived her
early adult life on an island made of dreams, pursued by a government intent on
dominating the world, imprisoned in a jail situated on stolen land, tried in a court
room built on the backs of enslaved peoples torn from the land of the ancestors that
was her birth.

She was deemed guilty until proven innocent, labelled before they knew her name,
persecuted with no crime to charge her for, taken despite refusing to surrender her
freedom, demonised because of her religion, misunderstood because of her
multicultural upbringing, rejected because of her ancestry, disregarded as a human
being and seen to be entitled to no rights upon this earth.

She refused to break when they tortured her, denied them the pleasure of seeing
her weep when her heart was breaking, refused to let them see her turning crazy
when she felt herself losing her mind, between the beatings, as she lay in solitary
confinement for days that were the same as nights, she comforted herself with the

recollection of words spoken by great philosophers and poets and memorised verses created out of the depths of her soul about the injustice of justice, remained resilient, determined and brave, held on to her belief that the truth would one day set her free because she'd been raised to value her worth.

Nalo Hopkinson

A Jamaican-born Canadian citizen, who grew up in Guyana, Trinidad and Canada, she is an award-winning writer of speculative fiction. Her novels—Brown Girl in the Ring *(1998)*, Midnight Robber *(2000)*, The Salt Roads *(2003)*, The New Moon's Arms *(2007)—and short stories such as those in her 2001 collection* Skin Folk, *often draw on Caribbean history and language, and its traditions of oral and written storytelling. Her writing awards include the World Fantasy Award, the Sunburst Award for Canadian Literature of the Fantastic, and the Norton Award. She is currently writing a serialised graphic novel in Neil Gaiman's Sandman Universe.*

Snow Day

The shovel bit through the foamy snow on the top stair of my front porch, then stopped with a clang. I scraped away the snow to see what was beneath. Ice. Serve me right for not shovelling after the snow had fallen last night. It had thawed, then the temperature had dropped into the deep freeze, and now the steps and the sidewalk were frozen solid.

On the street, a few cars and a bus slewed through the slush. The city had declared a snow day, so there wasn't much traffic out.

I sighed and began shovelling in earnest. I'd have to scoop all that snow into the road, then crack the layer of ice and start in on that. The small of my back was already twinging in anticipation of pain. I scooped the shovel under a big load of snow.

"You need to lift with your legs," said a voice behind me. It managed to sound both squeaky and hoarse. I turned. No one there. Just a raccoon, perched on my green organic waste bin. Damned things had been trying to figure out how to open it for months. Almost every week the bin had new tooth marks.

"Scram!" I shouted. I dropped the shovel, clapped my hands together to frighten the raccoon away.

The raccoon jumped off the bin and hid behind it. It peeked out at me. "Jeez, no need to get snarky. I was just giving you some good advice." Its mouth wasn't moving.

"All right," I said, looking around. "Who's the ventriloquist?"

I couldn't see anyone. Most of my neighbours were at work. And Granny Nichol, who usually spent the day at her window watching the world go by, had her blinds drawn today.

The raccoon stepped out from behind the bin and sniffed the air in my general direction. "Lady, it's no fun being able to understand you, either. It's creepy inside a human's head. Got any scraps? It's slim pickings out here in this weather."

"Shoo." I waved my shovel at it. If I could get it to go away, the prankster's trick would be spoiled.

The raccoon backed up out of the way of the shovel, but stood quietly watching me, though I could see its snout twitching in the direction of the green bin. I'd had fish for dinner, and the bones and skin were in there, right on top. I thought I could smell them, and they made my mouth water. I could imagine how they would taste, how the bones would crunch in my teeth, how I would save the head for last, holding it in my little black paws…euw. As if.

Suppose the raccoon was rabid? Should I call someone from the City?

The raccoon went over to the fence, swung itself up onto the palings, climbed to the top and crouched there unhappily. "You're just going to let them take that fish head away, aren't you?"

I ignored it. I scraped the snow off the icy steps, trying to pay no attention to the way I hungered for the offal I'd thrown away, the splintery feel of the wood palings under all four of my paws, the way that my eyesight seemed fuzzy and the sounds of the cars too loud. I wasn't thinking in raccoon, I wasn't. When I was done, I stood at the bottom of the five steps and looked up at them. The glare from the ice coating them hurt my eyes. I turned my head, backed up a bit.

"Watch out!" came the smoky voice. I heard a scraping, screeching sound and leapt out of the way just as a car skidded up onto my sidewalk, missing me by inches. My front steps stopped it. The stairs shook, but held, although all the ice splintered away. No crystal stair, not any more.

A man leapt out of the driver's side. "My god, I'm sorry!" he said. "Are you all right?"

"I'm fine," I told him. But really, I wasn't paying him much attention. I turned to the raccoon, still crouched on the fence. "Thank you."

"You're welcome," it growled. "Just consider it my payment for your tomatoes."

"That was you, then. You destroyed all my plants."

The raccoon shrugged.

"Lady," said the man, "I'm so sorry."

By then, a teenager had climbed out of the passenger side. "It's the brakes," she muttered.

"Your brake shoes just went." She looked at me and rolled her eyes. "1999 Passat. The rotors are crap. I told Dad he'd soon be singing the Ancient Volkswagen Blues."

"Never mind that," her father said. "Look. It's the same here, too." He was pointing to my back yard. From out of it—from everyone's yard, really—squirrels were climbing down from the trees and converging on the street. Raccoons came too, and the occasional deer. Mice. Rats. Cats and dogs. A moving carpet of snails and slugs. More bugs than I wanted to think about. Birds were massing in the sky, flocking to the electric wires and the lintels of houses. I saw a gazillion sparrows, a million pigeons and gulls. Even the hawks were flocking. Hawks don't flock. "It was like this on our street, too," said the man. "I got us out of there, but it's the same everywhere."

"What's going on?" I asked.

"Beats me, lady," warbled a starling from the railing of my abused stairs. "And can you open that plastic thing, already? Some of us are hungry here."

I heard a hollow crash and a tiny metallic tinkle. A bear had cracked the bin open with one swipe. Cautiously, the smaller animals near it moved in on the feast.

Now the people were showing up; in cars, on foot through the snow, in wheelchairs, on bicycles.

They gathered by the side of the road, leaving the street itself clear. That was important; I knew it somehow.

Granny Nichol's door opened. She let her dog Trevor out. "Good morning, everyone!" she said. She stepped onto her porch. She was carrying a bird cage. In it, a parrot shrieked and hopped from its swing to the floor of its cage and back again. "Shh, Billy, shh," she crooned.

"Get me the bleep outta here, lady!" it cawed. "It's time, can't you tell?"

"Yes, I can, dear. Just hold your horses."

Granny Nichol put the cage on the floor of her porch and creakily opened its door. The parrot leaped out. "Finally!" it hollered. Its wings were clipped, so it climbed, beak and claws, to join its avian cousins perched on Granny's eavestrough. Pets were exiting from all the houses, freed by their owners, who were also coming out onto the sidewalk.

"What about people's tropical fish?" the teenager asked. "They can't come out into this cold."

Nobody answered her, because just then, the sky directly above us went dark. "Is it the Apocalypse?" cried someone.

"Don't be an idiot," replied someone else.

If it was the Apocalypse, it was taking the form of a row of lumpy, somewhat spherical objects, each about four storeys high, landing soundlessly in the street in either direction as far as the eye could see. You know when an orange goes bad, and gets this kind of pretty blue fuzz on it? They looked like that. Funny; I always thought spaceships would be shiny and metal. Like in the movies. These looked like something I'd throw into my composting bin.

A bulge appeared in the side of each object. I wasn't scared. I don't think anyone was. We all just waited. The raccoon kept gnawing on the fish head it had retrieved.

Each bulge split open, and an animal or two stepped, slithered or flew out. I saw a hippopotamus, and a lynx, and I think a cassowary. A colourful butterfly clung to the alligator's brow, like a ribbon-bow. A human being came out of one ship, leaning on a goat for support. She was old—the human, I mean—and her features were African, and she was smiling.

They all came out, and behind them, their ships sealed, like those cool bandages. They all started talking to us, though no one's lips moved.

The ship in front of my house had disgorged some kind of cow, or antelope, or deer. No, too chesty for a deer, and too graceful for a cow. It had close, tawny fur, with deep brown stripes on its face and sides. Two long, thin horns stuck out from the top of its head. On its shoulder was a bird. The bird was smallish and plump, almost round. Its feathers were a deep grey with whitish flecks. It had a yellow beak with a reddish bit around its nostrils.

The beast picked its way carefully towards us through the snow. The bird on its shoulders wobbled, but hung on. They got close to us, stopped, looked us over. We looked back.

"So," said the antelope thing, "anybody wanna ride?"

"In that?" asked the bear. It got down on all fours, sniffed at the rotten orange ship.

"Yeah," said the bird. "You can come if you want to. It's a hoot."

An owl on a telephone pole above us hooted. The pigeons laughed.

"Where does it go?" asked the raccoon.

The antelope thing looked thoughtful. "Best I can describe it is, next door. You can visit, and if you like it, you can stay. Or you can come back here. Whaddya say?"

"Can we think about it?" asked the man who'd crashed into my front stairs.

"No. No time." The bird was addressing us over its shoulder. The antelope thing was already heading back to the ship. "Now or never. One-time offer only."

"Wait!" yelled a cat, turning in fretful circles at my feet.

The beast stopped and turned around. "We've discovered," it said, "that there are two kinds of creatures. The ones who come with us, we call them the Adventurers."

"And the others?" hissed the cat.

"We call them the Beautiful Losers. Because this Earth is beautiful and fearful, and it's a brave choice to stay, to never see anywhere but it. Just touch the skin of the ship, and it'll open for you." They disappeared back inside.

"Oryx and crake created He them," whispered the young woman.

"What?" I said.

"That was a spotted crake, and the thing it was sitting on was an oryx."

Birds were streaming into the ship. Granny Nichol was making her way to it as quickly as she could go. Her parrot, however, had clambered down to the porch and was headed determinedly back inside the house.

"Honey," said the man, "I really want to go. You coming?"

The young woman smiled at her father. "You go, Dad," she said. "I like being rockbound."

He hugged her tightly.

"But you have to come back, okay?" she said. "So you can tell me all about it."

She stood and waved while he disappeared into the ship's side. "Aren't you going?" she asked me.

Nearly every creature had made its choice. I saw smaller rotten-orange pods flying out of windows and doors. The tropical fish, I thought. And the shut-ins and the babies. I guessed that some of the ships had gone into the rivers, lakes, and seas. I looked at the snow shovel in my hands. Stay and shovel snow, or go and see what lay next door to this world?

The young woman gave me a gentle shove on the shoulder. "Go on," she said.

Delia Jarrett-Macauley

The youngest daughter of Sierra Leonean parents, she earned her PhD in English from the University of London and ran the first Black Women's Studies courses on the MA in Women's Studies at the University of Kent. She is the author of The Life of Una Marson 1905–1965 *(2019) and the Orwell prize-winning novel* Moses, Citizen and Me *(2006), as well as having edited* Reconstructing Womanhood, Reconstructing Feminism: Writings on Black Women *(1986) and* Shakespeare, Race and Performance: The Diverse Bard in Contemporary Britain *(2018). She has held fellowships at the universities of Warwick and London, has curated several creative programmes in Europe and Africa, presented programmes on BBC Radio discussing Sierra Leone and literature and spoken at numerous public events. She has taught and worked in academia, broadcasting and as a consultant. In 2016, she was appointed Chair of the Caine Prize for African Writing.*

The Bedford Women

It was a summer's day in 1968. I was a small child on a visit to London to see my sister, Daphne.

The train journey from Leicester to London had spun my excitement to dizzying heights. Now, we were making our way through the flurry of crowds in Regent's Park, its lawns resplendent in the sunshine. As we headed towards the creamy white buildings of Bedford College, we noticed how truly beautiful the swans were gliding on the still lakes of the Park.

Daphne was reading English at Bedford College, my mother had told me.

Nice, I'd thought. Because I couldn't imagine reading anything better.

All the way there, I'd been looking forward to seeing my sister. All year, I'd been longing to see where she sat and walked, and slept and read English.

And I was not disappointed. Inside the hall of residence, my breath stopped and a true awe gripped my heart. A world of style and study. On her return trips home, Daphne had brought back an assortment of books—Penguin paperbacks priced 2 shillings and 6 pence, leather-bound novels by Austen, Dickens and Wilkie Collins, and dictionaries of Old Icelandic, French and Middle English. She met us with laughter. In her person, she was glamour. Dressy, good with words, sharp. She owned a transistor radio. The song about love, love me do filled the room. I admired the flicked-back curl of her '60s hairstyle and the solid black gown hanging behind the door.

After hellos, it was time for me to play outside in the corridors. All afternoon I slid and skied along the polished floors, my patent-leather shoes finding their golden boards secretly magical in the same way that white swans and fast trains and old languages were.

Bedford College, London!

Big, brilliant London!

It was the middle of summer. Daphne was twenty. She had gone to London to continue her education, ordinarily a simple, personal venture. But Daphne, an African woman undergraduate, unwittingly or wittingly, was a figure in the social storm transforming university campuses in England, France and the United States. Only a few black African women were students at English universities during that decade. Their scarcity was an old deep pattern in higher education, a marked response to their gender and colour that had not yet found the global chorus to expose it.

1968 was a mould-breaking year: on university campuses from Paris to New York, students were protesting against the old order, against bureaucratic elites, against capitalism, sexism and racism and all forms of authoritarianism. One direct result of student protest was the birth of black studies programmes in such places as Cornell, Howard and Harvard.

Another brave new venture towards the close of that heady decade was the founding of the publishing house, Allison and Busby. Margaret Busby, from Ghana, had read English at Bedford College, and by 1968 was famous for being the first black woman to own a London publishing house. In tune with the zeitgeist, Margaret built a list of radical African and Caribbean writers, West Indian men such as C.L.R. James, who would probably have attended university had one existed in their region when they were young, and the Nigerian novelist, Buchi Emecheta.

The Bedford College Archives record that a century before Margaret and Daphne completed their studies, their first black woman student enrolled there.

In summer 1859, Sarah Parker Remond wandered through the streets of Bloomsbury. That was a sight to behold for the Londoners going about their normal business! An African-American woman walking across Bedford Square and into the liberal, non-sectarian college of higher education for women—Bedford College! Strange for Sarah, too, to be freely carrying an English novel in her bag when secondary schooling had once been denied her.

Born in Salem, Massachusetts, in 1826, the youngest of eight children in a successful family of freeborn people, Sarah passed the entrance examination to attend secondary school, but her stay was short-lived. After just one week of gazing up at the chalkboard, Sarah was sent packing. The segregationist committee would not allow her to remain in class among the white children.

Back on the steps of her family's hair salon, Sarah sat desperate to read. She devoured pamphlets, newspapers and anything else she could get her hands on. She had seen what her brother Charles, a gifted orator, could accomplish travelling to London, speaking on platforms. She wanted to be as successful as her parents, whose money came from catering and hairdressing businesses. She didn't just want to be charming. She wanted her life to count.

In spring 1853, when her brother Charles was called to Boston, Sarah and her sister Caroline agreed to accompany him. In Boston, they met with their friend William Neil who gladly bought four one-dollar tickets, by post, for a night at the opera. Donizetti's comic opera *Don Pasquale* was playing at the Howard Athenaeum with the brilliant German soprano Henriette Sontag playing Norino.

Sarah was thrilled to be going. Time off work, time off worry.

Sarah and Caroline dressed up in their finery. They wanted to be attractive and William was delighted to be escorting two gorgeous women on one excursion. The Athenaeum had boasted a sell-out opening show with Sheridan's *School for Scandal*, and on this evening, too, the Boston house was full. They had tickets for the Family Circle and were heading there, when William noticed the theatre manager, a Mr Palmer, signalling to them.

"You can't sit there," he informed them.

William showed the manager their tickets and insisted on their right to be seated.

Mr Palmer would not budge. "The Gallery or out!"

William refused to move and his guests stood by him, equally adamant.

Mr Palmer called for back up, which arrived in the form of Officer C.P. Philbrick, who ordered them to go. As the drama escalated, a mob gathering outside as voices were raised, Sarah was brutally knocked down the steps. Her dress was torn. Stunned, Sarah felt pain in her shoulder. She could not stand or move her legs.

The story hit the press when a lawsuit was brought. The refusal to desegregate the Athenaeum, in spite of private assurances to do so, cost the theatre $500, paid as compensation to Sarah. She also insisted on being given four good tickets for the opera. William C. Neil's assessment of the case appeared in the *The Liberator* on 17 December 1853:

> American colorphobia is never more rampant towards its victims, than when one would avail himself of the facilities of mental improvement in common with the more favored dominant party—as if his complexion was indeed, prima facie evidence that he was an intruder within the sacred portals of knowledge.

Bedford College, founded in 1849, was one of the few *sacred portals of knowledge* for Victorian women. Poor girls got no schooling. Girls from wealthy families had the benefit of home schooling and some attended boarding-schools. The few who went higher received vocational training, often to become governesses in their turn. For Black Victorians, traditionally excluded from the sacred portals of knowledge, access to them could be transformative. At Cambridge University, Alexander Crummell, another anti-slavery orator, laid the foundations for Pan-African thought in the 1840s.

At Bedford, Sarah demonstrated her love of learning by registering for several courses: ancient history, mathematics, geography, French, Latin, elocution and vocal music, and away from her studies, she socialised widely, making friends with English women whose hospitality and lack of prejudice she appreciated deeply. In 1859 she toured Britain, making speeches against slavery. On some occasions, such as the Dublin address, she focused on the plight of women caught up in slavery, demonstrating an adeptness in handling gender, race and class issues together. The Dublin speech was published in the *Anti-Slavery Advocate* on 3 November 1859.

The *English Woman's Journal* also recorded her views in "A Colored Lady Lecturer" in June 1861:

> My strongest desire through life has been to be educated. I found the most exquisite pleasure in reading and as we had no library, I read every book which came in my way, and I longed for more. Again and again mother would endeavor to have us placed in some private school but being colored, we were refused.

Sarah found a genuine welcome at Bedford. She boarded with its founder, the philanthropist Jesser Reid, at her home in nearby Grenville Street. There was much for these two women to discuss, their lives being so rich and full of purpose. Church, State, Darwinism? Europe, America? Social strife? Civil wars?

Why should we imagine they talked and talked?

Because it's not possible to imagine otherwise.

Jesser, born in 1789 to an ironmonger father and his wife, had become an extremely wealthy widow after just one year of marriage to her doctor husband; and in spite of prejudice and embarrassingly low student enrolment, she had written herself into the history books by founding Bedford College. She had seen first-hand what it meant to be voiceless. At the 1840 World Anti-Slavery Convention, she had met Mott and other women delegates who had been refused the right to speak. Now here was Sarah, a black woman, whose metier had been public speaking since the age of sixteen. Sarah had toured North-East America and Canada on the anti-slavery trail, and by the time she stepped over the threshold of Jesser's home at 6 Grenville Street, a single woman in her thirties, she had battled racial hostility at boarding houses, on steamships and in railway cars.

Unsurprisingly, perhaps, both women signed the 1866 Suffrage petition calling on the government to grant Women's Right to Vote. That August, Sarah arrived in Florence, Italy, via Switzerland. She was there to study medicine. Natural cures, attention to diet and the benefit of the housebound spending time in warm climes made sense to her, she discovered, while nevertheless, gaining her formal training at the prestigious Santa Maria Nuova, said to be the first truly modern hospital in Western Europe.

Sarah knew people in Italy. Mazzini, the founder of Friends of Italy, was an acquaintance. Also, Anne Whitney, the American poet and sculptor, who was struck by Sarah's "handsome dark person set off by a broad gold thread wound round and round her head, and a white shawl." Sarah enjoyed the more fluid European society and longed for the time when camaraderie between the races in the United States would become the norm. She had tried to make changes to the American way of life. Her failed attempt to have references to white males removed from New York State's constitution would have extended rights to black people and to women. That failure had drawn her back to Europe. In Rome, Sarah married an Italian from Sardinia, Lazzaro Pintor, in 1877 and her lifestyle, as a physician mingling with intellectuals and artists, granted her peace of mind and contentment.

We do not always know who has influenced our lives. The names of our foremothers are often lost. Women can thrive without their cultural history but like samples of DNA taken and retained way back for future testing, sources help to categorise their blood line to let the heart grow strong.

My sister Daphne was in her late twenties when she left London for East Africa. In Kenya and Egypt, she worked for development organisations and championed women's rights. Returning to England more than a decade later, she went into local government and in 2001 became the first black woman director of Social Services in the UK.

By that time at the start of the twenty-first century, Margaret Busby's ambitious collection of the words and writings by women of African origin and descent *Daughters of Africa* was almost ten years old.

Margaret and Daphne, two of Bedford's notable alumnae, had turned reading English into something global, explosive and urgent.

Why should we imagine they were compared?

Because it's not possible to imagine otherwise.

When Daphne turned up at Bedford College, her lecturers frequently addressed her as Margaret Busby, mistaking her for the seventeen-year-old West African who had preceded her as the only young woman of colour in the class, following in the solitary footsteps of Sarah Parker Remond a hundred years earlier.

Selected References:

Reyes, Angelita, "Allusive Autobiographical Performativity: Vicey Skipwith's Home Place and Sarah Remond Parker's Italian Retreat", in *Loopholes and Retreats: African-American Writers and the Nineteenth Century*, edited by John Cullen Gruesser and Hanna Wallinger. Vienna: Lit Verlag, 2009.

Catherine Johnson

*A British novelist and screenwriter, she is the author of several books for young
readers, including* Sawbones *(2013, winner of Young Quills best historical fiction for
children), and* The Curious Tale of The Lady Caraboo, *nominated for the Carnegie
Medal and Shortlisted for* The Bookseller YA Prize *in 2016. Her latest books are*
Freedom, *which has also been nominated for the Carnegie Medal, and* Race to The
Frozen North *(2018). She has also written for film, including the award-winning*
Bullet Boy, *as well as for television. Her radio play* Fresh Berries *was shortlisted for
the Prix Italia. She studied at St Martin's School of Art. She now has her own place,
by the sea in Hastings, and is looking forward again.*

The Year I Lost

I set out to write a memoir, capture a moment; something about being eight years
old, lying in the bed wedged into the end of a caravan and hearing the sound of the
blacksmiths' hammer from across the valley. About being brown and odd and never
finding anywhere I fitted in. But then the thoughts of now kept rushing in.

The void of now, which is where I have come to live.

I am at the end of a very long chapter in my life. Mourning for a life I had once, and
the very ordinary—in the run of things—break up of a thirty-four-year partnership.
It wasn't perfect, nothing is. In fact my daughter said I should have left him years ago.

Why didn't I?

Is it the devil you know? Is it the trade-off of being one half of something, of
having a secure—as much as any future can be secure—future? Of being smug in
my coupledom? I have been guilty of all that. And of taking him for granted. And
also of lessening myself, of walking softly, of not knowing so much, of turning down
work. Of trying to police what I wore and how I wore it. Not majorly. Subtly. Quietly.
Ordinarily.

I worked hard—too hard, he says now—and was always, always, contrite for that
one time twenty something years ago when I got drunk and kissed someone else.

Now I live in a spare room in someone else's house. My belated punishment.
What I deserve. After all, women like me, we are liars, neither one thing nor the other.
Untrustworthy. It's a fact. There are plays about us. Stories about us. Warnings about
us. In some lights I might pass as Mediterranean—what a joke. Or North African, or
South American. Something else I wasn't, something I am not. Because what I am is
uncertain, duplicitous. Two-faced.

I am fifty-six. I have two grown-up children. I have published twenty books and
written more. I've written one feature film that got made (others didn't) and won
prizes for my writing. I have grey hair and lines that cut into the side of my face.

In a previous life, only one year ago, I had a favourite duvet cover and some bowls my friend gave me for my birthday. I had a house and a room at the top to work in with shelves and a window that looked out onto the sea. A picture a friend drew of my daughter in France. Those photos of the children. The eggcups. The yoghurt pots I saved (what for?). The blanket my mother gave me and the jacket my father made for me. My knitting-needles, bundles of them, sharp and slippery, just like me.

The endless endless books.

Today I live in someone else's spare room. I have two suitcases. A few boxes of books. A growing number of bags, one for dirty washing, one for my swimming gear, one for my school visits when I have to appear like an author, clean and professional. Last year's accounts in a selection of shoeboxes. My marriage certificate and some soap.

I thought I'd be here for a couple of months. It's been ages now.

I've been mourning the future I thought I'd have, but learning to see a different one.

Of course I've been stupid.

"Don't text him, mum!" "Don't look at her Instagram!" But I can't help it. It's like picking scabs. And it shows me, reminds me, exactly what I am worth. Which of course feels like nothing. No thing.

He is reborn. Youthful, exciting and smug in his new love. I am bitter, old, empty. Two babies, four pregnancies. Those ghost children I murdered, is this their revenge? Have they moved in with their father? Are they sitting with him at night, leafing through photographs of her, listening to his sighs?

I have lost so much weight, my old clothes no longer fit. They belong to someone else. I tell myself it will be all right and if I say it enough, won't it be true?

A long time ago when our relationship first hit the rocks—that drunken kissing, remember? I was terrified of what I had done to him, of what I might have lost. The holes in the wall, the words he spat at me. Of course I knew how much I deserved each and every one. I consoled myself by thinking how successful I was in putting myself in between him and the children. Of course I know now I failed at that too.

I was always making excuses then. Smoothing things over, still not cleaning enough. Trying to prove how good I was. How sorry I was. Then at Tesco's buying long-life apple juice, I would read the date on the carton—it was always six months ahead. I would tell myself in six months I will be all right, we will be all right.

It is just me now.

And those ghost children are not my enemies. They were, are, happy not to be born. Both snug and secure in their never-being. After all, the youngest would be sixteen now and slamming doors.

One day, when I do get that place of my own, they will move in with me. Their flesh and blood siblings have moved on and there will be space. They will sit on the sofa or the kitchen chairs (I will have kitchen chairs) and sleep next to me in my bed, whispering in my ear through the night, telling me I did the right thing, telling me it will be all right. I will be all right.

Susan Nalugwa Kiguli

Born in Uganda, she is an academic and poet. She holds a PhD in English from the University of Leeds (UK), sponsored by the Commonwealth Scholarship Scheme, is an Associate Professor and has served as Head of the Department of Literature at Makerere University, Uganda. She was the 2011 African Studies Association Presidential Fellow, which gave her an opportunity to read her poetry at the Library of Congress, Washington, DC, in November 2011. The former chairperson of FEMRITE—Uganda Women Writers' Association, she currently serves on the Advisory Board for the African Writers Trust. She was the chief convener for both the second Eastern African Literary and Cultural Studies Conference, August 2015, and "Celebrating Ugandan Writing: Okot p'Bitek's Song of Lawino at 50", held in March 2016 at Makerere University. She is the author of The African Saga *(1998) and* Home Floats in a Distance/Zuhause Treibt in der Ferne (Gedichte) *(2012), a bilingual book in English and German.*

The Naked Truth or The Truth of Nakedness

(On 17 April 2015, elderly women in Apaa village, Amuru district, stripped naked before the then minister of internal affairs General Aronda Nyakairima, lands minister Daudi Migereko and a team of land surveyors as they visited the disputed boundary between Amuru and Adjumani districts in Northern Uganda.)

The Amuru women realise that they have nothing left
So they rise and stand without their clothes.
They advance to fight with their bodies
Against power that has nothing to lose
Because it will take everything.

The Amuru women surge forward with their bodies
Resisting inscription
Erasing branding
They whirl with what they have
Compelling the gaze away from the land
Which everyone thinks they are fighting for...

The Amuru women force us to look upon
The human body that lives on the land.
They make powerful vehicles stop

Because the women are moving as they are
To claim their lives.
They exhort us to read their bodies
As the history of belonging
As stories of ownership
As tales of taboo facing taboo.

If the land must go
The women of the land
Must strip
To rearrange the protocol of knowledge
The women of Amuru without their dresses
Read again the theory of decency.

The women get up separate from their clothing
To decry the forced fracture from their land,
Their history,
Their life.

The Amuru women move as if in dance
Without fabric, without even leaves.
They move forward
With their bare breasts,
Bare bellies, bare hips
Vulnerable and weak
But alarmingly unassailable
So the wave of invaders must halt their chase
Their cultural antennae prevail on them
Not to move, not to look…

The women keep time regardless
They flow with the motion of their rage
Their emptiness
They are set to lose nothing
Since invaders will take everything.

N.B. *the title of this poem is a favourite expression of my teacher,*
Prof. Timothy Wangusa.

Lauri Kubuitsile

She is the author of many works of fiction for children and adults, including the short-story collection In the Spirit of McPhineas Lata and Other Stories. *She was the 2007 winner of the BTA/Anglo Platinum Short Story Competition and the recipient of the Botswana Ministry of Youth and Culture Orange Botswerere Award for Creative Writing in the same year. She has twice won the Golden Baobab Prize for children's writing and was shortlisted for the 2011 Caine Prize. Her most recent novel,* The Scattering *(Penguin 2016) won Best International Fiction Book at the 2017 Sharjah International Book Fair. She lives in Botswana.*

The Colours of Love

He arrived with the spicy purple of the sunset, at the end of a long, hot, dusty day. They sat on the cool veranda and watched him walk up the side of the road into town.

"Where's he from?" asked Mma Boago, the owner of Mable's Takeaway, a takeaway that had never known a woman by the name of Mable.

"Don't know. What's that he's carrying?" asked Johnny-Boy, Mma Boago's perpetual customer and occasional bed-mate, squinting his eyes to get a better look.

"Looks like a guitar. Dirty long dreadlocks and a guitar. He's not bringing anything we need around here, that's for damn sure." Mma Boago turned and went back inside; she had magwinya in the deep fryer and couldn't waste time keeping track of unwanted strangers.

Warona was dragging her daughter, Kelapile, to the clinic when she spotted him. She wasn't one to believe in love at first sight and fairy tales with happy endings, having witnessed Kelapile's father's profession of undying love just before he slipped into bed with the neighbour. It was more than being heart sore, Warona's heart had been pulled out, knocked around for twelve rounds, and then placed back into her chest to perform only the bare minimum required to keep her moving. Some days she wished it would give up on that too.

"Hurry! They'll fire me if I'm not back in an hour." Kelapile's legs could only go so fast, decided by their three-year-old length. In frustration, Warona bent down and pulled the child up onto her back. When she looked up again, there he was.

"Do you know where I can find the guest house?"

Practical Warona didn't mention to anyone the way that her eyes went a bit funny the first time she saw him. She didn't mention the golden light that surrounded this odd stranger. It made her feel warm, and a barely held memory flooded over her, a remembered feeling, one that she had flung away deep into the folds and creases of the grey matter in her brain to be forgotten forever. It was joy; she felt a warm, orange joy.

"Are you okay?" he asked. His full lips and kind dark eyes overwhelmed with concern.

"I'm fine, thanks. The guest house? Come with me, I'll show you. It's near the clinic where I'm going."

As Kelapile fell asleep on her back, Warona, with each step, fell in love with this stranger. It was reckless and without sense, but irresistible. It was a curious, spooky magic and, against character, she welcomed it.

"I'm Silas," he said.

She smiled. "I'm Warona."

That was the beginning. The village looked on with jealous eyes as the pair flew high up to the clouds floating lazily in the silky blue sky, while the villagers stayed stuck to earth with their leaded minds and chained hearts. Resentment built against the couple and leaked out in words whispered in hidden corners and small actions made in public.

"Nothing good can come of that," Mma Boago cautioned, while the wisp of a wish hovered nearby.

Johnny-Boy nodded in agreement.

They knew only that love defined by the limits of a stingy life. Status-gaining love. Money-grubbing love. Security-seeking love. It had been so long since pure love had moved among them that all they could see was an outsider, an enemy. A threat.

Days passed. Silas played music while Warona hung bits of forest-green glass in the sunny window to create emerald patches of light that flicked around the one-roomed house. Kelapile danced. It was like that every day as they tried to circumnavigate the tricky path they had set out on.

Silas was happy where they were, but he spoke of other places where he had travelled, of the world out there where every step brought a new surprise and a new way to think about things. Aquamarine seas with white whip cream waves. Brown and gold beaches. Magenta mountains. Warona would lie in his arms and listen about those magical places and Silas would rub her head, opening her mind to make space for all of the pictures he created.

But it wasn't all smooth sailing. The fog of gossip filtered through their shell of private dreams and Warona was affected. She wondered if the rumours were true. When she slipped into the villagers' way of thinking, she fought against Silas.

"Stop it!" she'd shout. "What do you want from me? Go back where you came from, you know you will one day!" Tears flowed and she tried hard to make her heart a block of cold silver ice.

Silas was not troubled by this. He knew words backed down when you faced up to them and told it like it was. He would slowly reel Warona back in, pour warm love over her ice heart, and set her back on the course they were travelling.

Then one grey day, they disappeared. All three of them.

Mma Boago was cutting off chicken heads when Johnny-Boy came rushing in. He ran this way and that, his eyes wild with excitement. "I saw it myself!"

"Saw what?" Mma Boago said, as the cleaver came down with a thud, separating surprised body from instantly dead head.

"They're gone."

"Who's gone?"

"Warona, the baby, and that stranger. They walked down the road, back into the sun from where he came. Walked and then just…they were suddenly gone."

"Better. People were getting ideas. We don't need that kind of thing around here." Mma Boago raised the cleaver and slammed it down hard into the wood of the chopping-block.

Johnny-Boy pulled out a beer from the under-counter fridge, took a big gulp and nodded his head. Like always, he thought, Mma Boago was probably right.

Goretti Kyomuhendo

A Ugandan novelist and short story writer, she attended university in South Africa, earning an MA in Creative Writing from the University of KwaZulu-Natal in Durban. Her published novels include The First Daughter *(1996),* Secret No More *(1999),* Sara and the Boy Soldier *(2000),* Whispers from Vera *(2002) and* Waiting: A Novel of Uganda's Hidden War *(2007). She has also written two children's books,* Justus Saves His Uncle *(2008) and* A Chance to Survive *(2008), and is the author of* The Essential Handbook for African Creative Writers *(2013). She was a founding member and the first Programmes Coordinator for FEMRITE—Uganda Women Writers' Association and is the founder and director of the African Writers Trust, which works to bridge the divide between African writers in the diaspora and on the continent, bringing them together to promote synergies and to foster knowledge and learning between the two groups. She currently lives in London.*

Lost and Found

On Wednesday afternoon, when I arrive at Entebbe airport, I expect my whole family to be waiting to receive me; after all, I have spent seven years in America and I know they are as anxious to see me as I am to see them. But only Hajati, my big sister is waiting to welcome me.

"Where's everybody?" I ask Hajati.

Hajati says nothing and I repeat the question, trying to keep my calm, and wondering what could have happened to my mother, six siblings, their spouses, children and other extended family.

Hajati doubles her step instead, aiming for the vending machine to pay for the parking ticket. I am right behind her, and before she can insert the ticket into the machine, I grab her shoulder, forcing her to stop and look at me.

"They will see you next week," she answers, "I gave them the wrong date for your arrival."

"What do you mean?"

Hajati waits for the machine to discharge the ticket before answering. "I'll explain in a minute. Here, let me help you with the luggage, my car is over there."

As she pushes the trolley with my two suitcases: a medium sized one and my hand luggage, Hajati struggles to keep pace. I don't feel I'm walking as fast as I normally do but Hajati complains that my speed is too fast for her, and asks if I think this is America.

"Why did you give them the wrong date?" I press on, as I wait for Hajati to open the car. It is black and shaped like a coffin. I have not seen this type before. A Toyata NOAH, I read from the inscription on its rear.

"Is this all the luggage you travelled with?" Hajati asks me as I help her place the bags on the back seat. The NOAH has no boot.

"Yes," I nod my head, looking directly into her face. Her eyes, I notice, seem to be the only feature that hasn't changed about my sister since I left—and since she became a Muslim after marrying a Muslim man and started wearing the hijab. And we started calling her Hajati. Her eyes reveal the sister I knew then: collected, sensible, and forthright. It wasn't like her not to tell the truth.

"Why did you lie to them?" I'm still on Hajati's case, and I refuse to take any further step until I get to the bottom of this. Hajati is forced to tell me there and then, as we stand head to head on the hot, car park tarmac.

"It's that picture you sent me last month. I mean, what would people say? That you live in America or South Sudan? You will stay with me for a while. I have arranged for the salon woman to come over tomorrow to fix your hair, and nails, and face. They will see you next week. As for your weight loss…"

"I'm on a diet."

I've been struggling to lose weight for almost a year now and I'm finally happy with the results. And I want to protest about Hajati's plan of hiding me and the proposed makeover. But I don't. It's the way she talks—the way she carries herself; and perhaps it's the hijab, which I'm seeing her wearing for the first time. The hijab has created a barrier to our communication—and an uncertainty about how I deal with her. It's like I don't know who my real sister is any more.

People are like water. When did this city become so crowded? The cars stretch as far as the eye can see. The boda-bodas zoom past at unbelievable speed. And the potholes, eeiii! They are like fishponds.

"Yarabi Mungu!" Hajati swears as a she dodges a huge pothole that has dug a crater in the middle of the road. She swerves to avoid a boda-boda who nearly yanks off her driving mirror. Pedestrians pour onto the street as if they are fleeing the war.

"Wallahi, I'm going to crush someone," Hajati hisses. She drives on neither the left nor the right, but where there are fewest obstacles.

I hold on to the dashboard, grateful for the strength of the seatbelt.

They will see you next week, Hajati had said, when I arrived that Wednesday afternoon, and *not*: You will see them next week. I see what she meant now. After the salon woman is finished with me after two days of hard work, I feel like a trophy—ready to be presented.

On the first day, she worked on my face: shaving my eyebrows to a fine line with a new razor, which she opened in my presence to prove it was being used for the first time, and hence no possibility of spreading HIV. For the nails, I resisted the artificial ones, insisting on painting both my finger and toe nails with henna, which looked more natural against my black skin.

On the second day, she focused on my hair: soaking the dreadlocks in water first, then getting rid of the lumps and bends that had accumulated over time. Afterwards, she tightened and smeared the locks with natural almond oil, before crocheting them into a beautiful, tall pile.

The next day is Saturday and it's also Hajati's eldest son's birthday. He's turning fifteen. His mother had promised to take him and his siblings and classmates out to his restaurant of choice. But now the plans have changed because we can't risk going out in case someone spots me. Instead, Hajati has invited his friends to the house, and we're going to order a take away.

"KFC!" the birthday boy shouts.

"McDonald's!" the two younger siblings chorus together.

"Pizza Hut!"

"Chicken Tonight!"

"Café Javas!"

"Fang Fang!"

"What do you prefer?" Hajati asks me. "Don't listen to these children, you are the visitor and we'll go by what you choose."

"Gosh! I didn't even know there was a McDonald's in this country. I wouldn't want to put you to any trouble, and besides, the birthday boy should..."

"No trouble at all, we'll order online and JumiaFood will deliver whatever you want from any of these restaurants."

"I would like to eat something different..."

"This is different. We've been eating matooke since you arrived."

"I meant different to what I normally eat in…"

"Then try Café Javas. They have the best chips and…"

Chips! I should object. I'm on a diet.

In the morning, we shower like birds. There's only one bathroom in Hajati's house and we are rushing to beat the traffic so as to arrive at my mother's in time for lunch. This is the day that Hajati gave the family as my arrival date, and she told them she would be driving me from the airport straight to my mum's house, and we would all converge there for lunch. Hajati's children have been sworn to secrecy. This is how I remember my mother—when I was a nine-, ten-, eleven-year-old—accompanying her to visit my paternal aunt who lived not too far from our house. My mother, as I remember her then, talked with her hands, but mostly with her feet or face. My aunt always offered us food when we visited her, and my mother would pinch me on the leg with her big toe under the table, and the message could be interpreted to mean a host of things:

"Don't touch that food because it might be laced with poison. I know this auntie of yours very well. She smiles only on the surface but beneath, she's boiling with jealousy. Besides, everyone at church knows her as a witch."

OR

"Why are you not paying attention when your auntie speaks to you? She might think you despise her cooking."

OR

"Don't put too much food on your plate. It's bad manners to eat too much when invited to the table. Just put a little bit, and in any case, we're not going to stay long."

Over time, I had learnt to make the correct interpretation of the message my mother wanted to convey. On occasion, she would point to my aunt with her mouth, or kill one eye, and I would still have to decipher the meaning. I don't remember her taking any of my siblings to visit. It seemed it was always me who accompanied her. And it made me feel special. It made our bond stronger, especially because of our coded communication. I wonder if my mother still talks like that.

We arrive before everyone else and I go straight into the house to look for my mother. The large family room hasn't changed much and exudes the familiar, musky scent. The family portrait still hangs on the wall with all seven of us staring intently into the lens; a crooked smile here, a missing tooth there, a grin, a sombre face.

There by the mango tree, which still nestles between the back garden and the main house, I find my mother. She's sipping from a plastic cup and does not look up when I approach her. Hajati is hurrying to catch up with me. I'm standing right in front of my mother when she looks up and ululates.

"Yiii Yiiii Yiiii! Eyes cannot sleep hungry. Saiso?" She calls me by my childhood nickname, which I had almost forgotten. My heart swells with warmth, and the memory of my childhood, and of our time together. It's like I never left. As I make to go down on my knees so I can greet her properly, she takes another sip and swishes the water around her mouth before spitting it out. The water lands on my face.

"Mother!" I turn to look at Hajati, who is just standing there, watching us quietly.

"Her sight is gone," Hajati says.

"She's blind?"

Hajati answers "yes" with the nod of her head.

"But why didn't you tell me? Why didn't anyone tell me!"

"Tell you?"

"Yesssssss." I am yelling. "I have only been away and not dead. She's my mother, too. I could have done something. When did all this happen?"

Hajati shrugs.

"Saiso?" My mother calls again, flailing her arms, looking for me.

Patrice Lawrence

Born in Brighton and brought up in an Italian-Trinidadian family in mid-Sussex, she now lives in East London and is an award-winning writer, who has published fiction for both adults and children. Her debut Young Adult novel, Orangeboy *(2016), won* The Bookseller *YA Prize and the Waterstones Prize for Older Children's Fiction, and was shortlisted for the Costa Children's Book Award and many regional awards.* Indigo Donut *(2017), her second book, was shortlisted for* The Bookseller *YA Prize, was Book of the Week in* The Times, *the* Sunday Times *and* The Observer, *and was one of* The Times' *top children's books in 2017. Both books have been nominated for the Carnegie Award.*

Sin

Jacob turned into Five Aces community centre car park, locked the car and went in. He was still struck by the smell: damp clothes, powdered soup, hot metal and steam. He stopped by the notice board. Bric-a-brac wanted. One o'clock club with benefits advice and a Turkish interpreter organised in advance if required. The disabled riding school needed trustees. The Scouts were cycling to Berlin to raise money for a children's cancer charity.

The memorial service for Travis Norman was next Wednesday afternoon. The man had been only two years older than Jacob.

He found Miss Lynn in the kitchen arranging muffins on a tray. Her thick grey hair was twisted into Chinese bumps. He moved closer and kissed the back of her neck. She smelt of coconut oil.

"Jacob!"

"What's the problem? There's no one about."

She let him nestle, but when she pulled away to finish her cake arrangement, he felt stupidly resentful. He picked up the empty muffin box.

"No ginger cake? No coconut loaf?"

"Take up baking, Jacob. Then you can have a good supply."

"It's not the same."

She showed him her hands. The finger joints were swollen and painful. He reached to stroke her thumb but she shook her head.

He said, "You should use that mixing machine your daughter sent you from Canada."

She scowled at him. "I don't know why she sent me that thing when I can get the same from Argos. And she knows I prefer a good wooden spoon."

"That true, Lynette?"

She smiled. "I have to go. People coming soon."

They emerged into the sunshine two hours later. It was slow progress towards Leyton as the road people must have known Jacob's route and planted temporary traffic lights every few feet.

"Turn now!" Miss Lynn prodded his arm. "Now!"

Jacob swerved in front of a road sweeper into her parking area. He opened the passenger door for her.

"I'll only be a moment," she said.

"Why can't I come in?"

"It's my castle, Jacob. I'm the queen and I decide who can enter. And whatever you believe, my darling, you are not my knight in shining armour."

"Are you keeping a secret man in there?"

"Yes. He's tied to a table leg and I feed him home-made ginger cake."

She bent forwards, pushed against the car seat and eased herself up.

He sat with the car door open letting the sun warm his thoughts. Someone in the flats was cooking; he smelt garlic and coriander. A couple of planes were leaving long condensation trails in the sky like scars. The sun passed behind a cloud as big as a cruise liner.

His phone rang. "Jacob, come and help me with the food."

Miss Lynn was standing by the doorway, carrying two large straw shopping baskets and a heavy, alien walking-stick. She had changed into roomy dark trousers, but underneath he imagined thick, obstinate joints refusing to connect her to movement. He fumbled with the baskets. Her stick clopped on the concrete as they slowly made their way to the car. He loaded the baskets in slow motion to give her time to settle.

"Direct me, Miss Lynn."

"With pleasure, Mr Jacob."

They headed north. Again, she prodded. Again, he turned. He stopped and she gave him the key to open the padlock on the gate. It was hard enough for him. How did she manage the fiddlesome lock and the rusted bolt by herself? He returned to the car, drove them through and locked up again.

He looked around, savouring the rare warmth and stillness. Beyond the allotment, where he stood, lay the canal, sluggish and green with algae. He followed Miss Lynn, edging slowly between the plots. Vines thick with tiny purple grapes clung to makeshift supports. The sunflowers had dropped, but late-planted peas and clusters of stock belied the closeness of winter. A few steps ahead of him, Miss Lynn brushed away brambles, collapsing bean stalks and branches of shrinking damsons.

"It's all closing down," she said. "For the first two years, I followed the instructions on the seed packets and laid down crops every two weeks. And then I realised I didn't want to live off lettuce. And every day, there was a new battle with the slugs and the snails, sometimes other people. My neighbour planted an apple tree last year."

Miss Lynn turned to tell the story into his eyes.

"She didn't think she would get anything at all. But even though the tree didn't come up to so…"

She used the basket to indicate her hip.

"…she sees these little things, like ping-pong balls starting to show up on the branches. And she gets all excited, like she's expecting a child. So she starts coming by, checking every day, but she's not quite sure when they're ready. She picks a couple and they're sour, not ripe. Then she looks at another one, and as she's examining it, a small worm crawls out and shakes its head at her. She gets all frightened and throws it in the compost. And then the tree gets some sort of fungus or bug or something and it takes time to sort it out. Finally, there's just one apple left. If she could have found a snake to put in the branches to guard it, she would have done so."

Jacob rested his basket on the ground. "So what happened?"

"What do you expect? She came here one morning and the thing's gone."

Miss Lynn headed off again. Jacob stood still, thinking.

"Miss Lynn?"

She carried on walking, her stick stamping circles in the earth.

"Miss Lynn?"

She still didn't turn around.

"Lynette!"

"Yes!"

He slipped in front of her, barring the path ahead. "Miss Lynn, how did that apple taste?"

She stared back at him. "Jacob, it tasted like temptation itself."

Lesley Lokko

A Ghanaian-Scottish architect, academic and novelist, she says: "I live almost simultaneously in Johannesburg, London, Accra and Edinburgh." Her books include the edited collection White Papers, Black Marks: Race, Culture, Architecture *(2000),* Saffron Skies *(2005),* Bitter Chocolate *(2008),* Rich Girl, Poor Girl *(2009),* One Secret Summer *(2010),* A Private Affair *(2011),* Sundowners *(2012),* An Absolute Deception *(2012),* Little White Lies *(2013) and* The Last Debutante *(2017). She is Associate Professor and Head of the Graduate School of Architecture at the University of Johannesburg.*

"No more than three, please!"

As someone who occupies two quite distinct careers simultaneously—architect and novelist—I worry about the effects of one discipline on the other. After nearly twenty years I've found it more productive to think about the word "worry" in its secondary meaning, "to discover or solve something by persistent thought." To allow architecture to "worry" fiction, and vice versa.

I should say that I'm an academic architect (although I have built buildings), so the distance between the two disciplines is perhaps not quite so vast. Much of teaching is story-telling, constructing narratives, leading by example. I often begin my teaching year with this instruction to my students (quoting Steven Covey): "Live out of your imagination, not your history."

Of course, one's history is always intimately tied to one's imagination, but in the case of Africa, the weight of history is heavier than almost anywhere else. The artist's burden is to push *against* that weight, not be smothered by it. I'm writing this in South Africa, where I currently live and where the weight of history is different to where I'm *from*, which is Ghana, the first country in sub-Saharan Africa to gain independence in 1957, some seven years before I was born. In her wonderful collection of essays *Writing in the Dark: Whiteness and the Literary Imagination* (2003), Toni Morrison makes the point that "writers are readers before they become writers." In my case it's certainly true, and relevant to what I write is what I read.

My father was among the first cohorts of young Ghanaians sent overseas to study in the years after independence. He went on a government scholarship to St Andrew's University, returning some ten years later with a Scots wife and baby daughter. He took up a position as an army surgeon, posted to military bases around the country, and three more children followed, but Ghana's economy collapsed in the late 1960s and early '70s, and by the time I was seven or eight and of reading age, there wasn't a functioning bookshop in the country. On Saturday mornings, I drove with my father to the elegant Legon University Bookshop, only to find the shelves bare.

Salvation came in an unlikely form. For almost a decade, between 1972 and 1981, a network of parents, uncles and aunts banded together to bring back from their travels books for each other's children. An invitation to an overseas conference meant a suitcase full of novels shared among the fifty or sixty families who made up our universe. We child readers had no say in what was brought back, the upside being that we have some of the widest reading tastes I know. One aunt brought back nothing but Mills & Boon. Another would only purchase Penguins. We took what we were given gratefully. It was the blockbusters that had me hooked. Harold Robbins. Leon Uris. Arthur Hailey. Frederick Forsyth. Curiously, the authors were mostly male, their books seeming to combine two essentials: sex and history.

When I was seventeen, a Scots poet I met on a kibbutz gave me two books that changed my life forever. The opening line of *July's People* by Nadine Gordimer goes: "You like to have some cup of tea?" It was the first time I ever saw African-accented English in print. It gives me goosebumps to remember it. The second book was Toni Morrison's *Sula*, and on the inside leaf he scribbled: *"her strangeness, her craving for the other half of her equation, her tremendous curiosity and her gift for metaphor…"* He never explained what he meant by the dedication, but the words *"other half of her equation"* were powerful enough to make me seek out other works by Morrison; and she and Gordimer make up the lasting parentheses of my reading life.

Shortly afterwards, at boarding-school in England, I half-heartedly studied the classics, from Shakespeare to Trollope to Hardy, aware that the world(s) they described seemed to have nothing to do with mine.

An attempt in my mid-twenties to write my own Mills & Boon met with swift rejection, and I turned to architecture instead. But in my final year at architecture school I met someone who set my life on a course that would lead to both architecture and writing, but also—and perhaps more importantly—back to Africa. It was 1992. The UK was in the grip of a recession and we came 6,000 miles to southern Africa to find work. Namibia had gained independence in 1990 and was testing the boundaries and limits of its new-found freedom, and South Africa was gearing up for hers. We occupied quite an odd position: black and African, clearly, but European, too, on account of education and our London adult-student lives. We found ourselves at the centre of a dynamic between black and white: interlopers on the one hand, interlocutors on the other. I wrote a diary at night as a way of processing the encounters.

After eighteen months in southern Africa, we returned to London and I embarked on my Master's in architecture. To support myself through my studies, I worked as a temporary secretary during the holidays. One Easter, on my way to work in the City, I picked up a copy of *Time Out*, the weekly entertainment guide, and on the cover, in bold script, was the headline: "How to Write a Blockbuster!"

The article was wittily tongue-in-cheek. "A is for the 'arrogant male'; B is for the 'beautiful girl', M is for 'money—lots of it'", and so on. I read it from cover to cover, an idea forming.

That night I began the laborious task of turning my diaries into a blockbuster.

Two years and 200,000 words later, I began hawking it around publishers. In spring 2004, my first novel, *Sundowners*, was published and went on to sell 100,000 copies in thirteen languages. Of the many conversations between author, agent, editor and marketing director, one in particular stands out. It went something like this:

"Er, the thing is we don't want to be *too* prominent about it."

"About what?"

"Well, who you are."

"How so?"

"Well, what we *don't* want is to wind up putting you in the Black Interest section."

"What does *that* mean?"

"Three hundred copies sold if you're lucky."

"So what do you propose?"

"Let's play it down. The whole 'race' thing."

In 2005, Kenyan writer Binyavanga Wainaina published a controversial essay, "How To Write About Africa". With its uneasy combination of laugh-out-loud satire and biting sarcasm, it offers tips: "Always use the word 'Africa' or 'Darkness' or 'Safari' in your title. Subtitles may include the words 'Zanzibar', 'Congo', 'Big', 'Sky', 'Shadow', 'Drum', 'Sun' or 'Bygone'... After celebrity activists and aid workers, conservationists are Africa's most important people. Do not offend them..." Frustrated by the narrow bandwidth of tropes defining the African literary landscape, Wainaina turned each cliché on its head, establishing himself in the process as one of the continent's sharpest critical voices.

In the eleven novels I have published since 2004, I return to locales I know intimately: Ghana, Mali, Burkina Faso, Cote d'Ivoire, Togo, South Africa, Namibia, Kenya... At the heart of each is a cross-cultural, cross-racial relationship played out against the backdrop of well-known cities (London, New York, Paris, Berlin), lesser-known cities (Kuala Lumpur, Accra, Djibouti) and a few cities that sit somewhere between, popular in the Western imagination (Johannesburg, Cape Town, Singapore). There are many themes familiar to readers of "women's fiction", a broad, all-encompassing term—sex, power, relationships, family, secrets, fashion—into which "other" themes are woven: race, identity, history, politics. At first, I fancied myself a genre-buster, breaking out of the traditional mould by merging Africa and chick lit. It's fair to say that for the majority of my readers Africa remains exotic in a "safari-kind-of-way". Most love the detail, the colours, the descriptions of places they may never visit; few seem to *notice* that one or other of the characters is black. At one level, of course, it's heartening and proves *me*, not Wainaina, wrong. I began writing fiction with a half-formed intention to write a different kind of African into being: cosmopolitan, multicultural, modern, avant-garde, only to find that *he/she already existed*. Readers identified with the kinds of African characters I mistakenly believed I had invented. The revelation was not the readers; it was the industry.

In the mid-'90s, publishers were seeking to establish new categories that presumably would open up new sales "routes". Two of those, "faux-lit" and "bonkbusters", came closest to becoming literary movements in their own right and it was into the latter category that my books fell. Covers were always *pretty*, generally pink. A lonely girl in a sarong, walking down a deserted beach. Lettering was curled, gold, titles held ambiguous portent…hints of betrayals, by-gone days. *One Secret Summer*. *A Private Affair*. *An Absolute Deception*. *Bitter Chocolate*. The only title I ever chose, *Sundowners*, was intended to reference Gordimer's 2001 quote, "the sun has gone down on the last of the British Empire in Africa", though my publishers were firm: "It's a cocktail." Two conversations stand out, as uncomfortable for them as for me. The first had to do with plot:

"It's simple. Boy meets girl. Boy gets girl. Boy loses girl. Boy gets girl again…"

The second was exceptionally clear:

"It's not personal, of course…I wouldn't mind…but you're going to have to limit the number. The characters… We've had a little chat and…well, we think the best thing is to put a limit on it.'

"Limit on what?"

"Africans. The African characters. There's just too many. It's hard for your readers to…connect. So what we thought is, we'd keep to three. No more than three, please."

In J.M. Coetzee's novel *Elizabeth Costello*, published in 1999, the protagonist, a white South African novelist, says:

> The English novel is written in the first place by English people for English people. That's what makes it the English novel. The Russian novel is written by Russians, for Russians. But the African novel is not written by Africans, for Africans. African novelists may write about Africa, about African experiences, but they seem to me to be glancing over their shoulder all the time they write, at the foreigners who will read them. Whether they like it or not, they have accepted the role of interpreter, interpreting Africa to their readers. Yet how can you explore a world in all its depths if at the same time you are having to explain it to outsiders?

The relationship between intimacy (the solitary act of reading) and performance (the communal aspects of oral traditions) is one we continue to grapple with in Africa today. Coetzee is right: it is impossible to act simultaneously as interpreter and investigator.

Fast-forward to 2017. African literature, as it's called, is riding high. The roll-call is impressive: Chimamanda Adichie; Teju Cole, Aminatta Forna, Petina Gappah, Taiye Selasi, NoViolet Bulawayo… One must ask if the commercial category "African Writers" is equally a creative one. Scottish-born Aminatta Forna wonders why her novel, *The Hired Man*, set in Croatia, is in the "African" section of bookshops, alongside Teju Cole's *Open City*, which takes place largely in Manhattan. Chinua Achebe reflected that the famous June 1962 conference of African writers at Makerere University attempted and failed "to define African literature satisfactorily. Was it literature produced in Africa, or about Africa? Could African literature be on any subject, or must it have an African theme?" As Ben Okri has written, "I am a writer who works very hard to sing from all the things that affect him. Literature doesn't have a country."

It may not, but publishers certainly do. The tensions over classification are exacerbated by the fact that much African literature is published outside Africa, for audiences that may *include* Africans, but not exclusively, with everyone having a view on what it should be, what it should say, who can write it and who may read it. Yet the confusion and contestation are liberating. The "real" question is whether current and aspiring African writers will invent forms of their own.

At the recent inaugural Africa Architecture Awards, in the closing statement of the programme my words were: "Speak up, speak out, speak back." They've been variously interpreted as a "final call to arms" but their truth is simpler and more direct. *Speak up*: Experiment. Innovate. Invent. *Speak out*. Truthfully. Authentically. Confidently. *Speak back*: Cheekily. Irreverently. Playfully.

That's African literature. Or architecture. And probably no different for creativity anywhere.

Karen Lord

A Barbadian author and research consultant, she is best known for her debut novel Redemption in Indigo, *which won the 2008 Frank Collymore Literary Award, the 2010 Carl Brandon Parallax Award, the 2011 William L. Crawford Award, the 2011 Mythopoeic Fantasy Award for Adult Literature and the 2012 Kitschies Golden Tentacle (Best Debut) and was nominated for the 2011 World Fantasy Award for Best Novel. She is the author of the science fiction duology* The Best of All Possible Worlds *(2013) and* The Galaxy Game *(2014), and the editor of the anthology* New Worlds, Old Ways: Speculative Tales from the Caribbean *(2016).*

Cities of the Sun

The minister's secretary leaned forward and said, "We need a story."

The historian blinked. "Ah. Propaganda."

The secretary drew back. "Why would you say that?" he demanded, but his indignant stare shifted for a fraction of a second as if distracted by a slight and unexpected prick of shame.

The historian looked away, gazing instead at the pictures that bloomed and faded on the windows in a persuasive, soothing cycle. Faces, earnest faces of earnest people, asking to lead or to be allowed to continue leading. Words, slogans really, full-scale ideologies and intentions condensed to a glance-sized moment. It was a very festival of decoration, enhanced by the occasional glint and glitter as the solar cells in the windowpanes adjusted with minute efficiency to capture the sun's rays. Not unexpected in a ministry office, but these days she would see the same at the train stop, the fish market, anywhere that had walls and a large audience.

"What would you like to tell the people?" the historian asked kindly.

The secretary leaned forward again, but with caution, only halfway. "Tell them how we got here, and tell them where we're going—"

"And how you'll take us there? Your manifesto?" She chuckled at his annoyed expression. "I'm sorry. I'm a bit of a cynic these days. You want me to present our history, and our future…in a package like this." She waved a hand to the political messages—translucent, unobtrusive, yet insistent.

"If you can," the secretary replied stiffly. He stood, gave her a nod of stern farewell, and that was the end of the meeting.

The historian walked out into the daylight and paused to bask in the dappled glory of Heroes Square. Trees, natural and enhanced, filtered the sun with hungry leaves and eased the reflected brightness of the glass towers of a modern city. People moved within the innards of each building, dark pulses of collective life in constant motion, as hungry as the leaves and as numerous. What kind of retelling would move those crowds of singular souls from follow-foot compliance to fullness of choice?

"I can try," said the historian to herself.

They say I should tell it like it happened, so that the facts aren't forgotten, and the cities can rise again. I say no. If we want people to walk this path again, we have to tell more than facts. We must tell truths, root-deep, tree-tall testaments to understanding, because who knows who will build the cities, what they will be built of, where they will be constructed? Impossible to know in this present, impossible to know anything but the why. I will tell you this—*this* is why you must build the cities, and the why will bring forth the how, and the how will call to whomever can wield the power and the grace and the mercy of a steward.

May God send the means, as God sends the light of the sun. May God ordain the stewards, for a city needs stewards, not princes.

We were a hungry folk once, starved by design to make us a better fit for the machine that knew no rest, no satisfaction, but only a constant burning and turning. In this universe, perpetual motion comes not as a gift, but a cost, and so even our starved selves were insufficient fuel to keep the machine advancing.

A hungry mind in a hungry body knows no rest. It yearns, and that yearning extends from the birth of the elders to the last breath of the young. It spans lifetimes and timelines and makes demands of probabilities, pushing at the boundaries of the universe with a nagging finger: *is it time yet? Is it* our *time yet?*

We needed four generations, long enough to wash the taint of trauma from our genes. We wanted four millennia, not of supremacy, but of simple existence to give quiet, bold proof that our dream was possible. We managed four decades, and then enemies fell upon us.

Who was it tore us down? Men afraid to die alone, small without the bowed backs of others to stand on, weak without the coddling of servants, and poor without the labour of peasants. They made their civilisations like ever-expanding pyramids constructed from the bottom up, always dependent on the strength of a new, broader base. Destined to topple in time, they were doomed by design, and their people would turn to the conquest of others to delay the date of their own ruin.

But I tell it backwards. First, the dream. A city cannot be built in a day, but it must be built every day. Each cycle of decay must be countered by renewal, each new demand met with a new solution. The environment can be a partner to work with or an enemy to conquer, and the city itself a symbiont or a parasite.

You know the path we chose—the path our ancestors would have approved. And you know how difficult that was, with so many centuries of having strayed from that path, of having been lured and led from that path. But we wanted our future, and we worked for it. We planted the forests of baobab and banyan, taught them our names and our needs, our talents and our dreams. The eco/system kept it stored up for us, reminding us not only of ourselves but also of each other. Instead of consuming each other, we fed each other, and so the chains of commerce became a web of mutual benefit, and economy became ecology.

We celebrated our victory and vowed to work even harder, and yet there were matters beyond our borders that gave cause for concern. A few remembered that peace within does not always inspire peace without. We may claim to have tamed jealousy and greed among ourselves, but certain outsiders would be revenged on us for our brazenness. How dare we flourish, survive, exist!

But the dangers were yet over the horizon and the voices of certain elders were ignored. One elder said nothing. He quietly gathered a team of assistants and toiled away at saving the seeds of our forests and fields in a great vault. "But why?" the people asked him, and he replied, "Isn't it obvious? They will try to poison the trees."

Remembering now, I am thankful that no one laughed, but there may have been a few faces turned aside to hide a slight smile or an incredulous frown. Remembering now, it makes my heart cold to think how short were the days of peace that remained. The forests did not fall to poison, nor to blight, but to the wild malice of fire.

The audacity of our enemies is what saved us in the end. They struck with more haste than cunning. Had it been poison, had it been blight, the tainted soil would have taken centuries to recover. But forests know fire, and our knowledge and power was set unseen amid the roots below, waiting and ready for rebirth.

We needed no revenge and we took none. An overextended enemy is his own executioner, and we had only to wait. When we emerged from our strongholds below, the remnants of their shattered empire troubled us little, and then not at all.

So, the date of their ruin has come, and now that question *is it time? Is it now?* has an answer. Yes. Yes, our cities will be established again, slowly, day by day, unfolding like a tree that puts forth two new leaves for every one that dies. Yes, we will prepare for fire and also for blight, whether through chance or through malice. Yes, our generations will be strong and whole, our children will learn to be better than we are; yes, our civilisation will grow like a forest with strong roots and strong limbs, with leaves sunward, with hopes skyward. Yes.

I promised you truths, not facts. Not a manual, but a gospel; not a report, but a myth; not a request but an exhortation. I have told it as it happened, and as it will happen.

"I think he did not appreciate the manner of my telling, but I cannot be sure beyond the fact that I was never paid." The historian's voice was cheerful though a little cracked and weary, and her aged face was charming with the divine mischievousness of tricksters everywhere.

"Is that why you are in exile now?" the reporter asked, leaning forward eagerly.

The historian shook her head at his foolish bluntness. "This is not exile. This is retirement. The forests extend so far, there is no need to live in any city."

"Did you know what your story would do? That it would change everything?"

"What did I change? We still draw energy from the sun, we still preserve our names and deeds in the roots of the forests, we still remember how our enemies crept up on us while we were complacent."

"But you spoke of the enemy within. You warned us about our corruption."

"I only used the word 'blight' once. Maybe twice."

The reporter sat back, somehow satisfied within himself. "Three times. It was enough. It was the story that started the revolution, the rebirth that transformed us. You said enough."

"I cannot guess where lightning will strike, nor tell it to start a blaze...but two things I do know." She leaned forward and her eyes held the young man, not with charm but with authority. "A true tale is like clear water reflecting the hopes and fears of the listeners...and forests know fires; they will always recover in time."

The reporter mused on those two things during his return journey. He emerged from the transport, still thinking about the past and the future. He considered the cool, stone domes of a modern city, the hidden busyness of its citizens within, and, high above it all, the hungry leaves of trees tasting the sun to fuel and feed the people unto the fourth generation.

Jennifer Nansubuga Makumbi

A Ugandan novelist, short story writer, and lecturer, she now lives in Manchester, England, where she lectures in Creative Writing at Manchester Metropolitan University. Her first novel, Kintu, *won the* Kwani? *Manuscript Project in 2013 and was published to great success in Kenya. Her short story "Let's Tell This Story Properly" won the Commonwealth Short Story Prize in 2014, and is included in her new collection of stories* Love Made In Manchester *(2019). She was awarded a Windham–Campbell Literature Prize for Fiction in 2018.*

She is our Stupid

My sister Biira is actually my cousin.

Ever heard of King Midas' barber who saw the king's donkey ears and carried the secret until it became too much to bear? I stumbled on it five years ago at Biira's wedding and I have been carrying it since. But unlike Midas' barber—stupid git dug a hole in the earth, whispered the secret in there and buried it—my family does not read fiction. Bush grew on the barber's words and every time wind blew the bush whispered, *King Midas has donkey ears*. I've also changed the names. Of course, the barber was put to death. But for me, if word gets back to my family, death will be too kind.

Back in 1961, Aunty Flower goes to Britain on a sikaala to become a teacher—sikaala was scholarship or sikaalasip. Her name was Nnakimuli then. At the time, Ugandan scholars to Britain could not wait to come home, but not Aunty Flower, she did not write either. Instead, she translated Nnakimuli into Flower and was not heard of until 1972.

It was evening when a special hire from the airport parked in my grandfather's courtyard. Who jumps out of the car? Nnakimuli. As if she had left that morning for the city. They did not recognise her because she was so skinny a rod is fat. And she moved like a rod too. Then the hair. It was so big you thought she carried a mugugu on her head. And the makeup? Loud. But you know parents, a child can do things to herself but a parent won't be deceived. It was Grandfather who said, *Isn't this Nnakimuli?*

Family did not know whether to unlock their happiness because when her father reached to hug her, Nnakimuli planted kisses—on his right cheek and on his left and her father did not know what to do. The rest of the family held onto their happiness and waited for her to guide them on how to be happy to see her. When she spoke English to them, they apologised, *Had we known you were coming we would have bought a kilo of meat…haa, dry tea? Someone run to the shop and get a quarter of sugar… Remember to get milk from the mulaalo in the morning… Maybe you should sit up on a chair with Father; the ground is hard… The bedroom is in the dark… Will you manage our outside bathroom and toilet? Let's warm your bath water—you won't manage our cold water.* And when Nnakimuli said her name was Flower, the disconnect was complete. Their rural tongues called her *Fulawa.* When she helped them, *Fl, Fl, Flo-w-e-r*, they said *Fluew-eh.* Nonetheless, she had brought a little something for everyone. People whispered, *There's a little of Nnakimuli left in this Fulawa.*

Not Fulawa, maalo, it's Fl, Fl, Flueweh and they collapsed in giggles.

The following morning, Flower woke up at five, chose a hoe and waited to go digging. She scoffed when family woke up at 6 a.m. Now she spoke Luganda like she never left. Still, family fussed over her bare feet, *You'll knock your toes* chewing their tongues speaking English, *You're not used,* but she said, *Forget Flower; I am Nnakimuli.*

She followed them to the garden where they were going to dig. When they shared out the part that needed weeding, they put her at the end in case she failed to complete her portion. She finished first and started harvesting the day's food, collected firewood, tied her bunch and carried it on her head back home. She then fetched water from the well until the barrel in the kitchen was full. She even joined in peeling matooke. When the chores were done, she bathed and changed clothes. She asked Yeeko, her youngest sister, to walk her through the village greeting residents, asking about the departed, who got married, *How many children do you have,* and the residents marvelled on how Nnakimuli had not changed. However, they whispered to her family, *Feed her; put some flesh on those bones before she goes back.* Nnakimuli combed the village, remembering, eating wild fruit, catching up on gossip. For seven days, she carried on as if she was back for good and family relaxed. Then on the eighth day, after the chores, she got dressed, gave away her clothes and money to her father. She knelt down and said goodbye to her father.

"Which goodbye?" the old man was alarmed. "We're getting used to you: where are you going?"

"To the airport."

"Yii-yii? Why didn't you tell us? We'd have escorted you."

Entebbe Airport had a waving bay then. After your loved one checked in, you went to the top and waited. When they walked out on the tarmac, you called their name and waved. Then they climbed the steps to the plane, turned at the door, and waved to you one last time and you jumped and screamed until the door closed. Then the engine whirled so loud it would burst your ears and it was both joyous and painful as the plane taxied out of sight and then it came back at a nvumulo speed and jumped in the air and the wheels tucked in and you waved until it disappeared. Then a sense of loss descended on you as you turned away.

"Don't worry, Dad." She spoke English now. "I'll catch a bus to Kampala and then a taxi to the airport."

Realising that Flower was back, her father summoned all the English the missionaries taught him and said, "Mankyesta, see it for us."

"Yes, all of it," her siblings chimed as if Manchester was Wobulenzi Township which you could take in in a glance.

"Take a little stone," Yeeko snivelled, "and throw it into Mankyesta. Then it'll treat you well."

That was the last time the family saw her sane. She did not write, not even after the wars—the Idi Amin one or the Museveni one—to see who had died and who had survived. Now family believes that when she visited, madness was starting.

Don't ask how I know all of this. I hear things, I watch, I put things together and get to the truth. Like when I heard my five grandmothers, sisters to my real grandmother who died giving birth to Aunty Yeeko, whisper that Aunty Zawedde should have had Biira. Me, being young, I thought it was because Biira is a bit too beautiful. Aunty Zawedde is childless.

In 1981, a Ugandan from Britain came looking for the family. He says that Flower is in a mental asylum. Family asks, *How?* Apparently, she began falling mad, on and off, in the '70s. *How is she mad?* The messenger didn't know. *Who's looking after her?* You don't need family to look after you in a mental asylum. *You mean our child is all alone like that?* She's with other sick people and medical people. *Who put her there?* Her husband. *Husband, which husband?* She was married. *Don't tell me she had children as well.* No. *Ehhuu! But what kind of husband dumps our child in an asylum without telling us? How did he marry her without telling us?* Also, ask yourselves, the messenger said, how Flower married him without telling you. The silence was awkward. However, love is stubborn. Family insisted, *Us, we still love our person,* Nnakimuli might have been stupid to cut herself off the family, but she was their stupid. *Is her husband one of us or of those places?* Of those places. *Kdto!*

They had suspected as much. The messenger gave them the address and left. Family began to look for people who knew people in Britain. Calls were made; letters were written. *We have our person in this place; can you check on her and give us advice?* In the end, family decided to bring Aunty Flower back home, *Let her be mad here with us.* The British were wonderful; they gave Aunt Flower a nurse to escort her on the flight.

Aunt Flower had got big. A bigness that extended over there. She smoked worse than wet wood. Had a stash of Marlboro. *Yii, but this Britain,* family lamented, *she even learnt to smoke?* With the medicine from Britain, Aunt Flower was neither mad nor sane. She was slow and silent.

Then the medicine ran out and real madness started. People fall mad in different ways, some go silent and angry, some strip and scream, some attack people throwing stones, Aunty Flower was agitated, would not sit still, as if caged. *I am Flower Downe, Down with an e.* Who? family asked. *Mrs Downe.* Family accepted. *I want to go.* Go where? *Let me go.* But where? *I could be Negro or West Indian—how would you know?* They let her go. Obviously, England was still in her head. But someone kept an eye on her. All she did was roam and remind people that she was Down with an e. But by 6 p.m., she was home. After a month, the family stopped worrying. Soon, the bigness disappeared but not the smoking. Through the years, Flower Downe roamed the villages laughing, arguing, smoking. She is always smart, takes interest in what she wears. However, if you want to see Aunty Flower's madness proper, touch her cigarettes.

Then in 1989 someone remarked, *Isn't that pregnancy I see on Flower?* The shock. *Yii but men have no mercy—a mad woman?* An urgent meeting of her siblings, their uncles and aunts was called, *What do we do, what do we do?* There were threats, *If we ever catch him!* They tried to coax her, *Flower, who touched you there?* But when she smiled dreamily, they changed tactics. *Tell us about your friend, Mrs Downe.* She skipped out of the room. A man was hired to tail her. Nothing.

A few month later, Aunt Flower disappeared. When I came home for holidays, she was not pregnant. I imagined they had removed it. Meanwhile, Mum had had Biira but I don't remember seeing her pregnant. I was young and stupid and did not think twice about it.

There is nothing to tell about Biira. I mean, what do I know? I am the eldest—she is the youngest. She came late, a welcome mistake, we presumed. Like late children, she was indulged. She is the loving, protective, fiercely loyal but spoilt sister. We grew up without spectacle, close-knit. But we don't have strong family resemblance—everyone looks like themselves. Thus, there is nothing about Biira to single her out apart from being beautiful. But all families have that selfish sibling who takes all the family looks—what do you do? However, if you want to see Biira's anger say she resembles Aunty Flower.

Then Biira found a man. We did the usual rites families do when a girl gets engaged. Then on the wedding day, Aunty Flower came to church. No one informed her, no one gave her transport, no one told her what to wear, yet she turned up at church decked up in a magnificent busuuti like the mother of the bride. Okay, jewellery and makeup were over the top, but she sat quiet—no smoking, no agitating, just smiling—as Biira took her vows. And why was Dad and his sibling restless throughout the service? Later they said, *Flower came because Biira resembles her*. I thought, *Lie to yourselves*. Aunty Flower never came to any of my cousins' weddings.

That day of Biira's wedding, I looked at Aunt Flower properly and I'm telling you the way Biira resembles her is not innocent—I mean gestures, gait, fingers, even facial expressions? How? I have been watching Aunt Flower since. There is no doubt that her mind is absent—deaths, births, marriages in the family, do not register. However, mention Biira and you will see moments of lucidity in Aunt Flower.

Reneilwe Malatji

Born in Modjadji Village, she grew up at Turfloop Township in Limpopo Province, South Africa. She completed her BA degree, postgraduate teaching diploma in Education and a senior degree in Education at the University of Limpopo. She then served for 18 years in the Department of Education as a teacher, subject advisor and subject specialist in Limpopo and Mpumalanga Provinces. She completed a postgraduate diploma in Journalism and an MA in Creative Writing at Rhodes University in 2010 and 2011 respectively, going on to study for a PhD in Creative Writing at the University of Western Cape. Her collection of short stories, Love-Interrupted *(2013), won the Aidoo-Snyder Award and the South African Literary Award Nadine Gordimer short story category. She taught ELT students at Rhodes University (2012–13) and is currently a lecturer in Contemporary and Multilingual Studies at the University of Limpopo.*

My Perfect Husband

A man cheating on his wife in our community did not make headlines. Infidelity was as commonplace as taking a bath in the morning. In most cases, the girlfriend automatically assumed the status of deputy wife. The community accepted her as the official nyatsi even though the man did not marry her. She could even conceive two or more children with the man and he might provide a house for them. Then she would be accepted by the man's family, especially the parents and siblings. Any woman who left her husband because of a nyatsi was considered an idiot.

"Where does she think she can get a man who does not cheat? All men cheat, it's in their nature." This was always said in our township.

The more affluent a man was, the more women he would have. The chances of finding a man who did not have a nyatsi were as slim as winning the Lottery. Some women had tried to take it up with their mothers-in-law and all they got was: "He is better, he has only one nyatsi. His father had five nyatsis. And look! I am still here. You just have to live with it. Be grateful that he is still supporting the family."

Most women knew their husbands' nyatsis. Some women fought tooth-and-nail with them, but those who did not were considered to be well-mannered and mature. Most women lived with the pain of sharing their men and family resources with these nyatsis.

I was one of the few lucky women in Sibasa township. My husband Mashudu was a decent man. There were no official or unofficial nyatsis. He was a devoted father and husband. He had never been unfaithful. Most women regarded him as the model husband. If they could, they would have traded in their adulterous spouses for him.

"You are the luckiest woman in the world. If all these men were like Mashudu, this world would be a better place," my female colleagues often commented when they saw him dropping me off at work.

Mashudu was the kind of man that came home every day straight after work. He was also a sober-minded man who took neither alcohol nor cigarettes. If he was not at home I always knew exactly where he was. We went everywhere together: the shops, church, funerals and weddings. People called us the finger-and-nail couple. Up to now I could not even drive because he took me everywhere I wanted to go.

I was a teacher at Sibasa Primary School and Mashudu was the education circuit office manager at the Sibasa circuit office. He was a church elder at the Mbilwi Lutheran church and was also the chairman of the church building committee. In our house we all went to church every Sunday. After church he greeted everyone, offering the aged and disabled a lift home. His disarming smile displayed his perfect white teeth.

About a year ago, one showery Friday morning on our way to work, he told me he had been invited by the department to go to Pretoria that Sunday to attend an Outcomes-based Education workshop. The workshop was to commence on Monday morning and would continue until late on Friday. He told me that he planned to visit his uncle in Mapetla township, Soweto, on the following Saturday and would be home a week later.

That Sunday when he left for his trip my two sons carried his bags and the provisions I prepared for him out to our car. As he drove away, I watched him through our mesh wire fence with a feeling of misgiving that I could not explain.

"Don't forget to find out if they can keep the food in the fridge for you." These were my last words as he left.

Monday afternoon I went to the choir practice at our church as usual. My heart almost skipped a beat when I saw Mashudu's twin brother Ntakuseni. His tall figure with its large stomach blocked the door. All of a sudden I could not sing. It felt like there was something stuck in my throat. For a while I continued to hum the song. Then I recalled that Mashudu had not phoned the previous night to tell me that he had arrived safely. I was not worried about him because he was the kind of man that did not care for cellphones. Most of the time, he forgot his in the car.

I stepped away from the inquisitive eyes of the choir and hurried to where Ntakuseni was standing. He looked gloomy. He took my hand and directed me to the car. I left without saying goodbye to the choir members.

"Ah, *khotsimuhulu*," I greeted him, "why are you here? Is there a problem?" I said, expecting the worst.

"We shall talk at home. Mashudu is waiting for you there. My mother and father are also there," he said.

"What is wrong? Is everything okay? Is Mashudu okay?" I asked.

"Mashudu is fine, but there is a problem. Don't worry, it's a solvable one. But only you can solve it. We will talk at home," said Ntakuseni.

The five-minute drive felt like forever. I knew my brother-in-law well enough not to probe any further. I knew he was not going to tell me what was going on upfront.

Mashudu and his parents were sitting on the kitchen chairs and Mashudu was on the bed. His eyes were red and his expression grim. He was still wearing yesterday's clothes. His black trousers and white shirt looked soiled. When I came in, his eyes fell to the carpet. I could feel heavy words and thoughts in the air even before anyone said anything.

I knelt down, clasped my hands together, and bowed my head to greet my in-laws appropriately.

"Aah!" I said, still kneeling.

"Aah!" said my mother-in-law.

"Ndaah!" said my father-in-law.

"Khotsi a Tshiandze, why are you back so soon?" I said. I then raised my head but remained seated on the carpet. I had to look down because as a daughter-in-law it would have been rude to look my in-laws straight in the eyes.

"Tell her what happened," said my father-in-law to Mashudu.

"My dear wife," he began, his voice trembling.

"What is wrong?" I asked.

Mashudu looked down again and breathed heavily in and out.

"This is the most difficult thing I have ever had to tell you, but there is no other way," he said. "There has been a terrible accident. Our car is a write-off."

For a while I kept quiet. That was why his clothes were in such a state, I thought. The air was still heavy.

"Well, we must thank God. A car is nothing. We will get another one," I said.

He was silent.

"There is more. Tell her," said my mother-in-law.

"Someone else was in the car," said Mashudu. "She did not survive."

"She?" I asked.

"Yes. Mark Mulaudzi's wife, Matodzi," said my father-in-law.

"The accident happened last night, just before the Kranskop Tollgate. We were hit by a truck whose brakes had failed," said Mashudu.

"I see," I said.

I kept quiet and waited, hoping to get some answers.

"The major dilemma is that Mark and his family up till now have not been informed. Mashudu is the only person who has this information, other than the Bela-Bela police. Mashudu promised the police that he would inform the family in person, as we are all family friends. So he cannot go there alone to report this. It won't look good," said my father-in-law.

"I see," I said.

"It will look bad if they are told that it was just the two of them in the car. Mark might be suspicious or angry. You know how people are. They could interpret it negatively and Mashudu might be in trouble or, worse, they might even kill or bewitch him. My dear sister, you know how the Venda people are," said Ntakuseni.

I felt hot and cold at the same time, like someone who was having hot flushes. It was then that I understood what was going on.

"So we will all accompany him to the Mulaudzi home. The story is that you were with them in the car. It's the only way we can get out of this whole thing," said my father-in-law, as if we had all been part of what had happened.

The disturbing and sad part was that they were not even negotiating with me. I was simply given instructions on what I had to do.

"I need time to think about this," I said.

Sarah Ládípò Manyika

She is a writer, academic and overall lover of stories who was raised in Nigeria and has lived in Kenya, France, Zimbabwe and England. Her bestselling debut novel, In Dependence, *was required reading in a number of high schools and universities around the world, while her second novel,* Like a Mule Bringing Ice Cream to the Sun, *was shortlisted for the UK's Goldsmith Prize and the California Book Award. Her non-fiction includes personal essays and intimate profiles of people she meets from Mrs Harris to Toni Morrison. She was founding Books Editor of Ozy Books and a long-time lecturer at San Francisco State University. She currently serves as Board Director for the women writers residency, Hedgebrook.*

The Ambassador's Wife

Yétúndé hears the soft click of the thermostat followed by a rapid whistle of warm air blowing through the floor vents. Night has fallen. It's time to shut the wooden blinds to the cold and dark.

She returns to the oven which is hot enough now to heat the food. She reaches into the cupboard for a baking sheet and then, a surprise: four green bottles huddled together at the back. Oregano. Basil. Coriander leaf. Tarragon. Where have these come from? *Schwartz* they proclaim from labels circling their bellies. Only then does it dawn on her that this must be the work of her father. He must have bought them earlier and hidden them, knowing that, not long after his return to Nigeria, she would find them.

"Bless you," she finds herself saying, using his words. "Bless you, darling." She takes the four bottles and brings them to the edge of the stove where she places them in a row along the black granite counter, next to the white paper towels. "No," she says, returning the ready-made meals to the freezer. Tonight she must cook. He would like that. She will make penne pasta, the children's favourite.

She lights two candles, humming as she nudges the shallots round and round in a shallow pool of hot oil. The translucent, purple slivers turn quickly to a crispy brown, so she lowers the flame and sprinkles salt, ground pepper, and two pinches of cumin. She calms the noisy sizzle with the back of her slotted spoon and smiles, relieved to hear her youngest, now singing in the shower. His tantrum forgotten.

The herbs her father has left are not what he used when she was a child. Back then she remembers him cooking just one thing: àmàlà. And there was nothing about this staple food that she liked—not the dark colour, not the grainy texture, not the bitter smell, and certainly not the way he whacked the yam flour and hot water against the side of the pan with such vigour that it seemed to go beyond what was needed.

Take, eat. This is my body that is broken for you.

Strange how these words return. Words learnt from church where her father would assist with communion. Take. Eat. Broken. For this is how it feels sometimes—the body, broken for others. She wonders how he felt dishing out this very Yorùbá food to his half-American children. Take. Eat. To his two motherless daughters who, were it possible, would have held their breath, closed their eyes and swallowed without chewing. She wonders whether he interpreted their culinary dislike as cultural rebellion. As his two children pushing back on that which was Yorùbá. Or whether he regarded their wrinkled up noses simply as bad behaviour requiring discipline.

> *Four green bottles standing on a wall*
> *And if one green bottle should accidentally fall*
> *There'll be three green bottles standing on a wall*

He tried this once, maybe thinking that if he sang to them the way their mother used to, it might make things better. Yétúndé takes a deep breath, slicing determinedly through green peppers and plump shiitake mushrooms. "Good," she sighs, pleased at least to have wriggled out of tonight's event—more tedious, polite conversation-making at some other ambassador's residence. At least conversation with the children was never forced—none of the artificial, diplomatic smiles of Washington DC. She stirs until the mushrooms lose their soft white edges and then adds chopped tomato, a splash of water, and a squirt of tomato puree. In retirement, her father has expanded his repertoire. Now he too prepares soups and vegetables and experiments with herbs and spices. Whenever she returns home to Ìlọrin, she looks forward to his fried plantains and smoked catfish made with palm oil and hot peppers.

Leaving her pasta sauce to simmer, Yétúndé goes to the foot of the stairs and calls for her children to set the table. "Coming," shouts one, then the other. She passes the display cabinet on the way back to the kitchen where her father, on his most recent stay, had placed her framed, double first from Cambridge. And there it still stands in the crowd of family photos. He said, "Your mother would have been so proud of you," as he made porridge that morning, the way he always did—half a cup of oats and a generous gush of water taken from tap to saucepan. She had smiled and was about to reply when he splashed cold milk all over his oats and added, "She would have been so proud to see you now as an ambassador's wife." Yétúndé watched him then, in silence, as he prayed over his porridge, tea, and smattering of pills.

He had a tendency to bump into her when they walked side by side. He nibbled his fingernails and fidgeted in church when he needed to use the toilet. For all these things he was always saying sorry. He couldn't resist making notes in the margins of every book he read, no matter who the books belonged to. Little pencil ticks and bars by the side of pertinent lines. For this too he would sometimes express remorse. Markings that she followed, trying to guess what had moved him and whether it might move her too. But he never apologized for not understanding what her graduation certificate meant to her.

Her tears flow because she misses her father and cannot stand the distance that now separates them. The tears flow because she's content by the stove and happy to remember her father complimenting her on what an excellent homemaker she is. The tears flow because she has struggled, for so long, to be acknowledged for something more than this.

Ros Martin

Born in London, of Nigerian and St Lucian parentage, she is based in Bristol, UK. She is a writer, cultural activist, feminist, playwright, author, poet, digital artist and creative educator in schools in local African diaspora history and heritage which she links to active citizenship. Her practice is collaborative and socially engaged. She is published online and in the anthologies Marginalia *(Jerwood Arvon mentoring scheme Anthology vol. 2, 2011),* No Condition is Permanent *(2010) and* The Reality Is… the Bristol Black Writers Anthology *(1998).*

Being Rendered Visible in The Georgian House Museum, Bristol

1798, Valet to Mr Pinney, Pero / William Jones has just died. A distressed maidservant to Mrs Pinney, Fanny Coker, is visited by an ancestral spirit, "the Old Slave"

"Like the wind on the ocean, violent, then eerily absent.
Gone."
Events dot,
an ever-moving timeline
Here, now, time stands still,
a Georgian time,
This room, this house, this city, globally
Eighteenth-century gentility
merchandise extracted from cane juice,
the sinews of sugar cultivation
in field, in house,
Invisible woman
Objects,
These
Memories…
in clay pipes,
Smooth, meditative, comforting,
distract from rumblings in an ever-hungry belly…
Ancestral spirits come.

…"Shall I tell you what it is like, life in a mulatto skin? In this household, I am tragedy, I am a lie! I am to be eternally grateful. I am to say nothing, think nothing, feel nothing, be nothing, but answerable to endless whims. Be grateful for what?"

"To the gods not them," the Old Slave Spirit says.

She, Fanny Coker, can see nothing to be grateful for.

The Old Sage motions to the open window. He holds out his palm, an emaciated hand releases a feather. It floats before it descends.

"A symbol of our ability as humans to rise above problems, pains, heartbreaks, illnesses; to travel to another world, to be reborn, to grow spiritually is our freedom."

"Please…don't say that word! I am so free," Fanny says, "I have freedom papers issued me aged eleven, yet my mother remains in captivity. With this new 'freedom', my owners draw me closer to them. I am raped aged fourteen.

"Nothing of my will can contradict theirs.

"Escape? Where would I go? Who do I trust? I must stay with Mrs Pinney, when Mr Pinney dies, he says, or my annuity goes.

"I know nobody. What would be my fate? I have seen and heard all I need to know about England, her freedoms the coterie of Baillies, Tobins, Gills and their ilk, uphold.

"In and out, in and out, like ships in yonder harbour, the claret-faced coterie, go in and out the house, apoplectic with rage. They lobby Parliament to counter the abolitionists' petitions. Jubilations from church bells and firecrackers resound long into the night the slave trade bill is defeated. Hoorah!

"But what is there for me to do, but dress up in fine petticoats, take tea in bone china cups with Mrs Pinney, so my sisters believe…'Fanny will never wield a cutlass to sugar cane grass!'

"Enough! No more Fanny Cokering!

"I am defeated by all this madness like Pero…

"Ah! At least he's free…

"And I am?"

"Who are any of us?" the Old Slave remarks. "Why are we here, but to add or take away from the sum of humanity of our own free will? Don't let their demands imprison your soul. Be free in your spirit or your heart will sink."

"Like William?" Fanny laughs.

"So selfish of him!"

Pero/William, the barber, bought on an auction block aged twelve, alongside her mother Igbo Polly, also twelve, and countless other frightened children.

The Old Slave Spirit draws on his pipe.

"Maybe, just maybe, William didn't mean to…"

"Drink and kill himself?" Fanny says. "Just wanted to be rendered useless?

"Who would ever believe that of Pero?

"Pero the tooth extractor, Pero the trader, Pero the money lender, Pero the loyal valet who served Mr Pinney nigh on thirty-two years, now ungratefully and wantonly gives up. Why?"

"…Maybe, just maybe, he wished to be returned to Nevis, to comfort, to raise his motherless daughter, be reunited with his beloved sisters."

"Only, how would that ever happen?" retorts Fanny.

"Your mother?"

"Don't."

Igbo Polly the seamstress, the trader, a midwife, in possession of a shingle and board house on Mountravers sugar plantation…

"Quite remarkable that!" says the Old Slave, "to retain one's African identity in one's name."

"Yet she'll go nowhere," Fanny says bitterly. "Igbo Polly who survives the trans-atlantic passage, a motherless girl child herself, separated from loved ones, can't even purchase her own freedom, or prevent her younger daughter and son, from cutting sugar cane grass!"

"What is it?"

"My mother, my brothers, my sisters, will I…ever…see them again?"

Fanny knows what the silence means.

"How will she or I bear it?"

"With all that your mother has experienced, do you not think she sees, she knows and worries for you; how her fifteen-year-oldest daughter could leave all behind, make that tumultuous journey, traversing an ocean full of ghosts and unrested spirits, to a land full of strangers, praying the while, that you may yet meet kindly people."

"There is no one. Nothing comforts me but my Baptist church where I am known as Frances."

"O Frances! Motherless child of a motherless child, is your mother not doing the same as you, choking back tears, finding good cheer to lift you and keep you going, in three-monthly exchange of letters and gifts; keeping under wraps, all the heaviness in her heart?"

"I miss them so much, and here, my life is one of madness!"

"Let the madness stay where it belongs. For when you push people down to elevate yourself and are dependent on those you despise, what can this yield for posterity but more lies and deceit? So pity them, they who cannot love another like themselves, they who know the price of everything but the value of nothing."

"They are my family. How I hate them! I'm supposed to pretend everything is fine. I am favoured." Fanny laughs.

"Be a witness to your own truths, have faith in humanity. There are those who strive and are seeking truth here, find them. Let go of hate. The moon, the stars, the skies and trees see everything and are there to watch over you; wherever you are, take heart."

The bell for the breakfast room rings.

"Go forward, daughter of Igbo woman."

Fanny picks up the feather from the floor. She straightens her back.

"William didn't mean to kill himself. I am in captivity but will my spirit to be free. I will provide for my family as long as I breathe."

"That's right, Fanny Coker."

Gone is the Old Slave Spirit.

Gone in 1820 is Fanny / Frances Coker, aged fifty-two.

Survived by her sisters, and ninety-five-year-old mother, who survives the end of slavery; to witness her own emancipation.

Pipes
A Baptist memorial stone,
The Georgian House, Bristol
Greenbank cemetery…
Bones

Like the wind on the ocean, violent, then eerily absent,
Gone.

Karen McCarthy Woolf

Born in London to English and Jamaican parents she writes poetry and drama. Her collection An Aviary of Small Birds *(2014) was described as "extraordinarily moving and technically flawless" (Poetry Review), a "pitch perfect debut" (The Guardian) and was shortlisted for the Forward Felix Dennis and Fenton Aldeburgh prizes. She makes radio features and drama for BBC Radios 3 and 4, and has presented her work across the world, from the Americas and Europe to South East Asia.*

Of Trees & Other Fragments

—they all have names, Willow, Cedar, Oak, Elm…
                    mine is down a darker track
red pine shaved to skin-thick tiles

        Waterfall, by the waterfall, where spirits of the stream
race and dive from rocks, hold a small
child under—

one evening at dusk we mistake
a charred tree stump
—for a giant Man, with legs
        hidden in the brush

On Widbey Island
                        startled by a hummingbird
        I'm jumpy as a rabbit
the paths are tunnels and there's an axe
        struck deep

Mornings, at the retreat
        it's picking punnets
of sharp red strawberries, feeding rare-breed ducks
        rows of peas and chard

Victoria, dark-skinned and gamine, among candyfloss roses
and poppies, with her scarlet jumper
        and wicker basket—
she skips, almost
back to her angular, Swiss-style chalet
in a clearing, after dinner: Victoria in her little red…

*

you need to know that I don't
like
shadows and
        unidentified—
always being one step behind, behind…

*

        Jack's text says our cat
was sheltering under the mosaic table
from two jays

                I'm in Pike Place and witness
a crow attack, a blonde is dive bombed, then one more

—Is there any other language we understand?

*

In Warsaw E Annie Proulx
        writes me a note, To Karen, poet of trees, and climate change
and music, What are trees?

*

Last night Ed and I went for a walk in the dark with the moon, round
to the clearing. Last night Ed and I went for a walk,
it was dark, there was moonlight. He knew his way, in the dark,
along and off the path
        —When we get there, I slip my arm
around the rough-barked, slender waist of a young oak,
so companionable, and surprisingly warm

                              my fingers trace
adolescent names scarred into the trunk, a wonky
heart

*

At the reading I tell everyone *that horse chestnut was my friend*

*

a tree is a complex being
        that has relationships
        with soil, and air, and Jack reminds me,
mycelium
        as well as other trees'
        roots and branches
        and insects, with teeth

when thirsty a tree emits a
        noise, high and fast
        audible to humankind when slowed down a thousand times

a tree must
        deal with many teeth

a tree is a mass
        of tentacles in a sea of leaves

*

In the meeting we discuss a moment in Chapter 3, after
        Orlando marries
when she can't physically write:
        we don't need to hear the poem, it doesn't exist, the poem
        is called The Oak Tree.
                        It's a constant,
a companion, each era an annual, concentric ring cycle.
We know
we musn't write The Oak Tree. Not the poem. The tree
will find other ways to speak.
Surely we will welcome
the oak?

*

Are you wearing Eau d'Lancôme? the woman
with the long-haired
Alsation asks. Everyone has a dog. There are no women walking
in the woods without a dog. All the walkers are women.
Don't you have a dog?

*

This is how you learn to stay alive—
              sunlight streaming
through branches—
all young girls must remain
        alert. In the holly thicket, the Princess
from *Frozen* is deflated on a punctured balloon

other debris includes a red and white remnant
of crime scene tape

*

And then a breeze at last
        prompting leaf fall
        loud as fire
my youth flickering on and
off like
spiders' silk spinning in the sun
        among collapsed
fences, rotting stumps more than two
        centuries wide
a tiny, two-leaved seedling
pushing up

        O little seedling
you leave a deep and buried sorrow
even dancing can't derail

*

driftwood: great lobster claws
of rootlessness,
        whole palms, adrift and smoothed

what's wrong with roots? the wood asks

if trees were fully animate, surely they'd reach
down and squeeze
until we gushed like Sicilian oranges?

★

Yoga, under the ash and weeping willow
staring up into the canopy

        ash an unlikely synonym for green, verdant
against rare uninterrupted blue
no sign of die back
or other climactic disasters, two fat-breasted wood pigeons
roosting and quiet

        and I tell the story of how
I wasn't called Willow in the end, how
willow's chandelier teardrop drama
is overshadowed by its capacity for vigour
however hard you cut back

★

Jamaica, finally:
        at Devon House
        a whole class
        gathers, chitter-chattering, under a fruiting mango
                that reminds me of a tree at the hub
        of a village I passed through in Mozambique
                on the way to catch a ferry, its voluminous shade encompassing
                        at least four generations, three motorbikes
                        and a Vodacom vendor

★

The article describes
                the currently inexplicable
and multiple deaths of a dozen ancient baobabs
                some older than Christ

                        Thirst is a possible factor

★

Trees don't need to move
        to exact revenge, leave that to the crows

trees are now you see me, now you …
a long drawn-out, involuntary retreat
                              that ends in our asphyxiation

Meanwhile, give thanks for Sandalwood and Frankincense!

★

Can a fragment ever be complete——?

        Love shook my heart,
        Like the wind on the mountain
        Troubling the oak-trees

★

04.44
and I think of the bamboo in the hills
by Glengloffe
how the grove is many-stranded yet moves as one

and I think of Moxy
bamboo carver on the beach
outside the orthodoxies of the all-inclusive
who carves cups from the stems
with a Stanley knife, as well as
bongs and an instrument similar to a didgeridoo

        there's something hypnotic as curls of
green fall down onto white
sand, his hands worn, weathered
still steady—*no* he answers, *I never left Jamaica*

★

driftwood   a horizon of
        stars and stripes, flagpole after flagpole
one flagless, where a bald eagle perches

Useless Bay   shallow and
                        private, the water clear, the shoreline
littered with natural debris: for once a lack of plastic
        ·(so many billionaires own here)

> whole trees uprooted, bark stripped and polished
> to a grey sheen, smoother than pebbles, squid-like
> suckers groping cool air
> driftwood/
>   floating out to the ocean/ driftwood,
> bleached by the sun, whittled—

Wame Molefhe

A writer from Botswana, she has had her fiction published in local and international journals, anthologies and online. She has written a column for New Internationalist *(UK), as well as travel articles, and for television and radio. Her first book,* Just Once *(2009), is a collection of short stories for children. Her second short story collection is* Go Tell the Sun *(2011).*

I'm sure

You're sure in the way people from these parts mean when they say "Ahm sho". A grown-ass person will sniff the air and declare, "Ahm sho it's going to rain today." But it doesn't rain. Not this day nor the next nor the next. The drought slurps the land dry, exposing the dregs of dams: rocks, carcasses, broken bottles, cracked riverbeds, emaciated cows grazing on straw-coloured clumps of grass. The nation gathers at the dam wall to pray collectively for rain. Still, the liar doesn't apologise for leading people astray. Bearing no shame because his nose does not grow long; you feel the shame; you wear it. You resort to singing "liar liar pants on fire", but only in your heart.

That kind of "Ahm sho".

You're sure that if your Mama had called private parts by their name and not used a code decipherable by only you and your siblings, if she'd been able to make her tongue pronounce penis, and anus and vagina instead of calling them lavatory words, you'd have known to shout NO when you didn't want your most private parts touched. Instead you muttered eh-eh behind clamped teeth, or shrugged—even acquiesced, sometimes.

You're sure that if Mama hadn't averted her eyes when the aunty lifted the little girl's skirt, touched the little girl's front, making sneezing sounds, playing that "Hey-tia Motsoko!" game, you wouldn't have looked away either when you witnessed it. You would've slapped that witch's veined fingers away.

And perhaps if there was a word, in Setswana, a word other than "tshameka", to mean the act of sexual intercourse, maybe this act of intimacy wouldn't be treated as if it were a game to be played, a game in which there were winners and losers.

You're sure that if Mama hadn't instructed you to call all the men who visited your home "uncle", to always respect your elders or be clawed by vultures, you'd have slapped that uncle's yellow-nailed paw away when he brushed it against your breasts.

You'd have told Mama why you walked the winding car route to school. Maybe then she'd have understood why you arrived after the bell rang, instead of layering her whipping on the caning you'd already been given by the headmaster. You might've told your mama that you feared walking past the ogling men who sat by the roadside, zipping, unzipping their flies, cat calling you. You might've told her about the time one of them yelled, "ke itse yo o mo kgweding," and how you'd wondered how he'd known you were having your monthly. You'd tugged your uniform longer and pressed your thighs together, feeling them chafe like they did when you were pressed. That day you spent the Setswana, biology and domestic science periods silent, although you knew all the answers to the teachers' questions. You were just too afraid to ask to go to the toilet in case the boys heard and laughed, and said you were bleeding because you'd played too much, and that made you squirm with shame.

You'd have told Mama that one uncle—Papa's friend, actually—whispered that you were ripening as lusciously as the mangoes that he grew, and were almost ready to be plucked and sucked. He'd run his tongue over his lips like he could taste the sweet in his words, in you.

And you'd have told Mama that one uncle's son once showed you how he was going to play with you when there was no one home. You opened the outside tap on full blast like he told you to, then watched as the water drilled a hole in the earth and he plunged the hose deeper and deeper into the ground. He laughed with his lavatory mouth wide open, exposing his rusted teeth.

You never told Mama why you offered the kissing uncle with the prickly chin your hand in place of your lips and how he scratched your palm with his index finger when you did. And how when he thought no one could see, he clenched his fist and squeezed his thumb between his index and third fingers—thrust it in and out. But one day, your Papa was watching him through slitted eyes. And on that day, Papa leapt to his feet, like he'd been bitten by a snake and he marched that uncle out of our lives forever.

Then a day arrived when you met someone whose caresses warmed you in places with names you struggled to put your tongue around, you wondered again: what if your Mama had called private parts by their name and not used a code that only you and your siblings could decipher, perhaps you would be able to say I'm sure.

Marie NDiaye

translated by John Fletcher

Born in Pithiviers, France, to a French mother and Senegalese father, she published her first novel, Quant au riche avenir, *at 17. Her other works include:* Trois Femmes Puissantes *(*Three Strong Women, 2009*),* Ladivine: A Novel *(2013),* Self-Portrait in Green *(2006),* En Famille *(2007),* La Sorcière *(2003),* All My Friends *(2004),* Rosie Carpe *(2001),* Coração Apertado *(2009), and* Hilda *(1999).* My Heart Hemmed In—*the translated version of her 2007 novel* Mon cœur à l'étroit—*was released in 2017 to international acclaim. She was awarded the prestigious Prix Femina literary prize for her novel* Rosie Carpe *in 2001 and won the Prix-Goncourt for* Three Strong Women *in 2009, She is the only living female playwright to have a play* (Papa doit manger) *included in the Comédie-Française repertoire. She now lives in Berlin, Germany.*

From *Three Strong Women*

When her husband's parents and sisters told her, Khady knew already.

She had not known what form their wish to get rid of her would take, but that the day would come when she would be ordered to leave, that she had known or gathered or felt (that is to say, silent understanding and feelings never revealed had gradually melted into knowledge and certainty) from the earliest months of her settling in with her husband's family following his death.

She remembered her three years of marriage not as a time of serenity, because the longing, the terrible desire for a child, had made of each month a frantic climb towards a possible benediction, then, when her period came, a collapse followed by gloomy despondency before hope returned and, with it, the gradual, dazzling, breathless ascent day after day, right up to the cruel moment when a barely perceptible pain in her lower abdomen let her know that it had not worked this time—no, those years had truly been neither calm nor happy, because Khady never did become pregnant.

But she thought of herself as a taut, strong cord, vibrating in the restricted, impassioned space of this waiting game.

It seemed to her that she had not been able to concentrate on anything, throughout those three years, other than on the rhythmic alternation of hope and disillusionment, so that disillusionment—provoked by a twinge in her groin—might quickly be followed by the stubborn, almost ridiculous surge of hope regained.

"It'll perhaps be next month," she would say to her husband.

And, careful not to show his own disappointment, he would reply in a kindly way: "Yes, for sure."

Because that husband of hers had been such a nice man.

In their life together he had given her full latitude to become that desperately taut cord which vibrated with every emotion, and he had surrounded her with kindness and had always spoken to her with prudence and tact, exactly as if, busy with creating a new life, she needed to be surrounded by an atmosphere of silent deference in order to be able to perfect her art and give shape to her obsession.

Never once had he complained about the all-pervasive presence in their life of that baby which was never conceived.

He had played his part with a degree of self-denial, she said to herself later.

Would he not have been within his rights to complain about the lack of consideration with which, at night, she pulled him towards her or pushed him away, depending on whether she thought her husband's semen would at that moment be of use or not, about the way, during her safe period, she did not beat about the bush in making it clear that she did not wish to make love, as if the expenditure of useless energy could damage the only project she then cared about, as if her husband's seed constituted a unique, precious reserve of which she was the keeper and which should never be drawn upon in the pursuit of mere pleasure?

He had never complained.

At the time she had not seen how noble his behaviour was because she would not have understood that he could complain about—or even simply fail to accept as legitimate, obligatory and exalting—the ascetic self-denial (ascetic in a sense, though their tally of sexual acts was impressive) to which this wild urge to procreate subjected them.

No, certainly she would not have understood that at the time. It was only after the death of her husband, of the peaceable, kindly man she had been married to for three years, that she was able to appreciate his forbearance. That only happened once her obsession had left her and she had become herself again, rediscovering the person she had been before her marriage, the woman who had been able to measure the qualities of devotion and gallantry which her man possessed in abundance.

She then felt great unhappiness, remorse, hatred almost, about her lunatic desire to get pregnant that had blinded her to everything else, in particular her husband's illness.

Because surely he must have been ill for some time to die so suddenly, early one pale morning during the rainy season? He had scarcely got out of bed that day to open as usual the little café they ran in a lane in the medina.

He had got up and then, with a sort of choking sigh, almost a restrained sob, a sound as discreet as the man himself, he had collapsed in a heap at the foot of the bed.

Still in bed and barely awake, Khady had not at first imagined that her husband was dead, no, not for a second.

For a long time she would be angry with herself over the thought that had flashed through her mind—oh, a year or more later, she was, in truth, still angry with herself—over the thought that wouldn't it just be their rotten luck if he fell ill at that precise moment, because she had had her period a good two weeks earlier, and her breasts felt slightly harder and more sensitive than usual, so she supposed she was fertile, but if this man was so out-of-sorts as to be incapable of making love to her that evening, what a mess, what a waste of time, what a horrid let-down!

She had got up in her turn and gone over to him, and when she had realised he was no longer breathing but just lying there inert, hunched up, his knees almost touching his chin, with one arm trapped under his head and with one innocent, vulnerable hand lying flat, palm upwards, on the floor, looking, she had said to herself, like the child he must have been, small and brave, never contrary but open and straightforward, solitary and secretive under a sociable exterior, she had seized his open palm and pressed it to her lips, tortured at the sight of so much decency in a human being. But even then stupefied grief was battling it out in her heart with a still-unattenuated, still-undeflated feeling of exultation that enveloped her at the thought that she was ovulating, and at the same moment as she was running to get help, diving into the house next door, with tears she was unaware of pouring down her cheeks, that part of herself which was still obsessed with pregnancy was beginning to wonder feverishly what man could, just this once, replace her husband to avoid losing the chance of getting pregnant this month and of breaking the exhausting cycle of hope and despair which, even as she ran shouting that her husband was dead, she saw looming, were she forced to pass up this opportunity.

And it was beginning to dawn on her that this fertile period would be wasted, and the following months too, and huge disappointment—a feeling that she had put up with all that hope and despair for three whole years to no purpose—polluted her grief at this man's death with an almost rancorous bitterness.

Could he not have waited for two or three days?

Khady still, now, reproached herself with having entertained such thoughts.

After her husband's death the owner of the café threw her out to make way for another couple, and Khady had had no choice but to go and live with her husband's family.

Her own parents had handed her over to be brought up by her grandmother, long since dead, and after seeing them during her childhood at rare intervals only, Khady had finally lost touch with them altogether.

And although she had grown up to be a tall, well-built, slender young woman with a smooth oval face and delicate features, although she had lived for three years with this man who had always spoken to her kindly, and although she had been able, in the café, to command respect with an attitude that was unconsciously haughty, reserved, a touch cold and had therefore discouraged ribald comments about her infertility—despite such major pluses, her lonely, anxious childhood, and later her vain efforts to get pregnant, which, even though they had kept her in a state of intense, almost fanatical emotion, had dealt barely perceptible but fatal blows to her precarious self-assurance: it had all prepared her to find it not at all abnormal to be humiliated.

So that, when she found herself living with in-laws who could not forgive her for having no means of support and no dowry, who despised her openly and angrily for having failed to conceive, she willingly became a poor, self-effacing creature who entertained only vague impersonal thoughts and inconsistent, whitish dreams, in the shadow of which she wandered about vacantly, mechanically, dragging her feet with indifference and, she believed, hardly suffering at all.

She lived in a three-room run-down house with her husband's parents, two of her sisters-in-law and the young children of one of them.

Behind the house there was a back-yard of beaten earth shared with the neighbours. Khady avoided going into the yard because she feared getting sarcastic remarks thrown at her about her worthlessness and the absurdity of her existence as a penniless, childless widow, and when she had to go there to peel the vegetables or prepare the fish she huddled so closely inside her batik, with only her quick hands and high cheekbones showing, that people soon stopped paying her any attention and forgot all about her, as if this silent, uninteresting heap no longer merited a rude or jeering remark.

Without pausing in her work she would slide into a kind of mental stupor which stopped her understanding what was going on around her.

She then felt almost happy.

She seemed to be in a blank, light sleep that was free of both joy and anguish.

Early every morning she would leave the house with her sisters-in-law. All three carried on their heads the plastic bowls of various sizes which they would sell in the market.

There they found their usual pitch. Khady would squat a little to one side of the two others who pretended not to notice her presence and, responding with three or four raised fingers when asked the price of the bowls, she stayed there for hours on end, motionless in the noisy bustle of the market which made her slightly dizzy and helped her sink back into a state of torpor shot through with pleasing, unthreatening, whitish dreams like long veils flapping in the wind on which there appeared from time to time the blurred face of her husband smiling his everlasting kindly smile, or, less often, the features of the grandmother who had brought her up and sheltered her and who had been able to see, even while treating her harshly, that she was a special little girl with her own attributes, not just any child.

So much so that she had always been conscious of her uniqueness and aware, in a manner that could neither be proved nor disproved, that she, Khady Demba, was strictly irreplaceable, even though her parents had abandoned her and her grandmother had only taken her in because there had not been a choice, and even though no being on earth needed her or wanted her around.

She was happy to be Khady, there had never been any dubious chink between herself and the implacable reality of the person called Khady Demba.

She had even happened on occasion to feel proud of being Khady because—she had often thought with some amazement—children whose lives seemed happy, who every day got generous helpings of chicken or fish and wore clothes to school that were not stained or torn, such children were no more human than Khady Demba who only managed to get a minuscule helping of the good things in life.

Even now that was something she never doubted: that she was indivisible and precious and could only ever be herself.

Juliane Okot Bitek

A poet, her 100 Days *(University of Alberta, 2016) was nominated for several writing prizes including the 2017 BC Book Prize, the Pat Lowther Award, the 2017 Alberta Book Awards and the 2017 Canadian Authors Award for Poetry. It won the 2017 IndieFab Book of the Year Award for poetry, and the 2017 Glenna Lushei Prize for African Poetry. Her poem "Migration: Salt Stories" was shortlisted for the 2018 National Magazine Awards for Poetry. "Gauntlet" (the initial poem of the series these two poems are from) was longlisted for the 2018 CBC Poetry Prize. She is also the author of* Sublime: Lost Words *(The Elephants, 2018). She lives in Vancouver, Canada.*

genetics [1]

these[2] are[3] our[4] stories[5] the[6] ones[7] we[8] keep[9] to[10] ourselves[11]

---

1 so mail me a letter so I can tape the envelopes with your handwriting as evidence of things that held on to you

2 three four any amount you like as long as there's evidence in them that you were thinking of me so I can devise ways of organizing the world into those that left & those that held on to you

3 one strategy to maintain a collection of gestures & things that held on to you

4 separate beds curses the plush blue bathrobe behind the bathroom door memories that held on to you

5 that incubator in the back door that held on to you

6 long dreams that held on to you

7 gods with flaming tongues that held on to you

8 ordinary ones big ones the little ones we call idols everything that held on to you

9 fives & sixes laws & fixes everything was a balance that held on to you

10 insist on their stories would betray the ones that held on to you

11 these are lists to explain ourselves to no one

genuflections [1]

music [2]
european history [3]
physical education [4]
& that fresh-faced kid [5]
when royalty arrived [6]
when royalty arrived [7]
when royalty arrived [8]
when royalty arrived [9]
i too curtsied but just a little bit [10]

---

1 when princess anne came to our high school at gayaza we lined up to meet her

2 hobday

3 warren

4 cutler

5 & straight out of british a-levels a volunteer to teach us girls us African girls so we made it our business to keep his face in flush because none of us turned red with embarrassment & that also was physics but he probably was not there for the occasion but what's memory if we can't play inside it we kept his face red

6 at our school prefects for that day we were lined up to shake the hand of the daughter of the queen

7 who knew that we would could would have to witness whiteness as stratified categorized classed

8 hitherto as white people who loved us so much that they gave up all the thrilling possibilities of the good lives we'd read about what it was to be European to teach generations & generations of us african girls until the end of time about how to be decent educated good christian women

9 there they were all three of them in utter & complete adulation of the daughter of the queen & us prefects good girls still in the learning to be how do we be how do we be how do we be us who were being taught to be the good modern african christian women who did not worship idols or false gods or men or the daughter of the queen

10 because even with her white glove on even with our teachers on one knee she was no bigger than our elders for whom we went down on both knees

Yvonne Adhiambo Owuor

Born in Nairobi, Kenya, she was educated at Kenyatta University, the University of Reading and the University of Queensland. She is the author of the widely acclaimed novel Dust, *and won the 2003 Caine Prize for African Writing for the short story "Weight of Whispers", which the BBC described as a "...subtle and suggestive work of fiction that dramatises the condition of refugees." She was the Executive Director of the Zanzibar International Film Festival from 2003 to 2005. Her writing has appeared in numerous publications worldwide including* Kwani? *and* McSweeney's. *Her story "The Knife Grinder's Tale" has been made into a short film. She now lives in Nairobi.*

These Fragments

1.

Weeks later, a message comes with one of the boy soldiers who had gone to visit their illicit food supplier. A pink, scented card with a lily on the front. Inside,etched in gold ink:

> Dear Colonel,
> Your story seduces.
> The world needs to hear it.
> Please find me.
> *Safiya Fakhri.*
> *Filmmaker, Translator. 03/12*

The Colonel said nothing. A war-emptied man.

2.

Kalioyolipi. Place of temporary truces. Moonless night. Prickle of skin. Someone has been watching her. Yesterday, she could not sleep, at 2 a.m. needing the chill of a cold night wind that swept in from the dense forest river. Her hut was one of nine in a compound that, many years ago, had been set aside for paying foreigners. Yesterday Safiya had cried as she tried to wash the fecund stench of the African interior out of her thick, black-grey-streaked hair. Safiya waited. She studied the fireflies. She was being watched. Finally, she called out, her voice sharp: "Why don't you ask what causes a woman to cry in the density of night? Show your face, *putain!*" She half-rose, intending to check her camera batteries. Only then did a shadow shiver into life behind her.

"Tomorrow morning," a whisper said, "go to the market place. Wait inside the music stall."

Safiya turned. Nobody there.

3.

The market was beside a ravaged former military camp. Safiya lurked in a record stall wearing a white jumpsuit, and white high heels. Perfumed, she carried her camera bag. She waited. Nobody offered more than a greeting to her. She would be the last person to leave the market area. Her high heels marching on the uneven dirt road punctuated her rage.

4.

Cicada cacophonies in dark, green, sultry forest. Tea-coloured river water—black in the night. Escorted by four boyish guides carrying oversize weapons, a blindfolded Safiya lurched, shuddering at the screeching of a billion insects. One of her heels had snapped in half. A black cloud of insects hovered above her head. They had walked for more than five hours.

5.

Whispers. Receding footsteps. Sudden warmth and a calloused touch at Safiya's right elbow, a man's quiet *"Bienvenue,"* as if she were a dinner guest.

6.

He leads her into a cool space. The muffled sound of water. "Bend," he says. "A short crawl, then you can sit."

Her hands move towards her blindfold.

He squeezes her arm. "The mask...stays on." He says, "A chair...to your left." Safiya tumbles into a hard object, touches metal. A refurbished drum, foliage as padding.

Safiya says, "Colonel? I presume. You are...elusive." She tilts her head. "But you let me find you?"

"You asked."

"A risk."

"You baited the trap well."

She is engaging him with an overfamiliar ease. "My new project," Safiya says, "explores a theory of haunting about men like you." The Colonel watches her hands.

"Revolutionary affinity." She tosses, "And its consequences. Our need for vicarious atonement."

He inches closer. "Atonement?"

She says, "My father was guerrilla leader for the Ath-Thawra Al-Jazā'iriyya. His descendants inherited his unresolved guilt."

"Which war?"

"*La guerre d'Algérie*. The hero blew up people for The People until post-independence idiots in turn blew up him, and my three uncles, at a family function. Now it's just the women left."

He asks, "So what causes a woman to weep in the density of night?"

She turns. "You won't show me your face? I prefer the human gaze."

"That I cannot offer you, madam."

The forest is rustling its leaves. Safiya slips from her pocket a slender, silver, ten-centimetre long object with tiny gem-like green-orange-red-yellow light spots. "Mini-recorder."

The Colonel stoops to touch it.

She says, "There's a two point five million-dollar price attached to your head."

"Do you want it?"

"Yes."

"Make it four. I'll surrender to you."

Laughter.

She says, "But our topic today is 'Crimes against humanity'. Are you guilty?"

He grimaces. "What is human?"

"Bodies are strewn along the roads you pass. What does 'meaning' mean for you?"

"Victory."

"What's next?"

Staccato delivery. "Close our wounds. Build a sanctuary for my people."

She smiles with faux sweetness. "Your *orphans*? Do you hear them weep for mutilated mothers and fathers?"

He was weary. "Often."

He watches her hands move in the air. Her full-lipped mouth that tipped towards big laughter, which did not explain her tears.

Whine of a mosquito. She asks, "What's the hardest part of your war?"

"Loneliness."

Safiya depresses the audio recorder's switch. She is asking: "What do you want with your war?" He kneads the back of his neck. He used to know. She hurls a question at him, "Do you bear responsibility for the horror you create?"

His explicit, "Yes" drops her jaw. He asks, "Is this the interview?"

"No," she answers, perplexed by his "yes". "Yes," she corrects. "How did your war start?"

His mind searches for beginnings: "Went to Belgium. Studied flies. *Drosophila melanogaster*. Over 100,000 different species. Returned with a degree and an urge to grow my country…one insect at a time."

There is regret in her laugh.

He laughs because she laughs. He continues, "My people were so proud of me. My mother…" Lump in throat. A senior government scientist governing an underequipped over-heated lab, surrounded by shelves of textbooks, waiting for test-tubes that were never purchased, presiding over circular meetings that were only about what companies linked to which minister would win the lab supply tenders.

Outside, leaves rustle. Inside, the Colonel continues. "At twenty-nine, I met a grand one-eyed general—I was ready for a great fall. Had been a good boy for so long." Scoffing laugh. "Who doesn't want power when it's offered free?"

The Colonel moves away. He retrieves a metal jug of water. He fills a tin cup. "Except it's never free." He places the vessel in Safiya's hands. She drinks unquestioning. "You are too trusting."

She smirks. "As you are."

He watches her. "I became a professional sniper. Ninety-eight per cent first round hitter." He cocks his finger, *"Pttt.* I was that good. Flew up the ranks." He remembers. "Power is sweet. But the government changed. The new dispensation came for my General and me. We disappeared. They hunted out and…purged what belonged to us: families, friends. Gone."

The Colonel speaks in a rush. "We tried to repair blood with blood. In other years we might have been called 'Freedom fighters'."

Safiya says, "My father the Berber—not Arab—would be 'terrorist' today…you, officially, black and African, translate only as 'Warlord'."

Thunder.

It starts to drizzle. Safiya asks in a voice that is mere breath: "May I use my fingers to learn your face?"

He does not answer.

She turns, cool-voiced. "They seized your prophet. Helped by the 'allies', of course, in exchange for mining concessions and oil-drilling privileges. He's now dead. Did you know?"

The Colonel's dragged-out, hurting "Oooh."

She ladles out details. "His body on display. Shown on news outlets throughout the world. His desecrated corpse. An unmarked grave. No ceremony. Hoping he will be erased from memory. You are their next target."

7.

Later, he asked, "Do you still want to know my face?"

She did.

8.

They sat close together on the metal drum, as if it were a cosy sofa.

9.

None.

He has asked, her, "How much time do I have?"

10.

He carries out a final raid. A river man's homestead. His children, his wives. The Colonel had used his harsh voice and waved his rifle. When the Colonel leaves, he is wearing the second wife's dress and carrying the first wife's travel papers and her basket, which is filled with the family's groundnuts, and one of their eight red-headed chickens whose throat is tied to prevent it squawking. The river man had entered into the game, had giggled, but had wrapped the Colonel's uniform and rifle to toss into deep waters.

11.

They would catch the gaunt Colonel in the second town of another country. A police roadblock. His first captors would be balaclava-clad men with guns, and voices baying in assorted European accents. He would not fight back. They handcuffed him, stuffed him into a small blue car, which flew over roads, crashed through borderlands. He was hustled into a helicopter. They landed in a field in the capital city, where he was handed over to balaclava-clad men with African accents. They stripped him naked. They wrapped his body in chains. They bruised his head until it bled. They punched his lips and eyes. They shoved him into a cage, lifted it onto the back of a mud-green lorry. They wanted him to be seen by the public who, on cue, jeered and cheered and banged at his cage, believing they had been saved. He did not fight back.

12.

Safiya filmed everything. She did not expect that he would lift his bound, bleeding hands to salute her.

13.

The media resorted to superlatives to describe the happening: *Dark-souled pimpernel... Chameleon warlord...*they shared a word: *"Capturé!"*

14.

His body was in tatters, but it would heal. He was flown to The Hague, driven straight to hospital. Two weeks later, he was escorted into a detention cell. He had filled out forms; in the "next of kin" section he spelled out one name: "Safiya Fakhri". No diplomats came to visit him. Two pale-skinned ladies came from the International Committee of the Red Cross. He was impressed by their courtesy. Yes, he confirmed again that he would admit to the "Crimes Against Humanity". He had reduced his Defence team to one red-faced Afrikaner with a bad shave. After three months of trying to get the Colonel to reconsider, the Defence gave up.

15.

"The Prosecutor v. Xavier Aurélien Dikembe. The Chamber was satisfied beyond reasonable doubt of Xavier Aurélien Dikembe's guilt as an accessory, within the

meaning of article 25(3)(d) of the ICC's founding treaty, the Rome Statute, to ten crimes against humanity (murder) and five war crimes…committed between 14 February 2004 and 17 December 2012 during attacks on the villages of…"

Fifty-five years. He had wanted "Life". But the Defence successfully presented him as an accessory to a now-dead "real" criminal warlord.

16.

She strides into his prison world as "next of kin", red scarf sailing, a lemon-green trench coat skimming the tops of high-heeled brown boots. She approaches the red bench where he waits, legs crossed. She says in French, "They still would have got you. Once you allowed me in." She stoops to study his face. "They marred you. It must have hurt." She straightens, loosens her scarf. "You left me there. You could have killed me."

"Bad timing." He rubs the scars above his ears. They ache in the cold.

Safiya sits thirty centimetres from him. She shakes off snow from her woollen hat.

He asks, "What really makes a woman weep in the density of night?"

Snow flurries on the window. She speaks in jerking words: "One day. An ordinary family outing. A mama, papa, two sons. The mother drove, took a familiar bend—too sharp, too fast. The car soars off the mountainside. Bounces on rocks. Lands in the middle of an old European sea."

She looks at him. "There's a fine art to being broken; there's a finer art of having your fragments repaired. They used the bones and muscles of my husband and children to put me back together again." She shifts to lean against the man staring at falling snow. "Was a worker in one of those secret, special security centres. Programme Officer, Middle-East Desk. Imagine that. After I woke up in the hospital, I craved death. The agency offered me a place in an experiment from the book of Suicide Bombers and Trojan Horses. Added sensors to my body, barcodes that ping data to satellites and men lurking in shadows. My weapon," she turns to him, "is intimacy. You are my only survivor." She stares. "Are you warm? There was a ground blizzard when I drove in."

He adjusts his blue coat.

He says, "I wondered why you didn't ask for a way out of the forest. So, what does two-point-five million give you?"

She grimaces. "Repairs my nieces' fallen house in my father's name." She paused, "I may be doomed to live."

"Life imprisonment. That, *ma belle*, was what *I* desired."

She asks, "Next of kin. Revenge?"

"Yes."

Quiet.

She asks, "How is life?"

"I examine the cosmos of *Lampyridae*…" He looks at her. "Fireflies."

A window reveals skies obscured by whiteness. Inside the room, they smile at one another. Safiya reaches to pull off X. Aurélien's large black spectacles, wipes the lenses with her sleeve. She lifts her left hand and, closing her eyes, says, "May I touch your face?"

Winsome Pinnock

Born in London, to parents who were both migrants from Smithville, Jamaica, she was the first black female playwright to have a play staged at the Royal National Theatre. She has written for stage, radio and television. Her award-winning plays include The Wind of Change *(1987),* Leave Taking *(1988),* Picture Palace *(1988),* A Hero's Welcome *(1989),* A Rock in Water *(1989),* Talking in Tongues *(1991),* Bitter Harvest *(1991),* Mules *(1996),* One Under *(2005),* The Dinner Party *(2007),* Taken *(2011),* Clean Trade *(2015),* Tituba *(2017),* The Principles of Cartography *(2017) and* Rockets and Blue Lights *(2018) for which she won the Alfred Fagon Award. She is a recipient of the George Devine Award, Pearson Plays on Stage Award and Unity Theatre Trust Award. She received a Special Commendation from the Susan Smith Blackburn Prize. She was Senior Visiting Fellow at Cambridge University and is currently Associate Professor at Kingston University.*

Glutathione

Ginette and Simone, two young black women in a room somewhere. Sheets of newspaper laid down on the floor are covered with paraphernalia—needles and syringes, a medication case containing small vials. They both sit back on their heels, facing each other. Ginette takes two of the vials out of the small case and prepares two needles as Simone watches.

GINETTE: Me first then you.

SIMONE: Sweet.

GINETTE: Don't be nervous. You nervous?

SIMONE: I hate needles.

GINETTE: No one's forcing you, right?

SIMONE: Go on. I'm watching…

Ginette bends her arm and searches for a vein, but can't find one.

SIMONE: How many times you done this?

GINETTE: Loads.

SIMONE: And you can't find a vein?

GINETTE: Happens all the time.

SIMONE: Doesn't inspire me with confidence.

Ginette takes a strap and wraps it around her arm to raise a vein.

SIMONE: (*suddenly startled*) What was that?

GINETTE: What?

SIMONE: I heard someone. Coming up the stairs.

They both listen. They don't hear anything.

GINETTE: They won't be back for ages. Relax... Got it.

Ginette takes a cotton wool pad and cleanses the area around the vein. Simone covers her eyes.

GINETTE: There's no point if you don't look.

Simone watches. Ginette presses the needle into her arm.

GINETTE: See, nothing to it. (*sets timer on her watch*) Three minutes then it's your turn.

Ginette attaches a canula and drip to the syringe. Simone unwraps a sweet and pops it in her mouth, offers a sweet to Ginette who declines.

GINETTE: Took me a year to lose two and half stone. I'm not going back. I'm a passionate person, but I hate making other people uncomfortable. I admit it: I like to be liked.

Simone receives a message on her phone.

SIMONE: From Naomi. (*reads*) "Government's Audit lays bare racial disparities in UK schools, courts and workplaces" blah blah "...data shows disadvantages for black and ethnic minority communities..." blah blah "...if these disparities cannot be explained..." Cannot be explained? Blah blah..."disparities cannot be explained then they must be changed." Blah blah blah bullshit.

GINETTE: Disparities?

SIMONE: Racial disparities.

They both giggle.

SIMONE: It's working. You're definitely changing.

GINETTE: At least two shades. And that's only after four weeks.

SIMONE: Cool.

Slight pause.

SIMONE: What does it do, exactly?

GINETTE: It stops the…it halts the production of melanin.

SIMONE: And it's safe? Because I'm careful what I put in my body.

GINETTE: It's a hormone. You can't get more natural than that…

Slight pause.

SIMONE: Naomi ain't noticed?

GINETTE: What?

SIMONE: That you're different…

GINETTE: I haven't seen her. She's busy with her group.

SIMONE: She'd go ballistic if she knew about this, wouldn't she?

GINETTE: That's why you ain't telling her.

SIMONE: Feels a bit…

GINETTE: What?

SIMONE: Sneaky.

GINETTE: You don't have to tell her everything. You're entitled to a private life.

SIMONE: I suppose…

GINETTE: Course you are.

SIMONE: Does it *feel*…different? Do you feel, you know…lighter?

GINETTE: Lighter, yes. I'm changing and the world becomes…less heavy, you know? I'm definitely less anxious. And the people around me are less anxious too.

SIMONE: Cool. That's cool. I can definitely see it. I can see the change in you.

The timer goes. Ginette removes the drip from her arm as she speaks.

GINETTE: Now you.

SIMONE: I'm not sure.

GINETTE: It's your choice. (*slight pause*) You asked me, remember. Why did you come up here?

Slight pause.

SIMONE: It was that talk Naomi organised last week. That woman talking about her book…

GINETTE: *Living Free in a Microaggressive World.*

SIMONE: I'm thinking every word of this is true, but…

GINETTE: But.

SIMONE: I've lived all her examples. Like the one where the barista is cleaning the counter?

GINETTE: You know they've seen you, but they continue cleaning.

SIMONE: And you don't say anything because you know what they want. You know that they're angling for an explosion. So you stand there and wait. Someone else shows up.

GINETTE: That's when they stop cleaning.

SIMONE: They know you've been standing there, and they stop, they look at the other person and say—

GINETTE: Who's next?

SIMONE: I'm sick of it.

GINETTE: You're lovely you are. Do you know that? A really lovely person.

SIMONE: That's nice.

GINETTE: You wait. You'll soon see a difference. Everyone else will see it too.

SIMONE: I'd never have my nose done or anything like that. I like being me.

GINETTE: I like being me. I don't hate myself.

SIMONE: It's not like I wanna be light-skinned.

GINETTE: You can be an English rose, for all I care.

SIMONE: I love being black.

GINETTE: Black is beautiful.

SIMONE: I mean it.

GINETTE: We don't reject blackness. We reject what it signifies.

SIMONE: Do you feel anything? When the stuff goes in…

GINETTE: It feels good.

SIMONE: Relaxing, yeah?

GINETTE: Left or right? Up to you…

Simone takes a moment, then holds her arm out. Ginette swabs with cotton wool.

GINETTE: How many marches Naomi been on? You see her change anything? She's been banging on for years, and it hasn't made a single bit of difference. Me, I'm sick of identity. I refuse it.

Ginette picks up a needle.

SIMONE: Needle...

GINETTE: Don't be afraid. It won't hurt.

Ginette taps Simone's arm in order to find a vein.

GINETTE: You know the old saying about how you can't change the world, but you can change yourself? We're changing ourselves, Simone.

SIMONE: I don't deny my heritage. You understand that, yeah? Because that would be like a mutilation.

GINETTE: Of course. Where would we be without history? Little scratch.

Ginette injects Simone.

SIMONE: Ouch! You said it wouldn't hurt.

GINETTE: All done. Nothing to it. Can you feel it seeping into the cells, trans-forming them? We're not the only ones doing this, you know. It's a movement, far more powerful than Naomi's little group. A revolution of the body, that's what it is. Thousands of us, breaking free from history. We are a new breed, you and me. History used to be our puppet master, but now we're in control of ourselves. (*the drip is now in place in Simone's arm*) How's that?

SIMONE: I dunno, it's ... I suppose it's ... (*beat*) it's ... all right ... yeah ... I suppose ... it's all right.

ENDS

Claudia Rankine

She is the author of five collections of poetry, including Citizen: An American Lyric; *two plays including* The White Card, *which premiered in February 2018 (ArtsEmerson/American Repertory Theater) and will be published with Graywolf Press in 2019; numerous video collaborations; and is the editor of several anthologies including* The Racial Imaginary: Writers on Race in the Life of the Mind. *Among her many awards and honours, she is the recipient of the Bobbitt National Prize for Poetry, the Poets and Writers' Jackson Poetry Prize, and fellowships from the Guggenheim Foundation, United States Artists, the MacArthur Foundation, and the National Endowment for the Arts. She teaches at Yale University as the Frederick Iseman Professor of Poetry. In 2016, she co-founded The Racial Imaginary Institute (TRII). She lives in New Haven, CT, USA.*

From *Citizen*

July 29–August 18, 2014 / Making Room
Script for Public Fiction at Hammer Museum

On the train the woman standing makes you understand there are no seats available. And, in fact, there is one. Is the woman getting off at the next stop? No, she would rather stand all the way to Union Station.

The space next to the man is the pause in a conversation you are suddenly rushing to fill. You step quickly over the woman's fear, a fear she shares. You let her have it.

The man doesn't acknowledge you as you sit down because the man knows more about the unoccupied seat than you do. For him, you imagine, it is more like breath than wonder; he has had to think about it so much you wouldn't call it thought.

When another passenger leaves his seat and the standing woman sits, you glance over at the man. He is gazing out the window into what looks like darkness.

You sit next to the man on the train, bus, in the plane, waiting room, anywhere he could be forsaken. You put your body there in proximity to, adjacent to, alongside, within.

You don't speak unless you are spoken to and your body speaks to the space you fill and you keep trying to fill it except the space belongs to the body of the man next to you, not to you.

Where he goes the space follows him. If the man left his seat before Union Station you would simply be a person in a seat on the train. You would cease to struggle against the unoccupied seat when where why the space won't lose its meaning.

You imagine if the man spoke to you he would say, it's okay, I'm okay, you don't need to sit here. You don't need to sit and you sit and look past him into the darkness the train is moving through. A tunnel.

All the while the darkness allows you to look at him. Does he feel you looking at him? You suspect so. What does suspicion mean? What does suspicion do?

The soft gray-green of your cotton coat touches the sleeve of him. You are shoulder to shoulder though standing you could feel shadowed. You sit to repair whom who? You erase that thought. And it might be too late for that.

It might forever be too late or too early. The train moves too fast for your eyes to adjust to anything beyond the man, the window, the tiled tunnel, its slick darkness. Occasionally, a white light flickers by like a displaced sound.

From across the aisle tracks room harbor world a woman asks a man in the rows ahead if he would mind switching seats. She wishes to sit with her daughter or son. You hear but you don't hear. You can't see.

It's then the man next to you turns to you. And as if from inside your own head you agree that if anyone asks you to move, you'll tell them we are traveling as a family.

Leone Ross

Born in Coventry, England, she migrated as a six-year-old with her mother to Jamaica, where she was raised and educated. Graduating from the University of the West Indies in 1990, she returned to the UK and earned her MA in International Journalism from City University, in London, where she now lives. She has published two critically acclaimed novels, All the Blood Is Red *(1996) and* Orange Laughter *(1999). Her fiction has been nominated for the Orange Prize, the V. S. Pritchett Award, the Scott Prize, the 2018 Jhalak Prize and the Edge Hill Award. Her short story collection* Come Let Us Sing Anyway *(2017) was called "searingly compassionate" by* The Guardian. *She teaches at Roehampton University in London, and is also an editor and a writing competition judge.*

Why You Shouldn't Take Yourself So Seriously

the flesh and bone woman who is on a date with a lyrical man she met online is sitting in a yellow toilet cubicle in a mid-priced noodle bar wondering whether she should make a run for it whether she should go out and see him again whether she should finish eating the crispy duck rolls he might offer to pay for when the bill comes but if she doesn't go out again if she finds a way to exit the toilet then slip out and run down the road he will have to pay the bill by default and don't they say that's what makes women bitches and someone in the cubicle next to her farts and flushes at the same time to cover the noise she does that too in public spaces and sometimes even when she's at home and the sweet-mouthed man she met on the Internet seems to be the kind of man who wouldn't expect her to just leave would expect her to be a lady the truth be told she's pissed off by the way he uses the word lady he's been doing it all night when they met at the concrete theatre and he kissed her cheek and his breath smelled of cinnamon gum and he complimented her bright orange dress then again after they came out of the play him ushering her by the elbow and opening the door for her finally they were here together after weeks of increasingly liquid text messages and thoughtful phone calls that lasted until moonlight where they talked about the box sets they wanted to watch enshrined in someone else's arms fingers thick with salty buttery popcorn and the places they dreamed of travelling Reykjavik for her because she passed through once on a connecting flight and the mountains looked blue and like a place you could find unicorns and New York for him because everybody had to go once and he was a bit embarrassed he hadn't been yet and she actually told him she was lonely and then when the phone call was done she realised she'd picked off most of the Leave Me Blushing Scarlet nail polish on her left hand because she was so anxious about saying it but he was great and really honest when he explained he was over a year divorced and admitted he cheated yeah he could man-up and say it his wife she was a lady about the whole thing but the marriage just limped on afterwards then died the flesh-and-bone woman can't drop the feeling that it's a butter-knife kind of word seemingly harmless but if you stick it in hard enough it'll do you damage like any other knife and all evening he's been talking about how she's a beautiful *lady* choosing her pre-theatre drink for her a good Spanish shiraz she'll give him that and as he handed her the glass she thought his nails needed clipping chided herself for being fussy then admired his carefully groomed beard and thick eyelashes made her twitch a little you know where and this is why you have no man too contrary her aunties say fanning themselves and lip-curling and he told her about an upcoming art exhibition which seemed a reasonable thing to talk about on a date light and colour and emotion caused by art but did you like the play we just saw she thinks he's talking about getting books in the art gallery bookstore afterwards because that's half of the fun he said do you ever go and yeah she said but he's not listening then I like to walk my lady along the river after an exhibition or the theatre he said and she's aware that she's still sitting on this toilet worried about the crispy duck roll that she took one bite out of before she felt her stomach turning which seems strange she ate light today why's her stomach funny only had salad and chicken to keep skinny for this date and outside she's sure that the guy is waiting and wondering and checking his phone which might buy her some more time because everybody gets caught up in Twitter or whatever on a pause maybe he's even checking his dating profile to see if he has any more hits here is a girl with good tits here is a girl with big brown eyes here is a girl who says that she would like her neck squeezed tightly and how to do it here is a girl who says that she's the whole package here is a girl who says this is a recent photograph when it's not and here is a girl with a recent photograph with too many lines around her eyes and here is a girl who says she's bisexual never say that you're bisexual on your dating profile all you'll get are messages about threesomes or messages from men who say that they are socially conscious vegan polyamorous people or morally responsible multi-daters or some such and she doesn't trust men like that she thinks that it's all just a nice way to say they want lots of pussy and she wishes that men would just say that and the woman in the thin cubicle beside her is wiping she's intrigued that she can *hear* the wiping what kind of Velcro pussy does she have that you can hear the sound of toilet paper scraping on it and outside the lyrical man who she met on the Internet will probably be putting his phone back on the table by now wondering if she's OK and she has to make a decision she checks her own phone OK it's only been ten minutes ten minutes is fine most men expect a woman to be away for longer in the toilet especially if they're a lady and call it a loo and when this man first contacted her on the Internet she really liked that he didn't care for jumping out of planes or running for charity that none of his photographs had pictures of him embracing big cats or African children because that shit is all the same thing vanity and he said that what he wanted was a proper girlfriend a real girlfriend normal and he didn't use any puns and most important of all he never said he wanted a girl who didn't take herself too seriously that's the phrase she sees the most online sees it come up again and again and again and again and again profile after profile and she doesn't want to think about how many men's profiles she's looked at when she first started out she would read them carefully and respectfully but these days all she needs to do is look in their eyes to know whether they're stupid to know whether they're bitter to know whether they're funny to know whether they like women to know whether they're dangerous to know whether they only want sex to know whether they want a woman who doesn't take herself too seriously and she thinks if she isn't going to take herself seriously who is and why hasn't he talked about the play yet the woman in the cubicle next to her with the Velcro pussy flushes and then flushes again and the woman on a date thinks that the woman in the cubicle next to her must be stupid because the toilet chain's making wheezing noises and suddenly she realises that the woman is crying and without thinking about it she responds to the desperate sound because how could anyone ignore that barking pain are you OK she says and all she can hear is hiccuping and coughing are you OK please say something she says I'm sorry to disturb you I'm fine says the woman in the cubicle next to her I'm fine no you're not I can hear you crying it's not any business of yours and then there's a long pause and the woman on the date asks the woman in the cubicle next to her whether she's on a date and there is a shuffling and a sighing and I have to get out of here the other woman says and sorry to hold you up no it's fine but she's not moving and the woman who doesn't like being called a lady can see through the gap at the bottom of the cubicle that her neighbour's practical pink knickers are still around her ankles so she's not going anywhere fast but she isn't sure what to do next and she thinks about calling her best friend for an opinion but her best friend said she was going to see her ex today and everybody knows what a mess that is but her best friend is the kind of person who needs to sort through a mess's colours and textures to be sure that she doesn't want it any more and even though she's supposed to call anyway to say that the lyrical man isn't a serial killer she's been on so many dates recently that nobody expects her to call and talk about a serial killer any more and anyway all a serial killer would do is wait until the check-in call was done then get to the killing bit in the past she's been more likely to call and say a man is too tall and thin and since she's a fluffy woman she can't really be dating him because they'll look like a number 10 walking down the street next to each other or she's more likely to say that this other man has strange table manners and while she wants to make an excuse for him picking his teeth with the edge of his knife and then picking his own nose and eating it as if everything in this world should go in his mouth like he's a two-year-old isn't she entitled to say that's a reason not to date a man when he eats his own body waste and she's more likely to be calling her friend to say this other man over here only cares about money and only cares about clothes and she doesn't respect this other-other man because he shrugs at the environment and explains why we're all doomed anyway or he doesn't care about reading or he doesn't care about the upcoming elections and all the other men she's said no to who are becoming a blur now she can't remember how many of them have said don't get me started on the feminazis she's been noticing recently that you can type feminazi in your phone without predictive text protesting or changing it but you can never write fuck without the stupid thing changing it to duck or flock and seriously who is into birds on that level at all even though she does like birds she told one guy one time that she liked peacocks and swans and he said that wasn't a very black girl thing to do and was any of this good enough reason to be sitting on a toilet seat wondering about stealing away the girl in the cubicle next to her is clearing her throat and blowing her nose now yeah says the girl in the cubicle next to her anyway and she pulls up her knickers and unlocks the door and shuffles out and the girl who cares about swans thinks she should have asked more questions that she should've tried to be a better person but she's tired and she wishes she didn't get upset about things and wishes she had longer legs and wishes that she didn't want sex to mean something and she finally does what she came to do pulls her knickers down so she can see the torn lace and stare at the two spots of blood on the gusset that's what her aunties call it the other woman is washing her hands and leaving and she wants to call her back who told her to wear a skirt to meet a stranger she'll go back to the table now she's here with him after all she walked along the river with him pulling her really despite everything she didn't cry it's too late to make a fuss she might as well go back to the duck roll and who else was there to tell her what happened during the play

what happened

she missed it

in the dark

and everybody saying

shhh shhhhhhh shhh

Kadija Sesay

She is a Sierra Leonean/British literary activist, publisher and editor. In the mid-1990s she worked for the Centreprise Literature Development Project as the Black Literature Development Co-ordinator and set up the newspaper Calabash. *In 2001 she founded* Sable LitMag *and* Sable LitFest. *She has edited several anthologies of work by writers of African and Asian descent and published a poetry collection,* Irki. *She has also published short stories, essays, and articles in magazines, journals, anthologies and encyclopaedias in the UK, US and Africa; and has been broadcast on the BBC World Service. She is the co-founder of Mboka Festival in the Gambia. She has received several awards for her work in the creative arts, as well as an AHRC scholarship to research Black British Publishers. She is a fellow of the Royal Society of Arts, the George Bell Institute and of the Kennedy Arts Centre of Performance Arts Management.*

Growing Up ChrisMus

Before growing up in a "free-thinking" Christian/Muslim household, my brother, my sister and I grew up in a working-class British one in Kent.

We were placed in private foster care as babies, so our bodies and brains were raised on traditional home-made English food that consisted of pies and puddings throughout the week. For breakfast we would have sugared toast dipped in hot tea. How Mum made a sausage embedded into Yorkshire pudding become a "toad-in-the-hole" was never explained—it just was—and as long as it was covered in brown gravy, we didn't care. Apple crumble and custard followed for "afters"—we had the best of English. Our Friday night treat was a fish-and-chip "tea" with plenty of malt vinegar and "tommy sauce", wrapped in newspaper; yokey egg with buttered fingers made up breakfast at weekends (Dad was expert at that). Roast dinner after Sunday school was, of course, a special meal with the proper trimmings—lamb with mint or chicken with sage and onion stuffing are what my taste buds still remember.

Our brains were fed with plenty of books, sent by our birth parents, from *Dr Seuss* (which I flicked through in an hour) to boarding-school's bad boy Jennings, and I became fascinated and dreamy-eyed with *Sense and Sensibility* at the age of seven, but our parents decided that this was not the way they wanted their children raised.

Despite the difficulties for people of African descent finding a suitable place to live in London in the 1960s, especially with children, my parents removed us from the care of our foster parents to live on the first floor of a two-storey house in North London. We lived above Pakistani-born Danny who also had two rooms with his mum and two daughters. Upstairs were noisy people, and the bathroom. Danny's family had their own bathroom!

It was here that "real Mum and Dad" started to raise us as "real African children". All of our food came out of two pots—one with long-grain white rice, the other with stew—catering-sized pots filled with enough to feed a village, yet there were only six of us (my mum's youngest sister became my big sister). At weekends, the pot of stew was *plassas*: green leafy stuff—*crain-crain*, cassava leaves, potato leaves that soaked up the deep amber palm oil, liberally decorated with shiny red Trinidad peppers, that real Mum bought in the Indian-owned African shops in Finsbury Park. She dropped in sixteen peppers the first time that she used them and, even without stirring, it was so hot that she had to cook another pot of unspiced stew to mix with the first one in order to reduce the pepper burn. It provided a new gargantuan feast of wonder for my brother, who as the eldest child and the only son was fed like a king, and so loved everything hot and spicy with meat—chunks of beef and dried fish that he dug out of the *plassas*—that I wondered how he had survived his early years in Kent without it. My mother could see that she had done the right thing by removing him.

Our dining-room-cum-living-room-cum-kitchen turned into a bedroom for my brother at night. Next door, in the large front room that held our life belongings, we three girls slept in the queen-size bed, while Mum and Dad slept on the floor. We never questioned the arrangement that gave my brother a room all to himself. He was not allowed to sleep in the same room as the girls although we had just left a house in Kent where he fought over and won the top bunk bed. (Truthfully, I was the one who gave in, as I always did with my brother.) Things remained like that until we left those rooms a year later to move to a spacious, leaking, derelict house, waiting to be knocked down to make way for a new council estate. But my parents had a bedroom to themselves again and we had a garden in which we were allowed to play after we had completed our homework. That was our first proper home in London.

This was about the time when my parents really began to enforce certain harsh rules and conditions, as we saw it, although these were merely traditions and customs that my parents had carried with them from home and adapted to help them survive in England and to protect their family. We had an African household indoors, which our parents prayed would be sustained outside the home too. Private fostering was one of those customs that worked similar to the *men' pickin* system back home, whereby children were sent to another family member who could provide more for them than their parents could at an early age. My parents had migrated to England, and the best people to speak English were, of course, the English, and this was one reason why my parents, while working at least one job each and attending college in the evening, chose to leave their children with the descendants of their colonial masters.

And so my parents, with their mixed Christian/Muslim marriage, which is not unusual in Sierra Leone (or indeed in most West African countries), were unintentionally raising mixed-up children, believing that they would get the best start in life that England had to offer. Nigerian/British comedian Gina Yashere has referred to this type of relationship in her stage performances as "ChrisMus" because, in fact, we are happy to join in with the major religious celebrations of both religions. The Sierra Leonean term is "Marabout Krio" (the Krios, traditionally, being predominantly Christian, and the Marabouts traditionally Muslim holy people).

My mother's upbringing had been a typical Muslim one in West Africa, where religion was important to the infrastructure of the family, but hers was not as strict as it could have been. She was from a mixed Temne, Mende group of people in Sierra Leone. Both her parents raised her as such in the 1940s, when the colonisers were impacting on traditional life in a way that would make it appear beneficial for the locals, with their education system, Christian prayers and interference in local government. Her travelling trader father was broadminded enough to ponder the future of his daughter and decided to send his eldest child to a boarding-school run by American missionaries. My mother speaks about those days with brightness and fervour, although she has never talked to us much about her childhood before school. She has never mentioned *Bundu*, the women's secret society that "cut" girls in their puberty. I assume that she too was "cut" but there are certain things that correctly raised African children will never ask.

So, for the formative years of my life I had a "Mum and Dad" as well as a "Real Mum and Dad". People would look at me strangely or with pity when I described my black and white families; I was not to know until I was in my thirties that there were West African children who were privately fostered and abandoned by their parents—and here I was, boasting two complete sets! I didn't know or understand that foster care in England might have a negative connotation, signalling an assumption that we had been taken away from negligent parents to be cared for in the state system.

To ease the shock of leaving Kent, Real Mum would cook English roast dinners the way she had been taught at boarding-school, so that her children would not feel totally torn from what they had been fed since birth—we swore that her roast potatoes could not match Mum's—and she "seasoned" the roast chicken! No crispy skin, soaked in brown gravy, instead, she used the natural chicken juice to make a colourless thin gravy with herbs! Mum would try often to make jollof rice the way Real Mum showed her—but for English people to cook rice as well as they cook potatoes is challenge enough; to master the intricate ritual of cooking jollof rice—without scales—steaming till it peaked, adding onions, tomatoes, spices, herbs and various meats at the right time without a stop-watch—was just not going to happen.

I'm guessing that both mothers used their culinary expertise to woo and claim these three Krio Marabout Cockney children as theirs. Mum lost, and she and Dad moved out of the house on the corner, where we had zoomed down the hill in our home-made go-kart, a year after Real Mum and Dad moved us to a busy yet alien place called London, where Mum and Dad couldn't find us and take us back home.

Dorothea Smartt

London-born of Barbadian heritage, she is an internationally respected poet/live artist whose books are Connecting Medium *(2001),* Ship Shape *(2008) and* Reader, I Married Him & Other Queer Goings-On *(2014). She was formerly an Attached Live Artist at London's ICA, and has held residencies in the USA (Texas), Scotland and Barbados. Her poetry collection,* Ship Shape, *is an A-Level English Literature title. In recognition of her contribution to British cultural life, she was nominated for a Barbados 2016 Golden Jubilee Award.*

Poem Beginning With A Line From Claudia Rankine
(after Lisa Jarnot's "Poem Beginning with a Line by Frank Lima")

Your historical selves, her White self and your Black self
are in high relief, inescapable except maybe in those private times
you're both laughing at the tumbled laundry, the moody rain
your Black self skidding in the mud same way as her
White self drenched from the sweaty humidity broken by a
shower. You are both grabbing at clothes on the line with giggles
and soft slaps from flapping sheets her children attempt to rescue
a few. Her White self ankle deep as your Black self, hands
reaching out to steady you and the bundle as thunder
rumbles reminders of history unheeded in this moment your
Black hands holding her White hands tight. Her White self
breathing hard as your Black self, make it to the back porch
collapsing in embrace, children piling on top of wet kissed lips
in that private minute there's a shared look above their small
heads, up on your feet now, clothes discarded laundry abandoned
to the squeals of your boys and girl, purveyors of innocence lost
when her White self offers and your Black self accepts inside
the spring months the constant rain and futile laundry days
that have made you cry wipe tears of frustration from your Black
self held in the arms of her White self saying don't worry we'll
wash it all again together and you say, *Yes. Thank you, Ma'am.*

Adeola Solanke

She is an award-winning playwright, screenwriter, and founder of Spora Stories. She was a Fulbright Scholar at the University of Southern California where she earned an MFA in film and was an Academy Nicholls Fellowship semi-finalist. Her award-winning plays include the acclaimed Pandora's Box, *which won a Best New Play nomination in the Off-West End Theatre Awards in 2012 and was shortlisted for the $100,000 Nigeria Prize for Literature, Africa's biggest literary award. Her play* The Court Must Have a Queen, *produced by Historic Royal Palaces, was performed at Hampton Court Palace in 2018 and featured John Blanke, an African Musician in the court of Henry VIII. Another period drama,* Phillis in London, *about Phillis Wheatley, the enslaved prodigy who published the first collection of poetry by an African, has been performed in Gambia, Barbados and England. She's also developing scripts about artists in seventies Notting Hill, where she grew up, and nineties LA. She lectures in Creative Writing at the University of Greenwich.*

From *Pandora's Box*

Characters:

TOYIN: A London mother (late-thirties)

SIS RONKE: Her elder sister, a Lagos entrepreneur and socialite (forties)

MAMA-RONKE/ PANDORA: Their mother, a retired nurse (sixties)

BEV: Toyin's best friend (late-thirties)

BABA: Toyin's Uncle, Mama's brother (sixties)

TIMI: Toyin's teenage son (fifteen)

TOPE: Timi's cousin (fifteen)

PRINCIPAL OSUN: Principal of Tope's school (fifties)

This is a one-act play. The action takes place over one evening in late August, in Lagos, Nigeria. NB: Dialogue is often in Nigerian-English.

FROM SCENE 2

TOYIN: (*excited*) Gosh I don't believe it's actually opened.

SIS RONKE: What's the big deal? It's just a trunk. Everyone who comes back from London has one?

TOYIN and SIS RONKE crowd round as MAMA-RONKE dips in.

TOYIN: But I've never seen what's inside. It was like forbidden fruit. "Never go near my trunk. Don't let me see you tampering with my trunk…" Blimey I thought there were dead bodies in it.

MAMA fishes around and pulls out a dress. She unfolds it and holds it up.

SIS RONKE: I hope that's not for me.

MAMA-RONKE: What do you mean? It's a very popular style.

TOYIN: It was. A long time ago.

SIS RONKE: Ma'mi, we don't wear that sort of thing anymore.

MAMA-RONKE: (*indignant*) Oh, so this is not good enough for you? I bought this in C&A of Oxford Street.

TOYIN: C&A closed down years ago, Mum. It's a Primark now.

MAMA-RONKE: Na you sabi. It's your loss. (*folding it*) I'll send it to my people in Ibadan. They'll appreciate it.

RONKE fishes around inside the trunk. She takes out a doll. She jumps as TOYIN screams.

TOYIN: That's mine!

SIS RONKE: What?

TOYIN: (*pouncing and grabbing*) It's her. It's mine. She's mine. That's the doll I asked for when I was eight.

MAMA-RONKE: I bought it for you.

TOYIN: Then you said you hadn't bought it, but I knew. I knew I'd seen it in a bag and I thought you'd given it to someone else.

MAMA-RONKE: I bought it for you.

TOYIN: So why didn't you give it to me, Mum?

MAMA-RONKE looks tearful. She shakes her head. RONKE dips in again and takes out a dress. It's ghastly—lemon yellow taffeta with a petticoat.

TOYIN: And that dress…that's the…yes…that's the dress from Marks and Spencer. I begged you for it on my tenth birthday.

MAMA-RONKE is nodding again.

SIS RONKE: It's ugly, anyway.

TOYIN: No it's not. Everyone else in my class had one, except me. All the things I wanted. You bought them, and then locked them away! Why?

MAMA-RONKE: I don't know.

TOYIN: It doesn't make sense.

MAMA-RONKE: I know, but I didn't know what else to do. I wanted to be fair…to the two of you…but you were on two different continents.

TOYIN and RONKE look at each other.

TOYIN: Look at all the things I missed out on.

SIS RONKE: I'm the one who missed out.

TOYIN: Oh, please!

MAMA-RONKE: I don't know why… I thought I was being fair… Instead, maybe I failed both of you.

SIS RONKE: Yes, you did.

MAMA is stung and goes to leave.

TOYIN: No, she didn't. Mum, you didn't. Don't listen to her. *(to Ronke)* What's wrong with you?

SIS RONKE: She wanted to talk, didn't she? So let's talk.

TOYIN: Give her a break.

SIS RONKE: She's finally realising the damage she did. Good.

MAMA leaves, upset. SIS RONKE goes to follow. TOYIN grabs her.

TOYIN: She's been trying to talk to you since we got here. Now a few hours before we leave…

SIS RONKE: *(pulling away)* Oto oro o kan. *(Home truths are bitter.)* Some home truths are way overdue.

TOYIN: She did her best.

SIS RONKE: Ra, ra o! *(I disagree!)* It wasn't good enough. *(fighting free)* We're going to talk.

She exits. TOYIN is flummoxed, paces. We hear doors slamming. TOYIN charges after them, but before she can exit, MAMA-RONKE re-enters, RONKE hot on her heels.

MAMA-RONKE: From Taofiki to your sister. From your sister to me. Whoever you can vent your frustrations on. Well, I'm not your houseboy, nor am I your junior sister. You're quick to condemn Timi for lack of respect to his elders. What of you? Is this respect? I'm your…

SIS RONKE: Iya mi. My mother, abi?

MAMA-RONKE: (*deep breath*) You can refuse me as your mother, but don't forget this—I'm not your age mate. I won't tolerate your rudeness anymore! Don't let me say something I'll regret. I'm warning you. If I open my mouth, it will stick.

SIS RONKE: Do your worst. E se epe funmi te ba se! E so nkon ta ba fe so! (*Curse me if you like! Say what you want. Am I bothered?*)

MAMA-RONKE: (*superhuman control*) Ronke, let me pack my loads and go. I'm sorry I bothered you by coming here. I won't do so again. It's nearly eight. In no time I'll be leaving your house.

SIS RONKE: Yes, you're leaving. Leaving again. Well, the first time you left I was too young to speak up. But I can speak now.

MAMA-RONKE: And you've spoken. Very clearly. I failed. That's what you said. I'm a bad mother.

SIS RONKE: I've got some other things to say…

MAMA-RONKE: I don't have to explain myself to you or to anyone else. I am your mother. I did what I thought was best.

SIS RONKE: For you!

MAMA-RONKE: No, for you!

SIS RONKE: E duro na! (*Hold up! Wait a minute!*) That was best…leaving me behind? E fi mi fe le! (*You left me!*)

MAMA-RONKE: Yes, I left you behind. At the time, that's what I thought was best…

SIS RONKE: I want you to apologise.

MAMA-RONKE: For what?

TOYIN: Leave her alone, Ronke. She did her best

SIS RONKE: I want you to admit that you abandoned me. I want you to say you're sorry…

TOYIN: Leave my mum alone!

MAMA-RONKE: I've said it, haven't I?

SIS RONKE: No, you always say, "maybe I made a mistake" or "perhaps I was wrong". But it's not maybe, it's not perhaps. Both you and my dad left me and didn't come back.

MAMA-RONKE: We went to study. We didn't mean to stay.

SIS RONKE: Say sorry.

MAMA-RONKE: What was I supposed to do? I couldn't come, once I had Toyin and the others in London.

SIS RONKE: Say you're sorry.

TOYIN: Leave her alone. Mum, let's just go.

MAMA-RONKE: I couldn't be in two places at once. And I thought you were better off here.

SIS RONKE: SAY IT.

MAMA looks from one to the other, trying to find the answer. She sinks down.

MAMA-RONKE: I didn't succeed at all. I didn't even finish my studies. What I went there for, I didn't even achieve. I failed. And you paid the price. You're right. I'm sorry. Yes, I'm sorry.

SIS RONKE turns away. The apology she wanted isn't soothing.

MAMA-RONKE: (*picking up the dress*) Buying things and storing them up for years I don't know why. Because I was too proud to come home without my qualifications I did it all wrong.

SIS RONKE: I don't want your dolls, or dresses, or…

She starts tossing the dresses, dolls and other gifts back at the trunk, but they're flying everywhere but into it. She slams it shut. Finished, she slumps onto the sofa, a spent force.

SIS RONKE: Take them back I don't want them… I want…

She trails off. MAMA rises with whatever strength she can muster and stumbles out. TOYIN looks at Ronke, furiously.

TOYIN: You got your pound of flesh. Happy now?

SIS RONKE: I remember the day I met our dad. I was in form five. He came to my boarding house. I was called out of biology—it was near the end of the lesson—and when I got to the Principal's office, she said "there's someone special here to see you." And there was a tall, slim man, He was standing by her desk, looking out of the window, dressed in a gray suit. Wearing a red bow tie. I knew who he was straight away. He was visiting from England. He stayed for about an hour, we went for a walk in the gardens and he gave me some money, and then he left. And I never saw him again. He sent presents through his mum. For a few years. (*Pause*) Neither of them came back for me.

TOYIN: But you had Africa, the motherland.

SIS RONKE: (*crumbling*) But you had a mother.

She exits as BEV and TIMI return.

BEV: He wasn't in… I think he's at the polo club… (*taking in the chaos around her*). Hey! What happened here?

END OF SCENE 2

Celia Sorhaindo

Born on the Caribbean island of Dominica, she lived in the UK for many years and returned home in 2005, when she returned to her homeland to organise the Nature Island Literary Festival. Her poems have been published in The Caribbean Writer, Moko Magazine, *and* Interviewing the Caribbean *journal, and longlisted for the UK National Poetry Competition 2017/18. She is a fellow of the 2016 Cropper Foundation Creative Writers Workshop and 2017 Callaloo Creative Writing Workshop. She is currently working on her first poetry collection.*

Creation

Sometimes the only babies
us women subconsciously choose
to birth are our words.

Always a late developer,
mine scratched
on pregnant pause:

And forced their
way out of
tight lips.

Wayward, untidy, they
crawled naked into
the world;

I tried to catch
and tie them in
pink bows

but they wriggled out
to play,
confident, carefree,

and I smiled when Kahlil
and others whispered
they did not belong to me.

At night they crept
into my bed
and covered

my nakedness
with their awkward
limbs.

In muted nightmares—
neglected, bullied—
they disappeared;

Today I wake
relieved
and know
even in silence
words will
always be
tightly wrapped
around me.

In The Air

After the hurricane,
my grandmother,
who in her basement storeroom,
had hunkered down
and knelt
her knees raw with prayer
the whole long long lashing tail of night,
ascended slippery stairs
hoping by holy intervention
her home had been saved.
She stared from ruined room to room,

swaying like a punched drunk spirit,
mouth and eyes wide black holes of disbelief,
words gone as wounds appeared.
She walked on water,
treading over eighty years of floating debris,
then could do no more than silently thank
her saviour over and over for sparing her life.

After the hurricane,
after Mass,
tales of rampant looting
circled among them like hungry dogs;
after the turned-inside-out but well
clothed congregation,
still silent, had shared signs of peace.
No one appeared to conjure and divide
loaves and fishes between some people;
divided by good and bad luck or circumstance;
divided by ability or will to pad and prepare,
concrete seal, pantry stock, insure against calamity.
But having enough or not enough saved,
surely meant little then,
after all none were saved
from that almighty
hurricane that reined in our poor
island and had everyone drowning.

After the hurricane,
came the crazed lines for food…
for any kind of fuel;
came the tell tail spoors
of rats and roaches tracking rubbish;
dank despair
threading desperation through the dark.
At night my grandmother floated
in and out of light, nightmare-laden, sleep,
waiting for the chain rattle
of locked door;
for the bark signaling predators
had come for what little she had left.
She prayed for enough strength and grace,
to give the strangers what they came to take.

After the hurricane,
she said sometimes it felt
like man eat man survival,
every woman for herself.
Who had time, air, breath, breadth enough,
to free dive deep and long enough,
to understand
then these heads heaped,
backs breaking,
carrying stolen mud crusted sofas, sinks,
spirits,
through debris to homes
miraculously still standing?
To understand then the tragic
improvised or organised
bacchanal trashing of schools and stores?
Who could explain anything then?
Understand or explain anything now!

When she was able,
my grandmother told me
about after the hurricane.
Months later I flew home
and stood stone still
in the ruin of her home,
alone.
I thought fear, faith,
had been uncovered,
illuminated, as I watched
a mass of untethered particles
air-floating in the beam of
my head
lamp, from floor all the way above
my head
to the star spored heavens.

Survival Tips

When they start to shout at us
after saying come talk, trust us
this is a safe space,
tell us this is for our own damn
good little girls
little boys
but our guts
tell us this feels
bad
kicks and warns us
they are trying to ram
shame or guilt into our mouths
trying to hurt us
or Stockholm-syndrome smiles,
sparkles in eyes, confuse and dazzle us
Think—
we have been here before
Think—
they are not our star gods,
Think—
they are not
our father
or mother
Think—
even if,
we are no longer children,
Think fast;
should we prise fingers from throat
of our opinion
run run run
or fight
this time
or
be still—

decide
to do

nothing
because
we trust
even though we don't know we know…

Andrea Stuart

A Barbadian-British historian and writer, she was raised in the Caribbean and the US and now lives in the UK. She is the author of three non-fiction books. Showgirls *(published in 1996) was adapted into a two-part documentary for the Discovery Channel in 1998 and has since inspired a theatrical show, a contemporary dance piece and a number of burlesque performances.* The Rose of Martinique: A Biography of Napoleon's Josephine *(2003) was translated into several languages and won the Enid McLeod Literary Prize in 2004.* Sugar in the Blood: A Family's Story of Slavery and Empire *(2012) was shortlisted for the 2013 OCM Bocas Prize for Caribbean Literature in the non-fiction category and for the Spear's Book Award and was the* Boston Globe's *non-fiction book of 2013.*

A Calabash Memory

It is 2015, and I am on board a British Airways Flight to Jamaica, the island where I was born. I haven't been back there since I was fifteen, three decades ago, and I am excited and anxious all at the same time. I have avoided this trip back to my birth country because I did not want to awaken the grief I felt when I left the island, in my teens, so many years ago. None the less, I settle into my seat and notice immediately that the atmosphere on the flight is like a cocktail party, people wandering around chatting, drinks in hand. It is typical of the vivacity of the island I was stolen from.

The young guy sitting next to me is a Jamaican locksmith, with a bright gold-capped incisor tooth. He lives in Hackney and is returning to Jamaica to visit his mother, who lives there. He is hitting on me, and I am amused and a little bit grateful; middle-aged black women don't get much traffic in London. We start talking about England, our adopted country, and then he says, his gold incisor glistening under the plane lights:

"Tell me the truth, you ever felt really at home in England?"

There is a long pause. I can do nothing but shake my head. And I realize that after almost thirty years of living in England I still don't feel I belong there. The recognition is as if a knife has been twisted in my gut.

Nine hours later, we deplane into the heat and torpor of Norman Manley Airport. It is the late afternoon and the queues in passport control are hot and close. But when I get to the front of the line, the official, a dark-skinned man with a twinkle in his eyes asks me whether I am there on business or pleasure.

"I'm, a writer", I reply, "I'm here for Calabash."

There is a pause, he doesn't know what this is. I explain it is one of the Caribbean's coolest literary festivals, taking place every other year. The book fair is run by Justine

Henzell, an untiring cultural player on the island, whose father produced the iconic Jamaican film *The Harder They Come*.

"Have you read *Fifty Shades of Grey*?" the customs man, asks, roaring with laughter. "Now *that* is a good book!"

And instantly, I am reminded, once again of the irrepressible spirit that Jamaicans bring to every encounter.

After a brief wait, I and two other writers, a Scottish poet and an African novelist, are bundled into our car. Our driver is one of those beautiful Jamaican men, young, and dreadlocked, who are magnets for the female sex tourists flocking to the island to enjoy the other commodity—sex—that Jamaica has to offer. These renta-dreads, or "rastitutes", supplement their living by keeping company with women, often older, in exchange for their hard-earned cash.

Our chauffeur drives in JA style: that is as if he was training for Le Mans. Meanwhile the reggae music is so loud that the frame of the car is shuddering to the bassline. The artist we are listening to is Chronixx, the latest super-talented heir to earlier reggae superstars such as Bob Marley, who lamented so hauntingly the island's history of slavery and captivity. I am reminded again that music is the back-beat of this island, inescapable, and so strong that it pulses in your blood.

Our route from Norman Manley Airport goes along the Palisadoes, a sand spit parallel to Kingston Harbour, where Port Royal, the notorious sixteenth-century city, once perched. The town was once described as "the most wicked city in the world", until a mammoth earthquake sunk it beneath the sea. To this day some Jamaicans believe that the bells of the drowned city can still be heard reverberating beneath the waves.

As our driver speeds along, we talk about the state of Jamaica; specifically, about crime. He is both depressed and elated about the island's situation, genuinely regretful about what has happened to the island, whose currency has been devalued, and is riven by political unrest. But he is also proud of the islanders' spirit of derring-do that its populace always demonstrates in difficult times. He tells me that in Jamaica there are five women to every male, many men having been lost to emigration, imprisonment or death. Indeed, at the General Penitentiary, that we now drive past, and the other prison in Kingston, known as Tamarind Farm, men languish, four or five to a cell. So lawless is the island, he explains, that many local government spokesmen lobby to restore hanging.

Three or so hours later, we arrive at Jake's Hotel in Treasure Beach, where Calabash is to be held. It is in the parish of St Elizabeth, a part of the island that is not on the common travel path for tourists visiting Jamaica, who prefer the West Coast, and places like Ocho Rios, with their all-inclusives and private beaches. Instead St Elizabeth, as a parish, is somewhat rocky and neglected—and away from the majority of the island's tourists—but it has its own particular charms. Not least its sense of genuine privacy, intimacy, and calm.

The sun is setting, and I am sitting under a sea-grape tree, with its red velvet leaves and sprays of small green fruit, which will soon ripen to purple. It is evening now and I am at the bar, talking to one of the bartenders. He is one of the many casual employees who work the "tourist season" but then migrate overseas, particularly to the US, to do casual work such as serving at fast-food places, or as carpenters, or builders.

My new friend points out to sea and the moon-illuminated waters that fringe the coastline.

"See over yonder?" He points at a couple of boats. "That is the British Coast Guard," he says. "It has been seconded here to help with policing the waters. They have three separate craft there playing cat and mouse with smugglers, who have been shipping ganja to Costa Rica and coming back with guns."

I laugh out loud: "So it's like the pirates of old?"

"Yeah, man, it is just like the pirates old. When Port Royal was still the wickedest city in the world."

Then he tells me the story of the latest frauds that are afflicting ordinary Jamaicans: "One of them is acquiring people's card numbers by using spy machinery. The result of this is that boys of thirteen or fourteen years own two-storey homes, an arsenal of guns, and drive Jaguars."

We fall silent. I sense that he is worried that I may be put off by this lawlessness that he has recounted and reassures me that I am safe.

"Don't worry though," he says, "there is only one road in and out of St Elizabeth. And, anyway, most Jamaicans don't even know where Jake's or Treasure Beach is, or that it even exists."

A couple of days later, the literary festival begins. The seats are set out in a huge white tent, on the fringe of the sea. The venue could not be more alluring. And the writers who attend are genuinely varied and first-class. Salman Rushdie storms the stage, accompanied by the music of U2. Then there is Zadie Smith reading from her latest book. And the wonderful Colum McCann, reading samples of his own novels. The writing cast is truly international, some from the Slavic world, the Indian sub-continent, Europe, and Africa.

When it is my turn to read, I am so overcome by the stellar company, and my own nerves, it takes me a while to get into my stride. But I get a homegirl's welcome anyway and a memory that I will never forget. And it strikes me that so many people have written about Jamaica, many from what I call the "imperial perspective"—Englishmen who parachute down into the island, do some cursory research, and make their own convenient conclusions; and then fly out again, to tell their simplistic version of the island.

But none of these outsiders gives a real sense of what this island is truly like, with its extraordinary physical beauty, its hills and blue crested waters, its extraordinary green lushness, and its populace who never seem to lose their vibrancy. In truth,

Jamaica is like a grand soap opera; everything here is more intense, its scenarios more dramatic, the conflicts that it generates more lethal. So it is no wonder, then, that traveller and native alike fall in love with this island, as I do, once again.

Jean Thévenet

Born and raised in Kenya, and Sorbonne-educated, she now writes from Paris, France, a place she and her family call "home away from home". Alongside tea, the well-written and well-spoken word, she relishes moments that ooze a good story. She is a connoisseur of stylistics, literature and language which she studied and now teaches with passion in collège.

Sisters at Mariage Frères

Prelude:

Indigo watches Zawadi, who almost forgot her little red number, walk away. Both women saw the number at about the same time at the flea market. Zawadi says that she is classic: she wears blacks and whites. But that has changed now. Black skin goes with just about any colour. Black don't crack.

Prima volta/For the first time:

Indigo first met Zawadi on email. Zawadi's emails are not superfluous sprawlers. When writing, three things matter, Indigo can imagine Zawadi saying: word count, word count, word count. Each word counts. Simplicity and clarity of thought. Now she will be meeting Zawadi in person. Little sister meets big sister. Respect and courtesy.

Both women are genuinely looking forward to meeting each other. That is clear from their email exchanges.

Gare du Nord train station. Eurostar arrivals. Indigo is late; French late, not African late. She apologises all the same. Respect and courtesy. But it is the love at first sight that takes her aback. Zawadi feels very familiar. How unsettling. Indigo will later think that Zawadi doesn't sip life, she drinks in life; she not only seizes the moment but lives it to the fullest. Zawadi is so comfortable in her skin, so sure of her worth. How refreshing to be in the company of a sister who is not apologetic about occupying her rightful place on this good earth.

Travellers can once again leave their luggage in lockers at the train station. This hasn't been so for many years since 9/11. At the luggage locker, Zawadi riffles through her suitcase and produces a colourful cotton bag with pull strings. She takes out jewellery done by Jasper. Indigo gets to choose what she would like. Without hesitation she picks out a pair of fine carnelian dangly earrings. Zawadi is least surprised. She knew in her knower that these would be the earrings that Indigo would select. Shiver down Indigo's spine. Just before Zawadi puts back the cotton bag into her suitcase, she shows Indigo a beautiful Namibian bracelet that would perfectly match her new earrings. This bracelet goes well with the earrings, she tells Indigo, but you are not having it, she says, as she slips it back into the cotton bag. Indigo is so tickled. She knows precious when she sees it. It's been barely ten minutes since they laid eyes on each other and already Zawadi is precious. More precious than fine gold. Precious is what you keep for ever and beyond a day.

Counterpoint:

Zawadi likes flea markets and is looking for Mariage Frères tea, she wrote in one of her emails. Does Indigo know the tea? Of course she does. Mariage Frères not only sell teas but also have a salon de thé, a tea salon, a restaurant, a tea museum and a tea-tasting locale. With hindsight, it seems fitting to be having a tea-fest, what with the Queen's Jubilee on today. Mariage Frères cheekily surfs on the "British Empire" colonial aspect blended with present-day Parisian refinement and prestige. The clientele is urbane, cultivated but not snooty.

Zawadi and now Mariage Frères have Indigo thinking of Macomère. Macomère is Indigo's baby girl's godmother. She is Indigo's second self, her confidante, the one who has all the dirt on Indigo and the one who has earned the right to stroll through Indigo's heart, mind, spirit, and soul. Macomère will later write Indigo: "No surprise the instant bonding [with Zawadi]—I did all the hard work, remember, getting to know you both?" It feels fitting that Indigo is doing this "tea ceremony" with Zawadi. It is as if Macomère were here.

A piacere/At your pleasure:

At the Mariage Frères tea shop. Indigo helps Zawadi to look for a specific tea. A black tea with vanilla. Could it be *Thé de Lune*, a refined, mild, perfumed, vanilla-flavoured afternoon black tea with peppery overtones? They pick a sample tin, open it, and smell it. Zawadi shakes her head, no that's not it. *Black Orchid*? A smooth, silky black tea with vanilla and caramel notes? The same picking, opening, and smelling ritual. Noo, that's not it, but Zawadi rather likes it and will buy it. Indigo doesn't say so but the name of the tea appeals to her. Sooo Omar Sharif, soo Arabian Nights. A Mariage Frères employee in a white linen suit, probably made in a former British colony in the Far East, is sought out. He, a new employee, is not too familiar with all the Mariage Frères teas, but he does find the tea that Zawadi seeks: *Vanille des îles*, a classic afternoon black tea blended with Bourbon vanilla. Yes, the scent confirms it.

Mariage Frères use a sleek and unique packaging for their teas. Pre-packaged teas can be bought in striking round ebony-black canisters presented in gift boxes just as eye-catching. Loose tea goes into bags of the same colour. Black is class. Black don't crack.

Macomère's wedding gift from Indigo was teas from Mariage Freres: *Eros*, an afternoon black tea with a fruity and flowery bouquet and *Wedding Imperial*, a malty golden Assam with notes of caramel and chocolate. For the aphrodisiac factor, she also gave the marrying couple several assorted bars of extra dark European chocolate which the house help mistook for literature: she lined them up alongside books on the bookshelf. A delicious yet telling error: Macomère (like Zawadi) is a story-teller.

Andante grazioso/At a graceful steady pace:

Zawadi wonders if Mariage Frères carry black ginger tea. They do. Instead of tasting it, she will order it at the salon de thé. Both women stand in line and wait to be seated. As they wait, they study the menu. A colonial menu. They do not have long to wait. The head waiter proposes two seatings, the women choose a corner table. Zawadi sits facing the entrance so that she can appreciate the pastries on their glass shelves. She also has a gorgeous view of a stereotypically colonial poster while Indigo is granted a Marco Polo poster.

The two women study the brunch menu. It looks too filling. They, then, consider the lunch menu. Zawadi thinks she would like to have red meat: veal rib roast served with a brown gravy and Japanese green tea sauce accompanied by Brittany artichokes and raisins. Zawadi has her eyes set on the desserts even though she knows she is not being reasonable. Indigo is not decided. She is eyeing the duck breast with a sweet and sour sauce, cooked in *The Path of Time* (a flowery green sweet ginger tea) and served with curried French beans. Or will it be braised chicken cooked in *Lan na Thai*, a green tea from Thailand, and served with baby leek, baby onions, grilled almonds and lemon grass vinaigrette? Everything on the menu looks good.

A waiter in linen livery is ready to take the women's orders. Indigo is not ready yet, but Zawadi knows what she wants, or so she thinks. The waiter is kind and grants Indigo a few more minutes. The two women have been carrying on a food conversation spiced with ripples of laughter as they try to make their choice. They settle—finally!—for the afternoon tea menu. The club sandwiches look good. They will go the whole nine yards and order tea with their sandwiches, and round things off with dessert. Another waiter in linen livery comes to take their orders: two Club Louvre, with black ginger tea for one and *Thé des signes*, iced Dragon green tea for the other; it's the Year of the Dragon, after all.

The tea comes first. Indigo's iced tea surprises both women, coming in the biggest wineglass one ever saw. It has the women in stitches. Indigo looks at the tea, its colour, and knows that she will not like it at all, but it doesn't matter.

Zawadi pours her tea and both women look at its colour. Something about it is not quite right. Zawadi takes one delicate sip, then another. No, this is not what she asked for. Someone must have noticed, for they send a nervous waiter—probably a novice—who apologetically says that there has been a mistake. The *Marco Polo* green tea is replaced by another tea. Zawadi pours it and the colour still does not look right. More delicate sips. It doesn't taste right either. The novice waiter comes back. The tea is *Karikal*, a spicy green tea. The pot is taken away yet again. They get it right the third time, but there is no milk in sight, only a jug with water in it. Indigo is much bothered by this jug. Zawadi would like some milk, but doesn't ask for it, what with Indigo's no-you-can't!—because the French are such tea purists and this is Mariage Frères. Indigo seems to know what she is about. But what about this nagging jug of water? And she wants to enhance her concoction, but sugar will not do. Ask for honey, Zawadi urges. She does. Mariage Frères don't have any honey (too common?). Oh, well. Stiff upper lip, the Queen back in England would be chuffed.

Zawadi picks up the jug of water. She does not assume things are what they appear to be. She pours a few drops onto a teaspoon and takes a sip. Water? What water? This is clear corn syrup, ladies. Marco Polo, the Asian elephants, and the Englishmen in their uniform and colonial pith helmets gaze at these two black women who laugh crystal clear, making heads turn because they make no attempt to hide their mirth. The walls and tea-cups laugh along with the women, a laughter that goes on and on, tears coursing down the two women's cheeks. From then on, laughter will not be too far away. The tea-flavoured green salt will set them off, the green tea club sandwiches will set them off. But the jug, and the word "water" will be the mother. Serious conversation will be interspersed with fits of joy.

Onlookers must wonder what is so funny about what they have ordered since their laughter is plainly concentrated on what is on their table. They do not know the women's story, that they met that same morning, but that in the few hours spent together they have not only discovered a shared significant past but have also woven a rich tapestry of bonding memories. They do not know that these two women have bonded through a red dress, a marbled tea-cup, beads bought at the flea market; that they have bonded through tea, motherhood and stories of home. And even if they were to hear their story, would they believe the women? Impossible to skip all the stages of friendship and find yourself at intimacy.

Piano:

The waiters seem to understand that something magical is taking place. Zawadi charms the waiter at the dessert cart when she says she has travelled a fair distance to come to Mariage Frères. She, like the Queen, has a superb command of Molière's language. French waiters are partial to foreigners who respect their language. Mariage Frères waiters are no exception.

At a little before 7.30 p.m., a waiter places the bill on the table. He is apologetic. It is closing time. Indigo will look round at the *salon de thé* and realise they are the last clients and probably have been for a good while now.

The women will pick up their bags filled with memories; the waiters will bid the two sisters *au revoir*. It is rare for French waiters to forget to maintain that aloof and superior demeanour but the ones at Mariage Frères do. Their body language says *Karibuni tena*. See you soon.

Encore! Encore!

Natasha Trethewey

A two-term US Poet Laureate, Pulitzer Prize winner, and 2017 Heinz Award recipient, she has written five collections of poetry and one book of non-fiction. An American Academy of Arts and Sciences fellow, she is currently Board of Trustees professor of English at Northwestern University. She lives in Evanston, Illinois. Her writing includes the poetry collections Domestic Work *(2000),* Bellocq's Ophelia *(2002),* Native Guard *(2006),* Beyond Katrina: A Meditation on the Mississippi Gulf Coast *(2010),* Thrall *(2012) and* Monument: Poems New and Selected *(2018).*

My Mother Dreams Another Country

Already the words are changing. She is changing
    from *colored* to *negro*, *black* still years ahead.
This is 1966—she is married to a white man—
    and there are more names for what grows inside her.
It is enough to worry about words like *mongrel*
    and the infertility of mules and *mulattoes*
while flipping through a book of baby names.
    She has come home to wait out the long months,
her room unchanged since she's been gone:
    dolls winking down from every shelf—all of them
white. Every day she is flanked by the rituals of superstition,
    and there is a name she will learn for this too:
maternal impression—the shape, like an unknown
    country, marking the back of the newborn's thigh.
For now, women tell her to clear her head, to steady her hands
    or she'll gray a lock of the child's hair wherever

she worries her own, imprint somewhere the outline
    of a thing she craves too much. They tell her
to stanch her cravings by eating dirt. All spring
    she has sat on her hands, her fingers numb. For a while
each day, she can't feel anything she touches: the arbor
    out back—the landscape's green tangle; the molehill
of her own swelling. Here—outside the city limits—
    cars speed by, clouds of red dust in their wake.
She breathes it in—*Mississippi*—then drifts toward sleep,
    thinking of someplace she's never been. Late,
Mississippi is a dark backdrop bearing down
    on the windows of her room. On the TV in the corner,
the station signs off, broadcasting its nightly salutation:
    the waving Stars and Stripes, our national anthem.

Southern Gothic

I have lain down into 1970, into the bed
my parents will share for only a few more years.
Early evening, they have not yet turned from each other
in sleep, their bodies curved—parentheses
framing the separate lives they'll wake to. Dreaming,
I am again the child with too many questions—
the endless *why* and *why* and *why*
my mother cannot answer, her mouth closed, a gesture
toward her future: cold lips stitched shut.
The lines in my young father's face deepen
toward an expression of grief. I have come home
from the schoolyard with the words that shadow us
in this small Southern town—*peckerwood* and *nigger
lover*, *half-breed* and *zebra*—words that take shape
outside us. We're huddled on the tiny island of bed, quiet
in the language of blood: the house, unsteady
on its cinderblock haunches, sinking deeper
into the muck of ancestry. Oil lamps flicker
around us—our shadows, dark glyphs on the wall,
bigger and stranger than we are.

Incident

We tell the story every year—
how we peered from the windows, shades drawn—
though nothing really happened,
the charred grass now green again.

We peered from the windows, shades drawn,
at the cross trussed like a Christmas tree,
the charred grass still green. Then
we darkened our rooms, lit the hurricane lamps.

At the cross trussed like a Christmas tree,
a few men gathered, white as angels in their gowns.
We darkened our rooms and lit hurricane lamps,
the wicks trembling in their fonts of oil.

It seemed the angels had gathered, white men in their gowns.
When they were done, they left quietly. No one came.
The wicks trembled all night in their fonts of oil;
by morning the flames had all dimmed.

When they were done, the men left quietly. No one came.
Nothing really happened.
By morning all the flames had dimmed.
We tell the story every year.

South

> Homo sapiens *is the only species*
> *to suffer psychological exile.*
> —E.O. Wilson

I returned to a stand of pines,
            bone-thin phalanx

flanking the roadside, tangle
            of understory—a dialectic of dark

and light—and magnolias blossoming
            like afterthought: each flower

a surrender, white flags draped
                among the branches. I returned

to land's end, the swath of coast
                clear cut and buried in sand:

mangrove, live oak, gulfweed
                razed and replaced by thin palms—

palmettos—symbols of victory
                or defiance, over and over

marking this vanquished land. I returned
                to a field of cotton, hallowed ground—

as slave legend goes—each boll
                holding the ghosts of generations:

Hilda J. Twongyeirwe

Born in Kacerere village near Lake Bunyonyi, Uganda, she is a teacher by profession and has an MA in Public Administration and Management. Since 2007 she has been working with FEMRITE—Uganda Women Writers Association as Executive Director which has enabled her to participate in literary programmes aimed at amplifying African women's voices. She has received four Recognition Awards for contributions to Ugandan literature and women's emancipation from the government of Uganda, Women for Women Awards Uganda, Uganda Registration Services Bureau, and the National Book Trust of Uganda. In March 2015, she was named by For Harriet website as one of 18 African feminists to celebrate. She is a member of Action for Development and The Graca Machel African Women in Media Network. She serves on the Permanent Bureau of the African Asian Writers Union and the National Book Trust of Uganda.

From *Maisha Ndivyo ya Livyo*

Miriam lowered her bag on her lap and gasped…the earphone and power-bank charging cables dangled out of the bag like small intestines. Her mind raced through all the events of the morning, but she could not point at any suspicious act. That was Owino market.

She had just spent her morning there and all had seemed to end well, despite the overwhelming mud from September's El Niño rains—even stepping on the stones along the criss-crossing pathways between stalls splashed mud. It had rained again in the early hours of the morning, but Miriam still had to go to Owino because it was the only day she had for shopping before travelling to her village for the Christmas break. She knew Owino was the only place where she would get what she wanted. As she walked from one stall to another, hopping forwards and sideways to avoid bumping into people, she remembered what her friend Joy always said: that Owino market people walk in a to-whom-it-may-concern manner, as if other people are insects.

"It's their space," Miriam would respond.

"It's our space too."

"They're here because we come here."

"Look, we're here because they're here."

"But suppose we never came, who would they sell to?"

"Suppose they were not here, what would we come here to do?"

"Whatever! But this is a shared space."

Miriam had wanted Canon bed-sheets for her new bed. She was never sure about her ability to tell original quality from duplicates under the dazzling lights in shopping malls. Owino natural light worked better and, besides, she would get the original Canon bed-sheets at less than half the price quoted in main-street malls. She had hobbled to the stall of the bald-headed seller who always selected those bed-sheets for her that she never saw on other people's clotheslines.

"Oh, my friend. You have arrived," he greeted her. "You cannot exhaust my stock today."

"I want good quality Canon bed-sheets like the ones you always give me."

"I have them."

"I want a good price today."

"I always give you good price that I don't give to anybody else, even when they beg me. But for you, I always give you because you are my friend."

"Today I have little money."

"I have bed-sheets for all prices," he said, touching one pile after another. He selected a pair of white sheets with small pink flowers, cast it over her arm then dug out another pair, soft cream with a blue print.

"I want only one pair." But Miriam agreed with the bald-headed man. They were cute bed-sheets, soft and frothy. "I'll give you 20,000 for each of them," she told him.

"You people can insult."

"But that's what I have today."

"Then I will not eat your money today. You walk to other stalls and get bed-sheets for 20,000."

"Okay. How much?"

"80,000."

"I will give you 50,000."

"That is also money. I can get you another pair for 50,000. Those are for 80,000."

Miriam shook her head. "Please…" she said, looking at the shiny patch on the man's head where old age had already eaten away almost half of his hair.

"Put down my sheets and walk away." The man's smiling face was becoming several sets of furrows, belying the earlier declared friendship.

Miriam counted 160,000 shillings from her purse and paid for the two pairs of bed-sheets.

She had walked past several stalls looking for piles of jeans. She wanted some for herself, and a travel bag and a heavy duvet for her parents. As she walked, she found herself listening and smiling at the sale-songs that the vendors sang to attract or chase away customers:

Two thousand, two thousand, pick whatever you want.
It's two thousand whatever you choose.
If you don't have it, don't bend your back.
If you have nothing, you do'ot point your wire at the mandazi.
Two thousand, sweaters.
Do nor envy your neighbour's child's fat cheeks
Coldness brings kwashiorkor cheeks.

Nowadays Miriam avoided the cheapest heaps, however tempting the items. The last time she bought a sweater from such a heap, when she got home and tried it on, it had only one sleeve. Factory error, her sister had commented; but they could both see the sleeve had either been cut or had fallen off. On another occasion, her sister bought a flowered cotton dress, and after one wash the entire colour ran, leaving it a dirty brown thing that she could use only as a rug. Those cheap heaps were not to be trusted, yet they always drew the biggest crowds of buyers counting out hard-earned savings coin by coin to pay for the stuff.

Miriam stopped at the stall of two young men with welcoming faces. She never stopped at the stalls of mean-faced sellers; they could be a nuisance if you chose not to buy anything from them. Miriam looked at several pairs of trousers, tossing them back onto the pile. The sales boys became agitated. They drew closer and started gathering up and tidying the trousers she was throwing back.

"Are you buying or are you not buying?"

"What is your problem?" Miriam asked them.

"Hear how she opens her mouth. You don't just touch our maali and cast away, touch and cast away as if you are a witch."

"But I have to touch them in order to decide on what to buy."

"Just leave!" they shouted.

"Eeh. I will leave if you want me to."

"So what are you waiting for? Leave! You people make other people remain paupers because you put a spell on their maali and make it slip through their fingers. Go!" The voice was rising.

And leave she did. This was Owino. Very unpredictable.

She moved on towards the stalls ahead. As she negotiated her way around the mud, the scent of boiled rice and meat wafted through the air, reminding her that she had left home without breakfast.

A petite woman carrying a tray of food swung past. She could have been anything between sixteen and twenty-three years old. A white cap hid her hair. Her long skirt reminded Miriam of those days in her village when she would see women return from gardening during the rainy season, the hems of their skirts heavy with mud, flip-flapping against their legs. She loathed meeting those women; she did not want to be like them. Always returning in the evenings with soil-covered legs. There were a few women at the trading centre too but those were always clean. However, whenever she did anything wrong at home, her mother told her she was going to turn out like the women at the trading centre. Miriam did not know what was wrong with being like women at the trading centre. She admired them. They were clean. They were smart. They had time to just sit at the roadside and say "welcome back" to the women returning from the gardens. They had time even to talk and laugh with the men drinking amaarwa or those playing omwesho. Miriam smiled, remembering the time her mother said that the men in their village spent their days rolling their testicles on the bar benches, and Miriam had wanted to say that wasn't true, since the men just sat and played chanisi and other games without ever removing their trousers. Only much later did Miriam understand her mother's language.

Today, the food girl and other women with muddy feet in Owino, calling buyers to look at their wares, became the women in Miriam's village.

"See dress? Perfect for you." A woman on her left was tugging at her arm. "Come. I am not expensive. I will give you good price."

"Don't you see she wants children's clothes? Come. I have them," another woman was saying, with so much confidence, one would think she was Miriam's neighbour.

"Don't be confused. I know what you want. Come over here. See this?" Another woman was waving a pair of knickers almost in her face.

"Thank you. Another time," Miriam said.

The first woman was still looking at her. Her lips widened into a smile and she winked at her. She was still holding the dress.

"Office dress, madam. Come. You can try it. There is a dressing-room here," she said, spreading a multi-coloured kanga lesu, with a Swahili phrase printed on it: *Maisha Ndivyo ya Livyo*. Miriam smiled at the message: Life is like that.

"No, thank you."

"Please, madam, promote my business. I am looking for school fees for my children." The woman was now blocking her from continuing. Desperate. "And you need office wear." The woman's smile widened, her eyes rolling from one direction to the other.

"I said no, thank you." Miriam hoped that was not a betrayal.

The woman's lips slid back into a tucked-in position before she started jeering at Miriam.

Miriam hurried away. Struggle for survival sat at the wheel that propelled state of mind in Owino.

When Miriam got home her partner was cleaning the fridge, refilling it with his favourite beers, already in festive mood.

"What were you buying that took so long?" he asked.

"I wasn't long," she said, as she headed for the bedroom. He followed her. She placed the travel bag on the floor and the handbag on the bed. Through the razor-cut opening, she removed the book and placed it to the side. Next she took out her phone—a shimmering silver Sony that her girlfriends had nicknamed Sexy Sonny. She placed it on her chest and closed her eyes before putting it to her lips.

"Why the phone? And remember, you left me in bed," her partner said, closing the space between them, one hand reaching for her breast and the other trying to cup her chin to redirect her mouth from the phone towards his lips.

"Oh, please."

"What?"

"Not now," she said, louder than was perhaps necessary, as she disentangled herself from him.

"Okay, Madam Not Now. I am a patient man." He moved away from her but remained in the room.

Miriam ignored him. She reached for the bag again and picked out her cream purse, which she had bought herself on her thirtieth birthday.

"People are merciless," she murmured.

"Which people?"

"People people."

"Like you and me?" he said, leaning over her shoulder to see what she was looking at. "What's wrong with your purse? And your bag? What happened? Eeh! *Bakushara enshaho*? Jesus Christ! They cut your bag! You were robbed in Owino?"

"Yes."

"What did they take?"

"My power-bank and the Samsung tablet."

"Why did you take the tablet to Owino?"

"I wasn't taking it to Owino. I just wanted to do some work in the taxi on my way."

"You see! Now you have no tablet and no work. I always warn you about going shopping during the festive season. Everybody is looking for survival. How did they cut the bag?"

"How would I know?"

"What else did they take? Hmm? I always tell you, but you never listen."

Typical, Miriam thought. It was always: *I told you*. So how was she supposed to tell the story without feeling guilty and careless?

"Do you suspect anyone?"

"In Owino, it could be anybody."

But she could not tell him she had bumped into her former boyfriend in the market and he too was among the suspects. Why had he wanted to detain her longer than necessary? He had looked so unkempt… Yet it could as easily have been the boys at the jeans stall; they could have done it before urging her to leave their stall. Or they could have followed and robbed her without her noticing. The more she tried to recall at what point the theft might have happened, the more confused she became.

"Do you need anything?" Her partner's voice cut through her thoughts.

"No. Not now. But maybe yes."

"Yes?"

"A glass of water."

Letting the tip of his tongue play between his lips, he smiled and she knew exactly what he was thinking about.

Yvonne Vera
(1964–2005)

Born in Bulawayo, in what was then Southern Rhodesia, she went in 1987 to Canada, where she married, completed an undergraduate degree, an MA and a PhD, and taught literature at York University, Toronto. Her first book was a collection of short stories, Why Don't You Carve Other Animals *(1992), which was followed by five acclaimed novels:* Nehanda *(1993),* Without a Name *(1994),* Under the Tongue *(1996),* Butterfly Burning *(1998) and* The Stone Virgins *(2002). Her awards included the Commonwealth Writers' Prize, the Zimbabwe Publishers' Literary Award and the Macmillan Writers' Prize for Africa. For a while in the 1990s she was director of the National Gallery of Zimbabwe, but returned to Canada, where she was working on a new novel at the time of her death. She said: "I would love to be remembered as a writer who had no fear for words and who had an intense love for her nation."*

From *The Stone Virgins*

These women, lively and impatient, have secured a freedom that makes their voices glow. They know everything there is to know about anything there is to know, and have tasted their own freedom mature, because yes, it is truly theirs, this freedom. They have not misunderstood. They hold that freedom in their arms. With imaginations unencumbered they will have children called Happiness, called Prosperity, called

Fortune, called True Love, called Moreblessing, called Joy, called Ceasefire. Why not? The names will cascade like histories from their tongues…Beauty, Courage and Freedom. All their children will be conceived out of this moment of emancipation. Born into their arms like revelations, like flowers opening. It will be necessary to give their offspring middle names which will provide them strength…Masotsha, Mandla and Nqabutho. Names to anchor dreams.

These women are the freest women on earth with no pretence, just joy coursing through their veins. They have no desire to be owned, hedged in, claimed, but to be appreciated, to be loved till an entire sun sets, to be adored like doves. They want only to be held like something too true to be believed. They want to know an absolute joy with men who carry that lost look in their eyes; the men, who walk awkward like, lost like, as though the earth is shaking under their feet, not at all like what they imagine heroes to be; these men, who have a hard time looking straight at a woman for a whole two minutes without closing their own eyes or looking away; who smile harmless smiles which make the women weak at the knees and fold their arms over their heads; this man seems to say he has not killed anyone, that is all talk because the country needs heroes, and flags, and festivities, and the notion of sacrifice. Does she not know that? His tone is pleading for her to stop examining his wounds and hindering his view of the hills. At the start of each new day the question is on her lips, unspoken. Did he? Did he kill a white man?

He gives her a can of sardines and then a yellow ribbon to weave through her plaited hair, and asks her if she is going to be a school teacher and teach their children to say a e i o u…with their mouths shut. He does not stop there with his questions. He asks. Is it fine if he contributed to the making of these children, now, under this tree with its arm touching the ground, beneath this warm rock which has absorbed a whole day, under this syringe bush with its petals fanning the air, here, under this open sky, upon the sands of the Kwakhe River, the driest soil there is throughout Kezi and beyond, and surely, this river-sand sucking their feet in can keep any kind of secret including their own, he asks, and the woman surrenders all the freedom in her arms, nods her head within that softness of night, and she accepts those thighs which have climbed slippery rocks and the most severe hills of Gulati. Peace and calm pervades every nook, every crag, and surges through her waiting heels.

It is only when he sleeps, his arms flailing about, his voice darker than night and lit with stars, that the woman awakes and pins him down. Then she knows that her journey with this man is long and troubled, and that she cannot keep leaving him each night to his dreams. She is frightened, excited, lost. This man sleeps, but his eyes are open wide. In the morning she is not looking at him but at the circling hills of Gulati. She could never suggest it. Even if he smiled and told her the truth about everything, she could never suggest it. That he take her out there to see the hills up close, to touch distant rock, distant water and sky, to drop into the vast space where his mind has wandered through, falling, constantly, even as she moves her lips and whispers his name on her tongue. She could never suggest it, of course not. Not even without saying it, without thinking it. Not even if he said it himself. Lying next to him under the shadow of night is as far from Kezi as he is going to take her. As near to smooth rock and to the torrent of stars, out there. She cools his feet, unlaces, pulls, twists the worn and weathered leather boots off him.

The women who return from the bush arrive with a superior claim of their own. They define the world differently. They are fighters, simply, who pulled down every barrier and entered the bush, yes, like men. But then they were women and said so, and spoke so, and entered the bush, like men. To fight like men, and said so, to fight, like women who fight. They made admissions which resembled denials.

They do not apologise for their courage and long absence nor hide or turn away from the footpath. These women understand much better than any of the young women who have spent their entire life along the Kwakhe River ever could understand about anything or anyone and they tell them so, not with words, but they let them know fully and well, they let them speculate, let them wonder what those silent lips are about, what those arms, swinging from hip to shoulder, are about.

These women wear their camouflage long past the ceasefire, walking through Kezi with their heavy bound boots, their clothing a motif of rock and tree, and their long sleeves folded up along the wrist. They wear black berets, sit on the ledge at Thandabantu Store and throw their arms across their folded knees. They purse their lips and whistle, and toss bottle tops and catch them, and juggle corn husks which they toss at the young boys who leap to catch them before they touch the ground. They close their eyes and tuck their berets into the pockets along their legs, and button them up, and forget them. They watch, from this high plateau the young women who think freedom can be held in the hand, cupped like water, sipped like destinies. Who think that water can wash clean any wound and banish scars as dry as Kwakhe sand. These women whose only miracle is to watch water being swallowed by the Nyande River after the rain, if it rains, and they mistake the porous sands of Nyande for the substance of their laughters, their reckless joys, their gifts. These young women who possess intact and undisturbed histories, who without setting one foot past the Kwakhe River think they can cure all the loneliness in a man's arms, hold him, till he is as free as the day he was born, till he cannot remember counting the stars overhead, counting each star till he is out of breath and ready to hold his own screaming voice in his hands, to fight. With their immaculate thighs and their tender voices and unblemished skin they will make a new sun rise and set so that yesterday is forgotten. Time can begin here, in their arms.

The female soldiers marked with unknowable places on their own faces, with an unquenchable sorrow around their eyes, unaccustomed to a sudden stillness such as this, a sedentary posture and mindset, no longer wanderers, not threatened or threatening, these women hold their peace and say nothing to condemn or negate, but keep their distance a while to gather all the evidence they can about the other's cherished hope. This is a ceasefire. When they can they will avail themselves of destinations. The only sign they give of disapproval is to shake their heads sideways and look long and well as the young women walk into Thandabantu Store in their petticoats or with broken umbrellas to purchase some cream, some Vaseline, wearing leather sandals or with bare feet. They wait before they say anything or pass an opinion. They chew bubble-gum, bought by the handful, from Thandabantu.

They stay in their camouflage and pull out cigarettes and smoke while standing under the marula tree. They hold their faces up and seem amused either by the sky or by passers-by: their mothers. They walk leisurely to Thandabantu Store; slowly, as though they have a lifetime to consider what independence is all about, a lifetime, to place one foot after another, a lifetime to send a ring of laughter past the wing of a bird. They have no haste or hurry, no urgent harrowing hunger to satisfy, no torment they would rather not forget. Independence is a respite from war, the mind may just rearrange itself to a comfortable resolution, without haste, at the pace of each day unfolding and ending naturally, and opening again like a flower.

They sit on empty crates, like the men, then from here they watch the sun as though the watching of a sunset is simply a soothing pastime; but watching the sunset from Thandabantu Store and watching the sunset from the bush with a gun in your hand are related but vastly different acts. They are learning, with patience and goodwill, how it is to watch the sunset from Thandabantu. To watch a sun setting without a gun in your hand, so in this fair pursuit they forget that they are male or female but know that they are wounded beings, with searching eyes, and an acute desire for simple diversions. It is an intimate quest.

The men who for years have been going to Thandabantu to watch the sun, to summarise the day and what they have just heard of the war in the bush, who are part of the quality of this veranda and the sound of it and therefore an essential aspect of a place named Kezi because Kezi starts and ends at Thandabantu Store, these Kezi men have moved without reluctance or amazement at their displacement, moved to the marula tree and brought their hand-carved stools with them and from here they watch these women exude an elegance more spectacular than anything they have ever watched set or burn, their posture more genuine than their own feet on Kezi soil. They watch from the corner of their eye, feeling tongue-tied and charmed and privileged. And these men, whose feet have never left the Kwakhe River or wandered anywhere further than Thandabantu Store, lower their eyes frequently and efficiently, and their shoulders too, and pull their torn and faded hats further down. Thus contrite they glance at those military shoes, at those arms like batons, and look straight away, enchanted but not betrayed. They avoid those eyes or those hips under those clinging belts. The breasts, held carelessly up as though they are nothing but another part of the body where some human life just might be nurtured and survive, the breasts only a shape on the body, like the curve of the shoulder, a useful but wholly unremarkable part of the anatomy. The men know but dare not discuss how those breasts have held guns, have held dreams, and that they could never hold anything overnight less burdensome, less weighty than a broken continent.

Phillippa Yaa de Villiers

An award-winning writer and performance artist who performs her work nationally and internationally, she is noted for her poetry, which has been published in collections and in many magazines and anthologies, as well as for her autobiographical one-woman show, Original Skin, *which centres on her confusion about her identity at a young age, having been adopted and raised by a white family in apartheid South Africa, not knowing until she was 20 years old that she was half-Australian and half-Ghanaian. She writes, performs and teaches Creative Writing at Witwatersrand University, Johannesburg. She serves on the Editorial Board of the African Poetry Book Fund and has read and performed at poetry festivals in Germany, Denmark, the UK, Cuba, Sweden, Zimbabwe, Namibia and Ghana. Her poetry collections include* Taller Than Buildings *(2006),* The Everyday Wife *(2010) and* ice cream headache in my bone *(2017).*

Marriage

This is Afrika, you are the neck, your husband is the head.
—Traditional healer

My life as a pet sheep that I love and one day find out
my parents are fattening for slaughter. How else did they get me? My life
as a hardened chunk of cheese, forced to the back
of the fridge by fresh groceries. We want you to have more. My
life as that thick lump on an older woman's nape. You have to
work at relationships. My life
as a spare bicycle in case another child comes to play. My life
as a scorched shirt. My life as free plastic toys with every purchase
over R50 from Pick 'n Pay. My life as an empty house dreaming of people.
My life as the new cut, colour and style pour changer les idées.
My life as a suicide's favourite sweater. My life as
a rainy afternoon. My life cleaning out
my brother's room. My life as a tight, tiny skirt (pink). My life as a perfect lawn
whispering
beneath   your feet.

Foreign

I want to go into the world like an American girl, curious.

Savouring the sun on my body at Ellis Park pool, our world-class leftover from the bad old days when everything was for the whites and they descended, loud like ibises, two Americans talking.

I felt that pride of being indigenous, a snapshot of their experience, African woman sitting next to where the national swim team comes to train. Serious. And just around the corner the slum, unemployed men staying boys, still drunk from the weekend.

The one kid, chubby and shy, looked unsure about swimming. The Asian-looking one sized up the pool like she's got an appetite for it; like the pool's a man, a nice-sized man that's gonna make her feel her muscles, make her heart beat faster. When I was young I used to look at men that way, like I could give them a run around the block too.

The fat one squawked, surprised—the pool is heated. See? We don't live in trees. I ignored them carefully, diving in to start my routine 1km. No need to give them special attention. Let them have a story to tell.

After the swim I came out the shower as they entered the women's bathrooms. Yes, naked you know. From the shower. My mother used to look down on middle-aged women, telling me "Never let yourself go, sweetie." My round belly, momentous thighs, breasts still perky but less so than before confronted, they shrank into their young skins. I turned around slowly, turning the portrait to landscape, with texture.

They scuttled into the superintendent's room. Maybe I could have made them feel safe, disarmed them with smooth welcoming words, interpret this strange encounter for them and help us surf home on a wave of cheerios. But I didn't wanna. I wanted to be weird. I dried myself carefully, took my time to dress.

They were quieter as I swung my leg over the bike, I got a glimpse of them doing a selfie under that big fever tree by the entrance. An uber lurked nearby, waiting to gobble them up. As I blurred into the buzz of colour that is Troyeville, I wondered if they feel like they're elsewhere, or if everywhere feels like home. If they even curious about the difference, or wash it away in our world-class showers.

Heritage

The first time I saw my father it was like the whole continent was walking towards me. It was like his skin unzipped, opened up to let me in, and for the first time,
I was able to see my black skin as a badge of courage.

(*Original Skin.* For the woman at Goethe Institut
Accra, who wanted to know what that meant.)

First, you never denied me, even after I had summoned you out
of the blue yonder, father of three turned to father
a stranger. At the small provincial airport your eyes found
my shy, eager face, collected me with husband and son
swept us in, made place at the table, gave us clothes, fed the baby
his first solid food; took him from my breast and told him
that is good, but there is also turkey. You gentled my memories out
like handwashing underwear, a necessary task, without shame. You
faced the people who had raised me, listened to the legend of my rage, gave
thanks, especially to me for returning. Closed the
broken fence. From you I learned being in black skin.

Whole, unlike those dispossessed   *running from torment:*
of land, value, meaning

I am ~~white Coloured Cape Malay Griqua~~
~~Other coloured~~
~~a throwback your father slept with the maid~~
~~an experiment~~

Their children   stolen.   ~~aboriginal~~ *doll.*
Abandoned   not quite. *she never said "if your father had*
been white"

Now you, my child,   get over it already you
are different.

Song

River of my delight run on
the glint of the sun on your curves
scattering light in fragments feed us
your smile in the morning
the warmth of your hand in mine
the secret in your velvet gaze

tells me I am a treasure in your heart

unique your voice curls around sounds

names of all you love, dreams and memories

things and people wonder and your voice

beside me within me

river of my delight run on

beside me within me

river of my delight run on

never fear that you leave me behind

for I will always find my way

back to the river

back to our meeting place.

Kit de Waal

Born in Birmingham to an Irish mother and Caribbean father, she worked for 15 years in criminal and family law, for Social Services and the Crown Prosecution Service. She is a founding member of Leather Lane Writers and Oxford Narrative Group and has won numerous awards for her short stories and flash fiction. She has written two novels. My Name Is Leon (2016), her debut novel, won the Kerry Group Irish Novel of the Year 2017 and was shortlisted for numerous other awards including the Costa First Book Award and the Desmond Elliott Prize. The Trick to Time, her second novel, was published in 2018 and was longlisted for the Women's Prize for Fiction.

From *My Name Is Leon*

Right below the ball of his skull, right where his knuckly backbone pokes up towards his brain, Leon has a little dent. It's a groove that dips in between two hard bits and Maureen made it.

She must have made some kind of mark by now after six months of living with her. It's where she pushes Leon with her thick fingers whenever he has to do something, to go somewhere, to pick something up, to watch what he's doing. Go to bed. She never pushes him hard but it's always, always the same place, same spot, right on his neck. Leon's dad used to use funny words and he would have called that place his "neck-back" and then it would have been clear where it was. But Leon hasn't seen his dad for such a long time that he's nearly forgotten the things he used to say and the funny way he talked. Leon's dad used to say "Kyarell" instead of "Carol" and say "soon come" every time he left the house. That's when Leon's mum used to get annoyed with him because he never came soon and he never came back when he said he would. And now she's doing the same thing.

Leon's sitting back on the sofa with Jake asleep on his legs. Jake always gets hot and starts to sweat when he sleeps and beads of water on his forehead sparkle in the light from the telly. His curly blonde hair goes brown and two round pink spots appear on his creamy face.

Leon likes to watch Jake breathing. Jake breathes through his tiny perfect nostrils and lets the air out either side of his dummy. Then just as the dummy is about to drop out, Jake, in his sleep, draws it back in, sucks on it three times and starts all over again. Breathe in. Breathe out. Catch the dummy. Suck three times. Breathe in. Breathe out.

But sometimes, if Jake's dreaming maybe, he mutters something or cries out and the dummy falls on to his sleep suit and Leon has to be there to catch it and plop it back in for the three sucks before Jake notices and wakes up. Because if Jake wakes up before he's ready, nobody gets any peace. Least of all Leon because Jake always messes up Leon's games and Maureen nearly always sides with Jake and that's that.

"Up you come, sweetheart."

Maureen carefully lifts the damp baby off Leon's bare legs and as soon as she has Jake in the crook of her arm she pushes Leon towards the stairs. Pushes him in his neck-back. Leon realizes then that all his toys have been tidied away and the cushions have been rearranged while he and his brother have been sitting on the sofa.

Someone is coming. Leon knows who it is. The air is different. And there have been phone calls. And Sally or whatever her name is has come and bounced Jake on her lap and said how precious he is and that he has to have a chance. Maybe Carol is coming back. Maybe she's got better. And Sally has given Leon lots of sad smiles like he's sick or like he's fallen over and cut his knee. It's not Pretend Sad either. And Maureen keeps shaking her head and saying it isn't right. Maureen has been quiet for days and keeps looking at him and saying, "I don't know, I honestly don't. It's a bad, bad world."

The air has been different since yesterday.

"Upstairs with you, Leon, love. Upstairs and give that face a good going over and put a nice top on. Up you go. Quick as a flash. And wash your hands."

She fattens the cushions he's been sitting on and sits herself down in his spot, which is near the door where she can get up quickly and let the new social worker in. He watches her from the staircase snuggling her nose against Jake and he knows what she's doing. She's smelling the baby smell of him. The baby life of him. His perfection.

Maureen's broad back obliterates the whole of Jake and because she's just washed her orange hair it runs like wet snakes down the skin on her freckled back. It's hot in the house and Maureen's wearing a pink denim dress with no sleeves and one huge pocket at the front like she's a massive kangaroo. Leon comes down with a new face and a new top. He sits next to the social worker because every other social worker always says "Come and sit next to me" and this will save everyone the bother.

"Remember me?" she says. "Salma? I came yesterday to talk about you and Jake. Remember, Leon?"

It was only yesterday and since then nothing has been the same so of course Leon remembers her. She has the sad smile back on her face and also the look of fear. Maureen also has a different face. Leon knows that if the social worker wasn't here, Maureen would have rung her sister and said, "Know what, Sylvia? They've pissed me right off again, they have. Social Services? Waste of bloody space, if you ask me." But she never swears when the social workers are around. Neither does Leon.

Then Salma starts talking while Maureen bounces Jake on her lap. Maureen keeps shaking her head like she would like to say no, no, no but she doesn't say anything at all. Leon agrees with everything Salma says.

"Jake is still a very young baby."

"Yes," says Leon.

"He needs to be in a family."

"Yes," says Leon.

"Lots of families are looking for babies."

"Yes," says Leon.

"You love Jake, don't you, Leon?"

"Yes."

"Everyone knows how much you love your little brother. Even though you look very different, you can see you're brothers and that you love each other. Maureen's always telling me how you let him play with your toys and he will only sleep on your lap and no one else's. And that's lovely."

Leon nods.

"Wouldn't you like Jake to be in a family with a mum and dad of his own?"

"Yes."

"That's what we want as well. We want every child to have the best. You and Jake and all the other children who can't be looked after by their first family."

Salma takes one of Leon's hands out of his lap and he's glad he remembered to clean them.

"You're not a little boy now, Leon. You're nine. You're nine years old and so tall that you look about eleven or twelve, don't you? Yes. Or thirteen. A lot of people think you're older than you are. And you're very sensible as well. You had a long time looking after other people, didn't you, and that made you grow up very fast. Oh, I know you still like your toys and your games, but still."

Salma looks at Leon's hand and puts it back where it was. She then folds hers together and coughs. Leon sees her look at Jake. Then she looks at Maureen and he wonders if she's asked a question because no one speaks for quite some time.

So Leon says, "Yes."

"Leon, we've got a family that want to look after Jake. They want to be Jake's new parents. Isn't that good, Leon? Jake is going to have a new mummy and daddy."

"Yes."

"And soon, one day, a family will come along that will want you for their little boy."

Leon nods.

"Do you understand, Leon? Jake is going to be adopted. That means he's going to have a new forever family. But even though he won't be living with you any more you will still be able to get letters from him and find out all about him."

Leon looks at Maureen before he speaks.

"Jake can't write."

Salma laughs very loud and Leon knows she's pretending.

"Of course he can't! He's only ten months old! No. His new mummy and daddy will write the letter to you and probably even send a photograph as well. See!"

She has his hand again.

"I know this is hard for you, Leon. Very hard. We wish things were different but if Jake is going to have a chance…"

Maureen is up. "Thanks, Salma. He understands, don't you, pigeon?"

Maureen taps his neck-back and inclines her head to the kitchen.

"Curly Wurly?"

Leon gets up and goes into the kitchen. It isn't Saturday. It isn't Christmas and his room is very untidy, so why he's getting a Curly Wurly is a mystery. Then again, he has been very polite. He hasn't interrupted, answered back or tried to be too clever by half. There are three other Curly Wurlys in the cupboard and, as he's the only one in the house who eats them, Leon smiles. Maybe every time Salma comes and he doesn't lose his temper he'll get a Curly Wurly. He eats it in the kitchen but, before he's finished, Maureen calls him back in to say goodbye to Salma while she changes Jake in the bathroom. Salma puts her hand on his shoulder and shows him her sad smile again.

"You're a good boy, Leon. I know this is hard and you're a good brother to Jake but we have to think of his future."

"Yes."

Later, when Jake's in bed and Leon's watching the telly, Maureen asks him about what Salma said.

"She means it, you know, love. Did you understand that, Leon? Jake is going to be adopted."

"What's adopted?"

"Jake is going to have a new mum and dad."

"Why?"

"Because, love. Just because. Because he's a baby, a white baby. And you're not. Apparently. Because people are horrible and because life isn't fair, pigeon. Not fair at all. And if you ask me, it's plain wrong and—"

She stops suddenly and winks.

"Tell you what. Now His Nibbs is finally asleep, let's you and me get the biscuit tin out."

She comes back with a massive mug of coffee and the Golden Tin, which everyone knows is never allowed in the front room but this is, after all, a day of sad social workers and spontaneous Curly Wurlys so Leon says nothing. As she squashes a cushion into the small of her back, Maureen lets out a sigh that to Leon sounds a little bit shaky and he can hear something in her throat when she speaks.

"You stay here with your Auntie Maureen, love. Eh? We're happy enough, aren't we? You stay here with me."

Elizabeth Walcott-Hackshaw

A Professor of French Literature and Creative Writing at the University of the West Indies, she has published scholarly articles and essays on Francophone Caribbean Literature and co-edited several works including Border Crossings: A Trilingual Anthology of Caribbean Women Writers *(2012);* Methods in Caribbean Research: Literature, Discourse, Culture; Echoes of the Haitian Revolution *(1804–2004) (2009); and* Reinterpreting the Haitian Revolution and its Cultural Aftershocks *(2009). She has also published creative works, and her short stories have been widely translated and anthologised.* Four Taxis Facing North *(2007), her first collection of short stories was considered one of the best books of the year by the* Caribbean Review of Books. Mrs B, *a novel, was shortlisted for "Best Book of Fiction" in the Guyana Prize for Literature in 2014.*

Ashes

Sometimes leaves would fall from the trees, and sometimes ashes would just appear in the air, wriggling like black worms. I had just got home from a long day and was lying on a sofa on the veranda. Everything was complete now, the final payment made to the lawyer. Everything so easy, the secretary handed me the documents and explained carefully and slowly the next simple step. I handed over the final payment, she examined my cheque politely, with a cursory glance, assuring me that I was trustworthy, that it was fine, but all the while I was hoping that there would be a fault somewhere, something to cause a further delay, giving me just a little more time. The last documents were handed over with a gentle smile, a paper clip, and a manila envelope: "Could you sign here please?" "Is that it?" I asked. "Yes that's it," she said.

A divorce is like a death my good friend Sarah said to me, you grieve. But the difference from a real death? She had no advice then. We shared a friend who had lost a son, her only son, to a car accident, an unimaginable horror, "How do you get out of bed after that?" she said, "Especially if that was your only child," I added. The lights would have gone out with him, my world at an end; these were thoughts, I couldn't say the words.

We were having afternoon tea and there were tiers of cucumber sandwiches, smoked salmon sandwiches, scones, strawberry compote, clotted cream, and small sponge cakes. The waitress left a handsome wooden box of teas: Darjeeling, Earl Grey, English Breakfast. We both chose Earl Grey. We stayed in the cosy tea salon until dark and they were ready to close their doors. The owner said it was okay for us to stay on a little longer even though all of the waitresses, save one, had already left. We thanked her but felt we had really stayed on for too long, so we decided to move our little party to a bar that was not far away. There was still so much to talk about we joked, divorce, sex, death.

It was still early so there were only a few patrons scattered around the beautiful teak tables at the bar. Later in the evening, around seven thirty or eight the crowd would start to arrive. Sarah ordered a rosé and I got a beer.

"Since when do you drink beer?"

"Since last month, in London that was all I drank, all we drank." I had been travelling with my husband; and that "we" seemed to bother Sarah, her divorce still left a bitter taste, like my beer.

"If only I had known, how did I not see this coming?" She was looking directly at me when she said this.

"But you didn't know, you were friends, how were you to know that it would turn into what it did."

I didn't believe what I had said to her and neither did she; I knew it was coming but it made us both feel better so we pretended that Sarah was the real victim, not the husband that she had betrayed.

"We were never really happy, you know."

I shook my head as though commiserating with her but I didn't buy it; they were happy at one point because if they were only pretending then we all were, the entire group of us married folk would have been pretending. Something had to be true, I couldn't let her continue so I changed the topic, just a little.

"How is Maya coping?"

"At that age, all she knows is that Mummy and Daddy are now living in separate houses and Uncle Paul is spending a lot more time with Mummy than he used to." Sarah tried to laugh it off, and I smiled too, but none of it seemed really very funny.

"We never argue in front of her, we're really very good about that, so I'm not too worried, they say when you get divorced and the kids are young it doesn't affect them as much as if they were teenagers or, you know, more aware of what's happening."

I had no proof of this but I agreed, Sarah needed me to agree.

"When you get divorced wives don't invite you to their parties any more, I've been taken off of the list."

"I invite you to all of my parties," I said in mock defence.

"I didn't mean *you*. The others, you know who I mean, I think they think divorce is contagious, either that or they're afraid that I am about to steal their husbands."

"Or both." Yeah exactly and we both laughed. Sarah was beautiful and sexy enough to steal anybody's husband; I kept this thought to myself.

I ordered another beer, she was still nursing her glass of wine. Migrating was something we were both thinking about, and we shared dreams of setting up houses in London, Paris, Barcelona, New York, anywhere but the Caribbean. Sarah felt that Maya would have a better life, more options. I said yes but didn't totally agree, the Caribbean was still a good place to raise a child, and we had family and friends to call on in times of need.

"Would Barry let you take her?"

"Probably would put up a fight, but eventually he'd give in."

I really couldn't tell how serious she was about this although I knew that she had always wanted to live abroad. Having married at a young age, Sarah had never had the opportunity like some of her friends (I was included in that group) to have lived and studied abroad. Maybe now she was finally ready to go.

"This place can be suffocating," she said.

This time I was in total agreement, "Yes it can be."

"A small place," Sarah said.

I was thinking of Jamaica Kincaid's book which I was sure Sarah had not read, she had never been a reader like me.

"You know, like that book," Sarah said.

"What book?" I asked still unable to accept that Sarah had possibly read a book from cover to cover, far less a writer like Jamaica Kincaid, or even knew who Kincaid was for that matter.

"By that Jamaica woman."

"Jamaican you mean?" I was still unbelieving, and now deliberately trying to throw her off track.

"No, her *name* is Jamaica."

"Oh, you mean Jamaica Kincaid."

Of course, she always got names wrong, she offered. "We all do," I said condescendingly but Sarah didn't seem to notice the tone.

We stayed a little longer, and we saw the crowd begin to come in, all well dressed for an evening lime at a posh drinking hole. Sarah and I were still in our tea clothes, lighter colours as opposed to the black now filling the place. We recognized a few faces, said a quick "Hi" then "Goodbye".

By the time I got home the effect of the beer and the conversation with Sarah left me in a cloudy, uneasy state. That night in bed I kept replaying the Kincaid thing in my mind, how could she have known about Kincaid's *A Small Place*? It had to have been Paul's influence but I had never heard him refer to one single writer or book in the many years I had known him. And Sarah didn't even look as unhappy as I thought she would have. In fact, Sarah looked as though she had finally found the man of her dreams. In Paul of all people. Somehow Sarah had won again, the way she always had since our high school days, in a race that she didn't even know she was running.

Rebecca Walker

She is the author of the bestselling memoirs Black, White and Jewish *and* Baby Love; *the novel* Adé: A Love Story; *and editor of the ground-breaking anthologies* To Be Real, What Makes a Man, One Big Happy Family *and* Black Cool. *Her writing has appeared in the* Washington Post, *the* New York Times, Bookforum, BOMB, Newsweek, Vibe, Real Simple, Essence, *and* Interview, *among many other magazines and literary collections. She has spoken at over 400 universities and college campuses including Harvard, Facebook, TedXLund, and JP Morgan Chase.* Time *magazine named her one of the most influential leaders of her generation. She lives in Los Angeles.*

From *Adé: A Love Story*

We stepped off the bus with our backs kinked and mouths dry. The twists and turns of the road from the city to the coast, the loud yelling of the bus driver and his obvious addiction to an herb pulled obsessively from a wrapper of old newspaper had left us skittish and raw. The other passengers did not seem to notice the careening into darkness, the hypnotic beat of imported hip hop pumping through the threadbare seats, the angry outbursts of passing motorists.

Miriam and I tried to let our bodies sway with each lean and brake, tried not to conjure images of mangled bodies and buses overturned by the side of the road, but found we could not help ourselves. We sat the whole sixteen hours clutching metal bars crudely nailed into the sides of our seats, rivers of sweat streaming from our armpits. We glanced meekly from time to time at our fellow passengers, men and women who awoke from naps refreshed and took pity on us, offering cigarettes and bottles of hot cola as we quaked.

To finally climb aboard the ferry that took us away from the mainland of Kenya was to step into a dream. We were never so glad to leave tar and cement, metal and glass, profane music and men who did not take precautions. The boat was not big, but it was old and looked to us seaworthy, though of course there would have been nothing to do had it been otherwise. It was painted white and a calming pale green, and once it began to move, groaning loudly as the waters churned beneath us, it did not take long for the coastline to disappear, and for the fumes and chaos of the dock to fade from view.

I was worn out, but had never seen a swamp before, and certainly not the vivid mossy green of mangrove forests, the bent reddish-brown trunks rising up out of the muck, miraculous as lotus blossoms. Again, I felt a sense of belonging—the slow, irrational dissolution of the self I had known, and another, core truth of being emerging in concert with the landscape. I wanted to know about the small islands we were passing, were they inhabited, did food grow there? But I knew better than to talk to the women cloaked in black and laughing insouciantly at their own jokes, wrapping and rewrapping their coverings while staring nakedly at me as if I were no more than a life-size cutout of a woman, and not the real thing.

* * *

Soon, the landmass appeared on the horizon, and then all at once we were upon the tiny village, a string of flat, tin-roofed buildings, and the boat was roped to the hooks on the cement pier by a barefoot man old enough to be my grandfather. I noticed the Portuguese influence, the squat columned structures reminiscent of the slave trade, but it was not my first thought, nor did it take hold for long. I was already caught up in what was going on around me.

It was mango season, and mangoes were everywhere: loose and spoiling on the ground at my feet, carried in bulging sacks on the backs of men, bright orange and dripping in the hands of children along the sea front. Women were covered from head to toe in black, strolling unhurriedly in groups of four and five. Young, shirtless men with dreadlocks and surfboards were scanning the ferry passengers for rich white tourists. Older men in neat white shirts and embroidered skullcaps were walking briskly to and from mosques that dotted the small town.

I don't remember how we got from the pier to the guesthouse, but our bags were tossed onto the concrete, and we were escorted from the mouth of the boat onto the firm ground of the pier. Miriam and I stood there for a few moments amidst the orderly confusion, too tired to check the guidebook buried in our baggage, and too happy standing still to rush to movement. Then a young, brown-skinned man with thick-rimmed black glasses approached us with a mixture of boredom and pity, picked up our bags without a word, and led us through the narrow, winding streets to our new home, a few tiny rooms off a rooftop courtyard, completely hidden from the street but for a narrow stone staircase winding up from the curb.

Adé did not appear until many hours later, after the sun had melted into the sea and the sticky heat of the day had settled into a breezy cool. I had unpacked the contents of my bag into an old wooden chest that stood beside the thin mattress on the floor, and hung my brightly colored scarves on hooks pounded into the cracked, dry walls. The sheet on my bed was faded and flowery, and I stretched out on top of it in the dimly lit room, hearing the muezzin's call to prayer and thumbing through a book of poems, *The Captain's Verses*, by Pablo Neruda. The tightness in my neck and in the small of my back relaxed, and my mind began slowing to the pace of the island, downshifting from the screeching city chaos to the gentle lapping of the sea that beat like a pulse through the tiny town.

Gradually the opening and closing of doors and the shifting of furniture outside my door grew into laughter and talking and the sound of food and drink being served. It was Ramadan; the sun had gone down, and the music had begun to play. That night the fast was broken with a melodic Lingala, and I immediately put my book down and let my head fall back into my pillow. I had not heard Lingala music before, and the newness of the sound affected me. I was used to the haunting whines of the griots from Mali and Senegal, the polyrhythmic chants of pygmies from Central Africa. But Lingala was different. It was music born of African rumba, a child of Afro-Cuban fusion that took hold in the Belgian Congo in the forties, and made its way east to Kenya and Tanzania in the seventies and eighties, absorbing influences from Congolese folk music and Caribbean and Latin beats. On the Kenyan coast it leapt again, and with three or four guitars, one bass, drums, brass, and vocals, evolved a new offspring, benga, or the Swahili sound. Lingala was dance music, hypnotic and polyphonic, full of movement. It brought to mind the sound of bottles tinkling at a bar, and women and men sweating and dancing hip to hip under colored lights. The sound was so infectious, so sexy, it drew me out of my room and into the movement of it, into the ecstasy of its freedom.

I opened the door, and saw a man in the center of this exuberant stream of sound. He was inside the benga. Standing with his back to me, among a dozen or so other strikingly beautiful bodies, I saw his slender hips first, the clean white kikoi wrapped neatly around his waist, the tails of the turquoise button-down Oxford shirt modestly covering his behind. Adé's was the first body I saw, and then my eyes were captivated by others: a handsome African-American man I later learned was from Boston, a thin, olive-skinned beauty from Brazil, a serious exchange student from Tunis, five or six diffident-looking young men from the island. Everyone was talking, drinking, laughing, and sharing survival stories from months on the road.

* * *

I exhaled and looked past him at the moon rising, huge and luminous behind us, from the other side of the island. I motioned to it and he twisted around to see. We stayed like that for what seemed a long time, watching its ascent in silence.

Eventually he turned back to me and asked if I was hungry. I was not, but again, just as with the women in the boat, something stopped me from responding as I might have, loudly and without respect for the sanctity of the moment. I said yes quietly, almost in a whisper, and watched him carefully take the thin sheet of tin off of the plate. As I parted my lips and waited for the forkful of noodles he offered, I glanced at his muscular calves, and his large and handsome feet resting in sandals made from the faded black rubber of old tires. And then the spaghetti reached my tongue. It was sweet! It was cooked with sugar! It was one of his mother's favorite recipes, he said. It was special for Ramadan and meant to remind us of the sweetness of life, of God.

I nodded, pondering this new being before me, feeding me the taste of his mother's hands, her offering to God, and I had the urge to touch him, to feel that he was real. And then the sweet spaghetti was finished, and he said he had to work early the next morning at the woodshop. He was a fisherman first, but also a carver, he said, and chiseled rosettes into the massive wooden doors announcing the thresholds of the larger houses in town. We had seen some of them, I said, on our way to the guesthouse. He nodded. I wanted to kiss him, waited. He folded the square of tinfoil covering the plate and put it into his shirt pocket. I stood closer to him, and we walked together to the steps. He was taller than me by several inches, and I felt some indescribable protection there, in his imagined embrace.

After he left, I lay on my thin mattress thinking about the unusual potency of our attraction. I knew nothing about him and yet I wanted to see him again. I had too much power, I thought. I might consume him out of my own curiosity simply because I could. I could stay or go. He could not. He had too much power, I thought. He could reject me. He could break me in two.

Not long after, I heard a quiet knock on the door, and for a moment thought he might have returned. But it was Miriam who entered without waiting for my response. She spread out next to me, humming a tune from the Lingala, as I gushed excitedly about the moon and the sweet spaghetti, about young men giving money to their mothers. She talked about the invisibility of women in the Old Town, and the claustrophobia she felt walking down the narrow stone streets. She said that for the first time in her life, she missed seeing cars, a way out.

I tried to stay awake, but was tired and did not like what she was saying. I could not imagine we were on the same island. I started to say something, to defend this small place and its people, but I could not bring myself to do it. I had only just met this one boy. The story of the world was too big to reverse in one night. My mind and then my body grew heavy. I pressed myself against her, and drifted off to sleep.

Chimamanda Ngozi Adichie

An acclaimed Nigerian author, she has had her work translated into more than 30 languages and has contributed to numerous publications, including the New Yorker, Granta, The O. Henry Prize Stories, *the* Financial Times, *and* Zoetrope. *She is the author of the novels* Purple Hibiscus *(2003), which won the Commonwealth Writers' Prize and the Hurston/Wright Legacy Award;* Half of a Yellow Sun *(2006) which won the Orange Prize, was a National Book Critics Circle Award Finalist, a* New York Times Notable Book, *and was adapted as a 2013 film directed by Biyi Bandele, and* Americanah *(2013), which won the National Book Critics Circle Award and was named one of the* New York Times Top Ten Best Books of 2013. *She is also the author of* Dear Ijeawele, or a Feminist Manifesto in Fifteen Suggestions *and the 2009 story collection* The Thing Around Your Neck. *Her 2009 TED Talk, "The Danger of a Single Story", is one of the most-viewed TED Talks of all time. She divides her time between the US and Nigeria, where she was born.*

From *We Should All Be Feminists*

Okoloma was one of my greatest childhood friends. He lived on my street and looked after me like a big brother: if I liked a boy, I would ask Okoloma's opinion. He was funny and intelligent and wore cowboy boots that were pointy at the tips. Okoloma was a person I could argue with, laugh with and truly talk to. He was also the first person to call me a feminist.

I was about fourteen, we were in his house, arguing, both of us bristling with half-baked knowledge from books we had read. I don't remember what this particular argument was about, but as I argued and argued, Okoloma looked at me and said, "You know, you're a feminist."

It was not a compliment. I could tell from his tone—the tone with which someone would say, "You're a supporter of terrorism."

I did not know exactly what this word *feminist* meant; and I did not want Okoloma to know that I didn't know. So I brushed it aside and continued to argue. The first thing I planned to do when I got home was to look up the word in the dictionary.

Now fast-forward to some years later.

In 2003 I wrote a novel called *Purple Hibiscus*, about a man who, among other things, beats his wife and whose story doesn't end too well. While I was promoting the novel in Nigeria, a journalist, a nice, well-meaning man, told me he wanted to advise me. He told me that people were saying my novel was feminist and his advice to me—he was shaking his head sadly as he spoke—was that I should never call myself a feminist, since feminists are women who are unhappy because they cannot find husbands.

So I decided to call myself a Happy Feminist.

Then an academic, a Nigerian woman, told me that feminism was not our culture, feminism was un-African, that I was calling myself a feminist because I had been influenced by Western books (which amused me, because a lot of my early reading was decidedly un-feminist: I must have read every Mills & Boon romance published before I was sixteen. And each time I try to read those books called "classic feminist texts" I get bored, and I struggle to finish them). Anyway, since feminism was un-African, I decided I would call myself a Happy African Feminist. Then a friend told me that calling myself a feminist meant I hated men. So I decided I would now be a Happy African Feminist Who Does Not Hate Men. At some point I was a Happy African Feminist Who Does Not Hate Men And Who Likes To Wear Lip Gloss And High Heels For Herself And Not For Men. Of course, a lot of this was tongue-in-cheek, but that word "feminist" is so heavy with negative baggage. You hate men, you hate bras, you don't have a sense of humour...

Men and women are different. We have different hormones, different sexual organs, different biological abilities. Men have testosterone and are, in general, physically stronger than women. About fiftey-two per cent of the world's population is female, but most positions of power and prestige are occupied by men. The late Kenyan Nobel Peace laureate Wangari Maathai put it simply and well when she said, "The higher you go the fewer women there are."

Not long ago, I wrote an article about what it means to be young and female in Lagos and an acquaintance told me it was an angry article. Of course it was angry. Gender as it functions today is a grave injustice. We should all be angry. Anger has a long history of bringing about positive change. But I am also hopeful, because I believe deeply in the ability of human beings to remake themselves for the better.

Gender matters everywhere. And I would like today to ask that we begin to dream about and plan for a different world. A fairer world. A world of happier men and happier women who are truer to themselves. And this is how to start: we must raise our daughters differently. We must also raise our sons differently. We do a great disservice to boys in how we raise them. We stifle the humanity of boys. We define masculinity in a *very* narrow way. Masculinity is a hard small cage and we put boys inside this cage. We teach boys to be afraid of fear, of weakness, of vulnerability. We teach them to mask their true selves because they have to be, in Nigerian-speak, a *hard man*.

But by making them feel they have to be hard, we leave them with fragile egos. The *harder* a man feels compelled to be, the weaker his ego is.

And then we do a much greater disservice to girls because we raise them to cater to the fragile egos of males.

We teach girls to shrink themselves, to make themselves smaller. We say to girls, "You can have ambition, but not too much. Aim to be successful, but not too successful, otherwise you would threaten the man. If you are the breadwinner in your relationship with a man, pretend that you're not, especially in public, otherwise you will emasculate him."

But what if we question the premise? Why should a woman's success be a threat to a man? What if we decide simply to dispose of that word (and I don't think there is an English word I dislike more) *emasculation*.

A Nigerian acquaintance once asked me if I worried that men would be intimidated by me. It had not occurred to me to be worried, because a man who is intimidated by me is the kind of man I would have no interest in. Still, I was struck by this. Because as a female, I'm expected to make my life choices keeping in mind that marriage is the most important.

Marriage can be a source of joy and love and mutual support, but why do we teach girls to aspire to marriage and we don't teach boys the same?

We all internalize ideas from our socialization. The language of marriage is often the language of ownership, rather than the language of partnership.

Both men and women will say: "I did it for peace in my marriage." When men say it, it is usually about something they should not be doing anyway. It is something they say to their friends in a fondly exasperated way, something that ultimately proves their masculinity. "Oh, my wife said I can't go to clubs every night, so now, for peace in my marriage, I go only on weekends." When women say "I did it for peace in my marriage," it is usually because they have given up a job, a goal, a dream. We teach females that in relationships, compromise is what women do. We raise girls to see each other as competitors for the attention of men. We teach girls they cannot be sexual beings in the way boys are. We police girls. We praise girls for virginity, but we don't praise boys for virginity (and that makes me wonder how exactly this loss of virginity is supposed to work...).

We teach girls shame. *Close your legs. Cover yourself.* We make them feel as though by being born female they're already guilty of something. So girls grow up to be women who cannot say they have desire. Who silence themselves. Who cannot say what they truly think. Who have turned pretence into an art form.

Imagine how much happier we would be, how much freer to be our true individual selves, if we didn't have the weight of gender expectations.

Boys and girls are undeniably different biologically, but socialization exaggerates the differences, and then it becomes a self-fulfilling process. What if, in raising children, we focus on *ability* instead of gender? What if we focus on *interest* instead of gender?

I'm trying to unlearn many lessons of gender internalized while growing up. But I sometimes still feel vulnerable in the face of gender expectations.

The first time I taught a writing class in graduate school, I was worried. Not about the teaching material, because I was well prepared and was teaching what I enjoyed. Instead I was worried about what to wear. I wanted to be taken seriously. I knew that because I was female, I would automatically have to *prove* my worth. And I was worried that if I looked too feminine, I would not be taken seriously. I really wanted to wear my shiny lip gloss and my girly skirt, but I decided not to. I wore a very serious, very manly, and very ugly suit.

The sad truth is that when it comes to appearance, we start with men as the standard, the norm. A man going to a business meeting doesn't worry about being taken seriously based on what he is wearing—but a woman does.

I wish had not worn that ugly suit. Had I, then, the confidence I have now to be myself, my students would have benefited even more from my teaching, because I would have been more comfortable, and more truly myself.

I have chosen to no longer be apologetic for my femininity. I want to be respected in all my femaleness. Because I deserve to be. The "male gaze", as a shaper of my life's choices, is largely incidental.

Gender is not an easy conversation to have. Both men and women are resistant to talking about gender, or are quick to dismiss the problems.

Some people ask, "Why *feminist*? Why not just say you are a believer in human rights?" Because that would be dishonest. It would be to deny that the problem was specifically about being a female human.

Some men feel threatened by the idea of feminism. This comes, I think, from the insecurity triggered by how boys are brought up, how their sense of self-worth is diminished if *they* are not "naturally" in charge as men.

Other men respond, "I don't think like that. I don't even think about gender."

Maybe not. And that is part of the problem. That many men do not actively *think* about or notice gender.

Because gender can be uncomfortable, there are easy ways to close this conversation.

Some people will say, "Well, poor men also have a hard time." And they do. But gender and class are different. Poor men still have the privileges of being men. I learned a lot about systems of oppression and how they can be blind to one another by talking to black men. I was once talking about gender and a man said to me, "Why does it have to be you as a woman? Why not you as a human being?" (The same man, by the way, would often talk about his experience as a black man.)

Gender matters. Men and women experience the world differently. Gender colours the way we experience the world. But we can change that.

Some people say that a woman being subordinate to a man is our culture. But culture is constantly changing. Culture does not make people. People make culture. If it is true that the full humanity of women is not our culture, then we can and must make it our culture.

My dear friend Okoloma was right, that day he called me a feminist. I am a feminist. And when, all those years ago, I looked the word up in the dictionary, it said: *Feminist: a person who believes in the social, political, and economic equality of the sexes.*

My great-grandmother, from stories I've heard, was a feminist. She ran away from the house of the man she did not want to marry and married the man of her choice. She refused, she protested, spoke up whenever she felt she was being deprived of land and access because she was female. She did not know that word *feminist*. But it doesn't mean she wasn't one. More of us should reclaim that word. The best feminist I know is my brother Kene, who is also a kind, good-looking and very masculine young man. My own definition of a feminist is a man or a woman who says, "Yes, there's a problem with gender as it is today and we must fix it, we must do better."

All of us, women and men, must do better.

Zoe Adjonyoh

Born to a Ghanaian father and Irish mother, she is a writer and cook from London on a mission to bring African food to the masses. She deepened her understanding of West African cuisine after a trip to visit her extended family in Ghana. Described by The Observer *as a "standard bearer for West African food" and picked by Nigel Slater as one to watch on the topic of immigrant food in Britain, she has been making waves in the food scene ever since her first sell-out supper clubs in 2011. She has taken her fresh interpretation of classic Ghanaian flavours to pop-up venues across London and Berlin, as well as prominent street food festivals around the UK. Named as one of "London's hottest chefs" by* Time Out, *she launched her first fixed restaurant space in 2015, at shipping container community project Pop Brixton. Her debut cookbook* Zoe's Ghana Kitchen *was published in 2017.*

A Beautiful Story

Most women worry about turning into their mothers. I worry about turning into my father. Waiting outside Costa Coffee next to Woolwich Arsenal DLR station, I see my father—Charles—lumbering towards me. He is not hard to spot at six-foot-three, with his grey-speckled Afro. The burnt-orange corduroy suit with yellow striped tie and baby-blue shirt is hard to ignore. There is something dapper and reassuring about his appearance: it tells me he is feeling alright. He likes to dress up for an occasion and today, meeting me for coffee, appears to be that. His walk has changed in recent years: his once long, confident stride is now the heavy-footed shuffle of an old, tired man, though he is only fifty-five. He hasn't seen me yet so I pause to take him in. His limp seems to have worsened and his head dangles in front of stooped shoulders like a cartoon vulture. His hair, springing unevenly, needs a cut. I'll give him some cash later to get that sorted but now I watch how he looks at people, up and down, with narrow, critical eyes. *What is he thinking? Do I look at people like that? Who is that he just smiled and waved at across the street? They don't seem to know him.*

"Dad! Dad!" I self-consciously stick my hand in the air and motion him over.

"Hello, dah-ling—" His *"darling"* is always a spaced-out sing-song. His lips curl back and he smiles widely. I see the gaps where he has recently had several rotten teeth removed.

"How are you, my dah-ling—, what have you done to your hair? Did you comb it today?" he says, pulling at my Afro. "It looks different." He means it looks messy and he's right.

"Who was that you were waving at?" I ask.

"Just a friend."

I always have mixed feelings of dread and relief when we meet up. Dread because, after our initial greeting, little is said between us. We stare past each other, into a middle distance where we will never meet halfway. Relief because seeing him dissipates any guilt, however briefly, about neglecting his welfare—while he is in front of me, at least, he is fine.

In the coffee shop we exchange the usual "How are yous?" and monosyllabic responses once we are seated. I watch him empty five sachets of sugar into his cup.

"Five sugars, Dad?"

"They're only small," he says, laughing into the thick stir.

"That will be why you've barely got any teeth left—"

His laugh slips into a wry smile, which I read as *"I used to change your nappies you know…"*

I wonder what the woman who used to change *his* nappies, Cecilia Quansah, my grandmother, would think if she could see him as he is today.

I feel the small rush of air cloak us as someone enters the café—they appear to have captured Dad's attention. He eyes them like a private detective in a 1950s crime novel. Furtive slurps of sugary coffee between long, loud glances. He never could be discreet.

"Dad!" Despite feeling like an exclamation it's more of a stage whisper.

No reply.

"Dad? What are you looking at?" I glance back over my shoulder to cast my own suspicious eye over the elderly intruder. "Stop staring."

"Huh?" He rocks back into his chair like a judge who has just delivered a stern but fair sentence. His forehead gradually unfurls and he smiles.

"Anyway, Dad, what have you been up to?"

"Oh, you know…"

I have an idea but I don't *know*. What I do know is there's no point pressing him too hard, so we sit in customary silence after a short report on my journey here.

Some inane small-talk is about to flurry from my lips but then something makes me pause. His eyes brighten and he is half-holding, half-stroking my hand with his giant dry palms. *I should get him some moisturising cream*, I think. It is thanks to watching him smear Nivea all over himself when I was a child that I now have the ritual of lathering myself with cocoa butter every day.

"Give me your email address—" he says abruptly.

"Umm, why do you want it, Dad? What are you going to send me?"

"It's very important and I want you to have it."

I give a fatigued sigh. There are good reasons why I want to withhold it.

"Yes, Dad, but what is it?"

"It's my life story. It's a very beautiful story."

I am momentarily suspended in disbelief. I have attempted on a few awkward occasions to glean information from him about his childhood, his ever distant and mysterious family back in Accra. His standard response has been to remain mute or reply with detached puzzlement—"Why do you want to know?" Very rarely, nuggets of information have emerged with unexpected candour. A month ago when I came to visit him I blurted out the question:

"When did you actually come here, Dad—to England? I'd just like to know."

After only a moment's hesitancy and some searching looks at my inquisitive face he delivered a string of sequential sentences:

"Sixteen. I was sixteen. After school… I stayed with Auntie Beatrice. In Brixton."

"Auntie Beatrice? Who's that? I didn't know you had an aunt in Brixton."

"You've met her—haven't you?"

"No, Dad. I've never heard of her before."

"Oh." He laughs.

I later learn that "Auntie" and indeed "Uncle" are respectful pronouns in Ghanaian culture for anyone older than you.

Now, I wonder whether, through some father-daughter telepathy, he has read my thoughts as I've sat here measuring the creases on his face, pondering if I'll ever know anything real about him. *Has he been keeping a journal?* Where was this holy grail of a document? I wanted it then and there.

"Life story—" I say, pointing my head at him. "YOUR—life—story?"

He is nodding like a savant now, evidently very pleased with himself.

"How long have you been writing that then?"

"The last year."

"Really?" *Writing! I've always wondered where that pulse inside me came from.* I lean forward, staring at him with amazement. A sizzle of flashbacks: every promise ever made, every amputated attempt to ask him questions… *Could this really be true?* The devil of doubt sneaks up on me before I even realise.

"And *why* did you decide to write it?"

"For myself—and to share with you."

Time slows over the lacquered table-top space between us while the buses and people outside whoosh anonymously by. I feel the wells of my eyes trying to push up water. To think that some invisible, below-the-radar bond has formed between us over the past year where he understands what I want from him…"Dad—that's amazing!"

He is openly laughing now at my incredulity. I imagine that's why he's laughing, though he could be re-visiting a joke he heard years ago for all I know. I put aside everything I do know about him for the sake of everything I don't. My desire to have this information and believe that what he is telling me is true is overpowering. "Don't show it to anybody."

"Of course not." *Wait till I tell Mum about this.*

"When does it start from?"

"1957—," his date of birth, "well, the mid-'60s really, I suppose, in my childhood. You'll be shocked."

"Shocked?" He's included all the salacious stuff! Amazing.

"It starts now and goes backwards and forwards in time—"

I wonder what his style is like, probably quite formal, like his letters were.

"—do you want me to send you a preview?"

"Yes, yes, please!" I'm excited. "Thank you, Dad."

"But don't show anybody."

"OK. I won't."

"It's a very beautiful story. What's happened to us, our dreams and hopes for the future. Don't discuss it, though."

"OK, Dad."

As we say our goodbyes I palm him a twenty-pound note so that he can get a haircut, knowing it will only cost a fiver and that he will waste the rest of the money and the day in an Internet café. I suppose the cash is some kind of reward for his Good News. When we part company I feel as excited as when he had promised to send me to New York following my GCSEs as a reward for better than average results. In that instance the plan was foiled by the over-protectiveness of all my friends' parents who would not let any of them accompany me. He can do that even now, instil a sense of impossible hope. The success of his last recovery, his last sojourn into reality, his last version of a more ordinary life, had lasted nearly three years.

On the train journey home, I open my notebook and pen an account of the revelation. As I write in heart-racing scribble, my pen abruptly hovers and holds mid-air. *Can I trust him?* He's only been back on medication these last six weeks. He would have had to be writing it while still in the efflorescence of his particular madness. The chances of my opening an email from him that would fill in the last fifty-odd years of his life suddenly feels as remote as Mamprobi, Accra, where he is from and where I have longed for him to take me.

At home I don't rush to turn on my laptop. I tidy. I fidget. I pace. I scroll through the contacts on my phone and see "Mum" but I don't call. After fifteen minutes, three cigarettes and one and a half cups of tea I hunch over the open laptop, then stand up, then sit down, then open my Hotmail. My eyes scan the inbox—it's full of junk. There it is, from Charles Kabu Adjonyoh. I look at the subject line. *Wait, can that be it… U.N., START?* I click to open it. The text reads:

SEE PAGE 937 REFERENCE TO MUM (C.E.C.I.) AND APPLICATION FOR FINANCE TO 30 COUNTRIES (APPROVED) UN WEBSITE (START FILES)

What the—? Right. I see. C.E.C.I, as in Cecelia, Grandma. He thinks some United Nations directive has mentioned his mother and she's embroiled in some world finance conspiracy, no doubt. Bloody hell, Dad.

This is why I have purposely kept my latest personal email address from him: a fifteen-year-long deluge of emails with subject headers such as "READ THIS THEN DESTROY", the introductory body text of which summarily read: "Finished, exploratory examination of UN and world history and development. Love Dad. XXXX."

The contents of the attachments were always a balance of well-researched criticisms spliced with nonsensical verbiage detailing an investigation he had undertaken exploring some UN or EU Commission department, explaining where they had gone wrong and how it might be corrected, amended, fixed. At his behest I once read a fifty-page document of such nonsense, with a ten-page appendix implicating such A-listers as Kylie Minogue and Tony Blair in one of his conspiracy theories. This is how he now spends his days: looking up policy documents on the Internet seeking evidence to implicate major institutions in his own misfortunes. His current delusional state has convinced him that he is head of the World Bank.

There are two attachments. I can't bear to open them.

Within half an hour I get a call from Dad, asking urgently: "Did you get it?"

"Yes, Dad. Was it the email titled 'U.N., START?'"

"Yes. You didn't show it to anyone, did you?"

"No. I haven't shown it to anyone, Dad. And that's your life story, is it? The one you were telling me about in the café?"

"Yes."

"Starting with your childhood and all that?"

"Yes! Did you read it?" He's exasperated by my lack of urgency. "It's all in there… I told you. You need to read it." His tone has shifted from urgent to angry.

"Cool. Well, I haven't had a chance to read it properly, but I will."

"Make sure you do, yeah, but don't show anyone, not even your Mum."

Lisa Allen-Agostini

A writer and editor from Trinidad and Tobago, she is the author of the young adult novel Home Home, *which as a manuscript won third prize in the 2017 CODE Burt Award for Young Adult Literature. She is also the author of the book of poems* Swallowing the Sky *(2015) and the YA novel* The Chalice Project *(2008) and co-editor of* Trinidad Noir *(2008). Her poetry and fiction have appeared in* Wasafiri, sx salon, Susumba, Lightspeed Magazine, *and* past simple. *As a freelance journalist, she writes for* Trinidad & Tobago Newsday, Caribbean Beat *and other publications.*

The Cook

Prologue

I was always a loner. Between the gangs outside, the crack selling on my corner and the whores drinking in the rum shop, my father always wanting to be up under me, and my mother always busting my ass with licks, it was best to find a little corner and hide away, keep safe. In school it was the same thing. I mean, no Pappy to interfere with me and sit me on his lap but there was Sir, who was so very friendly all the time, with his breath in my face.

I can't wait to get away from them, from there, from that.

Modelling is my ticket out. I'm taking it. In Seaview I'm just the bony, ugly black girl with big eyes and thick lips, but through the lens of a professional's camera I am exotic, beautiful, sexy. I am the right size, the right shape, the right colour for once in my life and of course I'll take it. I can't wait until I get off this island for good.

Those fat pigs, slobbering on the chicken bones in their disgusting brown mess, they couldn't understand. KFC is meat. Meat is protein. Protein is good; carbs are bad. Models don't eat sugar and yam and flour dumpling.

I model off this island. It's too small here, and everybody is in everybody's business. For instance, I know about the lesbians, trying to hide what everybody can see plain as day, their relationship written like a billboard on the backside of the men's skinny jeans they wear. And I know all about these bitches and how many of them have been fucked in the back seat of the very car they are sitting in; they play innocent but we all know they aren't.

If that bottle had only touched my face, I would have killed the bitch who threw it. I took off for a while, cooling my head on the beach by myself before I did something I would regret.

I only came to the cook to get away from home for a day. Anything would be better than Seaview Road.

I.

I could feel the undercurrent of jealousy whenever she passed the other girls. It zinged, electric. She looked different from them, walked different, too, with a studied strut, tossing the silky, expensive hair extensions they could only envy but not afford. The other girls called her *"America's Next Top Model"*. Her lip-gloss was perfect, nude, and I think she was wearing BB cream. She'd had her eyebrows waxed and arched and well brushed and coloured in, not effaced and replaced in stark black pencil like theirs. You could see those perfect brows over her wide sunglasses, designer sunglasses like the girls wear in pictorials shot on beaches like this one, only they are flown in from Milan or New York, not driven here from Seaview Road, the worst neighbourhood on the island. And her shorts, a perfect size two, showed just a hint of her bikini bottom where the waistband hit the sloping curve as her abs met her hips. None of the other girls had that glamour. None of the other girls even knew what it was they didn't like about her, so deep in their self-hate that they thought she thought she was better than them.

I couldn't even tell why she'd come on this day trip—they call it a cook—in the first place. We'd gathered in town: the community college lecturer who had organised the outing for the hiking club; another guy on staff, his daughter and her girlfriend; and the students, eight teenaged girls. She was one of them. My friend, invited mainly to add another car to the pool, drove two other girls, her and me. She complained for the whole trip, two hours of winding road into the wilderness. She didn't like the long drive from the city, didn't like the company, didn't like the beach. After we arrived she spent the whole time by herself, sitting on the edge of a beached fishing pirogue; *Sea Lady* was its name. It hadn't touched the sea for years, its barnacles dried and crumbling, its paint flaking into dust. It sat behind a sand dune far in front of the thin woods where the group had gone to make the cook.

The men rolled together three heavy river stones, cut dry wood, gathered leaves and kindling, stacked the meagre twigs and bits of old paper and lit them with a match, blew on the small flickering and fed it until its flames blazed taller than the tops of the rocks, banked it until the fire licked lazily and low, just high enough for the pot to stand above. The girls poured brown sugar into the bottom of the pot, stirring it constantly with a long steel spoon so the sugar wouldn't burn as it warmed, melted into caramel, began to foam like a good stout, turned black and thin. They added a basinful of marinated chicken just before the browning burned, and others dropped in dumplings the size of a man's thumb, and chunks of peeled yam, sweet potato and green banana. Then they covered the pot with a sheet of steel and left it to simmer over that wood fire between the slender trees beyond the sandy beach.

She didn't help.

The other girls, while the brown down cooked, sat in the lecturer's car, playing music and dancing with him. She sat in the pirogue by herself and looked out at the sea. I never saw her talk to anybody except me before the fight started, so it couldn't have been her fault. But what do I know? I'm just a tourist.

II.

What them did fighting over? Who the ass know. Woman go fight for anything, for nothing. All I know is that when time come for food to share she take out she box of

KFC and start to eat. Them offer she a plate of brown down and she say she don't eat provision, but them girls and them say how she feel she too good for them, how she feel she is something, *America's Next Top Model* or something, when she is really just a nigger girl from Seaview Road and no better than none of them. How she dry and hard and how only dog does want bone, but man does want meat, and they roll their bottom to the dancehall blasting from how-he-name car, just to show that they have the fatness plus the wickedest wining skills, and how she don't have none. Me, I drink my rum and eat the brown down and hush.

III.

Me didn't see no fight. Me and my girl did over on the next side, on the beach, far past the boat, hugging up in the sand and trying to get a little privacy away from everybody who did watching we out the corner of their eye and quoting Leviticus 20 in their mind.

IV.

I did right in the middle of it. I leave the girls sitting inside my car and walk around to every man jack on that beach and tell them how she turn up she nose at we kind of food. I find the brown down was damn good. Damn good. And she didn't lift a finger. Like she too good to bubble a pot on the beach with the rest of we. She in she skimpy-skimpy bikini—all she breast showing, as if is a blues she in—and wouldn't shit on the rest of we. It don't surprise me that after food share, licks share. It was bubbling whole day, like the pot on that three-stone fire. Every time she sashay from the fishing boat she was sitting down in, the same boat what she dead in, and come over in we direction—without even turning she head to smile, to say, "Aye, Dog!", nothing—the fire get higher and them girls start to grumble louder and harder. By the time food share you coulda hear them, ain't even bothering to keep their voice down, "Who she feel she is?" and "Look Miss *Top Model* coming." It don't surprise me at all when one of the girls finally stand up and push a finger in she face to confront she about the food, about how she does play like she shit don't stink. Everything just come tumbling out because that one girl was talking for all them girls who was holding their hate inside for so long. It didn't take nothing for the bottle to fly.

V.

Everyone was drinking. I wasn't the only one with a bottle in my hand. You can look through my photos and see: Here. Here. Here. We had, nearly all of us, brought rum: Rivers, Clarke's Court, Fernandes Black Label. Who hadn't brought rum had brought Hennessy Cognac, Dewar's Scotch. And my daughter and her friend, well, they only came back after everything was over. So if you're asking me who threw the bottle at her, I really wouldn't know.

Afterwards everybody was tangled up, holding back the girls. Because those girls were out for blood, you could see it.

When we were all distracted, she just disappeared. It was only when we were packing up to leave that we found her there, strangled to death and laid out in the little beached boat.

Epilogue

she did tall and thin and black and she head did plait up in false hair hanging down all by she bottom and she did look like a magazine model or a girl in a nastiness picture on the TV not the white people nastiness with them blonde white girl with fake breast but black people nastiness with big bottom woman and man with wood like chair foot except she wasn't no fat woman she did thin and hard but she bottom did fat the only fat thing on she except for she mouth she mouth she mouth she had them thick rude lips and I hold she neck and squeeze and squeeze and stuff wood in she mouth force open them rude lips till she choke

Monica Arac de Nyeko

A Ugandan writer, she won the 2007 Caine Prize for African Writing with her story "Jamboula Tree". She had previously been shortlisted for the prize in 2004 for "Strange Fruit". She has an MA in Humanitarian Assistance from the University of Groningen. She is currently working on a novel.

Running for Cassava

The market is different now. Nothing is for free. Not bananas falling off bunches. Not oranges burnt by the sun. Not cobs of maize, with no sweetness. Not green sugarcane stalks. Not overripe mangoes. Not cassava. But, there was a time, when it was possible to get these things for free.

In those days, in the mornings or evenings, trucks came from up-country loaded with sacks of cassava. Those trucks were rusted. Their fuel gauges did not work. They looked like they would fail at the very next hill. And yet, they did not. For hours, they drove past districts and towns. They went up hills. They went down valleys. They went past children bathing in rivers and mud puddles. For hours, the trucks puffed. They heaved until they reached the city and the market. Then, the cassava brokers in the front and their truck boys seated on top of the sacks, got off. They stretched. They yawned. They welcomed the market with its promise of a big cassava profit.

In those days, my mother worked in the centre of the city. She was a copy typist at the national social security fund. All day long, she punched letters into the typewriter. She corrected errors with liquid white-out. Then she typed some more, until the copy was ready for the Director to draw his signature on the paper with a blue fountain pen. Soon after, the letters left the office to meet their owners—widows and heirs, sons and mothers. In black and blue ink, they declared the value of their beloved's life, what they had at the time of their death. The letters told heirs what they might expect by way of a better future, a better life.

As for my mother, by way of a better future, a better life for me, she sat in an office with sofa sets and typed letters. My mother drank tea in the morning. Office messengers brought her lunch to her desk in plastic containers. At the end of the month, she got her payslip. She thanked God for our blessings. In the middle of the school term when I got malaria, my mummy prayed, then she asked the nurse if I really, really needed the injections she was recommending, if perhaps the aspirin and chloroquine might be enough. In the evenings, my mother sat by the lamp to write down the things still left to buy after the day's demands. Cassava. Sugar. Tea. Exercise books. Pens. Pencils. School uniforms. Go-Back-to-School Bata shoes.

One day, on her way home through the market, when my mother was not even thinking about better futures, better lives, she saw the trucks of cassava in the market. They were many. The cassava peeped through the sacks. They were red, like the earth. After eight months in the soil, after that much sunshine, they were ready. My mother looked at the cassava. She watched the brokers haggling over prices with the market women. She saw off-loaders carrying cassava from the trucks. She saw also that when there were no sacks left to carry, there were small, broken pieces of cassava all over the truck floor and all around the truck. They were tiny. They were not saleable, but they were still as fresh, still as red. They would taste just as fine with hot oil and salt. With tea and plenty of sugar. With that much cassava, she would not need to add flour on her end of day list, ever. But, for now, they remained in the market, unclaimed. Later, much later on, the market cleaners would arrive to take them away. They would take them to the rubbish pit. There, they would be eaten by rot and time.

My mother left the market, thoughts of a better future, a better life in her mind, shining like light bulbs. At home, she changed into her slippers. She tied a scarf around her head. She took the sisal sack from the storeroom. She stuck it under her arm. She returned to the market. The sun was going down. It was red, the red of cassava.

My mother returned from the market when there was no sun. She poured pieces of cassava on the sitting-room floor. She told each of us to take a knife. She told us to start peeling.

In the night, with the light of the lamp, we peeled cassava. We cut it into pieces. We threw the now white pieces into water. We chewed raw cassava until our stomachs sang cassava tunes. It was sweet, as sweet as a better future, a better life. When we finished, my mummy washed all that redness, all that dirt off the cassava. In the morning, she put the cassava on the veranda. In a few days, my mother would take the dried cassava to the grinding mill across the main road. She would return with flour. For this entire season, we would eat cassava flour with eggplants or beans. At the end of the month maybe we would even eat it with meat or chicken.

My mother never asked me to go to the market with her. Not even once. But one day, when the sun was almost gone and she was not back home yet, a thought as bright as the gates of heaven shone in my mind. I took my mother's sack from the storeroom. I stuck it in my armpit. I crossed the road that separated the market from our house. I made my way through the shops, through the women seated under sun umbrellas with their cassava waiting for customers. I went to the open market where the off-loaders were already taking the sacks off the trucks.

Now that I was in the market, I did not know what to do. I stood, a distance from the trucks, thinking, waiting for a thought, bright, heavenly. It did not come, at least not as quickly as I needed it to. All that was left before me were the cassava brokers. They were everywhere. There were off-loaders heaving with the weight of the sacks. They were everywhere. There were women with wrappers, their money purses wrapped around their waists. They were everywhere.

I started to feel okay. I knew these off-loaders. I knew their faces. The women too. I knew them. My mother bought cassava from them. They were here now, everywhere, laughing, happy. Everyone was happy. Standing there, looking at all of them the thought, the one I had been longing for, arrived.

I stepped forward, towards a truck, a green one. It was newer. There was no rust on it. With each step, I took forward to my truck and to my cassava, the thumping in my chest went down until there was nothing left. Until there was only me, the truck and the brokers. They were happy. The women were happy. Everyone was happy.

With all this happiness, my feet were rapid, excited, they carried me forward swiftly until I was almost leaning on the truck. There was cassava all around me. This was cassava heaven.

I took the sack from my armpit. I squatted. I started to put cassava into my sack. My mother would be so proud of me. She would not need to come by herself to the trucks anymore. Maybe she would buy me some beads for my hair. Maybe she would tell everyone at church I was the bestest best daughter. Maybe I would get a dress for Christmas.

With my head down and cassava flying into my sack, I did not see the broker until he was next to me, his trousers almost touching my sack. I stood up. I stepped back enough to see him, the darkness of his skin. There were lines around his eyes from years of cassava broking. He was the height of the tallest building in Kampala. He had a bundle of money in his pocket for his better future, his better life. His trousers were the colour of cassava. He did not smile. His eyes were the colour of cassava. He looked at me. He looked at my sack. My heart started ululating.

"You!" the man said. "Stealing my cassava?"

What did he mean?

"You!" the man said. "Stealing my cassava?"

"Me?" I said.

"Yes, you!" The man said. "Who else?"

I stepped back. I did not let go of my mother's sack, at least, not right then. Not until the man stepped forward and stood in front of me.

"You!" the man said. "Thief!"

I did not wait for more. I just got on my marks. I got set. I ran.

Everyone knew exactly what happened to thieves. People threw stones at them. Traders took their clothes off. They kicked them in the eyes. Thieves did not return home to their families.

I hopped over gullies. I jumped over wheel barrows like it was the Olympics. I flew past potato sellers and their sun umbrellas. Past wives and their princess-dressed daughters. By the time they turned to catch the luminous green of my dress, I was not there. I was gone, poof, a ghost.

"Thief! Thief!" the market said.

"Thief! Thief!" the wind said.

"Thief! Thief!" the city said.

I ran until there was no market to run away from. No voices to escape. Until it was just the main road. It was just people coming from work. Wives buying supper for their husbands. I looked around then I bent down. I tried to breathe, just breathe.

At home, my mother was not there, hallelujah! There was only my uncle, the one reading for his A-level examinations. He was in the sitting-room on the sofa, his textbook on his lap. He still had on his school uniform, the white trousers and shirt. He looked up at me. He smiled.

"It was you, wasn't it?" he said.

My heart started to breakdance, like Michael Jackson himself.

"Eh?" I said.

"You heard me."

"Me? No!"

He smiled.

"Okay," he said.

But it was not okay. As soon as my mother arrived, my uncle told her about his passing through the market that evening. He saw a girl flying like there were demons racing after her. That girl looked like me. But he was not sure, not until he saw me standing in the sitting-room in my luminous green dress looking as if I just walked out of a twister. My feet were the colour of charcoal. There was sweat all over my face, perhaps even in my teeth. I had no slippers on.

"Oh," my mother said. "Is that so?" then they both started laughing, the kind of stupid laughter that only comes from stupid adults.

My mother and uncle did not stop laughing. Not then. Not even soon after. They asked me more questions and then they laughed some more. They laughed until tears flowed from their eyes. Until their stomachs were stiff. I just stood there, my face like a porcupine. They did not notice it. They just laughed even if my feet were bleeding, even if my dress was not luminous green anymore and my eyes were filling with water.

"All that running for cassava?" my mother said. "So funny!"

But it was not funny, of course. It was not funny at all.

Yemisi Aribisala

A Nigerian-born author, she is best known for her thematic use of food to explore Nigerian stories. Her award-winning first book, Longthroat Memoirs: Soups Sex & Nigerian Tastebuds *(Cassava Republic Press, 2016), uses Nigerian food as a literary substrate to think about Nigeria's culture and society. Her upcoming book on Nigerian feminism, identity, migration and Christianity, among other critical parameters for engaging Nigeria and the Nigerian, is to be published in 2019. She lives in London with her children.*

A book between you and me

He threw a toaster at her head. That's what she said.
She said,
"He threw a toaster at my head."
My response was
"A whole toaster?"

Let me talk about that response for a bit because I've spent many years shaking my head at it. Whenever I have a flashback to that day, I kiss my teeth under my breath in reprimand. In shame. I was one of the two women to whom she was telling the toaster-throwing story. She laughed as she related the build up to the episode. Laughed at the conclusion as if the story could be humorous. I couldn't laugh, but neither could I give an intelligent answer.

"A whole toaster?" What did I mean by "whole" as if it could be half a toaster. A quarter. Toaster minus cable and plug maybe was equal to something substantially diminutive therefore legitimate to throw at someone's head. Toaster model from the shop window made of cardboard and not a real toaster. Toaster minus the weight of chunks of day old sourdough bread...

Perhaps I was distracted by examining her head to see if it was true that she had been assaulted with the weight of a whole toaster. The word "whole" just kept interrupting like a pestilential tic. It was maybe a kind of exclamation that translated to "Is that so!"

I tried in vain to picture a grown man flinging a toaster across the room with the aim of hitting his wife's head. Perhaps, I thought, I would see a dent of some sort, like when a car brushes against the side of a stationary object. Brush, not collide—again the veneering of the stroke in question. Slight scraping and not the full collision was what my mind allowed so that it wouldn't catch in my throat on the way down, so it wouldn't snag at the barbed corners of my mind. The story was hard to swallow was the point. I'm not sure what exactly gave me the liver to utter such nonsense. Let's be frank: it was nonsense. I think it was shock maybe. That possibility of being taken unawares and therefore fashioning a bad response doesn't make me less ashamed.

I think it is like when you are in an airplane and there is terrifying turbulence. The plane drops and you press your personal gears under the chair in front of you. Or like when someone throws a paper plane at your head and you duck with the dramatics of someone avoiding a falling sky. An instinctive reaction to unexpected uncomfortable stimuli. Auto-pilot flaying. There is always shame after the response because it reveals something asymmetrical: a carelessly finished examination paper: immaturity: fear for yourself and your comfort more than the other person: a kind of ridiculous self-preservation: common sense that slipped in full view of others.

The "whole toaster" response had undigested grains of disbelief in it. I am even more ashamed of this fact. One justifiably wants to always hide the back end of the digestive process. This was a woman whose husband had beaten her so severely, on so many occasions, for so many different reasons, trifling or "defended"; a toaster thrown at her head was restrained going by his CV. I had no right, no precedent, no margin of foolishness or naivety to offer disbelief. Like many victims of abuse her bruises were there, on her face and in your face, broken, traumatised skin at the easy reach of your fingers if you couldn't believe your eyes.

My response was a request for evidence of abuse, and I didn't even know it or see myself well enough to make that crucial assessment. It was years later after layered moments of self-reprimands, after understanding the nature and logistics of a prologue to a head smashing...that was when I realised I had been asking for proof. If he had thrown the toaster and there was no dent in her head, no bruise waving for notice, no bald patch where hair had been extracted by the impact, then perhaps we could excuse and forgive him and wait... Wait till it was a "whole" table or a "whole" penetrating stiletto heel. I was asking for proof of insanity and wickedness. It had nothing to do with her laughter. I knew even back then that laughter was dialect for processing pain that made no sense.

I know it from hanging around men whom I seem to befriend more easily than women. Perhaps this is the problem, my soft-spot for my friends who are men. For their ability to cook violence with machismo and vulnerability until it was palatable. Their ability to mask heartbreak with blows. Boys decapitating lizards, knocking their heads against walls just to see their eyeballs fly out; strangling birds with simplicity, with primal innocence, you were both overwhelmed and dazzled. You were impressed by that ability that you so instinctively lacked. I didn't like animals but I felt sick when I saw a dying bird or a crumpled spider, or a bloody animal run over by a car.

My best friend in primary school was a boy called Hakeem. One day he asked to go to the toilet and the teacher said "No". He sat back down and put his head on the wooden desk and burst into tears. My heart melted into the hot stream trickling through his khaki shorts to the cement floor. I never told anyone he was my best friend. I honoured the cul-de-sac by forever and ever befriending heartbroken boys who mutilated animals in protest of pain and humiliation. I learnt from Hakeem and from my brother who allowed me to ride his much-better bicycle only if he was allowed to aim hard guavas at my head…how easy (easier) savagery was to boys and to men. I concluded with relief that I wasn't a wimp for sure when my teenage son's craniologist pinpointed with perfect accuracy the days when he had a surge of testosterone. On those days there was some form of violence acted out against someone. Or there was some attempt to fly from some elevated place and land four floors down. Some head-butting with walls.

Once I sat with some friends who were relating the story of a Lagos bus conductor who was decapitated by a passing truck. He had been leaning out of the bus door as bus conductors do, shouting hoarse abuse, apparently high on his morning shot of roots-in-ogogoro. The truck came past close and quick and…

And the men telling and listening to the story laughed riotously as if on cue. Laughed with tears and pounding of thighs. With knocking over of their chairs, scraping the terrazzo with metal chair legs, reeling backwards and holding their bellies. There was cold beer in the equation, in their bellies. A lot of it. I who hadn't had one drop laughed at the roguery of all of it. We weren't going to have the chance to laugh at our own deaths after all. So I laughed at all the things we didn't and couldn't say out of our mouths. For example, a bus conductor on a new sun-polished morning in Lagos had it coming didn't he? He'd had it coming for months or years. He had been daring death and he knew. He sauntered into it. Should we mourn? Should we laugh at that which is inevitable? Is there comedy in a tipsy stroll into extinction? A quick topple into that undocumented other side? I knew they laughed because the matter had passed the boundaries of weeping. I knew that kind of pain that blessed you with mechanically flung open gates of sounds from your insides because you had to process the pain and soon other doses of pain with some kind of anaesthetic…the raucous acknowledgement of death greased with inebriation, the relief that you could laugh because you had the animation of life to laugh. The sugar for the bitter medicine. We were laughing at all our executions scheduled for their own impromptu beautiful day. Life and death had a sense of humour that made no sense. What was the use of denying that sometimes the more moronic the joke was, the harder you laughed.

I had a problem with veneers of violence though. I did. Even though I had built agreeable cul-de-sacs of nice soft excuses for my friends who were men. I was not the only one guilty of that. The women in these men's lives were always making excuses for them, so they rarely had to pay for anything broken. Yes, I maintain that. Not only the women who were traditional and believed that men had to be men…whatever that meant. But also the feminists who denied the biology of men and demanded they do things like women did and that was just a terrible fairytale that was going to break the hearts of a few more generations of women to come. I wasn't the only one letting men off. I came from a family of women who for generations did so without any iota of demand for accountability from men for anything. Sometimes when a man said he beat his wife because she was rude to his mother, the women in his family ticked that off as justified. I had to learn to put my foot down and demand that my son control whatever biological motivations he had for violence. I owed him that. I owed the world I had pushed him out into that much. That was one of my first points of repentance from my "whole toaster" gaffe.

One of those stories that we loved to tell and retell for its comedic value was of the woman who told her mother-in-law that her husband never came home. That he slept out most nights. Mother-in-law answered her: "Is it your eyes he is using to sleep outside?" That was the punchline. We laughed hard and let mother-in-law and mollycoddled son escape the parable. Laughter with all its nuances, with its demonstrative convulsions, bops, stomps made full sense. The problem was we were all complicit to the notches of abuse and violence before that one that makes a toaster rebounding off your head "OK".

"After all he hasn't beaten you yet. When he does, we'll all deal with him." The first slap after that confident assurance of support…well…that one is just so-so, a tap, one-off, discussable in emotionless banter over a cup of tea like one is talking about the fluctuation of meat prices in the market; an aside of conversation, a hushed by-the-way, a "I deserved it this time".

…I quit the cul-de-sac eight years after my honeymoon in the Western Cape. A beautiful trip to a stunning country. We had stopped in Johannesburg for one or two nights before flying out to Cape Town, and I decided to buy Anthony Sampson's *Mandela* from a bookshop in Sandton. That year, the book was a big fat tall tome, unlike the shrunken fourteenth edition I bought this year (2017) in the Western Cape.

"You're not going to read that book, are you?" was the response from my husband to my purchase of the book.

"I am," I said.

"Why would you read a book on our honeymoon?"

"Because I'm always reading books"

"You bought the biggest book in the shop."

"Yes. So it lasts as long as possible."

"Well, life isn't all about things in books, is it?"

"No, it isn't, but there are millions and millions of books on things about life, so perhaps their presence and our attention to them signify something truly profound where not a lot else makes sense... In any case what's a book between you and me...one book?"

I was leaning so far backwards, I could feel the wall of the cul[ture]-de-sac. For years after I heard and experienced variations of the soft collision, the scrape that removes a little bit of paint every time; the knocks that grew in intensity until, as Fela sang, "suffering 'debaru[ed]' the head" and you were too confused to be coherent about anything.

"You aren't going to read in the car, are you?"

"Women who read too much inevitably feel they know too much."

"That's your problem...you think you know everything."

I always tried to say something clever in response, like: "Everything I learned is from the mad bad Jewish women in Jesus's bloodline that Nigerian women love to read about in the New King James Version."

I only ever got out limp comebacks like "A whole toaster. You mean a whole one?"

Somewhere among all the self-administered reprimands... I knew that veneered savagery over time meant one became inured to the meaning and true nature of violence. To its burrowing progress and its results. To death walking in something that seemed to still be alive. How can I explain it but to talk about seeing a man on fire, engulfed, but running with his hands held up over his head. You knew he was dead and that the motion was some kind of program running for a few more minutes before the crumpling of the hardware. It is easy to sit in a beer parlour and laugh at death, but when you see it progressing, there is nothing to laugh about. The anaesthetic of laughter doesn't work.

I had to teach myself the market-place response—that one you give the vendor who sizes you up for a fool. That is, the solidifying of every human pore into a towering wall of NO that cannot be beaten with bare hands. Loud bleating electronic alarm for the intruder sneaking into one's home at night. The wailing that accompanies the horrors of viewing, touching, cleaning up after death. The refusal of anaesthetic. The sprouting of powerful wings in elevation and flight. Not quiet levitation. The sensational soaring of the mechanics of wings—with sound and wind. This was my last conclusion. This is what I meant to say and feel. This is my response.

Yolanda Arroyo Pizarro

Translated by Alejandro Alvarez

An award-winning Afro lesbian novelist, short story writer, essayist, and feminist activist from Puerto Rico, she addresses both racial and gender issues, and sexual identity in her combative, non-conformist and creative works. She offers lectures about Afro-atheism, decolonial feminism, LGBTTQ issues and how to be an atheist and a black woman in today's society. She is also the Director of the Department of Afro-Puerto Rican Studies, a performative project of Creative Writing based in San Juan and has founded the Chair of Ancestral Black Women to respond to the invitation promulgated by UNESCO to celebrate the International Decade of Afro-Descendants 2015–2024. Her book Las Negras, winner of the PEN Club Puerto Rico National Short Story Award in 2013, explores the limits of female characters during the slavery period that challenged hierarchies of power. She also won the Prize of the Institute of Puerto Rican Culture in 2015 and 2012, and the National Prize of the Institute of Puerto Rican Literature in 2008. She has been translated into German, French, Italian, English, Portuguese and Hungarian.

Midwives (fragment)

To the historians, for leaving us out.

Here we are again…
bodies present, color in full force,
defying invisibility,
refusing to be erased.

I remember, half-awake, half-asleep, the bonfires during my escape with the Yoruba. We light pyres with pieces of wood and palm trees because it's cold and too dark at night. We manage to find some caves and hide there until we are sure we have lost our pursuers. Then we light torches, rest, and outline a plan for our return to the continent.

After hours of discussion, we give up. It will never happen. We would need resources—barges, weapons, supplies for the trip, and other necessities we do not have. We decide that dying would be better than bowing to the oppressor. We talk of some of our brothers who were experts in suicide; they had done it, and left instructions as their legacy. I mentioned Undraá, who was forced to cohabit with the white men on the ship that took us from the continent to the island, a woman who knew the sea and its species for she lived among the yellow fisherwomen for many years. She waited until the ship reached open sea, near the sharks' nests. Then she jumped into the water. The Yoruba mention other brothers. Bguiano, an expert tusk hunter, member of an army of men who continually sharpened their teeth and killed jungle beasts with their bare hands. He taught his skill to a group of newcomers at the plantation where he served. They all made an oath before Şàngó, and could rip out the most visible throbbing vein in someone's neck with a single bite. We remembered Zeza, spell-caster and brewer of potions, who knew the right combination of every poisonous herb in the region to close one's eyes and never open them again. And so we went on coming up with ideas, while some dozed off.

I yawn and make an oath to the gods of the wind: if I am ever caught again, the children shall pay.

Petro, the monk, gently taps my face to wake me. His pink, familiar look quenches my thirst. He puts water and medicine, made from painkilling herbs, down my throat to ease the pain in my body. "You were talking in your sleep," he says, and when the jailer passes nearby, Petro makes as if he is praying in Latin with his rosary beads. He then combines compound syllables to explain to me that I am not an animal. *Mbwa* / '*m.bwa* / *dog*; *tembo* / *elefant* / *thembo* / *elefante*; *ne.nda* / *not* / *no*; *you* / *toi*. The rebellious empathy in his voice that makes me believe him, even feel sorry for him. I mumble in French, and he freezes, surprised at my language proficiency. I repeat the phrase in Castilian Spanish and Igbo. Petro silences my mouth with this hand, so I'll not be found out. The guards are coming. They feed the other two women in my cell leftovers from the neighboring plantations; nothing for me. According to the public bulletin boards, I've been declared a Seditious and Subversive Black Woman, identified by a P-shaped mark made near my eye with a branding iron, a reward offered for my capture. When they leave, Petro takes out some casaba he had concealed, and puts it in my mouth, inviting me to chew it slowly, lest I choke. The other women share their water with me. Everything tastes like the candy made in the valley near our native river during the ceremony of masks.

With a clicking similar to tribal musical laments, fricative and guttural sounds, aspirated possessives, stuttering, short consonants, long vowels, Petro ensures me that he will keep my secret. All he wants is "to document the violence spreading all over humankind," he explains, "all this bestiality. There are friars in other islands chronicling these events; I want to tell your story. We act like friends to the crown, but it is not so. I swear I won't bring you any trouble."

"Do you swear it to your god?" I demand, and when he says that he does, I rebuke him: "Your god has no power; he is lazy, weak, useless. How can he let this happen?"

Petro nods and lowers his head in shame. He asks me who my gods are, if I believe in Babalú-ayé, Oiá, Obàtálá…

"I believe in none of them," and tears spring from my eyes. "They all abandoned us."

I swear I would rather die, Fray Petro, than be used as an animal. I swear that I wanted to kill them all, Father. *Nous allons reproduire une armeé, kite a kwanza yon lame.*

That is what I set out to do, what we women set out to do, and we spread the word through the beating of our drums. *Hebu kuzaliana jeshi.* We repeated it at music gatherings to the Wolof, Tuareg, Bakongo, Malimbo, and Egba. The news continued to spread in chant to the Balimbe, Ovimbundu, and the rest. Those of us from Congo, from Ibibio, from Seke or Cabinda, all of us women responded. *Hagámonos un ejército.* Let us breed an army.

The problem for those who oppress, Fray Petro, is that they underestimate the oppressed. I always take note of vitality or exhaustion on the faces of those who enter a woman without her consent. In my village, if something like that were to happen, the transgressors would be punished and fined. If a man raped a woman, he must pay with his possessions. And if he had none, he must pay by the chopping off, in cold blood, of an appendage—an arm, a hand, a foot, an ear, even the nose. We women were encouraged to defend ourselves, to hit back, bite, and tear out. Things have changed since Blacks started kidnapping other Blacks and selling us to the Portuguese or other whites, to ship us away. Now we are discouraged from defending ourselves because we belong to a master. Oppressors have such liberties, yet they underestimate us.

I always take note of vitality or exhaustion on the faces of those who enter a woman without her consent, Fray Petro. One afternoon, I am confronted with the face of an unknown night watchman, overcome with ecstasy just after forcing himself onto me. He didn't even care that Oshun's blood was running down my thighs on one of my lunar days. He closed his eyes for a second, exhausted. He tilted his head back, engulfed by the pleasure of his ejaculation, distracted. It only took a second to realize that he was alone… I bit him. I closed my teeth on his glans like a rabid dog. At first he tried to hit me. He fell, disoriented and in great pain. While he grabbed himself, moaning on the floor, I seized the keys from his pants, unbolted the cage, locked it behind me. I stopped at each cell, one by one, freeing ladinos, runaways, and native slaves. And the midwives, my sisters in battle.

Witch doctor, herbalist, bone healer, midwife. I have done every task of a domestic slave to gain access to white newborns. Following the instructions of a great Black witch stationed at a hacienda belonging to the Dominican cathedral Porta Coeli, I have blessed them with the sign of the cross and treated them for bellyaches. I smear my hands with concoctions and place anesthetic herbs on their gums when they are teething. I've had them suck on my breast until milk comes out, thus becoming their nursemaid. I read them stories; I untangle their hair with silver combs; I fluff skirts for rich girls and pants for the little masters. I cook for them and prepare their teas.

Gradually I gain their trust. We all do the same; we gain their trust gradually. Then I start helping newcomer Black slaves to bring their children into the world. Black women are the hardest to tame, say the whites. In essence, I am one of them, but I behave like a ladina, a native speaker. I speak Spanish and wear petticoats even when I work in the fields; I kneel at the right moment during mass, and at processions for imaginary Catholic virgins. No one knows I speak Hausa and Fulani, or that I stand behind walls and listen to the pronunciation of my master and his visitors from the militia, and later practise it when I'm alone.

On the twentieth day of my fifth imprisonment, I am taken from my cell for the physical punishment to be carried out in accordance with my sentence. The plantation's book lists my crimes: disobedience, defiance, insolence, vagrancy, inciting rebellion, and, finally, escaping—the worst crime of all. A mestizo woman ties my hands behind my back. She pushes me. She spits on me. The executioner says I belong to an animal race, soulless and heartless. A priest recites the prayers they have taught us so selflessly at our masters' homes. He orders me in Spanish to repeat after him. At first, I don't comply, until the lashing begins.

I remember the village shaman chanting to summon protection from pain, and I imagine that reciting "The Lord's Prayer" may do the same. In a final attempt at resistance, I manage to untie my legs and crawl, hands bound. The guards stop me and hit me harder, then ask permission to repeat the flagellation. But a high official will not let them, and they stop.

On the way back to the dungeon, I recognize Petro walking beside me. He extends his hand towards me, and I give him mine. I hear I've been sentenced to death by hanging. Then I faint.

On the day my sentence is to be carried out, someone comes to shave my head. Petro asks permission from his monastery to perform the last rites. They at least let him join the procession escorting me to the gallows where the noose awaits.

Petro touches my face and repeats the confession ritual: "Hail Mary, full of grace…"

"Bless me, Father, for I have sinned," I say.

"Tell me your sins, child."

I close my eyes, but there are no tears. "I have none!" I reply.

Petro hugs me, improvises some sort of sign of the cross, and tries to keep me on my feet. Everyone is watching—lieutenants, sea captains, plantation owners and their wives, pubescent children. A dozen Black midwives accused for the first or second time have been escorted by their jailers who are hoping to teach them a lesson through my plight. Owners who lost merchandise because of me applaud.

"Ndizi, what did you do to them?" Petro asks.

"It's my secret under seal of confession, Father," I tell him. "Forgive me."

And he insists, "What must I forgive?"

Silence.

Then a revelation. In a low voice, in our dialect—Fray Petro's and mine—I tell him:

"I drown their babies in the placenta bucket, Father. I press my hands into their little black throats and asphyxiate them. Or I suffocate them with their own umbilical cords, sometimes even before they come out of the womb. The mothers either don't notice or wish it so…have requested it, begged for it in a tongue unknown to the whites. The act can be quite subtle and seems normal to the keeper who is meant to ensure the survival of newborn future slaves. We all outwit him. If I can't do it at birth, I later feed them fruit tainted by the blood of women infected with tetanus from their chains. Or I collect diarrhea from dysentery outbreaks and mix it with puréed meals. Sometimes I smear my breast with the concoction and then breastfeed them. Or I put dry casaba close to their tonsils to block their breathing. I am not the only one. Many follow me. We have bred an army."

More silence.

I make a mental account of forgotten words. I repeat their sound. I articulate by touching the back of my tongue with the back of my soft palate. Suddenly there is narrowness in my air passages. Air does not pass. I feel a strong radiance at my uvula. I am a vibratory contraction. I am a choking pharynx—moon, energy, courage, eternity.

The last thing I recognize is Fray Petro's pink eyes.

Mildred K. Barya

Born in Uganda, she has authored three poetry books: Give Me Room to Move My Feet *(2009),* The Price of Memory After the Tsunami *(2006) and* Men Love Chocolates but They Don't Say *(2002). She has also published prose, poems or hybrids in* Tin House, Poets.org, Asymptote, Prairie Schooner, Per Contra, Northeast Review *and* Poetry Quarterly. *She holds a PhD in English from the University of Denver, Colorado, an MFA in Creative Writing from Syracuse University, New York, and a BA in Literature from Makerere University, Uganda. She is a board member of the African Writers Trust (AWT). She teaches creative writing and literature at the University of North Carolina-Asheville.*

Black Stone

Nyana Promise leans against the camp wall a few feet away from the maimed old women. Two lines of tears trek down her young face and she licks them when they arrive above her lips. She makes no sound. But there she is with wet eyes and a fisted hand concealing a black stone.

Other children do not call Nyana by name. They know her as the lone one, like the single mushroom growing behind an amputated tree. Women are afraid to use the mushroom for soup because mushrooms are supposed to grow in clusters.

Nyana goes to the children, thinking she should say goodbye. She wants to die. As usual, little Margo's nose is running. Her navy-blue dress is clean but probably will not survive three more washings. Nyana lifts the hem and cleans up Margo's nose. Margo thanks her and Nyana wants to tell her she can do it herself, it takes no effort, but she says nothing. Besides it's not even true; everything requires effort.

The kid called James Bond makes Nyana smile. He's always angry; his lips permanently in a pout, his eyes two red chilies. Nyana offers him a high-five and the kid frowns. On her way out she sees Kizito slumped in the folding chair, brooding. She searches for what to say. What eventually comes out of her mouth is a command: "Don't tell," then she walks away.

She knows she's breaking an unspoken rule; she's not supposed to walk alone but she couldn't care less. She imagines it would be a relief if the rebels killed her. She knows that when you die you die. Living is the tough part and her fear of getting kidnapped is worse than the fear of death. Because then she'd have to go on living. In the doorway is Hillary, her hands up against the frame. She is said to be the oldest but she doesn't look twelve years old. Obviously stunted, her stomach is big like a pregnant woman's, and Nyana thinks it's full of worms.

"Move," Nyana says.

Hillary drags her feet.

The women see Nyana leaving but they don't restrain her. There she goes again, is all they say to let the one who can't see know. Nyana walks down a short bend that connects to a broader, straight path. She arrives at a silent stream tucked away in the bush. She halts, then crouches abruptly and falls flat on her stomach. A group of armed men in military fatigues treads past her. Minutes later she rises to her feet but is uncertain whether to proceed to Gulu town or walk back to the camp. Two steps forward she hears: *Don't.*

Back at the camp, James Bond is missing, and one of the old women, Tasha, is on the ground writhing, her right hand holding back her intestines, trying to stop them from spilling and mixing with dirt. Her blood flows and merges with the dark soils of Acholi.

At night, Nyana dreams that Kony, the rebel leader himself, is trying to wrench the stone from her fist.

"Bastard," she screams. She kicks fiercely and lands on the floor.

"Nyana?" Modesta, the eyeless one, whispers and holds her. Nyana's back is hot with sweat. Nyana stares. She wants to know how the eyeless one has found her. How she can tell Nyana from the other children. Nyana peers into the empty sockets. She relaxes her tightened fingers and uncurls them.

"This is all I have of my people," she says of the small black stone, and guides the old woman's fingers to feel it.

"It's all right," the old woman says. She tilts her hand and closes Nyana's palm over the stone. "Nobody is going to take away your people. They're here and here," she says, touching Nyana's chest and forehead.

Nyana smiles.

"Try and sleep some more," Modesta says, helps Nyana back to bed and gently tucks her in.

Nyana sleeps coiled like a fetus in the womb.

At 4 a.m, there're more screams from the little ones. Modesta tiptoes to the makeshift kitchen to boil some tea. "Once it starts it starts," she says to Estelli, her colleague who lost her legs.

"Hmn, hmn," Estelli says, and hobbles along.

The screams have become a routine, a signal to start the fire and make tea. The two women fill small plastic cups and put them on a basket tray. Modesta carries the tray with Estelli in tow. Together they pass out cup after cup of lemongrass tea mixed with honey and chamomile flowers.

Modesta lost her home and eyes the same afternoon that Nyana's home was torched. Nyana returned from school and found their small house burnt to ashes. She tried to think she was in the wrong place, but an old man from the village called her name and told her the family line now rested with her.

"May the ancestors be kind to you. You're the only one left."

Nyana started to rake through the ashes, looking for remains of her family.

"You're wasting time, child. Come with me and I'll take you to a place where there are others like you."

Nyana continued rummaging, using both her hands and feet. She stopped when her left foot came into contact with a hard substance. It looked like a bead her mother wore, the one that her father had given her when she delivered the baby boy. The bead, which Olga loved so much that her mother had made her a promise that when she grew older and passed her primary leaving exams, the bead would go to her. Nyana picked it up. It had been green, now it was a black stone.

"It's getting dark and we have a long way to walk," the old man said.

Nyana did not move. The old man moved.

"Come," he pulled her gently and she followed.

When morning breaks, the women and children silently dig a grave and bury Tasha, whose intestines refused to go back inside, and whose blood chose the land.

Days later, Modesta and Estelli are seated on the large stones in the compound having a conversation. Their heads are covered with bright headscarves; gifts from the outside world. Keeping their voices low, they can't help wondering how Nyana stays out of harm's way when she's clearly courting danger.

"That girl will bring us trouble," Estelli says.

"We are like family," Modesta says. "She wouldn't betray us."

"I don't trust what I see."

Nyana walks towards them and stretches out her hand to touch Modesta's scarf. The woman ducks her head, making Estelli laugh.

Nyana murmurs, "How does she know what I'm about to do?"

"Senses," Estelli says. "Sometimes I walk but I have no legs, you see."

Nyana is about to sit when she smells danger close by. First there's a cry, then she sees red and yellow flames, a man on fire, running.

"Everyone take cover!" she shouts.

Modesta lies on her stomach begging Mother Earth for protection. Nyana leans against the mud wall, visible. She listens to the gunfire that's getting closer and more strident. This is it, she says to herself, looks around and notices the grass is not even tall enough to cover her people, and the small cactuses would not shield a rat. But the women and children keep their bodies to the ground, hugging Earth and praying to the all-knowing Protector to have mercy and preserve their lives.

Nyana waits for the rebels to appear, her heart beating fast but not wanting to hide anymore. What happens disappoints her. Every sound eventually dies until the only loudness is the emptiness.

"Bastards," she says, with renewed anger, and moves to rouse those in hiding.

She lays a hand on Modesta's shoulder. Modesta recoils in terror.

"They're gone," she says.

"Jesus," Modesta cries in relief, then stands on her feet and shakes the dirt off her body.

Nyana finds Hillary lying on her back. She taps on her stomach and it makes a tom-tom sound like a bongo drum. It hadn't occurred to Nyana that with such a tummy, Hillary might have difficulty lying on it. She taps on it again but suddenly withdraws her hand, horrified. Could she be heavy with a rebel's baby and not worms? What could be worse? She avoids looking at her face and goes to Margo.

Margo is weeping softly. Nyana picks her up and carries her to the women. Kizito refuses to acknowledge the pat. Rebels employ all sorts of tricks, he thinks. If they imagine you'll be scared with prodding, they'll prompt you nicely and when you open your eyes they'll whack your brains out. Nyana turns him over, and he remains rigid. Stone dead.

"Kizito," she says, "it's Nyana."

Eventually he rises.

The rest of the day, Nyana walks aimlessly, the fisted hand close to her lips and her tongue kissing the stone. It occurs to her that her family might be protecting her, wherever they are. If they're dead, they're saints praying for her. She perforates her stone and weaves through the hole a string to wear around her neck. When darkness approaches, she's far from the camp. A crescent moon comes out, resembling a tambourine. Nyana imagines a woman's profile shaking to music only she can hear as the moon moves. After several hours walking in step with the moon, she arrives back at the camp, goes to her bed and crashes.

That night the women decide to make tea before the crying hour. They awaken the children tenderly and pass out the cups. Nyana remains in the fetal position.

"Give it up, child," Modesta says. "Release your body so your people can freely move."

Nyana shakes her head.

Modesta strokes her fisted hand. It no longer holds the stone. There's anger in her fist, and the stone is around her neck.

"You have to imagine them safe in you but they cannot breathe, walk or move with you curled like that. Do you want to suffocate them or to keep them alive?"

"I want to keep them alive."

"Then ease up and your people will live."

"They're here and here," Nyana says, touching her chest and forehead.

"Good," Modesta says, and ambles back to her bed.

Nyana relaxes and remembers the half moon with the dancing woman. The woman becomes her mother and she has company. She is dancing the conga with baby boy, Papa and Olga. They move swiftly like beads along the thin line of the moon. Nyana begins to laugh, softly at first, then with bold joy.

Jackee Budesta Batanda

A Ugandan writer, journalist and entrepreneur, she runs SuccessSpark Brand Limited, an educational company that offers writing classes and ghost-writing services. She was the Africa Regional winner of the 2003 Commonwealth Short Story Competition, and her stories have been performed on the BBC World Service, BBC3 and radio stations throughout the Commonwealth as well as appearing in various international anthologies. She has written for publications including the New York Times, *the* Boston Globe, The Guardian *(UK), the* Mail & Guardian *(South Africa), the* Sunday Times, Sunday Independent *(SA) and* Al Jazeera. *She was the recipient of a 2010 Uganda Young Achievers Award, shortlisted for the 2012 Trust Women Journalist Award, named by* The Times *(London) in 2012 as one of 20 women shaping the future of Africa, and in 2017 was named one of the top 40 Ugandans under 40. The Africa39 initiative named her among 39 writers under 40 from Sub-Saharan Africa likely to shape the future of African literature. She is the winner of a Continental Award for 2018 from the Most Influential Women in Business and Government programme.*

You are a stammerer!

It is sunny this break-time. It is my first or second day at Kiswa Primary School. I am six years old, triumphant that I have crossed over from kindergarten to the primary section, where my older siblings are. The sound of children's laughter in the compound is like the busy hum of bees. Those who have already made new friends run around me playing in the sun. I am standing alone in the compound when a girl from a higher class comes over. She smiles and asks if I am Sam's sister. I nod, in awe that a big girl is talking to me. She asks where he is.

I open my mouth but nothing come out. In my mind I am saying, *I don't know*, but the words are teasing me, refusing to be spoken. I stand there with my mouth wide, breathing hard and stamping my right leg, in an effort to say the three words. And when I finally say, *I-I-I-don't know*, she is shaking in fits of laughter—the kind that brings tears to the eyes, stitches to the stomach and makes you pee a little in your panties.

She walks off and leaves me standing alone this break-time, even though the compound is bursting with children from all the classes. I stare down at the dirt ground. My heart is racing fast. I hold back the tears. I have recently joined primary school because I am a big girl and big girls don't cry. When I walk back to class, I stumble as the tears I am fighting blur my sight.

Later at home, Sam asks whether I had a chat with his friend. I nod quietly. He says she told him that she met me and spoke to me. She said I was funny.

I first learn the word from my cousin Kate. She lives with us sometimes. Her mother, Aunt Mary, is one of my father's younger sisters. Kate has come home for lunch. She studies at City High School, a low-level day-school in the upscale Kololo area. She is dressed in her uniform: a white shirt, smartly tucked into an orange pleated cotton skirt. She is a big girl and reads big-people books and maybe has big-people conversations.

We are seated at the new black mahogany eight-seater dining-table the company my father works for has recently added to the household refurnishing. Everything is new except, in the corner, the old non-functioning black telephone that sits majestically on a small side-table as decoration. It is the late eighties, the days when getting a phone connection comes with more bureaucracy than trying to meet a president. Life is more comfortable not trying to get the phone reconnected.

The sun seeps through the window and lands on the table. You can see a thin layer of dust if you look closely at the table surface. I am speaking to Kate. I don't remember what I'm saying. I remember sitting across the table from her, my feet dangling, when she announces in a matter-of-fact-way:

"You are a stammerer!"

"Www-haat is a ss-ss-stammerer?" Even as I speak, I am not sure I want an answer.

"Oh, the way you talk. You repeat words and take long to speak, so you are a *stammerer*. That is what you are," she says, and continues eating her food.

I sit back in the chair and stare at her. She has just shattered my world by giving my affliction a name. The word makes me fill with shame. I want her to take it back. But it cannot be unsaid. The word has grown its own body, comes to sit beside me and mischievously whispers, *I am finally here, mate. Now you know my name, let's get on with it.*

My mother maintains there is nothing wrong with me. When I tell her the children at school laugh when I talk, she says I should tell them that stammering is "contagious": that if they laugh, they too will stammer. I realize that she is only temporarily consoling me. I notice the classmates who continue to laugh at me never, ever stammer.

Years later, I am in a new school, Nakasero Primary School, in primary seven. My mother has been dead four years now and I have made it this far without transferring the stutter to the people who laugh at me.

It is a hot afternoon. I hate afternoon classes. I would rather be sleeping or playing. The Social Studies teacher stands in front of the class. He is one of only a few plump teachers at the school, with an egg-shaped head and very short-cut hair. He never tucks in his dark shirts, so they hang over his extended belly like a too-short dress. I don't remember his name now, though I can remember all my other teachers' names; I think my mind blocked his name after the incident.

We know he is tough. He talks with slaps. That is his language. He seems always angry about something. So when he asks a question, all hands shoot up in the air, whether we know the answer or not. We have learned the trick: when you raise your hand first, he never chooses you. So even if you have no idea what the answer is, you'd better be among the first to raise your hand.

Then he has this moment where he stares around the class and circles about us waiting to pounce on his unfortunate prey. We stare back at him, making it like a staring contest. All sixty pairs of eyes carefully watch him with bated breath as he searches for an unsure face before triumphantly calling out the name of the unfortunate who must answer. As soon as he calls out a name, all the other hands go down quickly in relief as if in a choreographed move.

I have raised my hand.

He meets my eyes in the staring game and bellows out, "BATANDA!"

Oh, God, my heart sinks. I sigh. I know the answer but know I won't get it out soon enough.

He walks over to me and says my name again. I open my mouth to speak, but there are no words even though my mind is screaming the answer. My mouth is open when he slaps me on the cheek. It is a hard slap, so loud it dims every other sound in the room. I feel heat building up in my cheeks. I hear the unison wince of my classmates. I stare at him and tell myself not to cry. I vow not to give him that satisfaction, so I stare at him coldly and close my mouth. I stop bothering to try to get the answer out. He moves on to the next person, who answers swiftly and flawlessly.

I sit hunched at my desk, feeling the sting of his slap on my cheek. For the rest of the lesson, my eyes are focused on my exercise book where I doodle away. My friend sitting adjacent to me, Yvonne Collins, whispers to me that she can still see the mark of his fingers on my cheek.

Years later when I learn that he has passed on, I feel neither sadness nor loss. I remember the slap.

The reason I love singing is that is the only time that my tongue loses its heaviness. I can belt a tune non-stop. It is the only time my mind relaxes and words come flowing out of my mouth without hesitation, as if they really want to come out in a melody.

My brother, Sam, asks me why I do not stutter when I sing. I tell him I don't know, because I don't.

My father's big brother, Uncle Sam, after whom my brother is named, pays my siblings and me for our singing when he visits. We are always excited about him visiting; it is a chance for us to show off our singing skills and get paid.

This time, our captive audience is Uncle Sam and our embarrassed parents. We move to the living-room, where we sing in flat monotone the boring songs we've learned at school. Swaying our bodies from side to side while moving our hands, we smile brightly as our school choir mistress has insisted.

Uncle Sam is a kind audience, the type every serious artist dreams of. He applauds loudly, then opens his black briefcase; he pulls out a wad of cash and carefully peels off a few banknotes to hand over to each of us, while praising our singing. He is overly generous with his compliments and we sparkle in them.

It is the early nineties when CNN first comes to Uganda. We, as a family and country, are excited. Paul Kavuma, the local anchor, always reports right in front of the swanky Sheraton Hotel with his trademark signoff: "Paaaulow Kaayvuumaaa, reporting for CNN in Kampala, Uganda." He speaks with what we call an American accent, rolling the words round his tongue. He is a "summer", as we call people who have lived abroad.

I am a teenager and easily impressed by Paul's accent. I begin to watch more news reporters on the little black-and-white TV of my childhood, and imagine myself reporting for CNN.

War is happening in the Balkans. Our shock at there being a war in Europe is fuelled by Christiane Amanpour's reporting. At the highlight of conflict, I grow to adore her, watching her for hours on our fourteen-inch black-and-white Sony television. Most of the homes in the neighbourhood have moved on to the more popular colour TVs, but we cannot afford one. Her voice provides enough colour for me.

I announce that I am going to be a television journalist—a war reporter like Christiane Amanpour—and work for CNN so I can travel the world regaling people with news stories. It is my brother Sam who wakes me up from my dream.

"But you stammer! You cannot be like Christiane Amanpour."

I agree; and resort to writing. No one will hear the stutter in my writing. Writing becomes my way to speak fluidly. I start writing for my high-school newsletter, which is very rudimentary—handwritten pages pinned on the main noticeboard. It is a weekly paper, covering the school's mundane stories in an (embarrassing) tabloid manner. It brings me a fan-base but also makes me lose friends because of the exposés that I pen. I am too busy enjoying the writing to realize what I am losing.

But I dream of reporting like Christiane Amanpour. In my mind I have clear and fluid conversations and can speak as eloquently as she does.

I dream of meeting her to tell her how she inspired me into journalism. The closest I have come is following her on Facebook and Twitter. She still inspires the fourteen-year-old girl in me.

"Should I wear a sad face?" he asks. His name is Gamali Adolph. He is an asylum seeker from Burundi and has lived in South Africa for over six years. We are seated in the shade of an acacia tree in a carpark in Pretoria. I am interviewing him for an article on the government's expenses in policing migration. I want to know his experiences with South African authorities since moving into the country.

"No", I say, "I'm not writing for international development aid agencies. This is a story about your life that needs to get out. I want to capture you in words and pictures."

We both laugh. Our laughter echoes above the sound of traffic in the distance. He obliges, and I engage him in further conversation. When he is free in his own skin and does not wear the sad face, I click, click, click, and click away.

I interview Voda from the Democratic Republic of Congo. We meet in a park in Rosettenville. After the interview, I get his permission to take his photograph. He sits and stares at the camera, but before I start clicking, he asks whether he should look sad and miserable. I tell him I want to capture his lovely smile. His baseball cap covers his eyes. When he smiles you can see the gold cap on his teeth.

It is nineteen years since I made peace with myself about what type of journalism to pursue: writing. My writing is my tool to connect with the world. I want to dig out the stories no one cares about.

I have previously covered stories in Uganda about refugee women living in the capital, Kampala. I have covered stories that never make the headlines of international media, about young Africans returning home from the diaspora to rebuild their countries.

Now based in South Africa, I document migrant narratives. I have had 6 a.m. breakfast with homeless asylum-seekers in Pretoria, spent the afternoon with women in informal settlements outside Johannesburg, spent the late morning with North Africans in Fordsburg. As they carefully weave their stories for me, like a multi-coloured reed basket, I have listened. I have laughed with them and when sad memories are brought back, I have paused with them. Moments of silence are what bring us together.

Ironically, what draws my interviewees to me is what has long embarrassed me. I start the interview, pausing on some words and breathing deeply—techniques I learned from a Nigerian I met at a conference in Harare back in 2004, who told me the trick of working through a stammer is to talk slowly and take deep breaths. If I stumble over words, I look the interviewee in the eyes and pause. That lingering moment always seems to form a connection. Interviewees interact more. I even let them complete my sentences, as seems to come naturally to many people when I falter. Their stories tumble out as from a loosened floodgate. Sometimes they pause and say, "This is off-record," in which case I turn off my digital recorder and just listen. These people who live under the radar of South African life willingly share their dreams and journeys with me, and as I write I know they will not die with their stories still hidden in them; each story adds understanding to our universe, coming from the inner spaces of hearts and souls.

Some speak of their ingenuity surviving in a country hostile to foreigners: "It's like we were thrown in the water and didn't know how to swim."

My writings capture their small beginners' swimming strokes, and the advanced butterfly strokes of those who have lived here for many years.

I listen as they talk, stories spiralling from the abyss where they have been buried too long.

Jacqueline Bishop

Born in Jamaica, she is now based in the US. Her most recent book, The Gymnast & Other Positions, *was awarded the 2016 OCM Bocas Award in Non-Fiction. She is also the author of the novel* The River's Song *(2007), and two collections of poems,* Fauna *(2006) and* Snapshots from Istanbul *(2009). She has received awards including the Canute A. Brodhurst Prize for short-story writing, a year-long Fulbright grant to Morocco, and a UNESCO/Fulbright Fellowship to Paris. She is an accomplished visual artist and has had exhibitions in several countries and is an Associate Professor at New York University.*

The Vanishing Woman

She tired of being a graduate student, tired of being a doctoral candidate. Was she even getting tired of the woman who came to visit every night in her sleep? Some days Denise found herself wondering if it was worth it, all this education. She was unlikely to get any big-time job, since there were so few positions in academia these days. Most of all, she tired of the quarrels over foolishness she kept having with her advisor. *Why didn't Noella just write the damn dissertation and call it her own?* Denise found herself wondering, as she crossed the street in downtown Kingston, near the Institute of Jamaica, where she was conducting research. It had all taken over her life, and she wanted her life back, to be the carefree girl who would go dancing most weekends. But these days so many women, so many voices, had taken up residence in her head, she could barely sort out her own thinking. This is what getting a PhD did to you. This latest dust-up with her advisor was so silly. She wanted to title her dissertation "The Vanishing Woman", but Noella kept insisting it should be "The Disappearing Woman", because disappearing implied you had a presence to be recouped. Denise was sure it was vanishing and not disappearing that she was after. The woman who came to her night after night to insist that Denise tell her story was not there when she opened her eyes in the morning. This nameless woman indeed vanished with the sunrise. But Denise could not explain this to Noella, who, when Denise first told her about her research topic had laughed.

"Say what? You want to research embroidery by enslaved women in the Americas? I can tell you, as a point of fact, that no such thing exists, and textile and fibres are my specialization. Embroidery was a leisure activity for *white* women during the time of slavery. It required resources, which put it out of the reach of even *free* black women. Maybe you could look at quilt-making?"

But Denise stood her ground. There was the woman who came to visit her nightly, embroidery hoop in hand. That woman, though she vanished at the first light of day, was real. Oh, so real. It was her job to tell this woman's story.

Noella told Denise that if she could find examples of any such embroidery, they would reconsider the topic. Denise left Noella's cushy office at the university that day knowing her advisor expected her to fail.

For a while she too thought that she would fail, despite the woman who came to sit in her mind every night, embroidering ornate and beautiful coloured herbals and bestiaries. Yet, Denise could find absolutely no documentary evidence that enslaved black women made embroidery. One museum curator after another told her no such thing existed in the records. Embroidery-making, it seemed, was a leisure-time activity that only white women engaged in.

"You not looking in the right places," the woman who came faithfully every night said. "I tell you where to look. But you have to make up your mind whether you believe in me or you don't. You can't be half-stepping. You believe fully in me, you find what you want."

The woman had a thimble in her hand and some rough-looking osnaburg cloth. This time she was making a piece that looked remarkably different from those Denise had seen her make before. It became so etched in Denise's mind that she was both surprised, and surprised at herself for being surprised, to come across that piece for sale on a website on the Internet a few weeks later, made by an "unknown Jamaican woman, possibly enslaved". It depicted a brown-skinned woman lifting a basket filled with tropical flowers over her head. Some flowers had tumbled from the basket and had sprouted, growing in profusion at the woman's feet.

That was the break-through piece that gave way to others. An enslaved woman had made a piece for Queen Victoria, whom she thanked for freeing the slaves. Another woman had made a piece for her daughter being sold away into slavery. And another woman, unknown, who made it into the Jamaican papers, for embroidering a piece of the island so sunny and resplendent that it caught the eye of the governor, who sent it as a gift to the Victoria and Albert Museum in London.

Noella could barely contain her astonishment. She had to concede that Denise was onto something, but the inability to name these women, track them down in records, was a problem for authentication and verification. Academia, after all, worked on facts, on what could be laid down in an orderly manner and examined.

That night as Denise lay in her bed she started talking to the woman. She felt stupid doing it at first, then, after a while, not so stupid at all. "Tell me your name," Denise heard herself saying out loud to the darkness around her. "Tell me anything you want. Tell me where to find you. I am here and I am listening."

Denise found herself in a darkened back room with the woman. There was an overpowering scent of sugarcane.

"It take you a long enough time to come," the woman began ruefully. "All the time I been the one visiting with you."

The woman was sitting hunched over, working by the light of the window. Yards of cloth were all about, and she squinted as her fingers moved, embroidering something. She was middle-aged, maybe older.

"Somebody important getting married," the woman continued. "The dress for the wedding come from England, but it not as pretty as they want, so they give it to my missus to pretty up. That woman can sew but can't do embroidery. All the embroidery on shoes and clothes and household things that bear her name, that people praise her for, I the one that does all of it." The woman looked up with rheumy red eyes. "Embroidery pretty, but it does make you go blind, you know. Nobody talks about that."

Denise got closer. The woman was wrapping silky white threads around a needle to create the most beautiful roses and rosettes, flowers that lifted off the delicate material to become three-dimensional on the pristine white wedding dress. Denise looked around the room. There were so many pieces of cloth, things the woman was working on: hats, gloves, aprons, bags.

"Missus glad when she buy me. All the way from New Orleans. She need somebody that can do embroidery good-good. I still youngish when I come. I getting old and tired now. I live longer in Jamaica than anywhere else. Missus ask me where I learn to make embroidery good so. I tell her they take me and my mother from the place with the big river where we live, and they separate we. One woman in Morocco buy me and I go live with she. That woman in Morocco in embroidery business, so that's how come I start learn. In Morocco, they have some beautiful beautiful embroidery. It different based on where you live in that country. I live with that woman in El Jadida, near Azemmour, and there it is all blue-and-white embroidery. I start to think it not so bad in Morocco, because I can make my way back to the big river; one day I can make my way home where I belong. But that woman she sell me to a man in Portugal, who keep me just a short time before selling me to another man in Spain. I stay there in Spain for a while, still doing the embroidery business. But these people, when business not so good, they quick-a-clock sell you to make money. Before you know it, I end up on a boat for a place call New Orleans, where a seamstress woman buy me for my skills. I liked New Orleans. Big river becoming nothing but a dream and a faraway memory. You know? Where you start to ask yourself if it really happen? In New Orleans, they have so many others like me, and I start form friends. My missus, she busy bad on Thursdays, Fridays and Saturdays, and I work my fingers down to nothing, so she give me Sundays and Mondays off. Boy, I used to be thankful for that, because by Sunday morning, I have no feeling in my fingers. In New Orleans you have these different nuns, black nuns, they had their own convent and everything. These nuns used to take in black girls and teach them skills, then find them good free black husbands. One day a nun come to ask me if on my days off I would teach those girls embroidery. I tell you, I jumped at the chance, no matter the state my fingers was in, because that would mean I could save up a little money to help myself, to free myself. But my missus was a wretch. One day when I save up about enough to buy my freedom that woman she ask to borrow my money and before you know it, I on a ship and I end up with a new missus and living in Jamaica."

The woman went back to her sewing. "Yes," she said, nodding her head after a while, "that was what that woman in New Orleans do to me. This new missus I have, she not bad. But I learnt long ago not to trust these people."

A pained awkward silence fell over the room.

It was then that Denise saw them, almost covered up by all the other pieces in the room. These were clearly works that the woman embroidered for herself, from bits and pieces of cloth and thread. The short fat stalks of heliconias and red gingers; the purple-blue blossoms of the national tree of Jamaica, which was now endangered; and oh, all the birds! There was the bird that islanders now called the rasta bird because of its red, green and gold coloring, many different kinds of hummingbirds with long tails that curved and met in something of a semi-circle. There was the giant yellow-and-black swallowtail butterfly, now hunted almost to extinction; and row upon row of sugarcane plants. A tapestry of a great house and people chopping cane, men and women working together. An overseer with a long dark whip. The heart-breakingly small children in the pickney gang. Here, too, was the woman lifting a basket full of flowers over her head. Denise carefully took up each work in the pile, studying each for the longest while.

Where had all the work vanished that this woman had created in whatever little spare time she had? She had told the island's history in embroidery.

The woman, still bent over her work, was talking again: "I forget the name my mother call me. I forget even what my mother look like. I just know she was tall and dark and a good basket weaver. I was from some place that had a big wide river. I loved playing in that river. They take me and my mother together from near that river. But no matter what my mother said, no matter all the begging and the crying, they did not keep us together. My mother she plant fruits and flowers, and when she put the basket with flowers over her head some of the flowers fall out all around her. She always loved pretty things, my mother."

The woman stopped talking, as if she had given as much information as she could give.

For years Denise could find no documentary evidence of the woman who visited her at night. But she kept at it, until little by little she was able to build a case, reclaim a history that everyone said was not there. The women had always been there, Denise showed; it was just that they ran afoul of the idea most people had of the kind of women who embroidered.

Denise dedicated her dissertation and the book that eventually followed to the woman who still came from time to time to visit with her, the woman who would be gone by morning, "The Vanishing Woman".

Malika Booker

A British writer, her work is steeped in anthropological research methodology and rooted in storytelling. Her writing spans poetry, theatre, monologue, installation and education. Clients and organisations she has worked with include Arts Council England, the BBC, British Council, Wellcome Trust, National Theatre, Royal Shakespeare Company, Arvon, and Hampton Court Palace.

The Conversation—Ruth & Naomi

Ruth go, sweet daughter-in-law leave me. *entreat me not to leave.* my son your husband is dead, leave. *whither you go I will go.* i am old fowl, a homeless chicken. *whither thou lodgest, I will lodge.* walk back to your people, go rest in your mother's bosom, leave while you still swing those hips, child. *thy people shall be my people.* child my body decays, age crawls me to death's muscled chest. *where thou diest, will I die.* her words prostrate before me. go leave, child. was this when she grasped both palms, pulled my body flush against her, my sagging breasts against her pert ones. my spread belly rolls against her stone wall belly. was this when she brushed lips at the side of my lips, a flicker, a whisper. was this when her palms splayed in the dip above my buttocks, then the feather tap of fingers. then the slide tickle of the dimpled dips. was this when we prostrate. was this when I found myself on the foor hollering, broken syllables like ughhh, like waaaaa, like…that night I found grace. that night "she had eat & was sufficed". that night. that night I heard my son's voice from the grave and he spoke about his wife.

Letter from Hegar to Sarai

Miss Sarai,

You say that we picked peas together? You are real demented, Miss Sarai. Woman, I picked peas and you sat in the room talking cobwebs and fireflies, I was your workhorse, vessel, whore, your ant to squash, grass to trample, slut, I was what you wanted. In your bed hands stroking me to cool your heat on the nights he don't call you.

That night you say you tucked me into his bed is all wrong. You dressed me like you, my dark cheek red with colour, my dress tied up so it ballooned around my hips, my pale blue drawers exposed, I was a black dot burning under an old man's disc, moving with gravity that night, screaming when my island was breached, then riding, being ridden, and for the first time I liked something, your old man's hand touching, sliding, stroking, no one had ever touched me that way. So I started to say "yes, oh God yes." Holla like you never did, whine like you never did, lying still like corpse under him doing your duty.

Why did you pin your ear to the door that night? What did you hear in my sighs to turn your face yellow, make you whip me each morning after, like you whipped your mule? So I had to run, Miss Sarai, run from the underworld of your hate. Run from the death planned for me in your eyes. Run to save this belly blooming here. Run from wildness to wilderness. I'd rather dry up in the desert than be gutted by you, hearing you sing hymns at me like you striking me with cuss word, something whispered "You better run." Run from sour face, run, place weight one foot in front of the other, run with awkward gait, O pregnant woman, hold that belly defy gravity and run. Seven nights I ran, a pregnant black cloud in motion.

Miss Sarai, I swear we looking at the same sky and seeing different motions.

Hegar

Eve Tells Her Creation Myth

(1)

That night we gathered, squatted
buttocks on thighs, toes tip toe.

that night rain lashed our bodies
sticking silk gown to nude skin.

that night salt packed into my cuts,
to sting, to heal. yea! that sexy salty pain.

that night our bodies uttered whale sounds
guttural grunts for my misunderstood pussy.

night said to me, this is a lullaby for your
cunt, with such logic & etiquette.

(2)

Yesterday   I
                   placed
        my
finger
                   into
        my
own
        wetness.
It   was
                   nasty
        and
sweetcake
                   at   once
yesterday   I
                   was
a
     finch
        beating
herself
        against
    a   wall
                     a
thumping
        mess

(3)

utterance I create you—ugh ugh ughhh,ughh
high   I   create you   sound

a sigh of breath   a punch of gut

sound   pattacake   this is how I define you.

(4)

so we squatted—white & lilac dresses
creased under sister moon. my depression
was wet rain water. wet sex juices. wet tears.
i dare. i dare. wet with the metallic smell
of blood. i drank my menstrual blood,
oh that taste of full body wine slipping
down my throat. I drank myself to heal.

(5)

they told me I was blue,
a dim sun
in morning.
I told them.
NO
i am a Black
fucking
horse,
all
fling mane
 &
striking
hoof
i told them
 i
am
utterance.

(6)

when he took the kids, after ice formed in our beds. an ice that would not
thaw, I never fight, after all my name is woman. my name is logic. my name is
hymn. my name is Eve. i gathered weeds, stool, and mud. I mold a doll into his
likeness. ribs and clay—i had learnt from the best. Then i broke him into little
pieces. ground him into dust. ashes and ashes and all that stuff. broke him like

the little piece of bitch he is. the next morning adam crawled to my gate our
kids clinging to his hair. He said *take them. take your offspring back. these are
no longer mine*. typical of man-kind to walk from his sperm. to sever his body
easy so.

(7)

I am rock salt
Yea I am thorns on a cactus
I am the moan of night
I am the estatic yes, yes yes
that rocks beds in nights eye, like
flies humming in clouds
I am movement, fire of flight.
I am that thing. Yea I am that thing.
A hushed cuss. Deadly. Sweet pink
grapefruit down there.
Pure water down there.
Oh sanctified pussy.
It's all ah that down there.

Saint Michael

He was last seen heading to Peckham on the 45 bus.
He left because shame was always the mongoose in the room.
He left his identity behind in an old fashioned briefcase.

He left to escape their muted rage.
He was last seen in pale blue denim jeans.
He left fed up with being the whispered rumour.

They last heard he had a job as a janitor.
His last words were a letter from Camberwell,
saying every road seems to be leading him back to jail.

He left an orange box of screwdrivers in a side drawer.
He left a mobile number on an answer machine
each time they call the number is engaged.

He was last seen on a street corner chatting with
guant, string beanstalk women, on the prowl.
He left because the family's silence was nasty.

He left because his mother was sick.
He was last seen leaving bent spoons in a bleached sink.
His family still tell people he is travelling the world.

He left because his family wrote him out of their wills.
He left convinced he sins no more.
He was last seen bawling on a 45 bus to Peckham.

Nana Ekua Brew-Hammond

An American-Ghanaian author of Powder Necklace *(2010), which* Publishers Weekly *called "a winning debut", she has had short fiction published in* Africa39: New Writing from Africa South of the Sahara, African Writing, Los Angeles Review of Books, *and* Sunday Salon. *She was a 2017 Aspen Ideas Festival Scholar, a 2016 Hedgebrook Writer-in-Residence, a 2015 Rhode Island Writers Colony Writer-in-Residence, and a Miles Morland Writing Scholarship Shortlistee in 2015 and 2014. She co-leads a monthly writing fellowship at Manhattan's Center for Faith and Work. Also noted for her personal style,* Essence *magazine and the* New York Times *have featured her fashion looks. Recently, she co-founded made-in-Ghana apparel line Exit 14. She is working on a new novel.*

After Edwin

Mawunyo Hodasi woke up to the familiar pam! of a tambourine accompanied by the sharp vibrato of her father Albert's experimental therapy children's choir. Poor, abandoned, or ravaged by rare and pitiable diseases, the kids' voices rang without doubt.

"Jesus loves the little children! All the children of the world!"

By now, Mawunyo thought, they had to know, Jesus's love notwithstanding, life didn't love them the same; the world loved some children more than others. But still they sang, employing all the elements of faith—desperation, determination, surrender, obedience, hope—in spite of life and the world.

"Hausa, Ga, Ewe, Akan! Rich and poor—yes, everyone! Jesus loves the little children of the world!"

For years, Mawunyo would roll her eyes at her father's earnest remix of the classic chorus as she watched the ragtag juvenile hospice chorales Albert started in different hospitals across Accra. Now, as she left her bed, she mouthed along, desperate for the song's heavenly truth to transcend the reality on the ground, her heart pounding with self-loathing and relief.

An eight-year-old was dead because of her. A little boy who, according to the death announcement posters plastered along Spintex Road, "never even hurt a mosquito." Yet the sinking, throbbing shame she felt was shadowed by an irrepressible feeling of invincibility.

In the immediate wake of the collision that had killed Edwin Ampah, Mawunyo had not had to submit to questioning. There hadn't even been talk of a breathalyzer. There had just been her mother and father flanking her, leading her into their car, ThyWill their driver waiting at the wheel to take them home; Uncle John—her mother had started teasingly calling him "Uncle Inspector" after he was named Inspector General of Police—leading the way in his Land Cruiser.

Every visit to Ghana, Mawunyo railed at her parents' easy acceptance of the serf-like hierarchy that entrenched Ghana's caste system. She confronted them about how guiltlessly they paid their maid the equivalent of $40 a month even as they gleefully did the math when their Social Security checks hit their accounts, simultaneously lamenting and rejoicing that the cedi's value had fallen again: 4.75 Ghana was $1 now. "What can that buy? Tell me," her father complained, because petrol was now 4.8540 Ghana per liter and the cars needed servicing and the roads needed tarring and the gutters needed rethinking and the street sellers needed removing and the government needed replacing because they were all chopping-oh. But now that her parents and Uncle John were "handling this business directly with the boy's family," Mawunyo went silent.

She trembled when she remembered Edwin's blood seeping like water from a punctured sachet, pooling around his opened face. She thought of Emmett Till, Trayvon Martin, Philando Castile, and the countless Blacks who had died without legal vindication. How many citizen justice petitions had she electronically signed demanding due process? How many Facebook posts and tweets had she liked and shared? In college, she had written reams of papers analyzing White Supremacy and the psychology of White entitlement, righteously prescribing the need for White people to give up their privilege for true equality to be had. At church, she petitioned God for justice. "Whatsoever you do to the least of My people, that you do unto Me," she had sung through tears of transfiguration the morning before she encountered Edwin Ampah.

She had meant it all—still did—until it meant her.

In that colorless hour between night and dawn, on the street without lamps just after the tunnel, when Mawunyo felt her car slam into body, bones, organs, blood, soul, and cement blocks, and, finally, a signboard advertising a new apartment complex with condos starting at $77,000; all she could think of was herself, her business, and the lone policeman at the checkpoint half a mile ahead.

On ordinary nights, when they approached the officer on the way home after an evening out, her father would suck his teeth. "If I refuse to stop, he has no car to chase me," Albert would say. "All he can do is radio the next checkpoint. He is powerless to do anything but collect bribes." Her mother would blink as she always did when she was faking a smile, then dutifully push the overhead light on and tilt her head out of the car as the officer shined his flashlight inside.

"Ɔkyena, me di something small bɛ ma wo, wai?" Harmless flirtation, Rosemary translated for her daughter.

"Complacency is the engine of corruption," Mawunyo would respond.

But that was B.E.

Immediately After Edwin, adrenaline numbing what she later realized was her broken nose, Mawunyo mentally counted the notes in her bag. She would give the checkpoint officer something big, if it came to that. She had not made the rules, she told her protesting integrity, and the rules would not be overturned because of her. No sense in allowing the levers of a warped system to churn her up when she had the option of exemption.

This was the pernicious privilege Mawunyo had picketed in college and sermonized her parents about, and she—young, Black, female, born in America, borne of Ghana—had the shadowy powers that be on her side. She was the euphemized "man."

Her status in Ghana had initially confused her. In the United States, Mawunyo had grown up certain of her place: inferior to whomever was White or rich; and she had spent the better part of her adolescence doing everything she could to achieve proximity to both. Among her first-generation American classmates from Haiti, Jamaica, Guyana, Guatemala, the Dominican Republic, Colombia, and Ecuador, she aggressively befriended the ones with the loosest curls and the straightest waves, the ones light enough to have freckles on their skin. She modeled her vocabulary, mannerisms, and tastes after White book and screen characters. She styled her freshly relaxed hair in cascading waves she regularly tucked behind her ears or tossed over her shoulders. She developed an obsession with golf, tennis, and surfing.

She wrote the hell out of her college application personal essay, conspiring with every exoticized notion of Africa she had seen or read, separating herself from all but the Talented Tenth of Blackness, campaigning as the ideal THANK YOU SO MUCH FOR THIS OPPORTUNITY & FINANCIAL AID candidate to secure a spot in one of the Best of the Whitest of schools, and she made it. She was accepted by Smith College, that old bastion of wealthy White femininity, where the daughters of slaveholders and suffragists converged in the intellectual mother of all finishing schools. It was the largest Sister of the Seven: Radcliffe, Vassar, Barnard, Wellesley, Mount Holyoke, and Bryn Mawr completing the number reserved for the richest, Whitest, historically women's colleges in America.

But at Smith she discovered more than how to be better at becoming an eternally inebriated, Feminine Mystique-quoting, White man's wife (should she be so lucky). Over four years of nailing her role as the STYLISH INTELLECTUAL WORLDLY GRATE-FUL HARD WORKING NEGRO, she found she wasn't the only one playing a part.

When the lights lowered, or drinks were served, when the music came on, she realized her White friends had been doing their own studying. Rapaciously singing along to whatever hip-hop track was the banger du jour, they always knew exactly when to go silent when the notorious "n" word appeared. In photos, they threw up gang signs they had seen in films or pictures, smiling at the irony, and captioned them with shrugging or marijuana leaf emojis.

Watching them perform what had been presented to them, and the world, as contemporary Blackness, it dawned on Mawunyo that her performances were minstrelsy too. There was no White or Black way of doing or being. Whiteness and Blackness were fabricated labels for invented identities, pernicious distortions of peoples and cultures to fossilize power and make money. Race was make-believe, and it was crushing every actor.

"Whites" were existentially undone by the masquerade of superiority, even (and especially) when they didn't know it to be a sham. They were nagged by the anxiety that comes with unmerited privilege: the fear that at any moment the ruse would be discovered, and everyone would stop playing along. They were bland with the ignorance borne of segregation and separatism; pickled by a legacy of myths their forebears had created to uphold their dominance; a fairytale that preserved them as uniformly powerful and rich, when most were actually struggling. But still, it was better brine than the one everyone else marinated in, and therein the privilege lay, and lied.

Meanwhile, "people of color"—"Blacks," "Asians," "Latinos," "Mixed Races"— were caged by the systematic invalidation of their identity and dignity; the severity of it moderated by their perceived proximity to Whiteness. To survive (and also to thrive), they were consigned to the schizophrenia of simultaneously inhabiting themselves and having to refute or play up some aspect of the many facsimiles of themselves permitted or peddled by White culture. And they were reminded again and again that neither wealth, nor extreme talent, intelligence, beauty, interracial coupling, acutely articulate diction, not even self-hate, offered total immunity—whether shopping under the surveillance of a following White eye, house hunting in a White neighborhood, or looking for a date online.

Every hand, every color, was cuffed by this concept that had flowered from a conspiracy of evil imaginations and financial interests into an evergreen global institution. Everyone was a victim of it, and victims cared first about turning their own fortunes around, even if doing so victimized others.

How ironic, yet apt, the term "race," Mawunyo often mused, set up so no one would ever be able to outrun it.

Then, Mawunyo went to Ghana for a visit; her first as an adult after her parents moved into the house they had built with their 401Ks to spend the rest of their lives in.

Speaking and thinking like the Ghanaian-American she was born and raised to be, half of her identity was dismissed and Mawunyo was summarily painted an "obroni"—White. With the almighty dollar in her pocket, and a blue passport in her name, she had the power to make grown men beg to carry her things, and she had the freedom—no humiliating visa interview to endure—to escape the survival mode setting life in Accra was permanently on, any time she chose.

It was intoxicating. Suddenly, Mawunyo inhabited a position America had made clear would eternally elude her: RICH "WHITE" GIRL. Inspired by the wealthy, White friends she had made at Smith, she played THE GOOD ONE to perfection, born for the role of CONSCIOUS RIGHTEOUS ENDEARINGLY TONE DEAF ADVOCATE.

Before Edwin, she had begun to drop parts of her act. After increasingly regular jaunts in Ghana, Mawunyo began experiencing emotional jet lag when she returned to the States. In Ghana she was the head. In America, she had to keep her head down and tuck her proverbial tail.

Formerly, code switching titillated her. She was a natural actress, and she took pride in her mastery of the subtle performance. But her onetime amusement at playing to the room—adapting into versions of herself palatable to the myth of Whiteness depending on the crowd—fermented into an acrid resentment. Deep anger slowly began replacing her need to be validated and affirmed by White people.

After Edwin, there could be no more pretense. Just as there was nothing inherently better about the White people or rich people she had been raised to worship, and nothing inherently worse, there was nothing good about the passive righteousness she practiced when she was in Ghana. There was just hypocrisy, and her conscious decision to love herself more than her neighbor.

Gabrielle Civil

A black feminist performance artist, writer and poet, originally from Detroit, Michigan, she has created 50 original performance art works around the world, including as a Fulbright Fellow in Mexico. Her writing has appeared in Small Axe, Art21, Something on Paper, Kitchen Table Translation, Obsidian, *and other outlets. She collaborated with artist Vladimir Cybil Charlier on "Tourist Art," an image + text work on Haitian cultural circulation and is the author of two memoirs in performance art:* Swallow the Fish *and* Experiments in Joy. *A graduate from the University of Michigan with Highest Distinction, she earned her MA and PhD in Comparative Literature from New York University. She currently serves as faculty in the MFA program in Creative Writing and the BFA program in Critical Studies at the California Institute of the Arts. The aim of her work is to open up space.*

From *Swallow the Fish*

"So, I'm doing a thing at Patrick's," Miré was saying. "I know there are hooks and water, but I'm trying to figure out the part with the fish."

"Fish?" Flávia asked, "Your piece is about fish?"

"No, it's about other things. But I was thinking about having a goldfish swimming in a bowl while I did the first part, then maybe do a thing with a rope and hooks or a knife. And then do something that transforms the fish, changes it."

"Oooh. A goldfish," I said. Lines from Rita Dove's "Dusting" popped into my head: "the clear bowl with one bright / fish, rippling / wound!" or "wound" to rhyme with around. I like it. Could you pour the fish from the bowl into a pitcher or something?"

"Or you could start with the pitcher," Flávia suggested.

"Then you could drink from the water."

"I think I need to do more than just sip the water. It needs to be a more powerful gesture."

"Swallow the fish," Colin said. "You know that's what you want to do. It's small and biodegradable."

"Eat a goldfish?" Evie interjected, eyebrows raised.

"You don't need to eat it," Colin continued. Or chew it or anything. Just swallow it."

"Colin," Flávia fussed. "Miré can't hurt animals for her art. That's not right."

Flávia's crickets had chirped blithely unharmed and she'd released them all at the end of her show.

"She doesn't need to hurt it. Just swallow it. And if it's necessary for the piece, then she needs to do it."

"Is it necessary?" I asked, repulsed yet titillated by the idea.

Swallow the fish? The whole thing had a new jack, lyrical black radical appeal, but was also old school performance art. Dramatic and crazy and slightly dangerous. Art at the level of life and death. Embodying the natural kingdom. Something indulgent and a little mean but tapping into another kind of power. Breaking taboos. Dancing the fine line between crazy and brilliant. Feeling something alien and alive move from transparency into your body, fish, rippling wound or wound.

But who would really do this?

"Hmm," Miré responded.

Swallow the Fish

I had never thought of myself as a fearful person, but performance art made me confront my fears. And also my desires. At the start, not the question, what would a performance artist do, because the answer was everything, anything. At the start, this question: who got to do those things? Who got to be a performance artist? Which people in which bodies?

I remember seeing Karen Finley in New York City. She hadn't swallowed any live animals (although it wouldn't necessarily be beyond her), but she had stripped down to just panties and put her feet in a basin of water which (as anyone who has ever stepped naked in water knows) gives you the overwhelming desire to pee. Karen Finley calmly told us that was what had happened to her, grabbed a bucket, and peed right there into it on stage. It was shocking, but also liberating. It was the brazen nastiness of white girls that had always intimidated me in my youth. (White girls, you know how they are… They'll do anything. Pee in the woods, walk around butt naked in the showers. They're loose, they're easy, they're crazy.) As a black girl, as a strong black woman, I was supposed to be appalled and superior to that kind of behavior. But at times, I was covetous. How come they got to do that? Where did they get that allowance? I had never seen a black woman do such things and wondered if it were even possible

Years ago, I had an artist show and tell at my house. I'd started moving from poetry into performance and had just gotten a big grant to turn my experience translating a long Haitian poem into a new performance art piece. When Colin suggested swallowing the fish, something rippled within in me. I wanted Miré to swallow the fish. I wanted her, a black woman to stare down craziness, to allow herself to be crazy, do something crazy on stage. Hell, I wanted to swallow the fish myself. To be as loose and crazy and unstoppable as those white lady performance artists like Karen Finley and Holly Hughes and Marina Abramovic. I wondered if I could do it.

"If it's necessary for the piece, then she needs to do it," Colin had said. The realization of need. Going deeper, taking it all a step further. I thought of the time I showed my landlords, my two great, gay godfathers whom I adore, some segments from Divine Horsemen, Maya Deren's documentary on Haitian vaudoun. One moment in the dance, the houngan, the priest, slits the throat of a chicken. You see its blood pour down to the earth below. That death is a necessary ritual that connects the worshippers to the spirit world beyond. My landlords were outraged at the violence; but, I felt honored, stirred. We were witness to the transfer of one life to another, one energy to another—not for entertainment or shock value but for transformation.

Swallowing the fish would have to be like that.

Making performance art as well.

To swallow the fish, you had to have something more than a reason. In a way, you had to reject reason itself. You had to have spirit (and perhaps spirits and the spirits too). Especially as a nice black girl, as a strong black woman. You couldn't just get away with whatever. Hell no. You could be crucified for that, or worse gain a bad reputation. Animal murderer. Race traitor. Nasty girl. Acting crazy. Acting up. Performing. Anything could happen to you. Anything could happen. It couldn't be pretense or something to do for kicks. It had to be real. There had to be some black art, some power, some need and conviction that warranted that kind of transformation. A particular kind of magic…

In the end, Miré chose not to swallow the fish or even to use a goldfish in a bowl at all. She passed a bucket with a freshly caught trout through the audience, a hook still dangling from its lip. She told a story in the accent of a fisherman displaced from his home, tying hooks into knots in a net. Then she masqueraded as a corporate raider with a clipboard, planning a new corporate development on the site. She only did the piece twice, one weekend at Patrick's Cabaret in Minneapolis, and hasn't revived it since.

In the meantime, that goldfish (rippling wound or wound), the challenge to swallow it, became mine. It belongs to anyone moving toward the form of performance art, struggling to figure out what it means, what is required to do it, what kind of body and spirit you would need.

Maxine Beneba Clarke

Born in Sydney, to parents of Afro-Caribbean heritage who migrated to Australia in the 1970s, she is a writer and slam poet. Her collection of short stories, Foreign Soil, *won the 2013 Victorian Premier's Unpublished Manuscript Award, the 2015 ABIA for Best Literary Fiction, the 2015 Indie Award for Best Debut Fiction, and was shortlisted for the 2015 Stella Prize. Her 2016 memoir* The Hate Race *won the New South Wales Premier's Literary Award, and her poetry collection* Carrying the World *won the 2017 Victorian Premier's Prize for Poetry. Her picture book* The Patchwork Bike, *illustrated by Melbourne artist Van Thanh Rudd, won the Crichton Award for Children's Book Illustration.*

Hurricane Season

Nico tucks his long dreads into his navy cap. The Melbourne summer heat itches his scalp. Getting too old for locks. Too old for a lot of things, really. Say forty's the new thirty, but Nico's tired: mind, body and bones. He tears the top off a hot chocolate sachet. Tumbles the fine brown powder into the mug. Tosses the crumpled packet into the plastic bin under the table.

Nico lifts the lever on the large silver urn, careful not to burn his knuckles again. Think they could afford an upgrade. Same urn's been in the meals room since the day he started driving. Nearly ten years. Been that long. *That long.* Taxi depot's almost empty. Nico's late this morning, because the dream came at him again. Dominica. Weeks now, he's been dreaming of home. When Nico woke an hour ago, he could feel the weather in the room with him, could smell the wet earth. Super-photosynthesis. Breadfruit and banana, fermenting wild on the branch. Luscious rot. Bounty. Decay. That foreboding something's-about-to-happen stillness he remembers so clearly from before the ground swallowed his Gracie. The ominous gathering of hurricane breath.

Nico scans the meals room. Old timers: hunched over drinks, or staring out windows. Slow-to-starts. World wearies. All swore they'd only be in the taxi game for a few years, like Nico did. Till they got their qualifications sorted to do whatever they used to do at home, or whatever they wanted to do here in Australia. Academics' minds. Carpenters' hands. Teachers' hearts. Their light blue cabbie shirts have faded to off-white now. Threadbare collars browned from decade-long wear no bleach can brighten.

Nico wraps his long brown fingers around the mug. Drink's making him sweat even more. Pulls out a vinyl-covered chair. Rocks precariously back on its pock-rusted metal legs. Cocoa. Mama Dominica. Home. Blushing khaki pods hanging unripe from roadside trees, the giant rough-skinned, teardrop shape of them. Their slow-darkening to raisin brown.

The smell of the hot chocolate is Nico, Gracie and Elias: bumping along towards town in the red open-air truck. Gracie's clutching Elias tight on her lap. Her hair's cornrowed down, in that zig-zag way she liked to do. The three of them, rambling down towards the spice factory in Elms Hills where Gracie worked, on Nico's day off from studying. Nico and Elias, perched on a wooden chair in the factory corner, watching Gracie dance the bean. One-two. Two-two. Her bare mahogany legs wrapped to the knees in plastic as she stands on the pre-fermenting racks. Dancing-dancing the cocoa. Swaying this way, swaying that. Laughing-laughing as she works. And Lord, the smell. Ginger-cinnamon. Nutmeg. *Home.*

Nico takes another scalding gulp. Got to get out on the road soon. His mate Ahmed's sitting near the window: shoulders slouched, grey beard almost touching the table.

"Ye okay, man?" Nico stops by him, on his way to the car.

Ahmed glances up, eyes so moist they look loose in their sockets, hands clasped. "Little Brother."

Ahmed's called Nico that since the moment they met. Ten years ago now. Twenty-nine he was, but Nico had still felt like a kid. He'd just arrived here with Elias: Gracie already gone, and him still wrecked with grieving. Black and righteous as Nico true-believed God was, he still couldn't figure why His Almighty would conjure a hurricane to send Gracie's way.

Driving was something Nico could fast-do to pay his rent on arrival. He'd been grateful for the job, but the *Little Brother* that Ahmed had whispered during his first shift had felt like a fist-bump in the darkness, an arm slung round his shoulder.

"I pick up a fare out to Belgrave last night." Fifteen years in Australia, and Ahmed's accent still sings *Somalia*. Same way Nico and Elias have somehow never picked up the local twang.

"Belgrave. Cha! In de country. Past de Dandenongs? Good fare, ole man."

Ahmed grunts. Stares down at the table. "Decent bloke. Suit. Tie and everything."

"Nice work, if it come te ye." Nico discreetly glances at his watch.

"Did the runner."

"No way. Ye chase him down?"

Ahmed's hands are shaking slightly. "I call the police on him."

"Ahmed…"

"The man rob me! I got a right to call." Ahmed rubs his palms together, as if his anger can be contained by the friction. "Policemen come. Two of them. White. Chewing their gum."

"Dem get ye money?" Nico already knows the answer.

"Say I'm trespassing. Told me *get moving*. Way they look at me, Little Brother. Down and up. You know how the way I mean," Ahmed's voice is all shake and anger.

"Motherfucker!"

"Watch that mouth, Little Brother." Ahmed's rebuke is like a friendly clip to the back of Nico's head. Like Nico used to do, back when Elias was small; deft at peeling back the stumps of Gracie's still-growing sugarcane, chewing off the tops before they'd ripened.

"Brother. You regret coming to here? Australia?"

Nico braces against his friend's question. Anchors.

"We never going to be like them. And they never going to like us." Ahmed is looking so deep into Nico's eyes that the pull feels inevitable.

"Sometimes. But den mi think of Elias, ye know. Young an cocky, like all-a dem brown boys. But dem *is* dis place. Dem kids: yours an mine. Australia dem home. An dem kids wid *opportunity*. Striving te make sometin of demselves. Is hard, my friend. But is dem why we come. We doing okay Ahmed. Doing good." Nico rests his hand on his friend's shoulder, leaning as much as comforting.

"Yeah."

Nico feels relief surge through Ahmed's body. Nico's not sure if it's true, or if he just wants it to be true. Been hard to raise Eli alone. *Spare the rod, spoil the child*, they say back home. Nico hasn't the hard heart or hands for that kind of fathering. Gracie would have known what to do with the boy at every turn. But he's raised the boy straight, Elias. Shoelaces always half untied. Natty afro hidden under dark hoodie. But chin raised. *Proud*. Like Nico was at seventeen. Not a bad thing. Straight As last term. Kid left the report on Nico's bedside table three weeks ago, when school let out. Praise don't come easy to Nico, so he never mentioned it, but it had filled his heart up. Took Elias to the pub for steak that night.

Nico starts his taxi shift down near the station. Habit so ingrained it's blood-ritual. This time of a Saturday morning Footscray wakes. Stretches. Launches itself bang into the weekend.

The smell of the fruit markets: plantain, okra, cantaloupe. The sour rot of fish guts, washing into street drains. Kids not that much older than Elias, rolling home clutching hangover pork-buns. Shiny BBQ duck hanging in the windows: whole glazed birds, beaks, eyes and all. Ethiopian coffee houses colourful with morning clientele, kitchens already herbing the air with Doro and Misr Wat on the boil.

The Sudanese men in the paved street mall are dressed a day early in Sunday best. Are *always* dressed in Sunday best. Scrubbed up king-fine. For home. For work. For the bottle. For church. Gliding aubergine-tall, history hovering in their walks.

Nico steers slowly into Paisley Street. The rank is empty of other cabs. But there's a woman, waiting. Neat bobbed haircut. Modest grey pencil skirt. Cream work blouse. Hot pink shoes clutched in hand, ridiculously heeled. She climbs in: bare feet blackened by concrete-wanderings. Something lacy's poking out of her small black handbag. Knickers, maybe. Unsteady on her feet. Furry bunny-ears headband. Nico can't quite pin a story to her. She looks familiar, somehow.

He sets the taxi meter, glances in the rear-view mirror as she lists the address. Been accused of looking too long before. Sometimes he can smell their fear—women riding alone. Specially at night. Eyes darting to check if the door's been deadlocked. Pretending to be on the phone.

The woman's gaze meets Nico's. She laughs at his expression. Tucks liquorice-black hair behind her ear. Smooths her crinkled blouse. "Bridal shower. Mine. Last night, after work. Could have done without it, to be honest. More for my sister than me."

Nico laughs too. The shake of his shoulders feels good. "Can't lie. Was wondering what-all was goin on." He brakes carefully at the intersection of Barkly Street and Geelong Road.

"You from Dominica?" Woman's staring back at him in the mirror now.

"Matter of fact, yes." Nico can't keep the surprise from his voice. "You de firs passenger get dat right bang on. Most de time dem say Jamaica." Nico's curious. "How ye know?"

"I went there once. Hiker's trip. *Breathtaking*. The *green*. Bags of sugarcane by the side of the road. *Rum and coconut* by the side of the road."

Nico laughs, louder this time. "Dem boys jus flag down de tourist, crack de coconut open in front-a dem an pour in a shot-a rum. Cheeky. Nobody on God's own earth can refuse dat!"

Her smile is tipsy-wide as the taxi barrels past the new Bunnings hardware store. Nico squints against the vicious morning light. The woman stares out the window.

"I teach. At the high school. Footscray City. Had a kid from Dominica. Came here when he was young, but that accent was still there. Good kid, but…" She sighs. "Must be hard. Coming here."

"What ye mean?" Nico can feel the heat, bouncing up off the black tar, reaching in at him through the open taxi window. He pushes the button to wind the window up. Presses the air-con on.

"I don't know," the woman rubs her eyes. "This kid. Smart. Everything seemed good. Just stopped coming to school." Her speech is still a little slurred. "Sometimes I think there's something missing in these boys. Who can say what it does to a person? Home is your heart, and all that. And this country is…*hostile*. You would know…" Her eyes suddenly meet his, in the rear-view mirror. "God! I *knew* I recognised you from somewhere. Mr Dawson? You're Eli's Dad?"

Nico wants to give the teacher a piece of his mind, let his thoughts rip. But the taste of wet earth is weighting his tongue. *Something missing in these boys. You would know*. Eli's neon shoelaces, undone and dragging. Afro hidden under hoodie.

Chin raised. Proud. Like Nico. A good boy. Straight As, just three weeks ago. Nico held the report with his own hands. Nico takes several deep breaths in.

"Sorry. I didn't mean to… I'm just…I'm gonna be quiet now, okay?" She pulls a ridiculously lacy bra from her purse, waggles it around, laughing. "Fricken hen's night."

The white lines on the road dance in front of Nico's eyes. First they sway this way, then they sway that. Laughing-laughing as he drives. Humidity rising. Black volcano grit flicking up in his eyes. Nico can hear Gracie screaming. "Get inside! What ye staring at, Elias? Hurricane ain't no pretty picture. Stare right into its eye like dat, it gwan come up an eat ye alive. Come! Come!" Elias. Seven years old. Running. Hiding behind her bright, smelling-of-nutmeg skirts.

"Are you okay? Sir! Pull over! Pull over!"

Nico's hands are shaky on the wheel. "I can't. I can't breathe."

"What?!"

"I can't…"

The taxi is slowly swerving into the next lane. The woman frantically unbuckles her seatbelt. Squeezes her body through the gap. Climbs clumsily into the front passenger seat. Leans over and grabs the wheel.

"You okay?" She steers the car wonkily into the side street. Pulls hard on the handbrake. "Should I call an ambulance. I don't… What happened?"

The pull inside Nico's chest feels like a landslide. Like Morne aux Diables volcano, dropping away to uncertain ground.

He can feel the weather in the taxi car with him, can smell the wet earth, that foreboding stillness he remembers so clearly from before the ground swallowed his Gracie.

The gathering of hurricane breath.

Black and righteous as Nico true-believes God is, he still can't figure why His Mighty would conjure this trouble his way.

Nadia Davids

Born in South Africa, her plays, At Her Feet, Cissie *and* What Remains *have garnered various theatre awards and nominations (seven Fleur de Cap Theatre Awards, and Naledi and Noma nominations) and have been staged internationally (in Africa, Europe, the US). Nadia was a part of the New York Women's Project Playwright's Lab (2008–10) and has held writing residencies at the Ledig House and at Hedgebrook. Her screenplay adaptation of her short story* The Visit *won best South African Film Project at the 2012 Durban International Film Festival. Her debut novel* An Imperfect Blessing *was shortlisted for both the 2014 UJ Prize and the Pan-African Etisalat Prize for Literature and long-listed for the 2014* Sunday Times *Fiction Award. It was named one of TIA's best African novels, one of three of Ozy's "Favourite New South African Books" and Radio702's 2014 "Book of the Year".*

From *What Remains*

What Remains is a fusion of text, dance and movement to tell a story about an unexpected uncovering of a slave burial ground in Cape Town, the archaeological dig that follows and a city haunted by the memory of slavery. When the bones emerge from the ground everyone in the city—slave descendants, archaeologists, citizens, property developers—are forced to reckon with a history sometimes remembered, sometimes forgotten. Loosely based on the events at Prestwich Place, *What Remains* is a path between memory and magic, the uncanny and the known, waking and dreaming. Four figures—The Archaeologist, The Healer, The Dancer and The Student—move between bones and books, archives and madness, paintings and protest, as they try to reconcile the past with the now. *What Remains* was first staged at the 2017 Grahamstown National Arts Festival, directed by Jay Pather.

Scene 1

A development ground, white floors, white set, smoke. The audience set up in the traverse, two banked rows facing each other, witnessing what is about to unfold.

The Student, The Archaeologist, The Healer are gathered, waiting to tell the story.

As they do, The Dancer, the ghost-body, emerges from the gloom. As The Student narrates, The Dancer animates her story; his body morphs, now the ghost, the bulldozer, the driver, the gathered crowd.

THE STUDENT:

This is a story in twelve parts.

Part One:

On a still, cool day in the east of a city by the sea, three sounds only: a bulldozer's engine, a forgotten song, a canon that tells the time.

Behind the bulldozer, a sign: Luxury Mall Coming Soon.

The vehicle rumbles, moves in, mouth open, teeth bared, ready to bite and spit. The ground gives easily, moves, tumbles, then suddenly, without reason, the engine switches off.

The driver tries to start it. Nothing. Again. Again. Nothing. Again, nothing.

He gets out. Inspects the vehicle. Circles it, runs his hands over the wheels, peers at the engine. Nothing. Finally, he looks at the debris stuck in the jaw of the bulldozer. In the dirt, splayed, smashed rocks, a sun-faded chewing-gum wrapper, frayed cloth—

A sense of foreboding, now,

of terror.

Wonder.

The faint sound of the song again, this time: almost words:

THE HEALER (*singing*):
Round our necks,
round our necks,
round our necks,
the amulets.

THE STUDENT:

He listens to the song.

Is made captive by the song.

Before the song ends, the engine switches on. By itself.

He jumps. To his left, a rustling. The wind is picking up. A rustling. He walks towards the sound, sees a movement in the ground, stops, bends down: in the earth, in amongst the broken things, something solid. A stick? Something. A thing doing that thing that things sometimes do; it is one thing, but it looks like another. This one looks like a finger. Like a middle finger. Like a middle-finger, out of nowhere, coming out the earth, telling it like it is. He laughs. He looks again.

He realises, holy *shit*, it is a finger.

THE ARCHEOLOGIST:

A finger's bone.

Right there. Pointing at him. At us. The ghost of a broken hand, rising through the earth and giving us all an old fuck you.

THE STUDENT:

Raw winds. Wild skies,
Foreboding—
Terror—
Wonder.

THE HEALER:

This, he knows now, is a burial ground.

Scene 2

THE STUDENT:

Part Two:

In the south of the city, lives a healer from a long line of healers. She, and those before her, before-her-before-her, before the ships, before the beginning of the terror, they know this city.

Know its past tense, its tense past, its future imperfect.

The Healer, knows that the underworld, the other place, the unseen country, has been disturbed. She has been up all night, talking the ghosts down from the wind—

In The Healer's house; a place of smoke, food, love and memory. As she speaks The Dancer follows her, moving, dancing, tumbling, sometimes she sees him, mostly she does not. The Healer is agitated, in a wild panic. She fears for the city, for everyone's safety.

THE HEALER:

—I've been up all night talking the ghosts down from the wind. A person can go mad listening. I knew in the afternoon already that the city would be chock full of spirits by the time the night came. I was hanging up the washing and one of the sheets took up, flipped and wrapped itself around me like a kafang, and that's when I knew, the dead were visiting. And that they would stay the whole week. You know how they say that guests are like fish—they stink after three days? Same for the dead. So I lit the house full of meang-stokies and I batjared in every corner I could find. I told my daughter that this night, this first night, is no time to tell them to go away. This is a night to welcome them. Light the corners, make things smell nice. Tonight, I tell her, tonight there will be so many you won't know what hit you. And they do hit. The nasty ones hit. So you want the good ones on your side. Because the others will come. Believe me, they will come. My daughter's eyes were big and dark in her head like two stones and she said, Mommy, Mommy, what will Mommy do if they stay?

They never stay, my child, I told her. Not for all time. They might stay till we die and join them but they won't stay forever.

Because in the end we are them and they are us.

So I start to make them food. A pot of rice. No meat. Those not of flesh will not eat flesh. A pot of rice, full of barakat, a pot that will keep going, keep giving and giving. We know this food, we know this magic, we can make the bone stretch and stretch for our children's soup, we can make this pot fill the emptiness. And I said to my daughter, Go and get some rest because it will be busy tonight.

And sure enough, whatever we thought was wind that afternoon was something else by the dark. The house is usually quiet by the early hours. The street too. Even one full of spite, like mine.

You may see stray cats, you may hear the beggars scratching for food, but otherwise, even the flowers are shut, tight-lipped, waiting for the light. But the noise tonight. The *noise*. The ghosts rush down the corridor and they take the TV cable and shake it and shake it and shake it so a person can't even watch something. And when the box does come on, they jump inside the TV anyway and all I can see is one of them standing behind the actors—just in the corner, in the shadow. See? You see?

So I'm up, I'm ready when they start to come. They start to walk through the front door, come through the windows, some of them faceless, some of them with just holes for eyes, lifting the lace curtains like brides, moving past the meangstokkies so the thin smoke follows them, breathing on the flowers so the petals fall off.

It is all one voice but there are a thousand of them. They come straight down the mountain wrapped in a cloud, they tip themselves over the edge and they streak and tumble. Oh God. Oh God.

Here they come.

They are grey.

The children are crying.

The women are screaming.

The men do not make a sound.

They do not.

I must fight air with air. Breath with breath. I pull in my own people—my mother, my sisters. I say, I need you now.

I need you.

We must talk them *down* from the wind.

We must stop the shrieking.

A person can go mad listening.

A person can go mad listening.

A person can go mad listening.

Camille T. Dungy

Born in Denver, Colorado, she is the author of four collections of poetry, most
recently Trophic Cascade *(2017), and the essay collection* Guidebook to Relative
Strangers: Journeys into Race, Motherhood and History *(2017), a finalist for the*
National Book Critics Circle Award. She has also edited anthologies including Black
Nature: Four Centuries of African American Nature Poetry *(2009). Her honours*
include NEA Fellowships in both poetry and prose, an American Book Award, two
Northern California Book Awards, and two NAACP Image Award nominations. She
is a Professor at Colorado State University.

From Dirt

For months now, I've been living through the grief of deaths, devastation, and
debilitating disease. I am naming none of these things in an abstract, global sense,
though they are pervasive conditions of our times. I am talking about the deaths of
family, the failure of this country to provide safety to dear friends. I am talking about
grief and exhaustion and auto-immune flares that make it difficult, daily, to get out
of bed. I'm talking about seeming to run out of prospects. But, this week, we pulled
several cubic feet of rock from our yard. Now the soil is ready to receive pole beans a
friend gifted me last summer, beans from a line of seed passed on by survivors since
the 1838 Trail of Tears. Soon, I will make a space in my garden for something that will
look, by autumn, like edible hope.

I'm getting ahead of myself. Working the land, I am always losing track of a
linear concept of time. What happens today is fed by what I did yesterday. What I
reap in the fall will recollect decisions made by the likes of Dr John Wyche—the man
who began to send out these heirloom Cherokee seeds to whomever showed interest
and sent postage—in a decade I was nearly too small to remember and which my
daughter calls the olden days.

If we were to start from the start, where would that take us? Black-eyed peas, a
staple food in West Africa, made the journey with enslaved people from that continent
into the American South. In their book, *In the Shadow of Slavery: Africa's Botanical
Legacy in the Atlantic World*, scholars Judith Carney and Richard Nicholas Rosomoff
tell us that these same people used the stimulating kola nut to manage the fetid water
they were given on slavers' ships. Later, that nut would make a key ingredient for
Coca-Cola. When I speak about garden-variety crops in this country, I nearly always
point toward simultaneous legacies of trauma and triumph. Watermelon, sorghum,
millet, sesame seed, rice: none of these would be what they are in America were it not
for the centuries of human trafficking we call the slave trade. The stories I've received
tell me some ancestor must have kept seed for okra in her hair through the long trial

of the Middle Passage and onto, then *into*, American soil. She must have secured raw peanuts in an unsearched scrap of cloth she kept near her body. Peanuts, like pole beans, like black-eyed peas, are both food and seed. You can eat them for power today or plant them for abundance tomorrow. People who came long before us carried the source of a new kind of flourishing through desolation most of us care not to fully comprehend. If I say my garden's story starts with the planting of a seed, to which seed am I referring?

I remember the first garden I planted as a married woman. It wasn't much to speak of, neither the garden nor the house in whose yard it was sown. The garden was a way to help me feel rooted in a place where we were struggling to begin our new life. I planted a few, sturdy starts: marigolds and nasturtium. I put in zucchini, mostly for the riot of its bright blossoms. I kept an artichoke for the same reason. The thistle flower delighted me, though it attracted an army of ants that quickly moved the artichoke beyond the possibility of human consumption.

Even if I had managed to harvest anything during our brief season in that house, I shouldn't have trusted the food that dirt produced. Fumes from the nearby freeway drifted over us all night and all day. Anytime they were touched, flakes of paint flew from the Victorian duplex's exterior walls. Soil tests in the area have revealed lead levels hundreds of parts per million above what is deemed to be safe, and I hadn't built raised beds. Still, I wanted to witness a plan come into fruition. I planted seeds, I planted starts, I watered, and I weeded, and I watched. I could say that my efforts were futile, but I won't. There had been little but dirt in that yard before I started digging. For the few months we lived in that house, we got to walk outside each day and appreciate a kind of flowering.

Not too long ago, I shared a few hours with a Salvadoran poet who walked across the desert into the US when he was nine years old. There is a great deal of hardship in his story. The landscapes he's walked across have delivered incredible pain. And yet, as we talked about the importance of writers of color celebrating the living world, he found himself recalling his grandmother's garden. There was joy there, he insisted. He wouldn't let his charge to document suffering stop him from recalling this pleasure.

There is sustaining power to be generated from claiming even complicated beauty as a peace we are entitled to enjoy.

Once, as I dug in dirt contaminated with legacy pollutants, a local nursery's discounted flowers in their black plastic pots nearby, a woman from the neighborhood stopped to watch me. Why would I bother to tend such a yard, she wanted to know. I remember feeling angry that she didn't believe our block, our rented house, deserved such a demonstration of care. I know it might take a lot of work, I told her, but I want to grow something beautiful.

On the property of Thomas Jefferson's retreat home, Poplar Forest, archeologists have discovered caches of food that give insight into the diet of the enslaved men and women who lived on that property. The very produce of the earth has provided a lasting record of who on that land had what type of access, autonomy and power.

The list of foods found in the storage pits reveals the epidemic of deprivation endemic to the institution of slavery—but it also reveals the strategies of a people insistent on nourishing themselves.

Archeological studies suggest that the people at Poplar Forest grew corn in their gardens. They probably grew sunflowers, mint, sweet potatoes, and violets. They might have grown the violets and sunflowers as ornamentals, but just as likely, they were using them for food. The violets could be a kind of replacement for okra and greens. Even the ornamental plants around the quarters were provisions the people who tended the land could eat. I like to think that the people appreciated looking at these plants as much as they appreciated knowing they could depend on them for physical sustenance when need arose. Archeologists have found the remains of wheat, oats, rye, sumac, blackberry, purslane, pigweed, poppies, and more. The people raised chickens, whose eggs they could sell, which they also might have done with some of the other produce from their gardens. But Jefferson made sure his son-in-law "put an end to the cultivation of tobacco" by the people he called property, who were growing it in their gardens. "There is no other way of drawing a line between what is theirs and mine," Jefferson admitted in a letter, than to forbid these men and women from growing for personal use the same crops they cultivated in his fields. Don't think I don't have histories like this in mind when I insist on growing what I please in the soil that surrounds me. There is power to be generated from cultivating whatever might sustain me, in whatever way I wish.

I grow sunflowers and sweet potatoes in my own garden. I plant what plants I desire, and I harvest or not as I choose. I grow mint and tolerate the purslane people these days tend to weed. As we learn in Lucille Clifton's poem "mulberry fields", sometimes unmastered growth reveals what it is our land most dearly needs. I grow poppies and let the wild violets flourish, for, through their flowering, time will progress.

It's been nearly a decade since I dug in the particular patch of dirt our neighbor questioned, but I still regularly encounter incredulity when I talk about coaxing beauty out of the legacy pollutants that haunt us every day. Not too long ago, a woman asked me how I could fancy myself an environmental writer when I write so much about African American history.

For a breath or two, I was speechless. I'm not sure I understand how it would be possible to talk about history without taking into account the environment out of which our history springs.

Living in the body I live in, I can't help but see the direct implications, the devastating implications, of the erasure of certain histories. When you dismiss lives from the record, you put those lives in jeopardy. There is a reason that freeways were so frequently run through one part of town (the black part of town) and not others. The reason is because the lives and the property of those who lived in that part of town were not valued as highly as others. The pollution of that indifference persists in the very ground people walk on today. Writing about the environment is a necessary political decision, just as finding a way to beautify the patch of dirt we called home was a necessity in that first house my husband and I shared. It is also why, once the ants announced their interest in the artichoke, I let them enjoy its substance while I settled for appreciating its splendor. I was not dependent on that artichoke for its nutritional value, and if my point is to see to it that things around me thrive, sharing with ants could be part of this goal. I refuse to take part in the segregation of the imagination that assigns greater value to some experiences than it assigns to others. If there is to be a flourishing that I can cultivate, I want its reach to be wide.

In our current yard, near where I'll grow the Cherokee Trail of Tears pole beans, there is some rhubarb that has greeted me each spring since we moved into this house. Rhubarb is a tricky plant, scorned by many but by others fiercely loved. The nontoxic stems of the plant are fibrous and nutritious, containing useful medicinal characteristics. For our contemporary taste, these stems are bitter. We typically add quite a bit of sugar to help the medicine go down, converting what might be considered a vegetable into something we use in simple syrups, cakes, and pies. Who were the people who put in this rhubarb? There is nothing else like it in the yard. The people who lived here before us poured river rock over most of the other patches that might have made a garden. But the rhubarb, in its three-square-foot bed, comes back each year to remind me of something. What? Where there appears to be only dirt, there may be the root system of some kind of insistent thriving.

I never know how much I need to see that rhubarb unfurling until it begins to unfurl. Rhubarb may lack the power to cure what truly ails this world, but, I am thankful, it brings me back to the recognition of wonder and of beauty; and that is not a gift to be dismissed. This year, for the first time, the rhubarb burst into flower. The many-headed bracts look like ten thousand snowflakes held firm on summer branches. I am supposed to lop off the flower heads to encourage the edible stalks to keep growing. They'll go dormant sooner if I leave these bold bids for pollination, and the plant will be of no practical use to me. But these enormous flowers are so lovely. I find it practical, as a matter of survival, to seek evidence of the wild wonder of the world. In this summer's full blooming, it's as if the joy I glean in this garden has erupted over every inch of my life.

Aida Edemariam

Ethiopian and Canadian, she grew up in Addis Ababa, Ethiopia, and now lives in Oxford, England. She studied English literature at Oxford University and at the University of Toronto, and has worked as a journalist in New York, Toronto and London, where she is currently a senior feature writer and editor for The Guardian. *She is a recipient of the Royal Society of Literature Jerwood Award for a work of non-fiction in progress, which was published in 2018 as* The Wife's Tale: A Personal History, *a memoir of her Ethiopian grandmother. The book was also a finalist for a Governor General's Literary Award for Nonfiction.*

Seven types of water

1.

A honeycomb of rooms, filled with steam. Tiled steps up to long low baths that in their gracious lines still held remnants of luxury and ease. Stripping, wallowing in water that arrived so hot out of the ground the main job was to cool it, splashing, shouting, setting off echoes. Here where nearly a hundred years before an empress had pitched her tent on a lush plain and turning to her rheumatic husband asked, may I build a house, here? Another, there, under that mimosa tree? And a palace, too? Bathing, here where the city began, because while there was plenty of rain, and the hot springs seeped from the earth as they always had, in the taps in our houses there was no water.

2.

Rain. High dark clouds massing, or already massed and already here. Walls of grey water moving across the horizon; a grey front chasing us down the street. The first drops—hard, singular, spreading into dark patches on dry ground. Drops doubling, tripling, hitting faster and faster until the roofs were a-roar with them. Rain running in the gutters, in the sewers, finding every nook and undefended cranny, rivers in the street. Rain to collect in cans, to heat on the stove, to wash in.

3.

Two hours, three, south of the city, pushing at the limits of available petrol, rationed and thus saved up for weeks. Under an archway and more hot springs, a long green pool surrounded by green. Steam curling across its surface, rising into the early morning. Bodies glistening, turning to catch the flow from communal showers directed out of a wall of rock. Bodies easing into the green, beginning to swim, vigorous, then slowed almost at once by the deep warmth of the water.

Playing, then, or drifting and twisting, limbs freed, faces blinking in the sun as it crests the trees.

4.

Another Olympic pool, in the city this time, not far from the springs where the capital began. A deeper green, and cooler, and thus exercise possible, especially in the early mornings or in the middle of the day, before schoolchildren, daunted by the full length of the pool, begin to fight themselves across its width, getting in the way. Or the later afternoon when young men, daring each other even when they seem not to be, begin to climb to the top of the fixed ten-metre diving board, so many steps in the ladder missing that the risk is as much in the going up, the possible fall backwards onto concrete, as in the dive itself. Once up, they divide into those who stride forward, bounce a little on the balls of their feet, then arc head first through blue air, and those who pause, making a performance of nonchalance: looking around at the ring of mountains, back toward the Jubilee palace, or forward, toward the football stadium and the asphalted expanses of Revolution Square. And then, finally, a jump, feet first, a flapping beat or two and a shouting, crashing entry into water so thick green, so deep, that looking for the bottom with one's feet feels distinctly ill-advised.

5.

Leaving the city, down a lorry and fume-filled road. Hawkers of guava, of sugar cane, of guava again. Dust and sun and thorns. And lakes. Old lakes, perfectly round, sides like inverted cones, gathering to a point in the middle, far under the water. Small boys swimming, or fishing for their supper where, some said, a plumb line, dropped, had simply kept dropping, and never found a place to rest.

6.

Airborne, and below, after the city, after the fields, after the rivers and the gorges, another lake—a vast brown mirror, blazing the sun back into the sky. The reflection of the twin-engined plane a dark dragonfly flitting across the shifting surface, the reed boats hugging the outer shores, the wooded islands and their quiet monasteries. And back to fields, a palette of greens and golds and browns sloping up, away from the umber lake, to a smaller city, its tall sycamores, and its castles.

7.

The day we left, a hailstorm. It arrived like the rain, with the same sense of gathered, delayed speed, but the impact was far harder; each ball of ice bouncing, then bouncing again, then clattering away. The path a forest of crenellations disappearing as soon as they were created. Hail as big as pulled molars ripping through the gladioli and geraniums, tearing the ferns, stopping up the spaces between the blades of grass and dancing down the pathway. Bobbing in the rivers that rushed past the rosemary bush until it stilled into glaciers, wide runs of pockmarked, granular ice.

Esi Edugyan

A Canadian novelist of Ghanaian heritage, she is author of three novels: The Second
Life of Samuel Tyne *(2004);* Half-Blood Blues *(2011), which won the Scotiabank
Giller Prize, and was a finalist for the Man Booker Prize, the Governor-General's
Literary Award, the Rogers Writers' Trust Fiction Prize, and the Orange Prize; and*
Washington Black *(2018), which also won the Scotiabank Giller Prize, and was
shortlisted for the Man Booker Prize, the Rogers Writers' Trust Fiction Prize, and
the 2019 Andrew Carnegie Medal for Excellence in Fiction. In 2014, she published
her first book of non-fiction,* Dreaming of Elsewhere: Observations on Home. *She
lives in Victoria, British Columbia with her husband and two children.*

The Wrong Door: Some Meditations on Solitude and Writing

I.

It is among the most fabled interruptions in literature: after an opium-induced
reverie, Samuel Taylor Coleridge regained his senses to discover that an entire poem
had written itself within his subconscious. It was one of those stunning and rare
visitations—the whole and complete knowledge of a work—and with great urgency
he sat at his desk to transcribe what had already been fully expressed within him. He
had just written down the fifty-fourth line of the poem when there came a knock at the
door: a person, come on business from nearby Porlock. The man would detain him
more than an hour; and when Coleridge was finally left alone again, his recollections
had completely vanished. He retained only the gist of the poem—a vague assembly
of words, a wavering idea—a few scattered lines, the rest, as he put it, "passed away
like the images on the surface of a stream into which a stone has been cast."

And so the great "Kubla Khan" was destroyed at the very moment of its making.

Except it probably didn't happen like that. Coleridge himself was known to
embroider and invent—the crucial letter from "a friend," for instance, that interrupts
the eighth chapter of his *Biographia Literaria* was in fact written by the author
himself. In the case of our person from Porlock, some scholars have suggested that
Coleridge merely invented him to explain away the fragmentary nature of his great
poem. Yet whether a bogey, an unexpected occurrence, or an actual flesh-and-blood
man, every writer fears these "People from Porlock"—which is to say, we fear the
sudden, thought-scattering disruptions that hurt our work. Indeed, these days such
disruptions seem the rule. One wants to board up the doors and dim the lights; one
wants to drop the blinds, bind the shutters and mount a sign at the entrance saying,
"The Wrong Door."

Silence necessarily plays a large role in creation. Privacy is something other than
silence, but is its near relative, I believe. Such notions may seem straightforward, at

first glance. But in a world where our ideas of self-hood and privacy are ever-shifting, an examination of their role in creation seems valuable.

The *Oxford English Dictionary* defines silence as "the state or condition when nothing is audible; [the] absence of all noise and sound; muteness; taciturnity." For the artist, I would add that silence is the state of being deep within oneself; it is the act of cutting out externals so that one may hear the internal. In this way, to greater and lesser degrees, Coleridge's reverie is how all art gets made. We open a door within ourselves and leave it open, so that the unexpected and the unknown may fill us. I realize this nears the language of the sacred; but that seems fitting, as there is something of the sacrosanct in the act of writing. We take what is percolating and unformed, and through some mysterious process turn the void into utterance. The word "lost" is derived from the Old Norse word "los", which literally means the disbanding of an army. This strikes me as the perfect metaphor for writing. We must break away from those we know, and go away alone, to lose ourselves in the unknown and miraculous.

II.

There is a second kind of solitude—a solitude other than the silence we carve out for ourselves amidst the roar of the greater world. It is needed if an artist is to stand behind his work, even in the face of the fiercest attacks. It is the solitude of certainty.

In a recent essay on silence, the novelist Shirley Hazzard tells a wonderful story that speaks to this necessity. To paraphrase: in 1572, the Renaissance artist Paolo Veronese was called before the Holy Office at Venice to defend himself against charges of blasphemy. He had painted a picture of the Last Supper, and along with the usual figures we expect to see in such a work, he had included random people in the background, dawdlers and loafers, men rambling by. There were people thoughtlessly scratching themselves, people with horrifying deformities, a man staggering with a nosebleed. These images, it was charged, had no place in a sacred painting.

Asked why he would depict such things, the artist replied: "I thought these things might happen."

It hardly seems a viable defense, but as an artistic statement it is enormously resonant. Veronese, in his few words, was arguing for the idea that the principal role of art is to depict the world at hand faithfully, and this includes what is unsavoury and ugly. Anything less than this is hagiography, or caricature.

If it is true that every reader has a favourite book, it is equally true that every book has a favourite reader. We write for everyone and fail to please across the board. And as artists, we must make our peace with the idea that this is alright; that in fact it is a welcome sign that we have challenged people, at least in the comfort of their sensibilities. *I thought these things might happen*, and so I wrote about them as faithfully as I could. This place of conviction can sometimes be lonely, but the work is all the truer for it.

III.

Privacy is something else again. It is interesting to note that the Chinese word that may come closest to the English word privacy, Si, means selfish. And indeed, there is that quality to it, a turning inward that is necessarily a rejection of others, the uncompromised protection of a sphere of silence from the violating whims of others. In our era of Twitter, Facebook and Instagram, notions of privacy are being shaped and reshaped by the hour, with some arguing that we live in a post-privacy world. The Internet yields all sorts of knowledge we are no better off for knowing.

The German futurist and film critic Christian Heller found himself relinquishing everything to this brave new world: he created a live site in which every quotidian detail of his existence was relayed online. "Privacy as a guaranteed personal space free from outside view is shrinking," he explained. "Long-term privacy will survive only as an exception, as a special case in everyday life." It was his belief that our only recourse is to confront the loss of privacy directly. One could read about what he ate that morning, how long it took him to get to work, et cetera. There were even links to his bank accounts, in which all his personal financial data was available for viewing. It was a staggering act of public intimacy, and like all long intimacies, gradually yielded to a wearying sense of banality.

I would argue that, above every other intrusion and interruption, it is a loss of privacy that has the greatest ability to destroy an artist. The knock at the door; the boiled-over kettle; the newborn's cry—for most (not Coleridge, of course), these interruptions are all surmountable because they are fleeting. They are nothing when compared with the irrevocable loss of a much-needed private sphere of creation.

I think it would come as a surprise to most readers to learn that most writers in their middle to late careers regard with nostalgia their days of obscurity. I remember being puzzled when a writing professor sat us down and told us to savour our collegiate days, because our motives for writing would never again be this pure. We dismissed her as jaded, and longed for the days when we would see our words bound and prominently displayed in the local bookstore.

How frustrated we were by that advice! So much of her meaning seemed to reflect her own anxieties over reviews and prize nominations. But I understand now too that what she was speaking of was a certain lack of privacy, a certain public spotlight that can begin to erode not only our artistic confidence but even motive, the very impetus for writing in the first place. I have spoken to a German writer who after publishing an international bestseller thirteen years ago struggles to write, paralyzed by the idea of tarnishing his own reputation with an unlikeable follow-up. I have spoken to an American writer who was so badly shamed for an extra-literary occurrence that she cannot bring herself to enter again the public sphere. All of these tragedies are tragedies of exposure, and they speak to the very fundamental need for an area of silence, a room of, yes, one's own.

As an extreme example, consider the fate of Elena Ferrante. The pseudonymous author of the Neapolitan novels takes as her subject the friendship between two bright girls in the harsh and limiting world of 1950's Italy. The novels are brash and intelligent and full of knowing and utterly authentic situations. All of this creativity was taking place under the dome of the most strict obscurity—the only thing the public knew about Ferrante was that she was likely a woman, and even that was unverifiable. In the very few interviews she had given, Ferrante had suggested that her very anonymity was crucial to her artistic process. Only under the cover of a pseudonym did she feel liberated enough to write with honesty. Said Ferrante, via an email interview published in *Paris Review* in 2015:

> Once I knew that the book would make its way in the world without me, once I knew that nothing of the concrete, physical me would ever appear beside the volume—as if the book were a little dog and I were its master—it made me see something new about writing. I felt as though I had released the words from myself.

Then, in the fall of 2016, the dreaded knock came at the door, in the form of a journalist called Claudio Gatti. In an investigative feat that enraged many, he revealed the likely author of the Neapolitan novels to be a Rome-based translator, with some probable input from her novelist husband. Gatti was said to have been blindsided and shocked by the vehemence of the public's reaction. He claimed he believed he was doing a public good, as Ferrante was slated to release a slim volume of memoirs that fall, which he had now revealed for a lie. Instead, he was castigated and jeered at on social media, cast unrecognizably to himself as the Person from Porlock, a lumbering, unthinking agent of creative destruction.

It is hard to know what to make of this man, Gatti. If he is sincere, then what he failed to understand was that the public had already consented to be lied to long ago. Indeed, the social contract between Ferrante and her readers was such that we accepted her constructed identity with all its attendant untruths. She had never claimed to have been born Elena Ferrante; we did not hold her to the fixity of that identity; we allowed her the fluidity to be what she needed to be. Where, in her relentless silence, we heard a voice—a true, authentic voice—Gatti saw only that last, curious definition of silence, "taciturnity," as if there were some personal spite in her desire to remain out of the public eye. Perhaps the greatest revelation to come out of the controversy was the frightening realization of how far we have come from our cultural consensus that privacy is a fundamental right.

Given the way of the world now, how do we best find quietude and preserve it? Survival lies, I think, in understanding the varieties of solitude, knowing what is available to us, and what is out of our hands. It is in accepting that the void is sometimes an echo chamber, and knowing it will pass. It is trusting that the silence still exists, out there beyond the spectacle, and that despite the noise the words are still in us, waiting to be made whole.

Zetta Elliott

Born in Canada, she moved to the US in 1994 to pursue her PhD in American Studies at NYU. She is the award-winning author of over 30 books for young readers. Her poetry has been published in We Rise, We Resist, We Raise Our Voices, *the Cave Canem anthology* The Ringing Ear: Black Poets Lean South, Check the Rhyme: an Anthology of Female Poets and Emcees, *and* Coloring Book: an Eclectic Anthology of Fiction and Poetry by Multicultural Writers. *"Women Like Us" is from her young adult poetry collection,* Say Her Name, *which is being published in 2019 by Disney/Hyperion.*

Women Like Us

Grandma couldn't kiss me and all her meals went through the blender because of the drug that once ran through her veins. Her kisses, puckerless and wet, were pressed with force but filled with love. Grandma couldn't kiss or chew, but her stories didn't cease. She passed on what she wanted preserved—tales told deliberately and arranged like the orderly jars of pulpy tomatoes she canned for future consumption.

Her brokenness embarrassed her but I hope she knew she was not to blame, that the darkness living inside of her was a curse *and* a blessing—an insistent invitation to seek refuge, towithdraw and find relief from pain's blinding glare.

I wish I had known at sixteen that I wasn't the first in our family to slide into the abyss. Over time I learned how to find my way out, buoyed by borrowed hope and the same frantic energy that wrung my grandmother's gnarled hands. In the abyss I find respite from the everyday hustle that grinds me down. I grind my teeth down with worry but when the darkness envelops me, I sleep with total surrender. When I wake, anxiety insists I get up and record my dreams. This is my uneasy balance.

There were some stories Grandma kept to herself. Years after her death, I learned my grandmother was a survivor. I hope it wasn't shame that censored her. I hope she knew I wouldn't have loved her less.

They say the dead never die so long as we speak their names; I proudly bear hers. I hope my grandmother knows that I am not ashamed of this inheritance.

I know what it cost a woman in her position to ask for help. She wanted to live with less pain. She charged me with telling our story.

Women like us may be wounded, but we can also heal. Women like us are not disposable. Women like us must testify.

Last Visit with Mary

trees outlive us
unless we cut them down
or a beetle determined like me
makes its way across the sea

walking the quiet streets
I'm reminded of my mother's
gated neighborhood and how I
always wonder which resident
will smile and which will scowl
at me

for breakfast I order
tea and a Bakewell tart
it takes longer to arrive
than the meals of other patrons

meanwhile Mary rests in her bed
slumber a respite from battling
the tumor taking up
too much space inside of her
and only yesterday I spoke
with Adrienne about gentrification
I'm the thin edge of the wedge
I told her
leaving Brooklyn to
try my luck in Philly
for the first time I'll be able to afford
a 2BR apartment—one room to sleep in
and another to write

you took an interest in me
and for that I am grateful
words I wrote in a card so Mary would know
the truth pitiful as it makes me feel
I'm not interesting to my own
but the universe has gifted me
other mothers who ask after my health
and read all my books and
question my career choices and
congratulate me when my decisions
bear fruit, no matter how small or sour

Christine sits in the sunroom
Mary once was her tutor and then
they became great friends
it's a comfort to Mary and to me
that she is so close by within
sight within reach within
earshot
Mary's still sleeping despite the whir
of a neighbor's saw and the visiting
nurse is due sometime today
but still there's that small prick of dread
what if what if what if

with the oak tree before me
I think of my father and
the shameful relief that came when
he went back into the hospital
becoming someone else's responsibility
so I didn't have to worry for one
night, maybe two

Jasmine is in Hastings with her
kids and her husband a survivor himself
bare feet scrambling over sliding rocks
to slip into the icy sea
for her, that same relief
respite for one
night, maybe two

and yesterday Adrienne took
me to lunch before heading to her
aunt's 80th birthday party
pancreatic cancer will claim her
too but for now they bought rose
bushes and planted them
in her garden

perhaps roses will outlive us too

5/26/18

Diana Evans

*A British writer and critic, born in London to a Nigerian mother and English father,
she is the author of the novels* 26a *(2005),* The Wonder *(2009) and* Ordinary People
(2018), with prize nominations that include the Whitbread First Novel (2005), The
Guardian *First Book, the Commonwealth Best First Book awards (2006), and the
Andrew Carnegie medal for Excellence in Fiction (2018). She has been a deciBel
Writer of the Year winner at the British Book Awards (2006) and was the inaugural
winner of the Orange Award for New Writers (2006). She holds an MA in Creative
Writing from the University of East Anglia and was a Royal Literary Fellow at the
London College of Fashion and the University of Kent. She lives in London.*

Thunder

"I'm going out," she said.

"Where?"

"To post a letter."

"We haven't finished talking."

"I don't want to talk anymore. We've talked about all of this before. I think half
our problem is we've talked too much. We've killed ourselves with words."

There were roses dying in the streets. It was early September, an angry summer.
Some days it rained and the wind was cold, others the heat lashed down, a violence
from above. On the high street there were groups of girls in their freedom clothes,
out of uniform. In the summer they found themselves, they were more, almost
frightening, the force of their lives. She remembered feeling like that.

She was wearing a long thin coat of a dark blue, which waved around her ankles. She had never liked revealing her shape. It was what Gene had liked about her in the beginning, how unexpected she was, in her warmth, her richness, the secrecy in her folds. Her hair was tied back, her lonely face jutting out into the world with all its difficult bravery.

Nowadays the people who worked in post offices always asked whether you wanted standard or special post. They were trained that way, to miss out the middle option, recorded. They made more money like that, but it was dishonest. She asked for recorded (it was a letter to her father, telling him she and Gene were separating; he would take it more easily with a letter, that they were separating even though they had never married). Then they ask if you want to open a post-office account, buy some envelopes, any currency. She pitied them. The cashier was a bald man in a white shirt in the late years of his working life. Money, the thirst for money, had charged the air with desperation. He couldn't do anything about it. He asked all the questions he was told to ask.

The road was thick with traffic. She hated it, the thunder of London, like an earthquake. She had wanted them to go and live with the children at the edge of Ankara, where she was born. She came here when she was nine, with her parents who were medical students. The country had never left her—the crooked horizon, the red hill behind the house, the unquestioning sky, the school classroom with its aisles of benches. She often thought of herself as still sitting on one of those benches, waiting for the next instruction, the next transference of knowledge. Here her mind did not retain things. She did not remember numbers or facts the way she used to. Knowledge slipped over her like a river going backwards. But she knew how she felt.

A white lorry paused in the road, its wheels like canons. She looked back once and felt a spot of rain on her forehead.

It had been like this for almost a year. He still loved her but love was incidental. They had decided to be together for the children, on the surface. Neither could give up the sight of one of them emerging from sleep in the morning, a dream still in their faces, drawing them back, into the lightness of their consciousness. There was a girl and a boy. She was sensible, a little nervous, occasional asthma. He was brash, more sure of himself than anyone they had ever known. They were both shy people, and they wondered where this confidence had come from. Was it that Asya had made him think of himself as a king, that he never bowed, for anyone? In this country they teach children to be afraid, of themselves and of the world, she said. And when I came here I became afraid like everyone else. You have never really known me, she told Gene. That's why it's never going to work. It never began, not as far as I'm concerned.

Gene stands in the living-room, looking out at the burning roses. Upstairs there is music playing. He is a stout man, thickly built, strong. He used to lift her off the bed after lovemaking, her legs wrapped around him, they would go to the window and see the cemetery where she liked to walk, observing the stones. He had felt like the maker of the earth, as if everything belonged to him, or at least, as if he had access to everything. There were no obstructions anymore. Love freed him from himself.

He met her in a church. She was walking out into the sun, it was winter, and he was walking in, looking for peace, which he saw instantly in her face, so immediately that he had to stop her. He said, "Where are you going?"

"Where am I going?" she said.

"Sorry. It's just that I feel like I know you."

Then she looked at him, studied him, frowning. A softer moment happened in her face, a little laugh.

She said, "You don't know me," and walked away, and he spent the longest week of his life hoping to come across her. He vowed never again to let a fundamental mystery go, no matter the humiliation of catching it. Embrace the light and hold it close when it finds its way to you. The next time he saw her he asked her to marry him and she said no.

Now the girl came into the room. Olivia. She had long braids and was wearing her mother's lipstick. He grabbed her and picked her up. "What's that paint on your face? Better wash your face this minute!" She tried to wriggle free but he was too strong for her. She suddenly flipped over so that she was upside down, the top of her head touching the carpet. You're the angel in my life, he told her most days, sometimes only in his head, if she had made him angry or if he was too tired to tell them of his heart. They demanded so much of him, their health, their souls, their security, their future, it was not always possible to make sure they knew that they were cherished. Especially now, that the love that had spawned them was dissipating, turning into ether. It terrified him, the absence of it. His freedom on the brink of return. To be faced again with himself, that dark image, that trouble. To walk on the common ground again like all the others, like beetles, looking for themselves, or a way out.

In the astrological twilight she had offered her lips to him, hungry. He melted in her magic. He gave her everything, his legs, his heat, his faith, his riches. Nights fell gently over Canning Town.

On this Thursday in the afternoon of the third decade of her life with the rain just beginning she stepped into the road as the lorry was turning. She was thinking that at the end of something there is a gift to salvage from the wreckage. There is a jewel, glowing out, a particular memory that makes a good carriage. And she was thinking of the glittered hours when the children were born and that this might be the carriage, that waking in the morning to the quiet snow and the lifting of the child for the first time, how these things will endure.

The big left-hand mirror flashed and blinded for a moment. A confusion of direction, a curse.

And last April, when she had walked the gorge in Crete, the mountains and cliffs heavenward on either side of her. The rocks and clear brooks and flat wooden bridges. Returning to Gene and the children in the hotel in the evening with the sun burning down, a swelling above the road. They had eaten dinner off silver trays on the terrace in the music of a man with a guitar.

Death did not warn her. It plucked her swiftly from the earth with no explanation, no reason. You disappear. You are a sudden small history lying in the road.

Gene is standing before the mirror, holding the woman's hair in his left hand, the scissors in his right. He cuts two inches. A black cloud falls to the floor.

"I don't want any off the top," the woman says. "Just trim it at the bottom, let it fall and meet."

She is a tiny woman. She tells him she has three children and he cannot imagine a pregnancy at her body, narrow, like a girl. He scans the women in this way; it is mostly women who come to him. There are frightened women, aspiring women, urgent women, women who cook for their husbands ("he won't eat if I don't feed him"), women who have been alone for centuries. They come to straighten their hair, curl it, blow-dry it, set it. To emerge from his door on to the street outside more brilliant, armoured by a temporary, nebulous beauty. He likes their company.

"My son is fourteen, my daughter is seventeen. They have to help clean the house or they're not going out. Simple as that."

There is a sharp tone in his voice when he speaks of them, a mixture of pride, compassion and disgust. He has spent all the years with them, so much time, it is impossible to separate that time from himself. He is the father, in the street, in the salon, in the house. He is one voice, one life. He has never had Asya's problem, that desire to preserve oneself, to keep a part of yourself safe from everything, from the intrusions of duty. Her absence has left questions over their lives. He has tried to teach them to be whole and present in the storm, to be strong right through.

"My daughter has very long hair," he says. "I plait it for her. Almost to her waist."

"She's lucky. A man who knows hair. You can teach her," the woman says.

He is thick around the middle now, rounder, but still strong. The muscles in his arms swell as he works. She has soft, natural hair, thinning at the temples. It is the activity, the art of it that he loves. You cut a dimensional shape, according to the face. You manipulate and arrange. The use of water, raining away the previous formation and giving way to another. He has looked at so many faces in the glass and witnessed the secret expressions of disappointment. It has always seemed important to him to enable the power of aesthetic beauty to bring a blanket to the continual problem of facing the world and carrying oneself through it.

"I didn't have a choice," he says, cutting another row. "Their mother died. She was run over. She went to post a letter and never came back."

The woman turns her head towards him slightly, to see his face. It is excruciating to him when they move even just a little. They must stay absolutely still.

"That's horrible," she says. "God."

He draws over a stool. At eye level he can achieve a perfect line. He thinks of Asya lying in the road. She is covered in a dark grey blanket, her left hand pummelled by the mighty wheel. He has wondered for years about her last thoughts, and where she went afterwards. Was it to a cool place or a hot place? She had believed in the concept of heaven and hell, and that your entrance is determined not by whether you have been good or bad, but whether you have manifested yourself, whether you have lived as the person you were intended to be, or whether you have lost your way and listened too closely to other voices. It didn't matter if you had not reached your full potential. That was beside the point. It was more to do with whether you were on the right path. Were you trying?

Olivia would stand by the window waiting for her, the long blue coat, the concentrating face. Whenever the doorbell rang she ran into the hall. In the end Gene dismantled the bell. People had to knock at the window instead. He missed deliveries that way, and had to keep going to the post office.

He is overcome now by a sea of tiredness. He wants to lean his head on the woman's small shoulder. He feels old as mountains, heavy as Jupiter. The red leaves of autumn are swirling in the street.

Deise Faria Nunes

Born in Porto Alegre, Brazil, she grew up near the border between Brazil and Uruguay. She discovered a passion for dance and traditional performance during her childhood participation in Carnival, and this was her earliest experience of artistic expression. In the mid-1980s, her family moved to Pelotas, where she studied electro-engineering, though her dream was to work in the arts. In 1999 she moved to Norway, where she freelanced as a performer, while studying literature, theatre and performance at the University of Oslo, going on to an apprenticeship at Odin Teatret in Holstebro, Denmark. She has since worked in theatre in Norway as a performer, producer, dramaturge, teacher and critic. In 2017 she established her company Golden Mirrors Arts Norway, focusing on black women in the arts, culture and politics.

The person in the boat

Some fellowships we do not choose: we are born into them. Others we walk voluntarily into, with our eyes wide open, even though we do not know what will meet us on the other side.

In the pantheistic, Afro-Brazilian religion *Candomblé Ketu*, with roots in West Africa, the initiation rites are so transformative that the whole process is seen as a new birth. The person being initiated is isolated in the temple, where s/he performs several rituals, led by priests and helpers. The process may last up to several months. The initiation is never individual, and the groups of novices are called *boats*. In a *Candomblé* temple—or *terreiro*—the members might say about each other: "I know her well. We were on the same boat." Then it is understood that these two people were initiated together.

One may be led to join a religious fellowship like *Candomblé* for many different reasons. Whatever the reason, it is a choice that means the devotee shall dedicate their life to the religion, and that the *Orishas*—a pantheon of sixteen dancing anthropomorphic gods and goddesses who reign over the forces of nature—will decide one's destiny in the near and remote future. There is no way of undoing an initiation—it is a decision for life.

I grew up in the time right after the twenty-one-year-long military dictatorship in Brazil. I believed in freedom and equality, not in inexplicable hierarchies where the gods and the fellowship created in their name rule over the individual. But I knew *Candomblé* was a part of my family history, so I wanted to go and see, I wanted to be there to challenge all my perspectives: the superstitious, Afro-syncretic, Catholic, South-American perspective from my upbringing; the politically awakened, freedom seeking and power challenging perspective from my youth, which had become coloured by the secular, sober, North-European way of thinking I had been exposed to after living in Scandinavia for nearly ten years.

As a child, I was told stories of deities.

I called it earth
They called it *Nana Buruku*
The eldest woman.
I called it a tree
They called it *Iroko*
The ravages of time.
I called it fire
They called it *Shango*
The lord of thunder.
I called it wind

They called it *Yansan*
The woman who dances with the dead.
I called it water
They called it *Oshun*
The river's body.
I called it sea
They called it *Yemanjá*
The mother of all fish.
I said: nobody owns the forest
They said: the forest belongs to *Oshosi*
The constant hunter.
I called it air
They called it *Obatala*
The wine loving sculptor.

I was thirty-six years old the first time I arrived at a place called Gantois, a hill in the heart of Brazil's black capital, Salvador. Gantois is the home of one of the best-known terreiros *in the country. I came alone. The ritual that night was dedicated to the creator god,* Obatala, *meaning that everyone was supposed to wear white from top to toe.*

The big ceremony room was full of people. The beautiful wooden floor was covered with leaves. Some of those in attendance were initiated in the religion, others not. The so-called open rituals are just as the name suggests, open, and they attract many people, both from the neighbourhood and around the world. The doors are open throughout the entire event and people can go in and out freely.

Three drums were placed at the rear of the space. As the main ritual instruments, they were embellished with white ribbons and green leaves. The biggest drum is called rum, *the middle sized one,* rumpi, *and the smallest one,* lé. *By the drums is a chair, also adorned with flowers and white cotton fabric: it is the seat of the temple's leader, the priestess often called* Yá *or* mãe *(mother). Behind her, a door that leads to the private rooms in the temple, where the rituals are prepared.*

We would soon move back in time. The drums would play the sacred, ancient rhythms and the deities would be called down. By possessing the body-mind of a few, well prepared ritual participants the gods and goddesses would enter the room to dance—both alone and with each other—and dramatically re-enact mythological tales, using specific costumes and objects.

The fellowship's highest values lie in the collective adoration of the gods. Is there a place for the individual in this context?

The people being initiated are divided in different categories, and the ritual varies accordingly, even if they are in the same boat. The categories are determined by the organizational structure of the religion and encompass several functions: some are helpers, some are chefs, some are musicians, some make tools for agriculture, hunting, fishing or slaughtering, some are butchers, some take care of plants, mixtures and teas. And some are mediums—the channels used by the deities to visit Earth. No matter their function, everyone has "their" god or goddess, who indicates their destiny through different sorts of oracles. The leader *Yá* possesses the knowledge to read the oracles. According to the North American theatre director and scholar Richard Schechner's thoughts on performance, ritual is not *self-assertive*, meaning it does not affirm the self; it is *self-transcendent*, it reaches beyond the self (*Performance Theory*. London: Routledge, p. 17. 2009 [1977]). Nevertheless, ritual has a transformative power that makes it both affirmative and transcendent of the self.

Since each individual has his or her own *Orisha*, to whom he or she is initiated, the deity's personality becomes a part of the individual's. The initiation empowers this unity, and makes it possible for each *Orisha* to have manifold manifestations. This in turn legitimates the function each person has in the rituals. The individual's spiritual development—which encompasses self-affirmative aspects—takes place through the performance of previously defined, codified and repeated ritual actions connected to the manifestations of the deities—the self-transcendent aspect. A composition of bodily, mental and emotional dimensions in a fixed sequence of actions in time and space creates qualities of presence that are unique to each person who actively participates in the ritual. Without this presence, the ritual cannot take place.

The fixed, strict, collective ritual frame is thus inseparable from the individual being.

Some *Candomblé* traditions have a strongly held belief that no woman can be initiated to *Osanyin*, the male botanist god who has all knowledge about herbs, plants and natural medicine. His few initiated devotees are men whose special function in the temple is related to cultivating, reaping and preparing plants for the ceremonies. They do not dance in the rituals.

That hot spring night in Gantois would turn out to be a long one. The ritual lasted longer and longer, with an increasing number of deities becoming manifest. After about five hours, the public started to leave. Only a few stayed. I did not want to give in to the tiredness I could feel taking over my body. It was at that moment that Osanyin *entered the ceremony room, in the shape of a young woman. I was thrilled and surprised. It was the first time I had seen it:* Osanyin, *a woman! And he who had become one with her, wanted to dance. The* Osanyin *woman danced their myths until late into the night. She was unstoppable. I sensed the sound of the drums and the heat of the room growing weaker. My presence disappeared into her intensity.*

Perhaps I was awakened by an extra powerful drumbeat or by a sound coming from the darkness outside the open window. I had slept for about an hour, but nobody around me appeared to notice my embarrassment. Osanyin *continued to dance. By embodying the destiny of a young woman, it turned out that the individual's existence in the religious context does have the potential to challenge the established practices of the fellowship.*

I raised my body and bowed silently to the dancing deities, the Yá, the musicians and the helpers, before I walked out.

Roxane Gay

Originally from Nebraska, she is an American journalist, novelist and critic. Her work appears in Best American Nonrequired Reading 2018, Best American Mystery Stories 2014, Best American Short Stories 2012, Best Sex Writing 2012, Harper's Bazaar, A Public Space, McSweeney's, Tin House, Oxford American, American Short Fiction, Virginia Quarterly Review, *and many others. She is a contributing opinion writer for the* New York Times *and the author of the books* Ayiti, An Untamed State *(2011), the* New York Times *bestselling* Bad Feminist *(2016), the nationally bestselling* Difficult Women *(2017) and* New York Times *bestselling* Hunger: A Memoir of My Body *(2017). She is also the author of* World of Wakanda *(2017) for Marvel and the editor of* Best American Short Stories 2018. *She is currently at work on film and television projects, a book of writing advice, and an essay collection about television and culture. In 2018, she won a Guggenheim fellowship.*

There Is No "E" In Zombi Which Means
There Can Be No You Or We

[A Primer]
[**Things Americans do not know about zombis:**]
They are not dead. They are near death. There's a difference.
They are not imaginary.
They do not eat human flesh.
They cannot eat salt.
They do not walk around with their arms and legs locked stiffly.
They can be saved.

[**How you pronounce zombi:**]
Zaahhhhnnnnnn-Beee. You have to feel it in the roof your mouth, let it vibrate. Say it fast.
The "m" is silent. Sort of.

[How to make a zombi:]
You need a good reason, a very good reason.
You need a pufferfish, and a small sample of blood and hair from your chosen candidate.
Instructions: Kill the pufferfish. Don't be squeamish. Extract the poison. Just find a way. Allow it to dry. Grind it with the blood and hair to create your *coup de poudre*. A good chemist can help. Blow the powder into the candidate's face. Wait.

[A Love Story]
Micheline Bérnard always loved Lionel Desormeaux. Their parents were friends though that bonhomie had not quite carried on to the children. Micheline and Lionel went to primary and secondary school together, had known each other all their lives—when Lionel looked upon Micheline he was always overcome with the vague feeling he had seen her somewhere before while she was overcome with the precise knowledge that he was the man of her dreams. In truth, everyone loved Lionel Desormeaux. He was tall and brown with high cheekbones and full lips. His body was perfectly muscled and after a long day of swimming in the ocean, he would emerge from the salty water, glistening. Micheline would sit in a cabana, invisible. She would lick her lips and she would stare. She would think, "Look at me, Lionel," but he never did. When Lionel walked, there was an air about him. He moved slowly but with deliberate steps and sometimes, when he walked, people swore they could hear the bass of a deep drum. His mother, who loved her only boy more than any other, always told him, "Lionel, you are the son of L'Ouverture." He believed her. He believed everything his mother ever told him. Lionel always told his friends, "My father freed our people. I am his greatest son."

In Port-au-Prince, there were too many women. Micheline knew competition for Lionel's attention was fierce. She was attractive, petite. She wore her thick hair in a sensible bun. On weekends, she would let that hair down and when she walked by, men would shout, "Quelle belle paire de jambes," *what beautiful legs*, and Micheline would savor the thrilling taste of their attention. Most Friday nights, Micheline and her friends would gather at Oasis, a popular nightclub on the edge of the Bel Air slum. She drank fruity drinks and smoked French cigarettes and wore skirts revealing just the right amount of leg. Lionel was always surrounded by a mob of adoring women. He let them buy him rum and Cokes and always sat at the center of the room wearing his pressed linen slacks and dark tee shirts that showed off his perfect, chiseled arms. At the end of the night, he would select one woman to take home, bed her thoroughly, and wish her well the following morning. The stone path to his front door was lined with the tears and soiled panties of the women Lionel had sexed then scorned.

On her birthday, Micheline decided she would be the woman Lionel took home. She wore a bright sundress, strapless. She dabbed perfume everywhere she wanted to feel Lionel's lips. She wore high heels so high her brother had to help her into the nightclub. When Lionel arrived to hold court, Micheline made sure she was closest. She smiled widely and angled her shoulders just so and leaned in so he could see everything he wanted to see within her ample cleavage. At the end of the night, Lionel nodded in her direction. He said, "Tonight you will know the affections of L'Ouverture's greatest son."

In Lionel's bed, Micheline fell deeper in love than she thought possible. Lionel knelt between her thighs, gently massaging her knees. He smiled luminously, casting a bright shaft of light across her body. Micheline reached for Lionel, her hands thrumming as she felt his skin. When he was inside her, she thought her heart might stop it seized so painfully. He whispered in her ear, his breath so hot it blistered her. He said, "Everything on this island is mine. You are mine." Micheline moaned. She said, "I am your victory." He said, "Yes, tonight you are." As he fucked her, Micheline heard the bass of a deep drum.

The following morning, Lionel walked Micheline home. He kissed her chastely on the cheek. As he pulled away, Micheline grabbed his hand in hers, pressing a knuckle with her thumb. She said, "I will come to you tonight." Lionel placed one finger over her lips and shook his head.

Micheline was unable to rise from her bed for a long while. She could only remember Lionel's touch, his words, how the inside of her body had molded itself to him. Her parents sent for a doctor, then a priest, and finally a mambo which they were hesitant to do because they were a good, Catholic family but the sight of their youngest daughter lying in bed, perfectly still, not speaking, not eating, was too much to bear. The mambo sat on the edge of the bed and clucked. She held Micheline's limp wrist. She said, "Love," and Micheline nodded. The mambo shooed the girl's parents out of the room and they left, overjoyed that the child had finally moved. The mambo leaned down, got so close, Micheline could feel the old woman's dry lips against her ear. When the mambo left, Micheline bathed, dabbed herself everywhere she wanted to feel Lionel's lips. She went to Oasis and found Lionel at the center of the room holding a pale, young thing in his lap. Micheline pushed the girl out of Lionel's lap and took her place. She said, "Just one more night," and Lionel remembered her dark moans and the strength of her thighs and how she looked at him like the conquering hero he knew himself to be.

They made love that night, and Micheline was possessed. She dug her fingernails in his back until he bled. She locked her ankles in the small of Lionel's back, and sank her teeth into his strong shoulder. There were no sweet words between them. Micheline walked herself home before he woke. She went to the kitchen and filled a mortar and pestle with blood from beneath her fingernails and between her teeth. She added a few strands of Lionel's hair and a powder the mambo had given her. She ground these things together and put the *coup de poudre* as it was called into a silk sachet. She ran back to Lionel's, where he was still sleeping, opened her sachet, paused. She traced the edge of his face, kissed his forehead, then blew her precious powder into his face. Lionel coughed in his sleep, then stilled. Micheline undressed and stretched herself along his body, sliding her arm beneath his. As his body grew cooler, she kissed the back of his neck.

They slept entwined for three days. Lionel's skin grew clammy and gray. His eyes hollowed. He began to smell like soil and salt wind. When Micheline woke, she whispered, "Turn and look at me." Lionel slowly turned and stared at Micheline, his eyes wide open, unblinking. She gasped at his appearance, how his body had changed. She said, "Touch me," and Lionel reached for her with a heavy hand, pawing at her until she said, "Touch me gently." She said, "Sit up." Lionel slowly sat up, listing from side to side until Micheline steadied him. She kissed Lionel's thinned lips, his fingertips. His cold body filled her with a sadness she could hardly bear. She said, "Smile," and his lips stretched tightly into something that resembled what she knew of a smile. Micheline thought about the second silk sachet, the one hidden beneath her pillow between the pages of her bible, the sachet with a powder containing the power to make Lionel the man he once was—tall, vibrant, the greatest son of L'Ouverture, a man who filled the air with the bass of a deep drum when he walked. She made herself forget about that power; instead, she would always remember that man. She pressed her hand against the sharpness of Lionel's cheekbone. She said, "Love me."

Hawa Jande Golakai

Born in Frankfurt, Germany, she spent her childhood in Liberia. After the civil war in 1990 she travelled throughout the continent. Her debut novel The Lazarus Effect *was shortlisted for the 2011* Sunday Times *Fiction Prize, and the University of Johannesburg Debut Prize, and was longlisted for the Wole Soyinka Prize for Literature in Africa. She is a laureate of the Africa39 Project, celebrating 39 of the most promising contemporary authors under the age of 40 on the continent. Her work has been featured by the BBC, Brittle Paper, Books LIVE SA, The Guardian (UK), Commonwealth Anthology,* Ankara Press, *The Elephant and others. She is the winner of the 2017 Brittle Paper award for her creative non-fiction essay "Fugee". She is also a medical immunologist and, with her son, lives in Monrovia.*

Candy Girl

"Grab her legs."

"I should do whetin? Haay, mah pipo lookah troubo. You nah serious for true."

Shaking my head, I wrestle Leonora by the shoulders, and holding her under her armpits prop her up. I nudge her cheek a little to avert her head because having to look at that clotted spit oozing over her peeling red lipstick and onto her chin is no wet dream. Then I crouch low and heave. My wife is no small woman. Once I've lifted her torso off the floor, I look up.

"Ciatta! Really?"

Was she serious? I'm breaking my back and my so-called girlfriend's over there with her arms crossed spectating like I'm nuts, like I just asked her to kill somebody. Okay, poor choice of words, considering the situation. I jerk my head wildly in the direction of Leonora's feet, urging Ciatta to jump in anytime and lift. She still doesn't budge, instead draws her arms tighter and juts a hip. "Cia, come on!" I lose it, then "Dammit!" when my back loses it, popping a tendon or something else that isn't supposed to pop. Grinding my pain between my teeth, I drop Leonora, who does quite an impressive face-plant into the carpet.

"Fineboy, chill, I beg you, before sumbady come buss inside heah and find out what we doin'."

"*We?*" I rotate my spine, coaxing it to unclench. "More like what I'm doing. You look ready to run the minute you hear *pim*. If you're not interested in saving my neck, I don't see why you're here."

"Mtssshw," she kisses her teeth the way only she can, and something sweet stirs in my heart. Alright, in my pants. "I don't blame you. I came, dah why you tellin' me nonsense."

She cocks her chin away from me, classic move when she's trying to control that sweep of hellfire she calls a temper. She's not pissed, not really, I can tell. Anger runs a whole different tier, in spectral shades, with her. She looks round the room, deciding if she approves, if I chose well despite the shitstorm this has turned into. From the tiny smile that crooks up the edge of her mouth, I did good. Clean and respectable but not high-end, romantic but seedy enough for debauchery. A tough combo in this nosy Monrovia. She beckons with the crook of her finger… I notice for the first time a French manicure with a tiny red heart stuck to each nail. Why would a detail I'd normally find so cheesy make me want her more? I go to her like a little boy.

"Dah whahappin?" she coos, massaging my head, neck and shoulders. Tiny knots dissolve like sugar to caramel.

"You see what happened—my wife's dead!" I point to the body, which I'm past the point of hoping will wake up, stagger to its feet and cuss my ass out.

Ciatta huffs. "Aay mehn, my eyeball dem nah bust. Whetin happin exactly? Tell me it." She flaps a hand. "*Articulate it*, in dah yor fine-fine white pipo book."

I ignore the gibe. She's no trash but playing up our differences (many) is one of her (again, many) little games and though I protest, that edge of forbidden frisson it adds…hot damn. Who knew I knew how to mess around. In looks, my *jue* is so like my wife I shouldn't have bothered. Night and day, though. Take for instance their outfits: Leonora, champion at making pretty love and eye contact, straight out of a corny rom-com with her red trench coat, fancy black frills underneath no doubt; Cia in the very *lappa* cloth I tore off her the first time we ravaged, with those hideous tiger-print heels that slaughter me every time they're up in the air.

"She was sitting on the bed when I walked in. I don't know how but she found out about the surprise I had planned for you and genuinely thought it was meant for her. What could I say?" I gulp. "Then she opened the box of chocolates…" My head slumps into my palms. "Once the reaction starts, it's unstoppable. She's so sensitive. She's always careful about carrying her EpiPen but—"

Ciatta questions me with her eyebrows. "You know, her medicine," I say. "She always has it on her but clearly, dressing like a common hopojo to surprise me took priority." I make a face. "This doesn't even suit her."

"Shut up. De woman didn't think her husband was gon kill her on Valentine's Day."

"I didn't—" I choke on a sob and she kisses me, silences me. For a moment. "We…we need to get rid of the body."

"What? No. Now'days, worst thing you can do. Uhn do nuttin wrong." I whimper. "You did not kill her, but let's get your story straight." She looms over my wife, unblinking. When she looks up her eyes glitter so dark and sultry in the twilight, like oil dancing on top of ink, that I know I'll wreck it all for her, now and always. "I came by the back way and nobody saw me, so dah part taken care of. But think. Pretend dis was like last year but sumtin went wrong. Don't make the lie too big, dah how pipo can get caught."

"How will that…" The clouds part. "*Yes, yes!* I always buy candy for you, my Ma and a special box for Leonora with no nuts. I'll say in my hurry to get here to meet my wife I grabbed the wrong box and that's how this catastrophe happened. Thank God the other boxes are safe at home. I'll destroy the extra one meant for you and produce the special candy as proof of the mix-up."

"Ehn-heeehhn, palaver fini. Who never made mistake?" She brought her hands together in a single clap of defeat and shook her head. "Dey say when bad luck call your name, ripe banana will break your teeth." She laughs at my awe. "O-o-o, you jek! Keep lookin' inside my mouf like my teeth made o' diamond. I nah only good for one ting."

She crosses to the bed and I drink in every muscle shifting under her thin wrapper. I shouldn't be tingling right now…why am I tingling?

"It been how long?"

I check my watch. "Twenty, twenty-five minutes."

"Good. More than one hour and it look bad. After I leave, be ready to give de performance of your life. *After* you give *me* de performance of your life." She drops the colourful *lappa*. Her body is heaven turned on its head. She picks a truffle from the box and runs it over her lips.

"Don't," I rasp.

"Why not? I nah de one who de got nut allergy. *Had*." She smiles.

"Why do you make me buy it? You always say it's too sweet."

Ciatta shrugs. "What woman can ever be too sweet?" The finger with the little red heart crooks at me again.

I'm going to hell a thousand, blissful times over.

Rachel Eliza Griffiths

An American poet and artist, her collections of poetry include Miracle Arrythmia *(2010),* The Requited Distance *(2011),* Mule & Pear *(2011), and* Lighting the Shadow *(2015), which was a finalist for the 2015 Balcones Poetry Prize and the 2016 Phillis Wheatley Book Award in Poetry. Her literary and visual art has appeared widely in publications including the* New York Times, *the* New Yorker, The Progressive, Tin House, *and* Virginia Quarterly Review. *Her video series of contemporary poets,* P.O.P (Poets on Poetry), *is featured online at the Academy of American Poets. Currently, Griffiths is working on her first novel. She teaches creative writing at Sarah Lawrence College and lives in New York City.*

Chosen Family

When you find your sisters you'll still look over your shoulder sometimes
to see if you're being followed. You're hoping one or two sisters you don't
know will want to see where you're going. When you find your sisters
they won't ask you where you came from because they'll already know
& if they don't they'll be busy putting good food on your plate & asking you
if you're hungry or broke. When you find your sisters, your people, they'll tell you
to use any bathroom you want, marry anybody you want, work side-by-side
together for long hours in close quarters without any fear of being harmed.
When you find your sisters they'll throw the ball to you, offer you
their love song & say you need to *listen to this track & dance with us*
whether or not you know all the steps. When you find your sisters
they'll say Do You Remember & you'll say Yes until you remember together
the different ways the whole thing happened. When you find your sisters
they'll say wear whatever you want, wear the tightest dress, wear the pants,
wear your birthday suit. They'll say we love your skin & drag & natural hair
& we love you naturally so please just live & don't let anybody kill you
or tell you they've killed you & you're just fine the dead way you are. When you
find your sisters don't leave them & don't let them off the hook when they are
in the wrong. When they are trying to take themselves out of the world
lay your hands on them & call them yours & yours & yours.
When you find your sisters be sure you've been preparing your heart
the entire way by loving your difficult self & what you pretend you don't know
but you do know so that when you see them smiling into your eyes, the soft
or tough flags of their hands covering yours in a truth so light & fierce you see
you all have been midair for some time & could go higher & burn some shit up
if you remembered what else is good everywhere
& everywhere you look.

Cathedral of the Snake and Saint

(for my mother and Maya Angelou who died two months apart)

Riverside Church in September one sunlit morning we gathered
to sing farewell to our sister, beloved poet, our warrior
from St Louis, raised in Stamps by her grandmother.
I thought it was too soon for me to go into a church. I wasn't civil
yet. I still crossed the street whenever I saw a sanctuary.
Then I would find myself, as if I had no luck, no choice,
crossing back again, searching for a quarter in my pocket or purse.
I would always light a candle. Couldn't bear to think
that if I didn't say a prayer what my dead mother might say or do.
& what she would have done that day (laughed & laughed)
to see her snake-headed daughter clapping & crying too loud,
carrying on like I was homeless, with a grief
only a god could wrestle from my soul. I shivered
on the white tongue of the holy spirit. Our people screamed
her name in the hollows. *Maya Maya Maya*
while she rose up & flew with wings so wide I was cold
from the brilliant shade they made. Indolent black angel
risen from her cage. There was that. But the singing. The singing!
I was shouting so wild & sad when Guy spoke at the finale
that the zipper of my dress snapped. My back exposed
right down to the black waistband of my panties.
The man behind me made a noise. I sat down fast in the dress
I'd worn to my mother's funeral. My good black dress with its snakeskin
panel down the front. A dress appropriate yet not animal enough.
I found it a few minutes after I chose my mother's burial suit,
an ivory Calvin Klein jacket & skirt. Feather-grey camisole.
Remembered once my mother said *Nobody will give you the skin*
off their back but me. I'm always going to love you. Because I'm your mother.
But that morning I died again in the pew. God against my skin, burning.
My entire body published like an unfinished deed to something, someone
I no longer owned. Clothed in her own grief, my best friend
could not give me her jacket. Could not allow the eyes of summer
to glare at her soft brown arms. Could not protect me
from the beak of death that still had not had enough (of me).
I rushed to the back of Riverside Church & flattened myself
against a pillar of stone. Wondered what would happen
if I started to hiss, go black upon my belly with my mournful fangs.
Friends went by, hugging & smiling after the tribute ended.
I could not move. Hugged nothing but stone. Too mad to cry.

Nothing between me & my God. Flesh, stone, immediate shame.
There went the great bright flock. Valerie Simpson who tore it up
earlier while performing *I'm Every Woman*. There was Toni
waving in a fine straw hat. & Nikki Giovanni & Hillary Clinton & Marie &
Jenisha. Then me, barely me, there against the stone, pinned
like a long, empty black tube of skin. I almost stepped right out of
the dead dress & why not? Again the edge of my mother's casket pulled
against the silk now split & hysterical. Everything ugly & sweet of me
exposed to the heavens. So funny I hoped Saint Maya would thank me
in her throaty chuckle, would hold me in her arms & promise
I Believe You Can Save Yourself.

Seeing the Body

She died & I—
In the spring of her blood. I remember
my mother's first injury. The surprise of unborn
petals curling light, red, around her wrist.
Some fruit she cut, some onion, some
body with skin & seeds. She fed me.
She listened & I—
She held We & I—
She kept speaking with those flowers
falling from her blood, taking her
across the sky to death. I remember
her voice like a horn I never want
to pull out of my heart. In the next life,
which is here & here, I gather every thing
that ever sang my mother's blues.
She burned & I—
She talked back hard at god.
O, she danced, unbroken, too.
Bale of grief on my back, opening
into something black I wear. A life of flesh
like a petal or fruit or burning.
I've carried everything & I'm tired.
She survived & I—
(But she did not live).
She told me Nothing & I—
She was waiting the entire time.
How does the elegy believe me?
Together, we crossed the sky.

There was a gate & we walked through
the world like that.
She wrote We & I—
She was last seen & I—
Eyes, without life, opened eternity.
When the air in her
stopped & I—
She was last seen dying. She was too silent
for the first time in her life. The spring
of my mother's blood hot & god the dark
dark beyond the closed door
that won't move again.

Joanne C. Hillhouse

From Antigua and Barbuda, she is the author of two picture books, With Grace,
a Caribbean Fairytale *(2016) and* Lost! A Caribbean Sea Adventure *(2017) and its
Spanish language edition,* ¡perdida! Una Aventura En El Mar Caribe *(2018); a teen/
young adult novel,* Musical Youth, *which was a 2014 finalist for the Burt Award for
Caribbean Literature; two novellas,* The Boy from Willow Bend *(2002) and* Dancing
Nude in the Moonlight *(2004), which has been reissued as an anniversary edition
with other writings (2014); and a novel,* Oh Gad! *(2012). She has also been published
in a number of journals and anthologies. She freelances full time—writing, editing,
training and more. Her passion for writing led her to start the Wadadli Youth Pen
Prize to nurture and showcase the literary arts in Antigua and Barbuda.*

Evening Ritual

"Emily?"

Veron's niece, who seemed to have grown again between morning and evening,
rushed in just in time to help her put away the last of the groceries. Probably hiding
that book she was always writing in, as if Veron didn't know she kept it stashed
between the mattress and the bedspring. Veron sat heavily.

"No, not there," Veron directed from the dining-chair when Emily opened the
fridge. "You know I don't like my sausage hard and cold. It take out all the spice."

She signalled for the salami, signalled again for a knife, cut through the plastic to
the briny meat, nipped a slice for herself, and another for her niece. Emily hmmmm'd
like there was nothing quite so salty and sweet, and Veron hmmmm'd with her. Veron

sucked on the casing after the meat was gone, reaching for the knife to cut them both another slice.

"We won't have any left for tomorrow," Emily protested.

Veron laughed. "Why leave for tomorrow what you can eat today?" Emily was right though. She directed her to wrap up the rest and stick it in a container in the cupboard.

"What you cook?"

Emily turned from the cupboard, set a fork and plate on the table, then brought the pot over from the stove. A one-pot rice and chicken seasoned with the last of the onion and some spinach plucked from the fence between their yard and the neighbour's.

"She didn't see you?" Veron asked, chewing on a piece of the spinach.

Emily shrugged.

"You eat already, right?"

Emily nodded.

Veron grabbed the fork and began eating directly from the pot.

"Auntie Veron!"

"What?" Veron scoffed. "My feet killing me, I don't need no extra work."

Veron worked as a waitress at the island's newest hotel, Sea Grape. Its beach was once popular for its seaside grape trees. Now as bereft of the juicy fruit as it was of locals. People fussed and protested in the beginning. As usual, government did what it wanted. "Politician will full dem belly but smadee ha fu work." Veron said.

The pay cheque wasn't much, even with the hotel being so lavish and the owner getting such a long tax holiday he might as well be on permanent vacation. "He red-shenky self," Veron and most of the staff grumbled behind his back.

"Red shenky" wasn't usually directed at white people. But "Sir" was local like them, just born on the right side of the whip. When it suited, he played up his island creds, as he stalked the property like a big shot. "Wha'happen, ole bwoy?" "Every t'ing good, sistren?"

At first, the island rooted for him, because black or white, seeing one of their own prosper in an expat industry made them feel like they were inching forward from 1834. He showed them who he was, though, when he cut the pay of those who didn't come out during the last hurricane. When she and the others had reminded bakkra—that's how they thought of him now—that the PM, the Met Office, and the media had advised all non-essential workers to remain indoors, he reminded them that tourism was what kept Antigua going. "Nothing tarl more essential than that." His lips twitched like it was a big joke. And when the union seemed like it wanted to put up a fight, bakkra went on the TV and said anyone who didn't want to honour their employee contract could leave. Next day, he and the union boss were laughing over Wadadli beers and the catch-of-the-day in one of the hotel's four restaurants. Veron served them with her own hands. She wanted to spit in their food, but her mother had raised her better than that.

Still, something was better than nothing, she told herself as she hung on. With Emily depending on her, she had to.

Emily had been with her since her sister had decided life was too much and found escape in a bottle. Emily's father, she called him the sweetie man, because that was all he gave, as if children didn't have needs day in day out. She remembered cursing both him and her sister to the darkest pits of hell when she discovered the state the now fourteen-year-old girl was in. It had been thanks to a nosy neighbor who'd reported that the child was barely going to school.

She had taken Emily to live with her then. Sat with her over her times tables and spelling words until she had not only caught up but was ahead of everybody. Emily was now an "A" student. A shame about those deep bowlegs, though; she'd never win any beauty contests with those.

"Want me to rub them for you?" Emily asked.

"Hm?" Veron replied.

"Your feet; want me to rub them for you?"

"Giirrl!" As if that was even a question.

The way the hotel was built—on a steep incline sloping down to the beach, so the tourists could have an unobstructed view of the Caribbean sea and the islands beyond—meant a lot of climbing when she was on room-service duty, which she tried to get out of when she could. No tips, rude guests; pass.

"Fix your face," Emily chuckled. She put on the kettle to heat up the water.

"Mind your mouth," Veron said, dropping the fork in the empty pot with a clatter. She let out a loud belch.

Emily made a face as she collected the pot and dumped it in the sink.

"What?" Veron said, "The food bang good. Compliments to the chef."

Emily rolled her eyes, turning back to the stove where the kettle was now whistling stridently.

"Don't understand how you work in hotel with that kind of behaviour," she grumbled.

Veron choopsed, "Me in mi home, where me cyan relax and be meself. Ah wha de world! Wha you be, Minister of Etiquette, Ms. Emily Post?"

Her niece could be so prissy sometimes, like someone who grew up in a mansion instead of a ghetto. "Ghetto is a state of mind," Emily would say whenever the topic came up, "you can have all the money in the world and still be ghetto, and I'm not ghetto."

Veron would just shake her head, both proud and mystified, thinking: "But where this gyal come from?" This girl, with a book in her hand and her head ever otherwhere seemed sometimes to her as new as when something she didn't even know she'd planted sprung up from the small patch of fertile land alongside their house. Their yard didn't grow much, the soil too tough and unforgiving for that. But there was a patch right at the corner, near the soakaway, where the soil turned easily enough and if she dropped seeds from their meal there, they'd come, all variety of things huddled up to each other like they were seeking shelter from the very rain that would help them grow, the very sunshine that would breathe life into them. Whatever sprang from that patch of dirt was always a nice surprise. Emily was like that.

The kind of girl she didn't have to check for, no ton of boys fishing around, no fear of picknee pulling down her belly. No, her niece had thoughts in her head, spark in her eyes.

"What homework you have?" Veron asked.

"Just history," Emily replied.

The girl shoved a bowl of snotty dumms toward her aunt, pulled another chair from the dining-table, seated herself, then lifted her aunt's feet up and into the pink plastic bath she'd already set between them. The water was more cool than warm but it would do.

"Hm," Veron moaned, feeling the weariness going out of her through her feet. "Tell me about it," she said, sucking lazily on the part-sweet, part-sour dumms, body going lax, almost like a child needing only a bedtime story to send their heavy-lidded eyes all the way closed.

"Well, Mr B. took us on a field trip today, out to Betty's Hope, the old sugar estate. It's kind of boring, to be honest, a lot of grass, and wild plants. That's where I got the dumms."

Veron's eyes snapped open. "Wait, is dead people dumms you have me here eating?" She didn't spit them out though.

"You want your foot rub or not?" Emily said.

Veron re-settled.

"The buildings are too crumpled to recognize as anything, especially the slave village where there wasn't no building at all—just grass and cassi…and dumms…" Emily said.

Veron hmmm'd.

"Yeah, dumms, and goats… Was all we could do to get some from the goats…or was it the ghosts?"

"Girl."

"OK, OK…there was a restored sugar mill, yes, but it don't spin or nothing, so that was kinda boring. The thing I found most interesting was the name, Betty; the owner's daughter apparently. Imagine naming a place like that, a place where you work people until they die, after your daughter."

Veron hmmm'd again. "I worked at a place like that once."

"A plantation?"

Veron's scoff was dry like ashum. "A hotel. The owner named it after his daughter… Hyacinth Hills."

Emily laughed. "Seriously?"

Veron hmmm'd again, eyes still closed. She opened them when Emily didn't continue speaking right away, to find her niece watching her. When their eyes met, Emily looked away.

"Well, anyway," Emily continued, "Betty got me thinking about women who didn't have slave plantations named after them, you know…"

"Women like us?" Veron said.

Emily's hands slowed, and she was sorry she'd interrupted. She wiggled her feet a bit to get the massage going again.

"Well, yeah…" Emily said. "I mean…inside the plantation museum they had some pictures showing the whole plantation business, the cutting and the boiling and the transporting on the loco line… In this one picture…with women packing the cane onto, like, a rail cart…two women stood out, one in a head-tie, and one in a straw hat, both in pink dresses. When Mr B. told us we had to write about the trip, I decided to write about these women who weren't Betty. I'd never heard about those women…when you hear 'bout the factory and field work cutting cane and them thing, is man you hear 'bout but there wasn't one man in the picture…except in another picture there was a man on a horse, in a long coat and a broad-brimmed white hat, that picture was black and white and could well ah been a different plantation, a different time…except for the women, packing the sugar cane, as he stood over them looking on… I had never read or heard their story and the Museum didn't have much…"

Emily's voice trailed off and it was the sudden absence of sound that brought Veron back to herself.

"That sound like a good story," Veron said.

Emily shrugged and smiled shyly at the praise. "Well, I'm still writing it," she said. She paused. "I guess I just never thought of it like that before."

"Like bakkra pon horseback, black man and black woman a bruk dem back?"

"No, just…I mean, yes…but just the way some get plantations named after them and some get…erased."

Veron told her the only truth she had. "Black woman hard fu rub out, them need some special eraser for that. Ent you see them?"

And Emily kept looking at her.

"Yeah, I see them," she said, just when her gaze was starting to make Veron uncomfortable.

Emily placed her feet gently on the patchwork mat they kept in the kitchen.

She opened the back door to dump out the grey water, came back for the bowl and dumped out the dumms seeds.

"Yeah, good story," Veron mused again. "You know what it put me in the mood for, though?"

"Huh?" Emily turned from the sink.

"Some sugar cane," Veron said, and Emily laughed out loud, shaking her head at her aunt and her long belly.

Ethel Irene Kabwato

Born in Mutare, Zimbabwe, she trained as a teacher and holds a BA in Media Studies. She is a founding member of the Zimbabwe Women Writers' Mutare Branch and a member of the Harare Branch. In 2004 she participated in the British Council Crossing Borders Writers project. She has read her work at several institutions including Rhodes University and the University of Witwatersrand, South Africa, and has been a guest of Cinema Without Borders at the Amnesty International Film Festival in Amsterdam. She has also participated in a reading and discussion of her work at the Hay Festival in Wales, UK. She works with Slum Cinema, a voluntary initiative to empower disadvantaged communities through multi-media work. She has been published in Writing Now, Sunflowers in Your Eyes *and* Writing Free. *Her poetry is included in* Between Two Rocks *and in* Ghetto Diary, *an anthology that is currently a set book for advanced-level literature students in Zimbabwe.*

After the Roses

After the champagne, chocolates and music
When the red, red roses have lost their bloom
…and the perfume has lost its scent…
When he sells
Your dreams to the devil…
After the red, red roses
Of Valentine's Day
Have withered
After a one-day wonder
Of hoping and dreaming
That he holds many honeymoons
In his hands
That "he is happy ever after" material…
She counts the scars on her back
She cradles the broken stems
Of roses in her arms
Long after the petals have gone…
After the roses
He is the custodian
Of broken dreams
She is the voice you hear crying at night
She is the faceless woman
You see everyday
…smiling but broken

Laughing but hurt…
Her words are under the tongue
Of one who steals
The dreams of women

The Missing

Sometimes I hear your voice
In places where we both
Have loved hanging out;
The Terrace, Café 263
The Flea Market
Sometimes I hear your laughter
In my sleep
And I know you are singing
The songs in my heart…
There are times when I
Run low in faith
And I go into the forest
Near your school
To look for signs of mass graves
But I know
When they brought out the dead
You were not among them
When they brought out the survivors
You were not among them
When they called out the missing
You were among the missing 43
The last one on their list;
Tell me that the voices
I hear each morning
Are speaking to my soul
Wherever you are
My free spirited one,
Sing the songs in my heart
Talk to me if you can still dream
Listen to the sound of the bell
At St Mary's Cathedral
It still rings at 7 a.m.
The time you always left home for school

Women's Day

I've seen you travel
The same road over the years
I've watched you pick up
The broken threads of your life
I've heard you sing
About the scars that you bear
But you have not faltered
I stand here and wait
For the sound
Of the African drum
Whose silence
Evokes a kaleidoscope of emotions
The haunting stillness
Of dreams
Yet to be realized
I've watched you dance
To the silent drum
But the sores on your feet
Are too heavy to take you through
To the last dance.
When you walk that same road again
Remember to take me with you.

Fatimah Kelleher

*A Nigerian and Irish-British women's rights technical adviser and strategist engaged
in feminist activism, research, policy and programming, since 2000 she has been
involved primarily in the areas of women's economic justice and empowerment,
education and health, providing feminist analysis and advice to varied stakeholders
including women's groups and local civil society, NGOs, UN bodies, and national/
subnational government organisations. She works and publishes at the international
level primarily on Africa, but also on South Asia and the Caribbean. She also writes
on diaspora issues, literature and the arts, and is particularly passionate about
increasing African and diaspora representation within the area of travel literature. In*

1997 she was the founder of Urban Griots, a popular open-mic night in London that was a key part of the spoken-word resurgence of that era. Her poetry has appeared in anthologies and in magazines such as Sable Litmag.

To Chew on Bay Leaves: on the Problematic Trajectory of Instrumentalist Justifications for Women's Rights

"You forgot to really emphasise how girl-child education will benefit society overall. Oh, and how much more *productive* an educated woman will be in the economy we want for the future. These policy makers need to be *convinced* you see."

The year is 2010 and I have just delivered an introductory address at a gender equality workshop. The person hastily mouthing these fervent words to me is a civil servant I'm collaborating with to deliver a training session in one of the government ministries I've visited in recent years. We are trying to make the case for Gender Responsive Budgeting at the national and sub-national levels and have lined up five days to regale a posse of largely recalcitrant government folk who have already communicated their irritation at being expected to learn all this "gender stuff". My opening salvo has focused squarely on women's rights to education, health, and economic resources as inalienable rights that governments should deliver as an ethical impetus. I have chosen to tone-down the "and also…" justifications of macro economic contributions that are often part and parcel of such sessions.

The civil servant's words are not a surprise. In fact, underscoring the economic and wider societal value of a woman's right to education has been one of my missions for years and I am certainly not opposed to highlighting them. But today, I've had enough. Not only of the constant necessity for such further justifications, but also of their growing ascendency over rights, *full stop*.

"So what if a woman wants to go and chew bay leaves in a cave somewhere afterwards?" I ask her.

Pause. "What?"

"Chew bay leaves. In a cave. After her education. You know…go completely off-grid. Perhaps to contemplate the meaning of life. Or just to sleep…even dispense with the need for a job. Can she still be educated then?"

Pause. Pause. A few baffled blinks, then: "So why would she need an education? What would be her use?"

And there it was. Ascendency had become primacy. Inalienable rights could not be championed unless they were instrumental to some wider output.

Looking back at this exchange years later, I know my question had been an irritated, rhetorical one. Compounded aggravation from a decade of dealing with recalcitrant folk who did not really give a damn for women's rights meant I was teetering on that dangerous brink where healthy cynicism becomes a plummet into despair. But her response was welcome in the end. Its confirmation helped to strengthen my own positioning not to become hooked into the instrumentalist premise that a woman's empowerment must always be *of use to something else beyond her simple right to have it*.

Instrumentalism has arguably always been a part of the women's rights agenda, and not necessarily without good cause; highlighting how women's access to education, healthcare and economic resources enrich and create a better society overall is important. However, the manner in which instrumentalism has become a critical part of justifying gender equality/a women's rights approach is also problematic, especially as it has become driven primarily by economic indicators, and often without any radical commitment to social and economic justice outcomes. Sometimes known as the "business case for gender equality", such terminology in itself smacks of the need to monetarily quantify first.[1] Even when rights-based arguments are put forward initially, it is often only a sentence or two before an instrumentalist positioning—such as women's contribution to GDP growth through increased economic participation—follows in order to "convince" stakeholders that rights and equality are value for money.

But this need to *convince* is a craw that eventually sticks in many a feminist throat. How much a woman's right to education/land/fair work/markets can equate to an increased dollar amount is now a common prerequisite when lobbying recalcitrant governments, indifferent private sector CEOs, and your common or garden misogynist everywhere. Somewhere along the neo-liberal line the mantra of economic growth latched itself to the women's rights and empowerment agenda. In one week in early 2018 there were three events on women's economic empowerment in London where the same McKinsey Global Institute Report—*The power of parity: How advancing women's equality can add $12 trillion to global growth*—was quoted by five different speakers with greater fervour than the moral impetus for women's rights alone.

Of course, for many it's difficult to fathom why such an impressive sum would be problematic to women's rights, and as a stand-alone piece of data it is indeed innocuous. But the problem with this focus is that beyond economic growth the debate around who controls and benefits from such increases in wealth is rarely engaged with. This in turn propagates the view that economic growth is a panacea in itself, distracting from those realities where per capita increases improve little when the cost of living is so steep citizens cannot comfortably keep a roof over their heads. As such, the fiscal charm of this figure starts to obscure the justice implications of what growth actually means for women and society overall.

For example, the question of whether women get to control their incomes as economies grow has often been secondary (if it comes up at all) to the simple focus on the contributory role of women's labour to global markets. Women's rights and gender equality subsequently become defined by participation, and economic

---

1   Chatham House (2010) "The business case for gender equality: key findings from evidence for action paper" Paris. Available at: www.oecd.org/dac/gender-development/45569192.pdf.

participation at that. A focus on Africa's economic growth for example has often been aligned with a "covetous eye" on African women's economic productive capacity, particularly within the agricultural sector.[1] Today countless organisational reports and media junkets utilise the African woman—often carrying a basket of produce—as the image of the continent's recent economic productivity as readily as she was once used as the face of the continent's battle with HIV and AIDS fifteen years ago.[2]

In the quest to see dollar increases as equivalent to empowerment, the reality that increased earnings do not necessarily lead to a fairer society is often skated over. Taking the time to radically unpack the word "power" in relation to either individual, societal, or corporate behaviour when using the word "empowerment" remains rare, while the patriarchal landscape itself is rarely systemically attacked. But as the feminist experience in the West has shown, patriarchal norms persist despite women's increased engagement in the formal economy. Unaddressed and nuanced inequities beneath the surface (such as a recent furore over gendered pay gaps) can become initially obscured as the simplistic goal of participation is celebrated. Without a "social upgrading"[3] the hype of women's increased formal participation and its macro contributions can water down feminist goals for decades as systemic prejudices remain intact even whilst a façade of progress is projected. The problem remains that rather than fundamentally challenging an unequal system, women are asked to simply join it.

Historically, this type of compromised social justice has often followed on the back of instrumentalist justifications. For example, today's economically developed countries universalized their education systems on the back of women teachers whose unequal status meant they were paid lower wages than men, and as such girls' education became cyclically instrumental to the maintenance of the education system in itself.[4] As women were mainly recruited for the primary sector, this also fed stereotypical expectations of women as automatic nurturers. Today, many of these teacher workforces are viewed as "feminized", with larger numbers of women teachers overall than men. However, hidden under the congratulatory mask of representation, women continue to face inequalities in career promotion and unequal presence in the secondary and tertiary sectors, while tabloid papers take periodic pot

---

1 Kelleher, F. (2017) "Disrupting Orthodoxies in Economic Development: An African Feminist Perspective", *Feminist Africa*, Vol. 22.

2 Kelleher, F. (2017) "African Feminism and the Struggle for Africa's 'Development'", presentation at the Africa Utopia Festival, July 15, 2017 as part of the session Africa: Feminism and the Future. Podcast avail. at: www.southbankcentre.co.uk/blog/africa-feminism-and-future-africa-utopia-2017-podcast.

3 Barrientos et al (2012) "Economic and social upgrading in global production networks: A new paradigm for a changing world", *International Labour Review*, Vol. 150, Issue 3–4.

4 Kelleher et al (2011) *Women and the Teaching Profession: Exploring the Feminisation Debate*, UNESCO, Paris.

shots at the perceived inability of women teachers to address moral panics in "boys' underachievement".[1]

This is a pattern not unique to women's rights alone: a core impetus behind the mass education of the poorer classes in late Victorian and early twentieth-century Britain was the call for an educated workforce who could fulfil the increasingly mechanized and service needs of an industrial society. Over a hundred years later the class inequalities of that time—despite having been blunted in the post-WWII era of the welfare state—have morphed but are yet to be eradicated. However, it often takes periodic financial crises and recessions and their resultant austerity policies slashing social safety nets to dissipate the mythical fog of a "classless" British society.[2] So whilst the instrumentalist premise did deliver on universal basic education, without a radical egalitarian premise first underpinning that education, the move towards equality has been a piecemeal endeavour.

But arguably some of the most conflicting evolutions of instrumentalist positioning around women's rights have been calculations around what violence against women monetarily costs public and private sector purses. Sometimes a valiant attempt to lobby for funding during a time of cuts to women's services, these approaches seek to demonstrate the wider economic impact of such violence, such as the cost to emergency response services.[3] More recently however the business case for why the private sector should also engage has become popular.[4] Decreases in a woman's productivity and resultant loss in profit for businesses when absent from work due to domestic and workplace violence are one feature of such calculations. And whilst the importance of public and private sector bodies tackling gender-based violence is certainly not in question here, the need for this focus presents a reductionist approach to women's experiences of violence that is heart breaking. When such economic rationales are also needed, it suggests that the human costs alone—the physical and emotional wreckage, the violation of body and psyche—are not enough.

It is this realisation that moral and ethical parameters are less attractive than instrumentalist ones that makes *the need to convince* using such arguments so

---

1 Matthews, A. (2016) "Rise of women teachers 'turning boys off education' as report reveals girls born this year will be 75% more likely to go to university" *Mail Online*, published 12th May 2016, available at: www.dailymail.co.uk/newsarticle- 3586401/Rise-women-teachers-turning-boys-education-report-reveals-girls-born-year-75-likely-university.html.

2 Glover, J. (2007) "Riven by class and no social mobility—Britain in 2007", *The Guardian*, Saturday 20th October 2007, available at: www.theguardian.com/uk/2007/oct/20/britishidentity.socialexclusion.

3 Ibrahim, Z. et al (2018) *Counting the Cost: The Price Society Pays for Violence Against Women*, CARE International, Geneva.

4 Beavers, S. & Kampf, B. (2013) *Violence Against Women Also Hurts Business and Development*, 29th March 2013 United Nations Development Programme, available at: www.undp.org/content/undp/en/home/ourperspective/ourperspectivearticles/2013/03/29/violence-against-women-also-hurts-business-and-development.html.

difficult to accept. More insidiously, they provide a silent legitimacy to the reverse scenario, where a world without rights and justice can just as easily provide economic growth; slavery, bonded labour, and unfairly remunerated work have all done so/ continue to do so in one society or another. An elementary question then must be asked: if the spread of rights provided no economic benefits at all, what would our arguments then be?

A return to that purely philosophical enquiry is now needed. The current trajectory of increased instrumentalist positioning around women's rights will not result in a feminist epiphany from economically driven stakeholders for whom women's rights have been tangential at best and irrelevant at worst in relation to their own goals. Having to convince people that furthering equality is good because it can also further an economic bottom line somewhere is not where we should be in the twenty-first century. A mushrooming of interventions on the back of this are not signifiers of success in themselves. Without the ethical underpinnings of rights and justice that fundamentally challenge core beliefs and patriarchal systems, the battle for a feminist future will continue to not only be piecemeal but arguably deeply compromised.

Rosamond S. King

A creative and critical writer and performer living in Brooklyn, New York, with family from Trinidad and The Gambia, she creates work that is deeply informed by her cultures and communities, by history, and by a sense of play. Her poems are collected in the Lambda-award-winning Rock | Salt | Stone *(2017), and appear in more than three dozen journals, blogs, and anthologies. Her performance art has been curated in venues including the NY Metropolitan Museum, the Encuentro Festival (Canada), and the African Performance Art Biennial (Zimbabwe). Her scholarly book* Island Bodies: Transgressive Sexualities in the Caribbean Imagination *received the 2015 Caribbean Studies Association best book award. She is Creative Editor of sx salon, President of the Organization of Women Writers of Africa, and Associate Professor at Brooklyn College.*

This is for the women[1]

Holds a gun like a claw
It would tear out your humanity if
it thought you had any
Holds a badge like a claw
to make your dignity bleed
to make you gag
this claw digs its blunt
into you—*swallow it*
or else

the badge tells you to get
naked and like it
flashlight pricks your belly
then asphalt grinds your knees
gun tells you to like it
so you like it better than prison
better than more flashlights
more badges more guns

laughter, like a claw
that never leaves you never removes
its pointy end from your
throat now stretched wide
a claw to suck the flesh off of
and your whole body
is your throat stretched
wide are you still screaming why
are you still screaming a receptacle
doesn't scream a waste bin doesn't
scream a throat filled with a claw
shouldn't be able to

a throat that is a whole body
resonates at an other frequency
sometimes in your everyday you feel
the earth thrumming with

---

1 For the women assaulted and raped by former Oklahoma City Police Officer Daniel Holtzclaw, who targeted Black women for his crimes because he believed if they told, no one would believe them.

the scream of a throat that is
a body that a claw tried to fill
and failed tried to fill and failed
the throat that is a body pierced
by the thing like a claw screams
and bleeds and the blood dries
but the scream goes on forever.
It does not become a song
But there is a song. The pierced hole
Is a second throat a doubled
sound scream is thrumming ground

song is ringing ears hear
? hear! *here*
!

(the hotbox and the flood)

The average human temperature is 98.6 degrees
; her normal is 101.3, radiating
heat through walls and her skin
, the woman who is not yet your
lover but wants to be

. This poem is aware
that *hotbox* might also refer to torture
devices in which humans are
first warmed, then cooked. There is
little of that here since the only
latch is internal

. She is the flood, her desire
crashing waves across your
modesty. They say a flood like
hers once drowned the world

— This poem does not know
the future, but it imagines
you two together
, the hiss and boil
that will ensue

Untitled Poems

each clump of grass or stone holds heat
(like) every imprint of my wide foot
smiling broadly at no one
look up; look up the view
from there is vast
and you do not know more than any stone.

very clean is the slate of your face
not smirking, your face not mean
this is my favorite; a photograph of water
propped on pillows before me
what were you thinking, you

———————————

scrub dark and soiled areas. scrub clean, scrub glee. pat dry.

sterility guaranteed if package has been opened or tampered (tampon, tamper away!). otherwise all openings orifices are productive and procreative.

child safe droppers, usually on the head. height and impact surface vary, though velocity is constant (provide velocity equation, using gravity).

our thick, elegant, nongreasy formulation will be absorbed by poors.
you'll never have to wash again.

———————————

I do not want to be a monster.
I do not want to be a cat.
If I want to be a sexy nurse or valet,
It will not be in public, where
My mask is used daily.
When it's off, the gaze
Sees caricature
In my skin.
Tell me,
What is it like to want
To be a monster?

for Isatou for Haddy for Adama for Elle

someone came looking for your kind and you looked at her
considered how much she is not from here
Asia all over her face and hair
her English worse than yours

and you opened your mouth

whispering in your own compound
            afraid still
but fear is as common as your own hair
    you wash it and comb it and
        plait it in rows

I am looking for you
    I am looking for our kind
will you open your mouth to me?
  we can scratch and oil each
   other's scalp
     if we only open our mouths
if we plait and unplait each
        other's heads
    we don't even have to speak

        it may never
    happen
you and I are dangerous
        to each other
    one whisper causes bush fire here—
you and I
    may even be cousins

if we never meet
if we never get to whisper together
it is enough that
    you opened your mouth
it is enough
    knowing
  that you exist

        my other
    in the long hours of doing
        and undoing your hair

listen to the whispers
> you will know
> it is me
> you will recognize
your own silent scream

Beatrice Lamwaka

A Ugandan-born writer who was recognised for her literary contribution by the Uganda Registration Service Bureau in 2018, she was also a recipient of the 2011 Young Achievers Award, was shortlisted for the 2015 Morland Writing Scholarship and the 2011 Caine Prize for African Writing, and was a finalist for the 2009 South African PEN/Studzinski Literary Award. The anthology of short stories Queer Africa, *to which she contributed, won the 26th Lambda Literary Award in 2014. Her children's novella,* Anena's Victory (2005), *is a supplementary reader in primary schools. Her stories have been translated into Spanish and Italian. She is working on her first novel,* NyapaRosa.

Missing Letter in the Alphabet

I am not supposed to be sitting in an empty bed, weeping onto a piece of paper on my wedding night. This has never been part of my dream. I have been waiting for this moment all my life. Michael is the person, my mind, my soul and my body wants to be with. I would have said "and my clitoris", I mean what is left after circumcision.

Maybe I should, maybe I shouldn't understand why he left. He wasn't supposed to leave. Not now. Not ever. He is my husband now. He promised. He promised to be with me, no matter what. But he should have known that I am a Sabiny and that I may not be whole in some places like Acoli woman.

My relatives and Michael's are still at the hotel singing and dancing. I can hear people speaking in Kup Sabiny and Leb Acoli. My mother winked as we came to the room. I know she loves Michael; she has been doting over him ever since she met him. She has often said, "Marry another tribe, so that your children will not be circumcised."

I am happy the wedding is now over. We have done it. It seemed hard in the beginning, but we did it. We got the orchids we wanted. The colours were perfect. The dim light in the evening made Serena Hotel perfect.

I am happy to say that my wedding was as I dreamt it would be. I worried about my gown, the food, the dancers and the musicians, but never did Michael cross my mind.

I almost want to believe my friend who said Sabiny and Acoli marriage can never work. "Chesha, my friend, don't get married to that Acoli man," she often said. I never listened. Of course, she knew I would not listen. I never listen to her, anyway.

I was hoping for a memorable wedding night that I would write about in my novel. I had never thought my wedding night would become something I can hardly recognize. I can still feel Michael's fingers sliding on my thighs. His lips warm against mine. I had imagined this scene in my head so many times that when it started to happen differently, I was too shocked to know what to do. "Baby," I murmured. Something I would never have allowed him before we were married.

I felt his finger go limp as he touched where my clitoris should have been. Yes, many years ago the word "circumcision" meant my husband would stay with me and trust me, but today I am not sure what the word means anymore. It never meant he would leave me in bed.

I don't know what I did wrong. All I know is I did what every girl in Kapchorwa did, and was proud of it. My parents never forced me but everyone was doing it. I wanted to be a woman just like my age mates.

I did get my clitoris cut, the source of evil. I had been prepared all my life. We didn't even listen to what the women from the NGOs were saying. How could they say circumcision wasn't good for us? It's what our ancestors have always done. It was much later that I realized that the women were right. My clitoris was already gone and I had to live with it.

But Michael should have known; did he think I wouldn't have done it since I was marrying him? I didn't know that when I was twelve. I wanted to belong so much. I would have sisters for life. I would be respected by everyone. Why wouldn't I get circumcised? There were too many promises for me to not consider getting circumcised. After I sniffed the herb, there was no stopping for me, I had to get circumcised. We danced. We sang about the glory of becoming a woman.

Circumcision was meant to keep me away from danger. With my friends, we said the word, but never imagined the pain we would undergo. Every time I think about the pain, I want to keep my legs together and never open them. Why didn't anyone mention pain? Why didn't anyone mention husbands walking away on wedding nights? Are they afraid of something?

I talked about it with my friends. We were excited. Teachers talked about it. We would be sisters forever with the people we were circumcised with.

It never occurred to me that when the day arrived, I would feel a tingle in my panties, or that it would be a near-death experience. My mother always brushed it off as something every woman has to experience. It was like childbirth: you celebrate soon after. I could see the lie in her eyes. So, every time I saw an older woman, I knew she had been circumcised. That something was missing, and it was already buried somewhere.

We were the alphabet and the C was missing. Our clitorises were the missing letter in the alphabet of the world. It's not a part of our bodies that we mourn. We celebrate its loss. The circumciser keeps it, bewitches us when we misbehave. That fear has always bonded me with the woman who caused me so much pain.

Everybody knows what happened to us as young girls. We walk around, and people from other tribes don't need to ask about clitorises. They know they are long gone.

I am an alphabet. My C is missing, and my husband is missing. Not my fault, but may be my fault. It is amazing how the husband quickly slides off the paper. When my friends teased me that Michael was my husband, before we got married, I often quickly corrected them. "He is my boyfriend," I said with a smile. Now I am calling him my husband, and he is nowhere to be seen.

I don't feel whole, not because I have a missing clitoris but because Michael has left me. I want to shout out: "I am whole," but I wonder who cares. And who cares that my clitoris is missing? I am whole. I am a woman. I am Michael's wife. I am me. I am Chesha.

I now sound drunk. Maybe I should have drunk a little bit of the white wine at the reception. My shoes kept squeezing my feet. I didn't want to deal with the consequences of the wine and the shoes as well. Then I didn't know there was a lot more I would have to deal with. I wish I could push back the time. Back to the time when I had a choice whether to drink the wine or not, but not whether Michael will ever come back to me or if our marriage was actually a marriage or something else.

Circumcision, the word is familiar to me now. Maybe it is actually mutilation. I remember the ordeal clearly. But it is the pain that will never leave. My wound healed fast, but the pain remained. I can still feel it, dream about it and it is so real. I don't know why my clitoris was cut, but I know that maybe I will have to deal with the pain of Michael walking away from me on our wedding night.

I remember the day Michael and I met for the first time. A month later, he sent me a friend request on Facebook. Soon afterwards, he said, "One day, I will marry you," and I thought, "Stupid man." And now I am the stupid one. I am waiting for a man who may or may not return and writing in my journal sober, maybe I should have been drunk—then I would feel less pain and sound more sensible.

He loves me. I love him. And what makes this wrong? Love plus love should be more love.

It is Michael who finds the weight I am trying to fight sexy, and my lips that I think are a little too big, good for kissing. He is the man I find easy to love. I can't get angry with him. He smiles, and I forgive him everything. I love that I love him.

I can't stop thinking about him. I should think about something else. The moon for instance, it's so bright. It makes me miss Michael more. He is my sugarcane. My fene. He is my everything.

I think, during one of our late-night chats on Facebook, I hinted to Michael that my clitoris was no longer there. But tonight shows that the words didn't hit home. It may have lingered on messenger and just reached him today. He has failed to be the Casanova he wanted to be, tonight.

I don't know how long I have been writing. I feel as if I am in a trance. I am hearing footsteps in the corridors. It sounds as if the person's shoes are pressing him. The steps are not the *kokokoko* you hear when a woman is walking on high heels. The person must be a man. I can hear the beating of my heart. If it is Michael, I will stop writing and will have to tell him I will be the best woman he will ever find.

The door opens, and there is my husband, holding his jacket in his hands. He looks very handsome. He smiles. I know he is willing to give it a try.

"Honey, I am back," he says.

Of course, I can see him. I have been waiting for him. I don't want to scream from happiness. Maybe, I should sweep the ground he is walking on. I can't let him know how happy I am. I feel a tear drop on my cheek. I will let it flow.

Lebogang Mashile

The daughter of exiled South African parents, she was born in the US and returned to South Africa in the mid-1990s after the end of apartheid. An actor, writer and performance poet, she appeared in the film Hotel Rwanda *(2004) and has performed in several theatre productions, including* Threads, *and recorded a live performance album incorporating music and poetry,* Lebo Mashile Live. *In 2005, she published her first poetry collection,* In a Ribbon of Rhythm, *for which she received the Noma Award. She was named one of South Africa's Awesome Women of 2005 by* Cosmopolitan *and was named Woman of the Year for 2010 in the category of Arts and Culture by* Glamour *magazine. She was cited as one of the Top 100 Africans by* New African *magazine in 2011, and in 2012 she won the Art Ambassador award at the inaugural Mbokodo Awards for South African Women in the Arts.*

Requiem for Winnie

Rip off the string
That keeps this fragile country
In its form
55 million petals separate
Serrated blades guarding your bursting heart
At the centre
What did your father know
When he raised you like a boy?
Which part of your face's perfection

Broke your mother and every mother
Howling behind mouths
No one dares listen to?

The little girl who holds a stick
And beats a man's world into submission
Is the woman who lays diamonds
On a murderous nation's neck
And then sets it ablaze
Who does not call this justice?

The queen draped in regalia
On a subversive courtroom catwalk
Is the prisoner stripped dripping blood
Paraded before men turned into beasts
Who taught our men to hate us?
If they hate us, can we call them ours?
In the hours of loneliness where your rivers
Burst onto pillows, sleeping children and concrete floors
Did we ever stop being yours?

They lie in your name
Despise in your name
Erase
Berate
Bludgeon
Belittle
Deny in your name
In the ravenous gorge between
What is written and what is true
An incendiary wall rises in your name

Like you,
they would cast us as monsters
Steal our gems
Then discard our carcasses
In the wasteland of the scavenged

Like you,
They would immortalize us
With the mouths they use
To say they love their mothers
In a country of contradictions

Mothers leave their children
Because they love their children
Men give women their names
Women give men's names meaning
Men carry this wealth out the door
As they are leaving

You are
Ever present and invisible
Amplified and silenced
Tortured and free
Married and abandoned
Elevated and degraded
Warrior and healer
Comrade and lover
Bleeding and beautiful
Playful and ferocious
Mary and Mary Magdalene
Oshun
Kali
Sekhmet
With life and death in the palm of your hand
You are gone
And
Everywhere

Invocation

We call on memories buried inside skeletons of the first people to walk the skin
     of the Earth
Who nursed and nested in the cradle and spread civilizations across the planet
     like seeds

Tell us of the air that flows through the heart of the land to all of life and
     creation
Tell us of breath, the first song
Tell us of words like constellations of ideas mapping our contribution to
     humanity
Tell us of infinity
How the universe lives in us
Tell us which stars bear our names
So that we no longer have to fear the night

Tell us of Earth
Of roots that course through the body of the land like veins through flesh
Tell us of the force that squeezed red sand like dough to form mountains
Tell us how to make communities strong like gemstones formed under extreme
    pressure

We call on the desert to remember when she was the bottom of the sea
Help us understand how to be fluid like water
How to be supple without losing our identity

We call on the volcanoes to inject us with flames of imagination
Once we carried tongues burping fire
We melted metals with our minds

Tell us what we have forgotten
We are not afraid of bones
Tell us what we have lost
We are not afraid of remembering
Tell us what has been erased
We are not afraid of time
Tell us who we once were
We are not afraid of ourselves

Isabella Matambanadzo

A Zimbabwean feminist, she was raised with a deep awareness of her country's struggles for liberation and self-determination, which has influenced her life's path. Her love for the arts won her a prestigious Reuters Foundation scholarship to study Journalism, Literature and Theatre Studies at Rhodes University in Grahamstown. In addition to working on the campus newspaper, serving on the founding team of Cue TV, the Grahamstown Arts Festival television channel, and broadcasting on the campus radio station, she supported herself by working as a waitress and reading audio books at a centre for the blind. She graduated with triple majors, summa cum laude and achieved Dean's List recognition and Academic Colours in 1999. She was published in the anthology Writing Free *(Weaver Press, 2011).*

A Very Recent Tale

The cubicles in her school library were hand-crafted from old teak, harvested from high on a *kopje* whose trees were once adored as sacred. They were the place where the ancestors were put. Upright. Swathed in generous constellations of frankincense. From the thickness of those far-away forests, their duty was to keep a watch on the next generations. And that is what they did. Until there were no trees left.

The adolescent girl, face framed by a pair of glasses, used her long hands to lever a reference book from its place on a wooden shelf. She sat deep in the cavern of a high-backed polished olive-green leather chair. Picking open the text, she inhaled odours of ancient things.

Her eyes paused at an entry:

> The *Gloriosa Superba* is Zimbabwe's national flower. It is among a variety of the protected plant species within the country. When Queen Elizabeth II visited Zimbabwe, then Southern Rhodesia, in 1947 she was presented with the gift of a flame lily diamond brooch. In traditional medical practice, skilled physicians use the plant to heal, induce abortion and as poison.

Flame Lily had been so named for her mother's favourite flower. She came into the world with a burst of incorruptible joy, brightening an otherwise gloomy season. The tendrils of her hair twirled into a globular gathering of deep yellows and warm oranges, just like the petals of her floral namesake.

Mama Senait, a middle-aged Eritrean midwife who had attended her home water birth, had obviously seen it all. "Mmmm", she exhaled, her expressionless face concealing her feelings, "she's a big and healthy one."

A migrant herself, Mama Senait was the community's midwife. She had left all sentiment behind her thirty years earlier when at fifteen she escaped from an unexpected war. Her friends had been less fortunate. They had been captured in the raids that took young girls from Asmara to the frontline, from where they were expected to strengthen the military ranks of the war that started in 1988 and continued till 2000. Girls became guerrilla women there, expected to dance in patriotic muteness to music that discounted what the men had done to them up there on the hills.

Mama Senait lived her life on two ingredients: prudence and pragmatism. Just as she had learned to perforate an amniotic sac, she had trained herself to cut off all emotion from her heart and live within her dead-end choice. Her only indulgence was bringing babies into the world. Her rudimentary spiritual theory was that for every brown life she pulled expertly from a womb reluctant to let go of its treasure, a wandering soul would finally find rest back in her once homeland.

Flame Lily emitted a spectacular fart in answer to her birth attendant's sobriety. It was an unmissable declaration of her arrival.

As her uterus emptied of its creation, Matireva Chiweshe, who had never planned motherhood for herself, was surprised. Her ears caught the fall of salty droplets, out of tune, into a champagne flute handed to her by a man she'd never wanted to love. That thought brought her hidden memories forward.

Flame Lily's name held a second tribute only revealed to those who probed about the stubborn, bounce-back kink in her full head of hair, and how at a summer's picnic, she would turn an enviable earthy hue. Nosey minds would learn that it was a tribute to her Zimbabwean roots. A country left somewhat unexpectedly. A place and time that had become forgotten in all but the soul.

By her early teens, Flame Lily's voice would be scrubbed clean of her mother's Zimbabwean influences. School took care of that erasure. Matireva looked at this paradox of her child, who was at once full of her being, but looked nothing like her.

By birth, behaviour and accent, Flame Lily was as English as could be. But in her dreams, a language she heard in her mother's songs played her imagination, pulling her to places she wished to be:

> *Vanorara musango*
> *Vachichema kwazvo*
> *Vamwe vano tsanya*
> *Vachigununguna*
> *Zviri kwamuri Mambo*
> *Chido chenyu itai.*
> *Chido chenyu here ichi? Pindurayi Mambo*
> *Chido chenyu here ichi?*
> *Pindurayi Mambo…*

The music rose in crescendos, causing Flame Lily to ask inconvenient questions. Her parents' secrecy with each other produced equally unsatisfactory answers. Yes, their meeting in November of 2017 was plausible, but was there romance? She demanded to know.

Her parents had both been invited, rather suddenly, to a dinner hosted by the Ambassador to Harare, Zimbabwe's weather-beaten, battered and bruised capital. It was the season for lavish, jubilant bread-breaking of this nature. The Biggest Man, for years viewed as an affront to all things progressive, had finally buckled. Not voluntarily, but under a disproportionate weight placed on him by his own Generals. Men he had once considered his trusted friends. He had no choice. After all, he had no guns; they had them all.

The country's lawyers argued publicly over whether an enforced resignation, tendered in an unsigned letter, was in fact a coup. Or not. Court etiquette, couched in faux-polite phrases such as *"my learned friend"*, fell by the wayside. Life-long friendships heaved against each other, intolerably strained over whether a weary old man who had outlived his welcome, even in his own political party, had been treated fairly or otherwise. Friends took jibes at the legal minds' contest for superior acumen. From the mixture of jest, jealousy and jingoism, "Not A Coup" rapidly gained hold.

The citizens of the country fell back on the safety-net of survivors' wit and parody. They wanted, some of them said in righteous rage, the Biggest Man to be put out on a bench in the square of the capital city's First Street. They deserved a chance to throw at him the rotten eggs they had stored, like precious gems, in disintegrating nests. Above all, they wanted the Biggest Man to return the billions he had stolen.

At the vast Embassy dinner table Matireva had no choice but to notice, positioned across from her, a tall, long-haired chap, whose skin gave off the unblemished shine that comes from generations of privilege. The rather awkward guest-list was an amalgam of ideology-less politicians, priests of the new and old order and protest types. Inconspicuous spies from both host and hosted countries sat carefully interspersed between those of opposing views. Someone who called himself an entrepreneur kept talking about money. It was a potent mix.

She spent most of the evening listening to predictable analysis of what had happened and how, remaining politely attentive; but in truth, she found this company boring and showy. She despised that her work as both owner and curator of The Clever Natives, an art gallery that took work from what a reviewer in a travel journal had called "unknown artists", required her to hobnob with expatriates.

Jonathan St John was the hurriedly appointed Cultural Attaché. He was charged with turning this unexpected political moment into one of artistic production. He was on the prowl for painters, photographers, theatre types and any artist with an appropriate story of struggle and creation. They had to be fresh names, he explained, who saw the mélange of existentialism and history as representative of a shared, hopeful future.

Matireva looked at this man with suspicion. He wanted underdogs who through his country's benevolence would be turned into global superstars. He also wanted first dibs on purchasing the most valuable art being created by hungry artists.

Jono, as his mates called him, had a disarming smile, flanked by even teeth that were the obvious beneficiaries of high-quality dental care. He claimed to have been born in Nigeria to Foreign Service parents. She suspected he was a spy.

The conversation was heated, fuelled by copious amounts of alcohol. Even the preacher men drank, she observed. She nursed her drink with caution, unwilling to be drawn into the dubious debate.

The mood of merriment continued until July of 2018, when the elections were to be held. By then, Jono had, quite uninvited, made her gallery part of his daily routine. His presence felt like a trap. Every day, he sprawled his long legs on the front lawn, occupying her space. His tools included engraved pens and leather-bound notebooks. He interviewed artist after artist. He appeared to have a limitless budget. He bought food, drink, painting supplies and cigarettes. Just like his ancestors, Matireva thought.

From the east-facing window of her office she watched the barely-there winter sun cut through end-of-day traffic that moved at the pace of an overfed *zongororo*.

Three weeks before Election Day, the city's walls were covered by glossy campaign billboards of candidates who promised that they were the beautiful ones, anointed to lead by the most powerful deity of all deities.

Jono cast a shadow over her view as he strode, unwelcomed, into her office. His proposition made her swallow nervously. How would she like, he asked without a question mark, to organise a dozen or so of the artists who exhibited in her gallery to travel to Britain, all expenses paid, for a couple of shows.

"I would not," she snapped, hoping the three little words would make him go away.

But Jono sweetened his deal. Scholarships for those whose works were most popular were already lined up, and post-exhibition support for those who would return home were certain to be confirmed. For a year, at the very least.

The community of artists around her had become like family. She knew that behind the vibrant colours of the post-*Not-A-Coup* creativity that drew on the country's flag were empty pockets and emptier stomachs. No one was buying art. Her accountant had suggested that if things remained this way, she should consider closing down.

So she said in a business-like tone, "Our company policy is that when an artist travels, he or she goes with his spouse or partner and their children. We don't separate families. We insist on medical insurance for everyone and that a quarter of the payment is made to the artist in advance. You also need to support the application costs for emergency passports. Not everyone has travel documents." Jono reached his hand out to shake on the verbal deal.

That was how, after voting on Monday, July 30, together with the artists and their families, she ended up flying across the ocean, with canvas loads of new works carried on board as hand luggage. In the small space between her departure from Harare and her arrival in London on August 1, things fell apart.

As they sat in the stuffy train from Heathrow Airport, Jono moved nervously beside her. "I suppose you've seen this," his questionless question, as he handed her his mobile phone. And she saw a woman's body, face-down, bullet wounds in her back, one foot shoeless.

Soldiers had been deployed downtown, to the side of the city where the gallery stood. They had opened fire on anyone in their line of vision. Her gallery, an old house her parents had left her, had gone up in a haze of smoke and flames.

A journalist for an international news agency, who had meandered off the election story beat at a nearby hotel, captured the events on his camera. The images made headline news. And because of the unplanned coincidence of her opening exhibition that evening featuring paintings of soldiers in a very different mood—in an overseas gallery that held other sacred things looted from the past, imprisoned in displays behind glass—she knew there would never be a return to the scene of crimes current and past.

Her stomach churned as she looked at clay pots taken, together with waist beads, from a maiden's trousseau. In that very moment she understood it was not only her dreams that had died, but the hopes of many of her generation. Born of war, their lives would forever be steeped in cycles of unfinished hate.

Maaza Mengiste

An Ethiopian American, she is the author of Beneath the Lion's Gaze *(2010), selected by* The Guardian *as one of the 10 best contemporary African books, and a second novel,* The Shadow King. *She is a Fulbright Scholar and recipient of a 2018 National Endowment for the Arts Fellowship. She was also the 2013 Puterbaugh Fellow and a runner-up for the 2011 Dayton Literary Peace Prize. She has been published in the* New Yorker, New York Review of Books, Granta, The Guardian, New York Times, Rolling Stone, Guernica, *and* Lettre International, *among other places. After her family fled the Ethiopian revolution, she spent much of her childhood in Nigeria, Kenya and the US. Both her fiction and non-fiction examine the individual lives at stake during migration, war and exile. She was a writer on the 2013 documentary film* Girl Rising, *and on* The Invisible City: Kakuma. *She serves on the boards of* Words Without Borders *and* Warscapes.

This Is What the Journey Does

From my table next to a large window inside a café, I watch the young man. The orange glow of a late afternoon sun drapes him in thick layers, lying across his shoulders and accenting his face. I recognize him for the East African that he is, a young man of Eritrean or Ethiopian origin with a slender frame, delicate features, and large eyes. He has the gaunt look of other recently arrived immigrants whom I have met, a thinness that goes beyond a natural state of the body. He moves differently from one accustomed to the space he inhabits; his gait is a series of cautious, jagged steps forward. He appears frightened, overly sensitive to those who brush past him. He seems as if he is trying to coil inside himself, shrink enough to avoid being touched. Though I can note all of these details, I know there is nothing really special about him, not in Florence, Italy. He is just one of the many refugees or migrants who have made their way here from East Africa, a physical embodiment of those now-familiar reports and photographs of migration.

Pedestrians amble past on the narrow sidewalk, casting long shadows in the golden light of dusk. They are caught up in their private conversations, lost in the steady rhythm of their exchanges. They are unaware of the young man I am observing, staring past my own reflection to get a better look. They do not realize that he is picking up speed behind them, his body stiffening with each passing second. He bends forward at the chest, slightly at first, then as if he might tip over from his own momentum. He moves that way for several paces before he starts to push past pedestrians, oblivious to those he nearly trips. He is a wild, wayward figure careening carelessly through the busy sidewalk, distracted by his own thoughts.

Then, abruptly, he stops. He is so still that curious eyes turn on him, this sunlit figure stepping calmly into the middle of the busy intersection. He stands there, immobile and slightly stunned as cars come to a halt and motorcyclists slow. Traffic waits for him to move. Instead, he begins to gesture, a conductor leading an invisible orchestra. His bony arms bend and extend, propelled by an energy only growing stronger. Each sweep of his hand pulls the rest of him upward then twists him in an awkward circle. He continues as observers pause, then shake their heads and walk on by. Soon, he is working his mouth around words, and even before he starts, I know he is about to shout.

I let everything else disappear so I can focus on the developing scene. People move past him, irritated but still polite. Motorists carefully angle around his intruding figure. Everyone ignores him as best as they can, treating him as no more than a mild disturbance, unremarkable. He continues gesticulating, his head turning one way then the other, his actions getting progressively faster. There is a strange kind of rhythm beginning, an erratic dance that is leaving him desperate to keep pace. While I watch, something squeezes against my chest and makes me take a sudden breath. I don't understand the ache that fills me. Or maybe I just do not want to recognize it. Maybe I do not want to find the words because to do so would mean to tumble down somewhere dark, far from this bright and busy street.

I have come to the café to escape the day's barrage of disturbing news. I have come with a notebook and my pen to distance myself from reminders of the turbulence continuing in America, in Ethiopia, in the Mediterranean, in the Middle East, in Europe: everywhere. I have come to find a way out of what I know in order to make my way toward a space where I can imagine, unhindered by unnecessary distractions. I have come to be alone, to write in solitude, free of the noise that has seemed to follow me for months, or perhaps it has been years. It is hard to know how to measure time, how to orient oneself when horror and shock begin to embed themselves into the pulse of daily life. It has become easy to live in the present moment, to spin from one disturbing event to the next, to move so quickly between disasters that entire days are spent in stupefied surprise.

Lazarus, I think, as I keep watching this young man: a defiant body refusing stillness, resisting quietness. A body using noise to stay alive, to move, to be seen. The waitress comes to take my order and smiles down at my notebook. I notice the couple next to me eyeing it warily, as if they are afraid I am taking notes on their conversation. No one seems to be aware of the drama unfolding outside the café where a young black man with unkempt hair is spinning in increasingly wide circles, motioning wildly, shouting incoherently at passersby. He is a spectacle without an audience. He is an actor in Shakespeare's tale, full of sound and fury.

He spins and flings his arms. He throws up a hand and snaps his wrist. He closes a palm over an ear and listens to his own whispers. He frowns and smiles, laughs alone, then twirls and catches another stranger's stare. There is anger in his spastic energy. There is sorrow and confusion in his eyes. He is breaking, I say to myself, and doing what he can to keep himself together. My reflection catches my eye and so I put my head down, and in my notebook I write: "You did not leave home like this. This is what the journey does." It comes again, that ache in the middle of my chest. For a moment, it is so strong that I am sure he can feel it. I am certain it is a tether binding us together and he will turn in just the right way and I will be exposed. If he looks at me, then our lives will unfold and in front of us will be the many roads we have taken to get to this intersection in Florence and we will reveal ourselves for what we are: immigrant, migrant, refugee, African, East African, black, foreigner, stranger, a body rendered disobedient by the very nature of what we are.

When I glance up again, the young man has quieted down. Now, he looks almost bored as he weaves between pedestrians while twisting a lock of hair around a skinny finger. He moves lazily, as if he has accomplished what he set out to do. From where I sit, it looks as though he is walking toward me, but he is simply following the sidewalk, and soon it will force him to proceed directly past the open door of the café where I am. As he saunters past, I notice a small bald patch on the back of his head. It is a perfect circle, as if a round object was placed on his scalp to burn away his hair through to his skin. I tell myself that I cannot possibly know what it is, that it could be an illusion, it could be just a leaf stuck in his hair, but that is not enough to keep myself from flinching.

Stories come back to me, told by a friend who crossed the Sahara to get to Europe by way of North Africa. He spoke of horrifying treatment at the hands of human traffickers and police in detention centers and makeshift prisons. He shared what he could and skipped the rest. In moments when several who made the journey were gathered, I would watch them point to their scars to help fill the lapses in their stories. Sometimes, there was no language capable of adding coherence to what felt impossible to comprehend. Sometimes, it was only the body that bore the evidence, pockmarks and gashes forming their own vocabulary. Staring at the busy intersection, I don't want to consider what this young man might have gone through to arrive in Italy, to be in the street on this day. That he is alive is a testament to his endurance. What he has been subjected to, what might have caused that scar, what was too much for his mind to accept—these thoughts lead the way to far darker realities than I can possibly know. I look back at the first note I took upon seeing him: "You did not leave home like this. This is what the journey does."

Lazarus was given the chance to walk again in the land of the living. On one hand, it was a simple proposition: he obeyed the command to stand up and he was able to live. The rest of his days paled in the brilliant light of this astounding miracle. It is easy to imagine that he moved gracefully through his new existence, a man pulsing with this exposure to divine grace and might. We want to think that when he rose from the dead, he did so untainted and unburdened. That it was a rebirth, free of unsettling wisdom. But Lazarus was an ordinary man who opened his eyes to find himself incomprehensible. Somewhere between the end of this life and his second chance, he shifted forms, became a miracle and a stranger, remolded from loved one to aberration.

Medical science understands death to be a process rather than a single event. Though death might seem a cataclysmic and sudden event, the body undergoes several functions before it no longer lives. The various organs that support it collapse one by one. They each must cease all activity for an extended period of time in order for a person to be declared dead. It is not sufficient for the heartbeat and circulation alone to stop, for example, they must cease long enough for the brain to also die. The end of life involves a journey, a series of steps before that ultimate destination. A body requires certain signposts to nudge it in the right direction. An abrupt shift in that progressive movement disrupts the order of things. It deforms a natural process and leaves behind something warped and unrecognizable.

Perhaps this explains Lazarus's complete silence in John 11 and 12 in the Bible. To give him a voice would mean to grapple with the messiness that his resurrection created. It would be to insert a complex, human component in a direct and potent lesson. Though the Sanhedrin wanted to kill him along with Jesus Christ, though his resurrected life and all that it represented was as much a threat to them as the claims of Jesus, Lazarus is not allowed to speak. He is a muted miracle, still alive today as a metaphor for uncanny second chances. We have found many ways to make use of his example, but we do not know what to do with the living man. In part, it is because the Bible reveals so little about him. His story ends when he is no longer convenient. But to assume that he became worthless once he stepped free from his grave is to shrink his life down to its most significant moment. It is to believe that nothing else can possibly matter after so great a feat. It is to embrace the idea that we are, all of us, simple beings relentlessly pivoting around the same occurrence, trapped by the enormity of an important event, as if it is both the sun that guides us and the darkness that leaves us spinning in uncertain space.

There is a phrase in medieval Chinese literature used to explain the biological phenomenon of an ailing body that revives, suddenly and briefly, only to collapse and die. It is *hui guang fan zhao*, translated as "last glow before sunset," that brief shimmer before night. I think of this as the café where I sit begins to empty and a new set of patrons streams in. A DJ near me starts to spin his music against the slowly darkening sky outside. Through the window at my side, I gaze past my own reflection to focus on the unbroken flow of pedestrians and motorists at the intersection. The young man I observed earlier is gone, and in his place, routine and repetition have stepped in. I see him for a moment, though, leaving home, wherever that might have been, and making the tortuous trek through the Sahara. I see him trapped in containers and overloaded trucks and crowded boats. I see him struggle with a deadening stillness, then step onto land to face the boundaries set up in Europe. The journey is designed to test the body's resilience. Its intent is to break a human being and rearrange him or her inside. Every inch forward is a reminder of one's frailty. You do not arrive the same as when you left. You will sometimes look at a stranger and recognize yourself reflected in that new life: impossibly alive, walking through the lingering glow of a splendid sun while trying to spin free of a permanent darkness.

Sisonke Msimang

*A South African writer and public commentator, who spent much of her youth
between continents and cultures as her parents' political life took the family from
Zambia to Canada, Kenya and Ethiopia, she is the author of* Always Another
Country: A memoir of exile and home *(2017) and* The Resurrection of Winnie
Mandela *(2018). Her work has appeared in the* New York Times, The Guardian,
Newsweek *and* Al Jazeera, *and she is a contributing editor to* Africa is a Country.

Black Girl in America

America gives me anonymity and gives me love. In that order. The two are intertwined
in my heart and in that place inside me that belongs to America. Anonymity comes
first and then—in the terrain of the unknown, this landscape where I am nobody
special, in the crevices and shadows of places where I have no birthright—I find love.

Until now, I have always been at the centre of the universe. I was born into an
Africa that was waiting for me, into a movement that needed children as emblems
of the future. We were totems not just of our parents' love but the ability of the
struggle to regenerate. It wasn't only us ANC kids. All across the continent were
Africa's promise, middle-class children birthed with the purpose of walking away
from the past with absolute confidence. The post-colonial children of the elite, whose
parents' hearts were filled with dreams, we carried the vision of a decolonised future
in our smiles.

In America I am given a new meaning. I am just a black girl.

In America I learn quickly that to be black is to be both unknown and unknowable.
As an outsider I see almost immediately that this society deliberately misrecognises
black people and the effect is to diminish them individually and as a group.

At first I marvel at the stories of mistaken identity. My friends were the best
and brightest in their schools. That's why they got plucked—into a private four-
year college. They are shining stars in their communities. The minute they step
beyond their drooping blocks into cities that gleam and glitter grandly, they become
invisible—a superpower they didn't ask for but know how to use to their advantage.
Sometimes their luck runs out. They'll be just walking, just shooting the breeze, and
suddenly they attract attention, like glow-in-the-dark figures.

They learn to creep, to walk close to walls, to put their hoodies up and keep their
heads slouched; to shrink so they aren't noticed. Attention aimed at ghetto children
is rarely positive.

In my first year I am assigned a room with a girl named Katie. She is half-white,
half-Sri Lankan. Everyone hangs out in our room a lot.

Someone says, "They thought my cousin was a guy on *America's Most Wanted*
so they shot at him."

Someone else says, "The clerk said I looked like a lady who had been in the store last week and stolen a watch so she kicked me out."

And another one: "That landlady said she forgot what I looked like. I just met you last week and you supposed to be tryin' to rent me an apartment! How are you gonna forget what a client looks like? My money's the same colour as everyone else's."

I learn quickly that to be black in America is to be looked through, passed over, or locked away. It is to be constantly misrecognised.

None of these experiences would be new to my compatriots who grew up in South Africa. They are not entirely new to me either. The years in Canada took their toll. Still, I have not grown up in the belly of the beast. When your individuality is denied, when you are constantly thought to be someone other than who you are, you either die or blossom. America shows me how this feels. I am grateful that it's too late for my soul to be killed by my encounter with American racism. I am even more grateful that, by the time I go back to South Africa, its worst edges will have been blunted.

So, because I have been raised to believe I am the centre of the universe, America does not threaten who I am. It makes me a soldier in a way I may not otherwise have been.

Before I went to America I was as politically aware as a high-school student can be. I was enrolled at the International School of Kenya, where I was on the student council and wrote for the school paper. My favourite classes were Social Studies and English and French because we read real books and grappled with ideas and our French teacher was a renegade and plucked his eyebrows and we didn't know yet what gay was but he was anti-authoritarian. And the carefully crafted multinational bubble made us feel special and loved and part of the politics of the country, even though we weren't.

So, it is only in America, in the fall of 1992, that I begin to understand the difference between being politically aware and politically active.

It begins with being made to feel small. In the first weeks after my arrival, I am followed wordlessly in shops in the mall. One night, as I'm coming home on a bus, an old man sidles up as he gets off and says softly in my ear—almost lyrically—"Nigger bitch."

I have spent eighteen years mainly protected from the psychological harm that comes of being looked through or past or over. Canada punctured but did not deflate my self-esteem and Nairobi put the air back in my tyres. So now, each time someone dismisses me, I grow stronger. I understand the power of having a lens through which to interpret the world. It signals the difference between drowning and swimming to safety.

America makes me brave because it forces me to fight for myself.

I make friends. There is LaKeesha from Gary, Indiana, Michael Jackson's home town. She is petite and wiry and intense. We talk through long nights, an inseparable, incongruous-looking, pair. I am tall with a big butt and a teeny chest, she is short but with boobs enough for both of us. We laugh about sharing our assets. Physical differences aside, we occupy space in the same way, filling every room with our preoccupations. When I am reading *Sula* everyone knows it. When we discover *for colored girls who have considered suicide / when the rainbow was enuf*, there isn't a table we sit at that isn't informed about it. We read aloud. Our sisterhood is kinetic. Then, there is Sharon. A year ahead of me, Sharon is from Natchez, Mississippi, but went to high school in Minneapolis. Her mother followed the river north, looking for freedom for her kids. Sharon is the hope of her family—hard-working, diligent, strait-laced. Yet all Sharon wants to do is act. When she is on a stage, nothing else matters. But college-educated black women with strong family ties don't become actors: they become accountants or lawyers or doctors. Sharon struggles with the decision, wedded both to the joy performing brings and to her commitment to being a good daughter.

And there is Simone from St Vincent originally. She too was raised by a single mother and, like the rest of us, cannot afford to mess up. Simone isn't prone to smiling, but she is protective and loyal, as good a friend as you can ask for in a hostile environment. There is Katie, my roommate. Her father is Sri Lankan, her mother white American. There is Marika whose pale skin and freckles belie her African and native American heritage.

The group of us become angry and eloquent spokespersons for diversity. We are intense. We read a lot. We talk a lot.

We form a poetry troupe, call ourselves Sistahs of the Rainbow. A year later we have become Sistahs 'n Struggle. Only the black members of the troupe remain. We scowl often and stage performances. Sharon and LaKeesha can really act and have talent. The rest of us are passionate but should probably not be on stage. It doesn't matter to us, though; our politics is our art. We rehearse earnestly, reciting Margaret Walker, Sonia Sanchez, Ntozake Shange, Nikki Giovanni. White students both love and fear us. We care a lot what they think even as we profess not to.

Soon everywhere we go on campus we are recognised and applauded. This makes us even angrier because the accolades don't change the attrition rate for black students on campus. It doesn't increase enrolment figures either.

We decide acting is not enough. We take on institutional discrimination. We scrawl graffiti on campus. We stage a sit-in at the president's office, demanding that the university review its policies on hiring black professors, admitting more students of colour and addressing the high dropout rate.

We win some concessions and we celebrate. A black professor is given tenure. A political science hire is made and he is African. We have not yet learnt—because we are so young—that institutional racism is a wily old beast, and that these are just superficial wins.

The casualties of racism on campus stack up. We cry a lot. The number of black students shrinks. One friend—Andre—turns into a shell of himself. He drifts. He acts in odd ways. He was hilarious. Then one day he is rambly. Then he is gone: dropped out. Our numbers are too small. Each departure, under circumstances unhappy and unplanned, shakes us.

I lose patience with other African students. They are full of excuses about how different Africans are from African-Americans. At first I simply nod. Like them, I knew the rigours of a nightly homework routine and not being allowed to watch TV until physics was mastered or essays completed. Intellectually I see little difference between the two campus communities, the small striving African one and the striving black American one, but there is a rift.

That first year of college, Spike Lee releases *Malcolm X*. Keesha and I see the movie on opening night. Our bellies are filled with fire. We read *The Autobiography of Malcolm X* over and over. "Listen, listen, listen!" I squeal: "I believe in the brotherhood of all men, but I don't believe in wasting brotherhood on anyone who doesn't want to practice it with me."

I am full of righteousness. I throw myself into more Malcolm X. I go back to Steve Biko. I read Stokely Carmichael. I read about the Black Panthers.

The poetry we perform is mainly by women, but the politics—the words that animate our conversations, and push us to act in the real world—these belong to men. It takes a while before I understand the effect this has on my own political sensibilities.

Had I been born into a Black Consciousness family my exposure to American racism at university might not have been so transformative. In our house, nonracialism has always been the quiet centrepiece of our politics. Mummy and Baba are proud and can stand up for themselves. They appreciate Biko but are grounded in a different sensibility. They are part of a Charterist movement, deeply connected to the idea that Africans are also intellectual and as worthy of respect as whites. Theirs is not a politics designed to question the very basis of white people's civilisation.

For the first time, I see my parents not as slightly naive. They have been duped by whiteness. Like Christopher Columbus, my friends and I believe that we have discovered blackness.

It is years before I understand bell hooks' ideas about radical love and discover Audre Lorde. It takes time for me to discover it is possible to embrace radicalism that looks and feels different from the radical ideas of women. And so it takes me longer than I would have liked to see that there are ways of being tough without being judgmental about the choices of others. It takes me even longer to realise that those with more moderate politics than mine were making choices that weren't necessarily based on being compromised. Mummy and Baba weren't ignorant of Biko. They had considered his point of view and differed—not on the basis of weakness, but on the legitimate basis of intellectual and strategic disagreement. I couldn't see that then, though it is plain now.

Blessing Musariri

A Zimbabwean author of short stories and poems, she has had some of her writing published in South African English textbooks for high schools, as well as in anthologies. She has published four children's titles, two of which have won national awards. She trained to be a lawyer but her active imagination took over after she was called to the English Bar in 1997, leading her to a more varied and fulfilling life in the world of arts and culture. She holds an MA in Diplomatic Studies from the University of Westminster. Over the years, she has worked as a freelance editing and proofreading consultant, an English teacher and a project co-ordinator for the British Council Harare.

Signs That You Were Here

A lonely cornflake, ousted from your cereal bowl for its unexplained deformity, now destined for a one-way trip to the rubbish. This, you leave for me to gaze upon and ponder your passing through the room.

On a coffee table in the living room, a cup of half drunk tea waits despairingly, knowing that it has become too cold to warrant your continued attention, it doesn't know it yet but you're not coming back and it's up to me to put it out of its misery.

In the bathroom, your toothbrush gloats and the damp towel flung carelessly in the corner luxuriates in the memory of your warm skin. They mock me as I set the room to rights. Through the open doorway, the bed sits in stoic despondency, resigned to the loss of your long, lean frame spread-eagled across the sheets, across me.

The mirror smiles and keeps her secrets to herself, tells me only that, which my eyes can see, indifferent to my wishing for something else, something…more, but here on the dresser is a sad cuff-link next to an empty box—the other is long gone to that place between then and now.

Then, you were right here in front of me, laughing as we said goodbye, sighing at the wonderful of it all, and now, the sound echoes faintly, whispering of your having been here.

The Poem I Wrote Standing Up—Indictment

We are proud to be Africans on distant shores,
learning ancient tongues, fighting for their survival,

while forgetting our own.
We adopt new inflections
and sing-song ways of speaking
to camouflage our origins,
hiding from the tainted brush.
We are the new Celts—darker, more robust.
We sanction our memories of sun and hunger
and hopeful hopelessness.
We unlearn our songs and disappear through our children—
the pristine generation, unmarked by unpopular citizenry.
We are not proud. We are not Africans.

On Platform 3

The 3.28 has been cancelled.
I've been dropped off and left alone,
no-one likes this side of morning—but I with my love of holiday,
left in singular dread, in a place unusually deserted.
After all, I am not a Lost Boy, wandering through Sudanese nights,
afraid of lions and land-mines. I am in Luton—
well-lit; a target for any passer-by,
who has issues with his mother, but,
it's the land of CCTV.

They are sorry to announce that
the oh three twenty-eight service to St Pancras
has been cancelled. They should have announced it in my dreams
so I could sleep a little longer.
Time doesn't tick, but lingers,
drones seamlessly in my ears, bites into skin,
slowing fingers, stiffening limbs,
nibbles at microscopic morsels in my gut until it grumbles.

There's no one here to answer my questions,
only machines, mouths open for my money.
I've walked for miles in tiny circles,
the killer has not come, and still, the tracks are silent.
They don't announce the loss of the 3.28 anymore,
they are over it now, but I am flying to sea, sun and sand,
I must sit and wait.

She, on the way to Monk's Hill

She knows everyone on the way to Monk's Hill,
stops to ask for mangoes—they are growing everywhere
it's almost a crime to pay.

At the overflowing bridge, men wash pink-skinned sweet potatoes
while the river steals a few,
she hollers hello and lets them know, tells me, they'll fetch them later.

Stopping for ginnip breeds nostalgia
of her childhood in Guyana—
plantain, sour-sop, breadfruit—
always free, from neighbours,

says her brother doesn't believe in apples;
he's never seen an apple tree, so doesn't trust the juice.
But her nephew, he eats strawberries in
banana cake and doesn't know the difference.

She careens through mud; a carefree cowboy, calling out the sights
arms wrapped around her waist, I am a jockey without her reins,
holding on to every word, bracing at every hurdle.

St John's, Antigua, 30 May 2010

Wanjiku wa Ngũgĩ

*Born in Kenya (into a family of writers that includes her father Ngũgĩ wa Thiong'o
and her brother Mũkoma wa Ngũgĩ), she studied in the US and has lived and worked
in Eritrea, Zimbabwe and Finland. She is a political analyst, the author of* The Fall
of Saints *(2014), and the founder and former director of the Helsinki African Film
Festival. She has been a columnist for the Finnish development magazine* Maailman
Kuvalehti *and her essays and short stories have been published in* Wasafiri, The
Herald *(Zimbabwe), the* Daily Nation & Business Daily, Pambazuka News, *and*
Chimurenga, *among other publications.*

Hundred Acres of Marshland

Even I find it hard to believe that I learned how to swim in a low-lying wetland with grassy vegetation. Down the hill from my house was what seemed like hundreds of acres of marshland. The sky with a blue so prominent that even when dark clouds gathered it was difficult not to make out the azure bouncing off the clear waters of the lagoon. I spent half my life swimming, even with passers-by who rested their weary feet in the cool of the water. A week after Ted, my now five-year-old son, was born, the lagoon was waiting for me to wash away the fatigue of motherhood. This was before I boarded the plane to the land where I began the wait. Waiting for Ted to join me. Waiting for my life to come together in the way I had envisioned so many times while lying on the green grassland by the lagoon. Like the photos I had seen of my neighbor's daughter's life in America.

These days there is hope only in my dreams, when someone gently pulls my hand and leads me towards my aspirations. And then I wake up in stone-cold Newark.

I mention the lagoon because lately I have been visiting it in my mind during waking hours. Mostly I wonder if Ted has been swimming. But on this particular morning, my attention is on myself. It feels as if someone is ripping my intestines out. I know it's the French fries. My body has waged a war with food in this new country. Not so new, its been a year already. Right now, I have an immediate problem. The thing is, although most of last night is a blur, I do remember that after the third glass of wine I made promises. To Au, my Thai friend. She is the one I blame for this revolution taking place in my head. I would much rather wallow in dreams about my grassy marshland than make social calls. I do sometimes feel the need to reach out. And then I feel guilty because I know it's his voice, my husband's, in my head telling me to make more of an effort. It's hard to describe how heavy my body feels these days. My pen is lighter. So I sit in a café and fill paper with haikus. A habit I have always entertained, and one my husband used to find endearing. Now he likes to be practical. His words not mine.

This morning, I watched him set off to work through my half-shut eyelids. I pretend to be asleep when his morning ritual takes place. Mostly so I don't have to listen to his rants, and his enduring wish to be in my position. Free. He says it as if it was an expensive virtue only available to some. What he really means to say is that two incomes are better than one. Many unpleasant words come to me for him, but I am bound by this contract I have with him, and to say them would only add to the wall we have been building between us.

In any case, on this particular morning, I have other things to worry about, like the djembe drumbeat playing inside my head, sounding like a hundred cracking bullwhips. And yet, I had made a promise to visit Au this morning. Where I come from, you just don't wave off an invitation. That's another reason I did not mention this to my husband. He would have thrown all that culture out, dismissed it like the American in him does. Or maybe it's his age. Add ten years to mine. I may regret not having his input on this visitation rite, though I suspect Thailand is like Kenya. The way you become friends with anyone tells you a whole lot about how they were raised. Take for instance my first meeting with Au.

I met her in my "Intro to Nursing" class. On the third week of class, she sat next to me. I only noticed her dark hair and lopsided walk later. In the moment she sat down, her presence was distracting, or rather the smell emanating from the bag at her feet. The lecturer's drawled words lacked the emotion needed to engage us, so it was easy to put one's attention elsewhere.

"Do you want?" The woman asked me.

"Want what?"

"The food," she said, pointing to the brown bag on the floor.

An hour later, sitting on the wooden bench outside the classroom, I leaned back on the hallway wall as the sweet spice mixed with pepper lingered in my mouth. The cook—Au from Bangkok. The other two smacking their lips were also foreigners. India. Nigeria. It was about six o'clock and it made sense to proceed to the bar located across the street from the metro trains. There is nothing like a watering hole located near transportation home. That was yesterday. And what a difference a day makes. Now I had a friend. And friends come with obligations.

Yet, on this morning my feet were dragging. I walked to the bus-stop, taking deliberate steps, because if I didn't, my feet would surely turn back home to the two-bedroom apartment that my husband was planning to eventually buy. Well, that is not what he had told me when I was wallowing in the countryside of Limuru in Kenya. The place I was born, opposite the marshes, where as kids we kicked and flapped in the water, a swimming technique frowned upon here in America.

I remember holding on to the reeds as I learned how to survive in the water, though in reality there was no danger of drowning, for my feet easily found the soft clay just beneath the water, which made it seem like walking on a soft mattress.

With every step I took towards Au's, I swore my jeans got smaller. Just the other day, as I slipped on the same pair of jeans, my husband had enquired about their size. Read *my weight*. Maybe they shrunk in the washing-machine, I said. He asked too much after my body. I knew what he really wanted; but I knew better than to have another child. Least of all before I had managed to bring Ted over. When Ted came I was going to take him to the local YMCA for swimming and hope he would enjoy it more than I had. You see, it was unlike the lagoon where we had spent hours chatting our lives away. That simple life now seemed a hundred years away. America was different. Besides, everyone worked three or four jobs. As my husband says: There is no time in America.

My husband's friends became mine when I first arrived. But I only saw them on Thanksgiving and Labor Day. I tried to make my own friends, when we made our way past midnight to the Shake'n'Drink night club in New York, where all the Kenyans in Newark drove once a month, to dance to songs of yesteryears. Kamaru. Madice. Kenny Rogers too: suddenly the entire club would be dream-dancing to his raspy voice that brought memories of the lagoon into focus. The air pregnant with memories; we screamed out the words, and those words we didn't know, we made up. But we kept up with the rhythm, one we knew so well. It was a rhythm of memory, of our country, of our childhood, of the place where we had crafted our dreams. In my case, back to the lagoon. For a few hours I enjoyed the connection to Kenya, but the feeling quickly dissipated after the last call for drinks. Then the shoulders stooped, and silence followed the walk to the trains and buses that sobered everyone up.

So I stopped going. Besides, Jack Daniels could come home to me, in the comfort of reality shows, in between my dreaded homework on nursing ambitions. They told everyone that America needs nurses. God knows my husband had said it enough times to me. If only I could run away. To where? That was the problem.

For no particular reason, the morning I trekked to take bus 45 to Au's house reminded me of the morning I left for the promised land. My mother, who single-handedly raised me, had thrown a party. The "my-daughter-is-going-to-be-someone-after-all" kind of party for those who had looked down on me when I stayed home before and after my Ted was born. That was the other thought I entertained on the way to visit Au. Would it better if Ted were here? He was born with a brain older than his years, so he liked to argue, and we constantly exchanged opinions, with me trying to get him to see reason. "He is very much your son," my mother would say. "Copyright," my aunt said. Whom else could they compare him to except me?

I met his father before I graduated high school, a year after he had. A Kenyan like me, he had done well on his university entrance exam. But that was not the only reason I took to him. He was cliché; tall and dark. Back then that was all I had on my list. So I gave in; but Ted had other plans, like being born to me at the wrong time. His father felt the same way and disappeared. My father had done something similar. "Men," my aunt said.

But I finally found a partner, not on university grounds because I never made it there. Out on the hundred marshes, I met him among a bus of white tourists. Looks were a thing of the past. He promised to support us—me, Ted and my haikus—since his dreams were already manifest.

That's why upon arrival, and the discovery that my husband had just been selling me his aspirations, I did not throw a tantrum. Besides, he had recently been promoted to manage the Starbucks near our apartment. That's where I did the writing. It will be something one day. Like a book. I knew this.

Just as I knew I was not a morning person. I had not communicated this effectively to Au. But halfway to her house, I entertained a change of mind. I would not wait for things to unfold in my life. I would not wait for someone to hold my hand in my dreams. Instead I was going to dive into America's bayou. Nursing. Writing. Ted. It all made sense. I would complete nursing school. I would write on weekends. I would bring Ted over. His dreams would be different. I would make them happen for him. It would also free my mother. Epiphany. Suddenly I was filled with the hope that had escaped me for so long since my arrival.

Elated, I arrived at Au's house. It was, like my house, sparsely furnished. A brown couch sat on a brown carpet. To the left was the dining-table. She asked me to join her there.

It was only 11 a.m. and the table was filled with food. Rice. Shrimps. Noodles. This was another thing I had not told her. I could only stand strong smells in the afternoon. That's how I found myself on the floor of her green-decorated bathroom—the toilet rug, shower curtain, toothpaste holder. In my house, blue was the color. I gave up the contents of my stomach before I had a chance to fill it with Au's food.

I asked her, later as I lay on the couch, if she had invited her other friends. Which ones? she asked. I understood her. Her quiet manner sprang from her. This other persona, the one who cooked for strangers, invited them to her house, was simply a symptom of America. She did not visit clubs, but she longed for home.

This occurred to me at the exact time I realized the throwing-up had been going on for over a month. And then it occurred to me. Another Ted was on the way. Clearly my dreams would have to wait.

Ketty Nivyabandi

A poet, human rights defender and social justice activist from Burundi, she has had poems published in several anthologies worldwide. She is an outspoken voice for justice in her country, and became a refugee in 2015, after she led women's protests in her capital city. She currently lives in Canada. In 2012 she was chosen to represent Burundi at Poetry Parnassus, the cultural programme accompanying the 2012 Summer Olympics in London.

Home

I once lived in a yellow little house.

Each morning, birds convened and sang at my bedroom window. The gate was indigo and inside the garden all kinds of flowers rose to kiss the sunny walls. The yellow nest was filled with cherished books, colorful art and sweet peace.

There was a little kitchen, with cherry-red cabinets made by the most business-savvy street artisan I have ever met. In the little kitchen, my daughters and I baked, giggled, danced and let our free-range souls be. Looking down on us was a Gael Faye poster, cooking books from the across the globe (including delicious Caribbean recipes by Maya Angelou), my daughters' early drawings, vintage photographs. And music.

Always music.

On the yellow porch sat a white high table where I would often pretend to write. Most of the time I simply soaked in the silence. And beside it, a long lounge chair, always tilted in the same, exact position: the only place in the house where one could spot the glistening, silvery lake Tanganyika. Between the neighbor's blue tin roof and two tall mango trees. On some mornings, after the skies had cried all night, I would witness the mighty mountains of Congo rise from the fog. And everything inside me would fall into place.

It is where I enjoyed the most joyful evenings with rowdy, tipsy relatives who sometimes popped in with red wine, some cheese, and impromptu dance moves. It's also where I often lay alone, by candlelight and let my heart breathe. Just above me hung a chalkboard, where my daughter once wrote: "Welcome home, where the sun is always free".

It was home, in every sense of the word.

Where one softens.

Where one belongs.

It was home until one sudden morning, when danger came banging at the indigo gate. Prompted me to drop the book in my hand, grab the closest bag and lock up the sunny nest. 'It's just for a couple of days' I thought. A couple of days later, danger spat me out of my city, out of the hills, out of the lake, out of the drums, out of the homeland I adore. Danger chased as I drove at the highest speed, through the coiled bowels of my beloved land, running away from the only place I had ever wanted to be. Running away from the yellow, the indigo, the cherry red, the morning birds, the splendid silvery lake, the scent of rain, the loud relatives, the red wine and impromptu dance moves, the sweet peace, the emerald hills, the sound of my daughters laughing in between two nap dreams, the escapades to my aunt's rural home, the smell of cow dung, of eucalyptus leaves, of freedom, the taste of isombe, the sight of bougainvillea on every street, the sound of church bells on Sundays and the muezzin at dawn, the scent of Arabica coffee beans, the voices of dear friends, the red soil, the green, the green, the green…

It was home until I crossed the border, looked back at the green sliding into red, and felt everything inside me falling apart.

(…)

"Thank God you are safe" they tell you. Not knowing that your heart was never more at risk, never more a wound, never more famished.

"You are so lucky you got out. Now you can rebuild your life." And you want to say that you don't want to rebuild, not here, not in this concrete greyness which leaves you out of breath. Not in these superstore alleys where bananas exude sadness, and remind you of the haunting look in the old lion's eyes, at the city zoo. The look of the displaced.

Not in this place where bananas refuse to grow, where parenting involves a strategic plan, where time is an investment, where couples debate what to have for dinner like a constitutional reform. Where a crowded commute ride screams with loneliness.

"You'll see, it will be great for the children." And you want to tell them that what is good for your children is napping with the scent of the rain falling on dusty ground, running barefoot in the grass with ten cousins, the taste of small and sweet bananas (how does one explain this?), the sun teasing the melanin in their skins, and the tender love and care they receive everywhere they go…

But you remain quiet, because there are no words to explain these mutterings in your veins. Because you should be grateful for being alive, even when your whole life burns. Because there is a certain indecency in not being grateful. In not acknowledging your fortune, the misery and fear of those who stayed behind, the kindness of your host country. Because you must, after all, reinvent (not rebuild, please, no) your life. Because your surroundings should not determine the state of your heart. Of course not.

And so you carry on, in a refugee camp, fetching wood with strangers who soon become your world, rising early to beat the maize distribution line, cutting deals to feed your babies, looking at this country within a country, not knowing when you will ever get out. Or in the homeless shelter, receiving food stamps, and explanations of how to proceed being given as if you were a five-year-old and wherever you came from requires things to be explained s.l.o.w.l.y.

You smile when kindness offers you used clothes and a cooking pan, you are overwhelmed by this warmth, these random acts of goodness but hold yourself from rupturing into a river. Because you are someone, you were someone, because you once had your own new clothes and plenty of cooking pans, thank you very much, and somehow this beautiful kindness also feels terribly unkind, unkind to your being, to your inside, to your life, and just makes you want to cry.

You overcome being called a refugee. A small, wounding word in which the world tries to squeeze you every day. As your vastness cries out.

You overcome the weight and inexplicable shame that comes with that word. The feeling of not belonging. As you desperately try to catch your dignity, flying away in the autumn wind.

You overcome becoming part of the diaspora, this warm, wide sea of people whom you now begin to resemble; always a little too distant, or too close to home. Never in balance. Almost like, but never quite "home".

You put one foot in front of the other, without thinking, forget thinking, forget any logic you ever had, because what kind of logic shatters a life into pieces in one single morning? You create normal out of the abnormal. For months, for years, until one day you surprise yourself laughing out loud. Find new blossoms in your heart. You learn to live with the scars of exile. To conceal them. Especially from yourself. You learn to "adapt". And when you finally receive your immigration papers, your new friends, your lawyer, your colleagues at the store, all rejoice: "All is well now!" As though a home, a country, a life could be replaced so easily, by paperwork.

You learn to oil the stretch marks that criss-cross your heart, to walk fast, not to smile to strangers, to do ten things at once, "to plan". You learn not to hear the voids in this wealth, the heavy silence on the crowded morning commute, the wails in the teenager's menacing eyes, the unraveling in the soccer mom's high-pitched voice, the insecurity in the suited man's walk. You learn to wear dark colors in winter, and not to miss the happy, organized chaos that is your hometown. You learn to unlearn yourself. To unlearn the organic joy, the carefree in you. And not see the dangers of this place where everything has a limit. Where your being feels tamed. Where life feels like a trap, and you don't understand why because everything "is well now". You learn because the alternative is too painful. Because to remember—to truly remember—is to hurt, and your stretch-marked heart can only stretch so far.

(…)

I still hear the yellow nest and the emerald hills, calling my name everyday. Sometimes on a merciful night, the moon will rise just as it used to, under my porch.

On such nights I close my eyes, and I am home.

Nana Oforiatta Ayim

A Ghanaian writer, filmmaker and art historian, she has contributed to publications such as frieze, ArtNews, Petunia *and* Accra Noir, *and her debut novel will be* The God Child *(Bloomsbury Publishing, 2020). She speaks to international audiences on cultural narratives and institution-building in Africa, and her films have been shown at museums including The New Museum, Tate Modern and the Los Angeles County Museum of Art. She founded the ANO Institute of Arts and Knowledge, through which she has pioneered a Pan-African Cultural Encyclopaedia, and a Mobile Museums project that travels into communities. She received the 2015 Art and Technology Award from LACMA, the 2016 AIR Award, and the inaugural 2018 Soros Arts Fellowship. She has been named one of the Apollo "40 under 40"; one of 50 African Trailblazers by* The Africa Report; *one of 12 African women making history by* Okayafrica; *and a Quartz Africa Innovator; and is a 2019 Global South Visiting Fellow at Oxford University.*

Abele, from *The God Child*

Abele, my mother sang at the dressing mirror, as I lay on the satin quilted cover on the bed behind her, watching.

Abele, she danced in her chair, the ends of her mouth turned half downwards in appreciation. *It's a pity my child did not take my beauty*, she told her reflection, putting cream on her face, caressing it into the softness, surveying the escarpment of cheekbones, the glow trapped in the amber recesses of her skin. She turned to me as if remembering, *you must always look more than perfect. Not just good enough, but perfect. You must always be better than them in everything you do, otherwise they will think you are lower.*

My mother came out, the smell of her powdery luxury encased me, watering my eyes. I opened them. She walked sideways down the stairs, her shoes clacking against the heels of her feet.

Would it arrive overnight, the desire for perfection, like the ability to smell expensive and wear fitted petticoats?

Maya, what is wrong with you, this girl? Do you want your father to come home and trouble my life? Ah.

I walked down the stairs, slowly, sideways, towards my mother, far like the rest of the world. When I reached her, she buttoned on my coat. My arms stuck out to both sides. I looked past her at my reflection in the mirror, half there, half in another place.

She was stepping back to look at me, edging towards the open box by the front door.

I closed my eyes, not wanting to see her fall.

Aich, she shouted.

I opened my eyes.

She was not sitting on top of the large new television, but suspended above it, her arms stemmed behind her against the wall, her legs spread out, skirt hiked up.

I began to laugh.

Ah! This time, her harshness came through her laughter. *Kwasiaa! Come and help me.*

I pulled her up, her weight threatening to knock me over.

She looked down into the box, turning the corners of her mouth down. *Hm*, she said, her skirt still hiked up around her thighs, *they shall see*.

I walked next to her, through the more than perfect neighbourhood of semi-detached red-bricked houses, made only less so by the African family camouflaged within one of them. Less than perfect, but not jarringly so, because he was a doctor and his wife was beautiful and his daughter perfectly groomed. Less than perfect, because they hung their washing out in the garden until the neighbour told them not to. Less than perfect, because their television was propped up with books and not a stand. Less than perfect, because the father deemed the new television with stand the mother bought with his credit card too expensive, and was having it returned. But still, separate from the men that stood huddled outside the Bahnhof and MacDonald's reeking of illegality; the women that sat in the Afroshops chatting in mismatched syncopated chorus as the hairdressers braided hair and the cloth sellers took out dotted, striped, stamped lengths of Dutch wax, like multi-coloured species of exotic animals.

I looked up at my mother talking too loud in her unperfected accent. People looked at her as she walked past, but she did not notice, because even if I had not taken her beauty, she did not understand that to be better than them, you had to be like them so completely that they no longer noticed your difference.

I do not know whether it was there from the beginning this knowledge that I was never just I, myself, but an I that was in me and also outside and that watched and witnessed all I did and everything around. When I later heard in words about the ancestors, I already knew, and when my father gave me the name—3no, grandmother—whilst almost still a baby, it was because he too could see, that what I saw and understood was not mine alone.

It began to rain. She wrapped me close to her, her pea green silk raincoat giving shelter to us both as we ran.

We reached the department store and rode on the escalator up past the electronics, the cosmetics, the household goods, and underwear, to the women's designer section. It was almost empty. Outside it was getting dark and the Germans were sitting down to their Abendbrod.

The sales lady looked us up and down as we passed, still dripping. My mother was weaving in and out of the racks, like a person drunk, her hands scanning silks, polyesters, sequins and feathers, taking down one after the other, until her arms were full, clothes trailing behind her on the floor.

The sales woman stood behind us now, but my mother still did not notice.

Kann Ich helfen? She asked in a thoroughly unhelpful tone.

My mother turned around now and laughed. *Ich will Alles kaufen*, she said, *Alles. Hier hilf mir*, she addressed the woman in the familiar Du, not the formal Sie, and handed her the clothes. She looked, vaguely left then vaguely right, brow furrowed as if concentrating, but her body movements betrayed no focus at all. She dropped her scarf behind her.

I looked at it on the floor, looked at the woman's frowning face as she bent to pick it up and followed my mother like a lady's maid. I turned towards the children's section. I ran my hands through the clothes like my mother, stopping at velvets and soft dark cords. I closed my eyes and saw myself in the cords, a perfect German girl, a young Romy Schneider running through the forest, arms outstretched towards a fenced-in deer, smiling like the girl on the Rotbäckchen 6-fruit juice bottle, cheeks apple red to match the kerchief on her head.

Guck mal! Guck mal der Neger!

It was a little girl's voice behind me. My hand stopped on the wine red velvet dress. I looked up to see who she meant, then turned towards her. She was pointing at me. She had mistaken me for a boy. Her mother looked at me angrily, took the girl's hand and walked away. I stopped to look in the small full-length mirror on my left. My hair was in four large plaits. It was true I was wearing trousers, but how could she mistake me for a boy? My father always told me to wear earrings and I did not. I touched my ears.

Beautiful, I heard behind me. *Yes.*

My mother was picking up the red velvet dress and another, peach with white lace ruches and a satin band. She was picking out white shoes and a white dress with strawberries on the left breast. She was picking cord dungarees and a matching shirt.

Ich bin Prinzessin, wissen Sie? She was saying to the sales woman, *Prinzessin Yaa.* She was telling her that where she came from her clothes were made of lace and gold and that she had servants and grew up in a palace.

The woman was looking a little frightened now.

My mother went into the changing room and I followed to be turned into a little princess-in-the-making, beauty's heir.

When we left with five plastic bags, there were four sales women tending to my mother. She paid with my father's credit card. They walked with us. They patted my hair. They helped my mother onto the escalator, *Tschüss Prinzessin Yaa. Tschüss.*

She did not look back. Her eyes were fixed downwards. I followed them and saw what she saw, a large commode full of plates of all sizes and depths, white plates with solid ink blue borders and swirls of gold that nestled inside the borders like gold-tipped swans at the side of a lake, bewitched.

We reached the floor and she headed towards them, not straight, but walking in a kind of zigzag. I looked around. No one was watching. She stood in front of the commode, and this time a man came to her side.

Ja? He said, his eyebrows raised.

Wie viel? She asked.

Wie viele Teller? He asked the eccentric woman wanting to know the number of plates.

Wie viel kostet Sie? She pointed at the plates.

The man looked confused. Did she want to know the price of one plate?

Sie will wissen wie viel alles zusammen kostet, I offered.

Ah, the man said, and went to the counter and opened a book. He came back with it and showed my mother, silently, looking up.

Ich kaufe, she said.

His eyebrows moved up higher. He closed the book and led us to the counter.

My mother handed over the card and told the salesman that the plates must be delivered in the day before six and not at weekends. She did not want my father to see.

Natürlich, the man said, smiling tightly. He handed her the receipt and looked down at me, *Du sprichts aber gut Deutsch*, he said, not a compliment so much as a statement of fact.

It always surprised them that my German was fluent.

I put on my broad little girl smile and shrugged my I don't know how it came to be so fluent either shrug, my apologetic and surprised by my own ingenuity shrug, so that he would not realise that I had worked at the mastering and not, like they assumed, acquired it by accident, or oversight. I smiled the smile that was rose patterned wallpaper over the extant unpapered cracks through which, if they looked hard enough, they might have seen a room within a room. A bulb, naked and alone. A table bare, covered in layered faded scrawl, its wood splintered and creviced. An empty chair. Against the wall a shadow of something or someone that had already long left. And at the far end, barely visible, but there, an open door.

Nnedi Okorafor

She is a Nigerian American author of African-based science fiction, fantasy and magical realism for children and adults. Her works include Who Fears Death *(currently being developed by HBO into a TV series), the Binti novella trilogy (currently being developed by HULU into a TV series), the* Book of Phoenix, *the Akata books and* Lagoon. *She is the winner of Hugo, Nebula, World Fantasy, Locus and Lodestar Awards and her debut novel* Zahrah the Windseeker *won the prestigious Wole Soyinka Prize for Literature. She has also written comics for Marvel, including* Black Panther: Long Live the King *and* Wakanda Forever *(featuring the Dora Milaje) and the Shuri series. Her science fiction comic series* LaGuardia *(from Dark Horse) was released in late 2018. She lives with her daughter and family in Illinois.*

Zula of the Fourth Grade Playground

In my fourth grade class, I was Zula from the second Conan movie.

In *Conan the Destroyer*, Zula was an African warrior who becomes one of Conan's loyal allies (What part of Africa? It was never specified). Conan initially comes across Zula as she's fighting back a mob of men. She was svelte but muscular and clad only in a sparse fur-trimmed leather outfit. Dark-skinned, beautiful, and powerful, Zula was played by the vibrant singer/model/actress/wild woman Grace Jones. Yeah, I was Zula, except I was nine years old, instead of fighting with a stick, I used my bare hands and instead of fighting a bunch of paler-skinned barbarians during some past ancient time, I was fighting a bunch of white-skinned boys of suburbia in the early '80s.

When I was nine, I went to a Catholic school and not only was I the only black person in my class, but I was also the only person of color. To top it off, to say that my school had a bit of a racial problem was an understatement. Nevertheless, though my parents were strong believers in peace and tolerance, I was not raised to take bullshit. I was baptized, had received my First Communion, and went to church every Sunday with my family, but I refused to "turn the other cheek."

My road to becoming Zula isn't hard to plot. I am the youngest girl in my family, my two sisters being a year and two years older than me. Not only am I the youngest girl, but though I am tall, I have always been the shortest and skinniest. Even my little brother, who is seven years my junior, eventually outgrew me. So, as I was growing up, it was either yield to the prowess of my Amazon sisters or fight like a banshee and earn their respect.

The fights I used to have with my sisters as we were growing up were not the "screech, scratch and pull hair kind of fights." Only my oldest sister had the long pretty nails and all of our hair at the time was so damaged by relaxers and jheri-curl juice that it only grew a few inches. Our fights were all out brawls. Our mother would let us go at it until we finished. So in this way, I learned how to fight and not fear those who were bigger than or outnumbered me.

And I've always had a sort of leadership quality. When I was in preschool, my mother received a call from my teacher. This teacher claimed that I had usurped her authority in the classroom; that the students were even coming to me to ask to go to the bathroom instead of her. I don't quite remember doing this but I can see myself being a sort of tyrant. Definitely. And mix that tendency with the lack of social skills of a preschooler…yes, I can certainly see this happening.

By the fourth grade, things started changing. More than ever, my classmates and I were aware of our gender. And this was most evident on the playground where the girls would only play with the girls and the boys with the boys. Nonetheless, once in a while, the two groups would meet and interact.

I usually led the girls' group. If not me, then Michelle Medoza, the "prettiest" girl in our grade. She had shiny red brown hair, pale skin, rosy cheeks and dark captivating eyes. So it was either Zula the African warrior or Jehenna the Princess, the powerful or the beautiful one as leader; there's a lesson in that, isn't there?

We'd all migrate to the back of the school where the playground monitors could not see us. To this day, I wonder why those teachers never noticed that two-thirds of the fourth grade class had momentarily disappeared. Usually there would be some sort of challenge from either the boy or the girl group and we'd all talk shit back and forth about why girls were better or boys were better, sometimes we'd talk about music or something on TV. Maybe someone would have a crush on someone else and a note would be passed. Or someone's parents had divorced and someone would comment on it. It wasn't about the conversation as much as it was about the girls getting close to the boys and the boys getting close to the girls.

And then there were the fights; these were what everyone really hoped for. They didn't happen often, but they happened often enough. I was always the one challenged and insulted. Never any of the other girls. The boys would treat the other girls—girls who were all white—with a sort of deference. These girls were potential dates, or they were girls that they'd grown up with, whose parents were friends with their parents. My family and I had recently moved into the neighborhood, so I had no real history there yet. Plus, I was that "ugly nigger black girl" with hair like a "crow's nest" (a phrase coined by my own teacher in the middle of class that year).

The boys would change during these times behind the school; they would become full-fledged villains. "I can kick your ass back to Africa," "Why are you so ugly?" "Are your cousins monkeys?" Then whichever boy had spoken would look to his male friends and laugh. Some of the girls would giggle, too. None of them would stick up for me.

"Come and say that to my face!" I'd retort, or some other challenging reply.

It was usually a boy named Joey who would step to my face. He was almost as tall as me but much stockier. Joey was the definite leader of the boys in my class.

"Nigger," he'd sneer, or some other racial epithet. Joey's parents were Polish. He had a brother named Edmond who was a year ahead of me, in my sister's class and he had a sister named Marta who was another year up, in my oldest sister's class. Edmond and my middle sister weren't friends, but they hung in the same group and they certainly didn't go at it the way Joey and I did. And my oldest sister and Marta were friends.

I don't know what it was about Joey. He was a white boy with deep dimples in each cheek and a lopsided smile that most of the girls thought was cute, including me (since everyone else did). It was Joey who took a rubber band and a sharpened pencil and accidentally shot the pencil into his left blue eye. He'd had to wear an eye-patch for a month. It was Joey who got all the boys in our grade to use erasers to rub the skin away on the backs of their hands. Some spelled their names, others etched satanic and anarchy symbols. Joey etched the word, "Fuck."

On the school bus, months earlier, it had been Joey who was the first to call me a "nigger," and then spit in my "ugly" hair. He went on to call his friends to do the same. I was so humiliated that the Zula-side of me retreated deep into my soul and I'd sat in my seat head down instead of kicking all of their asses.

It was Joey who pulled me aside and showed me a *Penthouse* magazine picture of some white woman spreading her legs. I'd stood there staring, feeling nauseous and wondering why the woman would do that, especially in front of a camera. When I'd glanced up at him, he was grinning.

And then there was that day in choir practice. Though I had a fairly decent voice, I refused to sing. For some reason, I hated our choir teacher. Whenever I looked at her, my eyes felt assaulted by her overly pale white skin and her voice sounded as if she had wet warm bread sitting deep in her throat. I hated when she sang. This day, she'd noticed that I wasn't singing. She stopped the class and tried to force me to sing alone but I refused, so she sent me out of the classroom. To this day, because of that teacher and how she embarrassed me like that, I can't sing in front of people. Oddly enough, it was Joey who came out after choir class was over, saw me standing there and said, "Don't worry about it. She's a bitch." And then he walked with me back to our homeroom.

This was Joey.

I'd lost count of the number of times that I pulled a Zula on him. After he'd get in my face and sneer whatever cruel racist phrases came to his mind that day (which he probably learned from his parents), I'd push him back. All the girls around me would move back and disappear from my peripheral vision and my thoughts. During these times, I was alone and I was fearless, I was Zula.

Joey would throw a punch back, but I was always faster than him. At some point, I'd grab his arm and start to swing him around and around. I'd swing him so hard that his feet would leave the ground. Then I'd let go and he'd go flying. Then another boy would come at me and I'd do the same to him.

I often wonder what was really going on with these fights. They were so satisfying to me, like I really did have warrior blood in my veins. (This is something I've suspected for a long time. My father was a nationally known hurdler and my mother was so good at throwing the javelin that she made the Nigerian Olympic team in that event. I inherited my swiftness and strong arms from my parents. And how different is a javelin from a spear?) I'd grab these boys with quick hands and sharp un-even fourth grader nails and swing them in a swift circle and throw them as far as possible like a discus.

The boys seemed to enjoy these fights, too. I think they liked being thrown by the lanky strong black girl. They would never try and jump on me more than one at a time. Even John the short Italian boy who had an enormous crush on me (I knew this because he told me and bought me all sorts of things like candy and Michael Jackson pins and posters), would get in line and allow me to fling him as far as I could.

It was as if these battles of me against the white boys would take place in a vacuum. No other kids or adults came to stop us and none of us reported the fights. And there were never injuries worse than scratches and bruises and grass stains and sore muscles. Was this some sort of playing out of racial aggression and guilt? A story that began long before any of us were born, long before my Nigerian immigrant parents even came to this country? Maybe.

The fight would usually end when the bell rang. Then we would all scramble to get into our lines of boys and girls. As always, I lined up next to Joey and we'd both glare at each other and then turn our heads forward, so that our teacher wouldn't yell at us.

My girl group would still be whispering words of awe and satisfaction. They were probably glad to have stood back and watched, been only mere audience to all the action. They'd rather be pretty than powerful. I had no choice because in our fourth-grade Catholic school world, I could not be pretty. I was too black, my hair was too coarse, my lips were too big. But I think even if I had a choice, I'd choose powerful…powerful and beautiful, like Zula.

Louisa Adjoa Parker

Of Ghanaian and English heritage, she lives in south-west England and writes poetry, fiction and black history. Her poetry collection Salt-sweat and Tears *and pamphlet* Blinking in the Light *were published by Cinnamon Press in 2016, and her third collection,* How to Wear a Skin, *is due from Indigo Dreams Publishing in 2019. Her work has appeared in a range of publications, including* Envoi; Wasafiri; Bare Fiction; Under the Radar; Out of Bounds *(Bloodaxe);* Ink, Sweat and Tears; Filigree *and* Closure *(Peepal Tree Press). She has been highly commended for the Forward Prize and shortlisted for the Bridport Prize. She has written for books/exhibitions exploring BAME history in the South West. She has also written articles for* Gal-dem, Skin Deep, Black Ballad *and* Media Diversified, *among other outlets. She has completed her first collection of short stories and is working on a novel.*

Black histories aren't all urban: tales from the West Country

The idea that black people only inhabit urban areas, and that the English countryside has always been white, is a myth. Yes, many black and brown people who came to the UK settled in our larger cities, but not exclusively—there are a multitude of rural histories which are yet to be heard.

The postcard image of the South West of England, with its rolling hills and coastline, evokes for some a nostalgic representation of Englishness, or rather, whiteness. Yet, as I discovered years ago, black history is rich within the land of this place; in spite of commonly held misconceptions, the region has numerous connections with Africa, the Caribbean and Asia. As a black British woman of English and Ghanaian heritage who has lived in the South West for most of my life, I had no idea about this history—locally or nationally—until one afternoon at university, while studying racism and migration, I heard there was a grave in Devon of a black eighteenth-century person. This knowledge sparked a curiosity in me, and since then I have carried out various research exploring the presence of BAME people in the South West.

This history is important—for people of colour who live in the region to see themselves reflected in local heritage; for the local white majority to understand that we belong, we are nothing new; and for those in urban spaces to understand that being black doesn't equal urban—we have lived all over Britain for thousands of years. Local black history helps us all understand that as humans we are connected, and migration is not a contemporary phenomenon.

The West Country has been home to people of colour for centuries. They came as slaves or servants, sailors, teachers, writers, visiting royalty, boxers, students, and entertainers. The two world wars brought soldiers, prisoners-of-war and refugees. Some of these people simply passed through, leaving traces of themselves behind (and in some cases, children). Others settled in the region. Numbers may be lower than in cities, but their stories matter: here are just a handful.

Some, although not all, of the research undertaken in places such as Devon and Dorset explores links with Transatlantic slavery. Although we tend to think of Liverpool and Bristol when we think of slavery, British involvement has its roots in Devon—John Hawkins of Plymouth is recognised as the first English slave trader. Many South West ports were involved in slavery, as were many local families. According to Lucy MacKeith, author of *Local Black History: A beginning in Devon*, "People at all levels of society were involved: sheep farmers, spinners and weavers who created cloth which was exported to Africa and the Americas, wool traders, bootmakers, food producers, metal workers who produced slave chains, shipbuilders… The list goes on." There are too many slave-owning families to begin to list. Names include the Willetts of Dorset and St Kitts; the Halletts of East Devon and Barbados, the Swetes of Devon and Antigua; the Draxes of Dorset, Jamaica and Barbados, the Calcrafts, the Joliffes, the Pinneys of Dorset, Bristol and Nevis, the Daveys, and the Beckfords.

Plantation owners often brought enslaved people with them when they returned from overseas. In Devon, Lady Raleigh, wife of Sir Walter Raleigh, was one of the first people in England to have a young African "attendant". My book *Dorset's Hidden Histories* includes black people recorded in eighteenth- and nineteenth-century Dorset Parish Registers. Many were children, for example, "Henry Panzo, a Black Servant to Lieut. Brine R.N. aged 12 years, Poole, baptised 1817." When Richard Hallett returned from Barbados to Lyme Regis in 1699, he brought "a retinue of black servants" with him. In 1702, Lyme Regis Town Court recorded that "a Black Negro servant of Mr. Richard Hallett called Ando" was accused of rioting in Broad Street. The way these people were treated would have varied according to the whims of their "owners".

Some "servants" were left money by their masters. For example, the will of Thomas Olive of Poole, 1753, includes the bequest of £900 to his "Negro woman", Judith, and their daughters. Others were respected enough to have their own gravestone, such as the aforementioned eighteenth-century black servant at Werrington Church, Devon. Philip Scipio was brought to England from St Helena by the Duke of Wharton. Scipio was buried in 1784, aged 18. He was described in the church register as "A black servant to Lady Lucy Morice." The bones of other black people must lie in unmarked (or as yet unrecorded) West Country graves.

After the slave trade was abolished in 1807 (with the help of abolitionists from the South West, such as Thomas Fowell Buxton) the government paid £20 million to British slave owners, who are listed in the Legacies of British slave-ownership database, as compensation for the loss of their "property". This wealth, along with the profits of slavery, helped build an infrastructure, still visible today in the form of manor houses, estates, buildings and roads. Many sites are named after slave owners: the legacy of John Rolle, who owned plantations in the Bahamas, includes Bicton

House (now Bicton College) and the Rolle Building at Plymouth University. Street names such as Drake, Hawkins and Raleigh also reflect this history.

There is much evidence of a continued black presence in the region post-slavery. Thomas Lewis Johnson settled in Bournemouth in the 1890s. Johnson was a missionary and former slave from Virginia, who spoke about Christianity and slavery and published a book called *Twenty-eight Years a Slave*. Black entertainers performed in the region. Historian Jeffrey Green compiled a list of West Country Blacks in Victorian times, which includes Daniel Peter Hughes Taylor, son of a Freetown merchant, who attended Wesley College in Taunton, in 1869. His son was the composer Samuel Coleridge Taylor. Not everyone was successful—like their city counterparts, many black people in the area were plunged into poverty, and spent time in workhouses.

When World War II started, a whole new influx of people transformed the region as American soldiers came to the UK in the run-up to D-Day. Estimates of the numbers of African American soldiers, mostly GIs, range from 100,000 to 300,000, with many concentrated in port areas. Although British authorities expressed concern about the arrival of so many black men (particularly with regards to them mixing with white women), British people generally welcomed them. It was ironic—the British didn't like the segregation the US Army brought with it, yet Britain was still steeped in a post-colonial racism. While they didn't object to a transient community, when it came to the offspring these men left behind it was a different matter.

The white Americans, often from the Southern states, were not prepared to see their black colleagues mixing with white women—a crime punishable by death under US law during wartime. Many fights occurred, and some black soldiers were killed. This didn't stop the African Americans mixing with locals, however, and many relationships were formed.

Across Britain a number of "Brown Babies" (as the children of black GIs were known in the press) were left behind after the war. Carole Travers, who first shared her story for my book *We Were Here: African American GIs in Dorset*, was the result of a relationship between her white mother and a black soldier stationed in Poole. Carole's mother decided to keep her child, but was already married, to a Scot with pale skin and red hair. "I had black hair and dark skin," says Carole. "Something obviously wasn't right." After decades of searching for her father, she recently discovered, through DNA testing, that he was Archie Elworth Burton, 1920–2004.

Not all the babies were able to stay with their mothers. Deborah Prior, who was born in 1945 to a widow from Somerset and a black American serviceman, spoke to Professor Lucy Bland on Woman's Hour. She spent five years at Holnicote House near Yeovil, a home for mixed-race children, after her mother was persuaded to give her up. This might seem remarkable in today's Britain, where mixed-race people make up one of the fastest growing demographic groups, but acceptance of relationships that cross communities has been a relatively recent occurrence meaning many people don't know about their heritage.

These stories are a mere handful showing that black history in the UK doesn't just have one narrative, even just in South West England it includes more than we would expect.

Learning about rural multi-ethnic history enables us to subvert ideas of a "golden age" when Britain was an all-white nation. This has never existed, except in some people's imaginations. British history—rural and urban—is intertwined with the history of non-white people. Black history is an integral part of British history.

There is already a plethora of information available, and yet more stories lie hidden in dusty records, waiting to be discovered.

Hannah Azieb Pool

An Eritrean-born journalist, author and curator, who writes regularly in the national and international media, she was a Guardian *journalist for more than 14 years, and has also written for the* Sunday Times, Vogue, *the* London Evening Standard, Grazia, *and other publications. Former Associate Editor of* Arise Magazine, *she is the author of two books:* Fashion Cities Africa *(2016), celebrating the fashion landscapes of four cities at the compass points of the African continent—Casablanca, Nairobi, Johannesburg and Lagos; and* My Fathers' Daughter *(2012), a memoir of her journey back to Eritrea to find her birth family. As Senior Programmer for Contemporary Culture at London's Southbank Centre, she led the annual Africa Utopia festival (2012–18) and was a Senior Programmer for the WOW (Women of the World) festival, including WOW Hargeisa (Somaliland), WOW Aké (Nigeria) and WOW Baltimore (USA). She is Artistic Director of the Bernie Grant Arts Centre and a trustee of LIFT (London International Festival of Theatre).*

Nairobi, from *Fashion Cities Africa*

It's 10 a.m., on a crisp, clear Nairobi winter's morning. Style bloggers Velma Rossa and Papa Petit, aka Oliver, are dressed down, in jeans, T-shirts and shoes that can take a good pounding, darting through tiny, crowded lanes that separate wooden shacks piled high with clothes. Velma and Oliver—better known by their blog title, *2ManySiblings*—are bobbing and weaving through the lanes, like fashion ninjas, stopping suddenly when a gem catches their eye—a denim jacket here, a vintage beaded purse there.

Welcome to Gikomba market, Kamukunji Road, Nairobi, Kenya. East Africa's largest second-hand clothing market, stretching out for approximately twenty acres (over eleven football pitches), where towering bales of second-hand clothes from Europe, North America and elsewhere, and cheap Chinese imports land daily, to be split open and sold for the highest shilling. Gikomba is not for the faint hearted.

"Wear comfortable clothes you can move around in," says Oliver, when they agree to take me to the market. "Dress like a street urchin so people don't think you have too much money," adds Velma. When we meet the next morning Oliver looks up and down at my scruffy jeans and T-shirt and says: "Great. You've dressed perfectly."

To the untrained eye, Gikomba is chaos, but once you get your head around the sheer scale of the place, it's not that different to Topshop on a Saturday afternoon. The bale houses are in one section, the stalls in another. Men with trolleys take the bales to the stalls, others carry them on their shoulders.

In many ways Gikomba mirrors any urban high street. Stalls are grouped by category. Womenswear, menswear, children's clothes, shoes and accessories each have their own, vast section. You'll find stalls selling only denim skirts, rows of belts and a huge mountain of white shirts, it goes on and on. In the midst of it all sit tens of tailors ready to do instant alterations. It's impossible to see more than the four or five stalls in your immediate vicinity. Luckily, this doesn't matter, because Velma and Oliver know exactly where they are heading.

For those in the know, there's an intricate system of runners—personal shoppers effectively—who'll bring the best stuff directly to you. After a quick phone call, Oliver meets a couple of his guys near the mountain of white shirts. One contact pulls a leather jacket and a pair of boots out of a rucksack for Oliver to look at. Velma is busy eyeing up the other seller's outfit. "How much for the jumper you're wearing?" she asks, with a cute smile that I sense knocks quite a few shillings off the price. Oliver walks away with the jacket, Velma gets the jumper later, when the wearer has found something to change into. The brokers melt back into the market and we carry on shopping.

Mitumba—second-hand shopping—is a key part of the Nairobi fashion scene. As well as Gikomba market, there's Toi, on the outskirts of Kibera, Ngara and many smaller markets dotted around the city.

The ability to buy good quality second-hand imports plays a key part in making fashion accessible, and if you've got the stamina it's a lot of fun. "I get lost, in Gikomba, it's like going to a casino. You're just there, spending hours and you don't notice," says Oliver.

Stylist and designer Franklin Saiyalel, is another fan of mitumba. "Everything I'm wearing, apart from the shoes is thrift," says Saiyalel who's blog KenyanStylista.com has won him the moniker "Kenya's best dressed man".

But Nairobi's fashion crowd have a mixed relationship with mitumba. Some see it as a great way to democratise fashion, enabling those with less money to buy essentials at knockdown prices and those with a good eye to pick up on trend bargains. Others see mitumba as damaging to local industry, flooding the market with other countries' cast offs and making it impossible for local designers to compete on price.

While many wear their thrifting skills with pride—Velma and Oliver for example bring *mitumba* to the cool kids, minus the mud and hassle with regular "Thrift Socials"—even those who love it are keen for Nairobi fashion not to be reduced to *mitumba*.

Back in downtown Nairobi, on and around Biashara Street, is the area once known as the "Indian Bazaar". Here you can pick up fabric and give it to a tailor who'll take your measurements and have an outfit ready in a couple of days for a few hundred shillings.

Roshini Shah, of Haria's Stamp Shop, and her family have been selling fabric on Biashara Street since the 1920s when her great-grandfather would import material from America and Japan. In recent years she's noticed a new generation coming into the shop buying East African fabrics such as *kanga* (a brightly patterned cotton cloth printed with slogans), *kitenge* (similar to *kanga* but with a different style of pattern) and *kikoy* (a striped, woven cotton fabric) to take to their tailor. For a long time, *kanga* was relegated in most people's minds as the cloth their mother wore to clean the house or wrap them in as a child. But along with *kitenge*, *kanga* are enjoying a new popularity as a fashion item, says Shah. "People are using African prints to pull off western looks," says Shah, who spoke on the history of *kanga* at the Smithsonian Folklife Festival in 2014. Given the culture of tailoring, the accessibility of *mitumba* and the dominance of foreign labels, Nairobi can be a tough place to cut your teeth as a designer. All of which makes the current fashion buzz in the city even more exciting.

"There's a renaissance happening in Nairobi. The creative industry is doing extremely well and that's affecting the fashion scene," says stylist Sunny Dolat, who runs Chico Leco, The Nest art collective's fashion hub, which won an award at the Berlin Fashion Film Festival with their short film *To Catch A Dream*. Starring one of Kenya's best known models, Ajuma Nasenyana, and eight of Nairobi's leading designers—Katungulu Mwendwa, Kepha Maina, Namnyak Odupoy, Jami and Azra Walki, Ann McCreath, Ami Doshi Shah and Adele Dejak—*To Catch a Dream*, is a celebration of local talent.

The film, alongside platforms like *2ManySiblings*, *This is Ess*, *Kenyan Stylista* and the rise of bands like Souti Sol (the video of the band dancing with Barack Obama went viral), who wear cutting edge local designers like Nick Ondu on the international circuit, shows how much Nairobi fashion has changed in recent years. "Kenyans are very conservative. Because of how we were influenced by the British, a suit and tie is what goes. If you walk in with something different, people don't seem to understand you or don't take you seriously. But things are changing," says John Kaveke, one of Nairobi's most established menswear designers.

The flamboyance that, for example Lagos or Accra might be known for isn't big here, says Sunny Dolat at The Nest. "Growing up, we were never really taught to express ourselves through clothes, we've been very conservative."

The blame for this conservatism lands squarely at the feet of the British colonisers and missionaries, who banned a lot of indigenous Kenyan clothing. This colonial fashion hangover meant that people were encouraged to aspire to foreign labels as a result the domestic industry suffered, says Dolat. "But people are starting to shift their mentality to see the value of investing in local designers and local brands." Hang out with the Nairobi fashion crowd and it's not long before you'll see *kanga*, *kitenge* and *kikoy* as well as West African *ankara* and *kente* worn with skinny jeans and trainers, styled as maxi-skirts and blazers or in other contemporary ways.

Higher end Nairobi labels such as Ann McCreath's Kiko Romeo and John Kaveke come with great tailoring and a fresh take on traditional fabrics. Accessories designers such as Ami Doshi Shah and Adèle Dejak are unashamedly rooting their brands in Nairobi by sourcing local materials to create bespoke pieces of such beauty that they smash the tired stereotype that Africa "doesn't do luxury".

Many are re-framing what it means to be a Kenyan designer by pairing fabrics like *kanga* and *kitenge* or locally sourced leathers, with contemporary silhouettes. You'll find patches of Maasai *shuka* blanket reworked into an evening clutch bag by emerging label Ziko Africa or *kanga* lining on a John Kaveke blazer. Designers like Katungulu Mwendwa ("Katungulu"), with her complex but clean structuring, or Nick Ondu ("Nick Ondu—Sartorial"), with his sharp menswear are giving this new breed of "experimental" Nairobi dresser plenty of options. Rising stars like Anthony Mulli are seeking out craftspeople, learning their skills and finding ways to modernise them for today's tastes. It's about changing perceptions of what constitutes African fashion, says Mulli, of his Katchy Kollections, which combine intricate Maasai beadwork with international seasonal trends to create bags that work as well in New York as Nairobi.

The notion of changing perceptions of African fashion, comes up repeatedly. "We don't do curios. Our whole ethos is to create beautiful products made in Africa," says Adèle Dejak, who has shown at Milan fashion week, collaborated with Salvatore Ferragamo and been featured in *Vogue Italia*. "Our pieces are all handmade, it's a piece of art," says Dejak. Of course you can find luxury in Africa, says Mulli, it's just a matter of how you choose to look at things. "We need to sensitise people to what we're doing and appreciating it."

Olúmìdé Pópóọlá

Nigerian-German by birth, she is a London-based writer of essays, poetry and fiction. Her novella this is not about sadness *was published in 2010, her play* Also by Mail *in 2013, and a short-story collection* Breach *(co-authored with Annie*

Holmes) in 2015. She also wrote the critically acclaimed novel When We Speak of Nothing, *published by Cassava Republic Press in 2017. She holds a PhD in Creative Writing and has lectured in creative writing at various universities. In 2018 she curated the African Book Festival Berlin, which focused on the themes of transnationalism and migration.*

The Swimmer

To look up from up from underneath, it made the sun blurry. The water swishing against my face, a thin layer, not enough to enter my nostrils. I was looking for him. I wanted to know the drowning, the losing your breathing to suffocation.

Of course, I didn't last. I didn't have enough drive to do it, actually I didn't have enough reasons. It is hard to take your own life. I think it is against your own body. Such an effort, incredible. I knew that before I jumped into the river Lea with my clothes on. You had to orchestrate the whole thing and pay attention to the variables. The only thing I had done was leave Mum's after the not so unusual but still weird morning. For some reason I went straight to Hackney Wick thinking, *Let's see this thing, drowning.*

Mum was stable as we both called it but on the unstable side of that. She had been rummaging through a big cardboard box packed tight with clothes. I thought she was looking for something that belonged to Jabori. It was ten years this year. I thought she was reminiscing, going to tell me a story I did or did not know about my dead brother. Instead she brought out a skirt. Something she had worn on a trip to Palestine in a completely different lifetime when she really worked as a photographer, as she said. I would have loved to know the story of the skirt. The story of the trip, the stuff mum had been doing when she included *really* in the telling but her voice already had that edge to it. I could sense that tone even in the tiniest whisper and knew exactly where she was on the spectrum of a manic episode. It was the same with hospital admissions. I would dream she would die and she would be admitted, without fail, soon after that. Sectioned mostly but sometimes she went of her own accord.

The person that had died was Jabori. I hadn't dreamt about him.

A couple of morning joggers slowed down when they saw me. They looked like one of those sharing hobbies couples.

It was still too early for most people. Mum and I had found ourselves in the kitchen at 4 a.m. She had woken early and I had not yet slept after leaving Temi in the club.

"Do you need some help?"

So much, I thought. But nothing you can sort out for me.

"I'm okay," I replied instead. "Just cooling off my high."

It wasn't truthful but then I hadn't said drugs. My eyes hadn't felt strained or hot or inflamed but the cool water was certainly soothing my eyelids. I was telling some version of the truth. It was promising, nice, the way the early sun was filtered by moving water before it reached my eyes, tiny leaves covering the surface. My long sleeve got covered in moss green. So cooling too, the green, the colour.

Temi had talked about someone we knew who had rearranged someone else's living-room.

"You get it, the woman went out to get some beers and came back to all the lamps rearranged, cushions moved about, armchair in a different spot, papers and books on a shelf instead of the table. All in the space of fifteen minutes. It was a completely different room."

I looked at her in a "and what" way.

And I said, "and what?"

"My friend lost it. She didn't know how to handle it."

I had gotten tired, very tired at that moment.

"Let's go to the other place," she said.

I followed because that's what I do. I follow Temi and let her let me touch her only to not hear from her for the following two weeks. And then we find ourselves in an all-nighter that lasts from Thursday evening until Monday morning if I can handle it. Lately I couldn't always make it through. Here I was Sunday morning, sober, alone, swimming without doing anything, really just lying on my back.

The joggers were still looking at me.

"Really. All okay here. I know it looks weird."

I lifted my head and showed them my perfectly healthy face. Issues, like everyone, but nothing that required institutional enforcement. At least I didn't think so. I even waved. And laughed.

"You wouldn't believe my night or morning. Honestly, I'm just cooling off."

"Oh, okay then."

They had been spot running through the whole exchange, one foot touching the ground, the other one lifted, arms moving along, held up close to the torso.

"We'll be back this side in half hour. If..."

"I won't be here, don't worry."

I hoped not.

Mum had waved the long skirt around, then draped it over her head, the fabric falling over her shoulders.

"Remember you used to do that, pretend your hair was moving when it was short."

It was 5.30 a.m. by then. I was tired.

"Mum, I was probably three or four."

"Yes," she replied. "My skirts were much too long."

She was laughing in that over the top way that you only know when you have a parent with serious bipolar. The shrillness that caught people's attention, but they couldn't quite place. The volume was turned up too high, the eyes had something in it that I could never explain. She pulled the chair close to the table.

Inside I went *oh-oh*. Two years ago she had climbed the chair, then the kitchen table, reached for the plant pots she had on the sill under the kitchen window, picked up the mint and thrown it against the opposite wall. Then the basil and the thyme, which was the heaviest, and the rosemary. I had been at hers because of another club night close to her flat. Not yet with Temi, not yet alone with her but with a bunch of friends that included her. A vase with dead flowers followed. When I shouted "why" from the kitchen door mum said she was repotting. It was spring.

She had gone on to throw many more things that were above hip level until the neighbours from underneath called the police. It wasn't that bad, a little loud, but they were always looking for a reason since the day the husband had helped mum out of the bathtub all naked. She had left the flat door open and he had come back from the terrace above, where he had his secret smokes, nothing exciting, just Superkings, and seen the light on at 2 a.m. Mum had fallen asleep in the bathtub. They'd had it in for us since then. Why did she have to be sectioned for throwing a couple of things in her own flat we had both asked. But the officer hadn't engaged. Of course, she had the shrill laugh then but there was no way he could know exactly what that meant.

Here we were two years later, another spring and a serious anniversary. I was bracing myself. I needed cooling down, something to keep me mellow.

She didn't climb the table.

I climbed down the river bank.

I should have done it face down. I should have tried to keep my face under water for as long as I could, submerged. But I already knew my face would turn out of the water the first chance it could. It's what the body does when it can, my body at least.

Mum had taken the skirt down and sat at the table.

"We should talk."

There wasn't anything I feared more than Mum's talks. They could be like the repotting. Anything could land on you, anything was up for being dismantled and thrown my way. Things I wasn't ready to hear, details I couldn't stomach. I left.

The long sleeve was pulling downward, so were my sweatpants. I moved my hands, back and forth, the fingers spread a little. The water was too cold to stay in for much longer, my lips had started to shiver. I was worried about the joggers. If I was still here when they got back, what would they do.

Temi had been rushing us, taking short cuts I didn't know, through back streets that smelled.

"Maybe it was the light." There was no telling if she was listening. "It could have been the light affecting her, that's why she moved the lamps. It happens with mania, light sensitivity."

I stumbled behind her. Her Doc Martens were almost echoing back from the arches we were under. Her long shirt was hanging over her ripped shorts moving around her legs where I wanted my hands to be. She stopped suddenly and pulled me close.

"It's not that I don't like you. I like you a lot."

Inside I was ducking. Were there pots coming my way?

She kissed me and I sucked on her lips until she pulled back.

"It's just, you don't talk. You are not really…here. You just disappear and hang on. Metaphorically."

Her eyes fixed on me as she walked backwards, her hands waving me to follow her. I did.

In the club we danced and kissed some more and she whispered something in my ear that I couldn't hear. When she went to the toilet I ran out of the club, and took the bus to Mum's. My head leaned against the window. I texted her about some emergency, I would catch her next time. It was the first time I had left first. It was also the first time Temi had talked to me like that. I had complained and complained about her non-committed ways. I had told my friends about her infrequent libido, or whatever it was, of her probably having a string of lovers, of her not knowing how to be close. She was stringing me along, she wasn't serious, she wasn't interested and called me only out of boredom. We, my friends and I, had chewed over it again and again.

To Temi I had only ever said, "Sure, I'm free, let's go out."

Before the skirt, Mum had asked what was wrong. And said that she hadn't expected me that night. How were things going with that young woman?

There was water everywhere. The river was full of it.

Twice in one night I had left a woman that I had complicated but deep feelings for.

I climbed back on the bank and sat on the bench with my knees close to my body, arms wrapped around the shins. It was dripping from everywhere, the water melted into the wood. I could see the joggers coming up. They were smiling when they saw me sitting on solid ground.

"I should probably get home, inside."

"Probably."

They were no longer running but had come to a full stop. The guy, it was a man and a woman, took my hand and pulled me off the bench. The woman flanked me on the other side. She picked up my phone, my oyster card and the keys I had left on the grass before the slope that led into the water.

"It might even be a warm day today."

"Yeah, looks like it," I replied.

We walked and my trainers made a slurping sound.

"How was the water," she asked. "Cold?"

I nodded. We passed the part where you had to walk up some stairs to the bus stop. I wanted to say something but it felt right, the walking.

Minna Salami

An author, blogger, social critic, international keynote speaker and founder of the multiple award-winning blog, MsAfropolitan, which connects feminism with critical reflections on contemporary culture from an Africa-centred perspective. She was listed by Elle *magazine as "one of 12 women changing the world" alongside Angelina Jolie and Michelle Obama. As an international keynote speaker, she has presented to audiences at the European Parliament, the Oxford Union, Yale University, TEDx, The Singularity University at NASA and UNWomen among others. She is a contributor to* The Guardian, Al Jazeera *and the Royal Society of the Arts, and a columnist for the* Guardian Nigeria. *She is Nigerian, Finnish and Swedish and lives between London and Lagos. She has a BA in Political Science from the University of Lund, and was awarded a distinction for her MA thesis in Gender Studies from SOAS. Her debut book,* Sensuous Knowledge: A Black Feminist Interpretation, *will be published in 2020.*

Searching for my Feminist Roots

This is an essay about a sense of loss leading to the discovery of self.

It starts with a cliché statement, which I am sure that every African woman who identifies as feminist has heard, namely "feminism is not African".

I am also sure that every African feminist, upon hearing this stereotypical statement, has felt exasperation. After all, if anything should be considered "not African", it is the oppression that girls and women are subject to. Also, the idea that there are parts of shared human culture that are "not African" is belittling. Africa is not a continent in outer space, it is part of the world. So long as feminism is a global movement, so long is feminism African.

But as I mentioned, this essay is about loss and self-discovery and not about whether or not feminism is African. The only reason I begin with the contention, is because these types of attitudes are what led me to the central figure in this essay, Oya, a woman who has significantly impacted my life.

Before I tell you about Oya, let me briefly explain why the "Feminism is not African" announcement nevertheless led me to her. It is because, apart from exasperation, what is implied in that statement always made me feel a sense of loss.

Why loss? Well put it this way, there are many influences that may shape a woman into a feminist; in my case first and foremost my mother, and the many books of feminist struggles around the world that she introduced me to. Furthermore, the experiences of oppression that one lives through as a girl and a woman shaped me into a feminist too. Moreover, I've always believed—if somewhat in jest—that I was born a feminist; in my earliest childhood memories, I was already the feminist person that I am now. But a key reason that I am a feminist is that I belong to a lineage of generations of women across the African continent who were feminist. I am sure that many of my colleagues share this last sentiment with me—we are feminists because there were women before us who were feminists. What causes the sense of loss, then, is that due to the invasion of Africa, the majority of historical records of these women are missing. So when someone says that feminism isn't African, we are reminded that we do not have the historical proof to show how continuous our presence is in the continent.

It is a similar sense of loss, I believe, that led Alice Walker to search for Zora Neale Hurston in her book *In Search of Our Mother's Gardens*; and it is a similar sense of loss that led Gloria Jean Watkins to take on her grandmother's name, bell hooks, as a pen name; I believe it is a similar sense of loss that inspired the publication of the first edition of this book, *Daughters of Africa*. As Margaret Busby writes in the introduction of the first edition, "Tradition and history are nurturing spirits for women of African descent. For without an understanding of where we have come from, we are less likely to be able to make sense of where we are going." Without doubt, it was this sense of loss that led me to Oya, who unlike any other figure in precolonial African history has expanded my purview of where I come from and of where I am going.

To readers who are familiar with Oya and who know her as an Orisha, that is, as a goddess belonging to the Yoruba pantheon of deities known as the Orisha where she is the "Goddess of Thunder", you may be thinking that it is pompous of me to imply that I am headed toward the status of a goddess. I assure you that I have no such aspirations, not least because I do not believe in any gods, or goddesses, for that matter. However, the Oya I have discovered was not a goddess, other than figuratively. She was an actual woman who lived many centuries ago and was a revolutionary feminist.

The eminent Yoruba philosopher, Dr Sophie Bósèdé Olúwolé, is one of a growing number of scholars who argue that "the word Orisha does not mean 'god' in the Yoruba language" as it has been sloppily translated, but rather something closer to "hero" or "heroine". She argues that from a Yoruba Classical Philosophy standpoint, the Orisha are actually human beings who made significant contributions to the transformation of society. She compares the Orisha to the Christian saints and Ancient Greece's philosophers such as Socrates. I would add that the Orisha are comparable to figures such as Gandhi, Mother Theresa, Martin Luther King, Jesus or the Buddha. I even like to think of Nina Simone as an Orisha!

The question is, were individuals such as Gandhi or Jesus spiritual figures or were they revolutionaries? The answer is that the line between the two is blurry. People generally think of spirituality as being predominantly about peacefulness, serenity, positive thinking, and so on. But can you truly be at peace if there is suffering around you and you do nothing about it? Resistance to injustice combined with compassionate action toward the self as well as toward society, is what it truly means to be spiritual. That is why, if you take a good look at any of history's perceivably most spiritual figures, you realise that what actually gives them an immortal status is that their radical, revolutionary as well as compassionate and wise ways diverted the steadfast progression of ignorance toward enlightenment, if only briefly.

The more I learn about Oya, the more the marriage between spirituality and revolution becomes clear to me. When it comes to Oya, she is on the one hand seen as the goddess of thunder, winds and lightning. She is held as the guardian of the realm between life and death, and as such, of funerals and cemeteries. She is worshipped with the colours red and purple and sacrifices of kola nuts and gin are made to her. These are all clearly spiritual—or you could argue—animist, readings of her.

But Oya is also seen as the patron saint of the marketplace and of women's affairs. She is noted as the one who fearlessly spoke truth to power no matter the consequences. She is recorded as a force of feminine leadership, and as both a sensual and a maternal figure driven to restore balance in society by all means necessary, even if by causing anomie.

In other words, while Oya is assumed to be a deity, embedded in her deification is the story of a revolutionary. The compendium of Yoruba philosophy, Ifa, includes a collection of verses dedicated to each Orisha including Oya. In one of the verses, Oya is described as "something [that] tore into the house and paralysed everyone with fright." In another she is, "the leader of freedom for women who unfreely praise the broken earth." Then there is the verse which begins with, "Vagina is highly intelligent" and goes on to say, "Oya, the complete fighter, massive woman up in the sky: pow, pow [...] whose uplifting strengthens me."

These incantations written many centuries ago carry echoes of more contemporary feminists such as Funmilayo Ransome-Kuti or Emmeline Pankhurst who you could say "tore into the house [or society]" and "paralysed everyone with fright"; or women like Leymah Gbowee or Malala Yousafzai who could be described as "leaders of freedom for the unfree". The altitude of transformation ushered by a "massive woman up in the sky" who lifts as she climbs could equally be plucked from a eulogy for a Harriet Tubman or a Simone de Beauvoir.

In 2015 I published an essay on my blog, *MsAfropolitan*, titled "Oyalogy—A poetic approach to African feminism". In the essay, I used Oya's divine status to build a feminist theory rooted in African mythology. But I needn't have deified the source of the theory. The extent to which Oya is a god, I now believe was bestowed upon her for her radical but compassionate uprooting of injustice in her society. I concede that this is a view that is open to interpretation: to some Oya will always be a supernatural being, but to me she was human being supernatural—a heroine. Whichever the case may be, what I found in Oya replaced a sense of loss with a sense of self-discovery; I had come upon the African feminist lineage I had sought for so long.

Noo Saro-Wiwa

Born in Port Harcourt, Nigeria, she was raised in England and is based in London. Her first book, Looking for Transwonderland: Travels in Nigeria, *was selected for BBC Radio 4's Book of the Week, named* Sunday Times Travel Book of the Year *in 2012, shortlisted for the Author's Club Dolman Travel Book of the Year Award in 2013; and nominated by the* Financial Times *as one of the best travel books of 2012. She has contributed stories to the anthologies* An Unreliable Guide to London, A Place of Refuge *and* La Felicità Degli Uomini Semplici. *She has written book reviews, travel and other articles for publications including* The Guardian, Financial Times, *the* Times Literary Supplement, City AM, Prospect *and* La Repubblica. *She was awarded a Miles Morland Scholarship for non-fiction writing in 2015. In 2018 she was among the judges for the Jhalak Prize for literature. She was awarded a Bellagio Center residency for 2019.*

A Fetching Destination

It's not every day I find myself eyeing up pornographic imagery with a Chinese man and a veiled-up African Muslim woman. The three of us were gathered around a counter and inspecting some aphrodisiac pills, the packaging of which displayed a photo of a man (with what I pray was a prosthetic penis) in session with a naked woman. Seized by embarrassment, my ears grew hot and I developed a phantom itch on my nose. The Nigerienne customer, however, didn't give a toss. She was here on a shopping mission and had little time to waste on coyness or prudery.

"Many, many," the lady told the Chinese seller, using the international lingo for wholesale purchasing. She ordered a thousand packets of Brother Long Legs, secured a delivery date for the merchandise then walked off with her friend, chatting away in French.

I was on the ground floor of the Tianxiu building in the southern Chinese city of Guangzhou, a magnet for African wholesale buyers. Dotted around me were glass counters stacked with all manner of "sexuality enhancing" products, sold by Chinese people who stood by nonchalantly while I checked out their merchandise. I saw vagina-tightening gels, and "extra strong delay sprays for long-lasting excitement" and—most intriguing of all—a "high-grade professional female oestrus induction toner" called Spanish Gold Fly. The packaging of another aphrodisiac had Arabic script printed on it and a photo of a black man being "entertained" below the waist by two white ladies. I scarcely knew where to put my eyes. The vendors slouched behind their counters and fiddled with their phones.

Very few things surprise Chinese manufacturers and wholesalers. They are the eyes and ears of the consumer universe. They know all our secrets and desires, and produce for them accordingly. Motivated by an all-consuming desire to make money (this non-Christian nation runs the world's biggest Bible printing press, after all), the vendors in the Tianxiu building were unoffended by my camera and time-wasting inquiries. So long as they made sales at some point in the day I was free to snoop, prod and ogle to my heart's content.

And so I checked out "hip lift" massage creams and hair wigs and Brazilian weaves. Some of the Chinese vendors had adopted the African method of hissing to get my attention—"Hello, my sista," they said, while showing me buttock-enhancing *yansh pads* and packets of Ginseng tea, formulated to strengthen one's kidneys, supposedly.

The second floor was the place to buy underwear. Some of the packaging displayed faces of famous footballers that had been photo-shopped onto Y-front-clad torsos: an improbably buff Zinedine Zidane showed off his bulge. Buck-toothed Ronaldinho looked especially pleased to be wearing his 100% combed cotton singlet. David Beckham, meanwhile, sizzled in a white vest and briefs, his hand cupping his crotch. But by far my favourite was the "Black Power Obama Collection"—a pack of men's underpants decorated with a photo of America's finest president, fingers on chin, eyes gazing eruditely into the distance. In the free-for-all that is the China-Africa small commodity trade, matters of image copyright do not enter the equation. Just shift the product.

China is Africa's largest trading partner, an economic relationship that has grown significantly since 2000. China provided huge loans to the continent when the IMF would not. It built infrastructure projects to replace the haggard modernist monoliths that sprouted during oil booms and colonial times. New bridges, highways, airports, stadiums and presidential palaces. The poorest of African countries were granted zero-tariffs on a sizeable chunk of their exports to China.

In turn, Africans were allowed to enter China and buy the small commodities that our low-manufacturing economies don't make or have stopped making. They began travelling here as traders on temporary visas, others settling there permanently. It is a relatively recent phenomenon in the history of global migration. For some, this relationship between China and Africa signified the start of a post-colonial epoch, free of Western mediation. No more finger-wagging "Wypipo" on their civilising missions. The Middle Kingdom's refusal to criticise or moralise was music to the ears of sensitive kleptocrats in Africa as well as some commentators, who saw a refreshing simplicity in this deal, this New Amorality.

While Europe narrowed its doors to Africans with non-essential skills, China offered a chance for Africans to live within its borders or visit on short-term visas in order to buy small commodities and other business. By 2008, up to 300,000 Africans were thought to be living in the southern city of Guangzhou, concentrated in an enclave known in the national media as "Chocolate City" (Chinese geographical nomenclature of all kinds often being indicative rather than artful).

From the Tianxiu building I headed to the busy Guangyuanxi Road in the Sanyuanli district. The smell of Chinese-brand cigarettes and egg waffles thickened the air. Visa overstayers leaned languidly against the railings while their fellow sub-

Saharans—the visiting traders—loaded boxes into taxis with contrasting verve. Two black men sat on roadside stools getting their shoes shined by Chinese women. The seventies buildings, the Anglophone shop hoardings, the concrete flyover colonised by creeping vines, resembled many a city in Africa.

Such a melanin-rich environment was too much to handle for some Chinese folks, who expressed their discontent with a frankness bordering on the comical. Take, for example, the online reviews for the Donfranc Hotel, which is popular with African visitors. Translated from Google, one review was bluntly titled, "Here are blacks". In another entry someone reported: "the hotel facilities are obsolete...the rooms are dirty, dimly lit, with no windows inside...guests predominantly black..."

Those African hotel guests come to Guangzhou to buy goods, particularly clothes, because the Chinese have undercut textile production back home. I could see their stalls diagonally opposite Canaan Market, run by friendly Cantonese ladies. The sight of them handling piles of African wax prints was to my eyes as culturally transgressive as those male shop assistants who handle ladies' underwear in Saudi Arabian lingerie shops. But that's the way of the world these days. Africa plays no part in the displaying of African attire either: manning the corridors of Canaan Market were white mannequins—fibreglass Vikings modelling kaftans and kufi hats; blue-eyed plastic children wearing faux-gold Africa-shaped pendants and Gucci knock-off T-shirts festooned with the kind of glitter that exfoliates your flesh on contact.

African buyers haggled with the Chinese for this stuff. It led to heated face-offs at times, due mainly to cultural differences. In Africa, bartering is an art form, performed with some banter and perhaps a smile. But some Chinese took it as a provocation. *Africans haggle too much*, they complained. *Always want things cheaper!*

"Nigerian market woman will pet you," one Nigerian guy told me. "She will tell you why it is costing this much—the trouble with her business... The Chinese? They just charge you."

The slightest hint of a negotiation sent certain Guangzhou vendors into a rage. I got a first-hand taste of this after requesting a discount for a rucksack. The shopkeeper reacted as if I had just pinched her arse. She was scary looking too: her fringe and pollution mask combined to cover her entire face save for two disgusted eyes. With shocking ferocity she waved me away, her calculator falling from her hand and clattering on the counter. End of discussion. I wasn't even allowed to improve my offer.

I walked on. There was nothing the Chinese didn't produce and sell, it seemed. Further down the road I could see that even Nigeria's election paraphernalia accessories were being manufactured and sold in Guangzhou. Shop windows were plastered with election bunting for Nigeria's two biggest political parties; bracelets proclaiming: "So-and-so 4 Governor"; stickers of election hopefuls such as Charles Kenechi Ugwu, whose face tilted righteously above the words: "The Lord's Chosen... Divine gift to Nsukka people". Rumour has it that the ballot papers for one of Kenya's general elections were delivered to Nairobi with "X"s already marked in the box for the ruling party. (I can believe it. While travelling in Kenya on trains built by the Chinese, I saw signs written in poorly translated "Chinglish"—proof that the government had abdicated supervision at the most basic level.)

Next to the election paraphernalia were displays of Nigerian police uniforms and badges. To my surprise, the vendor gave me prices on request. It made me realise I could clothe my own fake police force if I wanted to. One wholesale order—no questions asked—was all I needed to "establish my authority" on the streets of Lagos or Port Harcourt. Which was amusing but also alarming. That the apparel of such an important branch of Nigerian governance could be sold so casually in Guangzhou spoke volumes about the power imbalance between China and our Mother Continent.

In Africa, the Chinese have bought up huge tracts of farmland and mining concessions with the consent of the national leaders, but here in China, we and other foreigners aren't allowed majority ownership of so much as a hole-in-the-wall food stall.

I stepped out onto the street again. A trio of Nigerian "market women" walked past, wearing boubous and carrying bags of merchandise on their heads. Curly-mop hair weaves, eyebrows like painted caterpillars; dark lips contrasting ghoulishly against bleached skin. These ladies negotiated the streets of Guangzhou with the blinkered nonchalance of the business traveller. The vision of them sauntering along the road, butt cheeks dancing behind, could easily be transposed to their ancestral villages where, like their forbears, they might have trekked several miles to fetch water—a time-consuming task that drains productivity. Instead, they had "trekked" halfway round the world to Guangzhou on a trip costing upwards of £5,000. It's a long way to go to fetch life's everyday items.

The more things change, it seems, the more things stay the same.

Taiye Selasi

An author and photographer born in London and raised in Boston, she is of Ghanaian and Nigerian heritage. She holds a BA in American Studies from Yale University and an MPhil in International Relations from Oxford. In 2005 she published the seminal essay "Bye-Bye, Babar (Or: What is an Afropolitan?)", sparking a movement among transnational Africans. Her debut novel, the New York Times *bestseller* Ghana Must Go, *was selected as one of the 10 Best Books of 2013 by the* Wall Street Journal *and* The Economist. *The same year she was named on* Granta's *list of Best Young British Novelists. In 2014 she featured on the Hay Festival's Africa39 list of writers*

*aged under 40 with the potential and talent to define trends in African literature.
Her 2015 TED talk "Don't Ask Where I'm From, Ask Where I'm a Local" has
reached more than 2.5 million viewers, redefining the way a global society conceives
of personal identity.*

From *The Sex Lives of African Girls*

Begin, inevitably, with Uncle.

There you are, eleven, alone in the study in the dark in a cool pool of moonlight at
the window. The party is in full swing on the back lawn outside. Half of Accra must
be out there. In production. Some fifty-odd tables dressed in white linen table skirts,
the walls at the periphery all covered in lights, the swimming pool glittering with tea
lights in bowls bobbing lightly on the surface of the water, glowing green. The smells
of things—night-damp earth, open grill, frangipani trees, citronella—seep in through
the window, slightly cracked. You tap the glass lightly and wave your hand, testing, but
no one looks up. They can't see for the dark. It rained around four for five minutes and
not longer; now the sky is rich black for its cleansing. Beneath it a *soukous* band shows
off the latest from Congo, the lead singer wailing in French and Lingala.

She ought to be ridiculous: little leopard-print shorts, platform heels, hot-pink
half-top, two half-arms of bangles. Instead, wet with sweat and moon, trembling,
ascendant, all movement and muscle, she is fearsome. It is a heart-wrenching voice,
cutting straight through the din of the chatter, forced laughter, clinked glasses, the
crickets. She is shaking her shoulders, hips, braided extensions. She has the most
genuine intentions of any woman out there.

And they.

Their bright *bubas* adorn the large garden like odd brilliant bulbs that bloom
only at night. From the dark of the study you watch with the interest of a scientist
observing a species. A small one. Rich African women, like Japanese geisha in wax-
batik *geles*, their skin bleached too light. They are strange to you, strange to the
landscape, the dark, with the same polished skill-set of rich women worldwide: how
to smile with full lips while the eyes remain empty; how to hate with indifference;
how to love without heat. You wonder if they find themselves beautiful, or powerful?
Or perplexing, as they seem to you, watching from here?

The young ones sit mutely, sipping foam off their Maltas, waiting to be asked
to dance by the men in full suits, shoving cake into their mouths when they're sure
no one's looking (it rained around four; no one sees for the dark). The bolder ones
preening, little aunties-in-training, being paraded around the garden, introduced to
parents' friends. "This is Abena, our eldest, just went up to Oxford." "This is Maame,
the lawyer. She trained in the States." Then the push from the mother, the tentative
handshake. "It's a pleasure to meet you, sir. How is your son?" You wonder if they enjoy
it. You can't tell by watching. They all wear the same one impenetrable expression:
eyebrows up, lips pushed out, nostrils slightly flared in poor imitation of the 1990s

supermodel. It is a difficult expression to pull off successfully, the long-suffering look of women bored with being looked at. The girls in the garden look more startled than self-satisfied, as if their features are shocked to be forming this face.

But their dresses.

What dresses. They belong on the cake trays: as bright, sweet and frothy as frosted desserts, the lacy "up-and-downs" with sequins, tiny mirrors and bell sleeves, the rage in Accra this Christmas. It's the related complications—tying the *gele*, the headwrap; wrapping then trying to walk in the ankle-length skirt; the troubling fact that you haven't got hips yet to showcase—that puts you off them.

You can barely manage movement in the big one-piece *buba* you borrowed from Comfort, your cousin, under duress. The off-the-shoulder neckline keeps slipping to your elbow, exposing your (troublingly) flat chest. Absent breasts, the hem drags and gets caught underfoot, a malfunction exacerbated by your footwear, also Comfort's: gold leather stilettos two sizes too small with a thick crust of sequins and straps of no use. You've been tripping and falling around the garden all evening, with night-damp earth sucking at the heels of the shoes, the excess folds of the *buba* sort of draped around your body, making you look like a black Statue of Liberty. Except: the Statue of Liberty wears those comfortable sandals and doesn't get sent to go fetch this and that—which is how you've now found yourself alone in the study having stumbled across the garden, being noticed as you went: little pretty thing, solitary, making haste for the house with the shuffle-shuffle steps of skinny girls in women's shoes; and why you tripped as you entered, snagging the hem with your heel, the cloth yanked from your chest as you fell to the rug.

And lay. The dry quiet a sharp sudden contrast to the wet of the heat and the racket outside. And as sharply and as suddenly, the consciousness of *nakedness*. Eve, after apple.

Your bare breastless chest.

How strange to feel naked in a room not your own, and not stepping from the bath into the humidity's embrace, but here cold and half-naked in the leather-scented darkness, remembering the morning, the rain around four. This was moments ago (nakedness) as you lay, having fallen, the conditioned-air chilly and silky against your chest. Against your nipples. Two points you'd never noticed before but considered very deeply now: nipples. And yours. The outermost boundaries of a body, the endpoints, where the land of warm skin meets the sea of cold air. Shore. You lay on your back in the dark on the floor, like that, newly aware of your nipples.

Presently, the heart-wrenching voice floating up from the garden, "*Je t'aime, mon amour. Je t'attends.*" You sat up. You listened for a moment, as if to a message, then kicked off the sandals and stood to your feet. You went to the window and looked at the singer, in flight on the stage to the high note. "*Je t'attends!*"

Indeed.

So it is that you're here at the window when, five minutes later, he enters the room, his reflection appearing dimly on the window before you, not closing the door in the silvery dark. You think of the houseboys with their lawn chairs in an oval reading *Othello* in thick accents, Uncle watching with pride. Demand me nothing: what you know, you know. From this time forth I never will speak word. (Likely not. With the thing come together, the pattern emerging, the lines, circles, secrets, lies, hurts, back to this, here, the study, where else, given the fabric, the pattern, the stars. What to say?)

Enter Uncle.

* * *

He walks in behind you, saying nothing at all and not closing the door in the silvery dark. You turn around to face him. Full circle. Explaining, "I was fetching an album for Auntie. I'm sorry." Your *buba* slides down. You start to say more but he holds up a hand, shakes his head, is not angry.

"It's nice to be away from it all. Isn't it?" He smiles.

"Yes, Uncle."

"I'll bring her the album. Relax." He joins you at the window. Ever so slightly behind you. Puts a hand on your shoulder, palm surprisingly cold. In a very gentle motion he rearranges the *buba*. "Are you happy?" The question surprises you.

"Yes, Uncle."

"What I mean is, are you happy here? Happy living here?"

"Yes, Uncle."

"And you would tell me if you weren't?"

"Yes, Uncle."

"Meaning no."

"No, Uncle"

"'No, Uncle.' Better than 'yes', I suppose." He chuckles almost sadly. He is quiet for a moment. "Do you miss her?"

"Yes, Uncle."

He nods. "Yes, of course." Then you stare out the window, another couple at a painting. The singer is hitting a high note, clutching the mic as if for life. You look at the dance floor. You see Kwabena but not Auntie. The younger girls dancing with men in full suits. You look to the tables. There is Comfort, sitting stiffly. Iago, in a server's tux, approaches with drinks. He pours her more Malta; Comfort doesn't look up. You feel your breath quicken. Uncle's hand on your neck.

"You remind me so much of your mother." He leans down now. The hotness of rum and his breath on your skin. The *buba* slides off and he adjusts it again carefully. "She had this long neck. Just like yours," he says, touching. You stiffen. Not at the touch but the tense. He notices. "I frighten you," he says, sad, surprised.

"No, Uncle."

"Bloody hell. Is that all you say?" He speaks through clenched teeth. "It's a *question* for God's sake. Do I frighten you?" You are silent, unable to move. "*Answer me.*" Not gently, he turns you around. Unable to face him you stare at your feet sinking into the carpet, toe nails painted pink. But when he lifts your chin, whispering, "Look at me," you do—and don't find the anger you're expecting. None at all. You have never been this close to Uncle's face. You have never noticed its resemblance to your mother's. The dark deep-set eyes. And in them something familiar. Something you recognize. Loneliness. Loss. "I didn't frighten her," he says insistently, slurring the words. "I never frightened her. Do I frighten you?" Your chin in his hands.

You shake your head quickly. "No, Uncle," you mumble.

"I miss her so much." He cups a palm around your cheek. And when he leans down to kiss you, you know what he means. You feel his tears on your face, mixed with yours, warm; his cool. There is something sort of disgusting about the feel of his lips. But you bear it for those moments, as an act of generosity (or something like it), feeling for the first time at home in his house.

Still, you can imagine how it must look from the doorway when you hear Auntie, "How long does it take—?" Then sudden silence as she sees. "Oh, God," she splutters out in a horrified whisper. The only sound in the darkness. "Oh, God."

Uncle pulls away from you and looks at his wife. "Khadijeh." And there is Auntie, in the doorway. How she falls. She leans against the doorframe then slumps to the ground. She repeats the words, "Oh, God." Close to hyperventilating. In tears. Uncle smoothes his trousers with the palms of his hands. He touches your shoulder calmly before going to the door.

"Khadijeh," he says, kneeling, but she pushes him away.

"Don't touch me. How dare you? God damn you to hell." She hits him now, desperately. "She's your blood. She's your blood."

"That's enough," he says softly, as she kicks at his shins. He grabs her by the shoulders, standing her up on her feet. She flails at him, sobbing. He slaps her. Hard. Once. "This is *my* house," he says. Walks away.

In the dark and the silence you wish you could vanish, at least crawl beneath the desk without her noticing and hide. But she barely seems conscious as she sits in the doorway, her lace like a pile of used tissues, a cloud.

And that's when it hits you. Your mother isn't coming. Wherever she's gone it's a place without life. What life there was in her was choked out by hatred; whatever light in her eyes was the glint of that hate. And whom did she hate so? Her brother? Her mother? Your father? It doesn't matter. They live. She is dead.

This is what you're left with: a life with these people. This place and these women. Comfort. Ruby. Khadijeh. Who—it suddenly occurs to you, with an odd kind of clarity, as you watch from the window—mustn't be left to die, too.

So you go to her, stumbling over the hem of the garment as you cross the Persian rug and she looks up, face smeared. The kohl make-up runs down her cheeks like black tears. You sit down beside her, laying your head in her lap.

"Edem," she whispers faintly.

"Yes, Auntie." You start to cry. A familiar sound, peculiar: the sound of your name.

You put your arms around her waist. It is softer than you'd imagined it. You hold her very tightly, and she holds you as if for life. You wish there was something you could say, to comfort her. But what? In the peculiar hierarchy of African households the only rung lower than motherless child is childless mother.

Lola Shoneyin

*A Nigerian poet and writer, she graduated from Ogun State University in 1995. She is the author of three books of poems—*So All the Time I Was Sitting on an Egg *(1998),* Song of a Riverbird *(2002) and* For the Love of Flight *(2010)—and a children's book titled* Mayowa and the Masquerades *(2010), as well as her debut novel,* The Secret Lives of Baba Segi's Wives *(2011), which in the same year was nominated for the Orange Prize for Fiction and won the PEN Oakland/Josephine Miles Literary Award and the Ken Saro Wiwa Prose Prize. She is the founder of Book Buzz Foundation—an NGO devoted to promoting literacy, creating reading spaces, and organising cultural events such as the Aké Arts and Book Festival and Kaduna Book and Arts Festival. She recently founded Ouida Books, a new publishing house for the adventurous reader. She lives in Lagos, Nigeria.*

How We Were
(For Bade)

Hot afternoon.
You on the couch.
Me tapping keys.
You making music.
Me pacing the room.
You curling up with an ulcer.
Me stroking your cheek.
You saying how painful pain is.
Me saying that would suck on a sticker.
You shaking your head.
Me lifting your chin.
You looking up.
You winning.

Me getting the call.
Me thinking what the fuck.
Me calling your name.

You lying there.
You motionless.
You mouth open.
You mid-song.

Me stroking your cheek.
Me punching the wall.
Me kicking myself.
Me slapping the wheel.

Me speaking at your wake.
Me breaking down.
Me weeping at your wake.
Me swimming in memories.

You dancing at 'Politan Vibes.
You fluttering rainbow wings.
You belting out Kidjo songs.
You getting laid in New Orleans.

Me loving you.
Me losing you.
Me losing.
You.

Falling

I tell you of my darkness.
And every time you ask: there's more?
I cannot see your hand that reaches for me
when gloom outshines light.

I say I am near the end.
You watch me fret and fight the current.
It is the madness, not the method
that keeps me beneath the surface.

I am accustomed to the futility
of war against a water wall.

You tell me you are here.
You say I have to ride it.

I imagine myself on a magic carpet,
falling through the roof of my living room.
No doorbells, no doors, just a pink post-it note
to remind me that I am still here.

Buni Yadi

There will be no glory in this war, no victor,
no worn, torn leaves in history books,
no praise-song for homecoming kings,
no applause for the cause,
no clanging of swords,
no song for the cymbals.

When the North is nothing but a scrawl on a black board,
and the East is eating the South,
the West will pull out its teeth
and hold blood in its mouth.

Everyone will remember the days
when we knew the shoemaker
from the brush in hand,
the hand in bush,
the bush burning the hand at wrist.

Everyone will remember
when a school was painted with the blood
of sixty-nine boys whose names we never call,
Everyone will remember
when virgins hanged themselves by their hymens,
when three hundred girls slept with the snakes
of Sambisa—forest of the forsaken.

For God or for country,
the only moral for these mortals is loss.
In this lock-horn of cross and crescent,
smiths in red loincloth widen the needle's eye
for the chalked camel
on her dance to the riverbed.

Zadie Smith

Born in London to an English father and Jamaican mother (Yvonne Bailey-Smith), she published her first novel, White Teeth, *aged 24 in the year 2000. The book went on to win a number of awards and prizes, including* The Guardian *First Book Award, the Whitbread First Novel Award and the Commonwealth Writers' Prize (Overall Winner, Best First Book). It has been translated into more than 20 languages, was adapted for Channel 4 television in 2002, and in 2018 became a stage play, premiering at the Kiln Theatre. She is also the author of* The Autograph Man *(2002),* On Beauty *(2005),* Changing My Mind *(2009),* The Embassy of Cambodia *(2013),* NW *(2012),* Swing Time *(2016) and a 2018 collection of essays,* Feel Free. *She has been a tenured Professor in the Creative Writing faculty of New York University since 2010. She made the following speech when receiving the Langston Hughes Medal in November 2017.*

Speech for Langston

I am so moved to be here this evening that I knew I couldn't trust myself to speak off the cuff, so I've written it down. If you'll indulge me I want to tell you two anecdotes that I hope will explain what this prize means to me.

I came to the States about ten years ago. It was before my daughter was in school so I used to come for six months to New York to teach and then back to London again. This one time, I got off a plane at Heathrow very early in the morning, headed to Willesden, and reaching our house, found it dusty, cold and silent—as houses are liable to be if you leave them long enough. I put on the heating and the lights and the radio and started tidying up. On the radio I could hear four older white gentlemen having a conversation. They sounded pretty learned, like they were experts in something or another. And they were having a learned conversation about who gets to be British—who, in the final analysis, is *really* British. They spent a long time discussing this question: I'd filled the dishwasher, done a wash of towels and bed linen, and gone through all the unopened mail before they were done. But as I passed a cloth over my kitchen table they finally reached their learned conclusion. Turned out, you were only truly British if all four of your great-grandparents were born in Britain. That was their expert view. And I sat down, exhausted, and just started to laugh. It was sort of a crazy laugh—a mixture of laughter and tears, and if you'd heard it you probably would have thought it sounded unhinged. I sat there in my old neighborhood, in my new-ish house, and thought of all those years I'd spent as a child in England trying to prove that I was both Black and British; that I knew their plays and poems and history, that I could get into the finest institutions of education they had to offer, that I could perhaps even add a few words to the history of their literature—that I, too, was England. But something turned in me that morning and I realized I just didn't care anymore. The whole thing seemed totally absurd. The British could argue amongst themselves about who was or wasn't British but it just didn't matter to me any longer whether or not they included me in their narrow, claustrophobic self-definitions. And for the first time in a long time I felt free.

Six months later I flew back to New York, and one of the first things I did was visit that old Barnes and Noble on Sixth Avenue that's been closed now for about five years as no one can afford to pay the rent on that space, not even Barnes and Noble. Anyway, I was browsing in there, in the African-American corner of the store, when I spotted a book of mine, *On Beauty*, sitting snug in that corner, after Ms Morrison but before Ms Walker. And I started to laugh-cry again. I thought: well look at *this*. In England, they're still trying to decide if a person like me is really English at all. Meanwhile, over here in New York, I've been adopted! I'm in the wrong part of the bookstore, sitting alongside writers who have meant so much to me, and even though everybody probably knows it's not quite right, I'm still here on this shelf, a kissing cousin, an interloper, an admirer from across the sea, and nobody's demanding to see my passport, and no-one cares where my goddamn great-grandfather came from. Because in that corner of the bookstore, American wasn't the operative word. African was. That's also why, when I came to America, for the first time I heard people call me sister in the street, sister in the supermarket, sister in the airport or the bar. I had entered a broader consciousness in which national borders had little meaning. I was part of a historical and geographic diaspora that has penetrated every corner of this globe, and which no single passport can contain or express.

Receiving this prize makes me want to laugh-cry. With pride and amazement. I don't know what I am doing on a list of names that includes James Baldwin and Toni Morrison, Derek Walcott and Octavia Butler, but I am so grateful to find myself in their company. Growing up in England, in the eighties, these were some of the writers my mother gave me, to remind me that no country has the power to decide whether or not it will "tolerate" a black child or decide on her true identity, for the black child's inheritance is borderless and enormous and needs no such external authentication. Nor is it a monolith. At the root of blackness lies Africa, but from that rich soil spreads innumerable branches, each with its own character, own style, own struggles and victories. A diaspora is always by definition *E pluribus unum*, and that which spread from Africa is uniquely flexible, able to fit into its oneness a dazzling plurality while at the same time recognizing a sibling relation across time and space. My sister. My brother.

Despite all contrasts of history and nation Langston Hughes is also my brother. He was a mixed-up sort of person, of the kind I can relate to. He had black ancestry and white ancestry, native American ancestry and Jewish ancestry, he had men in his life and women, he was a communist and a capitalist, he was a poet and a playwright and a novelist, a believer in the uptown working man, and a lover of downtown intellectuals. He was always conflicted. He could write of the "eternal tom-tom beating in the Negro soul" and he could also write: "I was a victim of a stereotype. There were only two of us Negro kids in the whole class and our English teacher was always stressing the importance of rhythm in poetry. Well, everyone knows—except us—that all Negroes have rhythm, so they elected me class poet." He expressed these beautiful conflicts in everything he wrote. Are we truly a people of rhythm? Or is all that a myth? Are we a people? Are middle-class negroes still negroes? What does it even mean to be a negro? These are the kinds of questions he asked himself, and he was beautifully inconsistent in his answers, being a poet and not a politician. But the thing I really love about Langston is his insistence, from the very start, that black lives not only matter but are beautiful, ugly, sad, happy, angry, joyful, and finally undefinable because so complex and so various, just as white lives are understood to be. That's knowledge we need right now. In our benighted present it feels natural and necessary to reach back into the past for guidance. Jimmy Baldwin reminds us how to fight the threat we're facing. Langston reminds us what we're fighting for. The freedom to be ourselves, in all our wonderful variety. Langston put his arms around the whole diaspora, no matter how distant or mongrel, no matter how unlike we all may be in history or culture, and in this way he inspired diaspora artists of every subsequent generation and all around the world. In Langston's worldview black sibling-hood stretched the earth. And I am so thankful that tonight it has stretched far enough to include a Black-British woman like me, a freckle-faced woman like me, a mixed-marriage woman like me, a green-card holder like me, an immigrant like me, a second-generation Jamaican like me, a distant but not forgotten daughter of Africa, like me. Thank you.

Attillah Springer

Born in Trinidad, she describes herself as "a writer and jouvayist". She has a longstanding interest in social justice movements and has organised and taken part in events around climate change, women's rights and sustainability in Trinidad, England, Iceland and India since 2005, using Carnival and other indigenous festival arts as forms of protest or awareness building. She writes on culture and memory and has presented papers and written commissioned work on traditional mas, resistance and African spirituality. She is also a Director of Idakeda Group, a collective of women in her family creating cultural interventions for social change especially among women and youth in Trinidad and Tobago.

Castle in the Sand
25 May 2013

At a bend in the road, you turn right at the University of Cape Coast and the sight of the sea is startling. Not just for the sun shining silver on its surface. The row of coconut trees makes me feel like I've fallen asleep and woken up back in Trinidad, on the road to Manzanilla. And I remember all those times I have stood on the other side of the Atlantic, watching the same sun shining silver on the sea's surface imagining what the coast in Africa looked like.

But I am on West African soil, in Ghana and there is a lump in my throat and a sense of dread building in my ears. Elmina is a pleasant enough fishing village. Some of the inhabitants are light-skinned, a leave over legacy from 400 years of ownership of Elmina Castle by the Dutch, the Portuguese and finally the English. They say they came here first for gold. But as we enter the Castle and begin the tour our guide says they were always on a mission to trade in humans.

We go down into the dungeons where the stench of centuries of human decay is still palpable. We go down into the belly of the castle to meet the noise of ancestors screaming out in agony. The roar of the sea is distant as is the sun's light. He shows us where the Governor would stand and select women captives to rape. He shows us the death dungeon with the skull and crossbones over the door where no-one came out alive. By the time we get to the Door of No Return I am plotting ways to escape. The doorways are so very narrow, the final insult for those who survive the horrendous conditions to make the crossing is that you have to bend, practically crawl into the last dungeon.

We retrace the steps of millions of people whose names we do not know. Who died here covered in the filth of others. Who suffered every possible indignity known to humankind to make others wealthy. My mother, Eintou, gives me guinea pepper and white rum to stabilise my Ori. I hold the seeds and liquid in my mouth, focusing on the heat to counter the feeling that my head is about to explode.

To those who say it is time to forget, I say that the stench of 400 years of human waste is unforgettable. To those who say black people should get over it, I say we need more than ever now to understand that enslavement is real and present and as much a threat now as it was 170 years ago. Some of us choose enslavement now. To material things. And people. And the god of someone else's ancestors. And the drivel of politicians. And looking like someone else.

We have the freedom to choose these prisons. Far from Elmina. Far from the plantations. Far from the stinking, fetid dungeons and ships, we choose to be shackled to death and decay. It is history, but it still lives. The virulent strain of capitalism that runs the world right now will not think twice about reintroducing chattel slavery. And they might not ship us across the Atlantic anymore. But some of us don't mind the cheap labour that makes our laptops. The sweat shops that make our clothes.

Some of us don't see the connection between the material possessions that we crave that keep other people in grinding poverty. Elmina is Elmina. Elmina is also a clothing factory in Bangladesh that collapses under the weight of its own greed. Elmina is a mine in South Africa where police officers shoot to kill when the miners demand better wages and working conditions. Elmina is the scorn poured on trafficked women from South America in a police-run whorehouse in Trinidad.

Elmina lives and breathes and laughs in our faces. The dungeons are still full of the stench of our complicity in the enslavement of others for our benefit. I flee from the stench and the darkness. I run from the Door of No Return, hoping to never have to be there again. In that hot, dark place. Bent and broken.

With my modern mind that knows only this version of freedom I wonder whether I would have survived this place in that time. Whether I would have chosen death rather than face the uncertainty of the dungeons, the crossing, the plantation. Survival is a mark of defiance. I feel another surge of pride that I belong to them. They must have had serious belly. They must have been the bad-minded ones. I wonder if they didn't long to join the sea's percussion. Their bones the rhythm section for the waves' endless bass.

I feel another surge of pride that we made it. That the ancestors on whose shoulders I stand were strong enough to endure that hell that I shudder to imagine. So that I can stand here now. Free as ever. In the light at the top of this castle. Watching the sea and thinking about Manzanilla.

Valerie Joan Tagwira

By profession a specialist obstetrician and gynaecologist, she is also recognised as an accomplished writer of fiction who lives and works in Harare, Zimbabwe. Her first novel, The Uncertainty of Hope *(2006), won the National Arts Merit Award (NAMA) in 2008, and was chosen by the Zimbabwe School Examinations Council as a set book for Advanced-Level Literature in English. She also writes poetry and short stories, which have been included in publications such as the* Caine Prize Anthology 2010, *and* Writing Mystery and Mayhem *(Weaver Press, 2015). An earlier version of "Mainini Grace's Promise" appeared in* Women Writing Zimbabwe *(2008, ed. Irene Staunton) and was translated into Shona (by Charles Mungoshi and Musaemura Zimunya) for the 2011 anthology* Mazambuko.

Mainini Grace's Promise

Sarai's mother concluded that it was not the three successive funerals but her own subsequent illness that finally did it.

Since her disclosure, things had gradually changed. In time, the subtle became obvious. The extended family seemed to have conveniently forgotten about their existence. Their visits had been shrouded in an aura of something parallel to embarrassment and detachment, then had become erratic, before ceasing altogether. For Sarai, dropping out of school to become her mother's carer was inevitable. The family had washed their hands of all responsibility, dumping it carelessly into her fifteen-year-old lap.

Her vivacious and capable aunt, Mainini Grace, was the only one who kept in touch. She sent money for groceries from Botswana and wrote encouraging letters, filled with promises that she would visit. She promised to bring tablets for her ailing sister, as well as arrange for Sarai to go back to school.

Occasionally Mainini's list included the gloves that Sarai had requested for her mother's bed-baths, the bra she wanted so much because girls of her age had started wearing breast support; and sanitary pads because there were no pads or cottonwool in the shops.

While the letters were a beacon, little by little the fruition of Mainini Grace's promises became questionable. In the eleven months since the last funeral, she had not returned from Botswana. Despite this inconsistency, the letters continued. Sarai read them avidly, over and over again, longing for her aunt's return, wishing for her to share this experience.

In her replies to Mainini Grace, Sarai always expressed these sentiments, stopping short of hinting that the money she sent was never enough.

After the most recent letter, Sarai allowed herself to be optimistic. Previously, it had always been, "Soon, my dearest." But the imminence of Mainini's arrival was given life with her assurance of a date: Wednesday, the 17th July.

In the morning, Sarai woke early and tidied the shack. She wrapped her hands with pieces of plastic and gave her mother a bed-bath, just as the nurse had taught her. The raw bed-sores did not seem as daunting as before, and her mother's muted groans of discomfort when she rolled her over were not as heart-rending. It was a day with a difference, spent in happy anticipation of Mainini Grace's arrival.

But by early evening, Sarai knew that the coach from Botswana had long passed Kwekwe, was probably in Harare already.

"Do you think she will ever come?" she asked her mother, disheartened.

The older woman's brow creased for a moment, before she said slowly, "There must be a good reason. I know my sister. She will come soon."

Sarai looked at her mother, astonished by this lack of anxiety. She did not appear disturbed by her sister's slipperiness. What good reason could there be for Mainini Grace to make false promises? Sarai felt deceived and confused.

She wondered why she had been foolish enough to expect anything different. Misery was predictable, while its opposite was simply out of reach. Her aunt was not coming. Though her own desire to go back to school was not as urgent as her mother's need for medication, Sarai wondered, Will I ever sit in class again?

Despite her apparent complacency, Sarai's mother was more unwell than she had ever been. Nothing seemed to relieve her cough. Not the bitter juice from boiled gum-tree leaves that had given her husband temporary relief. Not the lemon tea and the Vicks chest rub. She needed proper medication, but there was none. It was three months since the last bottle of cough mixture ran out.

Although deeply tired, Sarai knew she could not sleep before her mother nodded off. Her place was right there, next to the older woman, who now lay huddled on a reed mat spread out on the floor. Only Mainini Grace could have shared this place with her. Her heart ached with love, and with profound loneliness.

Sarai mopped her mother's brow with a slow, gentle movement. Beads of sweat reappeared, no sooner had they been soaked up by the cloth. The older woman's forehead continued to glisten in the dim light.

Sarai sat in silence, overcome by a yearning for happier times. Reality swooped back swiftly to fill the temporary emptiness of her mind.

Her eyes strayed to the soot marks staining the wall. She must scrub it first thing in the morning, or risk the landlady's wrath. Mai Simba's rages were guaranteed to instil fear into any living soul, and eviction was a real threat.

Sarai had been warned several times about the hazards of fire in the shack, so now took care to make a great show of cooking outside, before sneaking the fire indoors for her mother at night.

Just yesterday, the care nurse had looked at the soot marks with displeasure. "You had a fire in here? How do you expect her cough to get better?"

Sarai had been contrite, but had wondered, *What else can I do?* Her disobedience came of necessity. July was cold and starting to get windy. Her mother's body was hot, but she often complained that the cold gnawed relentlessly into her bones. It was winter, after all.

Why aren't you here with us, Mainini Grace? Sarai stared blindly at the dying fire that mirrored the demise of hope.

The room was dimmer, now that the fire was almost out. Cold air was starting to creep in. She shivered. Just as they had used up the last of the firewood, they were also using the last precious candle whose lone flame looked as feeble as its source.

If Mainini Grace had come, maybe she would have brought a few candles from Botswana. Sarai's thoughts wandered again to her elusive aunt. Her mother's eyes seemed to be summoning her, pleading for something that was not hers to give.

Sarai strained her ears, at once reluctant and fearful of what she would hear. Instinctively, she knew the words before they were spoken.

"Be strong, mwanangu. It will happen soon. I know it." Barely a whisper, "Be strong. Be strong."

The words seemed to hang suspended between them, and then fell like the fading notes of an echo. A repetition was whispered through bouts of coughing. Her mother's voice was muffled, but still her wish seeped into Sarai's awareness. The words seemed to reverberate like a haunting refrain

"Find Mainini Grace. She will put you back in school. Don't end up like me."

She willed her mother to stop and reached out to hold her hands. Mainini Grace should have been there with them as promised, but it was simply inane to wish for her now.

The feverish hands quivered in her grasp, now so wasted they could have been a child's. Sarai remembered holding her young brother's hands in the same manner and thinking that they were like the feet of a tiny bird. ·

Her young sister's small hands had had a similar feel. Little birds' feet. The two little birds had flown, one after the other. But her father's journey had been slower and more agonising, almost like her mother's.

Sarai steadied herself. Her voice was strong, but gentle when she spoke.

"Don't worry, Amai. Don't worry."

In preceding years, she had perfected the modulations of these same words. Don't worry, Mary. Don't worry, Tafara. Don't worry, Baba. And now it was, Don't worry, Amai. She was the untouched; destined to be the survivor, the comforter.

It was two days since they had discharged her mother from hospital. Only two days, but the bleak medical ward and its caustic smells were already a distant memory. There had been no medicines in the hospital pharmacy.

"You will have to look after her at home. Our outreach nurses will support you," the doctor had said sombrely.

The words had fallen empty and meaningless.

Yesterday's follow-up visit by the care nurse had been no compensation. The woman came empty-handed. Although she counselled Sarai and told her what to expect, denial had been so much easier to embrace.

Making no attempt to disguise tactlessness, or simply lacking the skills to do so, the nurse had explained that there would be no need to call an ambulance. The hospital no longer had anything to offer.

Nothing.

Nothing.

In the dead of night, Sarai knew that they only had each other.

The wind howled eerily.

The nurse forgot to tell me about the pain I would feel. She forgot about me… Sarai found herself weeping silent, clandestine tears. Almost immediately she was resolute once more. Her mother should not see the tears that shimmered in her eyes, that rolled effortlessly down her cheeks.

Her mother appeared not to notice.

Though much quieter now, the insistent whisper continued: "Do not end up like me. Find Mainini Grace."

Sarai caressed her mother's hands, keen to reassure her but no longer confident of her ability to do so.

She nodded. They had been through enough to make them courageous. Words that her mother would never hear formed a lump in Sarai's throat.

The older woman had closed her eyes, her breathing rapid and increasingly shallow. Her words kept ringing in Sarai's head, distressing but at the same time strangely comforting because she knew that her mother wanted the best for her. She allowed herself to hope once again that Mainini Grace would come. Mainini Grace had a way of taking charge and making things happen. Sarai knew that if anyone was capable of putting her back in school and giving her a bright future, that person was Mainini Grace.

As Sarai sat, she heard the distant hum of a car engine. The sound became louder as it approached the dwelling. Then there was a brief silence followed by the resonance of doors banging. A dog barked. She heard hushed voices, mingling with the thud of footsteps.

Sarai wondered if the landlord, Mai Simba's husband, was back from one of his cross-border trips. He often arrived late at night. She pictured his children rushing out of the main house, falling over each other in eagerness to welcome him home. Jealousy surfaced. They had a father who was alive.

A soft knock on the door interrupted her musing.

Who could be calling so late? She hoped it wasn't Mai Simba coming to spy for evidence that might suggest that they had broken yet another household rule. Reluctantly, she stood up and dragged her feet towards the door. She pulled the handle.

The bizarre vision she encountered was of her mother standing at the doorstep. The right side of her body was concealed in shadow; the left side was harshly illuminated by the glare of an electric bulb shining from Mai Simba's veranda.

Sarai stood frozen in shock as she took in the sunken eyes, the gaunt cheeks, the emaciated form dwarfed by an oversized coat. At her mother's feet were three suitcases. She shook her head, confused by this peculiarity. She remembered weird stories of how dying people sometimes said goodbye to their loved ones in the form of apparitions.

"Amai? How did you…?" Her voice trembled in query and died in her throat.

The woman held out her hands and stepped forward. "Please don't tell me she's gone…" The voice was fearful. It was not her mother's voice. It was familiar, but unexpected, coming from this spectre.

Sarai found herself shaking uncontrollably. In that moment, she understood everything. Reality and reason merged, eliminating the need to demand an explanation.

And then came the realisation of what must surely have been fate's calculated conspiracy against her. All her expectations collapsed in that instant. She felt as if something had exploded in her head.

"No-o!" Screaming, she launched herself forcefully on the woman. She grabbed the scrawny neck and squeezed. They fell backwards in a writhing heap on Mai Simba's cabbage patch.

The woman struggled and gasped. "Sarai…please…no…."

Sarai thought she heard her mother calling out, but she felt something stronger compelling her to focus on squeezing harder. The buzzing in her head grew louder, drowning out everything.

It was her anguished hysteria that severed the stillness of night summoning Mai Simba and the neighbours. She felt hands pulling her from all directions, trying to break her hold on the woman who now lay on top of crushed cabbages, apparently lifeless, her eyes glazed.

"Why you too? Why you too, Mainini Grace?" Sarai sobbed brokenly, as they led her away to Mai Simba's veranda.

Jennifer Teege

with Nikola Sellmair

A German writer, she worked in advertising for 16 years before becoming an author. For four years in her twenties she lived in Israel, where she became fluent in Hebrew. She graduated from Tel Aviv University with a degree in Middle Eastern and African studies. She lives in Germany with her husband and two sons. A New York Times and international bestseller, her memoir My Grandfather Would Have Shot Me: A Black Woman Discovers Her Family's Nazi Past *(2015) is her first book.*

From *My Grandfather Would Have Shot Me*

It is the look on the woman's face that seems familiar. I'm standing in the central library in Hamburg, and in my hands I'm holding a red book that I've just picked up from the shelf. The spine reads: *I Have to Love My Father, Don't I?* On the front cover is a small black-and-white photograph of a middle-aged woman. She looks deep in thought, and there is something strained and joyless about her. The corners of her mouth are turned down; she looks unhappy.

I glance quickly at the subtitle: "The Life Story of Monika Goeth, Daughter of the Concentration Camp Commandant from *Schindler's List*". Monika Goeth! I know that name; it's my mother's name. My mother, who put me in an orphanage when I was little and whom I haven't seen in many years.

I was also called Goeth once. I was born with that name, wrote "Jennifer Goeth" on my first schoolbooks. It was my name until after I was adopted, when I took on the surname of my adoptive parents. I was seven years old.

Why is my mother's name on this book? I am staring at the cover. In the background, behind the black-and-white photo of the woman, is a shadowy picture of a man with his mouth open and a rifle in his hands. That must be the concentration camp commandant.

I open the book and start leafing through its pages, slowly at first, then faster and faster. It contains not only text but lots of photos, too. The people in the pictures—haven't I seen them somewhere before? One is a tall, young woman with dark hair; she reminds me of my mother. Another is an older woman in a flowery summer dress, sitting in the English Garden in Munich. I don't have many pictures of my grandmother, but I know each of them very well. In one of them she is wearing the exact same dress as this woman. The caption under the photo says Ruth Irene Goeth. That was my grandmother's name.

Is this my family? Are these pictures of my mother and my grandmother? Surely not, that would be absurd: It can't be that there is a book about my family and I know nothing about it!

I quickly skim through the rest of the book. Right at the back, on the last page, I find a biography, and it begins like this: "Monika Goeth, born in Bad Toelz in 1945." I know these dates; they are on my adoption papers. And here they are, in black and white. It really is my mother. This book is about my family.

I snap the book shut. It is quiet. Somewhere in the reading room someone is coughing. I need to get out of here, quickly; I need to be alone with this book. Clutching it close to me like a precious treasure, I just barely manage to walk down the stairs and through the checkout. I don't take in the librarian's face as she hands the book back to me. I walk out onto the expansive square in front of the library. My knees buckle. I lie down on a bench and close my eyes. Traffic rushes past me.

My car is parked nearby, but I can't drive now. A couple of times I sit up and consider reading on, but I am dreading it. I want to read the book at home, in peace and quiet, cover to cover.

It is a warm, sunny August day, but my hands are as cold as ice. I call my husband. "You have to come and get me; I have found a book. About my mother and my family."

Why did my mother never tell me? Do I mean that little to her, still? Who is this Amon Goeth? What exactly did he do? Why do I know nothing about him? What was the story of *Schindler's List* again? And what about the people I've heard referred to as Schindler's Jews?

It has been a long time since I've seen the film. I remember that it came out in the middle of the 1990s, while I was studying in Israel. Everybody was talking about Steven Spielberg's Holocaust movie. I didn't watch it until later, on Israeli TV, alone in my room in my shared flat, in Rehov Engel—Engel Street—in Tel Aviv. I recall that I was touched by the film, but that I thought the end was a bit kitschy, too Hollywood.

Schindler's List was just a film to me; it didn't have anything to do with me personally.

Why has nobody told me the truth? Has everybody been lying to me for all these years?

Chika Unigwe

Born in Enugu State, Nigeria, she has degrees from the University of Nigeria and the KU Leuven, and holds a PhD from the University of Leiden in Holland. She is the author of four novels, including On Black Sisters' Street *(2011) and* Night Dancer *(2007). Her short stories have appeared in several literary journals. Her works have been translated into a number of languages, including German, Japanese, Hebrew, Italian, Hungarian, Spanish and Dutch. She was the 2016 Bonderman Assistant Professor of Literary Arts at Brown University, Providence, Rhode Island. She lives with her family in Atlanta, Georgia, and is an Adjunct Professor of Writing at Emory University.*

Nchekwube

Mmeri runs her hands over the pair of wings in her lap. She has known that this day would come but she has tried to live like it would not. She cannot, she tells herself, let Nchekwube go. The girl does not understand.

You're just a lonely, sad woman! Nchekwube tells her mother. All the other girls are getting their wings and you won't let me have this one thing? I am turning eighteen and you want to keep me at home? What am I, a prisoner? You never let me do anything fun! You hover around. All. The. Time. You suffocate me! She lists all the other things her mother would not let her do: go to a pajama party at Nwamaka's for her tenth birthday (she had to hear the next day in class how everybody had fun, swimming in Nwamaka's parents' outsized pool all night long and camped out in their backyard where they were served croissants and moimoi and akamu in customized plates in the morning for breakfast); go on a school trip to Osumenyi (her classmates had stayed away an entire weekend and visited the nation's only floating museum); go to school by herself once she turned twelve and everyone else walked to school alone (which made her a laughing stock at school for a long time). The list of wrongs is long and each remembrance is steeped in bitterness and flung angrily at her mother.

Mmeri, the mother, accepts the words thrown at her. She feels their sting. It is as though a hundred bees have colonized her body. She is not unaware of the irony: that she who would love more than anything else to slide her daughter's wings over her on her eighteenth birthday (in a few days! What trepidation!) was being held back by love (for fear is a kind of love too!)

There are things she wants to tell her daughter but she does not know how to begin. From the beginning? From Godwin who loved Nchekwube before she was born but could not stand her afterwards? She has never met her father, does not even know his name. Yet Godwin had wanted to be a father more than Mmeri had wanted to be a mother. When she became pregnant, she felt guilty for not matching her husband in enthusiasm, and worked into that enthusiasm by throwing herself into preparing for the birth: painting the nursery, buying baby supplies, tussling over names with Godwin. After a while, that enthusiasm didn't need to be worked on anymore. She had willed it into being. When Mmeri went into labor, Godwin, on his way back from a trip abroad, was devastated to be missing the delivery. I'll come straight from the airport, Sweetie, he said. I'll rent a hovercar. Don't want to get delayed by traffic just to save a few bucks. Can't wait to see you!

When Nchekwube was born, she had slithered out so swiftly and smoothly that the doctor said had he not been quick she would have fallen straight onto the cold hospital floor. In all his decades of catching babies, he said, none had come out quite as rapidly as Mmeri's albino baby did. And had the baby fallen straight onto the tiles of the hospital room, it might have been an incidental act of mercy. *It would have freed you from making the choice*, he said to Mmeri, his voice soft like cotton, and in his eyes, something like compassion. The doctor placed the wriggly, slippery baby on Mmeri's chest. It was as if someone had stolen into her womb and rubbed lubricant all over the baby. Mmeri had to hold on to it with both hands so that it did not slide off her body.

What are you going to do? The doctor asked Mmeri, unfolding his words carefully, softly, while sprinkling talcum over the baby to provide traction, so that Mmeri knew that he was on her side. That he would not force her but that he trusted her nevertheless to do the right thing. And the right thing to do would be the merciful thing. She looked down at her baby, and even through the white powder covering every inch of it, making it look like some small-scale simulacrum of a fearsome *mmanwu* from a long-gone era, that yellow brightness of her sort was unmistakable. Babies like these were not allowed to live. And if they did, no matter how much you protected them, no matter how much you tailed them, one day they invariably strayed and ended as chopped-up body parts for a moneymaking ritual. How could any mother, the state governor said, when he first announced his plans for albino babies, want to put a child through that? Mmeri remembered her parents nodding their heads as the governor spoke. If she closed her eyes now, she could still see her father (dead in a canoeing accident thirteen years ago) nodding, dipping his hand into his eba and soup, and her mother saying, *No woman ever wants to carry a pregnancy and lose the baby. Mbanu! But this—what the governor is suggesting is kinder than the alternative.*

Mmeri held on to her baby and wondered what sound a baby's skull made as it shattered. If it made any sound at all. Perhaps it was as silent as the splintering of a heart. She told herself that letting the baby live would be selfish. Who had ever held on to an albino child for longer than twelve years? No one in recent memory. The doctor said what mothers in her position chose to do—if they did not want to use the smothering blanket—was to let the baby starve. They cleaned up and walked out of hospital so they did not have to see the babies die. Which was a gentle way to let go. They could carry on as if nothing ever happened. There were others who held on for a few days and then handed the babies over to the hospital to be smothered in the special blankets the government provided free of charge. Some mothers wanted keepsakes, footprints and pictures, but that just made things difficult, he thought. Easier to let go once and for all. Mmeri had a baby guinea pig as a child. One day while she was feeding the guinea pig, a carrot fell out of her hands and hit it smack on its head, killing it. She remembered crying for days. She could never imagine letting that guinea pig starve to death. A tear slid out of her eye, carving a line down to her chin. It dropped on her baby and she could swear the baby smiled at her. Toothless pink gums showing through red lips, as if they were the embers of a dying fire. Mmeri held on tighter. She could not imagine letting go. She might have held on too tight because the baby began to cry softly and then caterwauled, its mouth so wide open Mmeri swore she could see into its soul. The doctor stood beside her saying nothing. *I can't let go*, she snivelled. *I haven't even given her a name yet.* She missed her mother, practical and sensible, who would have given her the strength to do what she must do. But her mother had died parachuting from an airplane seven years ago.

When Mmeri was a child, hardly a day went by without a news report of an albino abducted and killed for juju. In cities and villages all over the state, albino bodies with missing limbs turned up in ubiquitous police raids. Sometimes only the heads were found. Even her next-door neighbor, Mercy, an albino girl Mmeri's age, whose eyes darted when she spoke but who squinted her way through excellent grades in elementary school, was carted off by two men on her way back from school. Mercy's brother, one year older at ten, ran behind the men, and when he could not catch up, ran shouting all the way home. *They've taken Mercy! They've taken Mercy!* By the time her parents contacted the police, the men had long vanished into the city's mist. Everyone knew that many of the state's wealthy wanting to get wealthier paid a lot for albino body parts. Even though the punishment for kidnapping was twenty years with hard labor, the rewards were tempting. As more albinos disappeared, the state sprouted new millionaires and flashy mansions sprang up like acne.

Mmeri's mother once told her that in her youth, the state had been a tourist paradise: the people came from far and near to admire one of its two waterfalls or to walk through the green parks of the city. Their city's zoo had been the best in the world—thousands of animals from across the globe and 150 acres of exhibits and gardens. It was now a sprawling estate with a huge shopping mall, the green parks destroyed to make way for casinos. In those days, her mother said, albino children were neither abducted nor killed. They were just like any other children. In fact, one of the state's best-known comedians and most successful womanizer was an albino called Cowboy Joe. A journalist asked him how many children he had and Cowboy Joe tilted his hat, gave a large grin, and said, *I'd be lying if I said I knew!*

Between the mother's youth and Mmeri's own, some juju priest had had a revelation that pulverized albino bones and secret incantations *magicked* money out of thin air. At first only two albinos went missing, one of whom was a homeless man so nobody cared. The second was a young woman who never returned home from shopping. It was thought that she had run away because her relationship with her parents was rocky. Her parents put up huge posters promising her they loved her. She never returned. It was not until two little girls went missing within days of each other, and the head of one (still with its newly beaded braids intact) was found in an abandoned warehouse, that people began to take notice. Mothers of albino children pulled them from school, and even then, all it took was one second of unwatchfulness for the children to be spirited off. Body parts turned up all over the state like pawns in a macabre treasure hunt.

After many unsuccessful attempts to curb the scourge, the state governor met with his advisers and landed on the genius idea that he announced on TV on that rainy Sunday afternoon when everyone was sure to be home. *Fellow citizens*, he began in the firm, rich voice that won him the elections years ago. *We can no longer bury our heads in the sand about the goings-on in our state. Tourism has been greatly impacted. Investments have fallen. Revenue allocations have been cut. Our state relies on all three. We have a solution to our problem and I hope that you all, fellow citizens, will see the value in it...* Killing albino babies at birth was the only way to stop the rampant abductions and clean up the image of the state. Mothers, especially, had resisted at first. How could they give the state permission to kill their young? Even animals protected their young, some woman protested on Facebook. But soon the protests died down. There was nothing, Mmeri's mother used to say, that one could not get used to. Women who had albino babies learned to leave the hospital with empty arms. In families with a history of albinism, many expectant mothers did not start painting rooms or setting up cots until the baby was out and was not melanin deficient. It was easier to deal with if one did not have to return to a room all set up for a child who would never use it. With no albino children to kidnap and kill, the state began to forget that it had ever had such a problem. Trade boomed once more and everyone said what a wise man the governor was and he could stay in power for life.

Mmeri has succeeded in keeping Nchekwube alive by keeping her close. How to let go? "Everything I have done, I have done for you," she tells her daughter. She sounds like a cliché, she knows, but she cannot bring herself to burden Nchekwube with the anxieties that have plagued her for years. What sort of life would her young daughter live if she carried the fear of attack every time she left home?

The first time Godwin laid eyes on his new baby, he flung the flowers in his hand away and let out a loud, long moan.

He held his wife and said, *I am so sorry*, as if the albinism were some mischief he had deliberately conjured up. He would not hold the baby when Mmeri held it out to him. *Let's go*, he said, his voice heavy with tears. *The doctor is waiting*.

Mmeri shook her head. And then with a tremendous effort, she said, *Godwin, the baby's coming with us*. She had not known until she said it aloud that that was what she had been thinking. But now it was out, her spoken wish solidified and she knew she would not be leaving hospital without this baby she already loved.

What... How? Godwin stammered.

We can keep her safe, Godwin. Maybe even send her abroad. We...

Mmeri. Sweetheart. Please. Give the baby to the doctor.

Godwin's voice was broken but firm and it was then that Mmeri knew that he would not support her. She had to choose: her beautiful new baby or her husband. The infant began to cry and Mmeri thrust a nipple in its mouth. She could not give it up.

Godwin stood undecided, and then his shoulders slumped and he walked out crying.

Mmeri wanted to call out to him, but the baby looked at her as if it already feared for its future. Nchekwube, Mmeri whispered into its ears. Hope. Hope destroys fear, she read somewhere.

How can I protect her once she gets her wings, free to go and come as she pleases? Mmeri thinks. A line from a poem suddenly flits into her head. *Hoping in the face of mountains, is a form of love too*. She begins to dust the wings.

Ayeta Anne Wangusa

A Ugandan writer and creative thought leader, she is the author of a novel, Memoirs
of a Mother *(1998), and short stories published by FEMRITE—the Uganda Women
Writers' Association. She is also a founder member of FEMRITE. She is currently
the Executive Director of Culture and Development East Africa (CDEA), a creative
think tank in Tanzania which hosts a Pan-African Writers Lounge with a focus on
providing a platform for visiting writers to attend writing workshops and hold
public conversations and readings in Dar es Salaam. She has participated in many
international literary festivals and served as a judge on literary panels.*

My Mouth Carries Few Words

The First Dream

The scars on my body are baskets that carry the memory of the past. Keeping tales
that have, over the years, sluggishly escaped through the gaping holes. Holes created
by sunrays digging into the walls of the baskets. The story of my past is hidden in the
blank spaces between the reeds. Sieved by His story and kept in the blank spaces that
give the baskets an oblong shape. These scars were born when the reeds and blank
spaces embraced one another to create baskets. Baskets that carry the tales of the
Bamasaaba.

When I slide my long fingers over these scars, I feel the stretched patches of skin,
firmly pinning my spirit inside my body. Patches of skin that were grafted from my
backside.

My navel is the deepest scar on my body. It is a tunnel that traces my mother
and her mother's MOTHER back to the crater on Mount Masaaba. A tunnel which
connects my father and his father's FATHER to the depth of the earth; the one who
crawled out of a hole on the mountain with a woman by his side.

I am that woman who crawled out of Masaaba with Mundu by my side, at a point
in my mind when there were no words spoken. A time wrapped up in mist, stored on
a shelf in my mind, when the universe was a world with no words. Mundu and I came
out of a crack on one of the icy ridges of Masaaba.

Mundu was frozen to the toes, so we held each other close, our legs interlocking,
keeping away the cold that was rising up the veins in our legs. Our mouths had been
filled with silence. But breathing through our mouths, gasping—we broke the silence
with our breath. Our bodies rubbed against each other like two ancient rocks in
the quest for fire. He thawed the frost in my veins with the warmth of his body
and together we were ablaze. The sun melted the frost on Masaaba's mountain and
we bathed in Manafwa as she flowed from the crater; the source of our life. Our
defrosted bodies were tributaries joining Manafwa River. We held onto each other,
lying on one of the rocks as our entwined feet dripped into the river. And we talked

to each other with our eyes. We bathed in solitude by the riverside, after an invisible hand had moulded the sun, moon and stars.

I did not talk to Mundu or the birds that circled above us or the wild animals for they ignored us. Each day I cupped my hands below my chin and blew my breath into the calabash that my hands had built. I breathed in and absorbed the smell that had come from me that now squatted in the calabash. I did not like the smell that had come from my mouth, the one that spread its arms wide in the calabash. I did not like the taste of my saliva in the mornings. So, I rinsed out the stale taste of my silence from my mouth using the broken waters from Manafwa's birth canal.

I savoured the clean breath around my tongue, which the sugarcane I had chewed had left behind. I rolled my tongue over my two front teeth and cherished the smooth surface. The sugarcane had eroded the food that had slept in my mouth overnight. I was tired. I lay back to rest on the grass, as I waited for Mundu to come lie down and rest, after he had cleared the bush around our cave.

He lay down beside me.

I watched the big brown bulge that had created the first distance between Mundu and I. I lay on my side, looking into Mundu's eyes as we waited for the next sunrise. As the half and full moons rolled over our heads, we watched the bulge I carried push Mundu further away from me. The bulge felt like a pod with a pea inside, moving and occasionally bumping on the walls of the pod. I wondered what it was. I wondered, with my hand cupped over the deepest scar on my body.

That scar, which had healed from a rope that had connected me to the pit from which Mundu and I had crawled. We had crawled out and when we reached the cliff, I had picked up a sharp stone from the side of the cliff and cut the rope. Mundu had done the same with the rope that connected him to the deep Ogre he had come out of, with me by his side. The spiral rope had snapped back into the valley of life, and we had moved on, with our navels healing, drying under the sun.

The pea inside me became as heavy as a stone. It could no longer float in the pot of water I was carrying below my navel. It started sinking, moving towards my thighs. It began to press harder, anxious to germinate, wanting to fall out and start its new life on the soil upon which I was standing. The pea was a stone grinding the bones inside me. It began to push the bones apart, away from my body. Mundu could see the pain in my eyes. He could see the tears that had settled around my mouth. The thing inside me was pushing me wide. Tearing me apart. Mundu could not stand the anguish around my clenched toes. He stood up, started walking away from me. Facing me but walking away from me. It was time for the thing inside me to get out, so I tried to get up from the bank of Manafwa and walk. I could not. I crawled to the river. I could feel it. The thing inside me had a pointed knife. It was hacking a road out of the rock of my body—then sawing me like a carpenter dividing a piece of wood.

On my knees I crawled to the river. The river rushed towards me. It reached below my navel. I burned with pain. I needed to ease the sting by soaking my body in the small river that had grown out of our feet. The river that now fell into

Manafwa. The wind was sucking breath out of me. I lifted my head towards the noise of the rushing waters ahead of me and drank the fresh air that the big river breathed out. My weak eyes rested on a giant rock ahead of me. I limped towards it and lifted my arms to place my exhausted hands on the smooth rock that jutted out of the water. The thing inside forced me to breathe out and in… Breathe in and out…until the tunnel, that the thing inside me had been digging, was wide enough to create an exit.

A sound burst out of my mouth. It had the colour of pain. It was deeper than red. It was deeper than tears. It was the colour of joy. It was the first sound out of my mouth.

A sound sprouted from the thing that had come out of me. The Little-thing that I had washed in the river because it was painted with blood. The thing that came out of me was still attached to me. So I impatiently disconnected the thing that came from the dark cave inside me with my teeth. I struggled with the cord until it was weak enough to be snapped by a sharp stone. The thin rope coiled back through the tunnel, leaving a small piece on the Little-thing for me to knot. Then, something else slipped out of me. Something from which the rope had grown; jelly-like, shivering. It sank into the river leaving behind a thick liquid, fiery like the sun falling behind the hills.

The Little-thing resembled Mundu. It had a tongue that vibrated like the small river that had grown out of our feet. It made a strange sound. Mundu came from behind the rock. When he saw me holding the thing that looked like him in body, his eyes told me not to worry. His eyes told me we had to watch the Little-thing's mouth; learn what it had learnt from the dark cave inside me.

The Little-thing began to cry and we watched its mouth for a sign. The sun and moon passed over our heads—the sun appearing from behind the mountain, the moon slicing through the blue sky—but still we did not know how to stop the tears. We did not know how to stop the sound from its mouth. I dropped a few droplets of water from Manafwa into its mouth, to stop the hiccups. My heart was boiling. It was heaving up and down under my left breast. The steam began to melt my heart. And the heat melted the frozen tears in my breasts. My long breasts began to cry, when my nipples stumbled over the Little-thing's lips. The young lips pressed hard and squeezed tears into its mouth. The Little-thing's tongue began to absorb the sweet teardrops from my swollen long breasts. And we learnt that this was food for it. Mundu looked at my mouth. It was smiling. I decided to move my long swollen breasts off my chest towards the little mouth. One long breast in one hand to the little mouth. The other long breast in another hand to the little mouth. The little mouth pulled at my cubical nipples, making sucking sounds. Pulled me towards it. I pulled the Little-thing towards me, keeping it warm in my arms, as it fed on the white fluid from my breasts.

When the Little-thing was not pulling at my nipples with its lips, it was talking to itself. Cuuu, cuuuuuu! It listened to the birds singing and watched them dancing above us in the sky, as it lay down on the grass. I stood at a distance and gathered fruits from the bush. The Little-thing listened to the white, black and grey birds, weaving songs with their beaks. The Little-thing began to sing with the birds. It began to talk with the winged creatures. *Nywinywi, nywinywi…* I watched the Little-thing curiously. It repeated the sounds that came from the birds. It looked at the hen that was warming its little-things with its wide-kind-arms.

The little-things sang one song, while looking their mother in the eye. *Mayi, mayi…* The Little-thing looked at the cock that had jumped onto the bird with wide-kind-arms, the one that had dropped into her a few seeds, and caused her to lay ten eggs.

The bird with wide-kind-arms had sat on the eggs and cracked them with her weight. And out of the eggs, came chicks singing a *qwe qwe* song. An ode about the cold they had found in the world. *Kwaaah! Mayi imbewo, kwaaah! Mayi imbewo.* And the bird with wide-kind-arms wrapped the cold little-things under her wings. And the Little-thing that came out of me, cried *Mayi imbewo, Mayi imbewo.* I understood. I wrapped the Little-thing in my arms, and shut out the cold.

Mundu was drawn to the Little-thing that came out of me because it resembled him in body. He was amazed at how the thing that came out of me could look like him and not me. So he carried it on his shoulders when he went to Manafwa to fish. The Little-thing sat on the bank of the river and listened to the river gurgling as it cascaded over rapids. Mundu played with the big river. Played with the river to make his Little-thing giggle when it became restless. He picked up a smooth pebble and at an acute angle hit the water's surface and produced a slapping sound. *Pa.* He did it again, two times over the water's face, when he saw the Little-thing chuckle. *Papa!*

Papa! Papa! The Little-thing called Mundu each time it woke up and opened its eyes to a new sunrise. *Mayi,* it called me, from the moment it watched the birds sing to their mother.

Mundu watched the birds flying across the sky. From east to west, returning home with fruits hanging out of their mouths to drop into their little-things' mouths. My Little-thing opened its mouth. Opened it to get some of the food from the birds. The birds descended to his mouth and dropped their songs into it.

My Little-thing grew tall. It yearned to grow taller and reach the sky. We saw the signs from the way it raised its arms and flapped them like the birds in the sky. We watched the future of its dreams. It wanted to be a bird and fly to distant lands beyond Masaaba. But its arms were too heavy to lift it into the sky to float about like the birds, so it resorted to being like us. It decided to imitate the way Mundu and I walked on the earth. But it refused to mimic our silence. It raised its voice when it saw the birds descend to their nests. Sang the songs that the birds had dropped into its mouth. *Nywinywi, nywinywi. Khanywinywi…* and so the bird was named.

Khanywinywi flew past the window of Susannah's Chariot and then climbed high into the sun-set sky at that moment when Kamau tapped her arm.

"Wake up my princess. We have reached Busia."

"Hmm, you just stirred me out of a weird dream." She blinked and lifted herself lazily out of her seat.

The newly-wed couple, Susannah Seera and Jonathan Kamau joined the line at the immigration desk. When she presented her passport to the immigration officer, he smiled and asked, "You are the writer?"

Zukiswa Wanner

A South African writer and publisher, she has published four novels, two children's books, a satirical non-fiction and a literary travel memoir, Hardly Working *(2018). In 2011 she was shortlisted for the Commonwealth Best Book and the Herman Charles Bosman Awards for her novel* Men of the South. *In 2014, she was recognised by the Africa39 initiative as an African writer under 40 with the potential and talent to define trends in African literature. In 2015 she won the K. Sello Duiker Memorial Award for* London Cape Town Jo'burg. *She was a 2018 Johannesburg Institute of Advanced Study (JIAS) Fellow. Although mostly based in Nairobi, she may be found in "any African city near you without notice".*

This is not *Au Revoir*

When I think of you and me. Of us. I think of postcards throughout the year from an African city with extreme weather conditions. Maybe Johannesburg. Yes. Definitely Johannesburg. Warming up in August and getting hotter towards the end of the year.

August, end of. When we first met again after so many years. I was with someone, then. Unhappily so. As unhappy with him as I am with you now. Soon you were the third person in our relationship with My Someone then. Never a third wheel. More the third line in a triangle. Giving us solidity and stability. The one we asked when you were around—why didn't you come to our life sooner? Always welcome by both of us. Everything happens just when it is supposed to, you would give your stock answer. Now that I have been with you, I know you don't have much original thought. I wonder whether you Googled even that clichéd statement? Is it the line from a song or the words of a poem that I do not know?

We would both complain to you about the other. Did you learn then how best to hurt me? Or had you had it in you from our uni days?

You welcomed me into your home in December.

Shall I talk to him? you asked.

I shook my head. There was nothing more to be said. When we first met again at the end of August, something in me towards My Someone then had already died. Sometimes I think I stayed with him as long as I did because you liked him. And I, I wanted the approval of an old friend I had cherished, had lost touch with and was meeting again.

And when I shook my head, it seemed something changed between us that night. It seemed as though all the days since we met again at the end of August, no, since I had known you in undergrad at Wits, had been leading to this. The raging of our bodies matched the Highveld storm outside. I think we both came the same second as the lightning bolt that struck the tree in your garden. I know so. Because when we looked at each other in wonderment, we were both lost, believing the noise had come from our bodies. It was only later, much later, when your neighbour texted to ask whether you knew that your wall was down that we realized that though our bodies may have roared inside, the noise was from your lightning-struck tree falling on a wall. There had been no plan on either of our parts. But you became My Someone then. And my Now No One accused you of stealing me from him.

Sitting together in the heat of our first Valentine's Day, we laughed at him. But patriarchy is a mofo, you said. I nodded and added—that in this age he could believe a woman is stolen instead of just going? We laughed. And I shook my head at My Now No One thinking I had no will of my own. You kissed me as I sat in between your legs while I marvelled at your hands. Afterwards we both proclaimed, I don't believe in Valentine's Day. And yet when the day came around, although we made sure that we did not wear red, did not say Happy Valentine's Day, did not buy each other gifts, we would spend the day together.

It seemed, as April approached, and Johannesburg started teasing us with cold weather, your ardour for me cooled. Or maybe mine did too. You stayed out later. You were too tired to make love, or I was too tired.

Then in July that horrible winter storm happened. It brought snow with it. Inside I felt colder than could be imagined despite the overpriced feather duvet we had bought and the thermal walls. It started with the criticism as you lay next to me in bed or were you lying on my lap on the couch? Your hand crept to just below my waist, and as your thumb and forefinger pinched me, you asked whether I was putting on weight. In my head the words of Grace Mugabe rang even before she publicly said them and I wanted to shout them out but did not. I did not say, *stop it. Stop it forthwith*. Instead I said, maybe a little. Then you kissed my stomach as I tried to suck it in and said, it suits you my sdudla mafehlefehle. This said while you rubbed your own belly and smiled a smile that did not quite reach your eyes.

Rich in every way coming from you, really.

Painful too, since you know my history.

The black girl who had to take a year off in uni for bulimia.

Private school girls trying to be white, I overheard as I was wheeled to the ambulance.

But. Shrug.

You said my weight suits me. And I am no longer in uni. And I was convinced you were different from *That* No One.

But then in a day or two you stopped being impressed with my potential sdudlaness. You instead started telling me that I seriously needed to lose a little weight. This as you ate a pork chop and pap I had prepared. No spinach babe. It irritates my teeth, you would say. Besides, I had a salad at work. Pork chop and pap, for you. Cabbage soup, for me.

You printed a diet that I should follow and stuck it on the fridge that July.

Just to remind you, you winked.

Summer bodies.

There are old cassettes of Tae-bo and yes, a still functioning VCR you told me. Billy Blanks would give me my exercise. If Tae-bo was not my thing, there was free WiFi. I could find a routine on YouTube. Or download something on my smartphone. The problem with you Naledi, you said stroking my chin affectionately belying the mean words you were about to speak. You always make excuses for staying fat.

You said the F-word.

Ignoring that you were at least twenty kilos heavier than I was.

I excused myself. Went to the bathroom. Stripped, and looked at my naked self. I did not need to suck my stomach in to see my mound of Venus. And yet I did.

So I left you as August approached.

Less than a year before that August end of, when we first met.

It was then that we established a pattern. I would leave. You would ignore me for a few weeks. Then return. Because you started communicating. Promising to change. Begging. In poetry. Antonio Jacinto's "Letter from a Contract Worker" which you know is my eternal favourite. Last year it was Koleka Putuma writing about making love and orgasming in an office. Because you cannot write your own poetry. Okay, maybe that is a little unfair. You have never claimed to be a poet. Just a lover of it.

But as I sit here now thinking about it, I think there is something that smacks of serious insincerity on your part. Using other people's words to lure me back. You whose own words are a casual, I'm sorry. Sometimes followed by half-hearted, babe, you know I love you. Never as heartfelt as the poems you sent trying to lure me back. But I used to always melt. And always came back. For the last three years.

Remember when I came to you that December and told you that it had died with my Now No One? It has died with you too and you can join him as Now No One.

No.

I am not going to anyone else as I came to you.

I need to be with me.

To enjoy this me with a will that both of you seem to believe does not exist. So this is not *au revoir*. This, No One, is goodbye.

I know when you read my note you will laugh as you always do. It is, after all, not the first time I have left you.

You'll call one of your friends and say, this Naledi.

Short laugh, your face sneering.

Her name went to her head, this Naledi. She thinks she is the star.

Longer laugh.

Cough.

And your friend on the other side will likely ask what Naledi has done now.

And you will tell your friend, she says she has left.

Laugh. She left a note. Something about me being a diseased penishead.

She gets things mixed in her head my Nana sometimes, you will say.

Because a woman cannot be a diseased penishead.

Jesmyn Ward

Born in Mississippi, where she still lives, she is currently a Professor of Creative Writing at Tulane University. She received her MFA from the University of Michigan and has received the MacArthur Genius Grant, a Stegner Fellowship, a John and Renee Grisham Writers Residency, and the Strauss Living Prize. She is the winner of two National Book Awards for Fiction: in 2011 for Salvage the Bones *and in 2017 for* Sing, Unburied, Sing *(from which the following extract comes). She is also the author of the novel* Where the Line Bleeds *(2008) and the memoir* Men We Reaped *(2013), which was a finalist for the National Book Critics Circle Award and won the* Chicago Tribune *Heartland Prize and the Media for a Just Society Award.*

From *Sing, Unburied, Sing*

3:

Last night, after I hung up the phone with Michael, I called Gloria and got another shift. Gloria owns the country bar where I work up in the backwoods. It's a hole-in-the-wall, slapped together with cinder blocks and plywood, painted green. The first time I saw it, I was riding with Michael upcountry to a river; we'd park under an overpass on the road that crossed the river and then walk until we reached a good swimming spot. *What's that?* I asked, and pointed. I figured it wasn't a house, even though it sat low under the trees. There was too many cars parked in the sandy grass. *That's the Cold Drink*, Michael said, and he smelled like hard pears and his eyes were green as the outside. *Like Barq's and Coke?* I said. *Yep.* He said his mama went to school with the owner. I called his mama years later after Michael went to jail, thanked God when it was her that picked up the phone and not Big Joseph. He would have hung up in my face rather than speak to me, the nigger his son had babies with. I told Michael's mother I needed work, and asked if she could put in a good word with the owner. It was the fourth conversation we'd ever had. We spoke first when Michael and I started dating, second time when Jojo was born, and third when Michaela was born. But still she said yes, and then she told me I should go up there, up to the Kill, upcountry, where Michael and his parents are from, where the bar is, and I should introduce myself to Gloria, so I did. Gloria hired me for a probationary period of three months. *You're a hard worker*, she said, laughing, when she told me she was keeping me on. She wore heavy eyeliner, and when she laughed, the skin at the sides of her eyes looked like an elaborate fan. *Even harder than Misty*, she said, *and she damn near lives here.* And then waved me back out front to the bar. I grabbed my tray of drinks, and three months turned into three years. After my second day at the Cold Drink, I knew why Misty worked so hard: she was high every night. Lortab, Oxycontin, coke, Ecstasy, meth.

Before I showed up for work at the Cold Drink last night, Misty must have had a good double, because after we mopped and cleaned and shut everything down, we went to her pink MEMA cottage she's had since Hurricane Katrina, and she pulled out an eight ball.

"So he's coming home?" Misty asked.

Misty was opening all the windows. She knows I like to hear outside when I get high. I know she doesn't like to get high alone, which is why she invited me over, and why she opens the windows even though the wet spring night seeps into the house like a fog.

"Yep."

"You must be happy."

The last window snapped up and locked into place, and I stared out of it as Misty sat at the table and began cutting and dividing. I shrugged. I'd felt so happy when I got the phone call, when I heard Michael's voice saying words I'd imagined him saying for months, for years, so happy that my insides felt like a full ditch ridden with a thousand tadpoles. But then when I left, Jojo looked up from where he sat with Pop in the living room watching some hunting show, and for a flash, the cast of his face, the way his features folded, looked like Michael after one of our worst fights. Disappointed. Grave at my leaving. And I couldn't shake it. His expression kept coming back to me through my shift, made me pull Bud Light instead of Budweiser, Michelob instead of Coors. And then Jojo's face stuck with me because I could tell he secretly thought I was going to surprise him with a gift, something else besides that hasty cake, some *thing* that wouldn't be gone in three days: a basketball, a book, a pair of high-top Nikes to add to his single pair of shoes.

I bent to the table. Sniffed. A clean burning shot through my bones, and then I forgot. The shoes I didn't buy, the melted cake, the phone call. The toddler sleeping in my bed at home while my son slept on the floor, just in case I'd come home and make him get on the floor when I stumbled in. Fuck it.

"Ecstatic." I said it slow. Sounded the syllables out. And that's when Given came back.

The kids at school teased Given about his name. One day he got into a fight about it on the bus, tumbling over the seats with a husky redhead boy who wore camo. Frustrated and swollen-lipped, he came home and asked Mama: *Why y'all give me this name? Given? It don't make no sense.* And Mama squatted down and rubbed his ears, and said: *Given because it rhymes with your papa's name: River. And Given because I was forty when I had you. Your papa was fifty. We thought we couldn't have no kids, but then you was Given to us.* He was three years older than me, and when him and Camo boy went flipping and swinging over the seat, I swung my book bag at Camo and hit him in the back of the head.

Last night, he smiled at me, this Given-not-Given, this Given that's been dead fifteen years now, this Given that came to me every time I snorted a line, every time I popped a pill. He sat in one of the two empty chairs at the table with us, and leaned forward and rested his elbows on the table. He was watching me, like always. He had Mama's face.

"That much, huh?" Misty sucked snot up her nose.

"Yep."

Given rubbed the dome of his shaved head, and I saw other differences between the living and this chemical figment. Given-not-Given didn't breathe right. He never breathed at all. He wore a black shirt, and it was a still, mosquito-ridden pool.

"What if Michael's different?" Misty said.

"He won't be," I said.

Misty threw a wadded-up paper towel she'd been using to clean the table.

"What you looking at?" she said.

"Nothing."

"Bullshit."

"Don't nobody sit and stare for that long on something this clean without looking at something." Misty waved her hand at the coke and winked at me. She'd tattooed her boyfriend's initials on her ring finger, and for a second it looked like letters and then bugs and then letters again. Her boyfriend was Black, and this loving across color lines was one of the reasons we became friends so quickly. She often told me that as far as she was concerned, they were already married. Said she needed him because her mother didn't give a shit about her. Misty told me once that she got her period in fifth grade, when she was ten years old, and because she didn't realize what was happening to her, her body betraying her, she walked around half the day with a bloody spot spreading like an oil stain on the back of her pants. Her mother beat her in the parking lot of the school, she was so embarrassed. The principal called the cops. *Just one of the many ways I disappointed her,* Misty said.

"I was feeling it," I said.

"You know how I know you lie?"

"How?"

"You get dead still. People is always moving, all the time, when they speak, when they're quiet, even when they sleep. Looking off, looking at you, smiling, frowning, all of that. When you lie, you get dead still: blank face, arms limp. Like a fucking corpse. I ain't never seen nothing like it."

I shrugged. Given-not-Given shrugs. *She ain't lying*, he mouths.

"You ever see things?" I say. It's out my mouth before I have a chance to think it. But at that moment, she's my best friend. She's my only friend.

"What you mean?"

"When you on?" I waved my hand like she'd waved hers moments before. At the coke, which was now just a little sorry pile of dust on the table. Enough for two or three lines more.

"That's what it is? You seeing shit?"

"Just lines. Like neon lights or something. In the air."

"Nice try. You tried to twitch your hands and everything. Now, what you really seeing?"

I wanted to punch her in her face.

"I told you."

"Yeah, you lied again."

But I knew this was her cottage, and when it all came down to it, I'm Black and she's White, and if someone heard us tussling and decided to call the cops, I'd be the one going to jail. Not her. Best friend and all.

"Given," I said. More like a whisper than anything, and Given leaned forward to hear me. Slid his hand across the table, his big-knuckled, slim-boned hand, toward mine. Like he wanted to support me. Like he could be flesh and blood. Like he could grab my hand and lead me out of there. Like we could go home.

Misty looked like she ate something sour. She leaned forward and sniffed another line.

"I ain't a expert or nothing, but I'm pretty sure you ain't supposed to be seeing nothing on this shit."

She leaned back in her chair, grabbed her hair in a great sheaf, and tossed it over her back. *Bishop loves it*, she'd said of her boyfriend once. *Can't keep his hands out of it.* It was one of the things she did that she was never conscious of, playing with her hair, always unaware of the ease of it. The way it caught all the light. The self-satisfied beauty of it. I hated her hair.

"Acid, yeah," she continued. "Maybe even meth. But this? No."

Given-not-Given frowned, mimicked her girly hair flip, and mouthed: *What the fuck does she know?* His left hand was still on the table. I could not reach out to it, even though everything in me wanted to do so, to feel his skin, his flesh, his dry, hard hands. When we were coming up, I couldn't count how many times he fought for us on the bus, in school, in the neighborhood when kids taunted me about how Pop looked like a scarecrow, how Mama was a witch. How I looked just like Pop: like a burnt stick, raggedly clothed. My stomach turned like an animal in its burrow, again and again, seeking comfort and warmth before sleep. I lit a cigarette.

"No shit," I said.

Tiphanie Yanique

A Caribbean-American writer from St Thomas, US Virgin Islands, she lives in New Rochelle, NY. She won the inaugural Bocas Prize for Caribbean Literature in the Fiction category with her debut book How to Escape from a Leper Colony: A Novella and Stories *(2010), and was one of the National Book Foundation's "5Under35".* Land of Love and Drowning *(2014) won her the Flaherty-Dunnan First Novel Award, the Phillis Wheatley Award for Pan-African Literature, and the American Academy of Arts and Letters Rosenthal Family Foundation Award. Her first poetry collection,* Wife, *won the 2016 Forward/Felix Dennis Prize. Her other accolades include the* Boston Review *Prize, a Rona Jaffe Foundation Writers Award, a Pushcart Prize, a Fulbright Scholarship and an Academy of American Poet's Prize. She has been published in the* New York Times, Best African American Fiction, *the* Wall Street Journal *and* American Short Fiction. *She is an Associate Professor in the English Department and Director of the Creative Writing Program at Wesleyan University.*

Monster in the Middle

Listen, daughter. There is no way to know anything for sure. And thank God for that.

Thank God for that New Year's Day, 1968. That day the monster was on my back. The monster has always been coming for me. I'm a warm-blooded person. Because of where my blood comes from. Island blood. Thank God for that blood and for that island. But I had never been so cold. The monster was in the air, trying to nyam me, eat me. But there I was. The kind of boy who would come to wear sweaters in the summers of South Carolina. Let my mother kiss my forehead that morning, then climbed aboard a plane. Nothing with me but one change of light clothes, suitable for the West Indies, a toothbrush and a razor…the last because my mother had heard there would be no one there who knew how to cut my black-boy hair. She hadn't thought about my needing a winter coat.

And thank God for that long plane ride where I was too excited to be scared and so watched the sky. And for that long sleepless bus ride where my sudden fear kept me from rest. Thank God for this St Thomas boy in a bus, me, not sleeping, but looking out of the window as it became winter before my eyes. Cold monster.

Did I clarify that it was New Year's Day? That the kiss was my mother's last? She was dying of cancer. Breast, though no one but me and a doctor from Puerto Rico knew. Sickness of any part of the body we call private—the parts we use to love, to make life—was a shameful thing. So I boarded that plane, climbed aboard that bus, feeling that I'd likely never see my mother again. But still, thank God for her kiss that let me know it was indeed goodbye.

I could tell you more about my mother. For even she is the monster—and her mother, too. I want to explain how this goes. It's a journey, but you're not alone, my love. None of us is. But also you take the journey because you don't want the loneliness. Maybe people go off to war because they want to be left alone. But alone and lonely? I didn't want either, baby. Don't be confused by all these lives. See, these lives are yours. Have I made it clear that I am thankful? Thank God for my memories and thank God for the memories that made me.

We can't out-run the monster. And did they make us run that first night! The winter air like pins in my nostrils. I had a bloody nose before a mile. But kept running. Because the drill sergeant was shouting and because everyone else was running. No matter that I was in short pants in air colder than I'd ever known. Thank God for the ash on my knees that looked like a disease, for the blood in my nose that guzzled out and coated my mouth and neck and shirt and scared the sergeants just enough.

That night I shivered. So loudly that a bunk mate threw his blanket on me. Generous monster. Thank God. I slept. But it started again. Every morning the blasted running. Every night the cold. And the sweating in the cold, freezing me. And the letter in the mail before basic was even out, telling me my mother was dead.

What is at the middle of it all? Doesn't matter. You'll still have to do the thing to know it. So what's there, at the middle? Myth and magic, both. We all know it takes a village to raise a child. But I can tell you honestly that it takes an ancestry to make a man or a woman. I would never have made it to my middle if it wasn't for my mother dying and my daddy being already dead.

My father had been fighting a war his whole life. A white man, he was. From the continent. A proper American. But not white-white. "Cajun," he insisted. Had fought in a war or two. Seen nothing but combat. Finally, too shocked in the mind and broken in the body, found himself stationed in the Virgin Islands. St Thomas. But it wasn't sunny for him. Lived on our island like he was done dead. Away without leave in no time. Made a half-breed baby who looked nothing like him—me. Then sat on the bench outside a rum shop praying aloud to die, until he did. But even that I'm thankful for. Thank you, old monster, thank you, dear suicidal Poppy. I went to the American war to out-war him. But then my mother died and it was so cold and well…

That wasn't my true middle. No. This right here is the middle. Oh, and I'm thankful. Because though everyone was heading to die in Saigon—I was not. It wasn't that I had connections. No Rockefeller father to save my backside. My own no-choice

choice. The base, cold as an ice chest. My lips frozen and my teeth knocking. No one could understand anything I said. I hadn't learned to talk yankee yet. So I didn't have to say a thing. All I had to do was fake sick.

I'd been living close to sickness for over a year. My mother told me she'd never breast-fed me. Baby formula just arriving on the island when I was born. Everyone thought the powder was better, best. So Mom scraped to provide it for new-born me. Even as a baby I'd never seen my mother as God created her. But as a grown man I had to face her breast. Care for it that long hot summer of love. The nipple sinking in. The huge red blister. I was there. Taking care of sickness. I knew it well. Thank you, God.

Black-boy bile, the officers called it. In America, I was the black boy, despite my half-blood history. Coughing up spit. All fake, but it fooled them. Remember, I'd bled so bad those first days. It wasn't that I was a coward. It was just that I realized I didn't want to war with the history of my old man, didn't want to hold up my life to his and see if mine was more worthy. I never really knew the man. He didn't live long enough. He was my first monster, maybe. And I knew he would follow me. But with a dead mom…well. I decided I wasn't going to 'Nam. I wasn't going to be the drink-till-I'm-dead poppy. But still. His story is mine because I lived against him. That made his life as much an influence as if I'd lived beside him. I didn't get that then. But now I just thank God.

America believed me, even though they couldn't always catch what I was saying. I'd been a good talker back home. Talked to the doctor. To my aunt about what to do with my mother's things—in the event. The Army officers believed I was too sickly to shoot a gun good. Me? My whole life I'd sprained my thumb once. Sick wasn't my thing. Until faking it so well made it real. Now that's how you know me. That poorly, hypochondriac papa.

Well, the war for me was no walking among tropical trees that might make me long for home. No blinding light before the rat-a-tat of a screaming enemy. No warm sweat in my face and pits. My war stayed cold and quiet.

I was put to ironing the uniforms of those who came back dead. I ironed alone and in air-conditioning. Had to keep the clothes crisp, ready for funerals. Easy work on the body. Hard on the mind. Because it was Vietnam times. And so you know about the many shirts I had to iron. And so you know about the many monsters that lived with me. I never fought in that war. I ironed. And still, thank God for every collar. For every sizzle of the metal when it kissed the starch. Thank God for the dead that came home for me to dress them.

Because what's going on with you is my fault. And my parents' fault. And Vietnam's fault. You are not your own fault alone. No one is.

You need to know that this monster is always coming for you. The undershirts hot from the drier? Yes. They came for me. And I was thankful for the heat in that cold-cold room. That was my whole war story. No jungle of grenades, just a landscape of stiff shirts, pants with creases that could cut you. Being sickly since is the small price

I pay. And I am thankful for my wife and my boys and for you, the daughter I chose, who cared for me best. I do thank God. I'm only sick now because I wasn't dead before. And there were so many ways to die in America that 1968.

So now it's cancer, the doctors say. Like my mother. Mine in the private prostate. The story of the monster on my back, the monster on your back, is not just of fathers and daughters but also mothers and sons, and mothers and daughters, and grandparents and aunties and first loves and second and third loves… It's all there. Meeting you in the middle, where you always are. This is how history works. And you and me and the whole of us aren't anything separate from history.

When the government released me there was the Serviceman's Readjustment Act, the GI Bill they call it now. Pushing an iron was the only skill I'd learned. Couldn't go back to our island of St Thomas; there was no home there anymore. So I wandered. Small jobs, medium jobs. King was killed. Then, Malcolm, too. By then I was American enough for that to matter. Took me years to get on a good path. But I didn't want to be lonely. So, eventually, I marched to Morehouse, where the black American boys went.

Yes, this is an American love story. Because on the first day of school orientation there was a speech for Morehouse men and Spellman women. The speaker said that thing I gather now the college presidents in America always say: "The person sitting next to you might be your future husband or wife."

I was at the end of the row. I was older than most and I'd been unsure about coming to the big meeting. I was a little ashamed at having been a solider at all. So, I snuck in late. On one side there was no one next to me. I stared at the empty space for a while. It had been so lonely ironing all those years. No buddies to grieve over because they was dead when they came to me.

But thank God for that New Year's Day. And for all the new days. I am thankful for every bit. Because there in the great hall I turned from the emptiness at my right. And there to my left? Your mother. Looking at me like she'd been on a long journey to get to that selfsame spot. And when she said "Good morning." I heard her accent. Imagine. A Virgin Islander. At her feet was a baby basket. What year was it? 1989, must have been. Because in the basket? You. Sleeping. Me? I didn't know yet how your mother could curse me like cursing could kill. How she could love like loving alone would make me live. How she could take a motherless man—me—and make a father and a husband. All I know was that I hadn't heard those St Thomas sounds in so long. Sounded like my own mother.

And then you made a noise. Like about to holler. And me and your mother both looked into the basket. Your eyes open. Looking at me like you already knew I'd be your daddy. Like you'd been waiting.

1980s

Ayòbámi Adébáyò

She has written for the New York Times, Wasafiri, Elle, *the* BBC, The Guardian, Grazia, Saraba Magazine *and others. She is the author of* Stay With Me *which was shortlisted for the Kwani? Manuscript Project, the Baileys Prize for Women's Fiction, the Wellcome Book Prize and the 9mobile Prize for Literature. It has also been longlisted for the International Dylan Thomas Prize and the International Dublin Literary Award. It was named a Notable Book of the Year by the* New York Times *and a Best Book of the Year by* The Guardian, *the* Wall Street Journal, The Economist *and others.*

From *Everything is Wonderful*

Tolani wonders if it's possible to drown in a tub, this bathtub. Just drown, sober, without the help of sleeping pills. Slashed wrists might help, but those would stain the white bathroom tiles. No, slashed wrists aren't for her. She has always kept a clean house, so clean that sometimes her husband, Yeni, jokes that he could eat out of their toilet bowl. Sleeping pills would be perfect, not that she's suicidal, she knows she isn't that sort of person, she just knows. On her last birthday, when the associate pastor who prayed called her "an ever-smiling ball of sunshine", murmurs of agreement had filled the church. No, she would never do something so drastic, it's just a thought. One that slinks into her mind more often with Yeni in Abuja and the children off to her parents' home in Akure for the holidays.

If she were to kill herself, God forbid, but if she ever wanted to, she would simply walk into the lagoon and never turn back, no ceiling fans or ropes, no cyanide or bullets in the head, just water. Once again, she sees it happen as she opens the jars of sea salt she's selected for tonight's bath. She sinks, then floats. Her body pretends she is swimming the way she once loved to, performing memory long after her soul is gone, bobbing on the surface, waiting to be found. For tonight, she has chosen lavender, vanilla and lemongrass sea salts. She sprinkles a handful of each into the bathtub then watches as the granules dissolve, colouring the water into a shade of blue that reminds her of swimming-pools.

The tub is her favourite place in the house. On Fridays, the only weekday she leaves the church office before nightfall, she spends hours in the water, mulling over her schedule for the weekend. She doesn't like any of the other fittings in this house. The wardrobes are too tiny and the shelves in the kitchen are way out of her reach. Not that she complains, not anymore, there is this wonderful bathroom with the perfect tub, enough reason to be thankful.

When Yeni preached about the importance of gratitude on Sunday, certain that the scriptures he was referring to were directed at her, she had kept her head down through most of the sermon. He thinks that because she gets moody around him sometimes, she doesn't appreciate their life together. He's wrong, of course. She knows how lucky, no, blessed, she is to be his wife. She is grateful for this house, which a church member gave them on their tenth wedding anniversary; it doesn't matter that the wardrobes are small. And now, whenever she climbs a stool to take spice jars off the rack before she begins cooking, Tolani prays: *I thank you, Lord, for the gift of this house. Bless the giver and reward him.*

She hums as she goes around the bathroom, lighting scented candles. Although she prefers to add essential oils, on the nights before Yeni comes back from a trip, she settles for candles alone because the fragrance from her oil burners could linger in their bedroom for hours after her bath and Yeni doesn't like that. Done with the candles, Tolani shrugs off her robe. She steps into the tub and takes a sharp breath, the water sloshes around just below her knees, stinging goose bumps into her flesh. Outside, her dog barks as a neighbour's generator sputters to life. She sits, leans back with her legs stretched out, careful to avoid the stopper's beaded chain. She's always loved the feel of water—how it pulls at her limbs and makes her feel she might sink, the way it ripples against her skin as she settles into it—she luxuriates in these sensations and the resulting tumescence that stops short of arousal. This is preparation, when her husband arrives tomorrow, she'll be ready.

She frowns at her toenails. She finally went to that overpriced spa Sandra is always raving about but she hates the colour their manicurist had convinced her would look "absolutely stunning". Yes, neons are in, but she doesn't like this shade of yellow and Yeni might think the colour makes her feet look like a hawker's or a maid's. Not that he would complain; he will insist that her feet look beautiful and she won't believe him. Instead she will believe Sandra, who said last week that Tolani's new hairstyle made her head look like a coconut. Since they met during their first year in secondary school, Sandra has never hesitated to voice her opinions about Tolani's choices.

She is startled by the knock. Her maid is the only other person in the house right now, but she isn't supposed to come into the master bedroom without permission. It can't be someone from church, Tolani steps out of the tub, nobody comes to their home for prayers when her husband is away. Maybe there's an emergency or it's someone who thinks Yeni is back in Lagos.

She stands on the bath mat. "Janet?"

"Yes, madam."

"Do we have visitors?"

"No, madam, nobody come visit. Na me, I wan talk, madam."

"Is something wrong?"

"Please, madam."

She sighs. At least, she won't have to convince anyone her prayers are as good as Yeni's tonight. "Wait, I'm coming."

She bends to pick up her bathrobe but decides against it and reaches for a towel instead. When she opens the bathroom door, she finds Janet on her knees. The maid's head is bowed so her face is hidden and Tolani can only see her hair, thick and lustrous, twisted into a fat braid at the nape of her neck.

"Janet," she wants to see the girl's face. "Stand up."

"Make I stay like this, madam, please."

"Well, then, shift and let me pass."

The maid moves out of the doorway without getting off her knees.

Tolani brushes past her to sit on the bed. "Come on, get up."

Janet shakes her head.

"Well, then, what is it?"

"I wan go my village tomorrow, madam."

"This tomorrow?"

She nods.

"Why are you just telling me now? I've told you to let me know at least one week before you need to travel."

"I no wan come back here, madam."

"I've made it abundantly clear that I need to know at least one week ahead because…wait, what? You don't want to come back here? Why?"

Janet is the first maid who has stayed on for more than one year. Even Tolani was surprised when the girl came back from the village after her first December break. She knows she's hard to please; no other maid could take washing the four bathrooms from top to bottom with a toothbrush twice a week. Some of her previous maids disappeared without giving her notice but Janet has been here for three years, and now Tolani realises how much she needs her. It might take another five years to find someone who could iron a skirt without leaving sharp edges on the sides.

"Do you want more money? I can increase your salary."

"No, madam."

She leans forward and touches Janet's shoulder. "Look up, look at me. See, you're a good girl, I can double your salary."

Janet shakes her head. "No, madam. I wan go village."

"But why now? Why?" She has never beaten any of her maids. This girl has her own room, with a bed, air-conditioning and a wardrobe filled with almost new clothes. She always gives her a Christmas bonus and even lets her eat at the dining table when they have guests.

"Look at me, Janet, why do you want to leave?"

"Mama is sick."

Tolani retracts her hand, stifles the desire to slap Janet's face—*Help me, Lord, I am slow to anger and quick to listen, slow to anger and quick to listen.* Deception always makes her feel so belittled and angry. She knows that Janet's mother died years before the girl came to work here.

"Leave my room, you lying...out!" Tolani points at the door. "You can go tomorrow if you want, do what you like, you hear? Just don't expect me to pay you one kobo for this month, not when you're leaving like this. Get out of here."

The girl runs out of the room.

Tolani is shaking. She grips her knees, shuts her eyes and begins to mutter verses from First Corinthians Thirteen.

"Love is patient, love is kind, it does not envy, it does not boast, it is not proud, it does not dishonour others, it is not self-seeking, it is not easily angered, love keeps no records of wrongs..."

"Madam."

She opens her eyes and sees Janet standing by the door. She doesn't trust herself to speak to the girl yet. She knows that her anger, already bordering on rage, would take over her mouth and hurl words sharp enough to shred the girl, it's happened before. Enough times to drench her in shame even now.

"Na Oga."

"My husband?"

"Yes, madam." Janet frowns. "Na why be that."

"My husband," she takes a deep breath and counts to five. "You're leaving because of my husband?"

"Before Oga travel, before him travel this time," Janet shifts on her feet and looks like she is about to cry. "Before Oga travel, he touch my breast."

Tolani tries to count to five again but she can't remember what comes after one. "You're a liar."

"I dey kitchen that night, I dey wash plate before I go sleep. Oga just come from back, put hand for my body like this." Janet pushes a hand through the neckline of her blouse. "He just dey squeeze am, squeeze am. Na so I push Oga, he con fall."

"Shut up, keep your rotten mouth shut. You're a liar, a liar." Tolani stares at Janet's chest; the girl has small breasts, perky breasts, but mere B-cups. In the eleven years since she got married, Tolani has hired only maids with small breasts. When she first arrived, before they changed her name from whatever it had been and rechristened her Janet, this one wore padded bras that pushed her breasts comically close to her chin and made them look twice their size. Tolani had bought unpadded bras for the girl before confiscating all the undergarments she had brought with her from the village. Her own breasts started their inevitable descent after her first son suckled for a full year but Yeni has told her several times that bulk has always mattered to him more than perkiness. No, impossible; no. This liar's tiny breasts wouldn't even fill his palm.

Harriet Anena

A writer from Gulu District in Northern Uganda, her work has been nominated for the Commonwealth Short Story Prize (2018), the Wole Soyinka Prize for Literature (2018), the Short Story Day Africa Prize (2017) and the Ghana Poetry Prize (2013). Her stories, poems and articles have been published or are forthcoming in the Caine Prize anthology, Jalada Africa, *the Short Story Day Africa anthology* ID: New Short Fiction from Africa, Enkare Review, FEMRITE *anthologies,* Babishai Niwe Poetry Foundation *anthologies,* Sooo Many Stories, Adda, Storymoja Publishers, *Popula and the* Daily Monitor *newspaper, among others.*

The stories stranded in our throats

I told my sister Okot slipped his tongue into my mouth
when I was 13. He kneaded my breasts
a year after they sprouted.

My sister said, why are you telling me this
17 years later?

I told my sister, I want to learn how to forget
the alcohol-ed smell of his breath and
stop feeling thuds in my breasts
whenever I see someone kneading dough.

My sister said, I'm going out to throw up.

I told myself, how lucky! My own vomit gets stranded
in my throat whenever mother calls Okot, in-law from heaven.

I told my sister, throw up for two.

My depression…

…is me avoiding eye contact coz I haven't mastered the art of looking friends
in the eye and lying about the darkness I carry; adding speed to my steps to
hide the sluggishness
of my spirit; storming out of office coz everyone turns on the tap in my eyes.

…makes me blink back tears in the presence of friends and sob on a stranger's
boda boda ride home; wakes me at midnight and keeps me up till morning like
thoughts about an on-off lover; drives me to a counsellor who I immediately
dislike and I leave, cursing all hospitals.

…is me cancelling calls and ignoring text messages; deactivating my Facebook and typing DON'T CALL OR TEXT in the family WhatsApp; flinging the phone across the room and cuddling pillows made warm by tears.

…makes me mute the TV from six to six coz voices of strangers stoke the voices in my head, and yet the sight of faces behind the screen keeps the world here. It helps me close the door to everyone knocking and makes me look at my darkness in the eye, admiringly.

…is me detesting dance. Even poetry.

…makes me eat everything I shouldn't coz its only food I can manipulate. It makes me crave the anti-deps coz they understand my love for sleep. It makes me listen to *Run* on repeat and pray for the sky to fall together with the rain.

…is me shutting out voices that ask; *You have it all together, what do you mean things are falling apart? You don't look it, are you sure?* …is me switching off the phone 30 minutes to girls' night out coz the thought of a crowd suddenly has me gasping for breath.

…makes me grope for words that can explain why work—like my life—is undone.

…is me thinking about what I'll say when the storm clears coz *I was just feeling low* no longer sounds convincing, even to me.

When it visited this time, my depression said life after here is a garden of flowers that bloom poetry.

Step by step

Josh finds me bent over,
pressing the blue and red buttons
on the water dispenser.

His hand and my ass meet
before my water bottle gets full.
They don't meet in bits the way long lost friends do,
stopping with a start, looking each other up and down
to confirm their surprise and
dissolving into an earnest embrace.

In our case, there are no introductions.
Josh grabs my ass. He squeezes. He lets go.

Later, Eva says it's no big deal.
It's not like he raped you or anything.
Plus, that note he left behind must be an apology.

I don't tell her the boss only wrote,
For what's worth, you have a happy ass.

Ayesha Harruna Attah

A Ghanaian writer born in Accra, she attended Mount Holyoke College, Columbia University, and in 2011 received an MFA in Creative Writing from New York University. As a 2014 AIR Award laureate, she was a writer-in-residence at the Instituto Sacatar in Bahia, Brazil, and also won the Miles Morland Foundation Scholarship in 2016. She is the author of three novels: Harmattan Rain *(2009), nominated for the 2010 Commonwealth Writers' Prize;* Saturday's Shadows, *shortlisted for the 2013 Kwani? Manuscript Project; and* The Hundred Wells of Salaga *(2018). She currently lives in Senegal.*

Unborn Children

Cells are multiplying with abandon in her womb. Splitting and fusing into balls of flesh, massing together into tissue with no other aim but to exist. They are ballooning, just because.

"How big are they?" she asks.

"You won't be able to have children if we don't remove them."

The doctor's windowless office will swallow her whole with its aged tobacco odour, with his grey-haired presence, with its loud jazz. His eyes, magnified behind glasses, make her feel responsible for what's befallen her.

The first time she realizes she has a body that is different from her brother's, she is seven. She has binged on toffee and chocolate and a white paste is oozing from down there. Her grandmother scrubs her raw, then makes her sit in a tub of diluted gentian violet. This procedure is done away from her brother, the person with whom she has always done everything. It makes her dislike having a vagina, a thing to be sloughed clean.

The second time she suffers a reminder of her body's feminine lines, her parents are away at a funeral in Kumasi and she and her brother invite over friends. They are in their parents' bed, king-sized, watching *True Lies*. Stacked liked sardines. Three boys on one side, two girls on the other. Packed next to her is her brother's friend, a fixture in her brother's room, forever glued to his Gameboy. She has never considered him until his fingers unbutton her shorts, slip under the lace of her panties.

She is eighteen. Her sexuality has stayed dormant since the combined emotions of terror and titillation gripped her during *True Lies*. She is in university now. After a dorm activity on sexual health—cervical cancer is not choosy; check NOW for abnormal cells—she signs up for a pap smear. Her first. The door is tattooed with flyers. Symbols of Mars and Venus. She is interrogated: when was your last period; how long did it last; how old were you when you first menstruated; how many partners have you had? The answers: last week, five days, fourteen, zero. The doctor taps the speculum lightly against her thigh to take away the element of surprise, and yet the cold startles her, pocks her skin. She inhales deeply and waits for the entry, which begins as a dull rubbery prod, then a metallic, bitter intrusion. She can taste the discomfort in her mouth. Her whole body stretches taut. She is a cat poised to attack, claws out, back arched. The speculum goes nowhere, because she can't unclench herself.

"You might want to consider desensitizing yourself before you come next time," says the nurse.

A semester abroad in Barcelona. For the first time, she is *looked* at. Sometimes, like a piece of meat. This regard, good and bad, makes her feel less transparent than she does in America. It makes her bold, less lost in her skin, sexy. She turns twenty-one and with one week left, she drinks a lot of wine. All the water she splashes on her face doesn't sharpen the blurred image in the mirror. But she is focused. She ends up in her roommate's bed. It is shrouded with blankets of some vague tribal origin; she is sure they have never been aired, but for all six months of her stay she has thought him beautiful and gentle. She has watched girls make their exits from this room, hair mussed, T-shirts crinkled, white All Stars unlaced and intentionally worn. She has envied their carefreeness. But most of all, she has appreciated how he's never said anything negative about them. If anyone is to be given the task of liberating her, it should be him. The wine lets her mimic them. Until she's naked. She has never been naked with anyone. And now she is touching skin with this creature, the stuff of romance novels, this type women all over the world have been conditioned to find beautiful. And yet, even wine doesn't unblock the fear that takes her body hostage as his hardened flesh tries to break her. She screams. He holds her in his arms and falls asleep not long after she tells him she needs time to further desensitize herself.

Possible root causes of fear: Her mother. Her mother's religion. Heaven and hell. Being pumped with the idea that sex before marriage will take her straight to hell's gates.

A year later, she is back home in Ghana. Her mother has dragged her to an all-night service in a church the size of an airplane hangar. This church has seized her mother's commonsense. This is the first time *she's* been to church in over a year. The pastor's voice is hoarse and he flails about, spinning like a Damba dancer. She finds it difficult to believe he's sincere. Add to the mix the Mercedes sparkling outside the church, under its own special awning, and the young, yellow wife in blood red lipstick sitting in the front pew. He is preaching on fornication. Her mother is lifting her hands to the sky, shouting Amens, proud her daughter is still a virgin. She wonders why her mother has fallen for such a cliché, why her mother has become such a cliché. She wonders what conversations her mother will have with this pastor and with God when she loses her special pearl of virginity.

She turns twenty-seven, a reasonable time to shed the special pearl, because she really isn't sure what purpose it serves any more. A red stain of broken hymen on white cotton isn't going to be paraded before a jury of old ladies, after all. If anything, it is keeping her away from love.

On OkCupid, she meets Promise—a fellow African transplant, working in a rival pharmaceutical company (seems like destiny), apartment in Queens, a G-train ride away from her place. She swallows a shot of whiskey to unclench herself. Then another and another. The next day she's sore, deflowered. She doesn't remember if she cried or if she enjoyed it or if she bled. She wonders if she now bears a stamp that lets people know. Can people sniff these things? She can never go back to before. The thought is sobering.

Like when she was seven, all is not OK down there. She walks into a women's health clinic, not far from her one-bedroom apartment. The air reeks of antiseptic mixed with something foul like urine. This time, the speculum slides in. She feels its full presence, tries to squeeze it out, but it stays. This time, swabs are swiped. *If you don't hear back from us in a week or two, all's clear, she's told.*

The dreaded phone call: "We would like you to come back to the clinic."

She phones her best friend, choking on tears. She should have stayed whole, shouldn't have slept with Promise, even if it was just once. It's going to be a brush with death, she knows.

It is an infection that is cleared with antibiotics. Most women catch it at one point or another. Even virgins get it. Promise breaks up with her after three dates. Dates that have taken weeks to schedule. Dates that have ended in disappointment, because he had to work the next day and wouldn't come back to her apartment or invite her to his. She'd wanted the experience with no masks, no alcohol.

"Also, how do I say this without sounding like a douche? It's the virgin thing," he says, as if he hasn't already snatched it away from her.

She cries on the train home.

Her friends have been talking about a church they all go to, one with young people and preachers-who-get-it. She goes. She enjoys the music, the congregation is bright and shiny and youthful. Beautiful. She likes the message of being and doing good, and yet she doesn't believe in heaven and hell any more, a life beyond here and now doesn't scare her. She concludes she's one of those people who isn't wired to believe. On the day she decides once again to quit church, she meets a man from Panama on her way home.

He is like the dress one wears to give girlfriends red-eyed envy. He charms, he dances like he is boneless. When he drinks, the charm melts away like butter on a hot day. He had started going to church to face his demons, but they are too much for even Jesus. He does not last long, but leaves her with an infection—this time, the kind that virgins don't get. Thankfully, it is treatable.

She adopts a new rule. The next person she lets into her body will have met her family and will have done the customary knocking rites, the traditional engagement, and a tasteful white wedding. He won't get to touch her until the honeymoon.

She fails at chastity.

There is a one-night stand on Valentine's Day with a ghost of a man; there are others that last a few months and fizzle out. She gives up on counting.

Thoroughly desensitized, she goes for vagina screenings every year. She is careful, becomes an expert at beating infections, and begins to think what they say about immunity and children is true. To make them immune, they have to play in muck, swallow some germs.

But now the gynecologist has unwrapped a condom, placed it around his transducer and inserted it into her body, waved it around like a wand. With his stale cigarette smell and loud jazz, he has kneaded her belly and knotted his brow. He has told her she has fibroids. His music is way too loud. She had liked that he played jazz music when she had first visited his clinic. Now, she wishes he would be more considerate to his patients.

She's never been broody. She's never really thought about how many children she wants. She's never really thought about her womb. Her vagina has been her preoccupation. She calls her mother.

"Mine went away with menopause," says her mother. "Most of your aunts have had them."

One even had a hysterectomy. She never married and lives in the Bronx. Over palmnut soup and fufu, Auntie says, "It's the black woman's curse. Fibroids are our unborn children." Auntie licks the line of palm oil snaking down her wrist and continues. "A long time ago, we used to have children much earlier. The fibroids we get now are sending us a message that we're being unnatural. Do the operation and then get pregnant as soon as you can."

Her belly is sliced open, scraped clean and sewn up again. When she comes to, her mother is hovering over her, lips moving non-stop. She shouts, "Praise Jesus! Praise Jesus!" Her mother tells her they took out forty fibroids.

The orderly, when no one is around, asks if she wants to see them. She hesitates, then nods. He dashes out and returns with a metal pan full of meat. Some as tiny as beans. One as large as a mango. Forty. She can't imagine what she's done forty times to warrant forty growths in her womb. Forty unborn children.

Jay Bernard

A writer, film programmer and archivist from London, their work is multi-disciplinary, critical, queer and rooted in archives. Recent works—inspired by the 1981 New Cross house fire, in which 13 young people died, and by archives held at the George Padmore Institute—include a short film, Something Said, *and the multi-media performance work* Surge: Side A, *which won the 2017 Ted Hughes Award for new poetry. Their 2016 pamphlet,* The Red and Yellow Nothing, *a queer-techno-medieval misadventure, was previously shortlisted for the Ted Hughes Award. They were elected as a Fellow of the Royal Society of Literature in 2018, along with 39 other writers under the age of 40.*

I resist the urge to destroy my own records by reflecting on archives, how I use them, and what they have meant to me

1.

Ask, then ask again
Work alone
Speak plainly
Show your working
Lucidity not obfuscation
Deep black on plain white
Write quickly, then edit
It shouldn't be expensive
Who is looking at what from where
Bring everything to the table
Source as structure
Be wrong
Tell your truth, not theirs

2.
Archives—that sacred upward vowel sound, striving and reverent. Then we are brought back down to earth. What is lovely is usually, often, locked away. I am interested in the act of archiving, in the poetics of archives, but I am not interested in any vision—creative or political—that derives value from locking people out.

3.
I used to be a bit of a club kid. Went to Scala, Egg, Bootylicious, Other People's Property, Twat Boutique, T Club, Bar Wotever. Suddenly it started to feel like I was in someone else's domain. Other spaces, like First Out, which was once full of queer people every day of the week, disappeared. So did the Oak Bar, where myself and a friend had one of our first (incredibly awkward) encounters with the queer world,

although we were too scared to go in. Candy Bar closed. So did the Glass Bar. Star Bar stopped being an especially queer establishment; when I walk past it now, I remember one night when myself and an old lover went in and had beers and were delighted to bask in the steely gaze of the lesbian behind the bar.

Things come and go. Whole neighbourhoods, establishments, subcultures, identities.

I used to be a bit of a psychogeographer. All criticisms considered, I used to like the term, the ideas, and made a zine for a short time called *Psychogeography for the Modern Black Woman*. I equated my gender with the city around me. I was not simply a woman, but a specific knot of places, perceptions, possibilities. It detailed my walks around London and mentioned the bookshops, squats and other spaces I used to go to—Silver Moon, Index, Kennington Books, New Beacon—locations that made me make sense. Only one of those, New Beacon, still exists.

Isn't that just what happens? Things disappear.

4.
Clearing my room, I find a magazine from 2013, a roundtable I participated in for the Black British issue of *Feminist Review*; myself and my interlocutor, Camel Gupta:

> J: I am regularly assumed to be trans. It's not that I mind, but I wonder. The fact that I use "she" is as troubling to some queers as my chin hairs are to my parents. I once had someone ask when I intended to have chest surgery. Why does that happen? Why is it so often your ID is broken into three parts, so you've got this beginning bit where you're clueless and then this middle bit where you're on your way to something else.
>
> C: And then you reach the promised land of your true self.

It's such a strange sentence—"I am regularly assumed..." I go back through all the text we produced for this roundtable, all the bits that did not make the final cut. I wonder why I have not expressed all the things I felt back then, about gender, about wanting to own my masculinity, about binding, about feeling suspicious of the binary categories of man and woman, even though I was happy to take on the label and the politics. I question how honest I was being at the time, and I question how much I am revising now to make myself fit a particular narrative of *always having known*.

I text my reflections to the third participant in the roundtable, Sita, who replies: "Zadie Smith has made a virtue out of changing her mind, I reckon the rest of us can too."

5.
The other day I watched footage of myself at the hospital in Brighton. It was ten days after my chest surgery. I was lying on the bed and the surgeon came over and pulled

the stitches out. What I was feeling in that moment was less an affirmation of my body or identity, more an affirmation of what was possible. I am not satisfied with or convinced by the notion that this latest phase in gender politics is the "last frontier" of civil rights in this country—a notion much beloved by the media.

For one thing, there are intersex people and a multitude of other genders and orientations that barely get a look in. For another, we seem to be waging war against migrants—the criminalisation of movement has been accepted to the extent that we as a nation are happy to let thousands of people drown at sea, and accept that we must show our passports now when we go to work, get medical treatment, try to rent a house. You can move between genders—hooray—but you cannot move across borders. Once upon a time it was the other way around. Either way, there is no final frontier.

You are not simply cis or trans. Whenever a binary is created, there will be people somewhere in the middle. For many years I identified as cis-gendered, because I thought that trans definitely meant surgery, hormones, dysphoria. I really understood something about trans people when I was about nineteen. I was on the 109 bus to Croydon, probably reading Pat Califia, and I said to myself, "You definitely have something in common with these people." But what did that mean? Years of battling with the NHS? Taking hormones? Coming out again? My experience as a woman had not been miserable, it had simply been. I felt no desperation to be a man, but I had always felt more like a boy than anything else. Then I realised you could be trans and perfectly happy with being totally misaligned. That you could in fact make a virtue out of oscillating from one thing to another, of changing your mind. The point is not that gender is a fun game of *Guess Who*, in which you might be wearing a moustache or a beret, but that I am black and therefore have never been fully a part of what someone means when they say "woman". And I have never cared to be.

6.

Archives exist as loci of queer identity in the absence of any respectable authority, also because so many of the other spaces have shut down. This requires a revision of the division between social and commercial and educational; as queer spaces of the past celebrated themselves, provided homes, romantic encounters, a sense of belonging, this new shift might be about finding spaces for reflection, spiritual growth, twinning of activism and education, and might re-orient the social figure of the queer person from hedonist to guardian of a more fully illuminated past, a more critical and loving present, some kind of hardy, compassionate, social fabric.

7.

I don't know how much longer I will be here, I probably won't have any children, I own nothing of any significant value. I am thirty. Maybe this new direction has come because I am—right on cue—beginning to fear death.

8.

I walk around New Cross—and London—with a sense of belonging that I do not feel anywhere else. I (often) feel myself to be English, of England, because I feel I have a very specific history here; I know where things used to be, I know the poems, I know the songs, I know who used to live where. I get a lot from imagining black queer people in the seventies, eighties, nineties on the same bus routes I travel now—having house parties in Loughborough Junction, Brixton, Streatham, Camberwell. I used to hang out at the Lambeth Women's Centre (now taken over by a school) and read my poems to a room full of delightful queer people—feminists, community activists, librarians for tomorrow. Britain is black/queer Britain.

9.

I am wedded to the history of the New Cross Fire. I made a film about it, *Something Said*, in which I wrote back to Yvonne Ruddock, the young woman whose birthday it was, and who died that night. I read all the interviews, in particular the ones of people who were not at the party but who witnessed the incident. For the first time I really *felt* a piece of black British history and saw its effects and remnants all around me—in short, the first time I have been haunted.

I sent an early version of the film to a friend who immediately responded: "You have put yourself in the story. Why?" I panicked. It was true. I had tried to tell the story from my position as a queer person looking back, but instead of expressing that notion of haunting, it just looked like me talking about my boobs in the same breath as thirteen dead children. I had a few weeks before I needed to turn the film in. I rewrote the script that night.

10.

From *A Stranger in the Archive*, 2017, after the Grenfell fire:

    A.   There is a mystery at the centre of both stories.
    B.   The people who died were not rich enough, in the eyes of the state, to be consequential.
    C.   The mystery is not how the fire started or why these people died.
    D.   The mystery is why we always find ourselves in the same place, the same moment.
    E.   A poet can't deliver justice but they can ask a different kind of question.

In the audience at the ICA, I'm watching films by Ngozi Onwurah; stunning films about what it was like to be black in the eighties: narratives of scrubbing her skin, dog shit through the letter box. A heated debate follows. Onwurah herself says over and over, things have not changed. Do I agree with that statement? One of the films, *The Body Beautiful* (1991) features Onwurah's mother, who had a mastectomy. Bravely, she appears on camera naked, and talks about what it means to have a mixed-race child, what it means to desire the love of a black man. I doubt that my perspective was on her mind when she was making that film, or the idea that someone like myself, nearly thirty years later, might be touched by it as the closest thing I have seen to the experience of black Britishness and the experience of losing (losing?) a breast uttered in the same breath.

11.

I suspect that one of the reasons I look to archives is that they have rules. To be broken, questioned, respected. These rules, these authority figures who are neither celebrities nor tyrants, might be the kind of authority we long for in this age of spiritual crisis.

In queer society we face a deadening of our own community in the tragedy that is pinkwashing, horrific racism, misogyny and proud ignorance in the commercial gay scene, in the gleeful and unrelenting destruction of queer and lesbian spaces, in the pitiless and vile attack on trans people in the media (even as we are media fodder), in the baffling cisgendered rage being exhibited by otherwise insightful feminists, in the gusto with which opposing factions tear each other apart, in the fact that much of this plays out on corporate platforms we do not own, manipulated by silent, indifferent algorithms which do not operate in our interests.

The irony is that this deadening might be remedied by the metaphorical liveness of the archives. I am now finding that this is one of the real sources of spiritual comfort I have. I never thought I would say those words and desire them: connection, groundedness, structured oneness with everything around you. A quiet place to be haunted.

Candice Carty-Williams

A British author and publisher, she studied Media at Sussex University and started work at the Guardian Guide, *before moving into publishing at the age of 23, working on marketing literary fiction, non-fiction and graphic novels. In 2016, she created and launched* The Guardian *and 4th Estate BAME Short Story Prize, which aims to find, champion and celebrate black, Asian and minority ethnic writers. She is author of the novel* Queenie *(2019) and contributes regularly to* Refinery29, i-D, Beat, *and more. Her pieces and commentary around identity, sexuality and race have been shared globally.*

Body Hair: Conversations and Conflict

I am only conflicted when it comes to one thing about myself and the politics of my body. I am not conflicted by being big, that doesn't bother me at all. I have always been aware of how I could lose weight if I wanted to, but the desire to be thin has never risen high enough for me to pay it any attention. I'm not conflicted about the hair on my head; I don't think it holds any more political weight when wrapped in a scarf than when it was straight and pulled into a tight bun at the top of my head.

The conflict that I feel so strongly, and hate feeling so strongly, is around the hair on my body. I'm going to blame my mum for my uneasy relationship with body hair. I remember, annoyingly vividly, sitting in my grandmother's house with my mum before I was a teenager. My mum's relationship with body hair has been, through stories I've heard from her and my aunts, more traumatic than mine could ever be. My mum's dad is Indian, was very hirsute when he had hair, and passed this on to my mum and her four sisters.

A conversation with my mum when I was eleven:
Mum: You're coming with me to my electrolysis appointment.
Me: What's that?
Mum: To get rid of my hair. Going to zap it all away.
Me: Why do you want to get rid of your hair?
Mum: Because it's not nice.
Me: Are you going to be bald?
Mum: No! The hair on my body! My arms and legs, look how thick it is.
Me: I hadn't noticed.

She is very talkative, my mum, but she wasn't after her appointment.

Me: Why are you crying?
Mum: It's really painful, Can.
Me: So why did you get it done?
Mum: You wait until yours starts growing properly, you'll want to get rid of it too.
Me: Not if it makes me cry, I won't.
Mum: I'll tell you what, you'll cry when people start making comments like they do to me and your aunts. We've *all* been called "werewolf" by different people at various points in our lives. You wait.

Four years later, I'd secretly shaved my legs with my grandad's disposable white and orange Bic razor because I'd been to a sleepover or two by this point and had the shock of my life when I realised that my white friends had *very* little hair underneath their tights, while I was already fully covered.

A conversation with my mum's sister, when I was fifteen:

Aunt: Do you think you'll laser, like I do?

Me: ...like laser tag?

Aunt: No, to get rid of all of my body hair! Arms, legs, back, face, (*quietly*) private area, everywhere.

Me: No? Why are you telling *me* that?

Aunt: You'll need to do it one day, I'm just letting you know! Just being helpful.

Me: Leave me out of it.

Aunt: You're lucky. Me, your mum, our sisters, we all have to do it. Grandad is Indian, Can, didn't you realise it runs in the family?

Me: No. I wasn't looking [*I had been looking*].

Aunt: We were bullied horribly at school, all the white girls in the class used to laugh at us. It'll come for you soon, then you'll be asking me how to get rid of it.

My grandmother is a very honest Jamaican woman. Nothing is off bounds to her. She is very logical and practical, so believes that when a problem (or what she would call a problem) is spotted, it is sorted.

A conversation with my nan, when I was nineteen:

Nan: It's happening.

Me: What? Are you okay?

Nan: (*Leaning closer to my face*) The family moustache is finally coming through.

Me: Oh, right. I didn't realise that was our "thing".

Nan: We'd all thought you'd dodged it, but here it is.

Me: Alright! Where's yours, then, if it's such a thing?

Nan: I've been waxing it since the year 1800, nobody has ever seen it. But it's lurking beneath, trust me.

I have still never touched what *she* might call a moustache.

When I was eighteen, I left my overbearing and overfamiliar family in London and went to Sussex University in Brighton, where I was one of about nine black people on campus at any given time. By this point, I was still doing the odd leg shave here and there but had upgraded from my grandad's disposable Bic razors to some sort of overpriced Venus one.

A conversation with my retail colleagues (all white) when I was twenty:

Me: So you're saying they took off everything? Everything?

S: All of it. Every single hair. No gross bush for me.

Me: Wasn't that painful?

T: A bit, but it was worth it. Haven't you ever had a wax?

Me: No. Shall I try it?

K: You're telling me *you've* never had a wax?

Me: No?

K: [*Grabbing my arm and inspecting its hair*] Never?

Me: You've got arm hair too!

S: But your hair is so *dark*, has nobody ever said anything about it?

Me: My family, I guess?

K: But what about guys? You don't want to scare them off with your arms before they get *down there*.

Me: Okay, Okay, I'll book it. It's quite fancy, though, isn't it expensive?

S: It's all right, we get a discount, tell them you work next door.

More curious than anything (and ignoring the comment about men being turned off), I took myself off to the beauty salon. It was incredibly plush and pink and soft in design, so my immediate thought was to turn around before even getting though the door because I didn't belong. I pushed through, though, propelled by this curiosity. I said hello, said quietly what I wanted done, and sat nervously in the waiting room, my mum's yelps and shouts from her electrolysis sessions loud in my mind.

And then, from the small room next to the reception desk, I heard a barely concealed conversation between the woman who would be my first waxer (white), and her manager (also white):

Waxer: …is there *nobody* else who can do it?

Manager: No, everyone else is in with clients.

Waxer: I don't think I'm best to do her, though, shouldn't she have someone who knows how to work with someone like her?

Manager: It's good experience for you, you'll have another coloured client soon and at least you'll know what to expect.

I sat glued to my seat with embarrassment and shame. I knew that as soon as I heard the use of the term "coloured" I should have stood up and given those women a piece of my mind and not given them my money, but instead, I stayed. I'm not sure why.

A conversation with my first waxer (white), when I was twenty:

Waxer: (Sighing) Now, if you could just take your tights and pants off, hop onto the bed and cover yourself with that towel?

Me: Okay, sure. Sorry, this is my first time, so I'm a bit nervous. How much is it going to hurt?

Waxer: It depends. For someone like you, probably quite a lot.

Me: Someone like me?

Waxer: Black. You're always hairier than white women.

Me: Oh, right. Sorry.

Waxer: It's okay. (Rolling up her sleeves) Good for me to get the experience, I guess.

Me: Okay, ready.

Waxer: (Lifting the towel) Oh! Phew! It's not so bad!

Me: Not so bad?

Waxer: I was expecting *loads* of hair, but this is fine! It's still more than I'm used to, but it's not, like, a *jungle*.

Eight years later, I'm still embarrassed to admit that I was grateful for her "praise". Though I didn't go back to any beauty salon for a long, long time.

Three years after that, I ended up going out with a boy I'd lived in the same halls with at Sussex. The relationship had its moments, but he could be very, very cruel. Never really about my body even though I was bigger than him, but he was definitely very cutting about everything else. When I recently moved house, I found a diary and almost cringed myself inside out over its contents, including one entry written a few days before I stayed over at his house for the first time that read:

Things I need to sort before I stay at [name redacted's] house:

—Nice pyjamas—maybe silk? Either way, cute shorts.

—Paint toenails.

—A discreet headscarf?

—I need a wax!!!!!!!!!!

Despite my size, I had (and still have) no issue with being naked in front of another person, but the thought of being seen to have *body hair* warranted ten (10) exclamation points. Unbelievable.

A conversation with my ex-boyfriend (white) when I was twenty-three:

Me: Oh!

Him: What?

Me: (Shoving my hand in his face) Look at this!

Him: What am I looking at?

Me: I've got loads of little hairs on my knuckles. I wonder if they were always there?

Him: EW.

Me: Pardon?

Him: Gross.

Me: That's not very nice.

Him: Sorry, I guess. But it's not *normal*, is it?

My group of friends from university are all white. Two brunettes, and two blondes. They're genuinely woke, and not performatively so. One of them is the only person ever to have gone chest to chest with a grown man for groping me in a club, and won.

She once almost punched a girl at Notting Hill Carnival for putting her hands in my hair. Anyway, they're all white, and all have different attitudes to their body hair, but they're all very pro body hair. Their body hair ranges from fine and light to thick and coarse.

A conversation with one best friend (brunette) when I was twenty-five:
Me: You're telling me you get your *friend* to wax you?
T: Yeah? Why not? That used to be her job.
Me: You don't mind her seeing you like that?
T: She's seen it all before, I guess. And I'm one of the most hairy, she says.
Me: You aren't that hairy, though.
T: Yeah, true, so it's over in about five seconds.
Me: Why do you bother then?
T: Good point. Look at [brunette] and [blonde], they've got loads of body hair and nobody ever says anything. Hold on, *you* get waxed too! Why don't we both stop doing it?
Me: You're all white, though. You lot can step out with unshaven legs and nobody can even see it because it's either blonde or it's so fine, if I don't shave my legs the hair looks like trousers.
T: Yeah, fair. I'd never thought of it like that.

I'd thought of it like that, though. I'd thought about it like that *a lot*.

In private, my attitudes to body hair are very different. I like having hairy legs. I don't find them ugly or unattractive. Whenever I've gone for a Brazilian and the waxer has taken everything off because she thinks "it looks better like that" I always feel robbed, bereft, infantilised. I like the hair on my face and even wish that my eyebrows were thicker. It's only when I see my body hair through the lens of others that the conflict begins to take hold and not loosen its grip until I walk into a salon and leave later, the parts that people will see smooth and acceptable. I hope that one day I can kick this fear of mine. One thing I do know, one thing that I have no conflict around, is that if I have daughter, she will never, ever follow me to a beauty salon.

Yrsa Daley-Ward

Born to a Jamaican mother and a Nigerian father, she was raised by her devout Seventh Day Adventist grandparents in the small town of Chorley in the north of England. In her teens she became a model, and worked in South Africa for three years, before winning recognition as a performance poet. Her published writing includes short stories and memoir, as well as poems, in which she notably addresses topics such as identity, race, mental health, and femininity. She is the author of On Snakes and Other Stories *(2013),* Bone *(self-published in 2014, new Penguin edition in 2017) and* The Terrible *(2018). She now lives in New York.*

What they leave you with—three poems

1) What IT leaves you with

I don't know what I am
or am not tonight.
The physics of my body are changing.
I am not a doctor
or detective
but I feel some part of me
gone. My head is Thirsty.
the liquid in my bones is Thin.

A four-letter word is haunting me.

My thighs are softer than usual.
I'm falling away.
I've fallen away.
I suck in my waist and distract people with my hair. If I make my lips redder
if I walk, swing hip
like this. If I push these breasts together and up,
up,
give these brows a stronger arch

if I blacken my lashes,

if I wear a tighter shirt
no one will know that I left the room.

I cannot feel my mouth.
Something is breathing
but it is not me.

2) everything is uncomfortable

But why the difficulty?
you wonder
You almost made it. You're pushing thirty. twenty. forty.

You never found a city large enough. Your palms are forever on fire. No
sooner do you put the rubbish
out or wash the dishes in the sink
there is always more waste
waste
waste
more to wash, either of the house or yourself. And when will the work end?
You ask yourself. When? It's a tough space now in life
you work and go to bed and wake up
and its as though it all begins again
as though it
all
begins.
Again.
You stretch. You run on the treadmill and try not to eat late. You kiss better
people than before and you're careful
(you're as careful as the lonely can be)
you're careful who gets in your bed.
All reasonable problems.
Nothing too dire
so why do you feel so dead?

3) not all families look the same
Two years after her funeral
her lover comes to visit.

Nice little place you got here
Where can I put my bike?

He parks it in the hallway.
It's the first time you've spoken since
he pawned all of her jewellery
and moved back to his mother's.

But everything is done now
plus
things,
we all know
are only things
and people,
we all know
are only people

He sits hunched, thin
one leg over the other

You ask what brings him back to
this side,
on this day. *Tings*, he says,
looking right at you
and not at you at all.
Work tings.
He tries to smile
twitches
and the flowers on the sofa
wilt.

It's getting late,

he sighs,
resting his hands on your writing desk
darkening the room with his breath.
Want a bump?

Even if you do
you know that drugs in a room with a man your mother loved
might finish you.

Later when he's gone
you lift the desk out on the pavement.
The room sits back on itself
and the moon swells.

Tjawangwa Dema

Born in Gaborone, Botswana, she is a poet and arts administrator, who received an MA in Creative Writing from Lancaster University. Her chapbook, Mandible, *was published in 2014 with Slapering Hol under the auspices of the African Poetry Book Fund, and she went on to win the 2018 Sillerman First Book Prize for African Poets for her book* The Careless Seamstress (2019). *Her writing has appeared in*

Cordite Poetry Review, The Ofi Press, Elsewhere Lit *and* Read Women Anthology.
Her poetry has been translated into Spanish, Swedish, German and Chinese.

Born Sleeping

I didn't know the child was coming
till it was gone.
I regret that more than the loss.
More than the wrench of loss
is loss itself—the thing never there
where it was before—
its miserly hand stirring at the smallest thought.
Its clench and yank;
no-use what-ifs strapped to the back like a newborn,
the spectre of sharp teeth tight at the nipple.

No one to say breathe,
just an upward punch through belly and lung.
The smallest nick
there
and there, a fistful of blood and more.
More than all the could've-beens
is the was.
A perfect face,
small in the mind's rear view,
coming,
coming, till it's gone.

Pugilist

Not yet thirteen
with your slipped jaw
dancing its talk of obvious pain,
bloodied nose glistening,

you come to our mother
with your broken mouth open—
certain you are no longer at ease
in this kingdom of boyhood.
Glad to meet its death
at your own hand.

Confinement

To make a child
narrow the berth.

When you have a baby
she'd place the words on her tongue like a thing that's done.
I'd think of now as never,
me thirty-six, arms empty and still frowning into cribs,
rubbing sleeping infants' cheeks to see if this wanting is catching.
I think I know when I became immune.
As a small child myself I'd been the one sent to fetch
when the new mom couldn't move,
confined as much by tight stitch as tongue.

Don't let anyone visit.
Don't eat from the family bowls.
Let no one but these women hold the child.

Often she'd stare at nothing except the baby in her arms
and the log at the gate meant everyone knew
only their good wishes could enter;
their bodies, their diseases, all that chatter they could keep
well outside the yard and its doughy new guest.
Even the father wouldn't see it till its knotted cord fell off.
He knew nothing of all the bloody screaming,
the noisy stench and mess of it all.

For three months there'd be this dance,
too much seeing by one and not enough by the other,
the language of ritual and taboo an old fence.

For years I frowned at the old ladies and their fraying ways.
How they kept the father out
dancing his own dance despite knowing
how sometimes a girl who'd never had other women
stare between her thighs with brisk empathy
would hold his eye and think him a ship in that distant light.
I know now
what the old women knew then—
how sore the new mother was
and how greedy the infant
and the one who helped her make it.

Edwige Renée Dro

A bilingual Ivorian writer, translator and literary activist, who worked in England for more than a decade before returning to Abidjan, she is passionate about bridging the literary communication gap in Africa. Her writings have been published by Bloomsbury, Africa no es un pais, Popula, *and* This is Africa, *among other places, and she also features in the new* Casa Africa *anthology. She was one of the 2015 judges of the PEN International Short Story Prize and was also a 2016 judge of the Etisalat Prize for Literature. She is currently working on her first novel and researching the stories of the Amazones of 1949, the women politicians who marched against the colonisers in Côte d'Ivoire.*

Courage Became Her Friend

The buzzing of the phone woke Sandrine. She stretched her arm to grope for it across the bed, the effort to reach it a struggle. She had only got home at 2 o'clock this afternoon, having done her nightly eleven-hour shift at the care home, grabbing a coffee at Starbucks at 6:30 that morning, then going to do her cleaning jobs. Beat wasn't even the word for how she felt.

Brrr–brrr! The buzzing noise carried on, regardless. For a moment, she thought it was her alarm but she had only just closed her eyes. She managed to grab the phone and quickly answer it before it rang out. At this precise moment, she hoped it was the agency calling to cancel her shift tonight. She would actually have paid good money for that to happen. OK, not good money, since she was trying to save the little she earned, although that was proving difficult. There was always something. The obvious things like rent and food, of course, but last week, she had had to buy new tyres for her bicycle. She'd hoped they would last a bit longer. Not so—and £80 went just like that!

Then there was the money she had started sending for her father's medical bills in Côte d'Ivoire, which she was glad to do. The last time she saw him, she had been eighteen. She was now thirty-two; in the years between, there had been only photographs, and his voice on the telephone. Nowadays, even that was becoming rare. Her mother was the one Sandrine spoke with, not her father: it was always that he was sleeping, he'd just popped out, he was taking a shower. Then when she called specially, with the express intention of talking to him, come what may, he was put on the phone.

But his voice sounded tired—*"Ah, Maman, tu vas bien?"*—and tears filled her eyes. How could she be well when she had not seen him in fourteen years and his photos no longer looked like him? Who was that thin, ashen man who had replaced her vigorous father? A few times, she had wanted to say *Fuck it* and just go there; but go and then what? Because she wouldn't be able to come back.

"Hello?"

"Allo? Sandrine…"

The line crackled but she recognized her mother's voice, and her mother called her Sandrine instead of Maman. She sat up and rubbed her eyes.

"Allo? Allo, Maman? Can you hear me?"

The line went dead and Sandrine cursed the phone. Now she had to go out and buy a phone card to call overseas, which meant that her sleeping hours were being eaten into. Perhaps just for tonight she would call in sick. This working all the time was killing her. In summertime, it wasn't too bad, but in these winter months she just wanted to stay under her duvet. The care home jobs, the live-in care jobs, the cleaning jobs—all cash-in-hand and none of them requiring any immigration status checking.

She threw a coat over her jumper and put on her Converse trainers, while keeping an eye on the phone. If her mother had tried calling her again, the call hadn't come through. And Sandrine wouldn't rest until she had spoken to her. Her mother had tried to keep the worst from her, but Sandrine's siblings kept her informed: about their father's blood pressure shooting up, about the comas he had been in, about the dialysis, about the fact that he had gone blind. For all those reasons, she dreaded getting phone calls from back home. She threw her scarf around her neck and went out.

As had also become a common occurrence lately, tears started flowing. Tired, that's what she was, but it had nothing to do with the crazy hours she was doing. At least if she was making something of her life here…but nothing. She was renting a room that was so badly heated she had to wear a jumper, woollen tracksuit bottoms and socks, and then throw a thick duvet over herself to be at all comfortable. She had just begun saving money when her father's illness came. *Tension*—high blood pressure. So her little savings had been sent back home, meaning that she had to stay here. Because if she couldn't save, she couldn't go. And courage became her friend. If anyone had told her that she would need courage to speak to her family, she would have called them mad. What was the need for courage there?

She wiped her tears. The wind was blowing and leaves littered the ground. During her first autumn in England, she had slipped on leaves similar to those and had fallen. Twice! And she didn't know why, until the following autumn, a whole year later, when she realized that her fall had everything to do with her shoes; with their soles smooth as a baby's skin, she had been destined for a fall. The reminiscence of it made her smile as she entered the shop with its familiar smell of dried fish, *akpi*, and palm oil. It seemed a new delivery of smoked pork meat had arrived.

"Good afternoon, *Tantie*!"

"Hey, Sandrine! You have become a stranger, *hein*. How are you?"

"I'm fine, *Tantie*."

"Ahi? All this time, I have been asking myself where has that girl gone? I even thought you'd gone back to Ouattara's country." *Tantie* laughed, referencing the Ivorian president.

The shopkeeper was a staunch supporter of his opponent, Gbagbo, although when she had left the country, Gbagbo was in hiding in France, travelling on fake passports.

"How's your aunt?"

"She is fine, *Tantie*. She greets you."

Sandrine had not in fact seen her own *tantie* in two months; she was avoiding the woman. It seemed as if since she was the one who had brought her into the country, *Tantie* was now expecting Sandrine to bail her out. *Sandrine, send me some phone credit. Sandrine, put £10 in my account. Sandrine, can you believe my electric card has run out?* The demands had stopped only because Sandrine has changed her telephone number.

"Ah, that's good. Next time she comes here, tell her to come and spend some time with me at the shop. If there's one thing I miss in Peckham, it's that. Here is the place of Ghanaians, and you can't be with them like with your own people. But at least, there's no *I'll pay later* with them," the shopkeeper said, and burst into laughter. Sandrine laughed with her for politeness' sake, before asking for the phone card she had come to buy.

"£10 or £5 one?"

"£5, please."

"How's your family?"

"They are all well."

"That's good. Greet them from me."

"They will hear."

It always puzzled Sandrine, that thing of sending your greetings to people you had never met and were probably likely never to meet. Even when she was still in Côte d'Ivoire she had, for some reason, thought that when she landed in England all that would disappear, along with the smell of *akpi* and plantains and *djoumgblé* in a shop. How terribly mistaken she had been, and taken in by the *Parigos* who descend upon Abidjan during the holidays, making out that they were all that.

Her own auntie had done the same, wearing jeans and little dresses, sunglasses always on "to protect her retina" or perched atop her head, French peppered with English words. Even she who was doing a BTS did not speak French the way *Tantie* Georgette—who hadn't even finished primary school—spoke. She approached her before her parents even had the idea. *Wêrê wêrê* or not, it was *Tantie* Georgette whose skin shone from living in Europe, and she couldn't have been that *wêrê wêrê* if she was still with the same man she met on a beach in Grand Bassam. Then, she was *wêrê wêrê* because she got up one day and decided that she was going to Grand Bassam to get her white man, and for three months solidly went without fail to Grand Bassam every week-end. But then when she put her claws into the white man, she stuck. And as Sandrine's parents acknowledged, were she such a *wêrê wêrê* woman, she would have left that man and got herself another man, and another man, and another man. "Georgette has come down. *Ahi*, can a person be and not settle down?" her mother had said. And the sentence had been the seal of approval needed to put into action the plan of *Tantie* Georgette.

"I can't be a guarantor for her visa, but you can send Sandrine on one of these *colonies de vacances* to England," *Tantie* Georgette told Sandrine's parents.

"*Colonie de vacances?*"

"Yes, there are travel agencies here who do that. To every country, and embassies aren't so particular about checking papers for things like this because only rich people's children go on this sort of trip…"

And the plan was made. Sandrine's father took a loan and the two million CFA Francs was paid for the three-week trip. At least, for the other rich kids it was three weeks, but for her, she was going for ever. On their first trip to London, after a week spent in Cornwall being bathed into English culture, she slipped into the McDonald's at Piccadilly Circus and went straight to the toilets.

"Sandrine!"

"My God, I didn't recognize you."

"Well, there you go."

Sandrine didn't say anything because she felt that, despite the bravado of *Tantie* Georgette, she was ashamed. The stylish woman who only left Abidjan some two months previously had been replaced by a woman whose weave-on seemed to have been thrown on her head, her jeans were too baggy to be a style and the once-shiny skin looked ashen. The trainers were proper running shoes with thick soles to match, and not the wonderful Converse trainers which she had come to associate with British casualness.

"You wait! In this country, you pound the pavements."

Although she now knew that to be true, Sandrine had refused to go down the road of chunky running shoes and cheap weave-ons worn because looking after afro hair in London cost a small country's budget. Sandrine had pair after pair of Converse shoes, and as for hair, her own hair that she twisted every weekend did the job.

Now she scratched the phone card and began to compose the number that would help her talk for more than an hour to her people back home. Her phone rang before she had even finished.

"Allo?" she picked up, bowed at the tantie shopkeeper and left the shop.

"Allo, Sandrine."

"Maman? Let me call you back. I had to go out and buy credit."

"Oh, don't worry."

Her mother's voice was so cold, and so distant and, as was always the case, Sandrine found herself holding her breath and gripping the phone. "Is everything all right?"

"Ahhh." Her mother sighed.

Sandrine stopped walking.

"*Qu'est-ce qu'il y a?*" What's the matter?

"*C'est Papa*. He's gone."

But even before she heard that other part of the sentence, she knew. *Parti*. Gone. Passed.

"*Je vais venir*. I'm coming."

Reni Eddo-Lodge

An award-winning journalist, author and podcaster, born and raised in London by a Nigerian mother, she was listed in 2014 by The Guardian *as one of the 30 most exciting people under 30 in digital media, and she appeared in* Elle *magazine's 100 Inspirational Women list, and* The Root's *30 black viral voices under 30. Her debut non-fiction book,* Why I'm No Longer Talking to White People About Race, *was published in 2017 to critical acclaim, becoming a* Sunday Times *bestseller, and winning the 2018 Jhalak Prize. The book was longlisted for the Baillie Gifford Prize for non-fiction, shortlisted for the Books Are My Bag Readers Awards (non-fiction), voted non-fiction book of the year for 2017 by booksellers at both Foyles and Blackwells, and was selected by actress Emma Watson as an Our Shared Shelf book club read in January 2017. Her podcast, "About Race with Reni Eddo-Lodge", premiered in March 2018.*

Women, Down your Tools!

A friend of mine once told me an interesting tale. Her mother had arrived home from a long day at work, only to be confronted by a sink full of dishes. Instead of asking her family why no one had lifted a finger to help, she calmly opened a kitchen cupboard, pulled out every piece of crockery, and smashed it onto the kitchen floor. The family ended up eating off paper plates for a while. "I think Mum's gone mad," my friend confided in me.

Looking back, I'd argue that that moment was the final straw on the camel's back.

Today, new research shows that women are still responsible for the vast majority of housework in the home—nearly twice as much as men. A poll of users of the parenting website Mumsnet has very similar findings. Nothing about this is new. In 1972, the legendary socialist feminist activist Selma James formed the International Wages for Housework Campaign. Together with founding members Brigitte Galtier, Mariarosa Dalla Costa, and Silvia Federici, Selma James argued that the running of a home forms the basis for all work in society. Children will not make it to school if they are not washed and dressed and fed. Husbands would crumble if they returned from work to an untidy house, with no dinner on the table. This labour underpinned all labour, yet it was heavily gendered, unpaid, and undervalued.

"We are seen as nagging bitches, not workers in struggle," wrote Silvia Federici in *Wages Against Housework*, published in 1975. Indeed, research by the BBC radio programme *Woman's Hour* has found that younger couples argue about housework the most. After being told that the world is for our taking, we find ourselves playing out the same acts as our mothers did a generation before us.

It was in 1963 that Betty Freidan identified this unpaid, undervalued labour as "the problem that has no name". White, educated middle-class women had been sold a lie. They were told that suburban housewife living would be fulfilling, that they were supposed to enjoy dedicating themselves to a life of unpaid work. In today's era, the twenty-first century, the dynamics of work have changed drastically.

We are all working now, while women who claim benefits are chided for their failed work ethic. Popular feminist struggles have switched from the struggles of women at the bottom to the concerns of women at the top—penetrating parliament, and occupying spaces on corporate boards. Fewer women are being raised solely with housewife aspirations. We are more likely to be able to make a genuine choice on the matter.

But the reality is, many of us are doing two jobs. In 1971, Selma James reported for a BBC documentary on women's labour called *Our Time Is Coming*. In it, a female shop worker explains: "I set my alarm at 6 in the mornings and do some of my housework. I leave home at 8.30 a.m., reach work at 9. Finish at 3.30 p.m., reach home at 4.30 p.m., start the cooking, and the rest of work I do until about 6.30–7 in the evening, until supper."

That's a thirteen-hour day, with only some of that work valued enough to be paid. Can we honestly say that this is no longer the case for many women? As *Woman's Hour* presenter Jane Garvey wryly comments: "Times have changed. Women are no longer trapped in the home. They can go out to work then come back and start the housework."

Of course, couples and families with enough disposable income can hire a cleaner. But that just puts a sticking-plaster over the problem, outsourcing to low-paid, working-class women who are overwhelmingly employed by agencies on zero-hour contracts. It is the opposite of feminist solidarity. Who is looking after the cleaner's kids, caring for her home? The answer is, too often, her friends, family, or in the worst-case scenario, no one. In late August, a busybody Twitter user broadcast a picture of a child cleaning a Hampstead branch of estate agency Foxtons late at night, calling it "child labour". Further investigation found that the girl was helping out her mum.

To assume that a woman's position in the home is unrelated to her social and economic capital is wilfully naive. The current set-up is unsustainable and structured for burnout. Selma James was organising to change society. She recognised that to ease the burden on women's backs, we needed a fundamental overhaul of gender roles to transform the home. Capitalism pulled its con trick by isolating women home workers—Selma brought them together in consciousness-raising meets so that they could realise they were dealing with a common problem.

Today housework is not talked about much among friends. But, as in the time of the Wages for Housework campaign, this disparate isolation is the basis of denying women labour rights. Housework is work. Have you ever wondered what amazing things you could have done with all the energy you've dedicated to housework, propping up the lives of people who don't even notice that you're doing it?

That is why today, as we absorb the news that women are still doing the lion's share of work in the home, I'm urging you to stop. Stop giving. Let the dishes accumulate.

Stop sacrificing your time. Stop waking up that little bit earlier to do the laundry. Down your tools. Walk out. Go to the pub. Go on strike. It is only through a collective withdrawal of labour that those who rely on us will realise how vital our work is.

Summer Edward

Growing up as a "third-culture kid" in Trinidad and the US, she is an alumna of the University of Pennsylvania. Her writing has been published in The Millions, Columbia Review, Horn Book Magazine, The Missing Slate, Kweli, Matatu: Journal for African Culture and Society, Bim: Arts for the 21st Century, Moko, sx salon, The Caribbean Writer, Obsidian: Literature in the African Diaspora, *and elsewhere. She is a Small Axe Fiction and Poetry Prize shortlistee, a Pushcart Prize nominee, and was selected for the NGC Bocas Lit Fest's New Talent Showcase that spotlights emerging Caribbean writers. Her work is included in* New Worlds, Old Ways: Speculative Tales from the Caribbean. *She is an editor of books for young people and editor-in-chief of* Anansesem, *an online magazine devoted to Caribbean children's and young adult literature. She divides her time between her adopted hometown, Philadelphia, and her Caribbean homeland, Trinidad.*

Love in the Time of Nationalistic Fever

I had no language for you then.

There in the waiting room,
the river fleeing
its settled frame
of darkening window.

No language
for the things I saw in that twilight
year of leaving you
to your nation of silence.

No language
for the single question we asked
of the countries between us.

Love I would,
were it not for this illness,
walk with you in lands
where only time has seen the hills.

For one like you,
I would break land like bread,
divide countries like war.

Friend, I am not silent.
I am sure you speak my language
like the river soon will speak
the language of the sea.

What is so different
now that you have seen me
cross the river, now that you have seen me
look through the pane?

Had I not met you
in the fever of our wakening,
I would not wait.

I would lead you
across this night
to the country I have found.

Old Year's Melody

Dry December days
preserve their fragrance
as memory jars
on each acropetal year.

May we always inspire
the lemon balm
of hours yellowed
like poinsettias,

follow the scent
of roots beyond
vetiver screens
of tradition and time,

find sachets of morning
glory among the faded
delicate clothes
of an incensed grandmother.

As this year burns
to its essential midnight, oil
runs down the temples

of wasted women; rose
hips sway to spicy waftures
of an anointed mandolin.

May I always distill
the fixative substance
of seven sisters,

mark the accent
of sorrel and citrus
peels parched
in a well-tuned kitchen,

never miss the stirring
of the pepper pot
as seconds sing
away the wrapped year.

Days, like potpourri,
will lose their freshness.
But now, we gather
from scratch our sage
songs.

Forest Psalmody

"Whoever moves within the forest can partake directly of sacredness…"
—from *The Island Within*

Oh let us hear, upon this rock,
the forest singing in its mass,

Sabbath tongue of tree and fan
leaves playing the wind,

organ ululant
strains of dark and light.

Let us, to the littoral niche
of islands named for saints,

—Saint Giles, unspoiled
as the Hermit's transfigured face—

tread our weary way.

On behalf of your congregations
of the migrant and the roaming,

I repent for roaming
too far. Our grandmothers knew

the forest, close
procession of canopies

humming godstongue to the sky,
how full the monastery of night

creatures grew in chorus
when silence was the God's truth of these isles.

Above, constellations
seared on a black anvil heaven,

but only the iguana scuttling through
the forest heard the forging

of our concrete history, naked
foot resting on a now-lost rock.

Let us go then as the Amerindian
to her sylvan worship,

hear the holy witness
of mora, the crappo's ancient

testimony, pause as black bodies

of tamanduas,
still as zemis before the dark

orison of a peccary, perhaps,
dying in the grave

and ritual circle of the guatacare
grove. Here,

a lamentation of macaws
haunts the bois mulatre.

Across the river's wide scroll,
bitterns write their lapidary scripture,

drill into moss-crusted stones,
gem the specular surface.

At shore, mangroves hunch over
studying the river's illumination

as priestly caimans prostrate
in silk tabernacles of water.

To this stand of sacredness
we come supplicant, from forgetful cities.

Shaking off the lonely sleep
of civilization, dead growth of revolutions,

we sing the great forest lyric.

Oh quivering librettos of undergrowth,
oh plainsong of the kiskidee,

oh musical ring of heartwood,
teach us to sing again in your language.

Our Lady of Acres, grant us your benediction.

Open the folio of foliage, each leaf
of the canticle turning

toward a new-blooming age,
wildlife of recollection.

The understory telling
our human chronicle.

Bell apple of our Eden
tolling in perennial light.

Eve L. Ewing

A writer and sociologist from Chicago, Illinois, she is an Assistant Professor at the University of Chicago School of Social Service Administration and author of Electric Arches *(2017) and* Ghosts in the Schoolyard: Racism and School Closings on Chicago's South Side *(2018). She co-wrote, with Nate Marshall, the play* No Blue Memories: The Life of Gwendolyn Brooks. *Her work has appeared in* Poetry, *the* New Yorker, *the* New York Times, *the* Washington Post, The Atlantic, FADER, *and many other journals and newspapers, and has received awards from the Poetry Society of America and the American Library Association.*

The Device

It wasn't like a George Washington Carver kind of thing where one brilliant Negro with a soldering iron made some magic and poof! A miraculous machine. It was an open source kind of situation. Thousands of high-school science-fair whiz kids, this and that engineering club at this and that technical college, the One Black Person at a bunch of Silicon Valley startups getting together with a bunch of other One Black Persons over craft beer and coding late into the night, even some government folks working off the clock (or so the rumors go). Not just one person. A hive mind of black nerds, obsessive types, scientists and inventors but also historians and archaeologists and the odd astrologer here and there. Project Delta Mother, they called it (goofy name tbh but it's whatever).

When the time came to flip the switch, the sentimental poetic ones who were in charge of communication and media and symbolism got the idea that it should be the youngest among them to do it. She stood at the front of the stage and seemed unfazed by how long the speeches went on, everyone wanting a moment at the podium to give a benediction or remember a lost comrade or shed a tear or play a short video that never turned out to be that short. She was a gangly one, a fifth-grader from Providence who had started showing up at the high school robotics team meetings when the afterschool science enrichment course at her own school got cut. Her grandmother had bought her a special dress for this momentous occasion, and she didn't want to wear it but didn't want to hurt Gramma's feelings either, so as the starched frill rubbed against the backs of her legs and made her itchy she tried to distract herself by counting the tiles on the ceiling. She was so engrossed and the speeches were so many that she almost didn't hear her name when it was called. The man in the lab coat whose name she had forgotten beckoned her toward the device, as the audience stood reverent and waiting. Their arms were all in the air to take photos and videos and she thought they looked like they were about to go down a water slide, and that made her smile, which made them smile.

She stood before the machine. It hummed at a low resonance, making her teeth feel funny as she got closer to it. Its ten thousand tiny lights popped into and out of momentary existence every few seconds, twinkling bravely though the theater was bright inside. She blinked at it, and began quietly humming herself.

The man in the lab coat watched her watching the device. After so many late nights with this hulking thing, seeing it in the light of day made him click his tongue. This day was no sleek reveal. No one would be gasping over pocket sizing and carefully beta tested user interfaces. The device was an inelegant hodgepodge, a reflection of the hands that made it. Bits and pieces stuck out of crevices where they should have been hidden—wire, shards of hastily sawn PVC, the odd patch of duct tape. It looked like in a hundred years it might be something you find at a yard sale. But of course, he thought after a second, wouldn't that be a success? Shouldn't the device come to be so average and commonplace that it ceases to be magic and comes to be part of everyday life for regular black people all over the country? Wasn't that the dream? He tilted his head slightly as though it might show him a new angle on the whole thing—just as the girl reached out for the switch.

In that split second, he realized for the first time that the machine might be dangerous. That having a child be the one to do it was symbolic, sure, and also very, very stupid. This was the thought that entered his head as the room filled with flashing lights, and he began to panic. The device was going to explode and kill them all, and the girl would be first to die, and he would live just long enough to see it happen.

But no. Those were flashbulbs. And a thousand journalists, official and not-so-much, captured the moment when the girl activated the device. It roared to life, its internal cooling fans whirring furiously, lights blinking faster and faster. People in the audience began to cry. One man, a pastor who had led a booming rendition of "Lift Every Voice", fainted. The girl stayed very calm. She had read the manual many times.

"Hello," she said. Her voice cracked, and she cleared her dry throat and repeated herself, loudly this time. "Hello!" Everyone else in the room fell silent. They waited.

The device's external speakers began to crackle, like a phone sounds when wind is blowing over the mouthpiece. And then the reply came back, loud and clear. Almost too loud. The man in the lab coat covered his ears. "Hello? Who—Lord, I have prayed for this day! I knew you would find favor with me as you have with my sister Willa. If you only guide my steps, I will be faithful."

The man in the lab coat looked, wild-eyed, at the girl. He began to gesture at her frantically, but she only nodded, unperturbed, and pulled a folded-up piece of paper out of her dress pocket. She had practiced for this. As the audience looked on in awe, she spoke, slowly and deliberately. Mostly she had it memorized, but she looked down at the paper every few seconds to be sure not to mess up.

"Hello. Please stay calm. This is not God, or a dream, and you are not going crazy. I am talking to you from many years in the future." She gulped once, and continued. "I am using a device built by the colored people of this country." She felt funny saying *colored*, but the history people said it would be better that way. "As you know, we were stolen from our homeland and brought here. We have had many difficulties and our families have been hurt and separated. In my time, we are not slaves. But we face challenges. We need help from our ancestors, but you have been lost to us. So we worked very hard and made this special machine. It allows us to talk to you inside your head, even though we are far apart. It is like yelling over a river." The poets had added that part and it hadn't made much sense when she first practiced that line, but now it seemed right. "I am your great-great-great-granddaughter. I am the first person in history to use this device. People from all over are here with me, watching. We have many questions for you. And other people will use the device to talk to their ancestors, too. So now, Grandmother, my first question is…"

She looked down at the paper to get it exactly right.

"What words can you offer us to help us be free as black people in a world that does not love us?"

The girl stared at the device as though a face might appear amidst the plastic and metal, then gulped again and folded the paper back up and stuck it in a sweaty rectangle back into her pocket. She turned toward the audience, seeing them as though for the first time. The device was crackling and humming and buzzing and shaking and so were they. People had their shoes off and feet up on the seats of the auditorium, rocking forward and back like babies. They wept. They grinned. They scribbled into notebooks and clicked photograph after photograph. They bit their nails. They grasped at each other's shoulders, holding each other up while they waited. And waited. The man in the lab coat sat cross-legged on the stage, leaning against the podium as though alone in his own living room, and stared at her with his mouth agape. She turned back toward the device, wondering if the connection had been lost.

"Grandmoth—" she began. But sound from the device cut her off, echoing across the auditorium, bouncing against brick and plaster and ricocheting in everyone's ears. It was laughter. It began hoarse and raspy and then unfolded into ringing peals and gasps, sounding and resounding louder and louder. The device sputtered and flashed and began to get hot, tape curling off and the smell of melting plastic curling forth from the rear vents, and the audience gasped, and the woman somewhere in America, sometime in America, laughed and laughed and laughed. And the little girl put her hands on her own cheeks and felt their warmth, and the woman laughed. And the lights in the auditorium began to flicker and fade, and still the woman laughed. She laughed, and laughed, and laughed.

home-going

I have endeavored to show that ants find their way home by virtue of
something which they acquire by experience and retain; in other words,
that they acquire from their environment impressions which influence
their home-going.

—Charles H. Turner

sprawled on my belly on
the hot sidewalk in front
of the house on Fletcher
that would later become
the old house, after the
old house which became
the old-old house. when
the others were jumping
fences or climbing over
rotted-out cars or putting
on lipliner i let my elbows
get ashy and scraped
on the cracked cement,
considering the ants
the business of the
mighty and unimportant
small black bodies
armored by god
up and down the creases
of my palm, tiny and
determined travelers
ants carry their dead
without ceremony
an ant is stronger than it looks
an ant can be replaced
some ants can fly
ants invented queens
an ant does not steal
an ant takes
back what you

Epistle to the Dead and Dying
for Eric Garner
(found poem after Paul Laurence Dunbar's "The Haunted Oak")

Pray you bare your veins
Pray you shudder
Pray you leave
Pray you leave
Pray you leave
Pray you leave
Pray you leave
Pray you free

Pray over me in the moonlight guiltless
Pray the moonlight down
Pray the the sore away
Pray you grow old old
Pray you fast fast

Pray a howl night wind
Pray a sky
Pray a raised hand beat steady
Pray a raised hand beat
Pray a steady beat

Do not stay
Do not be foolish
Do not weep

Pray you feel the rope
Pray you feel the weight
Pray you leave
Pray you leave
Pray you leave
Pray you leave a memory of your face

Vangile Gantsho

South African-born, she is a poet, healer and co-founder of impepho press. Unapologetically womanist, she has travelled the African continent and the globe, participating in poetry plays, events and festivals. She is the author of two poetry collections: Undressing in front of the window *(2015) and* red cotton *(2016). She holds an MA from the University of Rhodes and was named one of the* Mail & Guardian's *Top Young 200 South Africans of 2018.*

smallgirl

smallgirl with moths in her mouth
speaks anger in glances   knows the dagger of words
smallgirl   big voice   moves in silence
knows how earthquakes begin

in the rumbling of her stomach
entire families collapse

smallgirl cares too much   for such a small girl
smallgirl with treacherous eyes
carries too much feeling in her lungs
knows the sting of lonely
smallgirl sees too much   breathes too much
takes up too much air
smallgirl is too much mirror and   expectation
too much wanting more
smallgirl should know better than to try fight the sun

smallgirl with hands of spades
smallgirl dreams too much. hopes too much
wants to plant and grow
smallgirl thinks she is the ocean
smallgirl is a stream

smallgirl will break her heart with all this want
smallgirl is not even the wind

smallgirl must learn to swallow
and be pretty

Mama I am burning
for Fezeka "Khwezi" Kuzwayo

I am burning mama. Mama, I'm burning.

In a box. Set on fire while I slept.

I slept mama.

A girl faced the bullets head on. She caught a bullet in her eye.

She is blind mama.

Something is wrong mama. I kept pulling down my skirt.

Kept checking my lipstick. I was hiding in this box.

They found me hiding mama.

This fire is an uncle you trusted mama.

An uncle who promised to watch me while you were gone.

And while you were gone, in my sleep, the fire burned me mama.

While you were gone.

While I was sleeping.

I forgot to pull my skirt down. I put too much lipstick on.

I am burning mama. Mama, I am burning!

Her father's tractor
after Xidu Heshang "Fictionalising Her"

When she is nine years old,
she pretends the woman in the front seat with her hand on her father's lap does
    not exist.

When she is twelve years old,
she pretends the letter with a photograph of a baby boy in the cupboard does
    not exist.

When she is fifteen,
she pretends the mouth on her shoulder at her father's braai does not exist.

At eighteen,
she pretends the phone call from a girl three years older than her does not exist.

At twenty-one,
she pretends the shame in her father's eyes when she returns from the police
     station does not exist.

At twenty-four,
she pretends her stomach has never been pumped, and the woman half-dead in a
     motel with rum-soaked letters does not exist.

Three weeks into her twenty-fifth year,
she pretends the man shredded by a tractor plough does not exist.

Three days after they tell her,
she pretends she called to say happy birthday and her father's face on the funeral
     programme does not exist.

Three months into the ground,
she pretends the growing holes in her womb and her chest do not exist.

The day before her thirtieth birthday,
she pretends her longing to follow him, in footsteps and grave, does not exist at all.

zakia henderson-brown

Born and raised in Brooklyn, New York, she is the author of What Kind of Omen
Am I, *selected by Cate Marvin as winner of the Poetry Society of America's 2017
Chapbook Fellowship. She is a Cave Canem graduate fellow, was a 2016 Poets House
Emerging Poets fellow, and has received additional fellowships and support from
the Fine Arts Work Center,* Callaloo Journal, *and the Squaw Valley Community of
Writers. Her poems have appeared in* Adroit Journal, African American Review, Beloit
Poetry Journal, North American Review *and other outlets. She has been in residence
at the T.S. Eliot House, the Vermont Studio Center, and the Louis Armstrong House
Museum. She currently serves on the board of the Brooklyn Movement Center,
where she co-founded the anti-gendered and sexualised street harassment collective,
No Disrespect. She is an Editor and Strategic Partnerships Coordinator at nonprofit
publisher The New Press.*

unarmed

as in: has arms   dark flesh: an intact heart,
but they are   the city's   named prey
a shallow pond   fatal   to a foamed

still mouth at   wound   pistol, warm
dawn; a long   undressing   adrenal gland;
heavy rain.   itself—   a cold case.

A Man Walks into a Bar

Suspending the instinct   to fold a life into a palm
        then have it disappear   some animals
practice small-scale mercy: a hiss or spray as warning;

a nuzzle before drawn jaws.   I lived awhile
        just beneath   the knife of him
until the cold metal   became a porch light turning on.

Did I indebt myself to fire?   He claimed my pussy
        scrambled his wires   suggesting I was electric
if not already brain-dead   body moving in mime

until essential functions stopped.   His was a slow hiss
        one I itched   to drift toward:
melodic but   unmasked soon enough

as just a slurred word   behind a strong whiskey
        a finger on my lips, then   the smashed glass.

I Was Getting Out of Your Way
in memoriam, Sandra Bland

Just picked petunias sweetkiss my knuckles
Creating a genre of springtime. I succumb

To the urge to sing: *what gift* this small refuge
In my palm; the soft city wind, a lodestar.

Sudden rain catches me and I cinch
Like a ball of rubberbands, a noose thirsty

For air—then run, past an idle siren
Posing as a red vase: an empty vessel

Looking to transform whatever beauty.
It sees, in the skyline of my figure:

A smoking star; a token for what
Can bend or be taken, but breaks.

It determines, like a light turning green
That a wilderness   resides in me

ex-slave with long memory
after Dorothea Lange's

tunnels   under concrete
     bollworms lazing   in soil
pipes   guts and glaze
          of this beast—
     mine.   known   to wave
the long barrel   of an F
          for *Ef it*;
     it's all mine:
dirt   mucus   pavement
     spit: anything   i have
becomes silk   or bone—
     slay of the ax; air: mine
anything here   i want
          i loaned
     in the shed   of a house
          called roam:
     all these acres'   author
               i cannot
          be unknown.
     the sun: mime   bodies stacking:
          mine.   skeletons   over
     decomposed hearts   until the sky
          blackens—

Afua Hirsch

A writer, journalist and broadcaster, she was born in Norway, to a British father and a mother from Ghana, and was raised in Wimbledon, London. She studied Philosophy, Politics and Economics at Oxford University before going on to take a graduate degree in Law. She worked in international development in Senegal, practised law as a barrister in London, and was West Africa correspondent, based in Accra, Ghana, for The Guardian *newspaper, where she is now a columnist. She was the Social Affairs and Education Editor for Sky News from 2014 until 2017. She writes and makes documentaries around questions of race, identity and belonging—the subject of her 2018 book* Brit(ish).

What Does It Mean To Be African?

What does it mean to be African?

Some would define it, I think, as simply being someone who doesn't feel the need to ask that question. Isn't it a question only an outsider would ask? *What kind of black person*, I recalled being asked, in one of the lines in my book *Brit(ish)* that people seemed to find most entertaining, *writes a book about being black?*

I am a black person who writes a book about being black. I am an African who agonises over what it means to be African. I quote Kwame Nkrumah—who as president of Ghana led the first black African country to win independence—because he tells me what I want to hear: that I am African because I choose to be.

> I am not African because I was born in Africa, but because Africa was
> born in me.

I listen to Osagyefo Kwame Nkrumah—the title means *victorious in battle*—and I listen to all the sages. Maya Angelou told me it was a question of knowing your past:

> For Africa to me…is more than a glamorous fact. It is a historical truth.
> No man can know where he is going unless he knows exactly where he
> has been and exactly how he arrived at his present place.

Down the road from Wimbledon, the south-west London suburb where I grew up, the British-Trinidadian poet Roger Robinson said—writing in the heart of Britain's black community—it was a question of mental integrity, and purpose:

> People talk about toxic waste
> being dumped in Africa, but toxic
> waste has already been dumped
> in your minds. Some of you don't know

how you came to be in Brixton. Hell,
some of you don't know you're African.

(Roger Robinson, *The Butterfly Hotel*, Peepal Tree Press, 2013, p. 17)

But maybe the words that haunt me come from an earlier time. This exchange between expatriate American author Richard Wright and J.B. Danquah—one of the architects of Ghana's independence over decades of activism in the early twentieth century—is etched into my memory. They met during Wright's visit in 1953 to the then Gold Coast and Wright recounts in his book *Black Power* that Danquah starts by asking:

"How long have you been in Africa?"...
"About two months," I said.
"Stay longer and you'll *feel* your race," he told me.
"*What?*"
"You'll *feel* it," he assured me. "It'll all come *back* to you."
"What'll come back?"
"The knowledge of your race." He was explicit.
I liked the man, but not as a Negro or African; I liked his directness, his willingness to be open. Yet, I knew that I'd never feel an identification with Africans on a "racial" basis.
"I doubt that," I said softly.

(Wright, *Black Power*, 1954, pp. 218–19)

What does it mean to "feel" African?
That's not the same as what it means to "feel Africa". Tourists do that every day—exposing their senses to the immersive bath of sound, smell and energy, and finding it thrilling. *I just love Africa, it's SO colourful! The people are SO friendly! The bustle has SO much energy! The food is so spicy!...*

Everything my parents had to do required hard work: buying a house, raising money for school fees, creating the kind of home environment in which they thought—rightly—my sister and I would be able to experience joyful childhoods and emerge as functional, accomplished adults. My mother worked hard at everything, except sustaining an African identity, which seemed to require no effort at all. She has spent most of her life in a place that—as is the way of Britain—performs whiteness without knowing that whiteness is what it is. The leafy London suburb where I grew up is not multicultural like the rest of this great city of cultures, languages, cuisines and slangs; it is chronically preserved in a detached house, fruit-tree-populated lawn kind of Englishness, so attractive it has been commodified—in the guise of lawn tennis, and inflated property prices—and exported around the world. But my mother has navigated this locality, as is the way of her generation, surviving, without fussing or even vocalising the intensity of the experience, journeying silently to the nearest black place for hair products or fufu flour, fulfilling the functions of the eldest child in an Akan family, nursing herself on light soup when sick.

I don't think it occurred to either her or my father—who is British, and white—that Africanness was something that would be relevant to me. And so preserving for my generation a connection with our African heritage was not part of my parents' deliberate thinking. They were both secure in their own identities, which were cultural and national rather than racial. Identity was not the primary struggle of their lives—there were plenty of material things to worry about—and ours would take care of themselves.

But identities take on different strains when planted in new soil. It didn't occur to my parents that a mixed-heritage child, labelled casually as "black" by the loaded gaze of a white society, would crave substantial, positive messages about the source of her blackness. They did not know what it was like to be born and raised in a place where your identity is defined as a minority—by a sense of otherness and difference. They didn't foresee that beneath the blackness with which I was labelled, I—the second-generation, mixed-heritage, British girl—would feel my race. I was African. At least, that was my dream.

What did it mean to be African? Is it to bear a name?

Africans from the diaspora, reversing in the wake of the slave vessels by returning to the continent of their blackness, often find, when they land on African soil, that the first thing to do is to take a name. Some take on mine, if they were born on a Friday, as is the Akan way. Ghanaians often think, when I introduce myself by name, that I am African-American or Caribbean and have latterly chosen a new label for a newly African identity. *My name is Afua,* I say. *Oh! Are you sure?* they reply. *You know what that name means?* They school me. It's a lesson that causes me to wince. British people massacre my name. Ghanaians simply don't believe it is mine.

Is being African to live in Africa?

I thought it was. And I returned to the idea, like a creature bound by homing, that to heal one's identity was to journey to the place from which it springs. So one day, in my early thirties, bundling my then six-month-old daughter against the London snow, I packed up and moved to Ghana. My daughter would know this land first-hand, I decided, not as a narrative filtered through the British gaze, the still stale mess of a hopeless continent, ahistorical and doomed. She would, unlike me, understand the Ghanaian seasons and festivals, the pattern of a week where the emptied streets pour into churches on Sunday, where offices hum to the clash of local prints on Friday, where cryptic hand movements indicate the destination of a tro-tro bus, and where the fading of the light and the rising spice of kelewele frying fall with the rhythmic certainty of sunset. Maybe this would make *her* African, and—whatever happens to me—I will have given her that gift.

Is being African learning to speak?

Language gives structure to our thoughts, a fact not lost on the architects of the European imperial project of breaking the African spirit and disbanding the historic and cultural continuity of the peoples they overran. When I read of the short story by Ngũgĩ wa Thiong'o "The Upright Revolution: Or Why Humans Walk Upright", published in an unprecedented forty-seven African languages—a much needed attack on what Ngũgĩ describes as the problem of "intellectual production in Africa [being] done in European languages"—I applauded. Then realised that I, of course, would be reading it in English. And if the route to casting off the colonial legacy is embracing our African languages, where does that leave those of us—like me—who can't speak any? Learning to speak—and hence think—in a different way, may be the project of my whole lifetime.

My understanding of what it is to be African has been a process of elimination. I have been named in *Twi*, I have eaten light soup. I have worn kente and ankara, I have lived and worked across the African continent, I have studied languages, I have observed and repeated gestures, and intonations, rituals and gaits. I have done these things and they have shaped me. But if there is a tipping point at which the conditioning of this colonial power that raised me slips over into the African conditioning that I want to shape me, I don't know where it is.

The problem with the cultural delineations of what it means to be African is the temptation to fall into the trap created by the white gaze in which people like me have been immersed for most of our lives. Can we really escape the imperially stained nostalgia for the perceived Africa of the past—that loaded longing for a primordial world—that classic symptom of true outsider-ness? It is so tempting a tonic for those like me, who wish to connect with the Africa of their parents' memories, preserved as an antidote to an immigrant life in a hostile host nation, and who feel sentimental about the communal flow of life in the village where we have never actually lived. Our cousins who do live in the village are not romanticising ideas of "Africa". They are rooted in communities, regions and nations where the hustle is king—finding the power to charge their phones, struggling through school lessons taught by barely literate teachers, or trying to import Chinese fridges. They are urgently inventing the new.

No one is waiting, breath bated, for us to define what it means to be African. Yet still we continue to search for a reason to ask the question, for hope that an answer exists. And for a sense of purpose. "Africa," said John Henrik Clark, the Pan-African historian, "is our centre of gravity, our cultural and spiritual mother and father, our beating heart, no matter where we live on the face of this earth." Being African is to believe it. At least that's what being African means to me.

Naomi Jackson

Of West Indian parentage, she was born in Brooklyn and is a graduate of Williams College. She travelled on a Fulbright Scholarship to South Africa, receiving an MA in Creative Writing from the University of Cape Town, and subsequently studied fiction at the Iowa Writers' Workshop. Her debut novel, The Star Side of Bird Hill *(2015), was nominated for an NAACP Image Award and the Hurston/Wright Legacy Award, and longlisted for the National Book Critics Circle's John Leonard Prize, the Center for Fiction's First Novel Prize, and the International Dublin Literary Award. The Black Caucus of the American Library Association named it an Honor Book for Fiction. Her writing has appeared in* Tin House, Virginia Quarterly Review, Poets & Writers, The Caribbean Writer *and* Obsidian. *She is the recipient of residencies and fellowships from Bread Loaf, MacDowell Colony, Djerassi, Hedgebrook, the University of Pennsylvania's Kelly Writers House, Camargo Foundation, and the New York Foundation for the Arts.*

From *The Star Side of Bird Hill*

Dionne once had another idea entirely about how she would celebrate her sixteenth birthday. She and her best friend in Brooklyn, Taneisha, had their hearts set on a party hall on Church Avenue. Everybody was going to be there. Taneisha's Trinidadian cousins and uncles and sisters, their friends from school (mostly Taneisha's), and Darren, the boy that Dionne had been going with since he moved up from Jamaica three years before.

Dionne thought of Darren often in spite of herself, though she knew that attachment was the first step on the road to disappointment.

After her father left, Dionne witnessed a parade of men her mother entertained for as long as they would stick around. But while she could attract men, draw them into her web, Avril had trouble keeping them. In the last relationship, the one that ended the year before Dionne started high school, Dionne wanted to believe her mother's conviction that her boyfriend, Musa, would marry her. But something happened once her mother made her intentions for Musa clear, and every time he came over after that, he was always just about to leave again, as if her mother's desire for him had propelled him in the opposite direction. By his last visit, Musa wouldn't even take his coat off, just brought the books he'd promised to Phaedra and the *Vogue* fall fashion issue he'd promised to Dionne, kissed their mother, and left. Dionne had learned from her mother that if you wanted to keep a man, he should love you at least a little bit more than you loved him.

Avril's plan to send the girls back home for the summer, announced just one week before they left, had messed up everything—the party, working at V.I.M. to save up money for school clothes, Dionne's hopes of going into the city on Saturday nights with Darren and Taneisha and her girls. So, here she was in Bird Hill on her birthday, Saturday, July 16. And, as her grandmother Hyacinth would say, nothing at all go so. There would be no DJ making special shout-outs to the birthday girl, no adults hovering in the back alley smoking joints, drinking beer, squeezing past each other to heap their plates high with curry chicken and roti skins. No girls dancing front-to-front on boys, winding their waists as if their whole lives had made them move this way, talking afterwards about the boys whose dicks had gone hard, then soft on them.

Back in Brooklyn, the outfit that Dionne put on layaway—white jeans with a question mark in gold thread on the back pockets, a matching white top and jacket—still had $20 to go before it was paid off. Instead of wearing it, Dionne was sporting the new dress her grandmother made for her with "room to grow," a maritime number with a boat collar, white trim, and heavy navy fabric. Dionne thought that the dress was more fit for a box of powdered milk than a girl like her, with legs that started just below her neck, arms made for hanging on to boys rather than pounding nutmeg, and hands more fit for finger-snapping than housework of any kind.

Buller Man Jean was the one to whom most of the hill women turned to get their clothes sewn and, in a pinch, their hair done. He owed Dionne's grandmother a favor and so he gave Dionne a relaxer before the party that left her hair not quite straight. A night of sleeping in hard plastic rollers had given Dionne a neck ache and tight curls that didn't brush her shoulders the way she liked. But it would have to do. A lifetime of watching her mother closely had been nothing if not a tutorial in resignation and making do.

The party, if it was fair to call it that, was a joint one with Clotel Gumbs, a girl who wore glasses with lenses as thick as breadfruit skin, crinoline dresses that reached her ankles, and a mouth that seemed to open only to correct grammar or to quote Bible verses. Dionne thought Clotel rather unfortunate. And though in summers past the girls played together and ran as far as the hill women saw fit to let them, now it was clear that they had nothing in common besides a birthday. Where Clotel envisioned a life as a schoolteacher and homemaker, Dionne saw herself working in a fashion house on Fifth Avenue, selecting trends for the next fall collection. In Dionne's mind, her summer job selling sneakers and clothes at V.I.M. on Flatbush was a humble but legitimate step toward her career in fashion. Being stuck in Barbados, a place she might have described as sartorially challenged, was another step a world away from the life of glamour Dionne wanted for herself, a life full of style and free of the burdens of her mother's and sister's needs. These differences, simply matters of style when Dionne and Clotel were younger, were now big enough to constitute a wall neither of them could see over.

Both girls were new to the high heels that bore blisters into their feet. Dionne was painfully aware that she had finally turned sixteen, the age at which Avril said she could start wearing heels, and her mother wasn't there to see her wobbling or to show her how to walk in them. Dionne and Clotel shifted their weight as Father Loving said an interminable prayer, during which Dionne fluttered her eyes open to find the reverend wiping his brow and studying her breasts, which pressed insistently against her frock. After his incantations, Father Loving offered them each a new leather-bound King James Bible. Clotel seemed genuinely excited to accept her gift, while Dionne took hers reluctantly. She mumbled thanks to everyone for their gifts and kind words, all their variations on wishing her the best of life in Christ. Then she steeled her shoulders, readying herself for the inevitable conversations on one of two topics—books or baptism.

"So, now that you turn sixteen, are you going to give your life over to the Lord in service?" Mrs Jeremiah asked, her rheumy eyes taking Dionne in. She clutched Dionne's elbow between two firm fingers. The younger woman felt that Mrs Jeremiah's conviction about Christ could break bone.

"Yes, God willing," Dionne said. Her voice cracked. God's name felt like a word in a language she would never learn.

Dionne looked over the jaunty red feather in Mrs Jeremiah's hat and her gaze landed on her grandmother and Phaedra. She felt keenly the absence of her mother, who was in no small part responsible for her birthday turning out like this and should, she thought, at least be there to witness the disaster. The women kept bringing more and more food in aluminum pans out to the blue-flame burners. And Dionne kept expecting her mother to walk through the church hall's front door.

The people on the hill were Christians, and seriously so, but that didn't mean that they didn't like to have a good time. Lyrics such as "Get something and wave for the Lord" were made for Bird Hill, where any news was reason to have a party, and parties could start in the late afternoon and put the stars to bed the next morning. The Soul Train line sent women hobbling back to their seats with sweat on their brows and complaints on their lips about their old bones, the young children rubbing their eyes and seeking their mothers' laps.

Dionne and Trevor, who had been keeping each other at a respectful distance until then, came together in the back of the church hall, which doubled as a stage for the annual Passion play. They agreed to slip out separately and meet at their usual rendezvous location, star side. They'd named it that because of the way the moon and stars bathed the graves in the cemetery that sloped down behind the church in light, eliminating the need for flashlights that might lead prying eyes to their hiding place. "We'll call this our special place," Trevor whispered the night they named it, and Dionne, desperate for space that was not her sister's, not Avril's, not Hyacinth's, just hers, nodded, thinking he could give her what she needed.

It was hot outside, as if all the heat that had gathered during the day decided to stay the night. Sweat collected in Dionne's bosom, plastering her cotton bra to the top of her dress's wide collar. She'd worn the dress all evening with an air of self-sacrifice, but now, in the open air, she tugged at its buttons. She took a seat on Trevor's forebear's grave with the gift Bible tucked firmly beneath her, making a show of trying not to dirty her new clothes.

"You having fun yet?" Trevor asked.

"Define fun."

"C'mon, Dionne. You have to admit that seeing Sister B. do the pepper seed was fun."

"Yeah, I guess you're right." Dionne laughed. She remembered the old woman's shaking shoulders, the way that everyone was genuinely concerned about her teeth rattling out of her mouth.

"What do you think his life was like?" Dionne asked.

"Whose life?"

"His life. Trevor Cephus Loving. July 14, 1928–July 21, 1973."

"Probably the same as my father's. Baptisms, weddings, funerals. More food than you could ever eat in one lifetime."

"Same as yours? Do you want to be a reverend?"

"I guess I never thought I had a choice."

"Everything in life is a choice. It's not like you just wake up one day and suddenly you're Father Loving the third."

"Well, it's not like in the States, where you just decide what you're going to be and then you go to school and become that thing. Here on the hill, who you are is who your people have been. I was born the same day my grandfather died. Everyone said that was a sign I was coming back as him."

Dionne felt the door close on anything substantial between her and Trevor, but then also the urgency of their closeness in this moment. Dionne knew that any man whose life was already decided for him couldn't be hers. But here, where her spirit felt only halfway home, anchorless without Avril, she wanted something familiar to be close to, somewhere to land.

"Have you ever noticed that all these people died close to their birthdays? It's almost like the earth remembers them and knows it's their time."

"I don't know how your mind works, Dionne, but I like it. What would you do if you knew this was your last birthday?"

Dionne turned to Trevor and whispered in his ear something reserved for places outside polite company. Trevor was shocked that what he had been begging for all summer was finally being offered freely. He tried to stay cool. He placed a fiery hand on Dionne's thigh and did away with her blue panties with a deftness and care that indicated he knew that at any moment she could decide differently.

"Go slow," Dionne said, warning. She used her hands to guide him inside her.

Trevor made love to Dionne by moonlight, her bare feet planted on the crumbling gravestone while he entered her with sweetness she didn't know he could muster. Dionne remembered the roughness of Darren's hand inside her and braced herself for what Taneisha told her would feel like a pinch and then like the ocean opening inside her. She sighed, taking in the heat of him at her neck and the damp of the night air on them both.

When they were done, Dionne took her panties in one hand and her new Bible in the other and let the breeze when it came touch her where Trevor had before. She felt wiser somehow, and looking at the church lit up above, thought that maybe this kind of pleasure could be her religion.

Donika Kelly

An American poet, she is the author of the chapbook Aviarium *(2017), and the full-length collection* Bestiary *(2016), which won the Cave Canem Poetry Prize, a Hurston/Wright Award for poetry, and the Kate Tufts Discovery Award. A Cave Canem Graduate Fellow, she received her MFA in Writing from the Michener Center for Writers and a PhD in English from Vanderbilt University. Her poetry has appeared in journals including* Tin House, Indiana Review, Sinister Wisdom *and* Virginia Quarterly Review.

Sanctuary

The tide pool crumples like a woman
into the smallest version of herself,
bleeding onto whatever touches her.

The ocean, I mean, not a woman, filled
with plastic lace, and, closer to the vanishing point,
something brown breaks the surface—human,

maybe, a hand or foot or an island
of trash—but no, it's just a garden of kelp.
A wild life.

This is a prayer like the sea
urchin is a prayer, like the sea
star is a prayer, like the otter and cucumber—

as if I know what prayer means.

I call this the difficulty of the non-believer,
or, put another way, of waking, every morning, without a god.

How to understand, then, what deserves rescue
and what deserves to suffer.

Who.

Or should I say, what must
be sheltered and what abandoned.

Who.

I might ask you to imagine a young girl,
no older than ten but also no younger,
on a field trip to a rescue. *Can you*

see her? She is led to the gates that separate
the wounded sea lions from their home and the class.
How the girl wishes this measure of salvation for herself:

to claim her own barking voice, to revel
in her own scent and sleek brown body, her fingers
woven into the cyclone fence.

Where We End Up

Wonder why the grasshopper wells all point
east, heads dipped in sync at the rising sun.
Wonder too why we head west, what it means
to return home or someplace similar.
Probably don't mean much. There's only doing
and done and where we end up. So we keep
west until cliff and ocean, a seal dead
and bloating on the beach. I've been here before
and turned back. Then turned again to the same
place made different. Just another way of saying
this sand the same but smaller and more. This water
the same and new. This sun, the same one shine
here and wherever we used to call home.

Brood

My chest is earth

I meant to write *my chest is warm*
but *earth* will do
                    to exhume a heart

Beat

I meant to write
breathe

      Did you know I was alive the whole time

I was alive in the ground but torpor

    But torpor

Slowed beat

My chest filled like a jar with dirt

I mean
   dearth

For slow months at rest in the hole
I'd made in myself
     A frozen ground
A ground in thaw

I mean
     Spring is coming
I mean
   I push the wet dirt with my mandible
I mean *jaw*

  Jaw

     Y'all

I know I am not a nymph in exhumation

  but would you please explain
     this half-remembered light

Imbolo Mbue

Born in Limbe, Cameroon, she is a graduate of Rutgers and Columbia universities and currently lives in New York City. She is the author of the New York Times *bestseller* Behold the Dreamers *(2016), which won the PEN/Faulkner Award for Fiction, the Blue Metropolis Words to Change Award, and in 2017 was an Oprah's Book Club selection. The novel was named a Notable Book of the Year by the* New York Times *and the* Washington Post *and a Best Book of the Year by close to a dozen publications, has been translated into 12 languages, adapted into an opera, and is set to enjoy further life as a stage play and film.*

A Reversal

—When I die, do not take me back home, Papa said. I want you to bury me right here.

I sat up on my bed and rubbed my eyes, briefly looking at my phone.

—Papa, I whispered. What's going on? It's two o'clock in the morning.

—I needed you to know this right now, he said. I can't sleep. Whatever you do, do not take my body back to Cameroon.

I looked through the darkness of my bedroom, the light of a passing ambulance briefly illuminating it. I reached for the lamp but dropped my hand, deciding the darkness would be best for a conversation such as this.

—What did the doctor say at your check-up yesterday? I asked. Your blood-pressure medicine stopped working again?

—No, nothing like that. I'm fine. He says the way I'm going I may live to see the day when people go over to Mars just to have dinner.

I did not laugh. Neither did he, though he'd clearly made the joke for his own benefit.

—Papa, I have to be at work at 8 a.m., so please tell me right now why you're calling me in the middle of the night to give me this strange instruction.

He didn't immediately respond.

—Are you going to tell me now, or do you want me to drive to Brooklyn tomorrow…

He sighed.

—I just…

I continued waiting.

Why was he doing this to me, right now?

It had been a brute of a day at work. I needed my sleep, which had been slow in coming; my mind couldn't find rest, busy as it was ruminating on what a new client had said to me earlier in the day. The client had walked in, a man seemingly in his seventies, and the first thing he'd said to me, even before responding to my greeting, was where are you from?

—Where am I from? I said.

—Yes, yes, he'd replied, as if he needed the answer before we could proceed with his reason for coming to see me.

Take a deep breath, I told myself. A good long breath. That's right; take another one.

—I'm actually curious myself, I said to the man, smiling; where are you from? You have such a distinct, regal face.

He chuckled.

—As a matter of fact, he said, adjusting himself in his chair across from me at my desk, I'm from here.

—Me, too, I said smiling.

—Of course you are; you mean you were born here?

I nodded.

—And your people, where are they from?

—My people?

—Yes, your parents.

—Aren't we all from the same place, I said, still smiling. You, me, everyone in this country, everyone around the world, aren't we all from the same place?

He hadn't replied; he'd merely given me a look that suggested I was nowhere as intelligent as I thought I was. I realized then that I was never going to have him as a client. Our meeting hadn't gone long before his phone rang and he said he needed to leave. What was I to do? Let him tell me where I was from? For the sake of a commission? If Papa were sitting in my place, Papa would have told this man all about his ancestral village in Cameroon, the place he knew he was from. He would have told this man about his ancestors whose blood flowed in his veins. He would have spoken about the music of his people, and their food, and the dresses the women wore for celebrations. I'd never been able to claim any of that the same way.

—Papa, I said, you were right when you told us that this country would never be your country.

—It'll never be mine, he said, but it's yours. You have every right to it.

—I'm sorry, Papa. I'm tired, I'm confused; this conversation is going in a very strange direction. What is it you want? This is not your country, but you want to be buried here?

—I want to remain here with you and your sister. I have nothing left for me in Cameroon.

—There's nothing left for any of us in Cameroon, Papa. Except Mama's grave. And the graves of Mammi and Big Papa. Are you telling me you do not want to be buried next to them?

—Please do not try to shame me. I do not need any of that.

—I'm not trying to shame you! When Mama died we travelled for three days and drove on that horrible road so we could bury her in the village of your birth. And I'll do the same for you, because if there's one thing you've told me over and over it's that a man should be buried in his village, among his people—

—I go to your mother's grave every night. I sit there and tell her goodnight before I close my eyes. Every single night I do that.

He sniffed, and for a few seconds he said nothing.

I remained silent too, imagining him sitting alone on his bed, lights turned off, talking to the air, hoping that somehow his words would fly over bodies of water and hills and plains and valleys and arrive at Mama's grave. None of us had been to the grave since we buried her ten years ago. None of us had visited Cameroon since then.

—I promise you, Papa, I'll take you back home and bury you right next to Mama. If you're saying this to me because you don't want me to go through all this for you—

—I'm saying it because it's what I want. I want you to bury me right here in Brooklyn.

—You're telling me you want to be buried next to strangers when there's a place all set for you right between your wife and your mother?

—Yes, I'm telling you that you and your sister are all I have left. And until the day you both get married and have children, and even after then, I don't want you to be without me. Your mother is all the way in the village. I don't want to leave you here by yourselves, in another man's country.

Nadifa Mohamed

Born in Somalia, she studied history and politics at St Hilda's College, Oxford University. Her first novel, Black Mamba Boy *(2010), won the Betty Trask Prize, was longlisted for the Orange Prize, and shortlisted for* The Guardian First Book Award, *the John Llewellyn Rhys Prize, the Dylan Thomas Prize, and the PEN Open Book Award. In 2013 she was chosen as one of* Granta's Best of Young British Novelists *and in 2014 was on the Africa 39 list of significant African writers aged under 40. Her second novel,* The Orchard of Lost Souls *(2013), won a Somerset Maugham Prize and the Prix Albert Bernard, was longlisted for the Dylan Thomas Prize, and shortlisted for the Hurston/Wright Legacy Award. She contributed to the anthology* Reader, I Married Him *(2016, celebrating the bicentenary of Charlotte Brontë's birth), and writes regularly for* The Guardian, *the* New York Times, Lithub, *and* Freeman's. *In 2018 she was elected to the Royal Society of Literature and was awarded a Literary Arts Fellowship by the Rockefeller Foundation. Here she makes a rare outing as a poet.*

A lime jewel

A little girl,
a gold-wrapped
bonbon damp in
her cherry-skinned fist,
the mellow swirl
of another, whirling
in her mouth.
Lime.
Mango.
Banana.
Papaya.
The fruit of
the black soil
caught in a jewel of sugar.

Beneath her powdered feet,
rubble,
beneath the rubble,
pitted tarmac,
asleep beneath the tarmac,
black Jacobins.

She sucks,
They dream,
She appraises,
They dream,
She weeps,
They dream.

She tints the world with the lime of her bonbon.
Bitter. Sweet.
Wasteland melting into dreamland,
Cold, crystalline and curiously lit.

The light of Haiti,
once filtered
by palm fronds,
then cutlassed
by cane,
is now caught tight
in a lime jewel.

A symphony of blood
gushes in her,
her skin is the shroud
of saints,
dreams are breathed out of the earth,
and into her,
Cold, crystalline and curiously lit.

The symphony

You: Will you forget me?
Me: I will never forget you.
You: Do you remember the sweetness of my milk?
Me: Like the taste of my blood.
You: Can you feel the nape of my neck?
Me: It is hot to the touch.
You: Do you remember my eyes?
Me: I see the world through them.
You: You carry my soul.
Me: It is a burden.
You: Cast it off.
Me: Then I will be free, lost, unmoored.
You: Sing to raise the dead and give life to the living. *Nufyahay orodoo arligi
     qaboo, halkii aad ku ogeyd ka soo eeg.*
Me: I have lost your language.
You: It is in your footsteps, in the click of your fingers, in your howl of pain.
Me: I can howl no more.
You: Then sing.

Natalia Molebatsi

*Born in the township of Tembisa, near Johannesburg in South Africa, she is a poet,
singer and cultural worker. She is the editor of* We Are: A Poetry Anthology *(2008),
and author of* Sardo Dance *(2009) and* Elephant Woman Song *(2017). Her poetry
and music CDs include* Natalia Molebatsi & the Soul Making *and* Come as You Are:
Poems for Four Strings. *Her academic writing is included in, among other journals,*
Scrutiny2, Rhodes Journalism Review *and* Muziki.

a mending season

for miriam tlali
11.11.33—24.02.17

you are a song
singing in the deepest
voice of my people

a lullaby cusping tears
an amandla song
to every child of the storm

someone said that you
are the wind beneath
the broken wing of my people

another one said
that women like you
are the mending season of our aching

women like you give and give and give
their last breath to ignite fires called revolution
even when they force-fed you the rules of silence

you fought for your story to be told
in the season of your voice and inside your body
reside the melodies of your people

you with an uncontainable wail
that grew louder and larger
than the tight grip of oppression

with words that forced open
the doors of a world that was never
and will never be ready for our kind

it's time now for moon to night you
with your secret conversations
and moments of endearment

the same moon that will welcome you
on an orbit of black magic
woman wonderments

you will let this world know
that you loved her more
than she loved you

how do i thank you for your pain?
your banned and jailed
and unacknowledged dreams?

Your dreams are gifts to my bag of memories
through which i will craft songs
for tomorrow's healing

the healer
for sibongile khumalo and the song inside her voice

when the world burns she is cooling water
a breath of life and light this woman
a gift from her people to ours
when the cows are crying
and the children
and the dogs too
i close my eyes
to see her sound move
an entire world of oceans and bones
an affirmation that god lives here
in undertones and vibrations
wiping the heavy tears of this earth
the gods live here
inside the vein of this music

Melody
for fatima meer
12.08.28—12.03.10

there are memories of love and struggle
falling and flying off silent walls
you lifted silent things into screams
made them remember
marked them in place
as reference as lineage
hid colour and brush

in spaces of private touch and longing
rolled them up and smuggled them
in and out of bodies
these words are just a pact
to evoke your name and spirit
as a work of an open heart
another way of recollecting you
as a melody and a story of ours

Aja Monet

An internationally established American poet of Cuban-Jamaican descent, she was the youngest individual to win the legendary Nuyorican Poet's Café Grand Slam title, recognised for combining her spellbinding voice and powerful imagery on stage. She was a featured speaker at the Women's March on Washington, DC, in 2017 where she read the title poem of her book My Mother Was A Freedom Fighter. *In 2018, the book was nominated for an NAACP Image Award for Outstanding Literary Work-Poetry. Her other collections include* Inner-City Chants & Cyborg Cyphers *(2015),* The Black Unicorn Sings *(2015), and a collaboration with poet/musician Saul Williams,* Chorus: a literary mixtape. *She currently lives in Little Haiti, Miami where she is co-founder of Smoke Signals Studio and dedicates her time to merging arts and culture with community organising through her work with the Dream Defenders and the Community Justice Project.*

hexes

and there was a reckoning
for all the harm
and for all the evil eyes
and our strength was cute until it wasn't
and we were weak until we weren't
and your longing will be long
and your days will be numbered
and we are counting
on the stems who had their petals taken
in this spell for flowers
on the busted lips
and bruised cheeks

and there was loss
and our smiles will terrify you
because we will be laughing
and we will be cruel
and there will be no remorse
and your children will be ours
and we will make new ways without you
and you will miss who you could've been
admit you were never intent on loving
anyone but yourself
and sacrifice is the ego's kryptonite
and your heart is a tomb
mummified corpses
where we, are only body parts
and the thighs will haunt you
and the breasts will mock you
and the asses will shit wherever you lay
and the fists will find you
on street corners, in the alleys
or offices
in a titty bar or atop a lover
or below one
erotic and afraid
every where there will be a fist
and your knees will buckle
and there was a curse
some manner of sorcery
stanzas upon stanzas of stories
and we will feed you morsels
of your own medicine
pages and pages of feeds
and the pharmaceutical industry will go broke
and the doctors will all become witches
enter the roots of plants, sayings, and sorts of rituals
and banks will go bankrupt
values of play, a fair negotiation between gifts
and land will be unowned
where the mountains meet man
and hurricanes demolish your safety
and police will wither in confinement
with no commissary, mad sirens looped
fidgeting in the corridors of time

and developers will lose their hair and teeth
and supreme court will drown in menstrual blood
pages and pages of blood
and we are the book of revelations
and the end is near.
and this is where you pray
and this is where your god doesn't answer
and this god don't take bribes
unless
of course you repent
except repenting doesn't reverse nature
it cleanses
and only love
only love
only
love will get you through.

what riots true

if we don't talk about the moments
we fought back
the efforts to resist,
we will forever go down in history
as being complacent with our oppression
and therein complicit in the oppression of others

tell the stories of those who fought back and why
what compels a person
to anger
to radical love
they'll tell you militancy is
a story of soldiers intended to kill
and not of lovers intent on living
nor of the grass that uproots concrete pavement,
or storms that cleanse land
nature is militant toward survival.

we are taught a history of misconceptions
distorted partial truths
indifference is a deafening death
the scripts we live by animate us
with meaning, we argue from dawn to sunset

but if we are not united, we will be enemies tomorrow
if we do not have food we cannot think
full bellies let us reason
with nuance
hunger is a person not full
half empty people obey any hand that feeds them
do not argue with hunger
unless
you are prepared
to have your hand bitten off.

depressed as you may be
this too shall pass
everybody is mourning
its not just the family
no one owns the pain
everyone is terrorized
let go of yourself
you can only move as fast as you will
even the best of us is no better than the worse
once a word is spoken you cannot take it back

there's no such things as those children
its our children or its no children
when young people can't vote,
their political voice is protest
it's much easier to organize a rebellion
when all the tanks are pointed at the same place
then your identity is who am i
what kind of person will i become
it didn't occur to us that you can come back from a beating
until fannie lou

hypocrisy makes people happy
and truth makes them sad
compassion hushes wrath
a generation destroyed by facebook
the human face is undecipherable
and they can't read anything that doesn't look
like them
everyone can hear your thoughts before you think them
we quarrel with self
conversations are quiet mediations

poems wrinkled by loneliness
google maps the heart
passion is a prison of surveillance
emotions are actionless
and actions are emotionless

people expect comfort
more than freedom
and individualism becomes self-care
but the women are freeing their nipples
true or false

Glaydah Namukasa

Born in Uganda, she is a community psychologist, midwife and a writer: the author of one novel, The Deadly Ambition *(2006), and a young adult novella,* Voice of a Dream *(2006), which was awarded the Macmillan Writers Prize for Africa in 2006. Her short stories have been published in Uganda, South Africa, the UK, the US and Sweden. She is a recipient of the Rockefeller Foundation Bellagio Center residency in 2013, Mike and Marylee Fairbanks Fellowship in 2006, and in 2008 was awarded the title of Honorary Fellow by the International Writing Program, University of Iowa. In 2014 she was selected on the Hay Festival Africa39 list. In 2018 she received the URSB award for Ugandan Women in Literary Creativity. She has completed her third novel.*

The last time I played Mirundi

"Look Babirye, you have it between your legs," my twin brother Kato says and laughs.

I laugh too because one, Kato has a laugh which makes you laugh when you see it. Kato's laugh is like this: his upper lip goes up into his nose and his red red gum comes out and smiles. Two, I laugh because I think Kato is talking about the ball; our new jesa-milk-kaveera-ball. The bouncing ball we made for our Mirundi Ball Competition.

I am seated on the ball, holding up my pink tantantala dress. I want to test if the ball is very strong. Also to test if it can burst. We used only four layers of jesa-milk-kaveera and rubber-strings. Kato blew into the jesa-milk-kaveera until it became swollen and the blue words Full Cream Milk faded. Then he held the tip and I tied it with a small rubber string so that air wouldn't escape. The ball bounces better when the tube is blown to full. Then we wrapped the swollen jesa-milk-kaveera with four layers of buveera and rubber strings.

The ball is very strong. The ball can bounce.

Today is our Mirundi competition at Kadopado. Kato organized the competition for today because Jjaja will not be home the whole day. She will be at church listening to the Easter Carols. Kato organizes everything because he speaks well. I don't speak well. I stammer, and children say that I bark my words. But I don't bark all the words, no. I only bark the first letter of the first word when I speak. I don't talk much, but I do things better than many children. I am the best Mirundi baller in Bajjo but Kityo and Kalema and Apio say that Kityo is the Mirundi champion. Kityo says how can a girl be good with the ball? No girl in the world can beat him in the Mirundi game.

We play Mirundi all the time and each time I win. I can do fifty knees without resting, twenty feet without resting, ten heads without resting; I can do ninety knee-feet-head Mirundi without dropping the ball on the ground.

"Babirye you have fire between your legs!" Kato says.

I jump up like this and kick the ball at him but the ball goes up in the air, and I fall on my back, and my legs go up and my tantantala dress flies over my face. I wanted the ball to hit Kato and bounce off his head.

Why does Kato tell me that? For me I don't tell him those things which Jjaja told us. Jjaja told Kato to never play with girls because they have fire between their legs. And Jjaja told me to never play with boys because they have snakes between their legs. I told Kato that Jjaja doesn't know because she is very old. I told him that girls have girl private parts between their legs, not fire. Even boys have boy private parts not snakes.

I pull the dress away from my head and I see Kato with a face. Kato starts, taking the direction that takes you back to church. I think Kato has taken the path which branches off from the church maize garden to Kadopado field so that he will get there before me. I jump up, pick up the ball from the buyukiyuki where it fell and I run forward. This road passes our school, Mount Rahel's Junior School, and goes to Kadopado.

I get to Kadopado before Kato and find Lule, Kawuki, Tom, Kalema, Namu, Jjuko, Kityo, Tina and Naka doing Mirundi with a fibre ball. I stand behind the anthill where Kato and I hide to watch football when we are coming from school. I knee the ball, and then kick it and it hits Naka's back. It bounces off, and Lule gets it before it touches the ground. He starts: knee knee knee, foot foot foot foot, head head, knee knee knee. I come out from the anthill. Only Naka sees me. The others are counting Lule's Mirundi. I count, too. Twenty knees, twenty feet, five heads; the ball falls.

I foot the ball and make it fall in my hands.

"Ref is where?" Apio says.

"I I I don't know," I say. Now I don't want Kato to be the referee because he said bad things to me. I tuck my tantantala dress into my knickers and I start. I want to show them Mirundi before the competition starts for real. Knee, knee, knee, knee. Foot, foot, foot. Head. Knee…

"Look, Babirye, you have blood on your leg," Kawuki says.

I continue to knee up to fifty Mirundi because Lule did forty-five. I want to be the one on top. Then I let the ball fall. Kityo takes it. I start counting Kityo's Mirundi. I walk backwards to the anthill, counting. I pluck Kawunyira leaves, counting, I clean the blood off my thigh, counting. Everyone is counting. I hurry back to the game, counting. Sixty knee-feet-head. He drops the ball and I pick it.

"We wait for Kato," Apio says.

I start. I want to do seventy, because Kityo did sixty.

"But you Babirye what happened to you? You have blood on your legs," Apio says.

"Ayaa, even on her knickers. She did things of stupid with boys," Kalema says.

I knee the ball and make it fall in my hands. I throw it at Kalema. Kalema dodges it and it goes down the field. He laughs. Apio, Kityo and Tom run after the ball. Everyone laughs.

I run back behind the anthill.

On my left leg there are two blood strings. They are like small red snakes, crawling down to my foot. I pluck more Kawunyira leaves and clean my leg. There is some blood on my dress too. I bend like this to see where the blood is coming from. The middle part of my pink knickers is red red like Kato's gum. My heart starts. It beats faster than how I do rapid knees when I am playing Mirundi. I race back home. I want to hide in my bedroom and check if the blood is coming from my chuchu.

I hurry behind the kitchen to pick the key but I see that the door is open. I am afraid that Jjaja has come back home. Jjaja will see the blood and think that I have done bad things with boys. I hide and wait. I don't see Jjaja, I don't see Kato. I go quick like a lizard to the house, to my bedroom.

I stand behind the door and remove my knickers, and then I use them to clean my thighs. I touch my chuchu to check if I will feel pain, like the pain of a wound. No pain. Blood is just coming from my chuchu, I don't know why. Every day I play Mirundi but blood doesn't come.

I take off the tantantala dress, put the knickers inside it and I hide it under my mattress. Then I pick my purple-black dress from my suitcase, and I put it on. It is the ugliest of the clothes mummy sent me on my ninth birthday last week. But Jjaja says whatever mummy sends us is beautiful because she works so hard to send us money and things. I chose this dress because when blood goes on it it will not show like how the tantantala dress showed.

I get into bed and cry for mummy. I want her to come today and take us with her to America.

I hear Kato's voice saying, "Babirye where are you? Are you in the house Babirye?" He comes to my bedroom like someone has told him I am there. He pulls the blanket off my head and chest. I pull them back and cover my head again. "G G Go away," I say. "Y Y You left me alone at Kadopado."

"Just I saw blood on your knickers and I was afraid. Even I went to call Jjaja but I didn't see her because there were very many people at church."

Kato wants to cry.

"G G Go away."

"Naka is there outside. She said that Kalema said you did things of stupid with the boys." Kato's voice is crying.

"I I I didn't. J J Just I was playing Mirundi!"

Something moves in my stomach like a ball. It starts from the left side and crosses to the right side. Then it stays there and it pains me. My stomach is like it is going to burst. I turn and lie like a frog and press the ball with my hands.

Kato stays and cries for me. I don't want him to cry for me because Jjaja says when you cry for someone who is sick you can bewitch them and they die.

I press the ball very hard and the pain goes.

I uncover my head to see Kato. His face is like a fibre ball. His eyes are swollen, his nose is wet with mucus, and his cheeks are swollen. I think my face is a fibre ball too, because I have also been crying.

"I I I am not sick. J J Just the stomach was paining me but now it has stopped."

"Why did you have blood on your knickers?"

"L L Leave me alone."

Kato cleans the tears on his cheeks with his palm. Then he blows his nose in his shirt. He says, "Babirye, are you sick?"

"D D Don't tell Jjaja that you saw blood on my knickers."

Kato doesn't want to leave me alone. He goes and comes back with the food flask where Jjaja left our lunch and I tell him I don't want to eat now. He goes again and comes back and says he's going back to church to call Jjaja. I tell him don't tell Jjaja that there was blood on my knickers.

Jjaja enters the house singing azukidde tali muno yesu azukidde…

"Balongo bange? Balongo bange muliwa?" Jjaja says.

I hear more noises and I know that Jjaja is talking to Kato. I throw the covers off my head and pull out the tantantala dress from under the mattress. I use it to clean the blood from my chuchu, and on my thighs. Then I fold it and put it back under the mattress. I cover my head again and press my thighs very very hard so that blood will stop coming.

"Mulongo wange kiki ate?" Jjaja says. She has entered my bedroom.

I don't want to cry because Jjaja will think that I am sick.

"Bikira Maria Nyabo, Kiki kino?"

"Jjaja her stomach was paining her," Kato says. His voice is coming from the doorway.

I uncover my head.

Jjaja has my blood-pink knickers in her hand. She walks to the door and tells Kato to move away, and then she closes the door.

"I I I didn't do bad things with boys, Jjaja. B B B blood just came when we were coming from church," I say. "I I It's not stopping."

Jjaja throws the knickers down and she pulls away my blanket, saying, "Mulongo wange abadde ki?" She lifts my dress and then covers me again. She stands there, her face doing things: her eyes look from side to side, up and down; her lips knock onto each other. She starts counting on her fingers, one, two, three … she counts up to nine.

I cry because Jjaja's face is sad.

Jjaja sits on my bed. She lifts up my head and rests it on her lap. Then she moves her hand over my back, saying baasi baasi baasi.

When Mummy brought us to live with Jjaja, we were four years old and whenever we cried for Mummy, Jjaja put our heads on her lap, Kato on the left, me on the right side and then said, baasi baasi baasi.

The words mean that everything will be all right.

Selina Nwulu

A London-based writer, poet and essayist, she was Young Poet Laureate for London 2015–16, a prestigious award that recognises talent and potential in the capital. She writes for a number of outlets, among them The Guardian, New Humanist *and* Red Pepper, *and has toured her work in the UK and internationally. She has also been featured in* Vogue, ES Magazine, i-D *and* Blavity *among others. Her first chapbook collection,* The Secrets I Let Slip *(2015), was a Poetry Book Society recommendation. In 2018 she created a poetry series, in connection with the Wellcome Trust, called* "Who's Full?" *which looks at food justice and health.*

The Audacity of Our Skin

I

What does it matter?

> *…you don't worry about dirt in the garden because it belongs in the garden, but the moment you see dirt in the bedroom you have to do something about it because it symbolically doesn't belong there. And what you do with dirt in the bedroom is to cleanse it, you sweep it out, you restore order, you police boundaries, you know the hard and fast boundaries around what belongs and what doesn't. Inside/Outside. Cultured/Uncivilised. Barbarous/Cultivated, and so on.*
>
> —Stuart Hall discussing anthropologist Mary Douglas and her "matter out of place" theory[1]

1 www.mediaed.org/transcripts/Stuart-Hall-Race-the-Floating-Signifier-Transcript.pdf

I remember an empty seat next to me on a crowded train, my breath a plague. I remember walking easy in a quaint French village before being interrupted by the wrinkled nose of a passerby; *tu viens d'où, alors?* reminding me that foreign follows me like an old cloak lugging around my neck. I remember the breeze in Kerry's voice telling me, *I don't like the really dark black people, but you're alright*, the way horror grew in my chest like ivy that day (its leaves have still not withered). I remember Year 6, the way my teacher shuddered at a picture of my profile. How I first understood revulsion without knowing its name, tucking my lips into themselves to make them smaller, if only for a little while. I remember the pointing, questions of whether I could read whilst holding a book, being looked at too intently to be thought beautiful but blushing all the same. I think this is a love, but the kind we have been warned to run from. It owns a gun, yet will not speak of its terror; obsessive in every curl of my hair, the bloom of my nose, the peaks and troughs of my breath. I'd tell you who I am, but you do not ask for my voice. You've already made up your mind, haven't you?

II

Hostile, a definition:

Bitter; Windrush citizen: here until your skin is no longer needed
Cold; migrants sleeping rough will be deported
Militant; charter flights, expulsion as a brutal secret in handcuffs
Unwilling; women charged for giving birth after the trafficking, after the rape
Malicious; Yarl's Wood is locking away too many hearts, will not let them heal
Warlike; landlords, doctors, teachers conscripted for border control
Argumentative; hard Brexit, soft Brexit, Brexit means Brexit
Standoffish; do not fall in love with the wrong passport
Resentful; black and brown forced to prove their right to free health care
Unwelcoming; the number of refugees dying to reach you
Afraid;
Afraid;
Afraid;

* * *

how long must we make a case for migration? recount the times it has carried this country on its back so this nation could bask in the glory of its so called greatness? how loud should we chant our stories of beauty of struggle of grit? write all the ways we are lovely and useful across our faces before we become a hymn sheet singing of desperation? what time left to find a favourite café and a hand to hold? to lie on the grass in the park and spot clouds whose shapes remind us of the things we've lost? the souvenirs we can't get back?

III

Who are we to one another: a dirty secret

Here's the thing we forget as we age: we're not so different. Yes, there are some people whose clothes will never start a riot, those who will never know the grief of having a face made synonymous with a thug (the trauma of this deserves its own word). It is true that the things we experience are wrapped up in the life we are given. But when it comes to who we are, down to our most intimate core, aren't we all just a bit lonely, a little scared? Asking questions no one truly has answers for?

Consider this; many of us did not want to get up this morning, some of us couldn't. There is that dazed place we all inhabit seconds before fully waking that has no border, needs no passport. When the temperature drops to a chill, a body becomes its own shelter, shoulders round into a cave protecting itself. Some of our worst fears will come true, others won't. We are all still chewing on words we wish we'd said to someone, somewhere, and longing to swallow back the ones we've said in temper. A first love will make our bodies speak languages we didn't know we were fluent in and we all carry the heaviness of loss. How did we forget that we're all deeply connected on some level? Revealed only in moments like when a stranger falls ill in public; the way most of us will flock to help them, to remember ourselves.

Every day my computer scrolls through a news feed of angry people drunk on their ability to put others back in their place. There is a growing army of the righteous who tell us that there is a correct language to speak, an exact way to love, one acceptable altar to pray on. I watch a video of a man on the top deck of a bus screaming at another with a boiled kettle rage. He is all fist, spit in your face, *my-granddad-didn't-win-the-war-so-your-kind-could-piss-it-all-away*. I'm not sure it matters who the person on the receiving end of this rage is. In the video he is a chilling quiet, the kind many people of colour will recognise. It is a calculated silence, the kind where you are bargaining for your survival (and this too needs its own word). It does not matter whether he has a job he works hard at, the taxes he does or does not pay, if he tips generously, whether he is kind. That's the point, isn't it? Racism does not look for nuance, only the audacity of our skin. I wonder if with a different lens these two could be lovers, could be sitting next to each other as strangers on the same top deck. They'd realise they were listening to the same music and how this one track makes them each feel a particular kind of giddy as the bass drops, how as the bus jolts a headphone would fall from each ear and they would turn to look at each other and they would smile.

IV

What words have been left for us?

Words tell lies. This is difficult pill to swallow for a writer, but it is true, I think. We've inherited childish terms that shape the way we interact with one another. The words black and white are at their heart nonsensical, artificially packed with history and, all too often, too much meaning. And yet, still, these labels are seared onto our backs. You'll find this no better than in the language of terrorism, filled with a cruel rage reserved for people of colour, with the more noble and redemptive words, such as lone wolf and misunderstood, for white acts of violence. How we ourselves are living in a language that equates our colour to a shipwreck where all hope is lost. It is, after all, *a dark time*. Blackness, with all its pain and apparent innate knowledge of rap and knife crime and squalor embedded under its skin, stands with its back to whiteness, which in turn, knows fresh air and the best schools to get into. How boring this, but these terms of reference are as scorched in our minds as a national anthem. How then, should we come to understand ourselves with the language we've been given? To find meaning and truth in words that are the scraps of the dictionary?

* * *

Give us back our tongues and we'll give you an answer. It may not be a sound you'll recognise but it will be ours, all ours.

Half-Written Love Letter

I often imagine my parents came here
after hearing the sea of the British isles.
As if they put their ears to its shell
and the waves threw themselves tipsy
against conch, willing them to come over.

Then there were the things
we understood without words;

how sun in these parts is a slow swell,
the coastal path walks of Dundee,
graffiti hieroglyphics, damp shoes
against Sheffield cobbles and
the tastebud clench of a tart apple.

We learnt this country fiercely;
my father felt its knuckles crush his jaw
my mother delivered its children,
I have been kissed deeply by its tongue
it has licked Yorkshire on my vowels, left me
with the blushed cheeks of a first crush.

I am a half-written love letter
it does not know where to send.

So when go home
becomes a neighbourhood war cry,
we understand we are not what you wanted,
have been clean written out of your folklores.
But we have built here, loved here, died here,
already carry the heartache of leaving.
When we go home, we go back reeking of you.

Trifonia Melibea Obono

translated by Lawrence Schimel

An Equatorial Guinean writer and activist, she is the author of three novels in Spanish—Herencia del bindendee *(2016),* La Bastarda *(2016), and* La albina del dinero—*and a short story collection,* Las mujeres hablan mucho y mal, *which won the 2018 Justo Bolekia Boleká international Prize for African Literature.* La Bastarda, *translated into English by Lawrence Schimel, was published by the Feminist Press in the USA and Modjaji Books in South Africa. It is the first book by a woman writer from Equatorial Guinea to be published in translation in English.*

Let the Nkúkúmá Speak

The House of the Word is full of men: all arranged beside the nkúkúmá. Outside are the women, some seated on the ground, others on small seats brought from their homes.

"Something has changed in the village," people's gazes say, and the nkúkúmá, the chief of the tribe and the village, must make a declaration.

Adá committed suicide five days ago. The daughter of the nkúkúmá. Tradition is being questioned by the leader's own grandson, who lodged a suit against his mother's widow and his own grandfather.

The village is also waiting for the highest authority to reach a decision about a suit lodged against his first cousin Alogo to recover his brother's inheritance: the wife he left pregnant and the two girls she gave birth to.

The nkúkúmá is nervous. All the elders expect him to uphold the customs; like the political parties, they feel that traditional institutions must be conserved at any cost for the good of society. Alongside the elders of the village, are some of the youths: girls and boys who are barely in their thirties who sympathize with his grandson and demand justice. There are also some women, seated on the outskirts of this political institution, the House of the Word, who murmur that enough is enough, they want freedom. But they speak in low voices.

One voice comes from inside the House of the Word: "You should be in the kitchen, Women!"

At last the nkúkúmá reacts. He is wrapped in a popó outfit on which can be seen the image of the chief of state holding a torch with his right hand. He postpones for later the case of Adá's suicide and calls for the claimant against his cousin Alogo to state his case, who in turn summons his sister, eight months pregnant and seated with the women outside. Both of them sit on chairs made of melongo wood in front of the nkúkúmá, who asks if the matter cannot be resolved within the family.

"No and no," the plaintiff rejects, crossing his arm. "If you don't want to resolve the problem, give me back the money of the suit. I am in charge of two things and only one of them can be mine. As a Fang man, member of an honorable tribe that follows tradition, I demand that my brother-in-law comes to recover either on the one hand, my sister, her two daughters and the pregnancy, or the dowry on the other."

Outside, the women murmur about whether a person can be called a thing. The plaintiff continues his demand.

"Your cousin's brother died eight months ago in a traffic accident and nobody has come to recover the inheritance or the dowry. As far as I know, you are the only male remaining in the family."

The defendant takes the word and offers a motive: the woman rejected him as a man.

There is an enormous ruckus inside the House of the Word.

The men demand the woman opens her legs and follows tradition. The women outside slowly divide into two groups. Some support the men's version and others reject it. The nkúkúmá orders everyone to be quiet and offers the word to the widow, a shy woman who places her arms over her swollen belly.

"Finally, I am given the chance to speak. The protagonist of this case is me. Shouldn't I be the first to speak?"

The protest from the nkúkúmá is immediate, "You, no; your brother, yes. He had to speak before you, because he is your brother."

"So what? Am I a child? I am thirty-five years old, I work, I have a university degree, two daughters, a house in the city. I am not a child!"

"You are not a child. You are a Fang woman."

"And…?"

"Don't be a fool and don't make me waste my time."

"I am not a fool and…how am I making you waste your time. Are you not the representative of the entire village? Do women not form part of the village? If my brother wants me to disappear from the house of our parents let him say so here and now for everyone to hear. He is in charge of two things? I live by my own efforts and work, he doesn't feed me. And, by the way, I am a person, not a thing. For seven years, I was living with a man who unfortunately died. I loved my husband. If your brother now wants to take his place in my heart, something that seems impossible to me, let him conquer me. He only comes to my house at night because he wants sex. He says I'm obligated to copulate with him. Copulate with you? Not even if I were dead."

Angry, the nkúkúmá issues his sentence. He decides that the woman, as tradition mandates, is obliged to spread her legs accepting her brother-in-law as her husband or, alternatively, any other man of the tribe of the deceased, and if she is not in agreement, for her to return the dowry and the two girls of two and four years, when they've turned seven.

The woman's brother celebrates the sentence and when he gets up he gets a long applause from the members of his tribe and from the elders. His sister gets up and leaves crying, with the two girls, and from behind her back she receives jeering and a justification from her brother, "I'm just following tradition. It is my duty to respect and uphold the traditional institutions. I have the backing of the political parties. Maybe I'll be offered a position."

Silence spreads throughout the assembled group. Now it is the turn of Nsí, a young man of twenty-two years, grandson of the nkúkúmá and despised by the elders of the village. "He doesn't respect tradition," they hiss. He doesn't even wait for his grandfather to invite him to state his case. Directly he asks him if, when he applies and conserves the traditional institutions, he remembers that his mother was a woman, his wife is a woman, that he has three daughters and female friends, and that one of his daughters committed suicide a few days ago because of tradition.

The nkúkúmá falls silent and lets some teardrops fall. An elder calls him *obono fam*[1] for crying in public, and demands his immediate resignation.

"The position you hold is only for real men. The nkúkúmá doesn't cry. A Fang man doesn't cry. Since you fall short of the position, it is better for you to resign before we force you out."

His grandson does cry. He cries because he found his mother, Adá, hanging from the ceiling of the kitchen with a cord tied around her neck. She'd been dead for hours, two days after having threatened her father to kill herself if he gave her two children to a man who wasn't their father, but was still her husband because she hadn't returned the dowry.

Adá's marriage failed when she was declared sterile by her spouse and his tribe. She returned to the house of her mother and father and met another man. After a few months of relationship, she became pregnant with twins. Five years later, her still-husband appeared demanding the parental authority of the twins. Her own father, the nkúkúmá and honorable member of his tribe, applied tradition whereby

---

1 *Obono fam*: effeminate, a non-violent man, a man who acts like a woman.

a separated woman, if she doesn't return the dowry, the sons and daughters she has with another man belong to her still-husband because the dowry legalizes marriages in Fang tradition, its return annuls it.

Besides, the dowry determines the tribe the daughters and sons belong to and their biological or legal paternity.

Adá refused to return the dowry, alleging that her father had taken it. Her father the nkúkúmá also didn't return it and called his daughter "ignorant of tradition" because he wasn't under any obligation to fulfill the demand.

The one who barely opened his mouth was Adá's still-husband. He left before the verdict with the twins. The elders also left, accusing the nkúkúmá of not establishing order in his home as an authority, but first, they kicked out the youth who supported Nsí. The women likewise left, some crying because of Adá's fate and others in silence, but the boy's own grandmother stayed behind, and berated him,

"Your mother always exaggerated everything. The name Adá means exaggerated. Adá knew what would happen if she didn't close her legs before returning the dowry. Well…she should've kept them closed. Go on, go home and stop bothering your grandfather. Since when does a grandson denounce his own grandfather? You're a disgrace!"

"Did you know that the man who has taken away my young sisters is sterile?" the boy asked. "He was married three times before marrying Mama, and he didn't produce children in any of those marriages. Did you know that he has agreed to abandon the children, your grandchildren, in the hands of a distant cousin? Did you know that he brought his lovers home with him and ordered Mama not to leave their marriage bed but instead arranged for her to copulate with his lovers?"

His grandparents answered that they knew all that and that tradition took into account those behaviors.

"The children won't be returned and that's that," the nkúkúmá spoke. "Your mother always exaggerated everything. Her name was Adá."

Irenosen Okojie

A Nigerian-British writer, she won a Betty Trask Award for her debut novel, Butterfly Fish *(2015), and was shortlisted for an Edinburgh International First Book Award. Her work has been featured in the* New York Times, The Observer, The Guardian, *the BBC and the* Huffington Post *among other publications. Her short stories have been published internationally in collections including* Salt's Best British Short Stories 2017, Kwani? *and* The Year's Best Weird Fiction. *She was presented at the*

London Short Story Festival by Booker Prize-winning author Ben Okri as a dynamic writing talent to watch and featured in the Evening Standard Magazine *as one of London's exciting new authors. Her 2016 short-story collection,* Speak Gigantular, *was shortlisted for the Edgehill Short Story Prize, the Jhalak Prize, the Saboteur Awards, and nominated for a Shirley Jackson Award.*

Synsepalum

Manu was first spotted in the display window of the old sewing-machine museum touching holes of light on a Babushka costume. He seemed to have appeared from nowhere, a pied piper staging gowns as soft instruments, framed by gauzy street lights. His fingers were curled into swathes of the costume's bulbous ruby-red taffeta skirt on a mannequin, surrounded by elaborately designed sewing-machines poised like an incongruous metal army. A spool of gold thread uncurled behind him, drinking from the night. A wind chime above the blue front door argued with the soft falling of snow. The letterbox slot had a black glove with silver studs slipped into the slash like a misguided disruption. Manu gripped a large curved needle between his lips, and wiped his brow with a spotted handkerchief. The ash in his pockets felt weightless. He inserted the needle into the skirt's hem, unpicking a shrunken, smoggy skyline. He gathered two more mannequins standing to the side, naked, arms stretched towards the skylight in a celestial pose. Their eyes stared ahead blankly as though fixed on a mirage in the distance which could be broken apart then fed into their artificial skin, into cloth. He placed them in the display window, naked calling-cards waiting to be dressed. The spool of thread cut diagonally across rows of sewing-machines moored on metal stands, rectangular golden plaques identifying each one. There was an antique Singer 66-1 Red Eye Treadle from the 1920s, a Russian Handcrank portable number from the '50s, a 1940s Montgomery Ward Streamliner US model, a compact 1930s Jones model from Bucharest with a silver flower pattern crawling up the sides of its sleek, black frame. Manu gathered the thread slowly, a ritual he performed between each creation. A splintered pain exploded in his chest. In his mind's eye, the ash from his pockets assembled into feminine silhouettes. He needed to make more dresses, more corsets, more fitted suits, more gowns. He needed to find more ways to make women feel beautiful through his creations. The designs rose from dark, undulating slipstreams as if in resurrection. They were watery constructions, insistent, whispering what materials they needed, leaning against his brown irises until they leaked from his eyes onto the page while his fingers sketched feverishly. He walked to the atelier at the back, a hub flourishing under the gaze of light. There was a long, wooden work table, more sewing-machines dotted around it. A coiled measuring tape sat in the middle as if ready to entrap a rhinestone-covered, meteorite-shaped white gown that would crash through. Materials spilled from the edges towards the centre; rolls of bright silk, piles of linen, open boxes of lace, streams of velvet. There were jars of accessories, decorations winking in the glass;

zips, studs, feathers, small jewelled delights waiting to adorn the pleat of a skirt, the breast of a jacket, dimpled, soft satin. A black leather suitcase leaning against one wall spilled tiny grains of invisible sand from its gut. The air's pressure contorted a candy-hued ballerina-style dress carelessly flung over a guillotine.

It was on this night while leafleting that Noma was drawn to the seductive glow from the museum, orbs of light mutating in the front entrance's bubble of glass, a coloured small window in a door, a geometric code for the eye. A head in the window of that door on a winter's night could appear trapped there, bobbing in the glass curiously. Noma arrived at that moment through a triumvirate of migration from Swaziland, to Paris to the UK. Picking fruit to sell on the scorching roads of South Africa, homeless in Paris before working in a toy factory, leafleting in London which was repetitive, flexible, mundane but easy, bookended by daily returns to her tiny bedsit on the other side of Wandsworth, in a death trap with no fire exits just off the high street. Noma held a roll of leaflets in her right hand, a run of five hundred for a show about a woman trapped in a warehouse encountering a doppelganger at each exit every time she attempted to leave. She tugged one strap of her rucksack further up her shoulder, walked towards the museum door. Flakes of snow christened her like a black Venus in the cold. Spotting the Babushka dress in the display window, she pressed her face against the glass partition in the door, intrigued. The door opened. Manu smiled warmly, motioned her in with one hand, a ruffle of taffeta material in the other. It smelled like incense inside. The gentle ring of wind chimes multiplied in her eardrums, the low skyline from the Babushka costume bent over the sewing machines, the pressure of air made her skin hum, her senses were heightened. She felt sucked into a vacuum. Air seeped inside her like helium in the lungs. Mannequins facing the outside had drops of dew in their mouths.

"You have come for work," Manu announced, his elegantly handsome face wise in the light. Not even awaiting a response, he turned, rushing to the atelier.

Noma trailed after him, the roll of leaflets fell from her hands, becoming confetti in the view from the front door's bubbled glass partition.

She began working for him a week later, scouring shops for fine materials, measuring and cutting, learning to sew, hunting for unusual accessories. She visited millineries, procured fine hats the colour of quail eggs, the burnished gold of the Sahara, the hue of the Garonne at night. She watched his sketches come to life with a soft wonder in her throat, the outfits like architectural constructs waiting for bodies to invade them, her fingers spinning them slowly on a tailor's mannequin under the kaleidoscopic glow from the skylight, the quiet language of sand stealthily spilling in a corner, the chug of the sewing-machines temporarily silenced.

The pop-up atelier in the sewing-machine museum sprang up like a small utopia longing for the flurry of action. And the women came like drunken butterflies drawn to Eden, one by one until the atelier became a hive of activity, leaking laughter and excitable voices. The women were seduced by Manu; his beauty, his sophistication, the unpredictability of his style, his erudite tales and the assured rumble of his voice. He told them he was born in the Gambia, Namibia, Zanzibar. He was inconsistent, flamboyant. *Oh, but where was he from again?* No matter. He offered them Synsepalum, wild African berries, as if the fruit grew from the blade of the guillotine, the hands of the old grandfather clock on one atelier wall, the mouths of the mannequins. The break of sweet, exotic fruit flooded the women's tongues. They kept coming back for more; more Manu, more handfuls of Synsepalum, more Noma flicking through his sketches, fingering the lines of all they could be, if only. Aspiration captured in drawings. All the while, kernels of pain formed inside Manu, gathering into a mass.

The orders increased. Mrs Jovan, head of the town council, had a nettle-green Boudica gown made for her, which swished around her ankles romantically, Mrs Lonegran, owner of a chain of flower stores cooed in pleasure at the final reveal of her metallic Joan of Arc-inspired ensemble on the atelier floor. Mrs Hunt, a wine buyer, blinked at her image in an intricately designed pale off-the-shoulder 1920s flapper number with a crystal beaded beret to match, gasping as if she hadn't seen herself before, or at least not in this way.

Manu made women feel marvellous, valued, appreciated. He not only understood the female form, he celebrated it; every dip of the back, every arch of a neck, every individual flare of hips. He masked and he revealed, he obscured and he unearthed. He knew how to make the most ordinary of women feel like a goddess. This was his gift. Every woman had a quality of beauty of her own making lurking beneath the skin. Manu knew ways to make it bloom, how to tease it to the surface. And every night, Noma would return to her lonely bedsit bone-tired, fall into bed, unceremoniously woken up by the leak in her ceiling landing on her face, acting as an alarm for the next day's activities.

Five months passed. The women loved their new outfits. They danced in their hallways wearing them, spun in mirrors gathering mist the colour of Synsepalum. Their reflections were released, mimicking their poses in the poorer areas of town, the other side; a swish of silk skirt passing the window of a Turkish food hall that had shut down, a pantsuit limp against the keyhole of a gutted former Jamaican take-away, a squeezed flamenco dress sleeve brushing the iron gates of an abandoned youth centre that had lost its funding. Slipstreams followed each reflection like a watery shadow.

By June, the shots of pain Manu experienced had intensified, spreading through his limbs. His hands in particular were in constant pain. He woke up in agony, the fingers appearing gnarled to him. He couldn't keep up with the orders, with the monster he had created. The rise of sand from the suitcase in the corner of the atelier had become too much. The mannequins were pregnant with mirages, stomachs protruded splitting material. The glove in the post slot had swelled with blood. Designs from the periphery had begun to crash through the skylight in confused stupors, unsure of how their material versions would manifest. The chug of the sewing-machines in his ears was constant, till he found himself impersonating the sound sporadically in conversation. He had run out of ash. And his wild African berries no longer grew in the area for him.

On the third occasion the women wore their outfits, they discovered Manu had lied to them. They could only wear the designs three times. The third time, they couldn't get out of them. Seams tightened, buttons couldn't be undone, petticoats became silken cages. The women rolled around in the damp earth of their gardens, climbed onto their husbands, partners, lovers, hollering to get the scissors, knives, shears, anything to cut them out. They spilled out onto the streets.

It was on this morning Noma arrived outside the museum to find the crowd of women. Manu had disappeared, gone to the next place, the next set of women who needed to feel good, whose images of themselves he could manipulate like startled adult changelings behind a lens. The atelier was empty, the sewing-machines and mannequins forlorn in the void.

Noma spotted something glinting at the foot of the front entrance. She picked up the curved needle.

The baying women rounded on her. "Who will make us beautiful now?" they chorused, like a warped choir on the loose, faces strained, mouths drawn, teeth bared, closing in, scissors and shears gripped firmly, raised above their heads.

Noma almost dropped the needle just as the women began to turn to ash, the pads of her fingers sweaty, just as a bright red root bloomed in the eye of the needle.

Chinelo Okparanta

Born and raised in Port Harcourt, Nigeria, she is the author of Under the Udala Trees *(2015) and* Happiness, Like Water *(2013), each a* New York Times Book Review *Editors' Choice. She has won two Lambda Literary Awards, the 2016 Jessie Redmon Fauset Book Award in Fiction, and the 2016 Inaugural Betty Berzon Emerging Writer Award from the Publishing Triangle. She has been awarded residencies and fellowships by the Lannan Foundation (Marfa), Bread Loaf, the Civitella Ranieri Foundation, and Hedgebrook ("Women Authoring Change"). In 2012, she was chosen as one of Granta's six New Voices, and in 2017, was named one of Granta's Best of Young American Novelists and a Distinguished Immigrant by the Carnegie Corporation of New York. She is currently Assistant Professor of English Literature and Creative Writing at Bucknell University.*

Trump in the Classroom

The format of a writing workshop can vary. In my particular workshops, all students read a couple or more short stories, poems, or essays, and afterwards we discuss what the work is (or is trying to be), what the work is doing (or is trying to do), what the work's strengths and weaknesses are. The discussion often focuses on craft—narrative arc, voice, tone, characterization, etc. But the sociopolitical meaning of the story can never be ignored, because a finely crafted story with no message is hardly a story at all.

One day not long ago, I picked up a story written by a student in one of my workshop classes that caused me quite a bit of distress. In it, the author had created a whole new world—the future of our world. Earth was alive and thriving. In addition, a colony at a great distance from Earth had been created, a colony to which all the dark-skinned people had been banished. In this colony, unlike on earth, malaria still existed. Earth, of course, was where all the white people lived.

In the student's story, the colony—and all the black people in it—was suddenly set to be destroyed, because a few of the black people had taken to bringing up the issue of slavery. They were still living out the legacy and pain of it—an inherited trauma—despite the fact that this was hundreds of years after. This complaining was getting to be too much for the whites, so the whites had now arrived at a solution: blow up, destroy, obliterate all the dark-skinned people. Banishing them to a malaria-infested colony was no longer enough. Rather, put an end to the legacy of slavery once and for all, so that they would no longer have to listen to complaints, the inconvenience of guilt.

The student's story seemed to assert that black people had good enough lives in this colony, so why were they still protesting?

Context matters. Thanks to Donald Trump, people have for some time now felt empowered to speak honestly and proudly about views formerly denounced as racist, sexist, hateful. The area where I was teaching this class was heavily pro-Donald Trump. The student presented as a white male and hailed from what appeared to be a relatively privileged background, attending this somewhat elite, wealthy liberal arts college. Did I know for a fact his political leanings? No, but it didn't take me long to realize that, based on his background and on the content of his submitted story, in another world he could very well have been a younger version of Donald Trump.

There's a way in which the pulse quickens and the eyes tear up and the face burns with heat when one stumbles upon a story like this. If one is a particular kind of person, anyway. Say, a dark-skinned person reading about the destruction of herself by her very own student—the student she comes into contact with at least twice a week. The student she had no idea was capable of ever harboring such destructive thoughts, even in a fictional universe. I felt like a child skipping along a field of pretty green grass, dandelions and their clocks floating in the air, and suddenly realizing there were mines scattered all around me. I was one of the darkies this student's fiction was seeking to demolish.

In the classroom that day, standing in a sea of whiteness (only one black student—just the two of us, and she so quiet and hesitant, perhaps in the discomfort of it all), I felt my blackness profoundly.

"This is a very disturbing story," one white student whispered.

"Yes, I didn't know what to take from it," another white student agreed.

And yet, the story, with notable adjustments, could have been a satire. Perhaps, in a different world, it could have been parallel to Jonathan Swift's "A Modest Proposal," in which Swift encouraged readers to serve the children of the poor as food to the wealthy elites in order to help ease Ireland's economic issues. Or was it like Voltaire's *Candide*, an ironic rejection of false optimism? Or was it like Paul Beatty's *The Sellout*, which sought, satirically, to call for the return of slavery and segregation? If it were meant to be a satire, the tone was clearly off. Satire is notoriously difficult to master.

In my workshops, I insist that students not explain, defend, or apologize for their work. But in this case, I asked the student for just a tiny bit of clarification: had he, in fact, intended his story to be satirical?

No, he responded, without any visible pause or hesitation. But he added that he hoped people would see how sad it was that the father and his daughter were about to be destroyed.

So, what, then, to make of the story?

I tried to imagine the reason why my students and I were being presented with this narrative. Perhaps the young man had congratulated himself on coming up with a solution for dealing with all the annoying black people who keep whining about slavery. Perhaps he had forgotten, in all the whiteness of his semi-elite, super-wealthy liberal arts college, that his dear professor was a black woman. Perhaps he had grown used to airing these kinds of ideas with all those other whites who shared ideas like this one. Maybe his parents were responsible for bestowing the very idea on him. Only, they had neglected to warn him about how it would come off if he went on to dispense it to an audience that did not share his personal views. Maybe he himself hadn't thought of the story's implications. He'd perhaps gotten too caught up in his own cleverness to realize that a story like this is not just a story. Cannot ever be just a story.

But had the student really done anything wrong? Does one not have the right to write whatever he wishes in fiction? James Baldwin, in his defense of William Styron's controversial *Confessions of Nat Turner*, famously said, "No one can tell a writer what he can or cannot write." Even I myself have written stories that have been deemed, in some way or other, scandalous. Is fiction not just fiction?

What if my student had written his story with no bad intentions?

In response to Baldwin, Ossie Davis replied, "I respect [Styron's] right to write the book any way he wants to. But at the same time, the social consequences of a book do not necessarily always act out the good intentions of the writers themselves.

If we in our country have decided that race and color are nonsensical…and no longer need we concern ourselves with them, then I say to the book all success." Davis added: "Had we already solved the racial problem as we face it in this country, the whole question would be academic. I would read the book, like it or dislike it, and leave it at that." But clearly, racism and color were still plaguing the country then as now, and Ossie Davis feared the consequences—the destructive reactions by the masses of non-literary-minded people—of Styron's story being magnified on the screen.

Davis was aware that some were accusing him of overreacting in his censure of Styron's work. His response? "I will overreact as long as I am aware that racism is in our country and is a threat to me as a black man… I've been a black man all these years, and I cannot stop all of a sudden when my country has not stopped yet making me pay for that fact."

At this point I opened the class up to a discussion on social consequence, an issue I think of more and more these days. Much in the fashion of Ossie Davis, I explained that a story like this can have real-life damaging effects. It's the issue of power and hierarchies. Who has the control in any particular society? Because of power structures, it's not usually the same effect—or the same meaning—when someone who has all the sociopolitical control writes a story like this as when a person with little or no power/privilege writes it, especially given the lack of satirical intent. Power imbalances are the reason why things that begin as fiction, when constructed and given life by people in positions of authority, can progress quickly into reality—a group of people who are seen as a nuisance could very well be annihilated in real life by those in power, and have been annihilated many times over the course of human history.

In his preface to *Blues for Mister Charlie*, James Baldwin aptly wrote: "What is ghastly and really almost hopeless in our racial situation now is that the crimes we have committed are so great and so unspeakable that the acceptance of this knowledge would lead, literally, to madness. The human being, then, in order to protect himself, closes his eyes, compulsively repeats his crimes, and enters a spiritual darkness which no one can describe." This blind repetition was the horror that my student's story seemed to be seeking to enact.

Kill the blacks if they won't shut up might be better written by him as a satire, I told my student. (Here, I mentioned to him Swift, Voltaire, Paul Beatty). Or better yet, maybe kill the blacks if they won't shut up is not the story you really want to write.

Shortly after I dismissed the class, it occurred to me that maybe this story was exactly what the student should have written. Who was I to tell anyone what they could or couldn't write? At the tender age of twenty, maybe this was the perfect time for a white man to get that kind of story out—and maybe my fiction class was the perfect place to do it. Because if not now, and if not in this context, where we could openly talk about the horrors of such a mentality and the potential consequences of giving life to that sort of horror, even on the page—of breathing air into it by sharing it with other readers—then what happens when it is entirely too late, when he is forty or fifty or sixty years old and running for president, and perhaps has even won the vote, and is now hard and fast on his way to demolishing the "darkies"?

"We learn by discussion and by talk and by reasoning together," Ossie Davis said. Maybe my student did the right thing by revealing his thoughts in that relatively low-threat sort of way, and in a relatively low-threat sort of setting. By allowing me the opportunity to initiate a conversation with him, to dialogue openly and share my concerns; by allowing me to share my shock at the inhumanity of his story; by his being open to listening to my thoughts, instead of, for instance, blowing me up—perhaps he did precisely the right thing.

Yewande Omotoso

Currently living in Johannesburg, she is a Nigerian-Barbadian architect and author. She completed an MA in Creative Writing at the University of Cape Town. Her debut novel, Bomboy, *was shortlisted for the 2012* Sunday Times *Fiction Prize, the MNet Film Award and the 2013 Etisalat Prize for Literature. It won the South African Literary Award First Time Author Prize. Her short stories include "How About the Children" in* Kalahari Review, *"Things Are Hard" in the 2012 Caine Prize Anthology, "Fish" published in* The Moth Literary Journal *and "The Leftovers" in* One World Two. *She was a 2013 Norman Mailer Fellow and a 2014 Etisalat Fellow. In 2015 she was a Miles Morland Scholar. Her second novel,* The Woman Next Door *(2017), was longlisted for the Bailey's Women's Fiction Prize. It was also shortlisted for the Aidoo-Snyder Prize, the Barry Ronge Fiction Prize, the UJ Literary Prize and the International Dublin Literary Award.*

Open

He was boy-man. His body was boy, lean and taut. Surprisingly smooth when I stroked his skin. His face was boy. His lips plump, soft when they laid upon me, when he kissed my face and my mouth. His eyes weren't particularly large. They were hard but not man-hard, boy-hard, a hurt little person, a person that wasn't playing anymore. When he smiled he was beautiful but the wideness also exposed a black incisor, a detail that made him seem even more boy-like, a discarded boy. He'd been tired when he arrived. He'd driven six hours from Durban but I could tell his fatigue was from before then. Man fatigue, heavy with the weight of troubles. I was shy with him for only a few minutes. We hadn't seen each other in three years. The whole thing, his sudden presence in my bedroom, his small travel bag on the floor, had been devised so quickly, had settled into fact so suddenly, I was still adjusting.

"Excuse me."

I changed in my bathroom. Pulling off my clothes, wondering as I always did when I saw myself naked, why some bodies form one way and others another. Thinking of all that nakedness. Seven billion naked beings, so many ways to be naked. I pulled on a long-sleeve top, no need to put on leggings. In the room he'd climbed under the duvet. His trousers were on the floor next to his bag. I could see his bare shoulders and the top of his chest.

"Need anything?"

"I'm fine."

"Water? You're not hungry? After your long trip."

He shook his head. I put down the clothes I'd changed out of and got beneath the covers. I was aware of the hairs on my legs, long and soft, several months old. When he'd phoned to say he was coming, when he'd said it (not asked permission but simply told me) I'd worried that it was past midnight and I had no razors in the house. We would make love, I told myself. He would have me with the long hairs on my legs and that'll teach him to arrive unexpected. Or perhaps the lesson should be mine. Teach me to always be prepared. Or perhaps the lesson was even simpler—none of it matters.

"Sorry, I feel shy," I said and he smiled. Touched me underneath. "It's strange."

"Yes?" he said and moved closer. "What's strange about it?"

His softness surprised me, the succession of small kisses, like a tired moth stepping. He'd asked me a question that I wasn't required to answer. The act, the caressing would suffice, not as an answer to "what's strange" but as confirmation.

Afterwards he leaned over and switched off the lamp and, with my head on his chest, a wide chest, capable-like for all his boyness, I played back the whole thing in the dark. I'd somehow expected more but whatever disappointments were tempered by his grip around my body, so tightly was he holding onto me in the dark. His breathing slow, our bodies clicked together like a fit. I'd expected deeper kissing, more passion. His messages over the years had been plump with hunger, ardent, even violent in his insistence that we meet. I'd expected that. I laughed at myself, in the dark, held so tightly, I'd expected what he'd written which I keep forgetting is a mistake. I changed position, my back to his chest and he moved in closer, gripped me. It felt good to be naked in the middle of the night, with another naked person upon me, with the duvet over us both, with the darkness.

In the morning we slept in. The sun, timid at first, grew confident through the curtains, warming us. We'd separated in the night and found each other again with daylight. I wanted to pee. He was snoring. I thought I might have work to do. Felt muddled. His skin burnt against mine. My bladder forgot and I fell back asleep, slept deeply, woke up held, my nose at his neck.

"I need to get up," I said.

We tried again although it ended suddenly.

"Do you have a special person in your life?" I asked him. I'd seen it somewhere on Facebook about two years before, during a quiet spell in our correspondence. I'd been bored, he'd been texting me and I'd chosen to ignore him.

"Yes," he said.

"And a child."

"Yes."

I'd known, which is why the sadness I felt was curious to me.

"A girl?"

"Yes. She's two and a half."

"Lives with her mother?"

"Yes."

Perhaps he saw judgment in my face.

"Sometimes I take her. For a few days. For a weekend."

We were sitting up in bed. I hadn't offered him breakfast, there was nothing in my fridge. I thought, once we were clean and dressed, I'd take him out to a café nearby.

"Does she know you sleep with other women? Your girlfriend."

"Yes."

"And she doesn't mind."

He shrugged. He was boy-man. A slight but long body, a body that I (large as I am) had rested on. He was a boy with heavy adult ideas.

"She understands."

"And she can do the same?"

"She can do as she pleases."

"And you don't mind?" I wasn't clear what it was I wanted to fight for, so early in the morning, so doped by the tight caresses, as if an embrace was a drug.

"How?"

"I mean. Say for instance you see her. You run into her and her lover. How would that make you feel?"

He frowned.

"Won't you be sad? See, I don't understand it. I don't understand this way of living."

"Yeah. So we're conditioned. To think that this is how relationships have to go. We have this one-only model."

When he was awake and talking to me like this he was man. With short firm sentences. Clear things he'd decided that no one would ever change.

"We don't talk about it. You keep it to yourself," he said.

He spoke in such a way. Everything calibrated, no words escaped his lips without first passing through whatever measuring cup he used, whatever scale. I wanted something from him and I hated myself for it. He was not in any way the kind of man I would long for but he was here in my bed and I wanted something without units.

"Don't you think about it though? Because you love her."

"You know love as possession. I know it different. You know it as attachment. I know it different."

I wanted to touch his boy-face, kiss him maybe. I wanted to ask him why, in the night, we hadn't continued. Why, after three years, after finally being in bed together, why hadn't we spent the whole night looking at each other's bodies, inspecting our nudity, enthralled, disgusted, curious, nervous, embarrassed, whatever the feeling but something or all things. I wanted to ask if his spurts of lust were always so short. Did he enjoy it, I wanted to know. Did he like my body, had it been worth the long wait, the teasing, my prolonged reticence and final assent? Why this intricate philosophy for a life of polyamory if the actual love-making would end up so measly. Wasn't he hungry?

"Hungry?"

"Yeah."

I had the salad, he asked for a wrap and made a point of requesting fresh juice. The waiter frowned at the word "fresh" and brought something orange with no pulp or pips.

"It'll do," he said and took his first sip.

I'd once lain down with a man who'd insisted I stand in front of him first. Let me see you, he'd said. And then he'd said, after looking a few seconds at my skin, my naked torso, my hips with striations that I first discovered then learnt the word "cellulite"; he'd said, you're beautiful. I'd once gone to visit a cousin's friend whose mother had died. My cousin was unable to visit and I went instead and sat in the grieving man's living-room from afternoon till evening and he didn't turn the lights on. He told me he was supposed to go to a sex party the following night, he'd booked it before his mother's death and now he didn't know whether to go or not. A party where you leave your clothes in cellophane at the door. It only happens once a year, he said. Exclusive. He'd bought the tickets, he had two. I said no. Are you a prude he wanted to know. And after I denied this he asked, what would you do if I suddenly took all my clothes off. Not a big deal I said. So he took all his clothes off and several hours later we sat naked on his couch, him cradling my breasts. I once jerked a man off and he thanked me, asked me how I'd managed to do that—he'd never had a hand job in his life not even one given by himself; he looked at me as if I owned his life, could squash or pet it, whichever I pleased. One told me to hurry up, another took too long. One asked me if I knew what I was doing, another asked me what precisely was I doing. When I thought my relationship was over and what I ought to do was bring back the spice I spent hours in a lingerie shop, spent money on colourful lace I never found the right moment to wear. I bought expensive oils but when, after much begging, my boyfriend agreed to leave the TV and lay down on the bed, when I started to rub oil on his beautiful skin he sucked his teeth. You don't know what you're doing, he said. Lie down. He rubbed me all over, firm like a physiotherapist, then he went back to finish watching the game. I sent a man out at 2 a.m. to find a condom. Another time I ransacked my house mate's room for hers. I'd experienced intimacy once when my boyfriend cried in my arms, we were lying in bed, I was breaking up with him. I'd experienced intimacy once when, after I reached, I cried in a man's arms. I was in love with him and he was breaking up with me. What is it I search for that I cannot find.

"I'd—"

"Pardon?"

We'd finished our meals and his juice was half drunk.

"No, I was trying to say. I'd wanted something."

"What?"

"Last night. I mean. How do I put this? I'm glad you came through. Drove down to see me. And—"

"Oh. Yeah, me too."

"—I'd wanted something."

"What's that?"

"I don't know," I shrugged.

He gulped down the rest of the juice. He offered to pay but needed to draw cash from an ATM and there were none about. Later I would wonder why I didn't just suggest he pay with his bank card but at the time I told him not to worry. He asked if he could borrow my train card, he assured me he would return it. I dropped him at the station and he must have lost my number, he didn't call and it seemed we would never see each other again.

For many days after his visit I felt an odd mix of emotions. Some parts of my body ached from where I'd exerted myself, a sign not of how vigorous we'd been but rather how unfit I was, how unused those muscles were to working. Pleasant aches. I felt strangely revived. I went back to the recent memories of lying in bed with another warm body beside me. I'd so enjoyed that. The weight of his boy body, his smooth long arms gripping me. As the days passed and his silence filled them I felt duped. Not because I loved him, not even because I longed for him, wanted to call him myself or would even agree to see him again. I didn't necessarily feel duped by him, although in some moments I did. Rather I felt duped by something bigger than us both. I didn't regret seeing him but I regretted the pattern of my life, the incessant longing for something closer. The compromises for something lesser. I remembered long comfortable phone calls with lovers I no longer spoke to. I remembered the parabola love can make when it turns into hate, the burn of resentment, long nights awake, my heart loud in complaint and upset. I remembered feelings, what it is to weep for a human being that has forgotten you, what it feels like to be done with someone. I remembered pain. I remembered that I was alone, that I was mostly alone, had spent most of my adult life alone, even when I'd been together I was alone and I knew this like a truth and sometimes lived it like a blessing other times a curse. I didn't cry but when my phone rang my heart was several kilograms heavier with all the thinking, all the memories of all the people I no longer spoke to and all the dreams I'd disavowed.

"Hey, Beautiful. I have your train card. I'm still in town. Can I come over? I really need to see you."

Makena Onjerika

Born in Meru, on the windward side of Mount Kenya, she was the 2018 winner of the Caine Prize for African Writing. She is a graduate of the New York University MFA in Creative Writing program. Her work has previously appeared in Urban Confustions, Wasafiri, *the* Caine Prize Anthology *and the Storymoja website. She is working on a fantasy novel and a short story collection, both inspired in part by Nairobi.*

The Man Watching Our House

I

The night Maami first spoke of the death of her own mother, we were sitting in the dark, waiting out a power blackout. The hurricane lamp on the table magnified Maami's head tenfold on the wall. The night was full of cricket song, croaking frogs and a choir of dogs barking at each other, back and forth.

Maami said, "The day after we buried Marisera, we were in the farm, me and your Aunt Batha. We were digging and then we saw a man walking across our fields, coming from the river, where there were no roads or paths."

She sliced through the sharp smell of kerosene hanging over our heads and transported us back home to Meru, to a green, wet morning, pregnant with the medicinal smell of the eucalyptus trees. Black and white Friesian cows whipped their tails at pestilent flies and dropped healthy, warm blobs of dung. Smoke rose in cottony billows out of the metal-pipe chimney of my step-grandmother's kitchen.

Grandmother Marisera lies in an unweeded grave at the corner of my grandfather's homestead. Every June and December, coffee trees laden with red berries stretch their branches over a barbed-wire fence as if to greet her who weeded, pruned and harvested them for many years.

"He was a tall man with a thin face," said Maami. "In that sun his clothes seemed to be burning. We greeted him. 'Muugaa,' we said. But he went on walking across our land to the main road, without saying anything to us."

She widened her eyes at the man, standing tall and thin, right there in our sitting-room. "Who was this man walking on our fields the day after we put Marisera in the soil?" she asked.

"I ran home and asked your grandfather if the man had come to our homestead. I ran to the main road and asked everyone I met, 'Have you seen this man?' In that village with only one road, no one had seen him."

Her eyes become wet and glittery as she spoke. My brother was too young to see this. When he asked who the man was, she held herself as though she felt a wind we could not.

"Someone bewitched your grandmother. Someone sent that man to come see that the job was finished."

Her head grew larger on the wall as she moved forward to catch a mosquito buzzing close to my face. My blood was dark red on her palm.

Grandmother Marisera had died of breast cancer.

II

A story is told of a young man who lost his way in the forest as he returned from raiding a beehive. Instead of emerging at the edge of his village, he found himself at the field of the dead. He had not been there before, but recognised it immediately, the open ground in the forest where grass did not grow. This is where his father had brought what had once been his mother—the cold, wide-eyed but unseeing rukuu he found on her sleeping mat, one morning.

When he whimpered, his father spoke harshly. "Be quiet. She was good and has gone to sleep where it rains."

His father's father spoke with even more anger, addressing all who stood outside his mother's hut. "Are you waiting for the rukuu to poison us? Tie its feet and drag it to the mbiti. And burn that hut."

The young man had never seen the mbiti, only heard them laughing in the forest in the deep of night. Laughing, he imagined, as they tore apart rukuu and crashed their bones. It still pained him to think of his mother, and he was about to turn away when he heard a cry. Looking through the trees he saw a man squatting at one end of the field.

The young man could not see the stranger's face but guessed that he was a very old man; the top of his head was bald and his remaining hair all white. His people must have brought him out to die, so that the uncleanliness of his rukuu would not touch them. The young man pitied the stranger, but it was what had to be done.

The stranger cried again, this time as though he were a wounded animal. Pity affected the young man so greatly that he crept through the trees towards the stranger, intending to get close enough to comfort him while remaining hidden in the shadows.

"You are a good man; you will sleep where it rains," the young man intended to say.

But when he looked into the old man's face, he saw only himself, squatting there in the field of the dead. The calf-skin pouch in which he carried the honey fell from his hand. His people found it later, swarming with ants.

III

A devil entered my uncle, Maami's youngest brother, and caused him to burn down his house, one Sunday afternoon.

"Batha, is this not the devil?" said Maami into her mobile phone. "How is it that every time our brother harvests his wheat, every time he has money in his pocket, he goes mad?"

A few days later, she drove to Nanyuki for a fundraiser to help my uncle rebuild. It rained heavily all that morning and afternoon. The water roared and cut gulleys in the murram roads. When it was sunny again, I sat on the concrete steps outside our house—red ants buzzing electrically as they marched by—and tried to bring my uncle's face to mind. I had only met him once, at my grandfather's. During school holidays, Maami took us to visit our aunties in Meru and Isiolo, but never our uncles.

"They found witchcraft in his farm," whispered Aunt Batha's daughter, Gakiri, under the darkness of our shared blanket. I could still hear Maami and Aunt Batha gossiping in the kitchen about the past and the present, as they always did when Maami brought us to visit.

While Gakiri told me about the fundraiser, the wind howled violently outside, as if intent on ripping the corrugated sheets off the roof of Auntie and Uncle's house. I felt that we were sinning, talking about these grown-up affairs.

Gakiri said, "They brought a pastor who went round Uncle's farm praying, shouting verses from the Bible and commanding devils in the name of Jesus Christ. Everywhere he paused, he made the grown-ups dig. They found things buried in the soil. Bones tied together in bundles and pots full of rotten liquids and even clumps of human hair."

You see, there is a curse in my family; no one knows where it came from, but it has eaten all the men. "Eaten", that's how Maami says it.

"You tell me, Batha. None of our father's sons have succeeded. They got education same as us and the farms on top, but look?"

Years later, when I was already in university in America, Maami told me of the last time she saw her brother. Her voice came through Skype in pieces and screeches.

"I saw that he was running around in his head, looking for himself, but what could I do? I told them to go to church; I told them to pray; I told them to seek God. No one listened. Look what happened?"

My uncle drank a concoction of pesticides a few months after the fire and died howling.

IV

A young woman in a foreign country allowed her faith to slip out of her hands. She was at the Good Shepherd Church, watching Pastor John Wesley glide across the pulpit. He was sweating visibly from the effort of delivering his sermon. Big-hatted women, who referred to the young woman as "sister from the motherland", shouted halleluias, amens and "preach, preacher".

"We must be *booolllld*. We must rise up! Say it with me, rise up and lay claim to our inheritance." Pastor John Welsey was going hoarse.

Amen! The shouts clapped the young woman's ears, but the words did not sink in. She was already full of words. She was tired. She could take no more. She wanted to be light, to care less, to fear less, to be unencumbered. She asked to be excused and slipped out of the pew. Her church friend gave her a look, asking why she was leaving.

As she walked towards the door of the church and the light of summer, she began taking off her spiritual clothes. For many years, they had protected her, from demons, from temptations, from the world, from herself. And for all those years, she had been running around in her mind, trying to find herself. She stood spiritually stark-naked at the door of the church. The sun burned her thin exposed skin, but she was no longer afraid of fire.

V

"Kendi, what day is it today?" asked Maami, as she dug into her purse for church offering, squinting.

My first Sunday back in Kenya from America. A rainy day—the chalky smell of wet soil made me thirsty. My pyjamas were still warm from bed. Maami slapped her Bible on the table, said she wouldn't have an atheist in her house, broke a cup. My brother didn't make a sound in the adjoining room, his bedroom.

She asked, "Do you at least pray?"

Perhaps if I had said I prayed, she wouldn't have told me about the man. She said, "I knew it. From six months ago, I knew it, Kendi. Do you remember my cousin Boronica?"

She described this Boronica, her plumpness, her dark skin, her many children, the trickle of blood that connected us, but I refused to recall the woman. Outside, the various denominations within a kilometre radius of our house were shouting sermons at each other over mega-loudspeakers.

My mother pinched her brow with concentration: "Boronica called me six months ago. She said she met a man on the village road. A man she does not know. He addressed her by her name, and asked: 'Do you know Kareti of M'Mukindia?' Boronica did not know him, but he knew her and he knew me and your grandfather and he also knew you. He said, 'Tell Kareti I have a message for her, about Kendi.'"

I should have said, *"Shindwe!"* I should have quoted Psalms 23, but instead I sipped my tea and pretended calmness as I asked, "What was the message?"

Her keys clunked against each other as she went out the door and let it bang shut. The silence she left that day is still here, sitting beside me.

VI

In dreams I shout, "In the name of Jesus. In the name of Jesus. In the name of Jesus." But the demon chasing me through the darkest recesses of my subconscious pays no heed. I do not know what it wants or why it comes for me. It has neither face nor body, all I feel is its thick, shapeless malice, holding my legs even as I run, screaming soundlessly.

Each time, fear ejects me out of sleep and I wake disoriented and in two, body and spirit. My still sleeping spirit tries to pull me down towards the bed, back into the black oil of nightmare. And then, suddenly, I am one and panting into the darkness of my room. This darkness has real weight, infinitesimal, but real weight nonetheless.

Maami's words return to me on such nights: "I told them to pray; I told them to seek God. Look what happened?"

I know that one day I will meet the man who watches our house in the streets of Nairobi. I will know him immediately. He will wear a shabby suit and we will hold each other's eyes over the hurrying heads of Nairobians. Perhaps I will stop in my tracks. Perhaps I will try to run. My heart will clench into a fist and try to pound its way out of my ribcage. My throat will be parched. But he will be unperturbed by the honking cars and the shouting hawkers.

"Kendi," he will say, placing a cold hand on my shoulder. "I have been looking for you."

I will not resist him. I will simply turn and follow him.

Djaimilia Pereira de Almeida

translated by Eric M.B. Becker

Born in Angola, she grew up in Portugal, and lives in the suburbs of Lisbon. She is the author of two novels, Esse cabelo *(2015), winner of the Novos Prize 2016 and a finalist of the Casino da Póvoa Prize 2018, and* Luanda, Lisboa, Paraíso *(2018). Her portrait of a community of people with cerebral palsy,* Ajudar a cair, *was published in 2017. A graduate of the New University of Lisbon, she has a PhD in Literary Theory from the University of Lisbon. In 2013 she received the Serrote Essay Prize and in 2016 was a finalist of the Rolex Mentor and Protégé Arts Initiative. She is a contributor to the* Blog da Companhia das Letras *in Brazil, and her writing has appeared in* Granta.com, Granta Portugal, Revista Serrote, Revista Zum, Quatro Cinco Um, Revista Pessoa, Ler, *and* Words Without Borders. That Hair *is forthcoming from Tin House Books in the US in 2020.*

From *That Hair*

My mother cut my hair for the first time when I was six months old. The hair, which according to several witnesses and a few photographs had been soft and straight, was reborn curly and dry. I don't know if this sums up my still-short life. One could quite easily say just the opposite. To this day, along the curve of my nape, it still grows inexplicably straight, the soft hair of a newborn, which I treat as a vestige. The story of my hair begins with this first haircut. How might I write this story so as to avoid the trap of intolerable frivolity? No one would accuse the biography of an arm of being frivolous; and yet, it's impossible to tell the story of its fleeting movements—mechanical, irretrievable, lost to oblivion. Perhaps this might sound insensitive to veterans of war or amputees, whose imaginations conjure pains they still feel, rounds of applause, runs along the beach. It wouldn't do me much good, I imagine, to fantasize over the reconquest of my head by the soft-stranded survivors near the curve of my neck. The truth is that the story of my curly hair intersects with the story of at least two countries and, by extension, the indirect story of the relations among several continents: a geopolitics.

Perhaps the place to begin this biography of my hair is many decades ago, in Luanda, with a girl named Constança, a coy blonde (a fetching "typist girl," perhaps?), the unspoken youthful passion of my black grandfather, Castro Pinto, long before he became head nurse at Luanda's Hospital Maria Pia; or perhaps I ought to begin with the night I surprised him with braids that he found divine. I'd spent nine hours sitting cross-legged on the floor at the hairdresser, head between the legs of two particularly brutal young girls, who in the midst of doing my hair interrupted their task to turn some feijoada and rice pudding left over from lunch into a bean soup, and I sensed a warmth on my back (and a vague odor) coming from between their legs. "What a sight!" he said. Indeed: perhaps the story of my hair has its origin in this girl Constança, whom I'm not related to in any way, but whose presence my grandfather seemed to seek in my relaxed hair and in the girls on the bus that, after he was already an old man living on the outskirts of Lisbon, would take him each morning to his job at Cimov where, his back hunched, he swept the floors until the day he died. But how to tell this history with sobriety and the desirable discretion?

"Perhaps someone has already written a book about hair," problem solved, but no one's written the story of *my* hair, as I was painfully reminded by two fake blondes to whom I once temporarily surrendered my curls for a hopeless "brushing"—two women who, no less brutal than the others, pulled my hair this way and that, commenting aloud "it's full of split-ends" as they waged battle against their own arms (the masculinity of which, with their swollen biceps bulging from beneath their smocks, was the entire time my secret form of revenge for the torture they inflicted). The haunted house that every hair salon represents for the young woman I am is often all I have left of my connection to Africa and the history of the dignity of my ancestors. However, I have plenty of suffering and corrective brushings after returning home from the "beauty parlor," as my mother calls it, and of attempts not to take too personally the work of these hairdressers whose implacability and incompetence I never summoned the courage to confront. The story I can tell is a catalog of salons, with Portugal's corresponding history of ethnic transformations—of the fifty-year-old returnees to the Moldavian manicurists forced to adopt Brazilian methods—undergoing countless treatments to tame the natural exuberance of a young lady who, in the words of these same women, is "a good girl." The story of surrendering my education in what it meant to be a woman to a public space is not, perhaps, the fairy tale of miscegenation, but it is a story of reparations.

No blonde woman on a city bus ever gave my Grandpa Castro the time of day. Humming *bakongo* canticles to himself, Papá was the man whom you would never suspect of continuing the time-honored tradition he carries within on our side of the bus; the man of invisible traditions—and what a ring this would have to it capitalized: The Man of Invisible Traditions, an original notion. No one ever looked at him, this man who, by his own account, was rather cranky, "the Portuguese kid," as he was known as a young man, who was always shouting "Put it in the goal, you monkey," referring to black soccer players, and who categorized people according to their resemblance to certain jungle animals, even describing himself as "the monkey *type*," the kind of person who patiently waits for the conversation to come to a close before proffering his wisdom.

I come from generations of lunatics, which is perhaps a sign that what takes place inside the heads of my ancestors is more important what goes on around them. The family to whom I owe my hair have described the journey between Portugal and Angola in ships and airplanes over four generations with the nonchalance of frequent fliers. A nonchalance which nonetheless was not passed on to me and throws into stark relief my own dread of trips; a dread that—out of an instinct to cling to life that never assails me on solid ground—I constantly fear will be my last. Legend has it I stepped off the plane in Portugal at the age of three with my hair in a particularly rebellious state, clinging to a package of *Maria* crackers. I came dressed in a yellow wool camisole that can still be seen today in an old passport photo notable for its wide smile, the product of a felicitous misunderstanding about the significance of being photographed. I'm laughing with joy; or perhaps incited for some comic motive by one of my adult family members, whom I re-encounter tanned and sporting beards in photographs of the newborn me splayed atop the bedsheets.

And meanwhile it's my hair—and not the mental abyss—that day in and day out brings me back to this story. For as long as I can remember, I've woken up with a rebellious mane, so often at odds with my journey, far from the recommended headscarves for covering one's hair while sleeping. To say that I wake up with a lion's mane out of carelessness is to say that I wake up every day with at least a modicum of embarrassment or a motive to laugh at myself in the mirror: a motive accompanied by impatience and at times, rage. It's occurred to me that I might owe the daily reminder of what ties me to my family to the haircut I received at six months of age. I've been told I'm a "mulata das pedras", as they say in Angola, not the idealized beauty that "mulata" conjures for them but a second-rate one, and with bad hair to boot. This expression always blinds me with the memory of rocks along the beach: slippery, slimy stones difficult to walk across barefoot.

Alake Pilgrim

From Trinidad and Tobago, she has an MA in Creative Writing from the University of East Anglia, thanks to the Booker Prize Foundation Scholarship. Her short stories have received several awards, including a Small Axe Literary Prize and have twice been shortlisted for the Commonwealth Short Story Prize. She has had residencies at the Cropper Foundation Writers Workshop and the Community of Writers at Squaw Valley, and participated in the Bocas Lit Fest's New Talent readings. She is at work on her first novel.

Remember Miss Franklin

Catherine sits on the counterpane, fluffy and full of down, with the only daisies she will ever see in a field of white embroidered elegance. She runs her rough fingers over its smoothness. This counterpane came to Barbados in a British ship in the year of her Lord 1918. It has been with her these ten years, since the day her mother unwrapped the petticoat pressed flat under the mattress and counted the pound-notes kept safe for her only daughter's wedding, the only day for which she could buy this counterpane; the most expensive gift she had ever given or received.

Catherine lifts the counterpane from the bed slowly, drawing it into her arms. She had planned to do this washing the day before, but it had rained. Rain or not, she gets up in the cool air of dawn and kneels on the worn wooden floor to pray, then goes to the kitchen at the back of the house. She prepares her family's breakfast that leaves behind the smell of saltfish like clothes wet in sea spray, then left too long in an enclosed room. Each morning, she lays out her husband's ironed clothes, sleeves and pants' legs creased to perfection, collar stiff with starch.

Now, with her husband at work and son at school, the house is hers for a while. The tea she takes each morning stands beside the hot coal stove—verveine today to ease the upset feeling in her stomach. Did she already feed the fowls? Their clatter flies like pebbles against the turquoise walls of the house, capped with sheets of tin, coated red against the rust.

"Two times three is six, six into three, two!" rises triumphantly from the nearby schoolhouse. She stands still to listen, the counterpane gathered in her arms, paused before an island so flat, it feels like she can see from one end to the other. Barbados, the only place that she can call home: an island with few rivers to speak of.

"One one hundred, two one hundred, three one hundred, four…"

The sound of children counting takes her back to her childhood. She was a little girl looking for a place to hide. Behind the rocks there was a hole in the face of the earth.

"Eight one hundred, nine one hundred." At almost "Ten," she crawled inside. It was wider within. The counting stopped.

"Our Father," she whispered, not sure God would hear.

Ma had told her once, "Them caves full a ghosts, still hungry for they freedom."

Pa said, "Don't mind you mother's 'Nansi stories. Is once to die and after that the judgment. Jus' don't go near them caves."

He wouldn't say why. She went further in. She wasn't afraid of any old ghosts. She'd rather die than let Pips catch her down here by Harrison's Caves. Harrison, like the college Pips dreamed of entering; the one that was only for boys.

"Who don't have horse mus' ride cow," her father had muttered on her last day of school, scraping the mud from his hands. She had stared at his square forehead, his broad heavy cheeks, marked where the cane leaves had sliced him.

Catherine catches herself standing, staring out into the trembling air. The schoolchildren have stopped singing their times-tables. Why remember that now? It is years since her parents have crossed over and she is a grown woman.

The counterpane is a white mound in her arms. She walks carefully down the back steps and releases it into the stone sink behind the house. Where the time goes, she cannot say. Her son Obed is ten years old. When he was younger, she made housework a game. She swept the ground around him with a broom she made herself out of coconut leaves' dried spines. Heat came up through the soles of her slippers as she bent and swished, bent and swayed in a solemnly joyous dance.

"Bush-broom, bush-broom," he sang, a melody so unlike the sentences in his schoolbooks: John—and—Jenny—like—snow.

One day, when he is a man with thick black hair like his father's and solemn dark-coffee eyes, she hopes that he will remember the soft used pages of books, hidden in the folds of her skirts. Now, there is washing to be done. The rainwater collects in a drum at the side of the house. She adds lime so that she can use it to wash. She moves water from the drum to the stone sink with a metal pail, careful not to waste a drop.

With the rush of pouring water she is a little girl again, poised inside the entrance of Harrison's caves. Back then, it was the sound of water that drew her in deeper, after playing in the hot sun outside. At first she had seen nothing but a hole in the rocks, somewhere to climb up and in. A place to hide and make Pips pee his pants when she jumped out at him like a ghost. Then she heard it: water like a low gurgle in a baby's throat. She went further in, clinging to the wet walls so as not to fall, following that growing sound until it led her into a cavern crisscrossed with spears of sunlight piercing through holes from her former world.

She forgot about that drink. She was inside the earth's glittering heart. Above her, jagged teeth in blues and silvers and golds glistened and dripped. Out of the shadows, copper branches of rock reached down between misshapen pillars, while crystal trees struggled to break free from the earth and walk free into the light. She heard the river bubbling through, singing a forgotten language, but could only catch glimpses of it on the ground ahead, spots of reflected light.

She could have stayed there forever, been queen of that world. Now look how things had turned out. So many trips before the stone sink at the back of the house is filled. Sweat soaks the head-tie that keeps her short plaits in check. She pushes the counterpane under the water with both hands, holds it down, rubs it with blue soap, scrubs it over the hard ripples of the jukking board until her arms ache, thinking, *who else could I have been?* There, in that cave of wonders of her childhood, she could have been queen, but she does not want that now.

She remembers Pips on his way to the War. Phillip David Percy, the one and only, with his long-legged stride, turning heads in his brand new uniform.

"Turnin' all them girls' heads," she teased him.

"Every one except yours," he threw back in her lap and a silence fell between them.

Pips, with that leopard's smile wiped from his face, in the uniform so stiff and different that it felt like she was seeing him for the first time. He stood close enough to touch her, said: "I got to go now, Cathy." The only one who ever called her by that name. Now she grips the counterpane's wet softness, white as the fog he once described to her in letters, creeping over the stealthy river Thames.

The sun burns her face. It is time to get back about her work. She is not a child and Pips is no longer with her. Sweat seeps out of her pores. Her petticoat clings to her skin. Her head-tie slips to one side. The parts in her hair are like shallow gullies after the rain, before the sun magics the moisture back into the air.

When Pips was killed, it took months for the news to reach her. Some said he was part of a mutiny. Others said the West Indian soldiers had to fight two wars at the same time. She keeps the newspapers from that time in a box of old needlepoint shielded by the counterpane hanging over her bed. The pages are brittle from years of handling, till Pips' memory smells like black ink and dust.

She never had her mutiny. Even now, she imagines joining the Independence protests spreading up and down the islands. What a scene she would make, dancing through the street, Crop Over music and bottle and spoon beating in her feet, hips swinging, head thrown back singing, "This is mine, this is mine. Come an' steal a little wine, but doh get too familiar!"

Catherine stares down at the counterpane filling up the stone sink. Sometimes she can see Pips looking at her out of her son's eyes. One minute they're full of love—at other times, accusing. In their brown depths, everything changes. His face writhes in pain, breaking out in yellow blisters. It is Pips' face, covered in mustard gas, even though she cannot smell it. His eyes leak pus, but he does not cry out. Men groan in holes in the ground. Gunfire and echoes of bombs. Smoke clouds her vision. Pips' face alters. She sees the King in whose name they went to war. He is a head severed and unchanged, floating on stamps stuck on letters to London, lost at sea now. Ink blotting, running out.

She sees counterpanes and the Queen Consort in Buckingham Palace, marooned on her own kind of island. She thinks of all the women she could have been. Are they as afraid as she is of the darkness inside, of things buried deep, still fighting to come to light? She runs her hands along the edge of the stone sink. Her fingers graze the cracks webbing its surface. Her palms ride the washboard's unyielding ripples. She could break herself on this stone a thousand times.

Instead, she goes back to washing the counterpane, taking care of the delicate flowers. This counterpane must be cared for with gentle hands. It must be spread over her bed in the early morning light, when her husband has left for work. It must be straightened and pressed with hands that were once so smooth, to make her marital bed beautiful. It is enough. She sees the stains lift off into the water she has carried herself. Mrs Eleazar Conway Franklin she has become: to the Brothers of the congregation, a covered head bowed in prayer; to the Sisters, shared recipes and hand-finished clothes; to her husband, the memory of pink roses and white elbow-length gloves giving way to the smell of coconut bread and lavender baby powder. She is a decade of private caresses. She is the force that pushed her son out into the world and welcomes him back from it each day with warm food and a circle of bosom and arms in which he can, for a moment, feel safe. She is all these things and more.

Something vast and deep and unnamed keeps its head below the surface of the water. She can feel it rising in her throat, pressing up under her skin as if it is about to break through. The counterpane swallows water thirstily. Its soaking mass feels like the weight of a small child. She bundles it into her arms with straining care. Its weight forces her to inch her way across the yard to the clothesline, high and ready with waiting birds. She chases them away. Tired, sweating now more than ever, with that upset feeling pressing down on her chest, she consoles herself with the promise of rest when work is done. She pauses before the line and looks up into the sky kissed by clouds like white tulle. Then she stretches apart two fists clenched full of wet counterpane, and tries to lift it onto the clothesline to dry.

In Bridgetown, in a shop proudly marked FRANKLIN'S FINE TAILORING, her husband rolls out a piece of cloth. The shoe-store next door spits out a sudden blast of music. Bessie Smith sings the blues to Louis Armstrong's groaning trumpet. In the rumshop across the street a man bawls out songs by the calypsonians Shilling and Charmer. He screams out of tune: "Too Late Corkie, too late…!" Her husband's fingers slip, the pattern is spoilt. Little girls shriek as they run past her son in the schoolyard. She sees him through the veil that falls over her eyes.

They say it was the counterpane that killed her; too much weight for her weak heart. Her husband kneels in the dirt beside her. Her son cries, ink and dust on his face. A gaggle of men and women gather round her prostrate body to lift it into the house, no longer hers. At the funeral they file past the coffin weighted down with white roses so that she cannot just get up and walk away.

"Remember Miss Franklin," the Sisters squeeze out from lips closed with respect for the dead.

"Remember Miss Franklin," the Brothers intone, "a good wife, a good mother, a good keeper of her house."

"Remember Miss Franklin," mothers caution their daughters when initiating them into rites of womanhood.

Remember Miss Franklin. What will she remember? What was she thinking as she soared above her body and the earth?

She is a girl terrified by the sound of the river escaping its banks, by the pulse of her own heart, by the dark. She is a child lost in a cave, until she hears his voice, "Big Mouth! Cathy! You there? Big Mouth! You dead or what?"

He asks it first as a joke, then his voice gets shrill, "You dead, Cathy?" For death was something that only happened to big-people.

"No, I here, Pips! I here!"

He shouts back in relief, "Come quick, before night fall."

On the brink of following his voice out into the blinding light, Catherine waits... One thing remains. She turns around and goes down to the water.

Zandria F. Robinson

A Memphis-based writer and sociologist, she focuses in her work on race, popular culture and the US South. She is the author of This Ain't Chicago: Race, Class, and Regional Identity in the Post-Soul South *(2014) and co-author with Marcus Anthony Hunter of* Chocolate Cities: The Black Map of American Life *(2017). Her essays have appeared in* Oxford American, Rolling Stone, Hyperallergic, Scalawag *and* The Believer.

Memphissippi

Memphis is an exceptionally Mississippi-ass place. Some folks call it Memphissippi. I heard some white Memphis cops call it Memfrica. Some people say it's the biggest city in North Mississippi, but that's just them trying to sell Memphis short. Because if Memphis were a city in North Mississippi, it would be the absolute only one. Some folks say it's the capital of the Delta, like the Mississippi writer David L. Cohn who said the Delta starts in the lobby of the Peabody Hotel in downtown Memphis. It is true that Memphis is really an extension of the Mississippi Delta, with similar rates of blues and sadness and babies dying and diabetes. But it has the possibilities of black folks gathered in a place in close proximity and the magic that happens in the big city. If I had my druthers, I'd secede from Tennessee and make a new state out of the Black Belt, the Delta, Jackson, Mississippi, and maybe even the black folks on the other side of the river in Arkansas even though they act funny.

Seeing as I was born on the Tennessee side of things, I get more shame sometimes than Mississippi makes Mississippi folks. Tennessee founded the Klan, but when the Union came to Memphis, the Rebels just laid all the way down and surrendered like some punks. It takes eight hours to get from the southwest corner to the northeast corner of Tennessee, during which the physical landscape changes from delta to hills to mountains and the social landscape changes from predominantly black in Memphis to marginally black in Nashville, to even fewer black folks in Chattanooga and Knoxville to a smattering of black folks in Appalachian towns to straight up Klan country. And even though Tennessee, like everywhere in the world, is Klan country, Tennessee really loves being the Klan. If somebody threatens to take down Robert E. Lee's statue, the Klan is coming out to march and stop all of that. If someone says they are going to try again in a few years, even after we have had a whole entire black President, the state gone pass a law that says no one can remove statues of murderers, warmongers, rapists, and slaveholders. Tennessee gets to hide all of the time because it's not Mississippi Goddam. But to be clear, there ain't no border wall between Tennessee and Mississippi. The porosity means that the good and the bad and the brilliant pass through, both ways.

I have not been called a nigger to my face in Tennessee, though I'm sure someone in Tennessee has called me a nigger, perhaps on multiple occasions. Perhaps I have been called a nigger in every one of the contiguous United States. I have certainly been in Tennessee when I have received e-mails or tweets calling me a nigger bitch, which has a special poetry to it, or a nigger cunt or some such, which is kind of like to my face since the screen is in my face and the words are there yelling at me, but these white-on-black crimes are usually of the interstate sort. For instance, once someone called me a nigger in an e-mail, and I traced them to North Carolina. It seems like the FBI should have gotten involved in that. If the perpetrator has some kind of satellite Internet service, though, is that crime even on this planet anymore? Who has jurisdiction?

I was called colored once, though, directly to my little brown face in the early 1990s in middle Tennessee, and it felt like nigger because I was eight or nine and I had seen more confederate flags on the way to where we were going than I had ever seen in real life or on multiple television miniseries including Ken Burns' Civil War. From the fancy minivan that belonged to one of the parents, I looked out of the tinted windows and pushed myself further down into the seat, mad I couldn't read because I would get car sick looking down. To resist them I resorted to counting them, the flags, and I would keep a note of the tally and tell Mama how many I had seen as as soon as I got to use the car phone out of earshot. Mama always said that flag is about heritage, all right; a heritage of hate. And then she would cuss. The flags made me mad because they meant slavery and getting your foot chopped off and getting lynched and beat and jeered at and hosed and chased by dogs. From my window seat, they made me especially mad because no one else on the all-white-plus me chamber ensemble trip seemed to notice.

It didn't help that in our repertoire were Old South-signifying songs like "Millionaires Hoedown," "Rocky Top, Tennessee" and "Ashokan Farewell," pieces that had been added to our otherwise dignified classical repertoire to flatter our southern crowds. "Ashokan Farewell" had been in Ken Burns' *Civil War* and Mama said, "humph," when she found out it was written the year I was born. Some of my white counterparts lived in suburban neighborhoods called Plantation Oaks and Plantation Ridge and Plantation Peak and so forth, so I knew how white folks made up pasts and brought them to the present so they could feel comfortable. Mama and Daddy's nostalgia was old soul music and theirs was plantations and confederate flags and songs that sound like a sad Confederate soldier with a gangrene leg played them after losing a hard-fought battle with them damn Yankees when really they were written after Maynard Jackson had been mayor of Atlanta for over a decade. I wanted to sever the connective tissue, the sonic mark, the smells of this memory, or at least separate myself from it, because to be associated with such memories as a black girl would ultimately have consequences. I loathed those pieces because they demanded violins be fiddles, and I did not want anybody to mistake me for Fiddler and be reminded of slavery.

Those pieces also delighted white audiences, and I hated them because they brought white folks a particular kind of joy. When we started up the hoedown or Rocky Top, their eyes would widen and buck and they would clap their hands and raise knuckled knees to stomp off beat, afflicted by a sonic tribalism. It was the Holy Spirit of Whiteness that took them over, and I tried intently to watch only my black fingers move quickly on the ebony board, but they were white shadows that demanded an audience. I was known to push the tempo of pieces, a habit I developed in home practice to hurry up and get done that sometimes inadvertently spilled over into concert. But for the hoedown, I pushed it because I wanted the white folks to accidentally slap themselves red trying to clap and keep up and dance themselves and their bucked eyes into the ground. Our violin instructor, sometimes leading and facing us, would glare at me in the front row, her slender body, blue eyes, and stringy blond hair imploring me to slow down. Sometimes I returned her look with my own of confusion, to which she would immediately respond with incredulity. Other times I smirked a bit, changing my Resting Blackness Face just enough for her to know I knew what I was doing. Usually, I kept pushing, knowing

I would be scolded later, because I needed something to happen in exchange for my specific performance of these songs. If not reparations, perhaps winded white folks in worn-out patent leather.

It was the most earnest and unintentionally harmful thing that could have happened given the history of whiteness in America in general, and in middle Tennessee, in particular. The perpetrator looked white 90, so he could have actually been 199 years old and Robert E. Lee's first cousin for all I know given how white folks age like that picture of Dorian Gray. And of course Robert E. Lee's first cousin wouldn't know any better than to call somebody colored. He had made his way to the left side of the stage during the hoedown, his feet rising and falling in succession in a decrepit dance on the oak of the stage. The audience encouraged his dance, clapping in his direction as he added flailing spotted arms to the movement. We concluded and bowed, exiting the stage past him. "Play it again and dance this time," he had said. If I had tried to ignore that he was talking directly to me, he hobbled in front of me to make it plain. "Dance," he said, shortening the command. Oh, I don't know how to dance, I had said, looking down at my feet like I did when I lied, which was my way of refusing. "I never seen a colored couldn't dance," he said. Given as I was the only colored I had seen since we left Memphis and headed to Sewanee, I wondered how many coloreds he could have possibly seen and what kinds he had seen and in what capacities.

I was upset and wanted to go home, and I demanded to call my Mama to say so, even though the adult white folks with me said Robert E. Lee's first cousin didn't mean any harm. I wanted to call my Mama anyway so they would know if anything else happened everybody was gone be in trouble. I told her what happened and she said she was sorry that had happened to me, that somebody as old as Robert E. Lee's first cousin probably didn't know any better or any of the new terms like black and African American, and that at least he didn't say the n-word. Mama doesn't say nigga or nigger or any form of the word. I was about to protest about the implications about my ability to dance, about to say, but why does he get to assume that I can dance? And how many "CULLEDS" does he really know? but I was struck silent by the fact that I couldn't remember the exact final count of confederate flags I had seen to tell her like I had promised myself I would. There was an anxiety in my chest like I had forgotten something real important and was gone be in some big bad trouble. Hurriedly before the estimate disappeared, too, I blurted: also I saw approximately a dozen confederate flags on the way here. I couldn't remember specifically how many it was; I just know it was somewhere between half a dozen and half a million. "Heritage not hate," Mama said, mockingly. "Damn rednecks. Humph," she continued, chewing on something that I knew was better than anything I was gone eat until I got back to Memphis. Gotta go, Mama, I said.

Tennessee ain't shit. Ain't never been shit, really.

Namwali Serpell

Born in Lusaka, Zambia, she is an Associate Professor at the University of California, Berkeley, as well as an award-winning writer. In 2011, she received the Rona Jaffe Foundation Writers' Award, a prize for beginning women writers, and in 2014 she was named on the Hay Festival's Africa39 list of writers aged under 40 with the potential and talent to define trends in African literature. In 2015 she won the Caine Prize for African Writing (for which she was shortlisted in 2010) with her story "The Sack", which first appeared in the anthology Africa39: New Writing From Africa South of the Sahara. *Her first novel,* The Old Drift, *is due to be published in 2019.*

The Living and the Dead

Is it coming?

Yes, *bwana.*

Abdullah left the bedside and went to the entrance—the thatch was open where they had brought *bwana* in on the *kitanda.* Darkness had soaked the curtain of the sky, the fire under the tree gently ripping its edge. The boy, Majwara, heaved the kettle of hot water from its flames, the insides of his elbows flexing. A flock of shouts rose in the distance.

Is that our men making that noise? *bwana* called out, rising slightly.

No. Villagers, scaring off a buffalo.

Bwana grunted and settled back into the heady swamp of his cot. Abdullah beckoned for the boy to hurry. Grimacing with the weight of the kettle, Majwara barreled toward the hut, the steam shifting uneasily whenever he stumbled.

Is this the Luapula river? *bwana* croaked.

No. Chief Chitambo's village.

Majwara stood panting at the entrance, his knuckles knotted on the handle of the kettle.

Sikun'gapi kuenda Luapula?

Na zani zikutatu, bwana.

Oh, dear, dear.

Abdullah was in the middle of a dream about beetles when Majwara woke him again.

Bwana. Come, I am afraid.

Abdullah leapt up and was running before his eyes opened. There was only one candle lit inside the hut but he could make out the shape on the cot. *Bwana* was on his knees, curled over. Abdullah heard the others slipping in behind him. He had watched their *bwana* closely ever since his medicine box went missing, and he knew the effort it took for a sick man to kneel. Now, *bwana* was tipped forward onto his pillow as if falling, his face buried in his hands. Abdullah felt a sudden awe that would not admit touch. After a moment, he reached his hand to the *bwana*'s neck for the second time that night. It was cold.

At dawn, they carried the corpse out of the hut. Abdullah held the ankles, J. gripped the underarms, the body pitched in a vee between them. They lowered it to the ground inside the enclosure, then closed the entrance of the stockade to keep the villagers out. The limbs were stiffening in ticking increments. The arm that the lion had mauled years ago was already frozen. The skin was dull and waxen. A scatter of blood had risen to the surface, mottling it purple. Farjullah, the only doctor left among them, gave instructions.

Hold here. Now here.

Abdullah placed his hands on either side of the abdomen. Farjullah slid the knife into the skin's viscid layers. A blood clot, the size of a hand. Abdullah gagged once, twice.

Farjullah removed and poured water over each organ, then handed it into a large tin box. They watched, hypnotized, as he unraveled loops of purple and yellow entrail. By the time the body was empty, the sun was full. They bent the legs back and packed the trunk with salt. They buried the box of organs under the *mvula* tree and sat on the ground around it. Wainright read the service. The stockade was tall around them, nearly shadowless, blazing white at its center.

Who is here?

Chitambo's mourners.

J. let the two men from the nearby village into the stockade.

One mourner danced, the seed pods on his ankles rattling as he leapt and gamboled. The other mourner droned and played the drums. When the dirge was over, the older man asked for payment. Abdullah pulled out a sachet of beads.

Why do you not bury him here? the man asked out of professional curiosity.

He is an Englishman.

Still a corpse, the man grunted. He took the beads and started counting.

They wrapped the corpse in calico and a cylinder of bark. They sewed it in sailcloth. Finally they sealed it in tar. *Bwana* would have said to think of ethereal Heaven, the mortal coil shuffled off. That was before he left this rotting flesh for them to tend. It was impossible to ask him anything now. For days they debated whether to bury his body in the still, still forest, as he had asked, or to carry it home. In the end, they threw stones to decide.

It took five months and ten deaths before they reached Unyanyembe. Disease, lions, fights with hostile villagers, empty stomachs. We are almost cleaned out, J. warned Abdullah. And the fifty or so men left were bristling with mutiny. When they started tapping war ditties on their hollow rifles, J. took up his own and marched around the bearers carrying the corpse. Abdullah watched, listening to the creaking, purring sound of the wooden box on their shoulders. J. strode around the litter, his hammer clicking as he went from one man to the next. They turned their heads and showed their teeth. The last man stood upright and glared, but said nothing.

Bwana's geographical instruments were all cracked glass by now. How pointless to seize them. But the British never reason. There was no attempt at logic.

I *need* them, Susi. Searching for Livingstone these many months has made my case weaker—

Why bother searching for man you know is dead? thought Abdullah. Maybe at first there was money or fame to be had. What do you hope to gain now? He watched the white man marching in a small circle before him. Lieutenant Cameron was bemoaning the dwindling of his expedition.

We began with a large caravan, a search party, the finest men. Moffat died of fever. Dillon—

And me, I have only three caravan leaders left: Jacob Wainright. James Chuma. Farjullah—

And you? Cameron leered, his blistered cheeks flushing. Do you conceive that you have replaced your deceased master? This ridiculous funeral party you've formed—

We have lost our father. And you want to take his things from us. Force us to bury him.

Every day, putrefaction eats into that body. Soon enough, there will be nought to bury. In the territory through which we just journeyed, the Wagogo forbid carrying the dead…

Abdullah closed his eyes. Night. A man kneeling on the bed, his face buried, his neck bordered by a froth of white hair. He wears his old nightshirt. His hands are hidden.

Abdullah opened his eyes, opened his mouth, spoke over the *muzungu*.

We will take the Doctor home to England. We are so close to the coast, I can smell the salt.

J. lit a fire. The caravan leaders huddled inside the shack they had been granted—except Wainright, whom the colonial officers had taken in because his name was Christian and his English was good. The air in Zanzibar was silken and spicy. The sea was less than a mile away. From the doorway, Abdullah watched the sun's copper embers, the smoke-grey clouds. The day softened off slowly, but his thoughts were bitter and quick. He saw that the others felt the same. They were sitting on a blanket on the ground. Abdullah thought about their lives of catch-and-release. The Doctor had freed each and every one of them from slavery: broken their chains, sometimes with his own hands. Anointed them, hired them, trained them.

J. had brewed a pot of tea—hot water, leaves, no sugar—and was handing tin cups around. The inside of the shack was ripe with its metallic smell.

The HMS *Vulture*, said Abdullah.

What's that? Farjullah looked up.

The name of the ship.

It's here? J. said eagerly, putting his cup on the ground.

Yes. It will carry the body away by sea.

Farjullah wiped his hand down his face. It is done, he sighed.

And Wainright? J. demanded. Where is that bloody toady?

They only have room for one of us. They said they will send for the rest of us later. They've paid us—

They don't even know Wainright! He's only been with us for five years. He is not family. He is the help. J. sipped his hot tea and winced.

Wainright will go ahead, Abdullah said. We cannot afford to refuse the *bwana*'s people.

The sun looked spent in England, unhealthy. The light was more silver than copper here. But Newstead Abbey was lovely, with its lush green lawns and smooth stones like closed eyelids. J. sat across the dining table from Abdullah, in his blue serge jacket with its round bright buttons. He was stirring limp salad leaves with a fork. Abdullah watched without pity as J. pressed his thumb against the tine of his fork. They hadn't eaten British food in years, not since the Doctor had left them at Dr Wilson's Nassick School in Bombay while he scrounged money for a ship to replace the *Lady Nyassa*. Abdullah and J. were still called "Bombay Africans."

Their British host, Mr Webb, was leaning against the far wall, observing them, a hand on his hip. Abdullah's patience had withered: the man hadn't stopped staring at them for weeks. Mrs Webb, his wife, was seated at the table, shouting at a page.

Is it cooked? she asked sternly. Come here! Are you deaf?

The page moved hesitantly toward her and her hand fell heavily onto his arm. She often used the servants as props this way, displaying her might to her guests. Her accent rasped over words, shaving bits of sound off them. In the dull light of the chandelier, her eyes were tarnished coins.

We should take pictures! she panted at her husband. Souvenirs. We could show the Doctor's marvelous maps!

Mr Webb gaped, a laugh catching in his throat. That would be a dumb show indeed, my dear.

J. glumly pushed a tomato slice around his plate.

Abdullah had not thought they would be brought to Great Britain at all. The invitation was cold comfort a year after the state funeral. They had managed to get the great Doctor Livingstone halfway across the world, only to be plied with wreaths of pity: ornamental swords, thin ribbons, silver coins. J. gathered the medals in his hands like bounty and held them in Abdullah's face: Look! he said, his grin deepening the scar in his cheek where the *bwana* had once lashed him.

Their time in England stretched long. White men hosting them in big houses in every corner of the country, dragging them to yet another desolate mansion, a dark irregular trail across the land. Abdullah felt listless beside J. with his bloody felt hats—how far they had fallen, scraping and bowing for these whites. Mr Young made them build a thatch model of the hut where the *bwana* had died—a *kilanda* on its stilts inside. Reverend Waller took them to Leytonstone Church, and to the agricultural show, and on a tour of the workhouse. Abdullah thought with disgust about that awful speech J. had made to the orphans about slavery. The children had been so dirty. So very young.

I do not want to stay here, said Abdullah.

J. looked up from his plate. Are you a child that you must run home?

Abdullah stood and wiped his hands on his trousers. He crossed the stone floor of the old tollhouse where they had been put up for the week. J. kept on quarrying into his meal, humming. Abdullah crouched in front of his trunk and took out the book with the leather binding.

Not this again, J. muttered. I thought you were the wise elder.

Abdullah sat down. He inserted his dinner knife between the pages and the binding and cut the leather strap. He tipped the book open, pushed it across the table. J. continued eating in that slow noisy way of his.

Look, said Abdullah, pointing his knife at a page.

J. reached for a serviette to wipe his hands.

Who stole *bwana*'s medicine box?

You have it wrong, said J. I was faithful to that man, to the very end.

Faithful? *Nts.*

J. leaned back in his chair, his forearms, dark and thin, crossed over his striped vest. What word would you like? Obedient?

What do you know about that word? Abdullah sucked his teeth again.

J.'s cheeks were dotted with white crumbs. Oh, yes, *bwana*, he seethed. I know *nothing* about obedience.

Abdullah glared at him. Rage beat across the air between them. Strange food in a strange land, parading the Doctor's death around. This moldy tollhouse had rekindled something between them.

I did not steal that medicine box. J. released the words one at a time.

I have always suspected you and those—

No. I will not listen to false charges. I have dreams, *bwana*, J. spat.

He stood and paced the room with the easy vigour of an animal. His words cut through the smell of damp and stone, through the wind's whimpering.

I dream of Victoria, said J. The English name was steely in his mouth. My black hand in her white hand. The Queen's smile, true and full. Her crown like the sun, with jewels and gold. I ask: Will you honor us, Your Majesty? She nods. It will come to you when you accept it. Christianity, Commerce, Civilization.

Abdullah looked down and pulled the journal toward him. *January 20, 1867.*

The entry furred under his eyes. When he looked up, J. was gone. Abdullah closed the book.

You shouldn't talk about that medicine box.
    It's done.
    It's been done a long time.
    Bwana—
    Bwana is gone.
    Abdullah turned away in the cot they shared, gingerly hitching up his knees. The moonlight poured through the tollhouse window. Christian boys from Nassick do not need to be told not to murder, the *bwana* had shouted once. Abdullah still scratched invisible prayers to Allah in the sheets. Which God would be more forgiving?
    They carried the corpse to the coast to show their loyalty. They came to England to confirm their innocence. They even recreated the scene of the crime—the hut in the night where the great Doctor Livingstone died—to prove that they hadn't committed it. But Abdullah knew that a shackled man, once freed, is still shackled to the man who freed him. A slave learns early to weigh flesh against gold, life against life, death against profit.
    Abdullah felt J.'s breath in hot waves on the back of his neck. He thought of the times *bwana* shot at them for insubordination and smoking *bange*, for womanizing and caracoling. The moonlight swooned. Abdullah closed his eyes.

The first time he had touched the old man's neck that night, *bwana*'s eyes had opened, his hand scrabbling under his pillow for his bottle of calomel.
    The pain, he said, it pulses. Terrible pain, Abdullah. What is that howling?
    A screech owl, *bwana*.
    The old man sucked the calomel from the spoon like a child, then nestled the bottle back under the pillow. It wouldn't slow the fever's momentum. He had stayed alive as long as he could but his death began as soon as that medicine box vanished.
    Abdullah remembered how they shuffled through the dawn, carrying the corpse to the shelter before the sun rose, how it dangled between them, swaying as they stepped unsteadily between the trees. J. went backwards, and when he stumbled over a root, the *bwana*'s mouth opened with a sucking sound. They handed the body down piecemeal: buttocks, then torso, then legs.
    They stood looking at it for a long time. All of a sudden, J. pitched over the corpse, as if grappling it. A moan lifted, slipped, rose again to a jagged cry.

His eyes open. A face floats above like a stone: flat as day, dark as night. Now the hand around his neck. He clutches at it, fingers forming a bolus of flesh and bone. Slowly, it wrenches the air from its home. The living ebbs. As darkness comes sweeping through, he sees that there is no light. He's surprised to realize that this comes as a relief.

Warsan Shire

A Somali-British poet, her debut pamphlet, Teaching My Mother How to Give Birth, *was published in 2011 by flipped eye publishing. She won the inaugural Brunel University International African Poetry Prize in 2013. In 2014, she was appointed as the first Young Poet Laureate for London and was also selected as Poet in Residence for Queensland, Australia. Her poems have appeared in many publications, including* Poetry Review, Magma *and* Wasafiri, *and her pamphlet* Her Blue Body *was published in 2015. In 2016, she provided the film adaption and poetry for Beyoncé's Peabody Award-winning visual album* Lemonade.

Backwards
For Saaid Shire

The poem can start with him walking backwards into a room.
He takes off his jacket and sits down for the rest of his life;
that's how we bring Dad back.
I can make the blood run back up my nose, ants rushing into a hole.
We grow into smaller bodies, my breasts disappear,
your cheeks soften, teeth sink back into gums.
I can make us loved, just say the word.
Give them stumps for hands if even once they touched us without consent,
I can write the poem and make it disappear.
Step-Dad spits liquor back into glass,
Mum's body rolls back up the stairs, the bone pops back into place,
maybe she keeps the baby.
Maybe we're okay, kid?
I'll rewrite this whole life and this time there'll be so much love,
you won't be able to see beyond it.

You won't be able to see beyond it,
I'll rewrite this whole life and this time there'll be so much love.
Maybe we're okay, kid,
maybe she keeps the baby.
Mum's body rolls back up the stairs, the bone pops back into place,
Step-Dad spits liquor back into glass.
I can write the poem and make it disappear,
give them stumps for hands if even once they touched us without consent,
I can make us loved, just say the word.
Your cheeks soften, teeth sink back into gums

we grow into smaller bodies, my breasts disappear.
I can make the blood run back up my nose, ants rushing into a hole,
that's how we bring Dad back.
He takes off his jacket and sits down for the rest of his life.
The poem can start with him walking backwards into a room.

Novuyo Rosa Tshuma

A native of Zimbabwe, who has lived in South Africa and the US, she is a graduate of the Iowa Writers' Workshop, where she was a Maytag Fellow and a recipient of a Rydson Award for Excellence in Fiction. Shadows, *her short-story collection, was published to critical acclaim in 2013 by Kwela Books in South Africa and awarded the 2014 Herman Charles Bosman Prize for the best literary work in English. In 2017, she was a resident fellow at the Rockefeller Foundation's Bellagio Center, which supported work on her novel* House of Stone, *published in 2018. Her writing has been featured in numerous anthologies, including* McSweeney's *and* The Displaced: Refugee Writers on Refugee Lives, *edited by Viet Thanh Nguyen (2017). She serves on the Editorial Advisory Board of the* Bare Life Review, *a journal of refugee and immigrant literature based in San Francisco.*

Mr C

My fainting spells began around the time Mr C stopped replying to our letters about my father's estate. I was sixteen. They began as a rush of heat to my chest and a tingling coursing through my limbs, a surge of adrenaline that, on a hot day, would make me shiver, followed by a feeling of dread, and this is the only word I can think of that can come close to describing that sensation, so terrible is it, there are no words adequate to describe it. I would black out, whether from the terror of that sensation, as though death were at my heels, I don't know, but this is what I thought at the time, that the death that had taken my father was now after me. This is the feeling, and even though of course I've never experienced death, that is what these spells bring to mind, a sensation that is almost beyond articulation.

No doctor was able to diagnose what was wrong with me; all physical tests came back normal. I had to learn to live with these fainting spells; to anticipate them and try to abate them, this dread, which invariably plunged me into a terrible darkness.

I had loved writing those letters to Mr C. They were the strongest connection I had to my father, communication with this man whom I had first met at his funeral, dabbing his eyes with a checkered kerchief, his big hand warm on my shoulder, sniffling how so very sorry he was, so sorry, Frank had been his best friend, he didn't understand how this could happen. I felt the sour, steel taste in my mouth recede, then, but still I could not speak. I was eleven years old. I hadn't even been able to cry, ever since learning my father had died. He had been visiting Bulawayo from London where he lived and worked, and had been involved in a car accident on his way home from the airport. I had spoken to him on the phone just after he alighted from the plane.

"See you soon, Daddy!"

"See you soon," he had said.

And so I took great care with those letters. I would sit with Mum and together we would go over Mr C's correspondence, written in an extremely cold, lawyerly tone. I would help Mum draft our replies to him. I had taken care to research formal letter-writing, and where I thought of an ordinary word I would consult my father's thesaurus for a more severe-sounding synonym, so as to reflect back to Mr C his lawyerly tone. I thought this was the correct thing to do, but it irked him no end as, it later turned out, he thought I was being rude. But I was only trying to mirror him, matching him in both wording and tone. Instead of writing "things are not as you make them out to be", I would look for the appropriate wording and write: "matters are not as you purport them to be." I loved writing those letters; I laboured over them so, revising and revising and revising. I needed them to be perfect for Mr C!

But then, one day, he just stopped responding, and after a while, it became apparent that he had no intention of replying to any of my letters, which I imagine became less professional and more child-like, more *me*, with each unanswered correspondence. It was only natural that, when I turned eighteen, I decided to take over my father's estate. With a thrill, I realised this meant I would have to meet with Mr C.

Each time I telephoned his office to make an appointment to change the named executor of my father's estate from him to me, though, his secretary said he was booked up for months on end, and could not see me, and although she always assured me that he would get back to me, he never did. My emails to him went unanswered too.

I decided, then, to take the Greyhound bus from Bulawayo down to Harare and ambush Mr C right outside his offices. I thought myself terribly clever. And though I had come under the pretext of discussing my father's estate, what I really wanted was to see Mr C, to feel the reassuring weight of his hand on my shoulder again. I had with me the letters my father and I had exchanged when I was a child, and also an old copy of the *University of Zimbabwe Law Review* that he, Mr C, and my father had run while as undergraduates, during those days when my daddy, a sharp, pensive Marxist, had penned legal articles full of the passion of that age, the early twenties when one is full of ideals, and fueled as well by the politics of that time, the 1980s, just after Zimbabwe's independence, when notions of freedom and justice had run high, and our country had then had what had seemed a bright future.

Surely, seeing me, Frank's daughter, would soften Mr C. The sight of me would stop him in his tracks, for he hadn't seen me since the funeral. He would hug me, cup my face, run his thumbs over my cheeks, stare into my eyes and say, "You look just like him! You're the spitting image of Frank. Wow!" And I would beam and try not to blush and laugh that deep-throated laugh, full and chortling and free. Mr C would take us for coffee at a nearby spot, perhaps somewhere fancy like the Borrowdale Market, somewhere that was likely, during those terrible days of food-shortages and money-shortages and bloody water-shortages and a shortage of just about anything decent, to have banana bread or queen cakes redolent with that freshly baked aroma. We would sit side by side, and over milky, frothy coffee, the good kind that's bitter and sweet, I would show him the letters we used to write to each other, my daddy and I, and we'd laugh at his short, clipped sentences, their struggle to imitate a child's language.

I would ask him, Mr C, "What was my daddy like? I hear he loved to dance, he loved jazz—is this true? I hear he was also very pensive and took his work seriously and loved his alone time, like me. I'm very serious for my age and I like my alone time. Is it true that he was inspired to study land tenure law because of the pain of seeing how my khulu had to be away all the time as a migrant worker after those wretched Rhodesians took away his land during Smith's time?

"What was he like in university? I'll be going to university soon, myself. What kinds of things did he like? Did he have a temper? I have a temper. Everyone says he was brilliant. I'm trying hard to follow in his footsteps, although they are so very large and intimidating."

He would tell me how proud of me he was, Mr C, that I was more than enough to fill my father's shoes, that he had known Frank well and he would be proud of me and how I was turning out. I was his spitting image, after all, everyone said that. We would exchange memories of him, and I'd tell Mr C about my trip to Rome as a child, this trip I had played over and over in my mind because it was the last one I took with my father, and now it felt as though it was all I had.

I thought he would like to hear this, Mr C.

I must have stood for a good three or so hours on that quiet street of office buildings, leaning against the wall of his building, busy daydreaming. I went up the stairs to the first floor once, but balked when I got to the reception, and dashed back down the steps and out onto the street. And then he finally appeared, Mr C, not on foot as I had imagined, but in that sleek Jaguar I recognized immediately as it purred out of the office parking-lot. It halted, and I could see him looking first left, and then right, and I saw my chance. I straightened up, hesitated, then took a few steps towards the car. That's when he saw me, just as he was turning right, into the street, towards me. He must have seen me. I imagine he squinted behind his rimless specs. I certainly squinted, ducking my head slightly for a better view, trying to see him through his car window. I raised my hand, half-waving, half-waving him down. He craned his neck, and the Jaguar slowed down. But then it picked up speed. He did not stop; I thought at least he might. But the Jaguar purred past me, halted by the corner, turned left into Sixth Street and disappeared from view.

I stood for a long time in that street, on that road, looking this way and that, sucking on my lower lip. And then, finally, I turned and walked down Selous Avenue, towards the bustle of Sixth Street, headed back to my B&B, my shoes crushing the bell-shaped jacaranda flowers carpeting the road—it must have been late October—balmed, in a savage sort of way, by the sight of the boysenberry bruises my feet inflicted on those periwinkle Jacaranda petals.

I did receive, to my delight, a call from Mr C's secretary the next day, asking me to come and collect the documents I would need to change the executor of my father's estate from him to me. (So, he *had* seen me!) I remember, with a little shame, how so very excited I was, then, taking care to apply a little lipstick in the foggy bathroom mirror adjoining my single room at the B&B, dabbing my cheap-imitation Dolce & Gabbana perfume just behind the lobes of my ears, and on my collar bone as well, staining, in the process, my pin-stripe blouse, which went very well with my black pencil skirt. I looked, I thought, very professional and very grown up; the kind of woman Mr C wouldn't be ashamed to take to one of his fancy lawyer places for coffee; a version of Frank's daughter he would be pleased to see.

But when I went to collect the documents, I didn't get to go up to him, as I had expected I would, as I had all those times as a child, whisked welcomingly up to his office or the boardroom by his secretary. Instead, the documents were waiting for me at the reception. I asked if I could see him, and the lady at the reception called his office. She frowned slightly at me, the receiver angled to her lips, and then relayed the message that he would not be available that day. I said I would wait, I did not mind. After speaking into the phone again, she turned to me, shaking her head, and said I had to go.

I felt, then, those fainting spells creeping up on me, and I staggered, hoping to fall, to pass out right there, in Mr C's office. In my mind, I saw myself falling into his large arms, his face peering above me, his large nose trembling with concern. But I didn't faint, and though I tried, I couldn't will the full power of that dreadfulness, right at that moment when I needed it most!

I don't know if my eyes were brimming. I certainly felt like crying, though I tried very hard not to, swallowing hard, my throat throbbing with the sensation of suppressed tears. The receptionist winced, appraising me, I thought pitifully, and I could not bear that look of pity; I turned around and stumbled out of Mr C's offices, cluttering down the stairs, my head bowed.

Pre-1900

1900s

1920s

1930s

1940s

1950s

1960s

1970s

1980s

1990s

Yassmin Abdel-Magied

A Sudanese-born Australian mechanical engineer, writer and social advocate, she worked on oil and gas rigs before becoming a full-time writer and broadcaster. She published her debut memoir, Yassmin's Story *(2016), at 24, then became the presenter of* Australia Wide, *a national weekly current-affairs show on the ABC. After hosting the documentary* The Truth About Racism, *she created* Hijabistas *for the ABC, a series looking at the modest fashion scene in Australia. She is an internationally accredited F1 reporter and a regular contributor to the BBC. Her writing has appeared in publications including* Teen Vogue, *the* New York Times *and* The Guardian. *She founded the not-for-profit Youth Without Borders at the age of 16 and has since served on numerous boards and councils. She is currently based in London.*

Eulogy for My Career

I recently spent some time in my childhood home of Brisbane. As we drove around the soft bend leading up to my family's double brick house, I couldn't help but reminisce. I'd travelled on this road many a time on almost all forms of transport: driving in my new Alfa Romeo at 3 a.m. in the morning, sneaking back into the house from a late-night session (and by session I mean study session, OK? I was an actual certified nerd), walking to the bus stop when that Alfa Romeo lived up to its reputation by inevitably breaking down, and running 2km loops around the block when I was in that short-lived "maybe-one-day-I'll-do-a-marathon" phase.

Sitting in the passenger seat of the family car, my younger brother grown and behind the wheel, watching the familiar houses and trees glide by, I grew nostalgic.

How was fifteen-year-old Yassmina, running around this block, to know that a decade later, these streets would hold more than simple, happy memories of early morning jogging sessions accompanied by the soundtrack of feet lightly padding along the pavement, neatly wrapped in the still silence of suburbia?

How was twenty-year-old Yassmina to know that, five years later, her hard-won engineering degree would be the last thing that people knew about her, not the first? That six years later, she would have walked away from her dream of working on a Formula One team, ushered out of her job on an oil rig, squeezed out of her newfound role as a TV broadcaster, her mental health spiralling, reputation in shambles, and with a Wikipedia page that mostly talked about "controversies"?

How was twenty-six-year-old Yassmina to know that a year later she would be returning to the country of her citizenship to eulogise a career she didn't even know was coming to an end?

As my brother parked the black Honda Civic, I was overcome with a tidal wave of heaviness, a blanket made of lead that seemed to smother my soul. There was a strange metallic taste in my mouth that I couldn't quite name, and it wasn't until I lay in my bed that evening, the single bed I had lain in every night for over a decade, that it hit me. Moonlight was shining through the blinds, glinting on tears that threatened to spill. The weight was more than just jet lag—I was in mourning. What a strange feeling indeed.

I could feel my face furrowing as I tried to make sense of my emotions. I swallowed, allowing my tears to run down my cheeks and turn the pale pillow cover a darker shade of blue, and I attempted to reckon with reality. What was this deep, cavernous sense of loss that had opened up in my chest? What was this ache in my lungs, making every breath feel like I was drowning, trying to take in air through a snorkel that was rapidly filling up with water? Why did this whole house, this whole street, this whole city now feel foreign to me, like it was only a place I'd visited in my dreams?

This was grief, but it was not just my career I was grieving. I was grieving my past self. It was the baby Yassmina I had lost, a resolutely positive and perhaps blindly optimistic young person, a soul unburdened by the knowledge of what the world does to people who don't quite fit the mould and who want us all to be a little better. I had lost an innocence I didn't even know I had.

I wanted this eulogy to be funny. I wanted to bid farewell to a Formula One career that waited for all the lights to turn on but never quite got off the starting mark. I wanted to say goodbye to a professional engineering pathway that many don't know the details of, but that makes me very proud. I wanted to commemorate a broadcasting job that took us all by surprise, as it turned out that I was halfway decent at it. I wanted to talk about the highs and the lows, the bits that make me laugh, the times that gave it all meaning. And there are lots of those moments. But when I sat down to write this eulogy, all that came out was grief.

It poured out of my fingers and soaked these pages, like rainwater in a drought-stricken desert. It's actually annoying, really. I'm quite tired of this grief business. I thought I had bid farewell to this traveller. But grief is a visitor that overstays its welcome, and no matter how much subtle hinting at the time, it's still splayed out on your couch, eating nachos and getting guacamole on your carpet. Turns out grief does what it wants, and pays no attention to schedules or social niceties.

Grief will turn up when you least expect it—you're on your way out to a dinner date, and ding-dong, there it is, at your door, walking in uninvited. You're having lunch with friends, and then poof! It apparates next to you and dominates the conversation for the next hour, paying no attention whatsoever to what you were talking about before. Hell, you could be watching *Happy Feet Two* on a plane, and grief will pop out of the oxygen compartment above, wave its hands in your face and make you miss the rest of the damn film. Not that I'm speaking from experience or anything.

Part of me also doesn't want this eulogy to be about anything at all, because that would be admitting that those past versions of myself are gone. Done, dusted, finito. I'm not sure I'm ready for that. Are we ever really ready to let go? That's the thing about death. It's kinda like grief. A terrible houseguest. It just turns up, and you're expected to have the kettle on and the right kind of biscuits on hand. I mean, c'mon man. Cut a sister a break! Send me a calendar invite or something at least, so I can make sure I'm presentable. But no. Death, pain, grief: the bloody three musketeers that they are, they give zero fucks about your plans. It's brutal, but I guess it's the only way to ever really level up in this life. If you don't know, now you know, sister.

In Islam, when someone dies, we say *"Ina lilahi, wa ina lani rajiun"*. It roughly translates to: We are for Allah, and to him we shall return. I wondered if I could apply this to my past self, or my various iterations of careers, and then I mentally slapped myself for my indulgence. Girl, get a hold of yourself! You ain't dead yet! This is eulogy for your career, you indecisive millennial, not *you*. *You're* still here, alive and kicking Alhamdulilah, no matter how much some may wish otherwise. So act like it.

I got an Instagram direct message on Friday, just before I got the plane from London to Australia. It read as follows: "My Name Is Nelson, and I'm a big fan. Do you mind if I ask just one favour? Please Reply, I love You."

Then: "Go to Flinders St Station, Cut Your Wrists and Let them bleed out so we can all watch you die. Lest We Forget. Hopefully I'll be able to distinguish you from all the other Sudanese Niggers, but I know you'll be the only ape wearing a ridiculous towel over your head."

Nelson, I'm sorry to inform you that this specific favour will not be granted, darling boy, though I may be wearing a ridiculous towel on my head, because well, that's very on-brand. My past lives might be thoroughly dead, cooked, roasted, their remains served on a platter for all to feast on, but in this moment, I am not. I'm very much still alive, and that is a gift that I cannot bear to waste, and in the words of the great Hannah Gadsby, there's nothing stronger than a broken woman who has rebuilt herself.

I now think of the death of baby Yassmina as a controlled burn, in the tradition of the First Nations people who are the custodians of this land. They understood that sometimes for change and regeneration, you have to raze the existing growth to the ground and let the new take root. And oh, yes, those flames are searing and yes, sometimes, I still hear the crackle and pop of burning flesh.

But I'm starting to get used to it, as my careers have a habit of going up in flames. So why do I keep playing with fire? Well, perhaps my previous analogy was slightly off. This is no controlled burn, no regenerative wildfire. It appears that I live in a burning house. Death lives down the road, pain is my roommate and grief is always turning up uninvited. But we're friends now. We bicker, we fight, we make each other laugh. And I wouldn't be who I am today without them.

So bye-bye, baby Yassmina. Bye bye, straighty-180 engineer, toothy-smiled TV presenter, giggling Good Muslim Girl who thought that her trio posse of innocence, positivity and optimism were all she needed. I've got new friends now. But your old friends are welcome to visit, of course. Maybe, maybe they can even stay. Maybe, we can get to know each other. Come through, I'll put the kettle on.

Rutendo Chabikwa

*A Zimbabwean writer, poet and content creator, she was joint winner of Myriad's
2018 First Drafts competition. In 2012 she was awarded the Golden Baobab Prize
for Rising Writers, and in 2016 she sat on the panel as a judge for the prize. Outside
fiction, she writes about African art, as well as long-form socio-political analyses.
She is the host and producer of a podcast on diversity in academia and she recently
completed her MSc at the London School of Economics and Political Science in
Women, Peace and Security. The following extract is from a novel she is working on
called* Todzungaira.

Mweya's Embrace

I think I am hungry. Mweya always leaves me with an emptiness in my stomach. I
am not hungry. I lie on my back and stare at the ceiling in the dark. Dogs are fighting
over the garbage in the street. I think they are dogs. There is no barking or growling.
I hope they are dogs. I once saw a fox while walking home from the pub. It appeared
more scared of me than I was of it, though my heart still pounded heavily in my chest.
The dogs tip over a metal trash-can and I hear bags and glass fall out. I imagine them
tearing open a bag with their teeth, their snouts nuzzling into the filth. My attention is
drawn back to the empty feeling in my stomach. I get up, put on my bedside slippers,
stolen from a hotel I stayed in during a conference. I was there to present a paper on
embodying intergenerational trauma in the postcolonial subject. I shuffle to the door
and pat my way in the dark to turn on the light. I really need to buy a bedside lamp. I
could have used my phone but Mweya's visit tonight left me dull-witted.

Mhai tells me Mweya did not leave my great-grandfather that sharp either. Mhai
tells me that great-grandfather Chandapihwa was from kwaChiundura. He was only
twenty-three when, in 1944, he was forcibly conscripted into the Rhodesian African
Rifles and sent to Burma to help the British fight against the Japanese. Mhai has shown
me a picture. Chandapihwa was a tall, dark, lanky man with death in his eyes. Not
that he *was* death, but seeing so much death had displaced the life in him. He wore an
oversized wide-brimmed hat, khaki shorts, and an oversized khaki shirt with a badge
on his left arm. He saw death, when his fellow recruits dropped like flies around him
as they charged against the Japanese army. He felt the depth of pain when a bullet
tore through his leg.

He learned of companionship when he and other black men like himself were
flung into a war that did not concern them. He learned of affliction when, upon
returning home, all he received was ten pounds. The white regiments received land,
gold claims, and money for rehabilitation. They were given *his* land, *his* gold claims,
and money that *his* brothers and sisters had toiled for in the name of financing the war.
There was no parade, no hero's welcome. Black regiments were not made of heroes.

Chandapihwa found Mweya in Burma. She visited him each night as he lay awake in a cramped camp with other black soldiers. She sat and watched him recall the events of each day. She watched him as he remembered his brush with death. She listened to him sigh, dragging slowly across his mind the images of the bodies he had helped bury. She stared at him as he tried to remember all their names, hoping that if he lived to see home, he would tell about the bodies. She sat and watched him hope for a decent burial. Mweya stayed with Chandapihwa, her visits becoming more frequent. He felt her pull him back every time he moved forward. She held his head down every time he tried to float. She always held him close. Chandapihwa returned home from Burma with Mweya on his shoulders, death in his eyes, and a limp in his leg. He wore a heavy coat till he died. He would sink into it whenever he spoke—which was rarely—of the war that killed people like flies. Mweya followed Chandapihwa. She followed him to his job as a prison guard, the job that ended abruptly with no explanation. She trailed in his wake to construction sites that did not pay enough for the family he was starting. She shadowed him to the white farms that his damaged leg could not survive, where the weight of the work and Mweya on his back were too much to bear.

It is almost 3 a.m. now. I am in my kitchen and wondering what beverage one should drink at this time of the day, or night. It is too early for coffee and too late for wine. Water would be tasteless, and I forgot to buy juice. I take milk out of the refrigerator and I twist the cap off. The pungent smell punches my nostrils. I chuckle to myself, thinking that cultured milk—which I now call "bad"—used to be a favourite part of my cuisine. Mhai really knows how to prepare sour, or cultured, milk. Never too rancid, never too watery, just the right amount of mutuvi to add to the cream that rises to the top. But this milk I have in my hands right now, this is bad milk.

I drag my feet to my kitchen bin and throw the bottle in. I have not had fresh food in my house since the last time I fell in admiration. That was the last time I had any reason to have fruit, vegetables, and fresh milk in my house. He, like me, was from another country; came to this big city to try to make a living. Tried to understand what making a living in a dead place meant. We were both swimming against the current that is London, both without anyone to throw us life-jackets or teach us how to swim. So we floated towards each other and our half-living flesh and bones would occasionally merge in an act of loveless love.

But Mweya came along and ripped our tired bodies apart. Once, she held me in a corner for so long I could not move. I could not answer when he asked me what was wrong. Mweya sat on my lap and choked me, and told me that love was an illusion. With her foul cold breath in my face, I listened. She told me that, ultimately, we would all end up alone.

And so, he left, on a grey rainy Sunday afternoon when I had once again been unable to move. He had asked me, politely and apologetically, if he could stay and pry apart Mweya's scrawny arms. I stayed in her deadly embrace. The embrace that had once held my great-grandfather Chandapihwa. The same arms that had raised my grandfather VaMazivisa, long after Chandapihwa was gone. Chandapihwa had returned from the war with Mweya on his back and a limp in his leg. Only in a few moments, when Mweya was not sitting on his shoulders, and death had taken a short leave from his eyes, would he sit with a son who had learned to walk and talk while he was away fighting Britain's war.

VaMazivisa was a life made in the absence of death, a lightness not weighed down. Mhai says she cannot tell me much about VaMazivisa's childhood. VaMazivisa himself would seem to forget some parts of it when she asked, but Mhai was certain of one thing: growing up in a world that tried to whip him into something he was not made him embrace Mweya more. VaMazivisa grew up in the absence of Chandapihwa, who was always away trying his hand at one job or the other. At eighteen, VaMazivisa left Ambuya's compound for a job in the city. He joined his cousin in a township, Mbare, and they would occasionally exchange passes when they were leaving the neighbourhoods Black people had been relegated to, for the white suburbs where they would do menial jobs. Those days, Baba tells me, passes had no pictures, just a description of a feature, such as "birthmark on left arm". The pass they shared read:

> Name: Jairos Mutasa
> Date of Birth: 01 January 1941
> Village Chief: Mutasa
> Prominent Mark: Scar on right arm

Mhai tells me that VaMazivisa met her mother after three years of living in the big city. That was 1963. Mhai was already two years old at that point. Her biological father had passed away before she was born. Word that had reached Mhai's mother said it was a work-related incident in the industries. But Mhai tells me he was killed by the white police force during a strike. Mhai says her father was not the only one who lost his life then. Mhai was not born in the rural areas, her mother had moved to the city to clean houses and take care of white children to make a living. Mhai grew up with a void that even VaMazivisa could not fill. VaMazivisa was what the white people derogatorily called a "tea boy"; he worked in the kitchens of the headquarters of mining and insurance companies. He rarely returned to kwaChiundura, but he occasionally wrote to Ambuya and asked about Chandapihwa. He sent some money back, but the city was his home now. Mhai was his daughter, his daughter with a void.

A couple of years passed, and Chandapihwa passed on to another world. He died young. Life had long left his body by then. Death had made a permanent home in his eyes. Mweya had chained herself to him with metal too heavy to break. Everyone had tried. But every night Mweya would remind Chandapihwa of the time they met in Burma. She would drag his feet through fields of dead bodies. She would choke him, to remind him of the gas canisters that had been thrown at him. With every passing day, she used the chain to drag him to his grave, a journey he seemed to welcome more and more with every setting sun.

The funeral was the first time in a long while that VaMazivisa had returned to kwaChiundura. As Chandapihwa's body was lowered into the earth, Mweya loosened her end of the chain and embraced VaMazivisa. Her breath on his neck was cold. He felt uncomfortable, she was a new weight, but he carried her back to the city. He carried her to work, where she pointed out how he was treated by his superiors. He carried her on the street, where she reminded him that it was impossible for him to amount to much, that he might end up like his father. He carried her to the bottle store, where she held his hand as he drank one beer after another. He carried her home.

I settle on making some tea. I do not know why I had not thought of making tea before. Time is moving slowly. It is only 3:30 a.m. and sleep has completely left me. I could sit at my laptop and try to write a quick article for a blog or I could finish editing an audio project I recorded months ago. None of that sounds appealing. Nothing I could possibly write about has not already been written about; and if it has not, someone somewhere can surely write it better. As for the sound project, it sounded good while it was in my head—a combination of street sounds, poetry and song. It was an exploration of how I feel in this city. As soon as I finished recording each part, I realized the masterpiece I thought I had was worthless. So no, I am not going to edit that.

I half-fill the kettle with water and turn it on. I have only the option of either green tea or lemon and ginger tea. I should have bought that cranberry-raspberry tea they have at work. I snicker. I am here thinking about different tea flavours when, growing up, all I drank was black tea that had all the flavour boiled out of it, with ridiculous amounts of sugar and milk added. I miss that tea. Baba hates it. He says boiled milk makes him sick. I remember having that boiled tea every day when we visited Baba's mother in the rural areas. All the grandchildren would be rounded up and we would sit outside on the ground with metal cups full of boiled tea, and metal plates with two thick slices of white bread. Those days, my cousins were my siblings. That was before Mhai told me about the siblings that could have been. The siblings that Mweya took away.

Panashe Chigumadzi

Born in Zimbabwe and raised in South Africa, she had her debut novel Sweet Medicine *published in 2015, winning the K. Sello Duiker Memorial Literary Award. She is the founding editor of* Vanguard *magazine, a platform for young black women coming of age in post-apartheid South Africa, and a contributing editor to the* Johannesburg Review of Books. *Her work has featured in* The Guardian, *the* New York Times,

Washington Post, Die Zeit *and* Transition. *She combines reportage, memoir and critical analysis in her second book,* These Bones Will Rise Again, *published by The Indigo Press in 2018.*

From *These Bones Will Rise Again*

On 15 August 1991, my mother gave birth to me at the Mbuya Nehanda maternity ward of Parirenyatwa, Zimbabwe's largest hospital.

How fortunate to be born in a place named after the most famous person in Zimbabwe's liberation history, a political leader who defied expectations of African women's place by leading an anti-colonial war. A military tactician remembered in popular mythology for commanding, "tora gidi uzvitonge", take the gun and liberate yourself. A spiritual leader who held to her beliefs and refused to convert to Christianity. A visionary immortalized through her dying words, uttered as she faced execution for her role, "My bones will rise again".

How can I not be proud of this birthplace, when I have seen Mbuya Nehanda's restless spirit carried by many women, my grandmother Mbuya Lilian Chigumadzi, one of them. How telling is it that the word mbuya, or ambuya, refers to both grandmother and spiritual woman?

Having moved to South Africa in 1994, the year of its first democratic elections, I am a "born-free" of Southern Africa's two dominant former settler colonies. The thrusting of this title on the young is part of an understandable desire by the old to be free of their past, as if the mere passage of time will erase injustices. To grow up as a young black woman moving between Zimbabwe's post-independence and South Africa's post-apartheid eras is to understand that time does not erase history; so I seek guidance from these mbuyas who have led men and women in ways big and small, ahead of their time, defiant of the body's limits.

At the foot of a hill behind the homestead belonging to my great-grandfather, Sekuru Ifayi Dzumbira, there is rock art painted on granite outcrops, etched in vivid reds and brown. Hundreds, if not thousands, of years old, the images here are older than Zimbabwe.

It is 26 December 2017. We have driven almost 70km from my maternal grandmother Mbuya Beneta Chiganze's home in Makoni District. Our visit is to my late paternal grandmother, Mbuya Lilian Chigumadzi's surviving relatives living in Mutare, Zimbabwe's fourth largest city, located in the eastern highlands, on the border with Mozambique.

We begin 20km outside Mutare in Doradombo, a ruzheva, or what used to be called a "native reserve". This was where my father had always known his maternal grandfather Sekuru Ifayi Dzumbira to live, so he assumed this to have been her ancestral home. The homestead is tucked into a valley surrounded by towering granite mountains. As we approach, my father points to the adjacent mountain. "It used to be said that a njuzu lived on top of it." As the surviving children of my grandfather's second wife show us to Sekuru Ifayi's grave at the foot of a set of hills, they confirm that the menacing water spirit is there. They know, because whenever rain is about to fall, it is preceded by the sight of smoke at the top of the mountain where there is a stream. They take us to the cave-like overhang, under which Sekuru Ifayi practised his profession as an iron smelter. We pose for pictures with the remnants of his implements.

The perfect foundation for an origin story. A rock-solid moment on which to stake my family's claim to Zimbabwe and its history.

My own struggle for history begins in dislocation. Having grown up in South Africa, away from my extended family, I've always been at a physical remove from my culture. The kind of "loss" of heritage I experienced is maybe best understood through my relationship to my mother tongue. At some point, my brother and I had "forgotten" Shona. I couldn't tell you how exactly it happened. It felt swift and painless: I arrived at my predominantly white pre-school in the South African coastal city of Durban not speaking a word of English and, within a short time, I could barely speak any Shona, despite my parents speaking it at home.

By the time I was a pre-adolescent, Zimbabwe was dipping into crisis. Since independence in 1980, the government had been under pressure to deracialize an economy firmly invested in the domestic white landowning class allied with international capital. By 2000, liberation war veterans were fed up with the government's refusal to shake up an agricultural sector dominated by 4,500 white commercial farmers. Over that year's Easter weekend the war veterans staged a carefully organized campaign seeing 170,000 families occupy 3,000 white-owned farms. Initially opposing the move, the increasingly unpopular ZANU—PF government backed the veterans, sanctioning the chaos that Shona-speaking Zimbabweans refer to as jambanja, which spread to the economy; as inflation began to rise, the currency became worthless, and queues outside supermarkets, banks, fuel stations, hospitals and work places became longer and longer. Living in Polokwane, 220km from Beitbridge, which soon became the busiest of all the continent's border posts, we felt keenly the effects of this crisis, as every other weekend relatives would stay over to stockpile groceries unavailable on the shelves back home. I was now being called a "lekwerekwere", a pejorative for black foreigners, at school.

The stories we found in books and listened to from the mouths of my parents on frequent journeys back home held me as steady as they could against the onslaught of dislocation.

The struggles over history are complex, because the present continuously slips into the past, marking history as ambivalent, incomplete, a work in progress. History is like water—it lives between us, and comes to us in waves. At times, it is still and unobtrusive; at others, it is turbulent and threatening. Even at its most innocuous, water poses hidden dangers, enclosing contested histories, and so we are always living in the tension between tranquillity and tumult. When we walk along the water's edge, it's easy to take for granted the complex process of how that water reached our feet, to overlook what is washed away, what alters and what holds in the sands of time. It is history as a series of waves, always in flux, a site of discovery in the past, present and future, and not something stable, foreclosed, that is most troubling to nationalist agendas because it is too difficult to control.

In the midst of these moving waves, far from the sturdiness of Sekuru Dzumbira's granite boulders, the history I am trying to craft begins with a moment etched on a surface that is man-made and more flimsy. Perhaps less because of that fragility and more because of the dislocations and disjunctures across generations and space, this history begins with loss.

The unsteady surface is, or was, a studio photograph of Mbuya Lilian Chigumadzi as a young woman. I don't know whether it still exists. As a school child, this photograph was entrusted to my possession. I subsequently lost it, having, ironically, used it for a school project on family history. In it, she stands graceful, composed, sexy even. Her weight on her left leg and her right hip slightly tilted. A white cotton dress, stark against her dark skin, stretches a little over a rounded tummy and slim hips. A conical headwrap, the kind worn by Miriam Makeba, crowns her head. Lips part, revealing a cheeky gap to swallow the world. She doesn't smile. Eyes wide, she meets my gaze, demanding that I bear witness.

Her statement, if I hear her correctly: un-bought and un-biased. Just arrived in Umtali: with no young man preparing to persuade any uncles for cattle he has not yet worked to own; no white family with dirty kitchens and children which need cleaning and who need raising. Alone, unburdened, unattached, only Belonging to Herself.

Or so it is, in my imagining.

I look again. The photograph appeared to have been taken in the 1960s; she would have been my age, her early twenties. A black-and-white photo with contrasts softened by years of sun, sparks dulled by the weight of everyone else's future but her own. I bear witness to an epitaph that life has taught me: sometimes, dreams are colder than death.

To my knowledge, this was the only individual portrait taken of my grandmother for decades. Perhaps this is what I loved most about that picture: that she was alone. She stood with no baby in her arms or on her back or husband by her side. I was struck by the way she didn't look like the grandmother I knew. And perhaps this is the point; she is not my grandmother in that picture. She is not Mbuya Chigumadzi, Mai Chigumadzi, Mrs Kenneth Chigumadzi, Ma Rophina, Tete Lilian, Yaya Lilian. She just is. She belongs to no one but herself. She is Lilian. That is who I mourn, more than for my grandmother.

On the day Mbuya died, I felt the earth pull me down. I couldn't sleep, I couldn't read, I couldn't watch TV. I think I could accept the death of *Mbuya* because I had known that person. What I found difficult to accept was the death of the Lilian

Dzumbira I did not know. That is the person for whom I felt the deepest sense of loss. Unsure what to do, I wrote down some questions.

What were you like as a child? What about your mother, and your grandmother?

Mbuya Lilian met Sekuru Kenneth Chigumadzi when he was working as a clerk near Mutare.

Was it hard to live apart when he worked away in town? What did it mean to become a young widow with five children?

She had a stroke that paralyzed her twenty-three years ago.

Do you think your body was forcing you to rest after all those years of hard work? What kept you going all these years?

I don't have much recollection of her walking, except for the time she and Mbuya Chiganze came to visit us in Durban a few months before her stroke.

What was it like to take a bus and leave the country for the first time? What about seeing the sea?

You used to ask when we would come back to Zimbabwe. What made you stop asking?

My life, freed by almost limitless opportunities, and her life, limited by the circumstances of her day, seemed to exist planes apart. For years, I looked at her with eyes clouded by a disturbing shallowness not allowing for realities too far from my own experiences. It wasn't until I met the force of the unflinching stories of our mothers and grandmothers and aunts and sisters written by black women—Yvonne Vera, Tsitsi Dangarembga, Bessie Head, Ama Ata Aidoo, Alice Walker, Toni Morrison, Audre Lorde, Jamaica Kincaid, Edwidge Danticat, Maryse Condé—that I was compelled to ask more of my view of their worlds, to find an answer to the question: what did it mean to be a black woman in my grandmother's time?

Where I find myself in my writing, Mbuya found fulfilment in embodying a saying she often repeated: *"Mukadzi haa gariri mawoko."* A woman does not sit on her hands. With those hands, she built a rich world as caregiver, farmer, gardener, cook, baker, needle worker, doily-maker, cultivating a spirituality that is the basis of the worlds about which I attempt to write.

When we visited my grandmother she often had the radio on, listening intently to the news, the talk shows and music of the day. Sometimes, when I'd leave she would tease me, saying, "Panashe, we will talk on Facebook." When we lamented the changing weather patterns, she would comment, "It's this issue of global warming making this happen." Her little cell phone was always ringing, young and old alike calling for advice on this or that life matter. If it wasn't on the phone, they came to consult her directly in her bedroom that my family called the "head office" or "the court".

That is how she survived twenty-two years after a stroke. That is not the work of the body. That is the work of the spirit.

Anaïs Duplan

Born in Haiti and now living in the US, they are the author of a full-length poetry collection, Take This Stallion *(2016), and a chapbook,* Mount Carmel and the Blood of Parnassus *(2017). Their poems and essays have been published by* Hyperallergic, PBS News Hour, *the* Academy of American Poets, Poetry Society of America, Bettering American Poetry *and* Ploughshares. *As a music critic, they have appeared in* Complex *magazine and* THUMP, *and as a curator have facilitated artists' projects and exhibitions in Chicago, Boston, Santa Fe, Reykjavík and Copenhagen. Their video art has shown in exhibitions at Flux Factory, Daata Editions, the 13th Baltic Triennial in Lithuania, and the Institute of Contemporary Art in LA. They are the founder of the Center for Afrofuturist Studies, an artist residency program for artists of color, and currently a joint Public Programs Fellow at the Museum of Modern Art and the Studio Museum in Harlem.*

Ode to the Happy Negro Hugging the Flag in Robert Colescott's "George Washington Carver Crossing the Delaware"

I have waited all my life to find me find you
perched around my black neck in repose

songing of me in repose   your black legs
songing of me in repose

your black legs a dangle around me   I have waited to
find you find your black toes   to find them

sundering at the base   your black toes your black toenails hale and bright   your black feet a straddle around me

around my black waist a straddle I finding I was born I was
born who operated

in the white was born who was born
who operated in the white chapel

who found your black thighs in repose
songing to each other in repose

across

my chest   an extended black for blocks a
neighborhood song in repose

your crotch an extended black
at my neck   your black groin a straddle

around me in repose   what life what
there it is there   I had been looked at

there o lord sucked His black
thorax which spanned as a fracture
                              spanned as I

who grow up in you there as a fracture find your
black breast o lord quiescing

atop my head your other black
breast o lord hale and bright around me o lord

a pendulum o lord to my black ear
my black ear that finds you songing
of me in repose in your stature
toppling to one side of my one side

find your black shoulders a gaping
around me   death your body armless

around me   death none can
skirt it in your mother's way o lord

is finding black fingers there your black
neck is finding   lord is rising past

the cumulus-line an extended black
o lord is an extended black o lord

is thinking of self and thinking of self is
finding you there so that when I entered I entered
                              the pulpit I entered

"I Know This Is No Longer Sustainable," Etc.

You enter, in pain, a bestial marriage. Your head is a shroud at your neck. Your thought beckons to you. Your tongue is clipped. "I wish not to love you at all…"

There are birds of prey at the subway station. In all their bloodsoft. I will not come out on Friday. I will hold a paper bag tight. An apple juice carton, a bottle of kerosene.

You are too eager to get on with it. You haven't the blood of the sages. You plaster his face onto your faces. The inherent danger of strangulation.

I will tell you all of what happen to me. First I went to save him. Second he drowned. Prohibit that the earth be inflamed, o lord, by your bright animal nature.

The mountaintop is a blackhorse a'throttle in your mother. Your new haircut brings the black in closer. I even leaned forward—

How this people's fire must be reflexed in your teeth! The nude holograph of an unburdened sex. These are the commonplace things. I find your car keys in the freezer.

The flocked places inside of the train. You're either on the train or the train is on you, Marianna. The compulsive image of one prefigured violence.

I am the blue eyes at an evening ball in Mariona. My father in a ball gown, singing, "Mud is sweeter than money." I know this is no longer sustainable, etc.

A rural scene. My heart's in my hand, and my hand is pierced, and my hand's in the bag, and the bag is caught. Everybody clap your hands. In autumn, the sumac is wild.

Safia Elhillo

She is the author of The January Children *(2017), recipient of the 2016 Sillerman First Book Prize for African Poets and a 2018 Arab American Book Award. Sudanese by way of Washington, DC, and a Cave Canem fellow, she holds an MFA in poetry from the New School. In addition to appearing in several journals and anthologies, her work has been translated into Arabic, Japanese, Estonian, Portuguese and Greek, and commissioned by Under Armour and the Bavarian State Ballet. She is the recipient of a 2018 Ruth Lilly and Dorothy Sargent Rosenberg Fellowship from the Poetry Foundation. With Fatimah Asghar, she is co-editor of the anthology* Halal If You Hear Me *(2017).*

border / softer

in the new year or when i grow up or
if i live through the night i want to be

ungovernable   no longer a citizen
to any of the names assigned my body

& then how boundless could i make my life
which for all its smallness still exhausts me

balancing act of all my margins all my conjugations
of cannot if i live through the night i will bleed

into all my edges until i am no longer a stroke
of some careless man's pen   *after*

*a particularly liquid lunch churchill was said
to have created [   ] with a stroke of his [   ]*

& isn't a map only a joke we all agreed into a fact
& where can i touch the equator   & how will i know

i am touching it   & where is the end of my country
the beginning of the next   how will i know i've crossed over

how to say
after Agha Shahid Ali

in the divorce i separate to two piles   books: english   love songs: arabic
my angers my schooling my long repeating name   english   English   arabic

i am someone's daughter but i am american born   it shows in my short memory
my ahistoric glamour   my clumsy tongue when i forget the word for [ ] in arabic

i sleep   unbroken dark hours on airplanes home   & dream i've missed my
connecting flight   i dream a new & fluent mouth full of gauzy swathes of arabic

i dream my alternate selves   each with a face borrowed from photographs of
the girl who became my grandmother   brows & body rounded & cursive like arabic

but wake to the usual borderlands   i crowd shining slivers of english to my mouth
iris   crocus   inlet   heron   how dare i love a word without knowing it in arabic

& what even is translation   is immigration   without irony   safia
means *pure*   all my life it's been true   even in my clouded arabic

boys like me better when they can't place where i'm from

1
i tell a story   sometimes that
whitepeople love   it's about
summer in khartoum   in the
back   of a pickup truck with
my cousins   eating sunflower
seeds with the shells   dangling
from our dark lower lips   & we
played our favorite game which
was to yell into the street the names
we knew best the names   we all
had   *mohammed   ahmed*
omar & see   how many dozens
of strangers   would answer

2
do you like it do you like
the way i mimic my mother's
accent when saying aloud a word i
cannot pronounce & have only
ever seen written down

3
or is it   my diasporic stink
my halved tongue   wandering
forever at the borderlands   i

never learned the word am i   a
girl or am i an aperture   born by
the absence of a river   & broken
where the blue & white nile meet
the story is not new   nor is it
monogamous i was   not born i
was planted   at the place where
the world cracked in two   & crawled
from the wound as a new kind of tree
swaying forever back & forth for your
translated pleasure
                    in the harmattan wind

ars poetica

*Autobiography practiced in the enemy's language has the
texture of fiction.*

                                        —Assia Djebar, *Fantasia*

in ohio i tell a classroom of white students a story i mean to be beautiful
about my grandfather   retreating in his old age to his first tongue

in which there are no separate words for like & love   once at a restaurant
meaning   i think   to say i would like some tomato soup   repeats

to our flustered waitress   i love tomato soup   i love tomato soup
& the white students & the white professors like my story   they think i mean it

to be comic   the room balloons with their delight   they are laughing
at my grandfather & it is my fault   for carving tendernesses from my old life

without context   parading to strangers my weak translations
now they think i am joking & lap   at my every dripping word

& isn't this why i learned this language   to graduate
from my thick & pungent newness   my accent & my nameless shoes   to float
my hands like a conductor   redirect the laughter to a body not my own
for a moment of quiet inside my traitor's head

Ashley Makue

A writer and facilitator from South Africa, she was the Current State of Poetry South African National Slam champion for 2016/17. Her debut collection, i know how to fix myself, *was released in April 2017 by the African Poetry Book Fund as part of their* New-Generation African Poets Chapbook Box Set: Nne. *Her work has been included in multiple journals, including* Pain, *published by the Icelandic Partus Press. She was longlisted for the Sol Plaatje European Union Prize, and selected as a finalist for the 2018 Sillerman Poetry Book Prize. She writes for* AfroElle *magazine and freelances as a literary editor.*

mali

(blood)

The ancestry of sadness

to be born
by definition
to be blood
to begin
not at the very beginning
to begin
at lineage
to begin
before you begin

My mother, 'Mamaseko, bleeds with me. We cry on the phone together some days, bounded by torment, ribs bending together for (or against) agony. Our rocks cling together over the old country (Lesotho) and our loss is one colour (river border sand blue left to someplace else). We have both left. I crossed the bridge over a border drawn by a quiet river. She left, midnight in shoulder-deep Mohokari (river separating Lesotho from South Africa: water between home and what will become home). I was five years old. I ate fat cakes and drank sweet orange juice: easy transit. Ease of belonging here, and then there. But my mother, at sixteen, felt the old country leave her.

And I wonder what it means to be beings of blood: to relate by blood, and to live by blood.

My grandmother, Motlagomang, left South Africa to set up home in a country lent to her by marriage. She visits us every year and during these short visits, her body becomes sick with longing for the borrowed country. In a few months, I will move to my wife's birth country. And there, I shall stay—if I forget to run.

My great-grandmother, Josephine (after whom I was named), was a nomad. She moved around South Africa and died before naming any one place "home". Beyond our name, Josephine and I share a resemblance that is marked by circles around the mouth, knees knocking together and our yen to leave. We come together by (and through) a memory of loss (or the loss of memory), haunting my breathing body, and rattling her corpse—the loss of homes we did not choose, and the loss of the homes we almost found.

And I do not know if the inheritance of generational trauma has clotted our blood bonds. And if this clotting means anything for our relational identities. If I am my mother's daughter because of our blood, am I also her daughter for the pain we have shared: the loss of my father, and then a sister, and the scolding hands of a man whose jabs stayed in her heart, and so in mine? Am I my grandmother's for the homes we find in the countries of our spouses? Am I Josephine's to fulfil her name? To seek and never find? For the hunger we cannot fill?

our womxn
are known for their cry
and knee bent   wailing
impepho floating above them
from them   our men
look for girls   with large mouths
and husk over their   voices
and their tongues   split
between countries
of men   who are fathers
and men   who are trees
and their daughters are planted
by the blight   and they are starved
until they know how to plead
how to lie on their stomachs   and cry
until they are ours

My mother, and her mother, and her mother's mother have loved and married bad-mood men. My mother's husband punishes her mistakes (and other faultless acts of autonomy) with silence. He goes days, sometimes weeks withholding affection to make his displeasures known (and there are many). Much like my grandfather who left my grandmother for ten complete years—scapegoating an argument that got ugly. My great-grandmother never found a soft love. All of her affairs were with men who loved her as much as they hated her. And for many years my relationships followed this pattern. My lovers had the same incapacity for stable emotional tenderness.

Is it possible that I have inherited this way of love from the womxn who came before me?

I look for the root of my heart's constant sacrifice in the bending of my head, and my mother's, and my grandmother's and my great-grandmother's. And I know (how) to hold the edge of the sharp knife injuring my marriage. I know the hymn that quickens forgiveness. The apology that soothes the war and brings my bride into the warmth of our bed. I know the cup that runneth over, and I pour its honey over our burning for sprint and flight. I know how to bring softness back to her breasts. How to pull the lines that sweeten her mouth. I know how to put us out. And in the same way, I know how to drown us. How to hold against her, words said in(to) anger. I know how to heighten the flame. How to call my troops to battle. How to dress up in defensive armour. I turn cold for myself. And I turn cold for my mother, and my grandmother, and my great-grandmother. I set the table for five and I know my wife has no weapon for ghosts. But I am theirs, in sickness more than in health. And the blood that binds is heavy—falls clotted from my vagina.

sometimes love is a crowded place
a swollen stomach
water in the lungs
a dam
and algae
a room waiting to put both of its arms around you
to gather all its walls around you
sometimes love is a house
living in your ducts
even after you've left it
an old picture in circular motion
repeating itself
rehashing itself
a heart holding a past
a mind recreating a past
sometimes love is ghost
that will not go

We are sick. Habitually. I hold a hand over my head and it hurts. My mother cuts the tip of her finger and her blood ails. My grandmother presses her chest and it abates beneath her palm. The sugar rots my great-grandmother from inside her mouth and her stomach. And through the blood, we know how to erode on our feet. How to lie with wolves and wake before dawn to hunt for them.

If this is hereditary illness, will we find our medicine together? Will we drink aloe, eat cayenne pepper and heal at once?

in the year of healing
antihistamine shall
be a mirror
turned toward the heart
and the rot shall
be cached no longer
and the finger
pointed inward shall
pull out the dirt
and the leaving
of trauma will hurt
like any feet
turned against
the pain will flush
through you
and another death
shall take your father
and another country
shall steal your mother's
softness
and another night shall
begin and remain a year
and another ballot shall come
and you will not be the choice
the pus pressed out
shall be the memory
of a lover who could
only stay in your heart
the anesthesia shall
leave by the second loss
of a name of a face
and the completion
shall be a room
with all your sadnesses
and the sun rushing in

We are lonely. And sad. My mother engulfs herself in a husband and his children, pours herself into a Jesus so opaque she cannot see him. She leaves me, to complete the opening. To forget the face of the love that she lost. My grandmother flees her country, labours children and grandchildren to deter the quiet until her ears fail her. Until they begin to send the noise out. And by then, she is ready to lie still and sleep. My great-grandmother spent her whole life longing for someplace else, someone else, a new face, a new year. And I don't know how to sit still.

a body split
between countries
is a ship
standing
to be wrecked
the doors open
into landmines
and ghosts of
our fathers
and of girls
who came
and never left
who stayed
for the sad music
requiem for the womxn
who broke open
to labour children
psalm for the children
whose feet remained
in the womb
who toss and kick
but never begin
the treasures of
witchcraft venomoid
rusted under the clutter
of histories and recollections
dust settling deeper
into this day
and the doors creaking
open into daggers
into rope
into gas
into hemlock
into bullet
into ocean at night
calling the body
into itself
at the break of dawn
encircled by an army
of icebergs of lovers
and icebergs of friends

breaking in four parts
and then falling into
and remaining in

I am starving for strangers and a new country and faces I have never seen. I am starving for another day. For another body. Another face. I am starving for my mother's country. I am starving for my grandmother's womb. I am starving for my great-grandmother's heart. I am starving for the blood that makes me theirs. For the clotting. For the wounds that bring us together. For the losses that make me my mother's daughter, that make her my grandmother's daughter, that make my grandmother my great-grandmother's daughter.

And when I cry, they wear my face. The rift shortens. And we are the country we have lost, pulling us back but sending the wolves to eat our faces before we are home again. We are the men's wounding tongues. An accusing finger. A wild fire turned inside.

and my daughters
too
will know
the pain of the womb
which transcends
the blood cord
they will know
the grave melancholy
of breaking open
for another to be
and they that be
shall forever
know the wailing
of extraction
and then
the emptying
longing
the endless
wanting
the moonless sky
pining
insatiable anguish
unmediated
by a day of love
my daughters

will come to know
the little deaths
of waiting
and waiting
of being unwanted
by everything

and

the haunt
that came
upon us
will not go
unless we
go with it

Bridget Minamore

A British-Ghanaian writer from south-east London, she was shortlisted to be London's first Young Poet Laureate, has been commissioned by the Royal Opera House and the Tate Modern, and writes regularly for The Guardian *and* The Stage *about pop culture, theatre, music, race and class. She was chosen as one of The Hospital Club's Emerging Creatives, as well as one of Speaking Volumes' 40 Stars of Black British Literature.* Titanic, *her debut pamphlet of poems on modern love and loss, came out in 2016.*

New Daughters of Africa

You will get your hair done.

Your Auntie who's not your Auntie works from the hive of her high rise, seven stories up in the air. The lifts round here are always broken, so you climb: one step, two step, leap to avoid a puddle of piss, four step, five step, six step, manoeuvre around the boys who have colonised this stairwell, eight step, nine step, land on the tenth. Twist your body and do the same steps all over again—now you are on the first floor. Repeat six times. Arrive at a black gate, rusted but strong. Ball your fist and knock through the gap you find between two wrought strips of iron, wait for the door to swing open away from your body, wait for the gate to swing open into your face, look at the child who has opened both door and gate, step inside.

Time passes. Your Auntie who's not your Auntie is perched on the edge of a wooden hard-backed chair. She speaks into her mobile phone, the cracked-screen link to back home resting taut between her chin and collarbone; Aunties round here like to multitask. Aunties round here like to talk. She speaks a language you only half-understand, or, she speaks a language you don't understand at all, or, she speaks a pidgin hybrid that you understand more the more you listen to it. Her mouth is wide, her voice is wider. The sound of her speaking to someone who is not you fills the room, richochets off the highlife she plays on a loop from a weathered stereo, bounces around and settles a little too loudly inside your ears.

You are sitting cross-legged on a frayed, patterned cushion: bum sore, legs cramped, mind resigned. Your back is a solid mass against the warmth of her crotch—you and this woman have become so close you are now the same person, perhaps. Both machine and its end product. Your neck rests taut between her knees, your head, periodically pulled from side to side as she braids each weft of hair. Right-hand thumb and middle finger slip the strands together, index hooks underneath, wrist turns and pulls the hair under (never over), left hand and left fingers join in to mirror these movements, and now she has begun. Her fingertips are ballet-dancing in the air between your head and her breasts; your Auntie who is not your Auntie is making magic from and through and with your hair. For hour upon hour you stay here, in this spot, nothing to focus on beyond the volume of her voice, the hum of her music, and the yelps her two (or three?) (or is that four?) children make as they buzz by the back of the front door. Loud mothers breed loud daughters, loud mothers breed loud sons.

Products of our parenting. You sit, get your hair braided, watch the similarities across generations and wonder: is it this obvious when people see you and your own mother? Or your cousins and their kids? Or the girls from church and their children? Round here maternity feels mandatory sometimes, despite old stigma of young bellies weighed down with new life. These ends where babies seemed to be born before their mothers. Meanwhile mums rarely got credit for moulding and building their kids in a kiln of cracked pavement slabs. There are less of them now, you think, unripe teenagers, all baby hairs and too-early baby bellies. Still. You remember the newspapers from your own teenage years, large fonts and graphically close photos, headlines decrying these singular mothers, blaming them for the fact their children were being cut down like weeds. Why have we had no follow-ups? Front pages used to scream "Teenage mums in record highs" but no one has gone back to show the twenty-nine-year-olds you know feeding and clothing and preparing their own teens to go out into the world.

Still. Life turned out different for you. You might have read *Keisha the Sket* but you didn't act on it. You might have met the mandem down the park but never for too long, you kept your head down instead. Face-first in books back then, knee-deep in toil these days, because every day is workday. Grinding because if you don't, who will? You work as hard as your mother does: overburdened and underhyped. Find it easier to cross between worlds than your brothers can—dark boys who colonise stairwells on estates—often, their voices aren't allowed to codeswitch across postcodes like yours is. Their voices could be wrought against silver but they'd still fall on ears too beeswaxed to hear. Dark boys round here are heard as having dark voices everywhere. Yours, though? Yours is tempered by your gender. You are allowed to have a posh voice, and a road voice, and you are not sure which voice is yours. You have chipped away at your voice for so long you have forgotten what you actually sound like.

There are many of you. Black girls the wrong side of a line made of brown paper bags, parents low-incomed but hardworking, you new daughters of Africa born with expectation tattooed across your backs. You made your way to centuries-old universities in this new land—buildings so white your skin felt dirty—where elites commented politely on the way you mispronounced *hyperbole, epitome, segue*, but also *water, laughing, mother*. You would drop your Ts and Gs, find a V where there is none: waughah, larfin, muvva. Wrong, they would say. Wrong.

So you shaved your words into shape. You scrubbed your council flat from the flat of your tongue, you learnt to move your mouth and hands less, you convinced yourself your accent was a mess, and so you point-blank banished *blatently*, and *yeah but*, and *wallahi*, and *nah*, and *rah*, and *oh my days*. Years of being told you sounded white, or stoosh, or posh, but now? Now you are road. Now you are. You are. You. Posh-voiced. Bouncing between dialects depending upon who you are speaking to. You talk to people and you want to cry sometimes because you cannot tell if this is what you are supposed to sound like. If this is your real voice. Now you have forgotten your first language. Not the one your parents speak, or the pidgin hybrid that you understand more the more you listen to it. No, with every passing day you lose the language of your only true home, the words wrought from cracked pavement slabs, those weighted words spoken by boys who colonise stairwells.

Now you know how to speak   properly.

You will get your hair done, and you speak to your Auntie who's not your Auntie in an accent that mimics her own. You use the same strange voice that starts to appear somewhere down the high road, somewhere along your long walk to weave the strands that sprout from your scalp. Getting your hair done round here means navigating an obstacle course of women with babies strapped to their backs, women peering through shop windows and spilling from doorways. It means avoiding too-quick-to-see-until-it's-too-late grabs from taloned rows of French-tipped fingertip claws, it means ignoring the hissing meant to catch your attention. *Sssss, sssss, can I do your hair?* Sometime along this walk, somewhere inside your *No, I'm alright, I've got someone already* repeated response, your voice changes. An accent appears. It is involuntary, subconcious, and it happens every time you speak to an African elder.

You arrive at your Auntie who's not your Auntie's high-rise front door to get your hair done. This voice—your voice for today—is fully formed now, a voice wrought against the paving stones that surround this block. The lifts round here are always broken so you climb seven stories up in the air, sweat pooling at the base of your silk scarf-covered neck with each step. You have always had to work hard to make your hair work. One-step, two-step, leap to avoid a puddle of piss, four-step, five-step, six-step, manoeuvre around a group of boys who look, to so many, like men. The stairwell they have colonised smells like weed and opportunity because these boys are always working. You glance over them, a murder of navy and black, a shoal of Nike tracksuits and side bags. These flightless birds, these fish still swimming out of water. You wonder how hard it must have been for them to grow here, to sprout from the cracks in the paving-slabs.

You breathe in. Breathe in. Breathe. Let the grimey afrobeat trap drill rap beats that seep from their cracked screens fill the bottom of your lungs. What does it mean that the music they are making now sounds like what you were raised on? Or sounds like what their parents escaped from? Back home drum beats vs artillery fire. You go to raves with your mates and are reminded of Daddy Lumba ringing in your ears as your mother forced you to pass an uncle another bottle of Supermalt, petulance splayed across your face. You scour YouTube and hear gunshots. The music these boys play, loudly and proudly from phones in the corners of stairwells, is fresh off a boat that sailed straight from your diaspora childhood and you are in awe of it. Their music is London and Accra and Birmingham and Lagos and Leeds, their music doesn't need anything more than what it is, their music is settled in its chaos. You know they are as you are: desperate to connect with parents, and parents' parents, and parents' parents' parents, you and they are desperate to have a home somewhere. But. You know as they know this is perhaps impossible, so you and they want to at least sound like you've all found one.

You will get your hair done. Walking past boys who have colonised concrete they had no right to, you ascend: eight step, nine step, land on the tenth. Seven stories in the air, fist poised to knock through a wrought-iron gap, you assess the ways you have changed since the early days of coming to this home to get your hair braided. You are older now, your head is lighter now, less weighted with expectation and too-full braids. Still. Sometimes you look so heavy. It happens more the older you get. You wear a lot of jewellery because it's nice to be reminded there is something else that weighs you down. You keep your too-long acrylics on because being physically unable to do every single task you're asked to calms your anxiety. You took the earrings and nails off at university. Sent them away alongside a voice you once had that you're not sure is still yours, but now your jewellry and acrylics and voicebox have returned. As have you. Hair today, here tomorrow, and the next, and the next. Now you have accepted you are part of this place. Now you have accepted you are part of this. Now you have accepted you are. Now you are. You are. You.

Chibundu Onuzo

*Born in Nigeria, she moved to England when she was 14. She began writing her
first novel,* The Spider King's Daughter *(2012), at the age of 17 and it was published
by Faber and Faber when she was 21. The novel won a Betty Trask Award and was
shortlisted for the Dylan Thomas Prize and the Commonwealth Book Prize. It was
longlisted for the Desmond Elliott Prize and for the Etisalat Prize for Literature. In
2014 she was selected for the Hay Festival's Africa39 list of 39 Sub-Saharan African
writers under 40 with the potential to define future trends in African literature. In
2018 she was elected Fellow of the Royal Society of Literature in its 40 Under 40
initiative. Reviewing her second novel,* Welcome to Lagos *(2016), Helon Habila
wrote in* The Guardian: *"...her ability to bring her characters to life, including the
city of Lagos, perhaps the best-painted character of all, is impressive."*

Sunita

Dọlapọ twirled a strand of premium Brazilian hair around her finger, round and
round until the dark hair completely covered her nail. It was a tic for white girls, this
constant fiddling with hair, flicking pony tails, running hands through locks, tucking
strands behind ears, sweeping ringlets aside, tossing manes back, seduction rippling
in a million follicles. An ex-boyfriend had tried to run his hand through her afro once.
His fingers remained painfully stuck at the roots, his nail snagged on a tight curl.

Herbert would have been able to poke his pink fingers into her new tresses, rising
until he reached the contraption of cornrows and thread that held it all together.
It was a good weave. It was not stiff, proclaiming by its rigour that it was a helmet
of synthetic fibres, immoveable in the face of earthquake or hurricane. Her weave
bounced, swayed, flew into her mouth at the slightest gust of wind. Her weave was
smooth, silken, glossy, a buoyant advert for Pantene and yet she was dissatisfied with
her new look.

First, there was the unnaturalness of it. Real, human, hair from somebody else's
scalp now framed her face and rested on her clavicles. Then there was the cost of
three hundred pounds. There had been cheaper options, hair swept up from the
cutting floors of salons and stitched onto a double wefted track. Mongrel hair, her
aunties said, assembled from a hundred different heads, coarse strands, smooth
strands, blonde strands, red strands, grey strands all dyed a uniform black that hid
their imperfections. Get quality, her cousins said. You can reuse quality. Wear it, wash
it, use it again. Wear it, wash it, use it again.

There was nothing wrong with her new weave. John, a course-mate in whom she had
once harboured a vague interest, had said to her, "Love the new look, Dollop. Very
glamorous."

"Actually, I'm calling myself Dolly now," she had wanted to reply but he was gone, striding away in his Abercrombie shirt, body of a band lead, brains the consistency of hair gel.

She had been christened Dollop by the girls in her Wiltshire boarding-school, their slender, Anglo-Saxon tongues unable to wrap themselves round the chunky syllables of Dọlapọ. Dumpling Dollop, dimpled doughnut. She had been chubby back then, breathless at the sight of a lacrosse stick. She lost weight in the summer before university, sprinting on a treadmill for an hour each day, living on nuts and red berries like a squirrel. She had lost thirty pounds in two months. She should have lost her nickname as well.

"Don't tell me you introduce yourself to people as dollop?" her mentor Daisy had said in their first meeting. "That makes you sound like a blob of cream on the end of a spoon."

"No one can pronounce Dọlapọ."

"And nobody can pronounce Adaeze. Doesn't mean I call myself dazed. I walk into a room, confidently with my shoulders back and say, 'Hi my name is Adaeze, but you can call me Daisy.' Now go out, come back in and introduce yourself again."

Dọlapọ had been sent out of the room twice for introducing herself as Lapo and Olap. Finally she had come up with Dolly.

"Take a seat, Dolly," her mentor said. "Now we've given you a name, let's talk about your hair."

Dọlapọ loved the afro now hidden under her weave, loved its untameable, uncombable sprawl, loved the extra inches it added to her height, loved the mushroom silhouette of her head in photos, loved hair that grew up instead of down, gravity-defying, extra-terrestrial hair.

"That's fine if you want to work in advertising or publishing, or media, or fashion, or maybe even engineering, but certainly not banking," Daisy said.

"My friends like it."

"White friends or black?"

"Does it really matter?"

"White or black?"

"Mostly white."

"They think its funky, edgy and cool, don't they?"

"What's wrong with that."

"Never elegant, chic, glamorous; these are the adjectives we use for women in banking. These are the adjectives for success. As a black woman, let me be honest, when you walked into this room, what I saw was unprofessional, unkempt and unserious."

She had been paired with Daisy by Diversity Unlimited, a recruitment firm that helped companies fill up their ethnic minority quota. Daisy had worked for seven years in an investment bank. Daisy carried a red leather bag with slim, curved handles, discreet, silver, letters spelling out PRADA under the zip. Daisy wore structured dresses, thin black heels, milky pearls, minimal lipstick, dramatic eye shadow and cascading hair that swept below her shoulders. Daisy's hair cost a thousand pounds.

Dọlapọ's more modest purchase came in a black cardboard box, edged with gold curlicue. The hair lay lustrous on a bed of crepe, folded into itself like a small, sleek creature, a sable or a mink. Her aunt had gone with her to the salon, leafing through magazines as they wove Dọlapọ's afro into lines and then stitched the human hair to hers, tight-running stitches that made her eyes water. She skyped her parents in Nigeria once she got home.

"Ọpẹ o," her mother sang, her face large and happy on the screen. "Thank God you've finally gotten rid of that bush. Darling, come and see your eldest daughter." The tablet was passed to Dọlapọ's father.

"Dọla dearest, you look beautiful. You always look beautiful. Afro, weave-on, whatever. I'm so proud of you." He was the more emotional of the two, prone to bursts of affirmation, fed by his unvaried diet of American motivational books. You are what you eat, what you say, what you think, mantras he repeated like sutras.

"Thanks, Dad. I'm going to go to bed now. This weave is giving me a headache."

"Beauty is pain," her mother said in the background.

That first night, with her new hair tucked under a net, she dreamt she was on a cart, her legs dangling over the platform and trailing above short grass. Her tongue lay in her mouth like a pebble, smooth and dry. The cart swayed through the hot field, the wooden wheels creaking and rumbling on the axle, twenty noisy revolutions per minute. An ant crawled up her leg. Her calf was slim, thinner than she had ever wanted to be, almost wasted. She flicked the insect away. A bracelet of red, plastic beads stirred on her wrist. It was not her body she realised as she crossed from dream into her cold bedroom in Hampstead.

All through her lectures that day, the field rose before her like a sentimental painting, a bourgeois imagining of rural life: green grass, blue sky, wooden cart. The professor spoke of economic structures in medieval Europe, of peasant families and agricultural networks.

"You look so different," her friend Priscilla said, as they walked to the tube.

"Different how?"

"Just different. I liked your afro."

"It's under here somewhere."

"But how does it work? Whose hair is it?"

"Does it matter? I need to look this way to work in a bank."

Priscilla did not ask what she meant. Priscilla, with her corn-coloured, lank hair would never need to know what Dọlapọ meant. Instead Priscilla asked:

"Who studies history and goes off to work in a bank?"

"I'm not you. I can't just become the director of Daddy's luxury tea company."

Priscilla's blue eyes widened. "That's so unnecessary, Dollop. It's not like your parents aren't rich."

"I'm calling myself Dolly now," she said, as the barriers clattered open.

Dolapo had read somewhere that cheese gave strange dreams. That second night, she exchanged her bedtime snack of Brie and two crackers for carrot and hummus. She dreamt she was on the back of the cart again, fresh vegetables and fruit crowding around her. It had rained and the field had turned to mud.

"Sunita," someone said.

She looked back and saw two bullocks, their horns rising like pale crescents, sharp tipped and dangerous. They were pulling the cart, their shoulder blades rolling with each step.

"My name is Dolapo Owolabi," she said when she woke up. "My name is Dolapo Owolabi," she muttered as she rode on the tube, the ground beneath her a black mudslide. In the windows, she saw the marble eyes of a bullock.

The third night, she was afraid to sleep. Her first interview was tomorrow and she couldn't sleep. Daisy had called her that evening to ask what she thought of the falling oil prices. Dolapo had not heard.

"I've told you. You have to be going over the financial pages. Have you done your hair?"

"Yes. I was wondering, do you know where it comes from? Is it Brazil?"

"Well, it's called Brazilian hair but it's mostly from India. The women sell it to make money for their families. I read something about getting the hair from temples as well but I don't know if I believe that. Anyway, focus, Dolly, and tell me the difference between a stock and a bond."

When she got off the phone, she stared at the high Victorian ceiling of her bedroom. The house was hollow without her parents and two brothers. They were safely asleep in Nigeria. Who could she call? Her English friends wouldn't get it, her Nigerian cousins would tell her to get a grip. Get a grip, Dolapo, she said to herself.

This time Dolapo dreamt she was in a cool, dark room. She put her hands on the walls, pitted mud walls that her fingers slid into. There was an earthen bowl in front of her. She drank from it and tasted buffalo milk, fat and creamy, freshly squeezed from an udder that morning.

"Sunita, stop dawdling. Hurry so you won't be late for school."

She stepped into the sunlight, into a lane with other huts with brown walls and grey thatched roofs, thatch made from woven grass reeds and coconut leaves. There were other children emerging in blue and white uniforms.

"Sunita, where's your hair?" a little boy with dirty knees asked. She ran her hand over her scalp and felt the stubble of new growth bristling against her palm.

"Baldie," he chanted behind her as they walked to school. "Baldie, Baldie."

She waited until the huts were out of sight and then she flung her bag to the ground.

"Your mother is a baldie!"

She launched herself at her tormentor and they fell to the ground.

Dọlapọ woke with her legs still thrashing. She went to her dressing-table and brushed out Sunita's hair. She could still feel herself rolling in the Indian dirt, kicking and spitting and scratching. She hoped she won. Nobody messed with Sunita and nobody messed with her. She flicked her weave over her shoulder, glamorous for one last time and then she found a razor and began to slit the stitches that bound her and Sunita together.

Six hours later, Dọlapọ walked into a room in Canary Wharf, in a structured dress, thin black heels, a single strand of pearls and her hair combed out to its tallest and widest, a globe of an afro, space for Europe, Africa and Asia on her head.

"Hello, good morning. I'm Dọlapọ Owolabi."

"Morning, I'm Mike Jones. Is there a name you prefer to be called by?"

"Just Dọlapọ is fine."

"Please take a seat, Dọlapọ, and tell us why you want to work in banking."

Copyrights and Permissions

1992 *Daughters of Africa*

Opal Palmer Adisa
Abena Adomako
Ama Ata Aidoo
Grace Akello
Zaynab Alkali
Ifi Amadiume
Maya Angelou
Red Jordan Arobateau
Iola Ashundie

Mariama Bâ
Baba
Toni Cade Bambara
Valerie Belgrave
Gwendolyn B. Bennett
Louise Bennett
Julia Berger
Eulalia Bernard
Ayse Bircan
Becky Birtha
Valerie Bloom
Marita Bonner
Dionne Brand
Jean Binta Breeze
Virginia Brindis de Salas
Erna Brodber
Gwendolyn Brooks
Barbara Burford
Annie L. Burton
Abena P.A. Busia
Dinah Anuli Butler
Octavia E. Butler

Joan Cambridge
Aída Cartagena Portalatín
Adelaide Casely-Hayford
Gladys Casely-Hayford
Marie Chauvet
Alice Childress

Michelle Cliff
Lucille Clifton
Merle Collins
Maryse Condé
Anna Julia Cooper
J. California Cooper
Jayne Cortez
Christine Craig
Jane Tapsubei Creider

Tsitsi Dangarembga
Angela Y. Davis
Thadious M. Davis
Lucy Delaney
Noémia de Sousa
Nafissatou Diallo
Rita Dove
Mabel Dove-Danquah
Kate Drumgoold
Alice Dunbar-Nelson

Zee Edgell
Angelika Einsenbrandt
Zilpha Elaw
Elizabeth
Buchi Emecheta
Alda do Espirito Santo
Mari Evans

Jessie Redmon Fauset
Charlotte Forten Grimké
Aline França
Henrietta Fuller

Amy Jacques Garvey
Beryl Gilroy
Nikki Giovanni
Vivian Glover
Marita Golden

Jewelle Gomez
Pilar López Gonzales
Lorna Goodison
Serena Gordon
Hattie Gossett
Angelika Weld Grimké
Rosa Guy

Lorraine Hansberry
Frances E. W. Harper
Hatshepsut
Iyamide Hazeley
Bessie Head
Georgina Herrera
Saida Herzi
Merle Hodge
Billie Holiday
Bell Hooks
Pauline Elizabeth Hopkins
Amelia Blossom House
Gloria T. Hull
Marsha Hunt
Kristin Hunter
Zora Neale Hurston

Noni Jabavu
Mattie J. Jackson
Harriet Jacobs
Carolina Maria de Jesus
Alice Perry Johnson
Amryl Johnson
Georgia Douglas Johnson
Claudia Jones
Gayl Jones
Marion Patrick Jones
June Jordan

Jackie Kay
Kebbedseh

Caroline Ntseliseng
   Khaketla
Yelena Khanga
Jamaica Kincaid
Mwana Kupona
Ellen Kuzwayo

Alda Lara
Nella Larsen
Andrea Lee
Audre Lorde

Elise Johnson McDougald
Terry McMillan
Naomi Long Madgett
Lina Magaia
Barbara Makhalisa
Zindzi Mandela
Paule Marshall
Una Marson
Annette M'baye
Pauline Melville
Louise Meriwether
Gcina Mhlope
Mary Monroe
Anne Moody
Pamela Mordecai
Nancy Morejón
Toni Morrison
Mwana Kupona Msham
Micere Githae Mugo
Pauli Murray

Gloria Naylor
Citèkù Ndaaya
Womi Bright Neal
Lauretta Ngcobo
Grace Nichols

Nisa
Rebeka Njau
Flora Nwapa
Sekai Nzenza

Grace Ogot
Molara Ogundipe-Leslie
May Opitz

Marion Patrick Jones
Gabriela Pearse
Ann Petry
Marlene Nourbese Philip
J. J. Phillips
Ann Plato
Velma Pollard
Marsha Prescod
Mary Prince
Nancy Prince

Queen of Sheba
Christine Qunta

Joan Riley
Carolyn Rodgers
Astrid Roemer
Marta Rojas
Lucinda Roy
Jacqueline Rudet
Kristina Rungano
Sandi Russell

Sonia Sanchez
Simone Schwarz–Bart
Mary Seacole
Mabel Segun
Olive Senior
Dulcie September

Ntozake Shange
Jenneba Sie-Jalloh
Joyce Sikakane
Zulu Sofola
Aminata Sow Fall
Anne Spencer
Eintou Pearl Springer
Maria W. Stewart
Maud Sulter
Efua Sutherland

Véronique Tadjo
Susie King Taylor
Lourdes Teodoro
Mary Church Terrell
Lucy Terry
Awa Thiam
Elean Thomas
Miriam Tlali
Sojourner Truth
Harriet Tubman

Adaora Lily Ulasi

Bethany Veney

Charity Waciuma
Alice Walker
Margaret Walker
Michele Wallace
Myriam Warner–Vieyra
Ida B. Wells
Dorothy West
Phillis Wheatley
Zoe Wicomb
Sherley Anne Williams
Harriet E. Wilson
Sylvia Wynter

Index

Margaret Busby OBE, Hon. FRSL (Nana Akua Ackon) is a major cultural figure in Britain and around the world. She was born in Ghana and educated in the UK, graduating from London University. She became Britain's youngest and first black woman publisher when she co-founded Allison & Busby in the late 1960s and published notable authors including Buchi Emecheta, Nuruddin Farah, Rosa Guy, C.L.R. James, Michael Moorcock and Jill Murphy. An editor, broadcaster and literary critic, she has also written drama for BBC radio and the stage. Her radio abridgements and dramatisations encompass work by Henry Louis Gates, Timothy Mo, Walter Mosley, Jean Rhys, Sam Selvon and Wole Soyinka, among others. She has judged numerous national and international literary competitions, and served on the boards of such organisations as the Royal Literary Fund, *Wasafiri* magazine and the Africa Centre. A long-time campaigner for diversity in publishing, she is the recipient of many awards, including the Henry Swanzy Award in 2015 and the Benson Medal from the Royal Society of Literature in 2017. She lives in London.